Asian Money Markets

Edited by

DAVID C. COLE

HAL S. SCOTT

PHILIP A. WELLONS

New York   Oxford

OXFORD UNIVERSITY PRESS

1995

Oxford University Press

Oxford   New York
Athens   Auckland   Bangkok   Bombay
Calcutta   Cape Town   Dar es Salaam   Delhi
Florence   Hong Kong   Istanbul   Karachi
Kuala Lumpur   Madras   Madrid   Melbourne
Mexico City   Nairobi   Paris   Singapore
Taipei   Tokyo   Toronto

and associated companies in
Berlin   Ibadan

Copyright © 1995 by Oxford University Press, Inc.

Published by Oxford University Press, Inc.
198 Madison Avenue, New York, New York 10016

Library of Congress Cataloging-in-Publication Data
Asian money markets / edited by David C. Cole, Hal S. Scott,
Philip A. Wellons.
p. cm.   Includes bibliographical references and index.
ISBN 0-19-507429-7
1. Money market—Asia.   I. Cole, David Chamberlin, 1928- .
II. Scott, Hal S.   III. Wellons, Philip A.
HG1270.5.   A65   1995
332'.0412'095—dc20   95-4248

9 8 7 6 5 4 3 2 1

Printed in the United States of America
on acid-free paper

FOREWORD

The chapters in this volume are the result of a unique program of research involving the collaboration of scholars from ten different countries. They agreed to pursue a common research agenda in their study of Asian money markets and followed the original plan to a surprising degree. Their expositions of why some policies helped the development of money markets and others hindered it should be useful to all the many students and practitioners of monetary and financial policy in developing countries.

The close control of interest rates and credit allocation has slowed the growth of the financial systems of many less developed countries. In the last few years, however, there has been a general movement toward greater reliance on market processes to control financial activity. The financial systems of the Asian countries considered in this volume have led the way in those developments, and they have grown rapidly in size and scope. However, as the chapters in this book make clear, the relation between deregulation and financial growth is far more complex than appeared in the arguments for ending financial repression made a couple of decades ago.

The countries examined in this volume have pursued a variety of approaches to the development of financial markets and institutions, and accordingly, their financial markets have grown at different rates. The main objective of this book is to determine how those policy differences affected financial development.

The chapters in this book provide a realistic perspective on the development of those markets, but they offer much more than a description and history of market institutions. The authors are concerned with understanding not only what happened but why it happened. They are especially interested in the way that market development was influenced by government policy. In examining that question, they have followed a common methodology in analyzing the role of economic policy in guiding market development.

This book focuses on the development of money markets because they are at the center of financial activity. Most of the adjustment to cyclical and seasonal changes in the surpluses and deficits of businesses, households, and governments is made through these markets. And for those adjustments to be made effectively, the money markets must be broad enough and deep enough to maintain the liquidity of market instruments when various kinds of shocks strike the market. From a private trader's point of view, liquidity is the most important aspect of the market, but its role as a vehicle for a central bank's operations is equally important.

The IMF and other international agencies have been urging developing countries to move from the close, direct control of credit to the indirect control of its cost and availability. That is best done through central bank operations in the money markets. The experience of countries like Indonesia, which has recently moved to an indirect system of control, has proved to be especially valuable to banking specialists in countries now moving in that direction. So, too, is the experience of Malaysia, which has followed a different path toward the same objective.

The money markets also play a crucial role in the allocation of capital. The rates for short-term, riskless assets established in the short-term money markets serve as the base or reference rates for all the other instruments traded in financial markets and thus serve to unify the whole financial system.

The authors of the country studies examine how the policies of their countries have influenced the development of short-term financial instruments and the depth and resiliency of the markets for those instruments. In the same way, they look at the evolution of reference rates in those markets and the role of short-term money markets in monetary control. In doing so, they consider not only the impact of particular policy measures but also the effect of the policy regime in terms of its consistency and the extent of the government's commitment to the development of a money market.

To save readers from suspense, the editors have kindly summarized the main conclusions of the studies in the opening chapter. Those readers concerned with financial development can learn a good deal from that chapter, but they will learn much more by following the rich details of the same themes in the country chapters. Each chapter analyzes the interaction between market processes and institutional change to explain the complex and sometimes unexpected effects of government policy on financial markets. "The devil is in the details." The lesson of experience is there, too.

James S. Duesenberry
Harvard University

PREFACE

This book exists because financial experts in East and Southeast Asia wanted it and made it happen. The Program on International Financial Systems at Harvard Law School helped by suggesting a way to explore the impact of government policy on financial markets and by guiding the research.

The program emerged when its founders needed, for teaching and advisory work, a good analysis of developing countries' policies regarding their financial markets. The existing literature analyzed policy in one country or merely described financial markets in a number of countries. Complex issues thus forced scholars to review a wide range of policies at macro- and microeconomic levels and to understand how institutions worked. Differences among countries made comparisons difficult. Analyses of markets were rare. Harvard's program would promote good comparative financial policy research.

The resulting book has at least two audiences. Financial decision makers and their advisers, particularly in developing and transition economies, can be guided by the experience of these dynamic Asian states. One of the first questions that a finance minister contemplating reform asks is how well a suggested policy has worked in similar countries. Students of financial development should also learn from this book.

To start the research, the program designed a methodology for a comparative financial study drawing on the disciplines of law, economics, and business. The research team in each country followed this methodology. The question was in which countries and markets they should begin the research, and the answer came from the researchers themselves.

Three conferences shaped the research. The first, held in Sanur, Bali, in January 1988, was attended by a broad range of Asian financial specialists, in the public and private sectors, from Korea and Japan to Indonesia and Australia and from multilateral agencies like the Asian Development Bank, the International Monetary Fund, and the World Bank. These experts steered the research toward money markets as the most significant financial markets in the region. Researchers from universities, think tanks, and government agencies in seven countries agreed to write country studies following this methodology.

The second and third conferences, held in Singapore, refined the work. A conference held in August 1988 was attended by the participating researchers and a few country and regional specialists. They reviewed and sharpened the methodology based on their initial experiences. A conference in May 1989, attended by only the researchers, addressed the problems that the research teams discovered as they tried to obtain suitable consistent data. Even with these efforts to forge a common approach, local problems such as the availability of data or the peculiar characteristics of local markets inevitably created some variability in the final product.

Two more conferences aired the findings of the country studies and weighed their implications. One conference, hosted by the Japan Center for Economic Research in Osaka in June 1990, considered the central theme, the impact of government policies on the development of money markets. Another conference, hosted by the Federal Reserve Bank of San Francisco in July 1990, dealt primarily with the role of money markets in implementing monetary policy. These conferences sharpened the issues addressed and helped the authors of the country studies in their final revisions. Centralized editing of all the studies also contributed to a greater consistency of approach.

The editors extracted both the major themes of the research from these comprehensive country studies—many extending over two or three decades—and the comments of many participants, as well as Ouliaris's crosscutting econometric analysis of the efficiency and stability of money markets in several countries.

We are grateful to all who helped in this extensive scholarly research. Rarely can authors revise and refine their work to such a degree. Several sources, in addition to the Harvard Law School, supported the work. Major funding was supplied by the Ford Foundation, the U.S. Agency for International Development, and the Japan Center for Economic Research. The Asia Foundation, the Center on Japanese Economy and Business at Columbia University, Bank Bumi Daya, Bank Dagang Negara, Bank Negara Indonesia, Bank Rakyat Indonesia, and the Harvard Institute for International Development also provided important support.

We extend our deepest appreciation to the authors of the country studies who labored diligently, met most deadlines, and made significant intellectual contributions to the common effort.

We acknowledge the contributions of all the participants at both the preparatory and concluding conferences that helped to shape and improve the research, and particularly to Anne-Marie Slaughter and Angelos Tsichrintzis.

We express our appreciation to Betty F. Slade for her comprehensive editorial review of all the studies and for contributing to the organization of the whole project, and to Claire Brown, Patricia Walker, and Jeremy Hochenstein at HIID and Wendy Boyce, Lori Kelley, and Mary DeRosa at Harvard Law School for helping with the background research and preparing consistent final versions of all the papers.

Cambridge, Mass.   D.C.C.
June 1994   H.S.S.
                                                                                                              P.A.W.

CONTENTS

CONTRIBUTORS

Mohamed Ariff
National University of Singapore

Daniel Wai-Wah Cheung
Department of Finance
Chinese University of Hong Kong

David C. Cole
Harvard Institute for International
Development

Chung Tin Fah
Bank Negara Malaysia

Richard Yan-Ki Ho
Department of Economics and
Finance
City Polytechnic of Hong Kong

Basant K. Kapur
National University of Singapore

Mario B. Lamberte
Philippine Institute for Development
Studies

Lin See-Yan
Bank Negara Malaysia

Yu-Hon Lui
Department of Economics and
Finance
City Polytechnic of Hong Kong

Moon-Soo Kang
Korea Development Institute

Sam Ouliaris
Department of Business Policy
National University of Singapore

Shoichi Royama
Department of Economics
Osaka University

Hal S. Scott
Harvard Law School

Betty F. Slade
Harvard Institute for International
Development

Juro Teranishi
Institute for Economic Research
Hitotsubashi University

Amina Tyabji
National University of Singapore

Teodoro S. Untalan
Philippine Institute for Development
Studies

Josef T. Yap
Philippine Institute for Development
Studies

Philip A. Wellons
Harvard Law School

Ma. Socorro V. Zingapan
Philippine Institute for Development
Studies

Asian Money Markets

CHAPTER 1

THE ASIAN MONEY MARKETS: AN OVERVIEW

DAVID C. COLE
HAL S. SCOTT
PHILIP A. WELLONS

This book reports the findings of a study of money markets in eight countries in East and Southeast Asia. This first chapter summarizes and draws conclusions from the studies. It provides a general background of the overall study and then explores the nature and function of the money markets and their development in the region. The major findings of the study concern the types of government policy regarding the development of money markets and the effect of those policies on the markets' efficiency and stability.

THE MONEY MARKET STUDY: GENERAL BACKGROUND

The money market study investigated the effect of government policy on the development and performance of money markets in selected East and Southeast Asian countries. It is part of a long-range project to investigate the relationship between financial policies and financial systems in developing countries. We believe this can best be achieved by breaking the financial systems into various market components, such as capital markets, long-term lending markets, or money markets, which consist of particular instruments and participants. Over time, we seek to understand the role and development of each relevant market within a country, as well as the connections between markets, for example, the relationship of the money market to the capital market.

    The primary objective of these studies is to enable policymakers to determine which policies are likely to help them achieve their objectives and which are not. We are interested in understanding the reasons for success or failure. For this book, this meant that we had to take a longer-term view, extending back two or even three decades. This historical approach sets the context for policy initiatives in the 1980s.

The Asian money markets study covered the following countries: Hong Kong, Indonesia, Korea, (i.e., the Republic of Korea, or South Korea), Malaysia, the Philippines, Singapore, and Japan. Japan was studied in both its pre–World War II and contemporary periods. These countries provide a broad spectrum of levels of economic development, rates of economic growth, and patterns of inflation and financial development. Prewar Japan offers a fascinating case of a developing financial system in conditions that resemble those of some of today's developing countries. Contemporary Japan provides an alternative model of money market development that is less advanced than those of the North American or European countries.

Levels of Economic Development

The level of economic development among the eight cases can be most easily depicted by comparing estimates of gross domestic product (GDP) per capita, measured in U.S. dollars, as shown in Table 1.1. These estimates carry the well-known limitations of cross-country comparisons based on prevailing prices and exchange rates. In 1988, the year of comparison, most of the countries probably had mildly undervalued exchange rates, as evidenced by the substantial trade and balance-of-payment surpluses. Thus the comparisons are not badly distorted by unrealistically overvalued exchange rates. Prewar Japan is a special case in which the longer-term adjustment of exchange rates make the comparison more tenuous.

Table 1.1. Comparisons of per Capita Income, Economic Growth, and Inflation, 1980–88

	Japan	Prewar Japan	Hong Kong	Singa-pore	Korea	Malay-sia	Philip-pines	Indo-nesia
U.S.$ GDP per capita (1988)[a]	23,564	971[b]	9,782	8,150	4,081	2,047	648	490
Average real growth of GDP 1980–88[c]	4.0		7.7	6.6	9.7	5.2	1.0	5.2
Average annual rate of inflation 1980–88[d]	1.9		7.7	2.1	6.0	3.3	14.2	9.0

[a] U.S.$ GDP per capita is the 1988 GDP in local currency divided by the average exchange rate with the U.S. dollar in the same year.

[b] Per capita GDP for prewar Japan is the 1930 U.S. dollar value ($113.45) converted to 1988 dollar values.

[c] Average real growth of GDP is the compound annual rate of growth of real GDP between 1980 and 1988.

[d] Average annual rate of inflation is the compound rate of inflation in the Consumer Price Index between 1980 and 1988.

Source: World Bank, *World Tables 1992;* prewar Japan data supplied by J. Teranishi.

The data in Table 1.1 indicate that the countries differed significantly in their level of economic development. As of 1988, per capita income ranged from a high of about $23,500 in Japan, followed by Hong Kong at $9,800 and Singapore at $8,150. The lowest per capita incomes were in the Philippines and Indonesia, about $650 and $490, respectively. The economic growth records of all the countries, except the Philippines, were moderate to strong from 1980 to 1988, ranging from a high average annual growth rate of 9.7% in Korea to a low of 4.0% in Japan. These countries' average inflation rates, again apart from the Philippines, were also relatively modest.

Thus, except for the Philippines, all the countries had good to excellent growth performance and low to moderate inflation rates in the 1980s. And apart from the Philippines and Indonesia, all the countries had achieved moderate to high levels of real income. All these factors have been shown to be associated with high levels and rates of financial development (Fry 1988).

Patterns of Financial Development

The best available general measure of financial development for comparing countries is the ratio of broad money (M2) to gross domestic product (GDP). Narrow money, or M1, consists of currency in circulation plus banks' demand deposits, whereas broad money, or M2, is M1 plus banks' time and savings deposits. The International Monetary Fund provides standard definitions for these measures and publishes them for all member countries. These measures still have some problems, in that some countries are more apt to use foreign currencies in making domestic payments and the coverage of deposit institutions, as well as types of deposits included in M2 differ across countries. Recognizing these limitations, we use these ratios in Table 1.2 to give a rough indication of the different levels of financial development in these countries in 1980 and 1988 (1924 and 1930 in prewar Japan).

The ratio of M1 to GDP tends to reflect the degree of an economy's monetization, or the extent to which transactions are made in domestic currency rather than through barter or the use of foreign exchange. In relatively underdeveloped economies, the M1/GDP ratio is likely to be low due to limited transactions (high levels of home production and self-sufficiency) and continuing reliance on barter for exchanging goods. The M1/GDP ratio is also diminished by high rates of inflation and substitution of foreign for domestic currency. As economies develop, the M1/GDP ratio tends to rise somewhat until a "normal" level of monetization is reached, at which point it levels off. International financial centers tend to have higher "normal" M1/GDP ratios than do relatively closed economies.

The M1/GDP ratios shown in Table 1.2 reflect these patterns. Japan, the country with the highest income, and Singapore and Hong Kong, high-

Table 1.2. Per Capita GDP and Money Ratios, 1980 and 1988

Country	U.S.$GDP per Capita, 1988	M1/GDP		M2/GDP	
		1980	1988	1980	1988
Japan	23,564	0.29	0.31	0.86	1.12
Hong Kong	9,782	0.18	0.21	0.69	1.89
Singapore	8,150	0.24	0.25	0.64	0.88
Korea	4,081	0.10	0.10	0.33	0.38
Malaysia	2,047	0.18	0.20	0.53	0.72
Philippines	648	0.09	0.07	0.21	0.23
Indonesia	490	0.10	0.14	0.19	0.41
Prewar Japan	971	0.46	0.46	0.95	1.22

Source: World Bank, *World Tables 1992;* prewar Japan data supplied by J. Teranishi.

income countries that are also international financial centers, all have relatively high ratios. They are fully monetized economies, as was prewar Japan. The Philippines and Indonesia are at the other end of the scale, low-income countries that are only partially monetized. The M1/GDP ratio in the Philippines actually declined in the 1980s, probably because of rising inflation, political instability, and the substitution of foreign for domestic currency. Indonesia, on the other hand, experienced a significant rise in its M1 ratio, reflecting lower inflation and increased confidence in the domestic currency.

Korea and Malaysia are anomalous cases, in that Korea has a very low M1 ratio given its per capita income and Malaysia has a relatively high ratio. In the Korean case, the prevalence of erratic inflation and high short-term interest rates in the unregulated, easily accessible curb markets has conditioned businesses to economize on their cash holdings and make heavy use of postdated checks as a means of payment. A generally repressed and inefficient banking system led to the substitution of deposits at nonbank financial institutions for those in banks. In Malaysia, on the other hand, inflation has not been a serious problem; banking services are widely available, relatively competitive, and efficient; and businesses use the normal check payment system for transactions.

In contrast with the M1/GDP ratio, the ratio of M2 to GDP generally keeps rising with per capita income, as Gurley (1967) demonstrated many years ago, because of the increased propensity to hold financial savings in the form of bank savings and time deposits. Differences among countries are due generally to different rates of inflation and real interest rates, the availability and reliability of banking services, and the level of real income.

Among the countries covered in our study, Japan had the highest M2 ratio in 1980, but by 1988, Hong Kong's ratio had surpassed that of Japan. This reflects the fact that Hong Kong has become an important Asian dollar money center and that it includes both domestic and foreign currency deposits in its M2.

Singapore, another major Asian money center, does not include in its M2 deposit totals the deposits of special offshore banking facilities, the Asian currency units (ACUs). Thus, Singapore's M2 ratio in 1988 was only about half that of Hong Kong and not much higher than Malaysia's. If the deposits of the ACUs were included in Singapore's M2 ratio, it would be comparable to that of Hong Kong.

The large increase in Indonesia's M2/GDP ratio between 1980 and 1988 was due more to the change in its financial policies in 1983 (decontrol of bank interest rates and credit ceilings) and reduced inflation than to the growth of real income. It reflected a period of rapid financial development. The Philippines' ratio, conversely, increased only slightly. Korea's relatively low and only moderately increasing M2/GDP ratio was due in large part to the previously mentioned reliance on nonbank financial institutions instead of banks.[1]

Table 1.3 compares the percentage growth in the ratio of M1 and M2 to GDP in the countries from 1980 to 1988. The most extreme positive changes in money ratios were in Indonesia, where the removal of credit ceilings and interest rate controls in 1983 led to very rapid growth in the banks' deposits, and also in Hong Kong, where money center activity expanded greatly. In the Philippines, the deterioration in financial development reflected its poor overall economic performance during that period.

Prewar Japan had very high financial ratios, even higher than those of recent times. Even the fall of nominal GNP, due to the world recession in 1930, did not result in a diminution of its financial ratios.

Table 1.3. Percentage Change in Money Ratios, 1980–88

Country	M1/GDP	M2/GDP
Hong Kong	16.7	173.9
Indonesia	40.0	115.8
Singapore	4.2	37.5
Malaysia	11.1	35.9
Japan	6.9	30.2
Korea	No change	15.2
Philippines	(28.6)	9.5

Source: Calculated from Table 1.2.

A Comparative Approach to Policy Analysis

We used a comparative approach in our study to facilitate drawing general conclusions about effective government policy. Our hypothesis was that if the same policy worked or failed in a number of countries over time, one could have more confidence in evaluating the effects of that policy. We realize, of course, that our inability to control for all relevant variables influencing such outcomes may limit the precision of any conclusions reached on this basis. The studies used both quantitative and qualitative techniques to assess the effects of government policy on the performance of the money markets.

We have a very broad conception of policy that includes informal as well as formal government actions. Thus, we look not only to laws and regulations but also to government directives expressed through both administrative guidance and direct market operations. Measures of performance include growth, operational efficiency, and stability in the prices and quantities of various instruments.

THE NATURE OF THE MONEY MARKETS

The money markets in this study are broadly defined to include all financial instruments, easily converted to means of payment (M1), that are used by governments, financial institutions, and nonfinancial enterprises for short-term funding or placements. In the countries examined, they included government or central bank obligations, negotiable notes (including negotiable certificates of deposit, trade bills, and bankers acceptances), commercial paper, foreign exchange swaps or forward contracts, interbank loans, and repurchase contracts ("repos").

Bank time deposits (and NBFI deposits) represent a gray area because they are used for both short-term placements and longer-term savings by individuals and enterprises, including financial institutions. In general, they were not included in the study unless they were counted as interbank loans, that is, short-term deposits by one bank in another bank as an officially identified means of transferring reserves.

For the most part, we considered only instruments of less than one-year maturity as part of the money market. Longer-term instruments with deep secondary markets can also be considered as cash substitutes, but they did not exist in the countries studied other than postwar Japan.

The issuers of money market instruments (debtor or borrower) included governments, financial institutions, commercial firms, and, to some extent, individuals. Table 1.4 classifies the instruments according to issuers. Some money market instruments, such as spot foreign exchange and swap contracts, were denominated in foreign currencies. Later in this chapter we discuss the relative importance of different kinds of instruments in the various countries.

Table 1.4. Issuers of Money Market Instruments

I. Domestic currency–denominated instruments
  A. Government
    1. Bonds
    2. Bills
    3. Central bank bills
  B. Financial institutions
    1. Negotiable certificates of deposit
    2. Bankers acceptances
    3. Interbank loans
    4. Repurchase agreements
  C. Other domestic entities
    1. Commercial paper
    2. Promissory notes
II. Foreign exchange–denominated instruments
  A. Spot trading instruments
  B. Swap contracts

Government-issued instruments naturally tended to be most important in countries with significant direct government debt, for example, Malaysia and the Philippines. But other countries, recognizing that such instruments were important to the conduct of monetary policy, tried to develop quasi-government instruments.

Korea relied heavily on monetary stabilization bonds (MSBs), debt instruments issued by the Bank of Korea to implement monetary policy. The Indonesian government has not issued domestic bonds or bills to finance its budget. But Bank Indonesia, Indonesia's central bank, developed two substitute instruments, the SBI and the SBPU, for monetary policy purposes. The SBI, a liability of Bank Indonesia, is issued to absorb liquidity, and the SBPU, a standardized liability of banks that can be sold to Bank Indonesia, can be used to increase liquidity. The SBPU can also be used as an interbank instrument, and the SBI can be an underlying security for repurchase agreements between banks.

The investors in money market instruments consisted of financial institutions, institutional investors, commercial enterprises (both domestic and foreign), and individuals. For the most important money market instrument, short-term loans between banks (the interbank market or the call market), the only investors were banks, although in Korea there were some attempts to fuse the interbank and inter–short-term finance company markets.

Investment in government issued debt depended largely on whether the debt was issued at a competitive market price. When realistic market prices prevailed, investors were more diverse; when they were controlled, they tended to be financial institutions that were required to hold the instruments. Generally, market forces prevailed more with respect to the instruments issued by firms and individuals than those issued by the government.

Instruments also differed in terms of their negotiability. Some promissory notes and certificates of deposit are negotiable, but some central bank instruments are not. Some instruments had standardized terms: Government notes and foreign exchange contracts had standard maturities, but promissory notes and some commercial paper did not. Some instruments were pooled, as was the case with money market mutual funds or unit trusts, but most other instruments were not.

THE FUNCTIONS OF MONEY MARKET INSTRUMENTS

Money markets are generally recognized as fulfilling several important functions. First, interest rates on money market instruments serve as reference rates for pricing all debt instruments. Second, government or central bank instruments are used as tools of monetary policy. Third, money market instruments permit the liquidity management of economic actors, offering returns on short-term cash surplus positions and a way to finance short-term cash deficit positions. Fourth, short-term interbank markets finance longer-term lending when financial intermediaries transform maturities.

Although the role of money markets in the financial systems of developed countries has been broadly understood and extensively discussed,[2] their role and potential contribution to the financial development of developing countries were largely ignored in the early literature on financial development. But this pattern of neglect has been changing, and money markets have been receiving increasing attention in recent years as the approach to financial policy in developing countries has shifted from mainly direct controls to more market-oriented systems. So far, however, there have been few empirical studies of the actual functioning of money markets in developing countries or systematic analyses of how government policies affect their development.

In his pioneering study of financial development in low-income countries (1973), Shaw focused primarily on the banking system and ways of improving the banks' deposit mobilization and lending functions. He saw short-term, nonmonetary financial assets not as positive elements of a developing financial system but as indicators of imperfections and distortions in the monetary/banking system, and he suggested that governments should concentrate on eliminating those distortions. Shaw advocated (p. 69) "a lean selection of financial assets" centered primarily on those issued by the banking system.

Other early writers on financial development in developing countries, such as McKinnon (1973), Drake (1980), and Coats and Khatkhate (1980), also ignored the role of money markets. In his comprehensive review of the literature on financial development (1988), Fry does not refer to money markets (as defined in our study) until the final chapter, entitled "Policies for Financial Development." There, in connection with his proposal to let interest rates be determined by market forces, rather than be set by monetary authorities or bank cartels, he stresses the role of money markets (p. 437). He states that money "markets in which interest rates are freely determined by interaction of supply and demand are few and far between in the developing world." Then he cites Indonesia since 1984 as an example "of how to introduce and develop markets in short-term financial claims."

The World Bank's World 1989 Development Report, which focuses on "Financial Systems and Development," also suggests that money markets should play an important role in financial development, that such markets can "provide a noninflationary way to finance government deficits, allow governments to implement monetary policy through open market operations and provide a market-based reference point for setting other interest rates."(p. 108). It is perhaps noteworthy that none of the "background papers" commissioned by the World Bank in preparation for this report investigated the role of money markets.

This project was initiated, on the one hand, because of the growing awareness of the potential role of money markets in the development of market-oriented financial systems and, on the other hand, because of the lack of empirical studies of how money markets were functioning in developing countries.[3] Although the potential functions of money markets in developed countries are similar, some elaboration of their role in transitional developing economies is needed.

Reference Rates

The interest rates on money market instruments can serve as reference rates for pricing other forms of debt financing. Longer-term, more risky forms of credit are often priced as increments over a basic reference rate, for example, LIBOR (London interbank offering rate) plus 2% in the Eurodollar market. The reference rate must be a market rate if the goal is allocative efficiency. Otherwise, the pricing of debt and the allocation of funds from savers to borrowers will not be optimized. This was the situation in Korea for most of the 1980s.

In countries without foreign exchange controls, such as Indonesia and Hong Kong, the reference rate was an external one. The Indonesian reference rate for short-term domestic money market instruments was LIBOR plus a swap premium representing foreign exchange risk. In the swap transaction in Indonesia, a bank exchanged dollars for rupiah with Bank Indonesia (BI) at the current spot rate, with an agreement that BI would buy back the rupiah for dollars at some fixed time in the future (the redemption date) at the same spot rate. BI charged a swap premium that theoretically reflected the risk of depreciation of the rupiah against the U.S. dollar between the initial spot transaction and the redemption date. This premium was not always determined by the market, however. For most of the period, the swap premium was probably less than the difference between the spot rate and the future rate of the rupiah (at the redemption date) as anticipated by the market participants. This meant that BI was subsidizing its counterparties.

Since Indonesia's reference rate was not an actual market rate—because the swap premium was not determined by the market—the pricing of domestic debt within Indonesia, which keyed off the reference rate, was generally not at truly market-determined rates. This probably hurt the allocative efficiency of the debt markets. Indonesia might have developed a true market reference rate by allowing demand and supply to determine the rate of central bank bills, the SBI. The banks would then have tendered bids for the SBI based on their alternative use of funds in external markets at LIBOR plus their real expectations about the cost of holding rupiah, that is, the depreciation risk. This policy, however, would have let exchange rate expectations in the market determine domestic interest rates and would also have risked putting pressure on the spot rate of the rupiah since the SBI rate would have supplied a market judgment about the future dollar–rupiah exchange rate.

Instead, the Indonesian authorities preferred to use the fixed swap premium along with control of domestic interest rates and the exchange rate, and to accept the potential allocative efficiency costs that this entailed.

Hong Kong followed a different strategy. The Hong Kong reference rate was SIBOR (the Singapore interbank offering rate for the U.S. dollar), which usually was closely tied to LIBOR. Since October 17, 1983, there has been a fixed rate of exchange between the H.K. dollar and the U.S. dollar. The two note-issuing banks could issue H.K. dollar notes only by purchasing the rights (called *certificates of indebtedness*, or CIs) to issue such notes from the Hong Kong Exchange Fund at the fixed exchange rate (U.S.\$1.00 = H.K.\$7.80). The Exchange Fund agreed to repurchase the CIs and thus, in effect, all or part of the domestic note issue, at the same fixed rate of exchange.

Without any exchange risk of holding H.K. dollars, the reference interest rate for H.K. dollar money market instruments was purely a function of alternative opportunities, that is, SIBOR.[4] The fixed rate of exchange reduced the foreign exchange risk of holding H.K. dollars. Although an open foreign exchange market still existed, in which the H.K. dollar was allowed to float freely, arbitrage eliminated any significant deviation between the official fixed rate and the open market exchange rate. As the Hong Kong study observes, this resulted in the foreign exchange market exchange rate's stabilizing at a level close to the fixed rate of H.K.\$7.80 per U.S. dollar without intervention by the Exchange Fund. This meant that local money rates were determined by external market rates. Thus Hong Kong could achieve allocative efficiency in its local debt markets with an external reference rate and a fixed exchange rate.

Under such a regime, it was always possible that the official H.K. dollar rate could be changed as a result of significant political or economic changes. Chapter 2 describes how in 1987 and 1988 the market foreign exchange rate diverged from the official rate as a result of expectations that the H.K. dollar rate would be appreciated. This resulted in an increased demand for H.K. dollars: Speculators held H.K. dollars purchased at the official rate in the expectation that they could be redeemed for U.S. dollars at a more favorable rate in the future. The Hong Kong authorities responded with the announcement of an impending "negative interest rate" scheme that, if implemented, would have made customers pay the banks interest on the right to hold Hong Kong dollar credit balances in excess of H.K.$1 million. Since the Hong Kong dollar stabilized after the announcement, the scheme was never used. Thus, SIBOR continued to be the reference rate, and domestic money rates were determined by the market.

If the negative interest rate scheme had been implemented and expectations of appreciation had persisted, speculators would no doubt have invested in alternative money market instruments to avoid the charge on Hong Kong dollar deposits. This would have distorted the relationships among the various money market instruments and perhaps led to the extension of negative interest rates to other instruments, with adverse consequences for the money markets as a whole.

By the end of the 1980s, the money markets in most of the countries in our study provided reference rates to their financial systems. This was a major change from earlier periods. More specifically, Ouliaris's econometric study using unit root analysis concludes that effective reference rates were established during the 1980s in Singapore (SIBOR), Malaysia (interbank rate), Indonesia (LIBOR + swap premium), and prewar Japan (loan rate, discount rate, or overdraft rate). However, he finds no such reference rate in Korea or the Philippines, which he attributes to interference by monetary authorities attempting to manipulate the money markets.

Tools of Monetary Policy

A second important function of the money markets is that they can be used by monetary authorities to adjust primary liquidity in the domestic economy. Simply put, in a market-driven system, less liquidity means higher interest rates, and more liquidity means lower interest rates. In most developed countries, the purchase and sale of government debt by monetary authorities, through open market operations, are a key instrument for adjusting primary liquidity. As we already mentioned, many of the countries studied were in the process of trying to develop government or central bank debt markets for this purpose.

In the absence of government or central bank debt markets, countries depended on other means to adjust liquidity. They sometimes did this by discounting notes issued by the private sector, but the limited supply of such notes restricted the usefulness of this tool. In three countries—Singapore, Malaysia, and Indonesia—the central bank used purchases of foreign exchange swap contracts as an instrument for influencing liquidity. Alternatively, the central banks extended direct credits to banks or contracted such credits as a means of affecting liquidity.

Some countries imposed quantitative restrictions, particularly on interbank borrowings, in an attempt to tighten liquidity. This was true in both Indonesia and the Philippines. Such quantitative restrictions were effective means of adjusting liquidity but often resulted in shocks and severe disruptions to the money markets.

One theme that clearly emerged in the country studies was that governments constantly faced a common dilemma. Quantitative restrictions were imposed because the markets were not broad enough to be influenced by open market operations, yet these controls often impeded the longer-term development of the broader market that governments sought.

Indonesia is the best illustration. In 1987, the monetary authorities tried to maintain the value of the rupiah by forcing the repatriation of foreign exchange through engineering a rupiah liquidity squeeze. This was accomplished, in part, by requiring all banks to immediately redeem their SBPUs held by Bank Indonesia, even though Bank Indonesia had previously contracted to hold these money market instruments for varying periods up to at least one month. This measure undermined, for several years, the use of the SBPU as a monetary policy instrument.

Concurrent with the SBPU redemption, the authorities required several state-owned enterprises to withdraw their time deposits from banks and use the funds to buy SBIs from Bank Indonesia that could not be subsequently traded in the money markets but could be redeemed on maturity only by the issuer. Here again, forced purchases of these money market instruments undercut their acceptability as market-based monetary policy instruments.

Liquidity

The money markets can provide liquidity for commercial firms as well as banks. Interbank markets and central bank lending or discounting provide liquidity for banks. Commercial firms often have more restricted alternatives, particularly when the only alternative is to lend money to or borrow from banks at fixed rates.

Interbank markets were an important source of liquidity for banks in all the countries, but they were more competitive in some than in others. In Indonesia, state-owned banks were the suppliers of excess funds to private banks. State-owned banks had an advantage in attracting funds from nonbank depositors because their liabilities were perceived as less risky than those of private banks. This gave state-owned banks the potential, particularly when they were controlled by a common owner, the government, of exercising market power in the interbank market. In Hong Kong, the Hong Kong and Shanghai Bank dominated the supply side of the interbank market.

Private nonbank money market instruments, notably commercial paper, were particularly important in countries where the rates on these instruments were less controlled than those on bank instruments. Thus, in Korea, commercial paper accounted for 43% of the value of money market instruments in 1989, as compared with 2.5% for interbank call money. Among the principal issuers of commercial paper in Korea were nonbank financial institutions (NBFIs) that used commercial paper as a deposit substitute. Although the rates on commercial paper were ostensibly controlled by the government during the period studied, they were less rigorously policed and permitted to rise somewhat higher than the rates on bank deposits. In the Philippines, promissory notes of corporations and individuals were major money market instruments, accounting for over 47% of all trading in money market instruments. This was largely due to the presence of price controls on other instruments. On the other hand, commercial paper never developed in Singapore, where ample funding was available from banks at reasonable, market-determined interest rates.

Government instruments were not generally a good instrument for liquidity management, owing to controlled prices and the related lack of active secondary markets.

THE DEVELOPMENT OF THE MONEY MARKETS

Most of the money markets in our study grew not only in relation to the size of their respective economies but also, and more significantly, in relation to the size of the country's total financial system. Furthermore, the money markets did not just grow but also became more complex, encompassing more instruments and more participants. However, the studies generally reported less satisfactory development of their secondary markets than of their primary markets.

The Importance of Money Markets

Evidence of the growing size and economic importance of money markets can be gauged by the ratio of outstanding value of money market instruments to GDP (MM/GDP) as set out in Table 1.5. This table groups the countries into three categories indicating the basic financial policy stance of their governments, which is seen as influencing the development of their money markets.

By far the most developed and extensive money markets were in the international financial centers of Singapore and Hong Kong. Starting from a higher level than the other countries did in 1980 and growing more in absolute terms, they reached MM/GDP ratios of 8.95 and 3.14, respectively,

Table 1.5. Ratio of the Outstanding Value of Money Market Instruments to GDP, 1980 and 1988

Country	Domestic Currency						Foreign Currency		Total	
	Total		Government		Nongovernment					
	1980	1988	1980	1988	1980	1988	1980	1988	1980	1988
Financial centers										
Singapore	0.93	1.20	0.13	0.12	0.80	1.08	2.73	7.75	3.66	8.95
Hong Kong	1.18	1.34	0.00	0.00	1.18	1.34	0.39	1.80	1.58	3.14
Open exchange systems										
Malaysia	0.43	0.93	0.34	0.66	0.09	0.27	0.11	0.15	0.54	1.08
Indonesia	0.07	0.17	0.00	0.03	0.07	0.14	0.09	0.08	0.16	0.25
Japan (1924–30)	0.03	0.02	0.00	0.00	0.03	0.02	0.00	0.00	0.03	0.02
Closed exchange systems										
Korea	0.07	0.27	0.00	0.13	0.07	0.14	0.00	0.00	0.07	0.27
Philippines	0.20	0.25	0.11	0.23	0.09	0.02	0.00	0.00	0.20	0.25
Japan	0.10	0.28	0.02	0.03	0.08	0.25	0.00	0.00	0.10	0.31

Source: Based on country studies.

in 1988. Singapore's ratio more than doubled between 1980 and 1988, and Hong Kong's nearly doubled. Malaysia's ratio also doubled, but it started from a much smaller base than did the international financial centers. All other countries reported much lower overall ratios, despite some impressive gains during the period. Korea's money markets quadrupled in importance, and postwar Japan's almost trebled. Indonesia's grew by two-thirds, while the Philippines' rose only by one-quarter. Prewar Japan, however, had a rather lackluster performance.

Foreign exchange money market instruments accounted for much of the growth of Singapore's and Hong Kong's money markets, as one would expect from international financial centers. In contrast, money market instruments in foreign currencies were insignificant in countries relatively closed to cross-border capital flows—Korea, the Philippines, and postwar Japan. Even in relatively more open countries—Malaysia, Indonesia, and prewar Japan—foreign currency instruments were not important sources of money market growth.

Money markets based on domestic currency instruments grew at more rapid rates in the noninternational financial centers. Malaysia led with strong growth in both government and nongovernment ("private") instruments; its ratio increased from 0.43 to 0.93 during the period.

It is interesting to compare domestic money market (DMM) growth with the two other measures of economic and financial development that we used, GDP per capita and M2/GDP. Table 1.6 gives the results between 1980 and 1988.

Table 1.6. Financial and Money Market Development, 1980–88

Country	GDP per Capita		M2/GDP		DMM/GDP	
	U.S.$ 1988	Growth 1980–88	Ratio 1988	Change 1980–88	Ratio 1988	Change 1980–88
Hong Kong	9,782	7.7%	1.89	173.9%	1.34	13.6%
Indonesia	490	5.2	0.41	115.8	0.17	242.9
Singapore	8,150	6.6	0.88	37.5	1.20	29.3
Malaysia	2,047	5.2	0.72	35.9	0.93	216.3
Japan	23,564	4.0	1.12	30.2	0.28	280.0
Korea	4,081	9.7	0.38	15.2	0.27	385.7
Philippines	648	1.0	0.23	9.5	0.25	25.0

Source: Derived from Tables 1.1, 1.2, and 1.4.

The level and growth rate of domestic money market development did not always parallel the growth of GDP or M2/GDP. Consider the case of Korea, where the level of M2/GDP, 0.38, and the percentage growth in M2/GDP, 15.2%, exceed only those of the Philippines. Yet Korea had the highest real growth of GDP, 9.7%, during the same period. This apparent discrepancy between the real growth of GDP and the growth of the financial sector measured by M2/GDP can be explained in part by looking at the domestic money markets in Korea, which had the highest growth rate during the period, 385.7%. In turn, this reflects the role of NBFIs, which were raising funds by issuing commercial paper and other money market instruments, activities not reflected in M2/GDP.

A more accurate picture of financial activity and development is obtained by including money market instruments in addition to currency and bank deposits as captured in M2. This helps explain the limitations of analyses that rely simply on ratios of M2/GDP to measure financial development.

For example, the M2/GDP ratio for Japan in 1988 suggests that it had one of the more developed financial systems of all the countries in this study. On the other hand, the ratio of DMM/GDP indicates that Japan's domestic money markets were relatively underdeveloped. Japan's DMM/GDP ratio (0.28) was considerably below that of Singapore (1.20), Hong Kong (1.34), and even Malaysia (0.93). How can this be explained? Part of the answer lies in the importance of the Japanese banking sector. As both the Japanese studies point out, the banks were the key players in the Japanese financial system, so people and firms looked to banks for both short-term liquidity and long-term financing and as a place to put excess funds. Japan did not need to develop active money markets. Indeed, the Japanese story suggests that quite significant levels of real economic growth can be achieved without active money markets or, put differently, that banking systems and money markets can, to some degree, be substituted for each other.

The value of government and privately issued instruments in the money markets grew at significantly different rates among the countries included in our study (see Table 1.5). The money markets for government instruments grew in only three countries. Growth in government instruments accounted for much of the domestic money market growth in Malaysia, which reported a 0.66 ratio of government instruments to GDP in 1988, higher than that of any other country. Government instruments also became more important in the Philippines and Korea, where they served as instruments of monetary policy. But in four other countries, government instruments contributed little or nothing to money market growth. Singapore reported a lower ratio in 1988 than in 1980. Indonesia's and Japan's rose slightly, but only to 0.03. Hong Kong had no money markets in government instruments in either year.

Private sector-issued money market instruments showed strong or moderate growth in six countries. They grew fast in postwar Japan (the ratio quadrupled), Malaysia (trebled), and Indonesia and Korea (doubled). But their ratios to GDP remained low, ranging from 0.14 to 0.28. In the international financial centers, private instruments also grew, but at slower rates. Even so, the ratios reached much higher levels than elsewhere (1.08 in Singapore and 1.34 in Hong Kong). Two countries reported declines. Prewar Japan's private money markets' ratio fell slightly from 0.03 to 0.02 as the financial system and the economy declined during the late 1920s. The Philippine market dropped more dramatically, from 0.09 to 0.03. Between 1980 and 1985, the government needed to finance its large budget deficit, and two major crises wreaked havoc on the financial system. Not until after 1985 did money market operations begin to recover.

Japan between the two world wars emerges as an extreme case. In contrast with the other countries, Japan reported no money markets in either government securities or foreign exchange instruments. Despite efforts by the government to promote private money markets, they fell relative to GDP. As we shall see, Japan's experience was the result of important government policies.

The Creation of New Instruments

The core money market is the interbank market. Every country had one from 1970 on, though they functioned with varying degrees of efficiency. From 1970 to the current time, more instruments were added. Financial firms in Hong Kong, Singapore, Korea, postwar Japan, and Malaysia added bankers acceptances (BAs), and even prewar Japan tried to cultivate a similar instrument. Table 1.7 shows the types of instruments used in each country as of 1988. In most countries, the BA market remained small. Financial institutions in five countries added negotiable certificates of deposit (NCDs). NCDs gave investors more liquidity than holding regular time deposits, since they could sell the NCDs before they matured. In four

Table 1.7. Domestic Currency Money Market Instruments, 1988

Instruments	Countries							
	Postwar Japan	Singapore	Hong Kong	Malaysia	Indonesia	Prewar Japan	Korea	Philippines
Government								
Treasury bills	x	x		x			x	x
Central bank			x		x		x	x
Long government paper		x		x				
Private financial institutions								
Interbank	x	x	x	x	x	x	x	x
BAs	x	x	x	x		x	x	
NCDs	x	x	x	x			x	
Repos	x			x			x	x
Other								x
Private nonfinancial institutions								
CP	x	x	x			x	x	x
Notes					x			

countries, financial institutions began to enter into repurchase agreements, permitting financial institutions to lend to and borrow from other entities on a secured basis. Nonfinancial enterprises in six countries issued commercial paper, and in prewar Japan there was an unsuccessful attempt to introduce commercial paper. The existence of commercial paper allowed firms to bypass the banks for their short-term borrowing needs and to offer investors higher-yielding alternatives to bank time deposits.

New types of government securities also appeared during this period. Five countries report the equivalent of U.S. Treasury bills, but only in Malaysia and the Philippines were the markets significant. Instruments issued by the central bank or monetary authority became important in Hong Kong, Indonesia, and Korea, where they were used as tools of monetary or exchange rate policy. Longer-term government securities generally were absent during the period; only Singapore and Malaysia reported these instruments as part of their money markets.

Foreign currency instruments, though less prominent, were important in several countries. Starting in 1967, Singapore's Asian currency deposits were the most striking example of the growing market for offshore deposits in the region. Also, the Monetary Authority of Singapore began to use foreign exchange swaps as its principal instrument of monetary policy. Indonesia's central bank introduced the foreign exchange swap in 1979; starting as a device to protect foreign investors, it subsequently became a tool of monetary and exchange rate policy, as described earlier.

Patterns of Money Market Development

Diverse as the studied countries are, their money markets generally went through four similar stages of development during the 1980s: controlled system, initial liberalization, retrenchment following a crisis, and more aggressive development.

All countries started in the first stage with limited, heavily controlled money markets. The initial steps toward liberalization were to relax controls on interest rates or barriers to the entry of new participants into financial markets. Most of the countries took this step in the early 1980s: Hong Kong, Japan, Indonesia, the Philippines, and Korea. Singapore and Malaysia were the exceptions, starting earlier, in the 1970s. This earlier beginning helped their money markets become relatively more developed by the end of this period.

The third stage was a retrenchment following a crisis. The crises varied: speculative attacks on the Indonesian rupiah, a balance-of-payments crisis in the Philippines, recession in Malaysia, and excess liquidity in Korea. Fraud or market manipulation damaged the money markets in Hong Kong and Singapore and added to the Philippines' already severe problems. The common thread running through most of the crises was sudden, large changes in financial prices, either depreciation of the exchange rate or increases in interest rates that the governments were not prepared to accept. The response was to "shoot the messenger," that is, to curtail the money markets through which the price adjustments were taking place.

Under the pressure of the crisis, the governments changed the rules of the game, renouncing, at least temporarily, their efforts to withdraw controls on prices. The government of Indonesia drastically changed the terms of the contracts, requiring the banks immediately to redeem all their SBPUs that had been discounted at the central bank and concurrently requiring several state-owned enterprises to buy nonnegotiable SBIs. Several other governments forced players to take government paper at nonmarket rates. Malaysia instituted a deposit interest rate cartel among banks to control interest rates. The Philippines forced state-owned organizations to take government paper. Korea forced banks to buy central bank paper. The Japanese government did the same thing in the late 1970s. The overall effect was to undermine the demand for money market instruments and virtually to preclude active secondary markets so necessary for liquidity.

In the fourth stage, governments adopted more aggressive policies to free up and promote money markets after the crisis had passed. Each of the governments moved in this way, although the degree of commitment varied greatly, as we shall see. Gradual liberalization was Korea's response. Activating new secondary market participants in domestic money markets was Indonesia's and Malaysia's. The Philippine government developed new instruments and infrastructure. Almost all governments promoted indirect monetary policy tools.

Within this general sequence, the money markets evolved at different tempos. No case described a big bang, an abrupt and thoroughgoing change that turned the money markets around. No case reported money markets that had fully realized their potential; the transition is continuing in all the countries.

POLICIES AFFECTING MONEY MARKETS

As we have seen, despite experiencing broadly similar phases of development, the money markets in these countries grew at very different rates. At one extreme, Singapore's ratio of domestic currency money market assets to GDP rose from 0.93 to 1.20, up 35% from a high base (see Table 1.5). Malaysia's ratio rose from 0.43 to 0.93, up 116% from a lower base. What explains these differences?

Macroeconomic variables alone do not explain money market growth. Most notably, money market growth does not simply escalate with a growing economy. As we saw, Singapore, Korea, and most of the countries we studied reported moderate to strong growth in GDP, yet their money markets grew at very different rates. Perhaps a faltering economy does affect money market growth, however. The two countries with declining DMM/GDP ratios, the Philippines and prewar Japan, also reported very low rates of GDP growth.

Government policy, as we hypothesized, turned out to be the key to understanding the money markets' development in the countries we examined. Our studies reveal how a wide range of policies affected market growth. Governments helped create money market instruments: in Indonesia (the SBI and SBPU), prewar Japan (trade bills and treasury notes) and postwar Japan (CP and treasury notes), Korea (call market, CP, NCDs, repos, and Monetary Stabilization Bonds), and Malaysia (mortgage-backed bonds, government securities, BAs, and NCDs). A critical issue was whether the government rewarded innovation or prohibited new instruments from being introduced without its express approval. Policies regarding the pricing of financial services affected market development in most countries. The reader is encouraged to review the various studies for their details. A single policy's success or failure is very much a function of the context.

Governmental Commitment to Money Market Development

The governments made very different levels of commitment to their money markets. The studies reveal a constant tension between the policies needed to develop money markets and policies to deal with other, often more pressing, problems. Time and again, when confronted with the immediate prospect of serious difficulty such as a balance-of-payments crisis, a recession, or a financial crisis, the governments would sacrifice the money markets if doing so seemed likely to resolve the crisis. Yet some governments quickly returned to policies that would develop the money markets, whereas others temporized. As a result, in the late 1980s, although all the countries sought to strengthen their money markets, some built enthusiastically on a strong existing base, and others still worked with rudimentary money markets at a much slower pace. We shall describe this in the context of the development of domestic money markets for instruments of private-sector issuers.

The Commitment to Develop Domestic Markets for Nongovernment Instruments

The governments' commitment to develop the private domestic money markets fell into four categories: (1) Some governments fostered the development of their money markets consistently over a long period; (2) others tended to neglect them; (3) some took a stop/go approach; and (4) one government pursued severely inconsistent policies.

Table 1.8 relates the type of government commitment and the growth of these markets from 1980 to 1988.[5] Table 1.6 lists the countries by the increase in their private domestic currency–denominated money market to GDP (PDMM/GDP) ratio and parenthetically adds the base ratio and growth rate. A simple pattern emerges: The governments that continued in their commitment to money market development did achieve moderate to strong growth. Those governments that neglected money market development in favor of other goals achieved small to moderate growth. And those governments with a go/stop/go approach saw a small increase in their PDMM/GDP ratio or even a decline. The government with a basically inconsistent overall policy toward the money markets actually saw them decline relative to GDP.

A broad, continuous commitment to the growth of the money markets. Singapore and Malaysia demonstrated the strongest commitment over long periods of time. These governments slowly unraveled policies of controlling prices, volumes, and access and also offered encouragement so that over time various markets and instruments began to emerge. The process took a long time, starting in the early 1970s and still not completed by the late 1980s.

Singapore exemplifies the process of "managed liberalization." The government liberalized financial policy over the decade of the 1970s and into the 1980s. It gradually liberalized exchange rates and introduced new instruments in the 1970s. The early 1980s saw a financial crisis that led to tighter prudential regulations, but not policies that could damage money market mechanisms. By the early 1980s, government policy had promoted deeper markets, encouraging more sophisticated instruments like negotiable certificates of deposit denominated in SDRs, faster clearing and settlement, and a new government securities market.

Table 1.8. Changes in the Private Domestic Money Markets/GDP Ratio and Each Government's Commitment to Money Market Development, 1988

Changes in PDMM/GNP Ratio from 1980–88	Government Commitment to Money Market Development			
	Manage	*Neglect*	*Stop/Go*	*Basic Conflict*
Large increase in ratio	Singapore: 0.28[a] increase in ratio (from high base, grew 35%) Malaysia 0.18 (low base, grew 200%)	Japan postwar: 0.20 (low base, grew 250%) Hong Kong: 0.16 (high base, grew 14%)		
Small increase in ratio		Korea: 0.07 (low base, grew 100%)	Indonesia: 0.07[a] (low base, grew 100%)	
Decrease			Japan prewar: −0.01 (very low base, fell 33%)	Philippines: −0.07 (low base, fell 78%)

[a] Two examples of how to read this table:
(1) In Singapore, the PDMM/GDP ratio grew by 0.28 from 0.80 in 1980 to 1.08 in 1988, an increase of 35%.
(2) In Indonesia, the PDMM/GDP ratio grew by 0.07 from 0.07 in 1980 to 0.14 in 1988, an increase of 100%.

This is not a history of a government passively waiting for fledgling markets to appear and grow. Rather, Singapore's government promoted money market development directly through regulation and indirectly as a player in the markets. To maintain confidence in its capabilities as an international financial center, the government needed to provide effective but appropriate prudential regulation. To protect domestic banks, it initially limited the power of many foreign banks to operate in domestic financial markets, only gradually lowering the barrier. The government, however, had a presence in the financial system like an elephant in a small pond, so that bankers in Singapore reported the pervasive influence of the Monetary Authority even through informal directives. The government was a substantial supplier and user of funds in the money markets in several ways. It was a major producer in the real economy and had a monopoly in several sectors. It managed the enormous Central Provident Fund. It controlled intermediaries like the Post Office Savings Bank (POSB) and the Development Bank of Singapore (DBS), the largest commercial bank in the country. Its consistent fiscal surplus strongly influenced monetary policy implementation and the choice of money market instruments: The government did not need to issue its own securities to raise money. The government drew on large foreign reserves to intervene in foreign exchange markets as necessary. No simple neutral regulator, the government of Singapore actively managed the development of money markets. The story in Malaysia is similar.

A strategy of neglect. Three governments simply neglected the development of domestic money markets.

Hong Kong had little need for a domestic money market, since such a market's functions were met in other ways. Easily accessible offshore markets offered both a reference rate and a place to put or draw on excess liquidity. In Hong Kong, the government eschewed an active monetary role, so it did not need money markets as a tool of indirect monetary policy. Under these circumstances, Hong Kong had little incentive to develop domestic money markets.

Two interventionist countries that did little to develop domestic money markets were Korea and, particularly up to the 1970s, postwar Japan. They appear to have believed that activist economic policies, such as promoting export-led growth, required them to channel financial resources to key industries or firms. Since a deep money market might divert funds from the real sector, the governments in these countries did not encourage its development.

The Korean government did encourage private nonbank financial institutions (NBFIs) in the 1970s in an effort to draw funds away from the curb market, a large but uncontrolled alternative to the formal market that the government managed. The government tried to promote the use of some money market instruments by these NBFIs, but it also forced market segmentation among financial institutions. Instead of allowing all financial institutions to issue, hold, or trade new instruments, it allocated the new instruments among them: for example, CDs to banks, repos of non-public-sector bonds to securities companies, and cash management accounts to investment companies and later to merchant banks.

A go/stop/go approach. The commitment of two governments—Indonesia and prewar Japan—varied dramatically even over short periods of time. They made frequent adjustments and shifts in direction as circumstances changed, even though they did not abandon the goal of achieving stronger money markets. Whether the cause was external or internal, actual or anticipated, the variability prompted the governments to return to direct controls off and on over many years.

All governments occasionally drew back from policies of market development, as we described earlier. But Indonesia and prewar Japan did so with a frequency that sets them apart. The Indonesia chapter describes at least six distinct policy regimes over a seven-year period. Before 1983, offshore dollar money markets played a leading role. From June 1983 to August 1984 the government let an interbank market emerge by freeing interest rates, removing bank credit ceilings, and trying to balance the supply and demand for funds by state and private banks. Unfortunately, this market was seen to increase exchange rate instability. For two years from September 1984, the central bank managed money markets, limiting interbank borrowing and using SBPUs (bank-issued or -endorsed notes), along with SBIs (central bank notes), to intermediate and control money market operations. In June and July 1987, the government drastically contracted reserve money through use of the SBPU, and the SBI, hurting the development of these instruments. Over the next two and a half years the government tried to stabilize expectations through dramatic reforms that included lifting restrictions on interbank borrowing. As a result, the money markets grew rapidly, integrated, and became more flexible.

Although Indonesia's money markets continued to expand in spite of these shocks, the early Japanese money markets—trade bills and commercial paper—languished or died soon after birth. Japanese government policy tolerated and sometimes encouraged the growth of a few money markets between 1918 and 1927. It allowed the markets to grow before 1918, then tried to change them with a deposit interest rate cartel, and then relaxed some policies, only to tighten up after a financial crisis.

An approach with severe inconsistencies. During the 1980s, the Philippine government's strategy—if that is the appropriate word—was torn by contradictions. Tumultuous forces outside the money markets drove government policy. Poor performance and outright crises in the real economy, coupled with the need to stabilize politics and placate aid supporters, guided both the Marcos and the Aquino governments. Faced with a flagging economy, a serious payments imbalance, external creditors whose advice on policy could not be ignored, sophisticated financial agents skilled at circumventing regulations, and a complex financial system used for political purposes for a decade before the mid-1980s, both Philippine government regimes vainly tried to reconcile several conflicting goals. One was to get the economy into shape, which suggested freeing some controls on the financial system. A second was to service the external debt, for which the government needed to raise money. Another goal was to address, but not necessarily end, mismanagement and corruption. A fourth was to direct funds to politically important activities. These conflicting goals led to confused policy toward the money markets, whose development was actually reversed during part of the period. That is, domestic private money markets became shallower and less sophisticated because of government policy.

The Philippine government's policy toward pricing its own securities crowded out instruments in private money markets, starting in 1984. To deter capital outflows, the central bank issued Jobo bills, priced by negotiation at a rate much higher than that for other instruments. Transactions in private money market instruments (other than interbank call loans) quickly fell and never recovered. Although this is reminiscent of Indonesia's 1987 policies, the Philippine government did not later promote the private money markets as much.

The Commitment to Develop Markets for Government Instruments
The governments' commitment to develop markets for their own instruments was, with one exception, weak or mixed, and particularly so for secondary markets. The commitment did, however, intensify toward the end of the 1980s.

The numbers tell part of the story. Table 1.9 recaps the growth of the ratio of domestic markets for government instruments (GMM) to GDP.

Hong Kong had no market for government securities, and Japan's prewar market was negligible in size. Singapore's market was relatively large but declined during the 1980s. The markets in Japan and Indonesia remained very small. The data for the Philippines and Korea indicating high growth are misleading in that the growth results from extreme pricing policies, as we shall explain later. Malaysia's market, which grew the most, stood out as the exception and represented a case in which the government actively developed the primary market.

Table 1.9. Growth of Government Money Market Instruments Compared with GDP, 1980–88[a]

GMM/GDP 1988	Percentage Growth of GMM/GDP 1980–88[a]				
	No Market	Decline	Increase		
			Low	Medium	High
High					Malaysia (0.66 . . . 94%)
					Philippines (0.23 . . . 109%)
		Singapore (0.12 . . . −8%)			Korea (0.13 . . . up from insignificant base)
Low				Japan postwar (0.03 . . . 50%)	Indonesia (0.03 . . . from 0.00)
Zero	Hong Kong				
	Japan prewar[a]				

[a] Japan prewar is 1924 to 1930.

Government policy in many of the countries discouraged short-term government securities markets from serving the functions that they perform in developed countries. U.S. Treasury bills, for example, are key instruments for reference rates, monetary policy, and liquidity management, as well as tools of fiscal policy. Yet some governments in Asia could not use government securities for some of these purposes. A central government that is prohibited from issuing domestic debt, as in the case of Indonesia, or is unwilling to borrow, as in the case of Hong Kong, or does not need to borrow, as in the case of Singapore, cannot build a large money market in government securities.

Fiscal and monetary policies generally either hurt money markets or failed to promote them.

Government debt priced off the market. The studies record the damage to money market development when a government seeking to issue substantial volumes of debt tries to manipulate the markets by paying below-market interest rates. This occurred in Japan and Korea.

The Japanese government's goal in the mid-1970s was to fund a very large fiscal deficit. Japan allocated new government security issues to many financial institutions at negotiated below-market interest rates. The big banks and other financial firms forced to hold these securities found their portfolios distorted. Although the volume of government securities rose, trading was limited, and the markets did not develop.

The government of Korea used government bonds—the Monetary Stabilization Bonds (MSBs)—to achieve the monetary goal of reducing excess liquidity. The Korean central bank managed the issue of MSBs, beginning in May 1986, in order to absorb the liquidity generated by the trade surplus that began in 1985. The central bank assigned some of the new issues to banks (e.g., 20% in 1989), but most to nonbank financial institutions like life insurance companies (28%) and securities companies (14%). Pricing at issuance was negotiated and appears to have been below market, since despite frequent large variations in yields on the secondary market (and in the corporate bond market), MSB yields at issue rarely changed over much of the period. The primary market for MSBs grew, but secondary markets developed only slowly.

Monetary contraction linked to balance-of-payments outflows. To reverse the capital outflows, the governments of the Philippines and Indonesia used the common monetary tool of driving up domestic interest rates. Indonesia's use of SBIs and the Philippines' use of Jobo bonds to accomplish this increase has already been described.

In the Philippines, high interest rates on government bonds promoted the growth of its own securities market but crowded out private instruments long after the crisis ended. The government played by the rules of the game, manipulating the price of its securities rather than simply commanding others to buy them. By 1988, government securities accounted for 37%

of all money market assets, having had almost no share in 1980. We cannot describe this growth as healthy.

In Indonesia, state-owned enterprises were forced to buy SBIs by cashing in bank time deposits. This raised money market interest rates and forced a large inflow of foreign exchange to replenish the level of required bank reserves. This action reversed the speculation, at least in the short run, but it undermined the credibility of the SBI as a market-based monetary policy instrument.

Money market instruments as tools for indirect monetary policy. Building money markets to serve as tools of indirect monetary policy seems to have caught the attention of governments in the region, particularly from the mid-1980s. As they relinquished the direct tools of monetary policy, such as credit ceilings, the governments needed to be able to affect monetary aggregates and rates by buying or selling instruments in financial markets. For this, money markets were a prerequisite. Some efforts to develop these tools were more successful than others.

Some minimum market size is necessary for a market in treasury bills to become a useful monetary tool. Several country studies reported that the volume of such instruments was too small for a secondary market to develop in that country. The laudable conservative policy of minimizing the fiscal deficit collides with the potential development of a monetary policy tool.

The authorities in Singapore recognized the need for reference rates as benchmarks. Yet the government securities market was small and contracting (see Table 1.9) because of fiscal surpluses; indeed, no bonds were even issued between 1984 and 1986. Undaunted, the government in May 1987 launched a range of short-term instruments for regular and frequent issue through six primary dealers who also had to keep markets liquid. Denominations were set low ($5,000 for bills) to attract individual investors. Yet the secondary market did not grow because the outstanding volume was too small. The Singapore monetary authorities continued to rely on the foreign exchange swap as the primary open market instrument.[6]

The Japanese government faced a similar dilemma in February 1986 when it started to use treasury bills as an open market tool. To this end, the central bank introduced a six-month treasury bill to be issued in a competitive auction. Unfortunately, this coincided with a declining demand by the government for funds; indeed, the public sector's share of all domestic funds more than halved, falling from 44% between 1975 and 1984 to only 19% between 1985 and 1989. By 1989, treasury bills accounted for barely 4% of outstanding money market balances. Shoichi Royama (Chapter 9) found this market still not well developed. Chapter 8, on prewar Japan, also explains that the volume of treasury bills was so limited that no secondary market could develop.

The confluence of three factors seems to have produced a strong government paper market in Malaysia. The government wanted its securities as an open market tool. The supply of government paper, issued to fund the deficit, was adequate for a secondary market to develop: Government money market instruments were already 34% of the GDP in 1980 and grew to 66% by 1988 (see Table 1.9). The government also promoted the necessary institutional infrastructure for this money market.

Institution building by the Malaysian government took place over many years. For treasury bills, the government devised a system of weekly tenders as early as 1973 and set up a system of principal dealers as underwriters and market makers in 1989, thus promoting liquidity in the secondary markets. The dealers were rewarded with the exclusive power to implement open market operations and to tap the central bank's rediscount window. To promote trading, the government offered attractive rediscount rates. The central bank was the market maker, initially making markets at posted yields and then switching to market yields. It is unclear how effective these policies were, since the authors of the chapter on Malaysia (Chapter 5) still see secondary markets as thin.

Prudential regulations seem to have both promoted and impeded the development of money markets in Malaysia. Liquidity requirements stimulated primary demand by requiring financial institutions to hold high volumes of government securities. Discount houses had to keep most investable funds in short-term government paper. Commercial banks, merchant banks, and finance companies had to hold 10% to 17% of their deposits in liquid assets, mainly short-term government securities. These were ready-made primary markets. Secondary markets did not develop as rapidly, however, because in order to comply with the liquidity requirements, financial institutions often held securities from issue to maturity.

Three points emerge. The minimum size for government securities markets to be useful open market tools seems high: Malaysia's, at 34% of GDP in 1980, was clearly adequate; Singapore's, at 12% to 13% throughout the decade, perhaps was not. Second, an across-the-board effort to build a market infrastructure and promote a market orientation may be needed if a government wants money markets to serve as instruments of monetary policy. Third, careful attention must be given to the institutions and systems in the market as well as prudential regulation.

A COMPARATIVE EVALUATION OF THE EFFECTS OF POLICIES

The authors of the chapters in this book gathered and analyzed data that permitted a systematic comparison of policies and market performance across the countries. Many factors threatened to defeat a careful comparison. Countries presented data in different ways according to varying definitions. The macroeconomic, social, and political context was, to say the least, not the same from one country to the next. Policies addressed different problems, using different tools, in the countries. The common methodology was part of our solution to cope with these problems.

Methodology

The researchers agreed in advance to evaluate the way that government policies affected the efficiency and stability of the money markets in the country by using quantitative and qualitative tests.

Efficiency referred simply to operating efficiency. We did not test for allocative efficiency, an even more daunting task. The notion was that well-functioning money markets would equate the price of financial instruments with their investment value. We used several indicative measures to test for operating efficiency, since we realized we could not directly compare the cost and return on money market transactions. We asked, first, whether interest rates of important money market instruments moved with a reference interest rate. This required us to identify reference rates for each country, no easy task given the absence of competitive money markets in many countries and the barriers to using offshore markets that would have also given reference rates, such as LIBOR and SIBOR. Second, we asked whether high degrees of concentration or segmentation indirectly suggested a lesser degree of efficiency. We initially considered several other measures but found inadequate data across the countries.

Stability was defined in terms of the variance in prices in the market over time. Governments might seek stability in a financial market to protect the system itself and to promote real economic activity. Although one might believe that a market becomes increasingly stable as variance in prices decreases, absolute stability suggests price fixing that would impede rather than promote market development. Since the acceptable degree of stability would vary by country, we relied on interviews to learn whether very stable indicators suggested an inflexible market that failed to reflect changes in the underlying forces of supply and demand.

We used these measures of efficiency and stability for both quantitative and qualitative analyses. Quantitative analysis appears in the individual country studies as well as Ouliaris's econometric analysis, which used common tests for reference rates and efficiency in most of the countries. Qualitative analysis included case studies offering a chance to analyze key events, like a balance-of-payments crisis or a financial crisis, that called for responsive government policies. The authors examined the policies and their effects on the money markets.

Findings about Efficiency

Findings about market efficiency and the effect of government policy on it confirmed the story in the previous sections of this chapter. We distinguished between efficiency measured by rate integration and that measured by market segmentation and concentration.

Money Market Rate Determination: Integration with a Reference Rate

By the late 1980s, reference rates existed in most of the countries. In many but not all of the countries, the rates in at least some domestic money markets were well enough integrated with the reference rates for one to describe the markets as efficient by this measure. In some cases, this was due to the international character of the country's financial system.

As markets in several countries became increasingly internationalized, domestic rates correlated with offshore reference rates more closely. In Hong Kong after 1982, the Singapore interbank offer rate in U.S. dollars (SIBOR) drove the Hong Kong interbank U.S. dollar rate (HIBOR) but not the reverse, and HIBOR drove domestic money market rates. This indicates that external interest rates influenced local interest rates more after Hong Kong linked the exchange rate to the U.S. dollar. In Indonesia, rates in the market for thirty-day SBIs showed a close correlation (0.86) to the reference rate (LIBOR plus the central bank foreign exchange swap premium). The reference rate may also have influenced the seven-day SBI rate from 1988 on. But as we explain further later, rate movements in other domestic money markets did not correlate with the reference rate. In Singapore, SIBOR was a significant determinant of three domestic rates: the one-month interbank rate, the one-month fixed deposit rate, and the prime lending rate. All three domestic rates moved together and responded quickly, despite the high volatility in SIBOR. The interbank rate was a very good predictor of domestic interest rates in Singapore. Finally, in Malaysia, Ouliaris's comparative analysis found a fairly close relationship between the ex-post return on the potential foreign reference rate (SIBOR adjusted for exchange rate changes) and Malaysia's interbank rate, but not on the deposit rate or the average lending rate.

Some money markets were not integrated into international markets, even though the country was open to foreign exchange movements. In Indonesia, the interbank market correlated so poorly with the external reference rate that there was probably no relationship. In 1989 the interbank rate declined while the reference rate was rising. The authors note that during the whole period from 1983 on, the central bank was setting rates for the SBI, SBPU, and foreign exchange swap, rationing the latter two and at times limiting interbank borrowing by private banks. Interest rates on short-term time deposits at state-owned banks correlated better with the reference rate than did the interbank rate, but still not strongly (0.66). The correlation improved after 1987. In prewar Japan, short-term rates were independent of international financial markets. Finally, even in Malaysia, Ouliaris found overall that SIBOR had little if any significant influence on the deposit rate or the average lending rate. SIBOR was more variable, which suggested some monopoly power of Malaysian banks in the domestic money markets. Not surprisingly, researchers for countries with foreign exchange controls, like Korea, did not identify any significant foreign reference rates.

Some domestic markets were efficient despite reasons to expect the opposite. In Hong Kong, HIBOR was integrated with the bank lending rate (BLR). Unlike Malaysia, the licensed Hong Kong banks' market power, arising from their holding of 90% of short-term customer deposits, still was not sufficient for them to insulate domestic deposit rates from the foreign reference rate, HIBOR. In Korea, the government bond, commercial paper, and call market rates showed strong comovements from the mid-1970s through the 1980s, probably because of interest rate controls. The formal and informal or curb markets also were integrated, but statistical comparisons gave mixed results concerning the degree.

In Malaysia, money markets were found to be more efficient in the period before 1984 than after, measured against a domestic reference rate. The strong growth of Malaysia's money markets might prompt one to expect an increase in efficiency instead. Individual markets operated efficiently between 1979 and 1984, in that yields on any particular instrument moved randomly. The 1985/86 government antirecession stabilization policies—most notably the deposit interest cartel—reduced efficiency.

Some domestic money markets were not efficient. In the Philippines, Ouliaris concluded that the only real candidate for a reference rate, the treasury bill rate, was not in fact a significant determinant of rates in the other money markets he examined. The authors of the Philippines study believed that deregulation in 1981 increased efficiency, but they relied on an indirect measure of efficiency: liquidity, defined as the difference between the highest and lowest selling rates in the market. In Korea, Ouliaris found no reference rate and concluded that the Korean market was not very efficient. The authors of the Korea chapter identified the MSB rate as a source of the problems. The MSB rate did not move strongly with government bond, commercial paper, or call rates. In fact, the MSBs disrupted domestic money markets, pushing domestic interest rates above international rates because the MSB yields had to rise to keep them attractive. In Indonesia, the interbank rate correlated poorly with other domestic money market rates during the period that the central bank set rates on those other instruments. In prewar Japan, Ouliaris suspected monopoly power in the banks because even though demand and time deposit rates were relatively constant, the loan rate, the bill discount rate, and the overdraft rate moved and did so in tandem. The interbank rate, usually a proxy for the marginal cost of funds, was not integrated with the other rates, meaning that it would have been a poor reference rate. None of these findings is surprising in light of the discussion earlier in this chapter.

Efficiency Measured by Concentration and Segmentation

Another proxy for efficiency was the degree of market concentration and segmentation.

In Malaysia, incomplete interest rate integration was due to the banks' market power. Bank concentration declined before the 1984 recession but rose again during and after, when the government permitted a deposit rate cartel. Concentration continued after the policy ended, however, which suggests the tenacity of market disruptions. The banks' ability to pass on the entire cost of funds to borrowers also suggests the banks' market power. To counter these structural problems, the authors recommended structural changes in order to increase efficiency: allowing more new institutions in the interbank market, encouraging new instruments and bank mergers and acquisitions, and setting up an independent credit rating agency to help the commercial paper market.

In Korea, the authors examined the market for commercial paper (CP). For them, the question was how specific policies affected efficiency in this market. They measured the volumes and market share of the four largest dealers and borrowers and learned that efficiency was increased by policies introducing cash management accounts in mid-1984; permitting entry of new dealers in 1981, 1982, and 1983; and ending compensated balances, which liberalized prices, so that the CP rate rose 0.5% in the next month to become a reference rate for other money market instruments. Efficiency should have been increased by the policy promoting CP issued by small and medium-size industries, but the results were unclear. Efficiency was hindered by the policy of using MSBs, since the market share of the four top dealers grew.

These outcomes confirm what one would expect. Increased diversity of instruments, new entrants, and freer, more transparent pricing should, and did, increase market efficiency. The MSBs, which were not priced or managed according to market principles, not surprisingly may have damaged efficiency.

The Korean call market was so deeply segmented that the researchers concluded it was inefficient. As the segmentation decreased, the authors reported increasing efficiency. During the period labeled *financial liberalization,* from 1984 to 1989, government policies restricted the NBFIs' access to funds. Call market rates did not reach market levels. In late 1989, new policies partly freed the call market rates. In barely one year, the market more than tripled in size, but the NBFIs still paid much higher rates than the national banks did.

Operating efficiency in the Philippines may have been reduced by a policy that was supposed to increase it. In the securities trading market, fourteen institutions held a 55% share of the market in 1980 when the policy of universal banking was adopted. By 1987, only five institutions held a 55% share, in which no investment houses or finance companies were included. This policy, designed to strengthen the market, seems to have hurt efficiency.

Stability

General cross-country conclusions about money market stability and the effect of policy could not be subjected to meaningful quantitative analysis. The measures, periods, and markets varied enormously from study to study, making it very difficult to find a basis for useful comparison. Nevertheless, the findings from individual studies are interesting.

The stability of money markets within one country could vary widely. In Indonesia, the interbank market was highly volatile. The standard deviation of month-end rates from June 1983 to December 1989 was 4.74. By contrast, LIBOR's was only 1.42. The interbank rate was most volatile between 1984 and 1986, when the market was restricted. On the other hand, the SBI market was very stable, since the central bank managed the rate.

The policy of a country halfway around the world from Singapore may have contributed to the declining volatility of its money market rates. Volatility fell dramatically from 1983. The authors of Chapter 7 hypothesized that this was due to the U.S. Federal Reserve's switch from monetary to interest rate targets in the fall of 1982, which reduced the variance of SIBOR.

Internationalization seems to have fostered stability in Hong Kong. After the exchange rate was linked to the U.S. dollar, the deposit rate changed less often than it had before.

Successful macroeconomic policies fostered stability in Korea. Statistical comparisons of money market rate movements revealed that stability was a function of inflation. During the period of high inflation from 1976 to 1982, money market rates were high and volatile. In the period of low inflation that began in 1983, money market rates were lower and more stable in general. This was not true, however, for the call market, where rates showed less variance in the period of high inflation than after 1982. The authors of Chapter 4 speculated that collusion explained the stability in the earlier period and argued that one should expect the degree of variance in short-term rates that was found after 1982.

Government policies affected the stability of specific money markets for better or worse. The sudden, unexpected, and basic change in the central bank's rediscount terms profoundly affected Indonesia's SBPU market (for promissory notes). It disappeared for several years. Even while the market worked, the central bank had to set quotas for each bank in order to control the growth of reserve money. The introduction of MSBs clearly reduced the stability of Korea's commercial paper market, but the authors of Chapter 4 found no clear effect on stability from the policies that introduced CMAs, permitted the entry of new dealers periodically, or promoted CP issued by small and medium-size firms. This contrasts with the positive effects on efficiency.

The Relation Between Efficiency and Stability

At the outset of this research, we supposed that there might be trade-offs between efficiency and stability. Governments contemplating financial liberalization certainly fear new and extreme swings in market interest rates and returns. The notion is that as markets become more efficient, they respond to new information faster than before, which leads to greater variance in interest rates, at least in the short term. To some extent, the trade-off did exist. But the relationship was much more complex, with efficiency and stability sometimes moving together.

Malaysia offers a clear example of the trade-off between falling efficiency and rising stability. The deposit interest rate cartel in the mid-1980s reduced efficiency and increased stability. This was a clear choice by the government. On the other hand, we found no clear case in which a rise in efficiency led to a decline in stability, according to quantitative tests. This may seem remarkable, since this trade-off is one reason that governments object to liberalization. In part, this is due to the difficulty of measuring the short-term impact that policies have on efficiency. In 1984, the Indonesian government watched liberal policies lead to greater variability in interbank rates and then reimposed limits on interbank borrowing. We could not measure the change in efficiency in the sixteen months before the policy reversal, so we do not know whether efficiency grew in that short period.

We found no trade-off as both efficiency and stability increased in some cases. In Hong Kong, internationalization brought greater efficiency and stability during the 1980s. Perhaps this occurred because government involvement had been limited throughout, so there was no period of instability as the markets adjusted to a much more liberal regime. In Indonesia, as the SBI market became increasingly efficient (measured by integration with the reference rate), the rates were stable (i.e., had lower variance). In Korea, the introduction of the CMAs, the new entrants, and the end of compensating balances increased efficiency in the CP market without a decrease in stability.

In some countries where there was no trade-off, factors outside the money markets may have been important. In Singapore, domestic interest rates were determined efficiently against an external reference rate, and volatility decreased, possibly because of a change in U.S. monetary policy that made the reference rate more stable. Singapore's markets reflected this shift. In Korea, lower inflation brought more efficiency and stability to several markets.

Both efficiency and stability decreased in two countries. Indonesia's interbank market became less efficient (measured by integration with the reference rate) and was highly volatile. Korea's MSBs reduced efficiency and stability in other money markets.

Governments seemed to prefer stability to efficiency, at least when they believed that they had to choose. In Malaysia, the deposit interest rate cartel was government policy. The Philippines central bank preferred a stability that protected the oligopolists and inhibited money market development. But the Hong Kong government's preference for stability did not force a trade-off with efficiency. The authors (Chapter 2) reported that "the government does not seem to put the same emphasis on market efficiency as it does on stability. . . . It still maintains the . . . deposit interest rate cartel and until recently, has made no special effort to foster the . . . new financial instruments." They added, however, that stability was not gained at the expense of efficiency.

CONCLUSIONS

Some important conclusions can be drawn from this study:

1. The development of money markets is not purely a function of the level of economic development or even financial development as measured by the ratio of M2 to GDP. Money markets may grow in countries where banks are neither dominant nor efficient, as in Korea where NBFIs played a significant role, or they may be neglected where banks are dominant and perform well, as in postwar Japan. Development may also hinge on the need for the markets. Malaysia needed a market in government paper to finance its deficits and control domestic money supply. Hong Kong did not. The reasons for the development or lack of development of money markets are ultimately shaped by government policy, which responds to the needs of the country.

2. Money markets generally perform four key functions. Interest rates on money market instruments serve as reference rates for pricing debt instruments; government or central bank instruments are tools of monetary policy; money market instruments permit liquidity management; and short-term interbank markets can supply funds to finance longer-term loans when financial intermediaries transform maturities. By the end of the period we studied, most countries had developed reference rates, had not developed liquid government debt markets, and had diverse results in developing instruments that permit liquidity management.

3. Money market development, in terms of growth and size, was most significant in the international financial centers, Hong Kong and Singapore, but was largely built on the foreign component (dollar-denominated instruments). Domestic money markets, however, grew most significantly in nonfinancial centers, particularly Malaysia.

4. Diverse as these countries are, their money markets generally went through four similar stages of development during the 1980s: controlled system, initial liberalization, retrenchment following a crisis, and more aggressive development.

5. Policies affecting domestic money markets differed in content and impact with respect to nongovernment and government instruments. For nongovernment instruments, the key was whether the government was com-

mitted to the development of such markets: Singapore and Malaysia and, to a much lesser extent, postwar Japan had such a commitment. Hong Kong and Korea did not, and Indonesia and prewar Japan had stop/go policies. The Philippine government had no clear policy at all during this period.

For government instruments, countries without the need for central government borrowing (Hong Kong, Indonesia, prewar Japan, Singapore), naturally did less than those with significant government debt (Malaysia and the Philippines) did to develop these markets. But some countries that had no government debt saw the need to develop close substitute instruments as tools for monetary policy. This attempt was largely unsuccessful in promoting market-based money markets, because the markets were too small or the instruments were not priced at market prices.

The case of Indonesia demonstrates a dilemma for developing countries trying to develop quasi-government money market instruments: Their development may be sacrificed to short-term macroeconomic concerns.

6. Our study looked at the efficiency and stability of money markets. Hong Kong and Singapore had efficient markets, in that the rates on domestic instruments integrated with a reference rate. There was a mixed picture in Indonesia, where there was very poor integration of the major market—the interbank market—but better integration of the SBI market. The pictures in Korea and Malaysia were also mixed. Korea had covariance in the rates of domestic instruments but had no identifiable reference rate. The observed covariance might have reflected managed rate policy rather than market forces. In Malaysia, rate integration decreased after 1984 when the deposit interest rate cartel was established. The Philippines lacked rate integration throughout the period.

The stability of price and volumes in money markets was generally difficult to assess. Where the rates were stable the causes were varied: in Korea because of rate management and in Singapore because of U.S. monetary policy. Indeed, we found *no* necessary trade-off between efficiency and stability.

NOTES

1. If these deposits were included in the M2 figure, it would about double the ratio for 1988, bringing the ratio up to the level of Singapore and Malaysia.

2. The standard works on money markets in the United States are by Cook and Rowe (1986) and Stigum (1990). For the United Kingdom, see Shaw 1991. Most texts on money and banking or financial markets contain chapters on the role and development of money markets in the United States and other developed countries, for example Wood and Wood 1985.

3. A parallel study by Emery (1991) provides a somewhat different perspective on a similar set of issues.

4. Technically speaking, there was still exchange risk, but it was the risk of depreciation of the U.S. dollar against currencies other than the Hong Kong dollar.

5. Earlier sections of this chapter catalogue the difficulties of arraying countries' markets along some spectrum of growth. Even the simple measure PDMM/GDP generates problems for comparison. In one country, the ratio might grow fast — by even 200% — but from a very low base, such as from 0.01 to 0.02. In another country, the ratio might grow slower — by perhaps 33% — but from a high base, such as from 1.00 to 1.33.

6. The ample availability of a ready substitute, the foreign exchange swap, which served very well both interest rate and exchange rate objectives, made reliance on government securities for open market operations a second-best instrument.

REFERENCES

Coates, W. L., Jr. and D. R. Khatkhate, eds. 1980. *Money and Monetary Policy in Less Developed Countries.* London, Pergamon.

Cook, T. Q., and T. D. Rowe, eds. 1986. *Instruments of the Money Market.* 6th ed. Richmond, VA: Federal Reserve Bank of Richmond.

Drake, P. J. 1980. *Money, Finance and Development.* New York, Wiley.

Emery, R. F. 1991. *The Money Markets of Developing East Asia.* New York, Praeger.

Fry, M. J. 1988. *Money, Interest, and Banking in Economic Development.* Baltimore, Johns Hopkins University Press.

Gurley, J. G. 1967. "Financial Structure in Developing Countries." In *Fiscal and Monetary Problems in Developing States,* edited by D. Krivine. New York: Praeger.

McKinnon, R. I. 1973. *Money and Capital in Economic Development.* Washington DC: Brookings Institution.

Shaw, E. R. 1991. *The London Money Market.* 3rd ed. London: Heinemann.

Shaw, E. S. 1973. *Financial Deepening in Economic Development.* New York: Oxford University Press.

Stigum, M. 1990.*The Money Market.* 3rd ed. Homewood, IL: Dow Jones-Irwin.

Wood, J. H., and N. L. Wood. 1985. *Financial Markets.* San Diego: Harcourt Brace Jovanovich.

World Bank. 1989. *World Development Report 1989.* Washington, DC: World Bank.

CHAPTER 2
MONEY MARKETS IN HONG KONG

RICHARD YAN-KI HO
YU-HON LUI
DANIEL WAI-WAH CHEUNG

Over the past decade, numerous changes have taken place in the banking sector. Hong Kong has been effectively transformed into an international financial center where not only financial transactions but also actual operations are carried out. The internationalization also brought with it an influx of foreign banks in the 1970s, especially when the Hong Kong government lifted the moratorium on bank licensing in 1978.[1] Unlike Singapore, Hong Kong is an integrated financial center without any delineation between offshore and domestic banking business. Thus, foreign banks could always enter into the domestic market, provided that they had been granted a bank license.[2] This fact has created intense competitive pressure in the domestic banking sector.

The internationalization of banking came in the wake of China's open door policy, which started in 1978. One of the most important effects of this policy was the change in the competitive strategies of the Bank of China (BOC) Group, which is made up of thirteen sister banks owned by the People's Republic of China. Since 1979, the position of this group of banks has changed from highly conservative and stagnant to relatively aggressive and innovative. Their move intensified the competition in the Hong Kong banking market, which was long dominated by a locally incorporated but British-managed banking group, the Hongkong and Shanghai Banking Corporation.

Until recently, Hong Kong was well known for its lax government regulations. However, the laxity of the regulations, together with a sudden competitive shock from foreign banks and the "good" old British tradition of bank secrecy, also created an environment conducive to fraudulent activities and the banking crisis that ensued. One result of this banking crisis was undoubtedly the hastening of the regulatory process, which gave birth in 1986 to the Banking Ordinance and the many guidelines issued by the government.

The money market is an integral part of the Hong Kong financial system. It provides a source for short-term funding for deficit units and a short-term investment outlet for surplus units. In Hong Kong, the money market is composed of short-term deposits and loans with financial institutions, and money market instruments. Although Hong Kong is a major financial center in the Asia Pacific region, its money market is less sophisticated than those of most other Asian countries in terms of the number and types of money market instruments traded. In addition to direct deposits and loans with financial institutions, certificates of deposit issued by financial institutions and commercial paper issued by corporations are popular. Until March 13, 1990, there was no short-term government bills market because the Hong Kong government ran a surplus in its budget.

THE FINANCIAL SYSTEM

The banking structure in Hong Kong has a "three-tier" system because three types of institutions are authorized to take deposits from the public:[3] (1) licensed banks, (2) licensed deposit-taking companies (LDTCs, now renamed RLBs), and (3) registered deposit-taking companies (RDTCs, now renamed DTCs). As shown in Table 2.1, these institutions have different restrictions. The licensed banks do not have any restrictions except that they must comply with the interest rate rule set by the Hong Kong Association of Banks.[4] The LDTCs (RLBs) can accept only deposits of more than H.K.$500,000 per account, and the RDTCs (DTCs) may accept deposits more than H.K.$100,000 per account with a maturity

Table 2.1. The Three-Tier Banking System (Values in H.K.$)

	Licensed Banks[a]	RLBs[b]	DTCs[c]
Minimum capital	150m for local banks	100m	25m
Minimum deposit for an account	No	0.50m	0.10m
Maturity restrictions (months) on deposits	No	No	Not < 3 months
Interest rate restrictions	[d]	No	No

[a] The minimum capital requirement for locally incorporated licensed banks was H.K.$100 million before March 1989. For foreign banks there is a minimum asset requirement of U.S.$14 billion but no minimum capital requirement.

[b] Formerly known as licensed deposit-taking companies, with a minimum capital requirement of H.K.$75 million.

[c] Formerly known as registered deposit-taking companies, with a minimum capital requirement of H.K.$10 million.

[d] Need to observe the interest rate rule of the HKAB.

of not less than three months. All these institutions must comply with a minimum capital requirement, which is most stringent for licensed banks and least stringent for the DTCs.

On March 8, 1989, the commissioner of banking, Mr. Nicolle, announced the establishment of a new three-tier system, under which there are, again, three types of institutions: the licensed banks, the restricted licensed banks (RLBs), and the deposit-taking companies (DTCs). These three types of authorized institutions are equivalent to those in the old system, namely, the licensed banks, the licensed deposit-taking companies (LDTCs), and the registered deposit-taking companies (RDTCs). The minimum capital requirements for these three types of institutions are as follow:

Locally incorporated licensed banks	H.K.$150 million
Restricted licensed banks (RLBs)	H.K.$100 million
Deposit-taking companies (DTCs)	H.K.$25 million

There were three main reasons for adopting the new system. First, it was necessary to provide a different and yet respected status for the LDTCs (RLBs) vis-à-vis the RDTCs (DTCs), since they are not allowed to use the word *bank* in their promotional materials. Second, the government wanted to facilitate the establishment of RLBs.[5] And third, the government wanted to strengthen both the criteria for authorizing deposit-taking institutions and the protection of depositors.

The Licensed Banks

The licensed banks are the largest component of the financial system. At the end of 1989, they accounted for 91% of the total assets, 92% of the total loans, and 93% of the total deposits of all the authorized institutions (licensed banks, RLBs [LDTCs], and DTCs [RDTCs]). The licensed banks carry out the normal commercial banking business, that is, accepting various types of deposits (current deposit, savings deposits, and time deposits in both the local currency and foreign currencies); extending various types of loans in both the local currency and foreign currencies; dealing in foreign exchange and precious metals such as gold and silver; dealing in securities such as stocks, certificates of deposits, and commercial paper; and discounting trade bills and bankers acceptances. Some banks also provide financial and investment advisory services for both corporations and individuals. Of the three groups of authorized institutions, licensed banks have the fewest restrictions because they can offer checking accounts and accept small-denomination (less than H.K.$500,000), short-term deposits (less than three months).

Table 2.2 shows the licensed banks' balance sheet items in 1980 and 1989. Total assets had a compounded annual growth rate of 33.13% over

Table 2.2. Balance Sheets of Licensed Banks

| | 1980 | | 1989 | | Compound Annual Growth Rate (%) |
	H.K.$m	% in Total	H.K.$m	% in Total	1980–89
Liabilities					
Due to banks and DTCs in Hong Kong	55,760	18.90	410,255	10.59	24.83
Due to banks abroad	118,067	40.03	2,341,970	60.47	39.37
Customers' deposits	86,753	24.41	937,654	24.20	30.28
NCDs outstanding	2,041	0.69	31,019	0.80	35.30
Other liabilities	32,538	11.03	153,448	3.96	18.81
Total	294,979	100.00	3,874,345	100.00	33.13
Assets					
Cash	2,092	0.71	5,467	0.14	11.26
Due from banks and DTCs in Hong Kong	47,617	16.14	446,508	11.52	28.24
Due from banks abroad	78,366	26.57	1,979,330	51.09	43.16
NCDs held	4,106	1.39	17,641	0.46	17.58
Loans and advances	124,535	42.22	1,173,005	30.28	28.30
Bank acceptances	5,743	1.95	23,245	0.60	16.81
Floating-rate notes and commercial paper	1,766	0.60	54,679	1.41	46.44
Treasury bills and securities	7,425	2.52	71,763	1.85	28.67
Other assets	23,329	7.91	102,708	2.65	17.90
Total	294,979	100.00	3,874,345	100.00	33.13

Source: Hong Kong Monthly Digest of Statistics, various issues.

the nine-year period. The most important items are the "Due to banks abroad" and "Due from banks abroad," accounting for about 50% to 60% of total assets/liabilities and with a compounded annual growth of about 40%. These two items indicate the importance of the Hong Kong banking sector's international banking activities. The second most important items are "Customers' deposits" on the liability side and "Loans and advances" on the asset side, accounting for about 24% to 30% of total assets/liabilities but with a lower growth rate than that of total assets, indicating the declining share of these traditional items. The third most important items are the interbank items, that is, "Due to banks and DTCs in Hong Kong" and "Due from banks and DTCs in Hong Kong." These interbank transactions are the most prominent component of the money market in Hong Kong, and as will be made clear later, the local banks are usually the net lenders, and the foreign banks, especially the Japanese banks, are the net borrowers in this market. Items such as NCDs (negotiable certificates of deposit) outstanding, floating-rate notes, commercial paper, and treasury bills all carry little weight on the balance sheet, implying that these instruments may not be very important to the Hong Kong money market. But we also should note that these items grew very rapidly.

The Deposit-Taking Companies (DTCs)

The two types of deposit-taking companies are the RLBs (LDTCs) and the DTCs (RDTCs). The RLBs are actually merchant banks or investment banks, which provide a variety of services, such as accepting deposits (of not less than H.K.$500,000 per account), making loans, issuing and underwriting facilities, managing portfolios, dealing in foreign exchange and other securities, and offering financial advice. The DTCs are commonly known as *finance houses*. They accept deposits (of not less than H.K.$ 100,000 per account and with a maturity of not less than three months), offer installment-payment plans and leases, act as a middleman in business transactions, deal in foreign exchange, and make commercial and personal loans. Before the three-tier system was established in July 1981, those DTCs with a deposit share of more than 30% were not considered separately. Then, because the three-tier system prohibited the DTCs from accepting short-term deposits with a maturity of less than three months, deposits flowed back to the licensed banks. Thus in 1989, both kinds of deposit-taking companies accounted for only about 7% of total deposits and 8% of total loans. In other words, the three-tier system boosted the monopoly power of the licensed banks and created an extremely unfavorable environment for the deposit-taking companies, in particular for the DTCs. Table 2.3 shows the asset and liability items of the deposit-taking companies.[6] Note that the growth of deposit-taking companies' total assets was only 11.48%, much less than that of the licensed banks. Again, the three most important items on the liability side are "Due to banks and DTCs in Hong Kong," "Due to banks abroad," and "Customers' deposits." The three most important items on the asset side are "Due from banks and DTCs in Hong Kong," "Due from banks abroad," and "Loans and advances."

The growth rate of the traditional items such as customers' deposits and loans and advances is very low, indicating that these companies are becoming more wholesale oriented. Moreover, this sector has also become more dependent on the interbank market to fund its assets.

The Market Structure

A common method of categorizing banks is by the country of its head office's incorporation. Table 2.4 shows that a large majority of banks are incorporated outside Hong Kong. Indeed, banks incorporated in Hong Kong accounted for only about one-fifth of the total number of banks in 1989. All of its deposit-taking companies are incorporated in Hong Kong, and so the

Table 2.3. Consolidated Balance Sheet of Deposit-Taking Companies

	1980		1989		Compound Annual Growth Rate (%) 1980–89
	H.K.$m	*% in Total*	*H.K.$m*	*% in Total*	
Liabilities					
Due to banks and DTCs in Hong Kong	31,397	22.37	112,116	30.05	15.19
Due to banks abroad	49,961	35.60	86,408	23.16	6.28
Customers' deposits	42,101	30.00	70,004	18.76	5.81
NCDs outstanding	731	0.52	2,877	0.77	16.44
Other liabilities	16,168	11.52	101,713	27.26	22.67
Total	140,358	100.00	373,118	100.00	11.48
Cash	8	a	11	a	3.60
Due from banks and DTCs in Hong Kong	38,636	27.53	76,459	20.49	7.88
Due from banks abroad	24,251	17.28	98,630	26.43	16.89
NCDs held	3,648	2.60	10,138	2.72	12.03
Loans and advances	59,392	42.31	98,893	26.50	5.83
Bank acceptances	450	0.32	820	0.22	6.89
Floating-rate notes and commercial paper	2,061	1.47	38,379	10.29	38.39
Treasury bills and securities	4,427	3.15	20,213	5.42	18.38
Other assets	7,487	5.33	29,574	7.93	16.49
Total	140,358	100.00	373,118	100.00	11.48

a Less than 0.01%.

Source: Hong Kong Monthly Digest of Statistics, various issues.

banking commissioner differentiates them according to their affiliation with commercial banks. In 1989, most of the DTCs (RDTCs) and RLBs (LDTCs) were either subsidiaries of banks or bank-related institutions, with only twenty-eight DTCs and three RLBs having no bank affiliation.

Counting the number of banks by their place of incorporation also may have become less relevant given the wave of mergers and acquisitions that began in the late 1960s. Now it is more meaningful to group banks in Hong Kong according to the nationality of their ownership or management, although until 1986 there were no official statistics on the number of banks by country of ownership. Therefore, banking analysts and practitioners classified the banks in Hong Kong as belonging to one of four groups:[7] the Hongkong and Shanghai Banking Corporation Group, which includes the Hongkong and Shanghai Banking Corporation and a local Chinese bank (the Hang Seng Bank);[8] the Bank of China

Table 2.4. Percentage of Authorized Institutions

	1989	1986
Licensed banks		
Incorporated in Hong Kong	31	32
Incorporated outside Hong Kong	134	116
Unincorporated banks	3	3
Subtotal	165	151
Deposit-taking companies		
Registered deposit-taking companies		
Subsidiaries of licensed banks		
Local	30	35
Foreign	76	84
Subsidiaries of foreign banks not licensed in Hong Kong	46	51
Bank related	22	17
Others	28	67
Subtotal	202	254
Licensed deposit-taking companies		
Subsidiaries of licensed banks		
Local	3	3
Foreign	12	14
Subsidiaries of foreign banks not licensed in Hong Kong	7	9
Bank related	11	10
Others	3	2
Subtotal	36	38
Total	238	292

Group, which includes the thirteen sister banks owned by China; the foreign banks; and the local Chinese banks, very few of which remain since the 1986 banking crisis.[9]

In 1986 the Office of the Banking Commissioner started to publish statistics by country of beneficial ownership (with data going back to 1985). Table 2.5 shows that most of the licensed banks are from the Asia Pacific economies. Hong Kong banks had the largest number in 1985 but were superseded by the Japanese banks in 1989. The number of mainland Chinese banks was the same as that of Hong Kong (a total of 15). The number of Hong Kong banks fell to 15 while the number of Japanese banks increased to 30 in 1989. The number of European banks also increased, from 35 in 1985 to 50 in 1989, and the countries with the largest number of banks in this group were West Germany, France, the United Kingdom, and Italy. The number of U.S. banks declined from 24 to 20, indicating their loss in interest, especially in the retail market.

Table 2.5. Analysis of Authorized Institutions by Country of Beneficial Ownership

Country/Region	Licensed Banks		Deposit-Taking Companies[a]	
	1989	1985	1989	1985
Asia and Pacific				
Hong Kong	15	23	29	61
Australia	5	—	5	9
China	15	13	17	14
India	4	4	4	4
Indonesia	3	2	16	19
Japan	30	20	37	34
Malaysia	3	2	5	6
New Zealand	1	—	1	2
Pakistan	1	1	1	1
Philippines	2	2	7	6
Singapore	4	5	8	10
South Korea	3	3	9	5
Thailand	1	1	8	19
Others	—	—	1	4
Subtotal	87	76	148	199
Caribbean	—	—	1	—
Europe				
Australia	2	—	—	—
Luxembourg/Belgium	3	2	4	5
France	8	8	11	13
Italy	7	3	—	13
Netherlands	3	3	4	5
Norway	1	—	1	—
Republic of Ireland	1	—	—	—
Spain	3	1	—	—
Sweden	3	—	1	—
Switzerland	3	3	2	4
United Kingdom	7	7	13	18
West Germany	9	8	4	4
Others	—	—	2	3
Subtotal	50	35	42	52
Middle East				
Bahrain	1	1	2	2
Iran	1	1	—	—
Others	—	—	4	6
Subtotal	2	2	6	8
North America				
Canada	6	6	5	9
United States	20	34	39	
Subtotal	26	30	39	48
Others	—	—	4	3
Grand total	165	143	238	313

[a] Deposit-taking companies include both LDTCs and RDTCs.

Source: Commissioner of Banking, *Annual Report,* various issues.

Table 2.6. Assets and Deposits: Country/Region of Beneficial Ownership (in H.K.$ billions)

| | Assets | | | | | | Deposits | | | | | |
| | 1989 | | | 1986 | | | 1988 | | | 1986 | | |
	H.K.$	Foreign Currency	Total	H.K.$	Foreign Currency	Total	H.K.$	Foreign Currency	Total	H.K.$	Foreign Currency	Total
China	169 (19.40)	160 (4.74)	329 (7.75)	94 (18.80)	69 (4.18)	163 (7.58)	96 (21.29)	100 (17.95)	196 (19.44)	58 (21.25)	44 (15.83)	102 (18.51)
Europe	157 (18.02)	416 (12.32)	573 (13.49)	95 (19.00)	276 (16.73)	371 (17.26)	59 (13.08)	109 (19.57)	168 (16.67)	35 (12.82)	64 (23.02)	99 (17.97)
Japan	147 (16.88)	2,237 (66.26)	2,384 (56.13)	47 (9.40)	934 (56.61)	981 (45.63)	19 (4.21)	82 (14.72)	101 (10.02)	8 (2.93)	46 (16.55)	55 (9.98)
United States	73 (8.38)	183 (5.42)	256 (6.03)	56 (11.20)	144 (8.73)	200 (9.30)	28 (6.21)	72 (12.93)	100 (9.92)	20 (7.33)	43 (15.47)	63 (11.43)
Others, including Hong Kong	325 (37.31)	380 (11.26)	705 (16.60)	208 (41.60)	227 (13.76)	435 (20.23)	249 (55.21)	194 (34.83)	443 (43.95)	152 (55.68)	81 (29.14)	232 (42.11)
Total	871	3,376	4,247	500	1,650	2,150	451	557	1,008	273	278	551

Note: Figures in parentheses are the percentage share of the total.

Source: Commissioner of Banking, *Annual Report*, various issues.

In the total DTC category, the Asian Pacific countries had the largest number of firms, a total of 148 in 1989, but this number was much smaller than that in 1985. Most DTCs relinquished registration voluntarily because they were no longer active in the deposit-taking business.

Table 2.6 gives the distribution of assets and deposits by country of beneficial ownership. In 1989 the Japanese banks had a dominant share of total assets (56.13%), which was even higher than in 1986; but the share of the Japanese banks in total deposits was only 10.02%. Thus, Japanese banks had to resort to nontraditional sources of funds, such as interbank borrowing and issuing NCDs, to finance their expansion of assets. Japanese banks are using Hong Kong as a center for making loans.

The Hong Kong banks continued to have the largest share in the Hong Kong currency–denominated asset and deposit markets.[10] Their deposit share was also larger than their asset share, showing that Hong Kong banks had excess funds to lend to foreign banks to buy Hong Kong dollar assets.

A more vigorous measurement of market structure would be the Herfindahl index,[11] which uses individual bank data for all the banks in Hong Kong. But this approach is impossible, since foreign banks are not required to publish any information on their operations in Hong Kong. Nonetheless, we offer the following observations about the banks' market structure:

1. The banking market is generally concentrated and dominated by large institutions, especially in the licensed banking and the DTC (RTDC) sectors.

2. The banking market is heavily dominated by the licensed banks, a trend that may well persist in the future.

3. The Hong Kong dollar–denominated markets are heavily dominated by the Hong Kong banks. Foreign banks therefore must borrow from the local interbank market or issue NCDs to fund their Hong Kong dollar assets.

4. The foreign currency asset markets seem to be less competitive, with the Japanese banks taking the most dominant role. The foreign currency deposit market seems to be more competitive, with the market share more evenly distributed among banks of different countries.

5. The Hong Kong domestic banking market has created an indigenous market that is highly monopolistic and dominated by a few large banks, while the international banking market is more competitive, with the participation of many multinational banks. Thus, the local banks or the "grandfathered" foreign banks can obtain a monopolistic profit from operating in the local currency market, but they must compete furiously in the international banking market. Similarly, the foreign banks, especially the newcomers, may not be much interested in the retail market in Hong Kong, but their major objective for obtaining a foothold in Hong Kong is access to international banking activities such as foreign exchange dealing, money market activities, and project financing for the surrounding countries, especially China.

The Current Banking Structure

As we stated earlier, the Hong Kong banking system has the following features:

1. It is highly internationalized.
2. The deposit market is relatively segmented and heavily dominated by the licensed banks.
3. The domestic market is rather oligopolistic, heavily dominated by several banking groups, that is, the Hongkong and Shanghai Banking Group, the Bank of China Group, and the Standard Chartered Bank. The international banking market is more competitive.
4. In a society that is predominantly Chinese, there are relatively few purely local Chinese banks.

It is not, of course, easy to explain the evolution of such a structure, but we shall discuss briefly some of the reasons in the following sections.

Economic Growth and Technological Advances

Hong Kong started its enviable economic growth in the 1970s (especially in the late 1970s when the average economic growth was 12.3%). This trend was sustained into the 1980s, with the average growth rate for 1981 to 1988 at 7.1%. There is no doubt that such a strong economic performance could also lead to a rapid increase in the supply of deposits and in the demand for loans. Besides, as the economy matures, people will use more banking services; for example, they will use more bank checks to settle their transactions and will invest more in bank deposits as a means to store their wealth. Thus the demand for bank intermediation has been rising. On the other hand, the banking system has been adopting various types of advance technology, such as automatic teller machines and electronic banking, to increase the cost effectiveness and hence the supply of intermediation services. Both supply and demand factors are helping increase the size of the banking services industry.

Hong Kong is not alone in riding the tide of economic growth. The other newly industrialized economies[12] also had similar or even better economic performance in the 1970s and 1980s. In order to finance such rapid economic growth, some of the countries needed to borrow heavily from overseas. Accordingly, in the 1970s and early 1980s, Hong Kong served as a center for channeling funds from the European countries and the United States to the Asian Pacific countries. Notably, Korea has been a major borrower of funds from Hong Kong. In the 1980s, some basic changes in the economic environment altered the role of Hong Kong as a financial center. First, China began to reform economically, and it also changed its attitude toward borrowing from abroad. Hong Kong thus became one of the major centers for lending to China. Second, the United States' rising trade and fiscal deficits made it a net recipient of funds and turned some of the countries in Asia, particularly Japan and Taiwan, into net suppliers of funds. These economic and financial factors have made Hong Kong's international banking activities more important.

Government Policies

The predominant role of the licensed banks in the deposit market was not a natural outgrowth of market competition. Between 1966 and March 1978, the government imposed a moratorium on licensing new banks. Foreign financial institutions wishing to get a foothold in Hong Kong could not incorporate themselves as banks but had to form establishments like merchant banks or investment banks. At that time, too, some local firms converted to finance companies in order to lend money to people investing in the securities market and property market or to companies doing relatively high-risk business. Because these kinds of institutions were free of any regulations, their number rose very rapidly, to about two thousand in early 1970s. Then the government imposed the Deposit-Taking Companies (DTCs) Ordinance in 1976, which required a minimum paid-up capital of H.K.$2.50 million and deposits of not less than $50,000 for any one account. However, since these institutions were not controlled by the interest rate rule, they could still compete for deposits by offering higher interest rates than the licensed banks did, and their share in the deposit market reached almost 30% in 1980.[13] In order to have better control over the interest rate and better protection for depositors, the government then decided to establish the three-tier system, which effectively prohibited the DTCs from accepting short-term deposits and also enabled the banks to recapture their market share.

After 1978, although the government lifted the moratorium on licensing new banks, foreign banks that obtained a license after 1978 were allowed to have only one office in Hong Kong, which meant that they would find it extremely difficult to attract retail deposits. It is thus the government's intention to promote the status of Hong Kong as an international financial center but not to encourage competition with existing commercial banks for domestic business. Foreign banks therefore must depend heavily on the interbank market to get Hong Kong dollar funds to finance their Hong Kong dollar assets.

Banking Crises

The evolution of the oligopsonist nature of the banking system can also be traced back to the banking crises of the 1960s and 1980s. Some of the small and medium-size local banks collapsed between 1961 and 1965. The depositors' confidence was restored by a joint effort by the Hongkong and Shanghai Banking Corporation and the Standard Chartered Bank and by the acquisition of small and medium banks by the larger banks and foreign banks. Another major banking crisis also occurred from 1982 to 1986 when several DTCs collapsed and several banks ran into serious problems.

The government took over many of the commercial banks, and some large banks also granted emergency standby credit lines to the problem banks. As a result of the banking crisis, the small institutions have found it more difficult to attract deposits and have to rely more heavily on the interbank market to fund their assets.

The Regulatory Framework

Before the enactment of the Banking Ordinance of 1986, the Hong Kong banking regulations used to be relatively loose and did not comply with international regulatory standards. There were just a few noteworthy elements in the old regulations, including minimum capital regulation, a minimum liquidity ratio requirement, and a reporting requirement. The power of the Banking Commissioner was also very limited. Because of the banking crisis of 1982–86, the government decided to overhaul the whole banking regulation apparatus by seeking the help of experts from the Bank of England and by enacting the Banking Ordinance of 1986.

The Banking Ordinance of 1986 marked a monumental change in Hong Kong's banking regulations, which include the following:

1. The ordinance put both licensed banks and DTCs under the same set of regulations. Previously, these two types of institutions were governed by different laws.

2. The power and the duty of the commissioner was enhanced.

3. A minimum liquidity ratio of 25% must be maintained. The ratio is calculated as a ratio of liquid assets to qualifying liabilities. Liquid assets are short-term assets or any cash inflow items that can be realized within one month, and qualifying liabilities are the sum of net one-month interbank liabilities and other one-month liabilities.

4. A minimum ratio of capital to risk assets, or a capital adequacy ratio (CAR), of 5% must be maintained by both licensed banks and DTCs that are locally incorporated (the capital adequacy of an overseas institution is primarily the responsibility of the institution's home supervisory authority).

After consultation with an institution, the commissioner may set its minimum ratio above the level of 5% to not more than 8% for banks and at not more than 10% for DTCs. The need to comply with the ratio was a factor leading many institutions to reduce the size of their balance sheets. In 1988, the total assets of locally incorporated banks climbed by almost 20% over the previous year, and those of DTCs fell by 16%. The drop was particularly pronounced for the Japanese DTCs, which experienced a loss of assets of more than 25%. In December 1987, the Basel Committee published proposals to standardize the measurement of the international banks' capital and to set minimum levels of capital adequacy. Hong Kong is expected to follow suit. Starting on December 31, 1989, the minimum

CAR was changed to 8%, with a maximum of 12% for licensed banks and 16% for RLBs and DTCs.

Although the provisions of the Banking Ordinance of 1986 are much more stringent than those of the previous ordinances, they have generally been welcomed by the banking community because (1) they restore the confidence of local depositors and (2) they strengthen the role of Hong Kong as a financial center.

Government Policies

Hong Kong has basically a free market–oriented economy. Prices are generally not controlled, and market entry is relatively free. The same general principle is also applicable to the formulation of financial policies. Thus, the whole policy system is open and relies heavily on the market mechanism.

The Policymakers

There is no central monetary authority in Hong Kong; the governor and the Legislative Council hold the ultimate responsibility for financial and monetary affairs. The day-to-day executive decisions are made by the financial secretary and the secretary for monetary affairs, who also oversee the commissioner of banking in carrying out some of the central banking functions. Bank notes are issued by two commercial banks, the Hongkong and Shanghai Banking Corporation and the Standard Chartered Bank. Basically, the secretary of monetary affairs is responsible for all financial and monetary affairs such as monetary policy, exchange rate policy, regulations of financial institutions and markets, implementation of laws related to the financial sector, and the management of the Exchange Fund. The Exchange Fund was established in 1935 for the purpose of regulating the exchange value of the Hong Kong dollar. When the note-issuing banks wish to issue Hong Kong currency, they need to purchase certificates of indebtedness from the Exchange Fund. Before the establishment of the U.S. dollar–linked exchange rate system, the note-issuing banks had to pay the Exchange Fund in Hong Kong dollars. But with the establishment of the linked exchange rate system, the payment must be in U.S. dollars. The Exchange Fund is also responsible for managing the fiscal reserves of the Hong Kong government. Under the purview of the secretary for monetary affairs is the commissioner of banking, who is responsible for implementing the Banking Ordinance of 1986, registering DTCs, supervising banking operations, and issuing operation guidelines to banks and DTCs.

Allocation

The government does not have a deliberate allocative policy in the money market. That is, there are no guarantees against risk or failure in the deposit market, since there is no insurance to protect depositors. In addition, the taxation system is not geared to such a purpose. The banking·system does have some portfolio composition restrictions; for example, depository institutions are not allowed to invest more than 25% of their capital in real properties and to lend more than 25% of their capital to a single borrower or more than 10% of their capital to the directors of the bank, but such restrictions are not allocative in that they try to subsidize or penalize one sector of the economy against or in favor of the other. Moreover, there is no foreign exchange control, which in fact is a pivotal feature of Hong Kong. Over the past several years, any change in the exchange rate system has had to meet the criterion that foreign exchange will not be controlled. In general, therefore, the government does not use the money market as an instrument for allocative purposes; instead it relies on market forces to perform such a function.

Pricing
Since there is no foreign exchange control and the Hong Kong dollar is linked to the U.S. dollar through the linked exchange rate system, Hong Kong cannot adopt an independent monetary policy or interest rate policy in the long run. Under such a system, Hong Kong is heavily influenced by the U.S. money supply, and so in the long run, its interest rate level should not deviate too much from that of the United States. Hong Kong has an administered exchange rate system in that the price of the Hong Kong dollar is fixed, but the foreign exchange market is still open in that there is no exchange control. However, as we shall make clear later, the linked-rate system is not a fixed-rate or pegged-rate system in the traditional sense in that the government must intervene actively in the market in order to set the exchange rate. Rather, the linked-rate system relies heavily on the note-issuing banks' arbitrage operations with the Exchange Fund. Thus the system relies partially on the market and partially on the administrative power of the government.

An interest rate cartel, however, has been in existence since the 1960s. The Hong Kong Association of Banks sets the maximum level of interest rates on bank deposits of original maturities up to fifteen months less one day, with the exception of deposits of $500,000 or above with a term to maturity of less than three months, for which banks can compete freely. All licensed banks must comply with this rule. The government continues to allow the association to exercise such power in order to have more effective control over the interest rate. But it is doubtful whether such a cartel is still effective, because only small-denomination Hong Kong dollar deposits are controlled by the cartel, and many depositors are making foreign currency deposits or U.S. dollar swap deposits.

The withholding tax on interest derived from Hong Kong dollar deposits and foreign currency deposits was abolished in 1983 and 1982, respectively.

In regard to pricing, the interest rate cartel seems to be the only item that is heavily administered with the government's endorsement.

Supervision and Solvency
As we observed earlier, there are minimum capital and minimum capital adequacy requirements in the area of solvency requirements. In the cate-

gory of fitness and character, the Banking Ordinance of 1986 also requires that the appointment of directors, company secretaries, and controllers of authorized institutions be approved by the banking commissioner. But there are no provisions in case of risk or failure, although the government is trying to upgrade the quality of supervision to international standards in order to safeguard the soundness of the banking system. Although the current trend seems to be toward more restrictions and away from the "free-market" mode, this is an outcome of the banking crisis, and it is meant to remedy the regulatory measures that were outdated and unfit for the current and future development of Hong Kong as a center for international banking. Such a measure is just a long-overdue correction. Nonetheless, Hong Kong's regulatory mentality is still more lenient than that of its neighboring countries.

Institutional Structure

There is no active policy to promote the creation of instruments. The government usually responds slowly to demands to remove some of the obstacles preventing the development of new instruments. An example is the abolishment in 1989 of the interest-withholding tax on debt securities. This attitude may be changing, however, as the government began issuing some short-term government bills called Exchange Fund bills in March 1990. Nonetheless, probably the government's main reason for issuing such an instrument is to enable it to control the liquidity of the market more effectively, rather than to promote the development of the money market.

With respect to structural rules, the government does not follow a free-market philosophy. The three-tier system is clearly a market (the deposit market) segmentation policy favoring the licensed banks. In this respect, this policy conflicts with other policies. There are two reasons for establishing a three-tier system. The first is that the licensed banks were lobbying very hard to keep the finance companies out of the short-term deposit market. The second one is that limiting the scope of business allotted to the finance companies would lower the cost of supervision incurred by the government.

No special ownership requirements or payment policies are involved in the money market.

Information

The government seems to have adopted a semiopen policy in regard to information. Authorized institutions are required to disclose to the banking commissioners their financial information, such as assets and liabilities, types of loans, off–balance sheet items, foreign exchange exposure, and even inner reserves, but most of this information is not shared with the general public, who may read only the annual reports of individual banks and some aggregated figures pertaining to the whole banking system. The quality and quantity of information that the public can obtain are far from adequate to judge the soundness of a particular bank. One of the reasons given is that the general public may be too sensitive to individual bank data, that the release of unfavorable information about a particular bank may cause an unjustified run on it. However, the Hongkong and Shanghai Banking corporation may soon disclose its inner reserves, owing to its heavy involvement in the European market. Market forces would then force other banks to follow suit.

Generally, the government does not try to interfere with the free-market price mechanism in the money market or to achieve certain allocative objectives through the money market. But the government does seem to deviate somewhat from the basic free-market philosophy in regard to the three-tier system, perhaps because it lacks experience and resources in supervising the prudent operations of the financial markets. Obviously, the government is well aware of its weaknesses and has begun to gather more information and to employ international experts to improve the quality of supervision in Hong Kong.

THE MONEY MARKET

A money market is a market for short-term (one year or less) funds with instruments such as treasury bills, bankers acceptances, and commercial paper.

Owing to the absence of a central bank monetary authority and the lack of short-term government debt instruments, Hong Kong's money markets mainly comprise the short-term customer deposits, the interbank market, the commercial paper market, and the foreign exchange market. Although there also are certificates of deposit, bankers acceptances, and overdrafts, none of these is significant, and consistent data on these instruments are not available.

Short-Term Deposits

Short-term deposits refer to the deposits of maturity not longer than twelve months from customers of financial institutions. Surplus funds of individual persons and businesses are usually kept with financial institutions. In Hong Kong, only three types of financial institutions are authorized to take deposits from the general public. These are the so-called authorized institutions, namely, the licensed banks, LDTCs (RLBs), and RDTCs (DTCs).

Table 2.7 gives the total deposit liabilities of the three types of authorized institutions. For the years 1980 to 1989 (August), deposits had been growing very rapidly. Total deposits with all authorized institutions increased from H.K.$128.9 billion in 1980 to H.K.$928.2 billion in August 1989. The average annual compound rate of growth was 25.6%. In particular, deposits with licensed banks rose consistently from 1980 to 1989. At the end of August 1989, the licensed banks had the lion's share of 93% in

Table 2.7. Deposits from Customers (in H.K.$ millions)

	1980	1981	1982	1983	1984
Deposits with licensed banks					
Hong Kong dollars	76,132	85,870	107,876	124,674	158,005
Foreign currency	10,621	18,588	82,384	115,200	138,099
Subtotal	86,753	104,457	190,259	239,874	296,103
	(67.3)	(63.8)	(81.7)	(83.3)	(83.4)
Deposits with licensed deposit- *taking companies*					
Hong Kong dollars	..	..	3,455	5,264	7,734
Foreign currency	..	..	5,755	10,142	10,997
Subtotal	..	..	9,210	15,407	18,731
			(4.0)	(5.3)	(5.3)
Deposits with registered deposit- *taking companies*					
Hong Kong dollars	34,993	48,489	24,053	23,463	27,450
Foreign currency	7,108	10,678	9,243	9,300	12,680
Subtotal	42,101	59,167	33,296	32,763	40,131
	(32.7)	(36.2)	(14.3)	(11.4)	(11.3)
Deposits with all authorized institutions					
Hong Kong dollars	111,125	134,359	135,384	153,401	193,190
Foreign currency	17,729	29,266	97,381	134,642	161,776
Total	128,854	163,625	232,765	288,044	354,965
	(100.0)	(100.0)	(100.0)	(100.0)	(100.0)

[a] Except for figures in 1989, as of end of August; the other figures are as of the end of the year. Figures in parentheses are percentages of subtotal to total deposits.

total deposits, much higher than its 67.3% share in 1980. This increase in proportion partly reflects the establishment in 1983 of the three-tier deposit-taking system that favors banks in competing for deposits and partly reflects the growing confidence in banks since the deposit-taking companies were hard hit by the financial crisis from 1982 to 1985.

Table 2.8 shows the breakdown of deposits with the licensed banks. Among the three different types of deposits, time deposits had a dominant share of 73.4% in August 1989, a share that was significantly higher than that in 1980.

It is noteworthy that, as indicated in both Tables 2.7 and 2.8, the importance of Hong Kong dollar deposits declined. The proportions of Hong Kong dollars to total deposits with licensed banks and all authorized institutions were 38.8% and 39.5%, respectively, in August 1989,

Table 2.7. (*Continued*)

	1985	1986	1987	1988	End of August 1989[a]
Deposits with licensed banks					
Hong Kong dollars	174,121	213,337	278,494	313,969	334,742
Foreign currency	193,104	278,016	363,192	465,020	528,758
Subtotal	367,224	491,353	641,685	778,989	863,500
	(85.2)	(89.2)	(91.2)	(92.1)	(93.0)
Deposits with licensed deposit-taking companies					
Hong Kong dollars	6,948	6,496	7,840	9,888	9,392
Foreign currency	13,999	16,105	20,398	20,820	17,965
Subtotal	20,947	22,601	28,238	30,708	27,357
	(4.9)	(4.1)	(4.0)	(3.6)	(2.9)
Deposits with registered deposit-taking companies					
Hong Kong dollars	31,063	25,269	23,210	22,886	22,491
Foreign currency	11,577	11,428	10,477	12,937	14,846
Subtotal	42,640	36,697	33,687	35,823	37,337
	(9.9)	(6.7)	(4.8)	(4.2)	(4.0)
Deposits with all authorized institutions					
Hong Kong dollars	212,132	245,103	309,543	346,744	366,626
Foreign currency	218,680	305,549	394,066	498,776	561,568
Total	430,811	550,651	703,609	845,520	928,194
	(100.0)	(100.0)	(100.0)	(100.0)	(100.0)

Source: Monetary Affairs Branch, Hong Kong government.

substantially lower than the 87.8% and 86.2% in 1980. This decline in proportion reflects partly the shift in depositors' preference from Hong Kong dollars to foreign currency and partly the exchange translation effect due to the rapid drop in the value of the Hong Kong dollar in the early 1980s.

The Interbank Market

The largest and the best-established money market in Hong Kong is the interbank market, which is a wholesale market for short-term unsecured loans between local and overseas deposit-taking institutions. By nature, the interbank market has no physical location but, rather, consists of a complex and sophisticated network of telecommunication equipment connecting the dealing rooms of different authorized institutions.

Table 2.8. Types of Deposits with Licensed Banks (in H.K.$ millions)

	1980	1981	1982	1983	1984
Demand deposits					
Hong Kong dollars	14,709	13,921	14,644	15,564	20,078
Foreign currency	1,122	1,446	1,399	2,619	3,440
Subtotal	15,831	15,367	16,043	18,182	23,518
	(18.2)	(14.7)	(8.4)	(7.6)	(7.9)
Savings deposits					
Hong Kong dollars	40,031	48,073	61,907	58,704	66,241
Foreign currency	2,777	4,779	7,683	12,452	14,909
Subtotal	42,808	52,852	69,590	71,156	81,150
	(49.3)	(50.6)	(36.6)	(29.7)	(27.4)
Time deposits					
Hong Kong dollars	21,391	23,876	31,324	50,406	71,686
Foreign currency	6,722	12,363	73,302	100,129	119,750
Subtotal	28,114	36,239	104,626	150,535	191,436
	(32.4)	(34.7)	(55.0)	(62.8)	(64.7)
Total deposits with licensed banks					
Hong Kong dollars	76,132	85,870	107,876	124,674	158,005
Foreign currency	10,621	18,588	82,384	115,200	138,099
Total	86,753	104,457	190,259	239,874	296,103
	(100.0)	(100.0)	(100.0)	(100.0)	(100.0)

[a] Except for figures in 1989, as of end of August; the other figures are as of the end of the year. Figures in parentheses are percentages of subtotal to total deposits with licensed banks.

The participants in the interbank market are not restricted to licensed banks only; DTCs with a strong background may participate as well. Participants with surplus funds (in either local or foreign currency) may, through the market, lend to those with a shortage. In so doing, all participants may adjust their asset portfolios and balance their funding positions.

Deposit-taking institutions participating in the interbank market may transact with others in two ways. They may trade with other participants directly by means of telecommunication equipment. One party contacts another for a quote and then pays the price if appropriate. Sometimes participating institutions prefer to deal through money brokers, who are the middlemen between the two parties to a deal. These brokers collect bids and offers from various participants and help arrange transactions. As brokers, they do not take any position but earn brokerage fees from providing services. Under either method, a participant must establish reciprocal

Table 2.8. (*Continued*)

	1985	1986	1987	1988	End of August 1989ᵃ
Demand deposits					
Hong Kong dollars	24,949	32,305	49,061	49,381	47,915
Foreign currency	3,460	4,494	8,076	9,577	8,695
Subtotal	28,409	36,799	57,138	58,958	56,610
	(7.7)	(7.5)	(8.9)	(7.6)	(6.6)
Savings deposits					
Hong Kong dollars	81,216	97,949	138,612	118,951	118,851
Foreign currency	17,549	27,527	42,497	56,578	54,312
Subtotal	98,765	125,476	181,109	175,529	173,163
	(26.9)	(25.5)	(28.2)	(22.5)	(20.1)
Time deposits					
Hong Kong dollars	67,955	83,083	90,820	145,637	167,977
Foreign currency	172,095	245,995	312,619	398,865	465,751
Subtotal	240,050	329,078	403,439	544,502	633,728
	(65.4)	(67.0)	(62.9)	(69.9)	(73.4)
Total deposits with licensed banks					
Hong Kong dollars	174,121	213,337	278,494	313,969	334,742
Foreign currency	193,104	278,016	363,192	465,020	528,758
Total	367,224	491,353	641,685	778,989	863,500
	(100.0)	(100.0)	(100.0)	(100.0)	(100.0)

Source: Monetary Affairs Branch, Hong Kong government.

credit facilities with its counterparty beforehand and then can deal up to the limit designated by the facilities.

Money can be lent in the interbank market in any currency for periods ranging from overnight up to longer periods of six to twelve months. The market in foreign currency is one component of the global Eurocurrency market.

All transactions are made at prices set in the free market and determined by market conditions. The market prices are usually quoted in the form of bid and offer.[14] The difference between the bid and the offer is called a *spread,* which reflects the market's trading activities. When the market's trading is active with ample placing and taking, the spread tends to be relatively narrow.

Although the interbank market is the oldest established money market in Hong Kong, there are no official statistics on its trading volume. The government publishes only monthly statistics on the outstanding inter-institution liabilities.

Table 2.9 gives the consolidated inter-institution liabilities of all authorized institutions. From 1980 to 1989, the interbank market size (in terms of outstanding inter-institution liabilities) grew rapidly. By the end of September 1989, the total volume of outstanding inter-institution liabilities was H.K.$529.8 billion, about 6.1 times of that in 1980. The average annual compound rate of growth was 22.9%. The interbank market has been widely recognized as a major channel of liquidity for authorized institutions. A significant proportion, about 12.9%, of their total liabilities (as of September 1989) was inter-institution borrowings. In particular, more than one-quarter of their Hong Kong dollar funds was obtained from the market, evidence of the market's significance as a source of funds for deposit-taking institutions as a whole.

Table 2.10 breaks the total inter-institution liabilities into different components. Several points are worth mentioning here. First, among the four activity components, the interbank liabilities grew in importance. Its proportion of the total liabilities increased from 30.7% in 1980 to more than 60% in September 1989, and the proportion of the other three components (banks' liabilities to DTCs, inter-DTC liabilities, and DTCs' liabilities to banks) declined. This indicates that banks are more active participants and find it easier to deal in the market than DTCs do. There are two

Table 2.9. Consolidated Inter-institution Liabilities of Deposit-Taking Institutions (in H.K.$ millions)

	Inter-institution Liabilities (i.e., amount due to banks and DTCs in Hong Kong)			Total Liabilities			%		
	H.K.$ (1)	Foreign Currency (2)	Total (3)	H.K.$ (4)	Foreign Currency (5)	Total (6)	(1) — (4)	(2) — (5)	(3) — (6)
1980	51,240	35,917	87,157	202,916	232,422	435,337	25.3	15.5	20.0
1981	76,366	57,943	134,310	271,522	361,260	632,782	28.1	16.0	21.2
1982	83,256	87,234	170,490	297,521	565,586	863,107	28.0	15.4	19.8
1983	96,982	129,679	226,660	341,155	774,307	1,115,462	28.4	16.7	20.3
1984	114,276	154,397	268,673	384,723	884,935	1,269,658	29.7	17.4	21.2
1985	129,188	179,179	308,367	437,656	1,117,967	1,555,623	29.5	16.0	19.8
1986	149,319	277,409	426,728	503,172	1,647,119	2,150,291	29.7	16.8	19.8
1987	172,842	312,443	485,286	606,780	2,611,010	3,217,789	28.5	12.0	15.1
1988	189,853	270,994	460,847	695,818	3,002,158	3,697,976	27.3	9.0	12.5
1989[a]	234,038	295,775	529,813	786,814	3,306,350	4,093,164	29.7	8.9	12.9

Average Annual Growth Rate (End September)

1980–89	19.0%	27.2%	22.9%	16.8%	35.5%	29.2%			

[a] The figures for 1989 are as of the end of September; other figures are as of the end of the year.

Source: Hong Kong Annual Digest of Statistics, various issues.

possible reasons for this. One is that many active DTC participants were forced to withdraw from the market in the financial crisis of 1982–85. Another reason is that after the crisis, banks became more selective when dealing with DTCs. As a result, the DTC participants became less active.

A second point is that in 1980 and 1981, banks' liabilities to DTCs were greater than DTCs' liabilities to banks, indicating that banks were net debtors to the DTCs. This reflected the banks' use of their subsidiary DTCs to compete for deposits. However, the trend started to reverse in 1982, when the DTCs owed the banks a net amount of H.K.$21.263 billion, an amount that rose to H.K.$40.986 billion in September 1989. This change was due to the establishment of the three-tier system, which made it more difficult for DTCs to attract deposits and thus made them more dependent on banks for funding.

Third, the proportion of Hong Kong dollars in the total inter-institution liabilities fell consistently from 1980 to 1986. This decline in proportion may reflect the increasing importance of Hong Kong as an international financial center. As banks accept more foreign currency deposits from local residents and neighboring countries, they have more excess foreign currency funds to lend in the market. Nevertheless, the decline has reversed in recent years, because the market is quite concerned about the pressure to revalue the Hong Kong dollar. More investors switched deposits from foreign currencies to Hong Kong dollars, and there was also some speculative money flowing in, thereby increasing the Hong Kong dollar's liquidity in the market.

Another important feature noted in Table 2.10 is the terms of the market activities. The bulk of market activities was mainly in time deposits, which accounted for more than 70% of the total volume. Not only is this evidence consistent with the terms of customers' deposits mentioned in Table 2.8, but it also shows that participants rely on this market more to finance longer-term assets (such as loans) than to balance their short-term liquidity position.

Table 2.11 shows the interbank lending of authorized institutions by the country or region of beneficial ownership. Among the five groups, Japanese banks were the most active participants in both placing and borrowing. At the end of 1988, they had a net borrowing of $425 billion. The major fund suppliers to them were China banks and Hong Kong banks (included in "Others").

The Commercial Paper Market

Commercial paper (CP) is a short-term unsecured promissory note typically issued by large corporations to finance short-term working capital needs. In recent years some firms have also used CP as a source of interim financing for major investment projects. As the maturities for CP are very short, usually ranging from 30 to 365 days, CP is classified as a money market instrument and so is issued on an unsecured basis. In other words, the issuer pledges no assets to protect the investors in the event of default. Therefore

Table 2.10. Component of Inter-institution Liabilities (in H.K.$ millions)

	1980			1981		
	H.K.$	Foreign Currency	Total	H.K.$	Foreign Currency	Total
Interbank liabilities						
Demand and call	4,885	646	5,531	5,622	1,000	6,622
Short notice	3,325	1,350	4,674	5,117	3,564	8,681
Time deposits	8,723	7,857	16,579	15,982	14,412	30,394
Total	16,933	9,852	26,785	26,721	18,977	45,698
	(33.0)		(30.7)	(35.0)		(34.0)
Banks' liabilities to deposit-taking companies						
Demand and call	2,273	800	3,073	11,009	1,474	12,483
Short notice	9,095	759	9,854	2,328	2,007	4,335
Time deposits	13,295	2,753	16,048	21,466	4,266	25,732
Total	24,663	4,312	28,975	34,803	7,747	42,550
	(48.1)		(33.2)	(45.6)		(31.7)
Inter-deposit-taking companies' liabilities						
Demand and call	265	75	340	362	322	684
Short notice	924	1,021	1,945	1,630	1,622	3,253
Time deposits	2,104	5,719	7,823	2,728	8,276	11,005
Total	3,294	6,815	10,109	4,721	10,221	14,941
	(6.5)		(11.6)	(6.2)		(11.1)
Deposit-taking companies' liabilities to banks						
Demand and call	710	425	1,135	980	378	1,358
Short notice	1,702	1,842	3,543	1,815	1,892	3,707
Time deposits	3,939	12,672	16,610	7,326	18,729	26,055
Total	6,350	14,938	21,288	10,122	20,999	31,120
	(12.4)		(24.4)	(13.2)		(23.2)
Total inter-institution liabilities						
	51,240		87,157	76,367		134,309
	(100.0)		(100.0)	(100.0)		(100.0)
		58.80%			56.90%	

Notes: The figures in parentheses are percentages of the component total to total inter-institution liabilities. The figures for 1989 are as of the end of September; the other figures are as of the end of the year.

the issuer must be a large, well-established firm of very high credit standing (low default risk) in order to gain investors' confidence to subscribe. In countries with well-developed credit markets, there is a systematic credit rating system that compares and ranks various securities (e.g., commercial paper, notes, bonds) in terms of the issuers' credit risk.[15] The ratings provide a useful indication of the issuers' credit quality for investors. On this basis, investors can decide what yield they require in order to lend funds to a specific issuer. Generally, the higher the rated issuer's credit risk is, the higher its borrowing cost will be. Since Hong Kong's credit market is still developing, such a system does not exist; rather, the burden of credit rating usually falls on the shoulders of the merchant bankers concerned.

Table 2.10. (*Continued*)

	1982			1983			1984	
H.K.$	Foreign Currency	Total	H.K.$	Foreign Currency	Total	H.K.$	Foreign Currency	Total
4,528	1,156	5,684	4,060	2,055	6,115	4,904	1,980	6,884
8,793	4,614	13,408	9,829	10,676	20,505	10,564	14,642	25,206
23,090	20,299	43,389	27,654	30,559	58,213	36,875	44,199	81,074
36,411	26,069	62,481	41,543	43,289	84,833	52,343	60,820	113,164
(43.7)		(36.6)	(42.8)		(37.4)	(45.8)		(42.1)
6,123	1,590	7,713	7,420	1,650	9,071	7,408	1,017	8,425
2,717	4,121	6,837	2,724	3,996	6,720	2,473	5,025	7,498
13,647	7,034	20,681	17,431	13,682	31,113	17,398	14,998	32,396
22,486	12,745	35,231	27,575	19,329	46,904	27,279	21,040	48,318
(27.0)		(20.7)	(28.4)		(20.7)	(23.9)		(18.0)
852	1,229	2,081	398	202	600	326	348	674
948	1,875	2,823	605	1,790	2,395	600	2,380	2,980
2,442	8,938	11,379	1,693	8,485	10,178	11,292	8,144	19,436
4,242	12,042	16,284	2,696	10,477	13,173	12,218	10,871	23,090
(5.1)		(9.6)	(2.8)		(5.8)	(10.7)		(8.6)
1,341	562	1,903	987	396	1,383	615	813	1,428
2,133	2,252	4,385	2,152	5,413	7,565	2,169	5,259	7,428
16,642	33,564	50,206	22,028	50,774	72,803	19,651	55,594	75,246
20,117	36,377	56,494	25,168	56,584	81,751	22,435	61,666	84,102
(24.2)		(33.1)	(26.0)		(36.1)	(19.6)		(31.3)
83,256		170,490	96,982		226,661	114,275		268,674
(100.0)		(100.0)	(100.0)		(100.0)	(100.0)		(100.0)
	48.83%			42.80%			42.50%	

Sources: Hong Kong Annual Digest of Statistics and *Hong Kong Monthly Digest of Statistics,* various issues.

The history of commercial paper in Hong Kong can be traced back to 1977, when the first CP issue appeared.[16] Nevertheless, the market did not start to flourish until 1984, when two sources of momentum emerged. The first source was the introduction of the tender panel mechanism to CP issuance facilities, which will be discussed later. The second impetus was the clarification of the CP issue's legal position. Before November 1984, raising funds from the public via an issue of securities (including CP) was considered similar to taking public deposits and thus contradicted the DTCs Ordinance. Therefore, before any issue, an exemption had to be sought from the authorities on an individual basis. This formality prevented the issuer from launching an issue at the most appropriate time and remained a major

Table 2.10. (*Continued*)

	1985			1986		
	H.K.$	*Foreign Currency*	*Total*	*H.K.$*	*Foreign Currency*	*Total*
Interbank liabilities						
Demand and call	4,635	2,109	6,744	4,142	1,198	5,339
Short notice	13,349	14,367	27,716	18,737	25,594	44,331
Time deposits	39,697	53,863	93,559	47,369	116,622	163,992
Total	57,680	70,338	128,019	70,248	143,414	213,662
	(44.7)		(41.5)	(47.0)		(50.1)
Banks' liabilities to deposit-taking companies						
Demand and call	9,232	1,573	10,804	6,363	2,176	8,540
Short notice	3,729	7,088	10,817	4,001	7,780	11,781
Time deposits	19,129	15,228	34,357	20,914	21,714	42,628
Total	32,089	23,889	55,978	31,278	31,670	62,948
	(24.8)		(18.2)	(20.9)		(14.8)
Inter-deposit-taking companies' liabilities						
Demand and call	443	613	1,057	187	397	584
Short notice	635	1,870	2,505	823	2,052	2,875
Time deposits	12,876	9,619	22,495	12,962	6,182	19,143
Total	13,954	12,102	26,057	13,972	8,631	22,603
	(10.8)		(8.4)	(9.4)		(5.3)
Deposit-taking companies' liabilities to banks						
Demand and call	668	3,349	4,017	2,064	2,520	4,585
Short notice	3,134	11,171	14,305	4,536	18,654	23,190
Time deposits	21,662	58,231	79,993	27,221	72,520	99,741
Total	25,465	72,850	98,315	33,821	93,695	127,516
	(19.7)		(31.9)	(22.7)		(30.0)
Total inter-institution liabilities						
	129,188		308,369	149,319		426,729
	(100.0)		(100.0)	(100.0)		(100.0)
		41.90%			35.00%	

Notes: The figures in parentheses are percentages of the component total to total inter-institution liabilities. The figures for 1989 are as of the end of September; the other figures are as of the end of the year.

obstacle to the development of the market. This problem was not resolved until November 1984, when the government announced that a CP issue was not regarded as equivalent to taking public deposits, so application for exemption was no longer required. Accordingly, the market was stimulated.

At present, the issue of commercial paper is mainly subject to the regulations of the Protection of Investors Ordinance. This ordinance aims to protect investors by prohibiting the use of fraudulent or reckless means to induce investors to buy or sell securities or to take part in investment arrangements, and it regulates the publication of information in promotional or other related material. Accordingly, prior authorization must be obtained from the commissioner of securities before any CP is issued.

Table 2.10. (*Continued*)

	1987			1988			1989	
H.K.\$	Foreign Currency	Total	H.K.\$	Foreign Currency	Total	H.K.\$	Foreign Currency	Total
8,177	998	9,175	3,007	3,990	6,997	2,940	1,870	4,810
16,716	32,713	49,429	26,278	31,053	57,332	36,775	45,508	82,284
64,162	126,979	191,141	82,961	125,177	208,137	114,820	132,890	247,711
89,054	160,691	249,745	112,246	160,220	272,465	154,535	180,269	334,804
(51.5)		(51.5)	(59.1)		(59.1)	(66.0)		(63.2)
5,863	1,826	7,689	5,617	962	6,579	4,336	897	5,223
4,869	8,407	13,275	4,927	7,991	12,919	4,063	6,545	10,608
24,458	26,643	51,101	26,216	26,271	52,487	29,723	29,240	58,963
35,190	36,876	72,006	36,761	35,223	71,984	38,122	36,681	74,803
(20.4)		(14.9)	(19.4)		(15.6)	(16.3)		(14.1)
194	379	574	97	32	129	79	36	115
853	1,903	2,756	267	614	880	350	499	849
8,173	5,864	14,037	2,922	3,122	6,044	1,632	1,821	3,453
9,220	8,146	17,366	3,285	3,768	7,053	2,061	2,356	4,417
(5.3)		(3.6)	(1.7)		(1.5)	(0.9)		(0.8)
2,627	995	3,622	2,959	1,862	4,821	500	1,762	2,262
3,798	18,947	22,745	3,661	8,746	12,407	5,133	22,671	27,804
32,954	86,789	119,743	30,941	61,176	82,117	33,688	52,035	85,723
39,378	106,731	146,109	37,561	71,784	109,345	39,320	76,469	115,789
(22.8)		(30.1)	(19.8)		(23.7)	(16.8)		(21.9)
172,842		485,286	189,853		460,847	234,038		529,813
(100.0)		(100.0)	(100.0)		(100.0)	(100.0)		(100.0)
	35.60%			41.20%			44.17%	

Sources: Hong Kong Annual Digest of Statistics and Hong Kong Monthly Digest of Statistics, various issues.

Since that CP is issued on an unsecured basis, it has no way of protecting investors in the event of default. In view of its high risk, the commissioner stipulates that a minimum denomination of H.K.\$500,000 is required for each CP in order to prevent unsophisticated investors from participating in this unsecured market.

Owing to the requirement of a large denomination and the subsequent absence of small individual investors, the CP market is almost entirely a wholesale primary market. The major investors are professional institutional investors such as banks, finance companies, unit trust funds, and insurance companies that purchase the CP and hold it until maturity. A secondary market is virtually nonexistent.

Table 2.11. Interbank Lending of Authorized Institutions by Country/Region of Beneficial Ownership (in H.K.$ billions)

Other Regions	China	Europe	Japan	United States	Others (including Hong Kong)	Total
1986						
Placement	92	249	669	122	230	1,361
H.K.$	41	40	15	16	67	178
F/cy	51	209	654	106	163	1,183
Borrowing	42	242	855	126	148	1,412
H.K.$	25	40	32	23	51	171
F/cy	17	202	823	103	97	1,241
Net lender/(borrower)	50	7	(186)	(4)	82	(51)
H.K.$	16	—	(17)	(7)	16	7
F/cy	34	7	(168)	3	66	(58)
1986						
Placement 129	327	1,228	134	279	2,097	
H.K.$	43	47	17	14	78	199
F/cy	86	280	1,211	120	201	1,898
Borrowing	60	318	1,608	129	172	2,287
H.K.$	25	50	42	19	64	200
F/cy	36	268	1,565	109	108	2,087
Net lender/(borrower)	68	9	(380)	6	107	(190)
H.K.$	18	(3)	(25)	(5)	14	(1)
F/cy	50	12	(354)	10	93	(189)
1986						
Placement	169	313	1,475	126	307	2,390
H.K.$	60	47	26	13	75	222
F/cy	109	266	1,449	113	232	2,168
Borrowing	87	310	1,900	115	181	2,593
H.K.$	49	54	68	19	52	242
F/cy	38	257	1,832	96	129	2,351
Net lender/(borrower)	82	3	(425)	11	126	(202)
H.K.$	11	(6)	(42)	(6)	23	(21)
F/cy	72	10	(383)	17	103	(181)

Source: Hong Kong Commissioner of Banking, *Annual Report,* 1987 and 1988.

Firms issuing commercial paper may sell it to investors directly using their own sales force or indirectly using dealers that are financial institutions (mainly merchant banks) responsible for credit rating, pricing, and marketing the CP. The major incentive for direct placement is that the issuer is able to save the 0.125% dealer's commission. But because the issuing firms in Hong Kong are mainly nonfinancial corporations without any expertise in the market, dealer placement is more common.

Marketing arrangements may be made on an individual or a rollover basis. Under the former, the dealers' responsibility for marketing the CP is once and for all. Most of the CP issued in Hong Kong is on a rollover basis. A facility is first set up by the dealers' syndicate, which agrees to submit bids continually for any CP drawn by the issuers within a certain period of time (say, three years). The most popular form is the revolving underwriting facility (RUF) through which the (underwriting) syndicate guarantees to discount the amount of shortfall at the underwritten margin, subject to an upper outstanding limit. The RUF offers flexibility to the issuer in that it allows the issuer at any time to draw short-term CP for sums needed for current liquidity. This releases the firm from using a long-term debt for short-term finance and accordingly makes fund management more efficient. Moreover, since funds are obtained directly from investors, the cost of borrowing in this way is less than the cost of bank loans.

Although the maturity of CP is short, there is always the risk that an issuer might not be able to pay off or roll over[17] the mature paper. Therefore, in most cases issuers need to back up their CP issue with a standby credit line from a commercial bank. The standby lines ensure the availability of funds in the event that the firm experiences a cash flow problem or encounters a tight credit market. From a practical standpoint, most investors do not buy CP unless it is backed by a bank line. Of course, the banks receive a fee for providing backup lines.

Table 2.12 provides some statistics on the Hong Kong dollar–denominated commercial paper issues from 1984 to 1989.[18] The market was very rudimentary in terms of the issues' number and value.

The Foreign Exchange Market

Hong Kong has a mature and efficient foreign exchange (FX) market in which the local currency and major international currencies are actively traded. As an integral part of the corresponding global foreign exchange market, Hong Kong is especially advantageous because of

1. Its advantageous time zone location.

Table 2.12. Hong Kong Dollar–Denominated Commercial Paper Issues Under RUF

	Financial Institutions		Commercial		Total	
	Number of Transactions	Amount (H.K.$ millions)	Number of Transactions	Amount (H.K.$ millions)	Number of Transactions	Amount (H.K.$ millions)
1984	3	1,050	3	1,350	6	2,400
1985	5	860	15	8,000	20	8,860
1986	—	—	7	3,725	7	3,725
1987	2	600	7	4,950	9	5,550
1988	2	600	5	4,550	7	5,150
1989	2	1,000	2	1,750	4	2,750

Source: Schroders Asia Limited.

2. Its large volume of trade and of other external transactions, with the resulting demand for and supply of foreign currencies.

3. The absence of foreign exchange controls.

4. The existence of a highly advanced telecommunications system.

5. The well-established financial infrastructure.

6. The presence of a large number of international banks with experience in foreign exchange dealings.

Like the interbank market, the FX market does not have a centralized physical location for dealings. In essence, it also is a complex, sophisticated network of telephone and telegraphic communications among the dealing rooms of financial institutions operating in various financial centers throughout the world.

The major participants in the Hong Kong market are the authorized institutions, namely, the licensed banks, LDTCs (RLBs), and RDTCs (DTCs). These participants trade on their own accounts and act as interest arbitragers, speculators, or hedgers. They participate in dealings not only to cover commercial demand but also to speculate. At the end of April 1989, there were 407 authorized institutions in operation. More than half of them were actively participating in exchange trading. Since the financial crisis of 1982 to 1985, however, many DTCs, especially those not affiliated with banks, have become less active because participants have become more careful in selecting their counterparty.

Among the participants, foreign banks are relatively active in foreign currency dealings, particularly in trading connected with their home currency. The reason is that these banks have more experience in foreign exchange transactions and may also benefit from closer access to the money markets of their home country.

Deals among the participants may be executed in one of two ways: directly or indirectly. In direct dealing, which is based on the principle of reciprocity, participants simply call each other through telecommunication equipment. One dealing bank makes a market, that is, stands ready to buy or sell a currency to another bank on the understanding that the second bank will also make a market for it. Indirect dealing occurs via foreign exchange brokers, who act as middlemen between the two parties wishing to deal. As of April 1989, there were eleven brokerage firms, all of which had to be the members of the Hong Kong Foreign Exchange and Deposit Brokers Association. Membership is granted with the official recognition of the Hong Kong Association of Banks (H.K.A.B.). Of the eleven brokers, eight are international brokers, and their presence strengthens the link of the local market with the international ones.

Table 2.13 displays the aggregate statistics on foreign exchange transactions by counterparty in April 1989. Most of the foreign exchange transactions (89%) were interbank (including banks and DTCs) transactions.

Table 2.13. Foreign Exchange Transactions by Authorized Institutions' Counterparty Analysis (April 1989)

Counterparty	Average Daily Turnover (U.S.$ equivalent, millions)	% share
Interbank	43,730	89
Direct with authorized institutions in Hong Kong	3,774	8
Direct with banks abroad	22,803	46
Through brokers	17,153 [a]	35
Nonbank sector	5,418	11
Active market participants [b]	834	2
Other customers	4,584	9
Total	49,149	100

Note: Figures may not add up to total because of rounding.

[a] This figure includes transactions arranged by overseas brokers.

[b] Includes active participants in the wholesale foreign exchange market and prime customers enjoying rates similar to those in the interbank market.

Source: Monetary Affairs Branch, Hong Kong government.

Although 8% of the dealings were directly between authorized institutions in Hong Kong and 46% were directly with banks abroad, indirect deals through brokers accounted for a considerable share of 35%. Direct dealings are more popular, partly because of the existence of a brokerage commission and partly because they enable participants to handle a very large amount in a short time with less price variation than in indirect dealings.

The Hong Kong FX market is primarily a spot market, as a significant proportion (62%) of dealings are spot transactions (see Table 2.14). Swap and forward markets, though well developed, are less active in comparison with the spot market.

Table 2.14. Foreign Exchange Transactions by Authorized Institutions' Transaction Analysis (April 1989)

Type of Transaction	% share
Spot	62
Forward [a]	38
Maturity up to and for one month	29
Maturity longer than one month but not more than one year	8
Maturity longer than one year	[b]
Options and futures contracts	[b]
Total	100

Note: Figures may not add up to total due to rounding.

[a] Including swap deals.

[b] Less than 0.5%.

Source: Monetary Affairs Branch, Hong Kong government.

All convertible currencies can be traded in the market, although the trading volumes for different currencies vary greatly. As indicated in Table 2.15, which shows the currency composition of exchange transactions in Hong Kong, the most actively traded ones, in order of their turnover, are Japanese yen (JY), deutsche marks (DM), Hong Kong dollars (H.K.$), sterling pounds (SP), and Swiss francs (SFR).[19] The level of Hong Kong dollar dealing fell following the introduction of the linked exchange rate system in 1983, because the relatively stable exchange rate environment reduced opportunities for speculation. Nevertheless, the foreign exchange market for Hong Kong dollars is still vital to the export-led economy.

The foreign exchange market in Hong Kong has grown rapidly and has been internationalized since 1978, when the lifting of the moratorium on bank licensing caused an influx of international banks. Most of these foreign banks had expertise in foreign exchange dealings. According to a survey conducted by the Monetary Affairs Branch of the Government Secretariat in April 1989, the daily average turnover in the Hong Kong market was about U.S.$49 billion, which was below Japan's U.S.$115 billion and Singapore's U.S.$55 billion in the Asian Pacific region. Hong Kong is thus ranked as the sixth-largest FX–dealing center in the world.

It is noteworthy that the conduct of participants in the market is not regulated, though some guidelines are being drafted by the banking commissioner. Basically, the whole market is completely unregulated and is

Table 2.15. Foreign Exchange Transactions by Authorized Institutions' Currency Composition (April 1989)

Currencies	% share
U.S. dollar against	
Japanese yen	26
Deutsche mark	21
Pound sterling	13
Swiss franc	11
Australian dollar	5
Canadian dollar	2
Others (except H.K. dollar)	3
H.K. dollar against	
U.S. dollar	14
Others	1
Cross currencies [a]	5
ECU denominated	[b]
Total	100

Note: Figures may not add up to total because of rounding.

[a] Direct trading between two currencies not involving the U.S. dollar or the H.K. dollar.

[b] Less than 0.5%.

Source: Monetary Affairs Branch, Hong Kong government.

dependent on economic and social incentives for orderly behavior. It is very important for a dealer to keep his word on the contracts that he has made, as failing to do so will result in his elimination from the market. As the industry puts it, "A dealer's word is as good as gold."

The guidelines propose to control the risk of foreign exchange trading with authorized institutions. Central to the proposal are limits on overnight open positions, which should be linked to the capital base of the institutions involved. The intention is that the limit should not exceed 10% of the capital base in any single currency and 15% for the aggregate portfolio. Any limits exceeding 5% must obtain the commissioner's prior blessing. The restrictions would be applied mainly to locally incorporated banks and DTCs. The local units of overseas-incorporated institutions—either branches or subsidiaries—would be under the jurisdiction of the authority of their parent countries.

EVENT STUDIES

Banking Crises

The Liu Chong Hing Bank had the first serious bank run, in 1961. The run was stopped after a joint support program was announced by the Hongkong and Shanghai Banking Corporation and the Standard Chartered Bank. Later, in 1965, a more serious banking crisis occurred. A small sole proprietorship bank, the Ming Tak Bank, and a medium-size bank, the Canton Trust and Commercial Bank Ltd., collapsed. The panic soon spread to other local banks, which also were subject to a run by depositors. In order to restore the depositors' confidence, the largest and the most successful local Chinese bank, the Hang Seng Bank, was acquired by the Hongkong and Shanghai Banking Corporation. Other smaller local Chinese banks also sought an injection of foreign capital in order to maintain their depositors' confidence. Foreign banks were more than willing to acquire local Chinese banks, simply because no new bank licenses were granted during this period.

There was another major banking crisis from 1982 to 1986. Jao (1988) proposed three main reasons for the crisis:

1. Imprudent management or even fraud committed by directors or senior executives of banks or DTCs.

2. General economic recession, political crisis, and the rapid fall in property prices and in the Hong Kong dollar exchange rate.

3. Overly loose banking regulations at that time that were inappropriate to handling a banking system expanding at such a rapid pace. Some of the government officials were also not well trained, and the Office of the Banking Commissioner was not capable of supervising banks and DTCs.

The crisis began in September 1982 when depositors began a run on the Hang Lung Bank, which was suspected of having a high risk exposure. Several leading banks quickly supported the Hang Lung Bank, and there was not a serious panic. Two months later, two large property firms revealed their financial difficulties, and several DTCs that had large exposure in the property market encountered insolvency problems. In November 1982, a number of RDTCs failed to repay their bank loans, and so the banks stopped extending loans to some of the RDTCs that had problems and lowered their credit limit to other RDTCs. This aggravated the RDTCs' financial situation, as the government had already imposed restrictions on them in July 1981 under the three-tier system in regard to receiving short-term deposits. Existing RDTCs were told to phase out their short-term deposits over the following two years, and by July 1983, no RDTCs would be allowed to hold deposits that matured in less than three months. Thus, many RDTCs had to rely heavily on banks and money market borrowing to finance their assets. This left the independent RDTCs (those not owned by banks) especially vulnerable to the withdrawal of credit lines. By early 1983, the registrations of seven RDTCs were revoked by the banking commissioner, and they subsequently failed, causing heavy losses for their depositors.

In September 1983, the Hong Kong dollar dropped precipitously, and there were rumors again about the soundness of the Hang Lung Bank. In order to restore confidence, the government announced on September 25 that a currency stabilization plan was under consideration, and on September 27, 1983, the government took over the Hang Lung Bank. Later, in June 1985, the government also took over the Overseas Trust Bank, which was one of the largest locally incorporated banks, and its subsidiary, the Hong Kong Industrial and Commercial Bank. Survival funds were also supplied by the government to several problem banks, including the Ka Wah Bank, the Union Bank, the Wing On Bank, and the Hon Nin Bank. Later, the Ka Wah Bank was acquired by the China-owned China International Trust and Investment Corporation; the Wing On Bank was acquired by the Hang Seng Bank, which also belonged to the Hongkong and Shanghai Banking Group; the Union Bank was acquired by the Modern Concepts Ltd., which is a joint venture between the United States and the China state-owned China Merchants Steam Navigation Co.; and the Hon Nin Bank was acquired by the First Pacific Group. Thus, after all these crises, only a handful of purely Chinese banks remained.

Because of the banking crisis, the government had to tighten its regulations on the banking sector, and the new Banking Ordinance was enacted in May 1986. The Banking Ordinance of 1986 marks a monumental change in Hong Kong's banking regulations. The major innovations of the new laws are as follows:

1. The ordinance governs both banks and DTCs, and the commissioner of banking supervises both types of institution.

2. The power and the responsibilities of the banking commissioner are enhanced.

3. A minimum capital to risk assets ratio requirement is instituted.

4. The commissioner is also empowered to issue from time to time guidelines for banking operations.

The minimum capital adequacy ratio requirement is probably the most innovative regulation in Hong Kong's banking history. When it was first made effective in 1988, the minimum ratio was 5%. In December 1989, the requirement was raised to 8% in accordance with the international norm. Such a regulation was introduced partly because of the trend in the area of international banking regulation to adopt a more uniform capital requirement and partly because of the banking crisis in the 1980s that clearly demonstrated that all the institutions that encountered problems were undercapitalized relative to their assets.

Although most of the licensed banks could meet the minimum capital adequacy requirement when it was first instituted, a number of DTCs could not meet the 5% minimum requirement. In 1988, thirty-nine DTCs, especially the Japanese-owned ones, added H.K.$3.2 billion in cash to their equity, and there were five issues of perpetual subordinated debt. Other institutions that could not increase their capital base tried to meet the requirement by reducing their assets. During the same year, the total assets of DTCs decreased by 16%, and those of locally incorporated banks increased by 20%. The assets of the Japanese DTCs suffered the greatest fall, of more than 25%.

The Linked Exchange Rate System

In 1983, Hong Kong confronted a severe financial crisis. The uncertainty surrounding the territory's political future after 1997 led to a significant capital outflow, and this, abetted by a strong U.S. dollar, unsettled foreign exchange markets worldwide, and speculation created a heavy downward pressure on the exchange value of the Hong Kong dollar. The currency depreciated from 6.10 against the U.S. dollar at the end of August 1982 to 7.595 on August 31, 1983, nearly 25% in just twelve months. The situation got worse when the Hong Kong dollar continued to slump afterward, reaching an all-time low of 9.60 on September 24, 1983. Against a background of the continuing depreciation and increasing instability of the Hong Kong dollar's exchange rate, the government decided, effective on October 17, 1983, to alter the arrangements for issuing notes and consequently to change the exchange rate system from a freely floating to a linked one.

The new arrangement centers on the certificates of indebtedness (CIs), which are issued by the Exchange Fund[20] to the two note-issuing banks, to be held as a backing for issuing Hong Kong dollar notes. Before that date the CIs were issued and redeemed against payments in Hong Kong dollars. Under the new arrangement, such payments are made in U.S. dollars at a fixed exchange rate of U.S.$1.00 = H.K.$7.80. The Exchange Fund promises to issue and redeem the CI at a rate of H.K.$7.80/U.S.$1.00, and the note-issuing banks agree that they should provide notes to, and accept notes from, other banks on the same basis as they themselves deal with the Exchange Fund, that is, against payments in U.S. dollars at the rate of U.S.$1.00 = H.K.$7.80. In other words, an interbank market for Hong Kong dollar notes at a fixed exchange rate was created.

In the open FX market, the exchange rate of the Hong Kong dollar is still allowed to float freely, and the value of the Hong Kong dollar should therefore be determined by market supply and demand. Nevertheless, any significant deviation between the official fixed rate and the open market exchange rate will result in profitable arbitrage opportunities for the banks. Their forces of competition and arbitrage between the two markets will ensure that the FX market exchange rate converges to a level very close to the fixed rate, without any intervention by the Exchange Fund in the market.

Appendix 2A provides some statistical tests for the variability and efficiency of the FX market immediately before and after the establishment of the linked-rate system. We found that the linked-rate system has greatly reduced the variability of exchange rate changes but that the market remains practically efficient (in the weak-form sense).

The Negative Interest Rate Scheme

Between November 1987 and February 1988, the linked exchange rate system faced a challenge because there was a huge amount of hot money flowing into Hong Kong and there were widespread rumors that the Hong Kong dollar would be revalued. Its market exchange rate hovered around 7.77 during this period and at times went above 7.75, which was about 0.6 percent higher than the official rate of 7.80. The six-month forward rate was once over 7.60. Law (1988) showed that since the introduction of the linked exchange rate system in October 1983, it was challenged by market forces five times and the pressure for revaluation occurred four times (see Table 2.16). We next summarize these four cases.

Because of the continued speculation favoring an upward revaluation of the Hong Kong dollar, the government announced the "negative interest rate" scheme, which had two parts. The first part was a charge payable by licensed banks to the Exchange Fund on incremental balances of their credit balances at the clearinghouse. The second part was a charge on customers' credit balances at licensed banks in excess of H.K.$1 million. However, the Hong Kong dollar soon stabilized after the announcement of the negative interest rate scheme, and the scheme was never implemented.

Table 2.16. Challenges to the Linked Exchange Rate

Period of	Highest Value vs. U.S. Dollar	Reduction in Best Lending Rate	Major Causes of Pressure
Feb. 15, 1984– Mar. 10, 1984 (about 30 days)	7.77 (+0.48%)	3%	The market considered the official rate to be too low.
May 10, 1995– Aug. 10, 1985 (about 90 days)	7.72 (+1.0%)	3%	U.S. dollar declined very rapidly.
Jan. 10, 1987– Feb. 5, 1987 (about 25 days)	7.75 (+0.6%)	1.5%	Baker said that the United States could not accept the large trade deficits with the NIEs.
Nov. 20, 1987– Feb. 10, 1988 (about 80 days)	7.75 (+0.6%)	1.25%	U.S. and European governments strongly attacked the linked rate.

Source: C. K. Law, "Forum on the Negative Interest Rate Scheme," *Hong Kong Economic Papers* 19 (1988): 75–78.

The New Accounting System

In the afternoon of July 15, 1988, the Monetary Affairs Branch and the Hongkong and Shanghai Banking Corporation (HSBC) jointly announced a new accounting arrangement between the Exchange Fund and the HSBC. This change requires the HSBC to maintain an account with the Exchange Fund. The purpose of the new arrangement is to enable the government to exercise more effective influence over the availability and price of money in the interbank market.

Under the old system, the HSBC was the ultimate clearing bank, since it was not necessary for the HSBC to hold an account with any outside entity. The transactions of the HSBC with other banks would affect the net clearing balance of other banks with the HSBC. If the HSBC purchased (sold) assets from (to) other banks, it had to credit (debit) the other banks' accounts, and so the net balance would increase (decrease). Such a net balance would have widespread implications for the interbank market. Banks that ran a surplus could lend to banks that had a deficit, and the interest rate or the interbank rate would be determined by the supply of and demand for funds. An increase in the net balance would mean an increase in the net supply of liquidity, and the interbank rate would fall, whereas a decrease in the net balance would cause the interbank rate to rise. Any sustained change in the interbank rate would ultimately affect the decision of the Hong Kong Association of Banks to change its deposit rates, and the leading banks would then change their best lending rate and the mortgage rate. In more technical jargon, the HSBC could use its own liabilities to inject liquidity into or extract it from the economy. There is, of course, a limit to such an effect because the supply of high-powered money, that is, the CIs, was constrained by the supply of U.S. dollars under the linked exchange rate system. But there is no doubt that the HSBC did have some leeway in manipulating short-term money market conditions.

Effective on July 18, 1988, the new arrangement was worked out between the Exchange Fund and the HSBC.

1. The HSBC is required to maintain a Hong Kong dollar account with the Exchange Fund and should try to maintain a balance in that account at not less than the net clearing balance of the rest of the banking system.

2. The Exchange Fund does not have to pay interest to the HSBC for credit balances in such an account. However, the HSBC does have to pay interest to the Exchange Fund if the balance is less than the net clearing balance or if the net clearing balance is in debit.

3. There are two scales for the interest rate charged. Up to a certain amount, the Exchange Fund charges a basic rate, that is, the best lending rate or the interbank rate, whichever is higher. Beyond that amount, a premium of 3% is added to that basic rate.

4. The Exchange Fund can use the HSBC account to settle its transactions with either the HSBC or other banks.

In addition, the Treasury also must maintain an account with the Exchange Fund, and it may be asked to transfer its balances with the banking system to such an account in return for interest-bearing debt certificates issued by the Exchange Fund. Thus, the Exchange Fund account has two funding sources: the net clearing balance of the banking system and the fiscal revenue from the treasury.

Under the new system, the Exchange Fund effectively replaces the HSBC in the provision of liquidity to the banking system. When the Exchange Fund borrows funds from the HSBC, the HSBC's account with the Exchange Fund is debited, thereby causing a shortfall relative to the net clearing balance of the rest of the banking system. In order to avoid an interest penalty, the HSBC then tries to borrow a corresponding amount from other banks to make up the shortfall by debiting other banks' clearing balances with the HSBC. The net effect is a reduction in the net clearing balance. If the Exchange Fund chooses to borrow from other banks, the Exchange Fund will debit HSBC's account, and the HSBC will debit the account of other banks by the corresponding amount, leading to a reduction in the clearing balance in the banking system. These transactions will then drive up the Hong Kong interbank offered rate (HIBOR) and support the exchange rate. Lending activities by the Exchange Fund will lead to an increase in the net clearing balance, a decrease in the HIBOR, and a weakening in the exchange rate. In effect, the new system enables the Exchange Fund to extract liquidity from the economy by issuing its own liabilities and to inject liquidity by retiring its own liabilities. Thus, the Exchange Fund has effectively assumed part of the central banking functions. That is why this new arrangement is a fundamental change in Hong Kong's financial system and should have wide implications for the HSBC and the financial markets. Between July 1988 and March 1990, the Exchange Fund intervened fifteen times (Table 2.17).

Generally, the Exchange Fund intervenes in the market to keep the parity of U.S.$1.00 = H.K.$7.80, but there are some exceptions to this rule. On June 5, 1989, the Exchange Fund deposited H.K.$194 million in the market to cover the large withdrawal from the Bank of China during the June 4, incident. The Exchange Fund also intervened to alleviate short-term liquidity shortages in the market.

Although the new system has already widened the scope for control, the menu of instruments available to the Exchange Fund is still very limited, which is why the government introduced short-term treasury bills on March

Table 2.17. Record of Intervention by the Exchange Fund Since July 1988 (in H.K.$ millions)

Date	Balance in the Account	Scale of Intervention
1988		
Sept. 7	1,100	−150
Oct. 11	950	−150
Oct. 12	880	−70
Nov. 30	860	−20
Dec. 6	1,060	+200 [a]
Dec. 7	860	−200
1989		
Jan. 5	728	−132
Jun. 5	922	+194
Jun. 12	923	+1
Aug. 7	728	−195
Dec. 30	978	+250 [a]
1990		
Jan. 2	728	−250
Jan. 5	528	−200
Mar. 14	524	−4 [b]
Mar. 21	510	−14 [b]

Note: "Minus" signifies a withdrawal; "plus" an injection of funds.

[a] Overnight assistance. The invervention on Dec. 6–7, 1988, and Dec. 30, 1989–Jan. 2, 1990, covered the H.K. Telecom share issue and the liquidity shortages over the long holiday weekend, respectively.

[b] Interventions associated with the issuing of the Exchange Fund bills.

Source: Asian Monetary Monitor, March–April 1990.

13, 1990. Every Tuesday, the government auctions off between H.K.$200 million and H.K.$300 million in ninety-one-day Exchange Fund bills. The government also appointed a group of fourteen money dealers to be the market makers who bid directly for the weekly issue; other institutions and investors have to bid through them. Initially, only H.K.$3 billion to H.K.$4 billion in bills will be outstanding at any one time. The first weekly auction took place on March 13, 1990, and the tender for H.K.$300 million of thirteen-week Exchange Fund bills was vastly oversubscribed (by more than sixfold, with H.K.$2.01 billion in bids received). The average accepted yield of 8.04% was well below the day's three-month HIBOR of 9%, with the highest successful yield coming in at 8.37%. The government has made it known that the bills are issued only for the purpose of intervening in the money market but not for the purpose of financing the government deficit.

THE PERFORMANCE AND BEHAVIOR OF THE MONEY MARKET

The Spread Between the Lending Rate and the HIBOR

Table 2.18 shows the spread between the best lending rate (BLR) and the three-month HIBOR. The HIBOR is the cost of funds for the banking institutions, and the BLR is the cost of funds for nonbank institutions. Our

Table 2.18. Spread Between Best Lending Rate (BLR) and Three-Month HIBOR (%)

Year	Mean	Standard Deviation
1980	0.6094	2.11
1981	0.7708 [a]	0.95
1982	1.4010 [b]	0.75
1983	1.4271 [b]	1.30
1984	1.6198 [b]	1.22
1985	1.2656 [b]	0.70
1986	1.1667 [b]	0.66
1987	1.1771 [b]	0.87
1988	0.9233 [b]	0.66
Jan. 1980–Oct. 1983	1.0443 [b]	1.41
Nov. 1983–Dec. 1988	1.1969 [b]	0.92
Jan. 1980–Dec. 1988	1.1512 [b]	1.16
T-test	−0.44	N.A.
F-test	N.A.	2.42 [a]

Notes: T-test tests the means between the two periods; F-test tests the variances between the two periods.

[a] Significant at the 5% level.

[b] Significant at the 1% level.

analysis covers the period from January 1980 to December 1988, which is divided into two subperiods: January 1980 to October 1983 and November 1983 to December 1988. Table 2.18 shows that there was an increase in the spread in the second period but that it was statistically insignificant. There was also a decrease in the standard deviation of the spread, and the F-test indicates that the decrease in variability was significant. Table 2.19 gives the mean and standard deviation for the BLR and the HIBOR over the years. Like the world trend, the interest rate level fell until 1988, and the variability of interest rates seem to have followed the same trend. Thus, the results indicate that interest rates became more stable after the linked exchange rate system was implemented, but there is no significant increase in the spread.

Causality Relationships

Next we examine the causal relations among the SIBOR (the Singapore interbank offered rate), the HIBOR, the BLR, and the three-month deposit rate (BD). We used Granger's (1969, 1980) definition of causality and the Akaike (1969, 1970) final prediction error (FPE) criteria to determine the optimal lag structure, and we used the likelihood ratio test to see whether the coefficients of the additional variables in a bivariate VAR model are equal to zero. The bivariate VAR models we considered are presented in Equations 1 to 6:

Table 2.19. Best Lending Rate and HIBOR, by Year

	BLR		HIBOR	
Year	Mean	S.D.	Mean	S.D.
1980	13.58	2.45	12.97	3.09
1981	17.42	0.95	16.65	1.24
1982	13.79	2.06	12.39	2.34
1983	12.58	1.74	11.16	2.10
1984	12.38	1.95	10.76	2.32
1985	7.96	1.45	6.69	1.01
1986	7.00	0.50	5.83	0.98
1987	8.06	1.64	7.14	2.23
1988	6.42	0.91	5.24	1.45
Jan. 1980–Oct. 1983	14.38	2.68	13.29	3.12
Nov. 1983–Dec. 1988	8.53	2.64	7.33	2.75
1980–1988	11.02	3.93	9.87	4.14
T-test	11.22 [a]	N.A.	10.21 [a]	N.A.
F-test	N.A.	1.04	N.A.	1.30

Notes: T-test tests the means between the two periods; F-test tests the variances between the two periods.

[a] Significant at the 1% level.

SIBOR (RS) and HIBOR (RB)

$$RS = \alpha + \beta^m{}_{11}(L)RS + \beta^n{}_{12}(L)RB + \varepsilon \qquad (1)$$

$$RB = \alpha + \beta^m{}_{21}(L)RS + \beta^n{}_{22}(L)RB + \varepsilon \qquad (2)$$

HIBOR (RB) and best lending rate (RL)

$$RB = \alpha + \beta^m{}_{11}(L)RB + \beta^n{}_{12}(L)RL + \varepsilon \qquad (3)$$

$$RL = \alpha + \beta^m{}_{21}(L)RB + \beta^n{}_{22}(L)RL + \varepsilon \qquad (4)$$

HIBOR (RB) and deposit rate (RD)

$$RB = \alpha + \beta^m{}_{11}(L)RB + \beta^n{}_{12}(L)RD + \varepsilon \qquad (5)$$

$$RD = \alpha + \beta^m{}_{21}(L)RB + \beta^n{}_{22}(L)RD + \varepsilon \qquad (6)$$

where α is a constant; L is the lag operator (i.e., $LX_t = X_{t-1}$); $\beta^m{}_{ij}$ and $\beta^n{}_{ij}$ are the polynomials in L of order m and n, which are estimated by the minimum FPE criteria; and ε_t is a random error term with a zero mean and constant variance.

Table 2.20 summarizes the causal relations. In the earlier period, there was a two-way relation between the SIBOR and the HIBOR. But in the latter period, the SIBOR caused the HIBOR unidirectionally, indicating that external interest rates have had more influence on the local interest rates since the linked rate was established. The causal direction between HIBOR and BLR is also clear, in that the HIBOR caused the BLR. The results with the RD (three-month deposit rate) were less consistent: There was no relationship in the earlier period, but there was a two-way relationship in the latter period. However, judging from the variance decomposition results given in Appendix 2B, we can conclude that the causal effect running from RB to RD is stronger than that running the other way round.

Serial Correlation of Interest Rates

A market is efficient if all the relevant information is used in forming the current price, and thus the historical price would not be useful in predicting either current or future prices. This type of efficiency is usually referred to as *weak-form efficiency*, and people usually resort to serial correlation to test for the randomness of the logarithmic price relatives. In this study we used the Box–Pierce Q-statistics with five months lag to test for the randomness of the logarithmic interest rate relatives, and the results are shown in Table 2.21. In the overall period, all the Q-statistics are not significant, demonstrating that all the interest rate series can be treated as a random variable. The analysis can also be done by delineating the period into two: one before and the other after the establishment of the linked exchange rate system. One interesting point that can be detected is that in the case of the HIBOR, the Q-statistics in the latter period are

Table 2.20. Result of the Likelihood Ratio Tests and Causal Direction

Models (period)	Null Hypothesis	Chi-Square Statistics/ Conclusion	Causal Direction
RS–RB			
	$\beta_{12}^{1}(L) = 0$	4.12 [a]/Reject	
1980–Dec. 1988	$\beta_{21}^{1}(L) = 0$	12.85 [b]/Reject	RS↔RB
	$\beta_{12}^{11}(L) = 0$	22.70 [c]/Reject	
Jan. 1980–Oct. 1988	$\beta_{21}^{1}(L) = 0$	9.53 [b]/Reject	RS↔RB
	$\beta_{12}^{4}(L) = 0$	4.91/Accept	
Nov. 1983–Dec. 1988	$\beta_{21}^{2}(L) = 0$	12.10/Reject	RS→RB
RB–RL			
	$\beta_{12}^{4}(L) = 0$	2.88/Accept	
Jan. 1980–Dec. 1988	$\beta_{21}^{3}(L) = 0$	30.31/Reject	RB→RL
	$(L) = 0$		
	$\beta_{21}^{4}(L) = 0$	2.11/Accept	
Jan. 1980–Oct. 1983	$(L) = 0$		RB→RL
	$\beta_{21}^{3}(L) = 0$	7.43 [a]/Reject	
	$\beta_{12}^{4}(L) = 0$	7.05/Accept	
Nov. 1983–Dec. 1988	$\beta_{21}^{8}(L) = 0$	45.84/Reject	RB→RL
RB–RD			
	$\beta_{12}^{4}(L) = 0$	3.74/Accept	
Jan. 1980–Dec. 1988	$\beta_{21}^{1}(L) = 0$	23.12 [b]/Reject	RB→RD
	$\beta_{12}^{4}(L) = 0$	2.96/Accept	
Jan. 1980–Oct. 1983	$\beta_{21}^{4}(L) = 0$	7.71/Accept	RB⊥RD
	$\beta_{21}^{6}(L) = 0$	27.91 [b]/Reject	
Nov. 1983–Dec. 1988	$\beta_{21}^{11}(L) = 0$	62.54 [b]/Reject	RB↔RD

Notes: X→Y means that X causes Y. X↔Y means that X causes Y, and vice versa. X⊥Y means that no causal relation exists between X and Y. RS = SIBOR, RB = HIBOR, RL = BLR, RD = deposit rates.

[a] Significant at the 10% level.

[b] Significant at the 1% level.

[c] Significant at the 5% level.

Table 2.21. Q-Statistics of Interest Rate Series (five-month lag)

	Jan. 1980– Dec. 1988	Jan. 1980– Oct. 1983	Nov. 1983– Dec. 1988
HIBOR			
One-month	8.87	5.11	5.84
Three-month	7.40	5.03	2.41
Six-month	4.66	3.83	3.47
Deposits			
One-month [a]	7.62	3.53	7.36
Three-month	11.06	5.02	11.61 [b]
Six-month	8.01	4.77	10.18
Lending rate			
	6.29	4.69	6.68

[a] Data for the one-month deposit rate cover July 1982 to December 1988.
[b] Indicates significant at the 5% level.

of the same magnitude as or even smaller than that in the earlier period. However, in the case of the deposit rates and the lending rate, all the Q-statistics in the latter period are unanimously greater than that in the earlier period and the Q-statistic for the three-month rate is also significant at the 5% level. The reason is probably that after the establishment of the linked rate, the Hong Kong dollar exchange rate stabilized, and the interest rate in Hong Kong was also linked to that of the United States; thus the Hong Kong Association of Banks was under less pressure to change the cartel rate in order to defend the Hong Kong dollar. Thus, after the linked rate system was established, the deposit rate was changed less frequently than previously, leading to a higher serial correlation.

CONCLUSIONS

Hong Kong is unique in that it has no central bank and yet it has been able to survive various financial crises. The lessons offered by the Hong Kong financial system may be valuable to other emerging economies.

As a small and open economy, Hong Kong is constantly subject to severe shocks, which are further aggravated by the uncertain political future of Hong Kong. The most obvious example was the currency crisis in 1983. It is also difficult, if not impossible, for Hong Kong to have perfect control over its money supply. It is thus more meaningful for it to peg its currency to a hard currency. In the case of Hong Kong, the U.S. dollar was chosen in 1983 as the currency to which the Hong Kong dollar would be linked. One special feature of the linked currency system is that it does not rely on direct government intervention but instead operates on an automatic system of cash arbitrage. Hong Kong's experience tells us, however, that such a system is not perfect and that a mechanism for active management of liquidity is still needed. That is why a mechanism was implemented in 1988 to enable the Exchange Fund to influence the money supply after the repeated speculations from 1984 to 1988.

In a system without any kind of deposit insurance or safety net, the government obviously has to resort to other means of maintaining the stability of the financial system. A segmentation program thus was adopted in the deposit market, which imposes maturity and minimum deposit restrictions on the deposit-taking companies (DTCs). These restrictions caused a rapid shrinkage in the DTCs' market share, and it also reduced the cost of supervision and the cost of any DTC failures. But this policy does not seem to serve the purpose of maintaining stability, at least in the short run, as many (marginal) DTCs encountered problems in the early 1980s soon after the policy was adopted. Thus, it seems that a system without any deposit insurance does not necessarily lead to the more prudent management of financial institutions. Moreover, it may be the government's intention to trade short-term stability for long-term stability, in that it takes time for the dust to settle.

Apart from such a segmentation policy, the government is also relying on the major private banks, especially the Hongkong and Shanghai Banking Corporation, to bail out problem banks during financial crises. Although this practice did work quite well in the 1960s, the Hongkong and Shanghai Banking Corporation did not seem to be enthusiastic about handling financial crises in the 1980s, and the government had to resort to its own means to help problem banks. The reason may be that the Hongkong and Shanghai Banking Corporation has become an international conglomerate, and it has become increasingly unfair for its shareholders to shoulder the responsibility of maintaining Hong Kong's financial stability. Moreover, a quicker response by the government was needed to combat instability in the financial market in the 1980s. This is crucial, as Hong Kong has become an important link in the international flow-of-funds network, and any problems would certainly tarnish the image of Hong Kong as an international financial center. It is crucial that the government provide at least an implicit guarantee of the safety of the system, in order to maintain the viability of the financial center.

The adoption of the minimum capital adequacy ratio in 1986 further demonstrates that the segmentation policy alone cannot safeguard the stability of the financial system. In fact, the segmentation policy may increase the riskiness of the system by blowing up the size of the licensed banks' balance sheets. In retrospect, the government should have adopted the minimum capital adequacy ratio at the same time it implemented the segmentation policy. But this criticism may be too harsh, as the issue of capital adequacy has only recently been considered seriously in international banking circles.

Finally, the government does not seem to put the same emphasis on market efficiency as it does on stability. That is, it still maintains the interest rate rule (the deposit interest rate cartel) and, until recently, has made no special effort to foster the development of new financial instruments. It is fortunate that stability has not been gained at the expense of efficiency, probably because of the principle of maintaining an open system and the fact that Hong Kong is still the integrated financial center of the Asian Pacific region.

In the area of money market development, the Hong Kong market remains relatively simple. Hong Kong's money markets mainly comprise the short-term customer deposits, the interbank market, and the foreign exchange market. Although a variety of other instruments such as commercial paper, certificates of deposit, and bankers acceptances also exist, they carry relatively little weight on the balance sheets of banks and deposit-taking companies.

The short-term customer deposit market is also highly monopolized, with the licensed banks maintaining more than 90% of the market share. This outcome is partly due to the government's segmentation policy and partly due to the financial crisis in the early 1980s. Such a policy also has an important impact on the interbank market in that the licensed banks have become the net lenders and the DTCs have become the net borrowers. Moreover, within the licensed banking sector, the local banks usually act as net lenders of funds to foreign banks, because, of course, it is usually difficult, if not impossible, to intrude into a retail banking market that is already very oligopolistic. Another, minor, reason is that the new foreign banks that obtained their licenses after 1978 are allowed to operate only one office in Hong Kong.

Unlike the domestic currency market, the foreign exchange market is a totally free, except that the Hong Kong–U.S. dollar rate is administered by the Exchange Fund. Although survey statistics show that the market turnover in Singapore is higher than that of Hong Kong, the Singapore government's involvement in terms of intervention by the Monetary Authority of Singapore (MAS) is also very great, whereas government-related dealings in Hong Kong are relatively minor.

The development of the Hong Kong money market in regard to the variety of instruments is still very slow, because the secondary market is very thin and there are no government securities. But this may change very rapidly, as the government has already issued short-term Exchange Fund bills of up to twelve months. Longer-term instruments of two to three years are also being planned, to raise funds to finance the infrastructure projects in Hong Kong. Thus, it is in the interest of the Hong Kong government to help develop a secondary market. With such stimulation, it is expected that the breadth and depth of the Hong Kong money market will improve.

NOTES

This chapter was prepared in connection with the Research Project on Money Markets in Asia, organized by the Program on International Financial Systems of the Harvard Law School and the Harvard Institute for International Development. This chapter is not to be circulated, quoted, or cited without the express written approval of the authors.

1. A moratorium on issuing new bank licenses was introduced in 1966 in order to avoid fierce competition among the banks, but it was lifted in 1978 in view of the development of Hong Kong as an international financial center.

2. Foreign banks obtaining a license after 1978 can maintain only one office in Hong Kong, making it extremely difficult for the newcomers to compete in the retail market.

3. These institutions are governed by the Banking Ordinance of 1986 and are collectively known as the "authorized institutions" in the ordinance.

4. The "interest rate rule" means that an interest rate cartel sets the maximum interest rate on deposits that has to be observed by all "licensed banks." But since the DTCs are not members of the Hong Kong Association of Banks (HKAB), they are not bound by this rule and so can freely set their own deposit rates.

5. Previously, it was necessary for the former LDTCs first to become an RDTC before becoming an LDTC. This was an irrational requirement, as the RDTCs operated mostly in the retail market, whereas the LDTCs operated mostly in the wholesale market. Thus, the experience of running a RDTC would not benefit the operation of an LDTC.

6. The government did not report the two types of financial statistics separately until recently.

7. This is the categorization adopted by Jao 1974.

8. The Hang Seng Bank also acquired 50.3% of Wing On Bank's share holdings in 1986.

9. There are ten fully independent (with less than 50% capital owned by a foreign institution) or semi-independent local Chinese banks: the East Asia Bank, Dah Sing Bank, Tai Sang Bank, Tai Yau Bank, Hong Kong Industrial and Commercial Bank, United Chinese Bank, Commercial Bank of Hong Kong, Shanghai Commercial Bank, Wing Lung Bank, and Liu Chong Hing Bank.

10. In addition to the Hong Kong banks, "other banks" include those from other Asian Pacific countries (excluding China and Japan) and from Latin America, Africa, Eastern Europe, the Middle East, and the Caribbean. It is believed that the share of banks other than Hong Kong banks is extremely small. This item should be heavily dominated by banks from Hong Kong, especially the Hongkong and Shanghai Banking Group.

11. The Herfindahl index is calculated as $\Sigma\ S_i2$, where S_i is the share of the ith bank in the market under consideration.

12. The newly industrialized economies include Hong Kong, Korea, Singapore, and Taiwan.

13. This might be an exaggeration, as some of the DTCs were also owned by banks.

14. The bid rate is the market's borrowing price at which participants may, through brokers, place (lend) funds to the institution bidding at that price. Participants with a shortage of funds may take (borrow) at the offer price (the so-called HIBOR, or the Hong Kong interbank offered rate).

15. For instance, in the United States there are two agencies rating CP: Moody's Investor Service and Standard & Poor's. From highest to lowest, CP ratings are P-1, P-2, and P-3 for Moody's; and A-1, A-2, and A-3 for Standard & Poor's.

16. The issue was made by the Mass Transit Railway Corporation (MTRC) in the form of negotiable bills of exchange with a maturity of 360 days in the value of H.K.$500 million.

17. Rolling over paper means that the issue sells new commercial paper to get funds to retire maturing paper.

18. Owing to the lack of data, we restrict our discussion to the Hong Kong dollar–denominated instruments. But there have also been issues in other currencies, notably U.S. dollars, Australian dollars, and, to a lesser degree, Canadian dollars. Issues in these currencies tend to be opportunistic in terms of prevailing exchange rates and perceived investor demand, and as such they tend to have peripheral effects compared with the ongoing progress of the domestic markets.

19. Of course, the U.S. dollar is the most actively traded currency because of its nature as a medium of exchange in the market. As a market practice, all currencies are usually traded against the U.S. dollar.

20. The Exchange Fund is the official organization responsible for maintaining the stability and convertibility of the Hong Kong dollar and managing the government's financial assets placed in the fund. The fund is under the control of the financial secretary and is used for such purposes as the financial secretary deems suitable, affecting, either directly or indirectly, the exchange value of the Hong Kong dollar, and for other incidental purposes.

REFERENCES

Akaike, H. 1969. "Fitting Autoregressive for Prediction." *Annals of the Institute of Statistical Mathematics* 21: 243–47.

———. 1970. "Statistical Predictor Indentification." *Annals of the Institute of Statistical Mathematics* 22: 203–17.

Chan, Daniel. 1987. "Hong Kong Bond Market: Difficulties and Feasible Solution." *Securities Bulletin* 14 (June): 32–33.

Cheung, H. 1988. "Capital Market Instruments in Transition." *Securities Bulletin* 24 (April): 19–20.

Ghose, T. K. 1987. *The Banking System of Hong Kong.* Singapore: Butterworths.

Granger, C. W. J. 1969. "Investing Causal Relation by Econometric Models and Cross-Spectral Methods." *Econometrica* 37: 424–38.

———. 1980. "Testing for Causality: A Personal Viewpoint." *Journal of Economic Dynamics and Control* 2: 329–52.

Ho, Y. K. 1985. "The Money Market and the Foreign Exchange Market." In *Hong Kong's Financial Institutions and Markets.* Edited by R. H. Scott, K. A. Wong, and Y. K. Ho, pp. 79–103. Hong Kong: Oxford University Press.

Hurst, M. K. 1989. "A Review and the Prospects for Hong Kong Capital Market." *Securities Bulletin* 33 (January): 20–22.

Jao, Y. C. 1974. *Banking and Currency in Hong Kong.* London: Macmillan.

———. 1988. "Monetary System and Banking Structure." In *The Economic System of Hong Kong.* Edited by H. C. Y. Ho and L. C. Chau, chap. 4. Hong Kong: Asian Research Service.

Law, C. K. 1988. "Forum on the Negative Interest Rate Scheme." *Hong Kong Economic Papers* 19: 75–78.

Lee, S. Y., and Y. C. Jao. 1982. *Financial Structures and Monetary Policies in Southeast Asia.* London: Macmillan Press.

Lui, Y. H. 1988. "The Information Content of the HIBOR." *Hong Kong Economic Journal Monthly* 12 (July): 93–96.

———. 1988. "The Variety of Hong Kong Capital Market Instruments." *Hong Kong Economic Journal Monthly* 12 (November): 95–103.

———. 1989. *The Hong Kong Financial System.* Commercial Press.

McBain, R. E. 1988. "Hong Kong Capital Market Since October 19." *Securities Bulletin* 24 (April): 21–24.

APPENDIX 2A

EFFECT OF THE LINKED EXCHANGE RATE SYSTEM ON THE EXCHANGE RATE

To investigate the impact of the regulatory change on exchange rate behavior, we performed a statistical analysis on the interbank daily closing spot selling rates for U.S. dollars against H.K. dollars. The data are for January 4, 1982, to December 31, 1984. This period was chosen to cover the time around the day (October 17, 1983) that the linked-rate system was established. There were a total of 733 trading days for the entire period concerned, of which 434 were before and 299 after the commencement of the linked-rate system. Our statistical tests were performed on the daily changes in the natural logarithm of spot rates,

$$X_{t+1} = 1nS_{t+1} - 1nS_t$$

where S_t, S_{t+1} are the spot rates at the end of day t and $t+1$, respectively.

Summary statistics of the distributions of daily exchange rate changes are reported in Table 2A.1. When considering these sample moments, it is important to note that the distributions do not appear to be normally distributed. Sample skewness moments are 0.4046 before and 26.8001 after the change; the sample kurtosis moments are 16.1570 and 50.4881, respectively. Not only are both distributions markedly skewed to the right and highly leptokurtic, but also the skewness and peakedness increased after the regime was changed.

We performed stationarity tests by plotting the exchange rate change series in Figure 2A.1 and also by dividing each of the two samples into two distinct subsamples.[1] We then examined the variances and means of these subsamples to determine whether any temporal drift in the series emerged.

Two features of the data are evident in Table 2A.1. First, the exchange rate series is not stationary over the complete sample period (January 4, 1982 to December 31, 1984): The parameters of the distribu-

Table 2A.1. Summary Statistics of Exchange Rate Changes

	Before Link 1/4/82–10/12/83	After Link 10/17/83–12/31/84	Null Hypothesis (H_0)	Test Statistic	Probability Value
Mean	0.00088	−0.00007	$\mu_B = \mu_A$	$t = 2.53$ [a]	0.01
			$\mu_B = 0$	$t = 2.38$ [a]	0.02
			$\mu_A = 0$	$t = -1.00$	0.32
			$\sigma_B^2 > \sigma_A^2$	$F = 39.83$ [a]	N.A.
Standard deviation	0.00770	0.00122			
Sample size	433	298			

Subperiods	B1 (1/4/82– 9/24/82)	B2 (9/25/82– 10/12/83)	A1 (10/17/83– 9/26/84)	A2 (9/27/84– 12/31/84)	Null Hypothesis (H_0)	Test Statistic	Probability Value
Mean	0.00046	0.00113	−0.00009	0.000026	$\mu_{B1} = -B2$	$t = -1.00$	0.32
					$\mu_{B1} = 0$	$t = 1.38$	0.17
					$\mu_{B2} = 0$	$t = 1.95$	0.05
					$\mu_{A1} = \mu_{A2}$	$t = -1.16$	0.25
					$\mu_{A1} = 0$	$t = -1.01$	0.31
					$\mu_{A2} = 0$	$t = 0.57$	0.57
Standard deviation	0.00441	0.00930	0.00136	0.000365	$\sigma_{B1}^2 \leq \sigma_{B2}^2$	$F = 4.45$ [a]	N.A.
					$\sigma_{A1}^2 \leq \sigma_{A2}^2$	$F = 13.88$ [a]	N.A.
Sample size	176	256	233	64			

[a] Significant at the 5% level. The significance level is overstated because the distribution of the exchange rate changes fails to satisfy the assumption of normality.

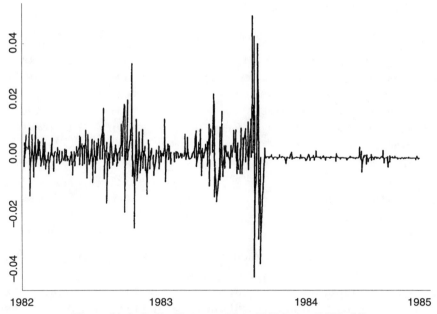

Figure 2A.1. Daily Changes of Spot T. T. Rates (1982–85)

tions are significantly different in the floating and linked periods. But the insignificant differences between the subperiods' parameters suggest that the series was stationary within each period. Second, the introduction of the linked-rate system seems to have greatly reduced the variability of the exchange rate changes.

We also carried out runs and serial correlation tests. The runs tests have the advantage of avoiding the distributional assumption of normality. The results of the runs tests are shown in Table 2A.2. The null hypothesis that the daily rate changes are independent can be rejected at the 5% level in the floating-rate period but not in the linked period.

The results of the serial correlation tests are reported in Table 2A.3. The sample coefficients, either before or after the link, are quite small in absolute value: All but one is smaller than 0.16. For the floating period, there are six cases in which the coefficients are significantly different from zero at the 5% level. For the linked period, all but the first-order coefficient are less than 0.08 and not significantly different from zero at the 5% level, indicating that successive rate changes do have some "memory," albeit a memory that is short lived and weak. No significant systematic patterns in terms of signs and lags were found in either period. It appears unlikely that these small serial correlations, though statistically significant, can be used as the basis for formulating substantially profitable trading strategies.

The first-order serial correlation in the linked period is quite large but arguably may not provide a potential for profitable speculation,

Table 2A.2. Runs Tests of Daily Exchange Rate Changes

	Before Link	*After Link*
Number of positive (+) sign changes	217	119
Number of negative (–) sign changes	194	113
Number of zero (0) sign changes	22	66
Total number of sign changes	433	298
Expected number of runs of all signs (under H_0)	237.21	194.01
Actual number of runs	212	196
Standard error	9.9451	8.0386
Z value	–2.485	0.309
Probability value (under H_0)	1.30%	75.66%

since the mean exchange rate change is very small (only -0.00007, or -1.75% annually).

On the whole, the results indicate that the linked-rate system could reduce exchange rate volatility without impairing the weak-form efficiency in the exchange market. As a matter of fact, throughout the more than six years in operation, the regulatory change stabilized the Hong Kong dollar against the U.S. dollar at a level close to 7.80,[2] despite the volatile fluctuations of other major currencies in the world against the U.S. dollar. This reflects both the effectiveness of the new system and the return of confidence in the local currency.

Table 2A.3. Serial Correlation Coefficients of Daily Exchange Rate Changes

	Before Link (floating period) N = 433		*After Link* (linked period) N = 298	
Lag	r_k	(+)2 S.E.	r_k	(+)2 S.E.
1	0.136954 [a]	0.096225	0.346280 [a]	0.116052
2	– 0.107340 [a]	0.096337	0.032260	0.116248
3	0.027812	0.096449	0.017580	0.116445
4	– 0.054271	0.096561	– 0.039758	0.116642
5	– 0.159271 [a]	0.096674	– 0.036105	0.116841
6	0.041327	0.096787	– 0.022462	0.117041
7	0.048402	0.096900	– 0.030890	0.117242
8	– 0.082628	0.097014	0.030362	0.117444
9	0.144958 [a]	0.097129	– 0.070298	0.117647
10	0.039828	0.097243	– 0.014512	0.117851
11	– 0.031762	0.097358	0.031659	0.118056

Table 2A.3. (*Continued*)

Lag	Before Link (floating period) N = 433		After Link (linked period) N = 298	
	r_k	(+)2 S.E.	r_k	(+)2 S.E.
12	− 0.054624	0.097474	− 0.025133	0.118262
13	0.051108	0.097590	− 0.045053	0.118470
14	− 0.006242	0.097706	0.023420	0.118678
15	− 0.014672	0.097823	0.010471	0.118888
16	0.018323	0.097940	− 0.064659	0.119098
17	− 0.035169	0.098058	− 0.054174	0.119310
18	0.005768	0.098176	0.032440	0.119523
19	0.018059	0.098295	0.041977	0.119737
20	− 0.107862 [a]	0.098414	0.004904	0.119952
21	− 0.099301 [a]	0.098533	− 0.012815	0.120168
22	0.034526	0.098653	0.035384	0.120386
23	0.057138	0.098773	− 0.021070	0.120605
24	0.016996	0.098894	− 0.030021	0.120824
25	0.045467	0.099015	− 0.004370	0.121046
26	− 0.057825	0.099134	− 0.023461	0.121268
27	− 0.045878	0.099258	− 0.012175	0.121491
28	0.020142	0.099381	0.031886	0.121716
29	0.013926	0.099504	0.068539	0.121942
30	− 0.034704	0.099627	0.007855	0.122169
Q–statistic	59.404 [a]		46.252 [a]	
positive	16		14	
negative	14		16	

[a] Significant at the 5% level.

NOTES

1. The dividing point in the floating period is September 24, 1982, which was chosen because on that date the sensitive words — "China's sovereignty over all Hong Kong is unequivocal" — first appeared in the official statements of the Chinese government just before the end of Prime Minister Margaret Thatcher's visit to Beijing. The dividing date chosen in the linked period is September 26, 1984, the time at which the draft agreement concerning the colony's future after the lease expires in 1997 was signed and announced.

2. So far the Hong Kong dollars has fluctuated within a narrow range (+1.28%) of 7.8. Its highest and lowest levels against the U.S. dollars were 7.74 and 7.90, respectively.

APPENDIX 2B

Table 2B.1. Decomposition of Forecast Error Variances, January 1980–December 1988

RS–RB				RB–RL			
Forecast Error Variance of	Steps Ahead	Explained by		Forecast Error Variance of	Steps Ahead	Explained by	
		RS	RB			RB	RL
RS				RB			
	4	95.51	4.49		4	100.00	0.00
	8	91.54	8.46		8	100.00	0.00
	12	90.72	9.28		12	100.00	0.00
	16	89.97	10.03		16	100.00	0.00
	20	89.68	10.32		20	100.00	0.00
RB				RL			
	4	29.73	70.27		4	87.44	12.56
	8	41.49	58.51		8	93.55	6.45
	12	47.95	52.05		12	95.05	4.95
	16	50.90	49.10		16	95.61	4.39
	20	52.47	47.53		20	95.87	4.13

RB–RD			
Forecast Error Variance of	Steps Ahead	Explained by	
		RB	RD
RB			
	4	100.00	0.00
	8	100.00	0.00
	12	100.00	0.00
	16	100.00	0.00
	20	100.00	0.00
RD			
	4	88.23	11.77
	8	93.40	6.60
	12	94.63	5.37
	16	95.05	4.95
	20	95.22	4.78

Notes: RS = SIBOR, RB = HIBOR, RL = BLR, RD = deposit rate.

Table 2B.2. Decomposition of Forecast Error Variances, January 1980–December 1988

RS–RB				RB–RL			
		Explained by				*Explained by*	
Forecast Error Variance of	*Steps Ahead*	*RS*	*RB*	*Forecast Error Variance of*	*Steps Ahead*	*RB*	*RL*
RS				RB			
	4	63.71	36.29		4	100.00	0.00
	8	47.75	52.55		8	100.00	0.00
	12	46.74	53.26		12	100.00	0.00
	16	43.81	56.19		16	100.00	0.00
	20	44.30	55.70		20	100.00	0.00
RB				RL			
	4	20.29	79.71		4	82.34	17.66
	8	22.36	77.64		8	88.88	11.12
	12	25.00	75.00		12	91.05	8.95
	16	24.91	75.09		16	92.01	7.99
	20	25.36	74.67		20	92.50	7.50

RB–RD			
		Explained by	
Forecast Error Variance of	*Steps Ahead*	*RB*	*RD*
RB			
	4	100.00	0.00
	8	100.00	0.00
	12	100.00	0.00
	16	100.00	0.00
	20	100.00	0.00
RD			
	4	79.77	20.23
	8	79.77	20.23
	12	79.77	20.23
	16	79.77	20.23
	20	79.77	20.23

Notes: RS = SIBOR, RB = HIBOR, RL = BLR, RD = deposit rate.

Table 2B.3. Decomposition of Forecast Error Variances, January 1980–December 1988

RS–RB				RB–RL			
Forecast Error Variance of	Steps Ahead	Explained by		Forecast Error Variance of	Steps Ahead	Explained by	
		RS	RB			RB	RL
RS				RB			
	4	100.00	0.00		4	100.00	0.00
	8	100.00	0.00		8	100.00	0.00
	12	100.00	0.00		12	100.00	0.00
	16	100.00	0.00		16	100.00	0.00
	20	100.00	0.00		20	100.00	0.00
RB				RL			
	4	41.41	58.59		4	87.23	12.77
	8	58.61	41.39		8	91.25	8.75
	12	62.66	37.34		12	92.61	7.39
	16	64.31	35.69		16	92.94	7.06
	20	65.08	34.92		20	93.05	6.95

RB–RD			
Forecast Error Variance of	Steps Ahead	Explained by	
		RB	RD
RB			
	4	90.40	9.60
	8	87.12	12.88
	12	73.39	26.61
	16	71.15	28.85
	20	69.60	30.40
RD			
	4	71.04	28.96
	8	72.78	27.22
	12	60.12	39.88
	16	56.32	43.68
	20	54.70	45.30

Notes: RS = SIBOR, RB = HIBOR, RL = BLR, RD = deposit rate.

CHAPTER 3
MONEY MARKETS IN INDONESIA

DAVID C. COLE
BETTY F. SLADE

Money markets are markets for short-term financial instruments that are close substitutes for money. Such markets and instruments provide a means for adjusting liquidity positions—acquiring or disposing of funds— for short time periods, and they usually carry a limited risk of illiquidity or large changes in the asset's value. All entities that have access to the money markets can use this liquidity adjustment function, but it seems to be especially important to financial institutions in developing countries.

A second main function of the money markets is as a conduit, or channel, through which monetary policy is implemented by the monetary authorities. If money markets are functioning effectively and are well integrated with the other financial markets, then the monetary authorities can indirectly influence the money markets to adjust the primary liquidity (reserve money) of the banking system and thereby affect the total supply and price (interest rates) of liquidity in the economy. If the money markets are not functioning well or if they have limited depth and breadth and therefore cannot absorb large transactions and shocks, then the monetary authorities usually have to rely on some form of direct, nonmarket controls to implement monetary policy.

A third function of money markets is to provide information about the cost of capital and the nature of expectations. Again, if they are functioning properly, the money markets can generate a reference interest rate and a yield curve for high-quality, short-term obligations that can serve as a basis for pricing many other types of longer-term financial instruments. Furthermore, movements in the reference rate and changes in the slope of the yield curve give the monetary authorities an indication of changing market conditions and expectations.

In performing these three functions, money markets are metaphorically the heart of the financial system, receiving funds from its many parts and then quickly pumping them back out to other parts, and in the process giving signals as to the pulse rate and pressures of demand and supply from various parts of the system.[1]

In this chapter we focus on the role of government policies in the development of money markets in Indonesia between 1983 and 1989. We are not trying to assess how well those markets have been used for managing liquidity, for implementing monetary policy, or for obtaining information from the participants in the markets but, rather, how and why those markets have grown and developed and how various policies have affected that process.[2]

Financial policy in Indonesia is ultimately decided by the president, based on recommendations of the Monetary Board, which is chaired by the minister of finance and has as its members the governor of Bank Indonesia and other ministers representing trade, planning, and possibly others. Bank Indonesia is responsible for the day-to-day management of monetary policy, but when major decisions on monetary policy or other aspects of financial policy must be made, the Monetary Board and other key economic policymakers are drawn into the process. This broader group was responsible for formulating the basic policy directions described in this chapter.

Before 1983, Indonesia had an unusual combination of a directly controlled, nonmarket-oriented domestic financial system, dominated by the central bank and five large state-owned banks, along with a very open, market-driven foreign exchange payments, or foreign capital account, system.[3] There were rigid controls on bank credit and bank interest rates, but banks—and others—could freely purchase foreign exchange and hold foreign exchange accounts in domestic banks or banks abroad. The consequence of this set of policies was that foreign exchange accounts, either at home or abroad, became the primary money market instrument and the main form in which banks, businesses, and individuals held any kind of short-term liquid balances. These foreign exchange money markets had no role in the implementation of domestic monetary policy, which was managed solely through the imposition of domestic credit ceilings on each bank.

In June 1983 the Indonesian government began a process of financial reform that is still continuing but that has already had a major impact on the form and functioning of the whole Indonesian financial system, including the money markets. The financial reform in Indonesia has been neither a one-time change of policies nor a continuous smooth process of policy adjustment. Instead, it has followed a pattern of two steps forward then one step back then eventually several more forward steps, with the shifts in direction often determined by some form of crisis. These shifts in policy have caused sudden shocks and corresponding adjustments in the financial markets that offer good opportunities for studying the effects of government policies on the functioning of markets. We use this varied experience since 1983 to demonstrate the linkages between government policy actions and market response in the Indonesian money markets.

The Indonesian money markets that we analyze in this chapter are the following:[4]

1. The central bank's short-term debt certificates (SBIs).
2. Short-term bills eligible for rediscount at the central bank (SBPUs).
3. Interbank loans.
4. Bank Indonesia's foreign exchange swap facility (the "swap").
5. Foreign exchange accounts.
6. Short-term (one- and three-month) time deposits.

In analyzing the impact of government policies on money market developments, one approach is to try to construct a general model of policy variables, prices, and quantities of money market instruments and major exogenous factors affecting the money markets; to fit this model to the whole period under study; and then to estimate the effects of the different policies on the outcomes. We considered this approach but decided not to use it because such a general model is not only difficult to estimate with any degree of reliability but, more important, because such an approach sacrifices much of the interesting short-term detail that gives more robust indications of the effectiveness of policy changes. These details are better captured by a descriptive analysis and by simpler forms of quantitative analysis covering shorter time periods that focus on fewer significant variables.[5]

The major shifts in monetary or money market policy since 1983 are as follows:

1. June 1983: The removal of ceilings on bank lending for all banks and on most types of interest rates charged or paid by the state-owned banks.
2. September 1984: The imposition of restrictions on interbank domestic borrowing by commercial banks, and a more active use of money market instruments (SBIs and SBPUs) by the central bank.
3. September 1986: A major devaluation of the rupiah and the removal of ceilings on the foreign exchange swap facility between commercial banks and the central bank.
4. June 1987: The forced redemption of SBPUs by commercial banks and the forced purchase of SBIs by state-owned enterprises to bring about a sudden reduction in reserve money for the purpose of stopping a large outflow, and inducing a return flow, of foreign exchange.

5. October 1988: The PAKTO 27 reforms, including a major reduction in reserve requirements and compulsory purchase of SBIs by commercial banks
to offset the reduction in reserves, a shift from a fixed to a market-based
premium on swaps, the encouragement of a secondary market for SBIs, and
the removal of restrictions on interbank borrowing.

6. May 1989: The imposition of net open foreign exchange position limits
and the removal of limits on foreign borrowing by commercial banks.[6]

These fundamental shifts in policies have strongly affected the markets for the various money market instruments, sometimes stimulating
them and at other times repressing them. From 1983 through 1987 the development of the money markets was periodically sacrificed to the more
fundamental objective of containing crises of confidence in the rupiah.
But the various policy measures adopted since October 1988 have been
particularly noteworthy in terms of improving confidence in the rupiah.
In turn, this confidence encouraged a shift from a reliance on foreign exchange–denominated money market instruments to the greater use of the
domestic rupiah-denominated instruments and has led to better integration, stability, and growth of the money markets.

THE INDONESIAN FINANCIAL SYSTEM

Broad Trends, 1968–89[7]

The Indonesian financial system has experienced two growth spurts since
recuperating from the destructive effects of hyperinflation in the mid-
1960s. These longer-term trends are best indicated by the ratio of broad
money (M2) to the gross domestic product (GDP), as shown in Table 3.1.
The first growth spurt was from 1968 to 1972, when the M2/GDP ratio rose
from 6.0% to 13.0%. During this period the monetary authorities set relatively high nominal interest rates on bank time deposits, and the government gave a partial subsidy on those interest rates. Over the next decade
the M2/GDP ratio showed a mild upward trend, reflecting a rise of about
two percentage points in both the M1 and the quasi-money ratios.

The second important growth spurt started in 1983 and continued
through 1989. This latter period of rapid growth was manifested initially
by a drop in the M1/GDP ratio and a large increase in the quasi-money
ratio, resulting in only a moderate increase in the M2/GDP ratio.[8] Subsequently, the M1 ratio stabilized, and the quasi-money ratio continued to
rise rapidly. This second growth spurt resulted mainly from the removal
of credit and interest rate ceilings in June 1983 and from the growing competition among banks to attract deposits, especially time deposits, since
that time.

In the two decades since 1968, the ratio of narrow money (M1) to GDP
approximately doubled. Since narrow money is primarily a means of pay-

Table 3.1. Monetary Ratios, 1968–89

Year	Currency (CU/GDP) (1)	Demand Deposits (DD/GDP) (2)	Quasi Money (QM/GDP) (3)	Narrow Money (M1/GDP) (4)	Broad Money (M2/GDP) (5)
1968	3.58	1.86	0.57	5.44	6.01
1969	4.27	2.50	1.84	6.77	8.61
1970	4.79	2.96	2.47	7.75	10.22
1971	4.56	2.77	3.39	7.33	10.72
1972	5.09	3.80	4.12	8.90	13.02
1973	4.99	3.91	4.23	8.90	13.12
1974	4.13	3.71	4.31	7.84	12.15
1975	4.48	4.48	5.22	8.97	14.19
1976	4.62	4.86	6.08	9.48	15.56
1977	4.78	5.02	5.50	9.80	15.30
1978	5.11	5.15	5.45	10.26	15.71
1979	4.45	5.26	5.27	9.72	14.99
1980	4.40	5.81	5.51	10.21	15.72
1981	4.40	6.76	5.56	11.16	16.71
1982	4.70	6.70	6.33	11.40	17.73
1983	4.29	5.45	9.13	9.74	18.88
1984	4.14	5.43	10.42	9.56	19.99
1985	4.58	5.85	13.47	10.43	23.91
1986	5.21	6.18	15.59	11.39	26.97
1987	4.64	5.54	17.02	10.19	27.21
1988	4.48	5.84	19.80	10.32	30.12
1989	4.63	7.22	23.52	11.85	35.37

Sources: Bank Indonesia, Monthly Report, various issues; Bank Indonesia, Weekly Report, various issues; Central Bureau of Statistics, Indonesian Statistics, various issues.

ment, this suggests that the monetization of the economy roughly doubled over this period. On the other hand, the ratio of quasi money, or time and savings deposits, to GDP increased from almost zero to 20% in the two decades. It was the rise in this ratio that accounted for most of the growth in the two spurts. Since quasi money is mainly longer-term deposits, it is more indicative of increases in financial savings held in the form of claims on the domestic banking system.

Both these measures are limited in that they do not include other means of payment and forms of financial saving. One of the more important of these, in the Indonesian context, are the deposits and other claims held abroad. Part of the spurts in domestic time and savings deposits in the high-growth periods may reflect the repatriation of claims held abroad, but we have no reliable way of estimating the magnitudes involved.

It is noteworthy that the periods of high domestic financial growth were not necessarily correlated with the periods of high real growth of the Indonesian economy. The initial period of financial growth occurred at a time when the economy was growing quite rapidly, but mainly recovering from a long period of mismanagement and deterioration. Then, during the decade of high economic growth and high investment prompted by the oil boom, the domestic financial system languished. Finally, after the bloom went off the oil boom and real growth slowed, domestic financial growth accelerated.[9]

We can obtain a broader measure of financial development by looking at the total assets of various types of financial institutions. These inevitably include some double counting because, for example, the assets of financial institutions include deposits at banks, which in turn are matched by bank assets. Of greater significance, a sizable portion of the assets of Indonesia's central bank (henceforth referred to as Bank Indonesia) is composed of loans to deposit money banks (DMBs) which they then lend to their customers.[10] Another distortion arises from the likely overstatement of the real, or market, value of many financial assets, such as banks' bad loans, and, on the other hand, the understatement of the market value of real assets. Despite all these limitations and the gaps in the data for earlier years, the data shown in Table 3.2 and in Figures 3.1 and 3.2 indicate the relative size and growth of various types of financial institutions in Indonesia over the past two decades.

The best overall measure of financial size and growth is the ratio of financial assets to GDP (Ratio B), because this ratio omits Bank Indonesia loans to deposit money banks and thus avoids one source of double counting. This ratio rose from about 23% of GDP in 1969 to 76% of GDP at the end of 1988.

During the initial growth spurt (1968–72), the deposit money banks (DMBs) raised their share of total financial assets relative to those of the Bank Indonesia (BI). This is seen most readily by comparing "Total assets of DMBs less loans from BI" with "Total assets of BI" in Figure 3.2. In 1969 the DMBs' net assets were equal to roughly half of the BI's total assets, but by 1972 they were about 25% greater than the total. By 1982, however, "Total assets of DMBs less loans from BI" were once again less than the BI's total assets. After the second growth spurt (1983–present), this rose again to 117% of the BI's total assets.

Note that there also was substantial growth in the total assets of other financial institutions, namely, insurance companies, leasing companies, pension funds, nonbank financial institutions (NBFIs), and the State Savings Bank (BTN), as discussed in the next section. Although data for these other financial institutions were not available for the earlier period, they were probably of negligible importance. Their recorded growth in recent years, however, has been very rapid and has accounted for an important part of the rise in the ratio of financial assets to GDP.

Table 3.2. Assets of Financial Institutions, Selected Years (in billions of rupiah, end-of-year data)

	1969	1972	1977	1982	1987	1988	Sept. 1989
1. Bank Indonesia[1]	417	675	3,003	13,706	35,554	42,445	38,880
2. Deposit money banks (DMBs) A[a1]	291	983	4,030	15,922	48,202	63,284	85,929
a. National foreign exchange banks	217	735	3,199	12,724	37,499	50,051	67,409
b. Foreign banks	37	126	370	1,172	2,779	3,215	4,626
c. Development banks	7	66	288	1,336	3,699	5,046	6,384
d. National non–foreign exchange banks	30	57	172	690	4,225	4,972	7,510
3. Deposit money banks B[b1]	211	834	3,349	12,180	37,941	49,812	71,656
4. State Savings Bank (BTN)[1]	N.A.	N.A.	30	451	1,883	2,272	2,704
5. Nonbank financial institutions[2]	N.A.	N.A.	125	805	2,497	3,063	3,564
6. Insurance companies[2]	N.A.	N.A.	N.A.	587	3,457	3,906	N.A.
a. Life insurance	N.A.	N.A.	N.A.	173	677	799	N.A.
b. Loss insurance	N.A.	N.A.	N.A.	355	1,013	844	N.A.
c. Social insurance	N.A.	N.A.	N.A.	59	1,768	1,930	N.A.
7. Leasing companies[2]	N.A.	N.A.	31	73	1,626	1,751	N.A.
8. Pension funds[2]							
a. TASPEN	N.A.	N.A.	N.A.	277	920	1,105	N.A.
b. Other[c]	N.A.	N.A.	N.A.	N.A.	N.A.	224	N.A.
9. Securities[3]							
a. Listed bonds[d]	N.A.	N.A.	N.A.	N.A.	536	856	1,417
b. Listed equity shares[d]	N.A.	N.A.	3	96	133	190	794
10. Total financial assets (A)/GDP[e] %	26.04	31.07	35.29	51.09	76.13	85.44	N.A.
11. Total financial assets (B)/GDP[f] %	23.10	28.27	31.96	45.10	67.89	75.78	N.A.
12. Total financial assets (C)/GDP[g] %	10.69	18.41	20.61	29.15	47.58	55.00	N.A.
Other Data:							
13. Bank Indonesia[1]							
a. Gold and foreign assets	65	239	1,057	3,730	13,442	11,724	9,862
b. Claims on DMBs	80	149	681	3,742	10,261	13,472	14,273
14. Deposit money banks[1]							
a. Foreign assets	24	203	578	4,013	7,806	8,397	8,156
b. Foreign liabilities[h]	57	222	457	2,403	5,415	7,683	7,200
15. GDP current prices[4]	2,718	5,339	20,469	62,476	124,539	139,452	159,977

[a] Based on consolidated balance sheets.

[b] Equivalent of line 2 minus line 13b.

[c] Only partial data available.

[d] Values at initial offerings.

[e] Total financial assets = Sum of lines 1, 2, 4, 5, 6, 7, 8, and 9. GDP is from line 15.

[f] Total financial assets = Same as footnote e minus line 13b. GDP is from line 15.

[g] Total financial assets = Same as footnote e minus line 1. GDP is from line 15.

[h] Since 1983, total foreign exchange liabilities are the sum of foreign currency deposits and foreign liabilities from BI, *Monthly Report*, Table 1.g.

Sources: 1. Bank Indonesia, *Indonesian Financial Statistics*, various issues; 2. Ministry of Finance, Directorate of Financial Institutions and Accountancy; 3. Capital Market Executive Agency, *Fact Book of the Indonesian Capital Market—Statistical Supplement*, various issues; 4. Central Bureau of Statistics, *Indonesian Statistics*, various issues.

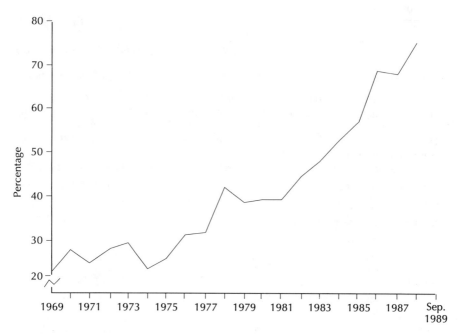

Figure 3.1. Ratio of Financial Assets to GDP. *Source:* Table 3.2, line 11.

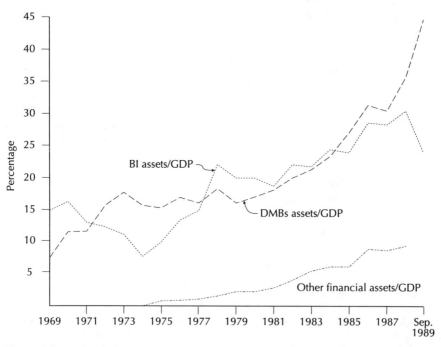

Figure 3.2. Ratio of Financial Assets to GDP by Selected Categories. *Source:* Table 3.2.

THE MAJOR FINANCIAL INSTITUTIONS AND THEIR ROLES

Table 3.2 lists the assets of the major financial institutions for selected years since 1969 to show the longer-term development of the domestic financial sector. The domination of the deposit money banks plus Bank Indonesia is clear throughout the period, but by the 1980s other financial activities were beginning to make inroads.

Table 3.3 gives a more detailed picture of the structure of the formal domestic financial system in Indonesia as of 1982 and 1989.[11] The deposit money banks, on the whole, dominated throughout this period, but the private national commercial banks' assets grew faster relative to those of the state-owned commercial banks.[12] Recently, the nonbanking sectors have grown quickly, especially the capital market and related types of activities. The recent development has been mainly in response to the PAKTO 27 (Oc-

Table 3.3. Financial Institutions in Indonesia, 1982 and 1989

	Number		Total Assets (Rp billions)	
	Dec. 1982	Sept. 1989	Dec. 1982	Sept. 1989
Central bank[a]	1	1	13,707	38,880
Deposit money banks (DMBs)[1a]	119	140	15,922	85,740
State banks[a]	5	5	11,529	51,450
Joint ventures[2a]	1	12	N.A.	N.A.
Foreign bank branches[a]	10	10	1,172	4,626
Development banks[a]	28	28	1,336	6,384
BAPINDO	1	1	804	3,886
Regional development banks	27	27	532	2,498
Private banks[a]	75	85	1,885	23,469
Non–foreign exchange banks	60	64	690	7,510
Foreign exchange banks	15	21	1,195	15,959
Rural financial institutions	5,807	7,713	86	579
Existing before PAKTO[b]	5,807	7,236	86	55
Established after PAKTO[c]	0	477	0	524
Money changers[a]	N.A.	300	N.A.	30
Pawnshop (state owned)[3d]	1	1	80	152
State Savings Bank (BTN)[a]	1	1	451	2,531
State Securities and Investment Fund (DANAREKSA)[e]	1	1	149	298
Nonbank financial institutions[f]	13	13	805	3,564
Development finance institutions	3	3	137	837
Investment finance institutions	9	9	654	2,413
Housing finance (Papan Sejahtera)	1	1	14	314
Insurance[g]	91	130	587	3,906
Life insurance	13	30	173	799
Loss insurance	62	77	355	844
Social Insurance[4]	5	5	59	1,930
Reinsurance	3	4	N.A.	333
Adjusters	8	14	N.A.	N.A.

Table 3.3. (*Continued*)

	Number		Total Assets (Rp billions)[6]	
	Dec. 1982	Sept. 1989	Dec. 1982	Sept. 1989
Pension Funds[g][5]	79	130	278	1,329
TASPEN	1	1	277	1,105
Others	78	129	1	224
Securities companies[g]	0	7	0	N.A.
Brokers/dealers[g]	39	129	N.A.	N.A.
Nondeposit financial institutions[g]	17	154	N.A.	N.A.
Leasing companies	17	101	114	1,195
Factoring	0	14	0	N.A.
Venture capital	0	7	0	N.A.
Credit card	0	11	0	N.A.
Consumer finance	0	21	0	N.A.
Securities exchange activities[h]	23	90	20	5,540
Listed stocks	23	68	20	3,980
Bonds	0	22	0	1,560

[1] This item includes Bank Indonesia claims on DMBs.

[2] These banks are joint ventures between Indonesian and foreign banks.

[3] There is one pawnshop office with 487 branch offices.

[4] Includes ASABRI, the military employees social insurance fund.

[5] Excludes an unknown member of pension funds not registered with the Ministry of Finance.

[6] Valuation at public offering price.

Sources: a. Bank Indonesia; b. Bank Indonesia, total assets as of September 1988; c. Bank Indonesia.; d. Ministry of Finance, as of December 1982 and December 1989; e. Ministry of Finance, as of December 1989, consolidated balance sheet; f. Ministry of Finance, as of September 1989; g. Ministry of Finance, total assets as of December 1982 and December 1988, when available; h. Capital Market Executive Agency, as of December 1982 and January 8, 1990.

tober 1988) deregulation and opening up to new entrants and new financial products. In fact, the growth of most activities accelerated over this period, as did the development of new financial products.

The Central Bank

The central bank (Bank Indonesia, or BI) is sole issuer of Indonesian currency; it implements monetary policy through open market operations and reserve requirements, extending credit to banks and setting the exchange rate; it supervises all banking institutions including the NBFIs; it serves as the government's banker; it manages the nation's international reserves; it participates directly in financial institutions; it provides special credits for targeted sectors (known as *liquidity* credits); and it helps finance the government's price support and stockpile programs.[13] It is the issuer of the Sertifikat Bank Indonesia (SBI), the rediscounter of the Surat Berharga Pasar Uang (SBPU), the seller and buyer of spot foreign exchange, and the provider of the foreign exchange swaps facility (known as the *swap*). The SBI and SBPU are used as instruments of open market operations in pursuit of monetary policy targets. BI sets the indicative foreign exchange rates and publishes daily its "swap" premium.[14] It also sets reserve requirements on deposits.[15] Clearing regulations are set by Bank Indonesia, which also provides the actual clearing services for the interbank market (through the Jakarta Clearing and its network of branches).

The General Banks

The general banks in Indonesia (which have the broadest authority) are often categorized according to their authority to carry out foreign exchange transactions, their ownership (state owned, private national and foreign, and private joint ventures), and the "restrictions" on other activities. In regard to foreign exchange operations, new foreign exchange licenses once were difficult to get, but since PAKTO 27, they are generally available to banks of larger size and soundness. Table 3.3 gives the numbers and asset sizes of these categories. (Note that all the state-owned Banks are foreign exchange banks.) In regard to ownership, the distinction among state-owned, private national and foreign, and private Indonesian–foreign joint ventures remained intact during this period, even though joint venture bank entry and branching had been severely restricted before PAKTO 27. But now new commercial banks can be established with relative ease, with the exception of foreign "branches" and subsidiaries. Banks wholly owned by Indonesian citizens can open branches throughout Indonesia, whereas foreign and joint venture bank branches are restricted to seven major cities and Batam Island. No new foreign "branch banks" were allowed to enter during this period and thus are restricted to the existing number of ten. Eleven new joint venture banks (with up to 85% foreign ownership and a minimum capital of Rp 50 billion) were licensed in 1989. As far as other restrictions are concerned, all general banks have the same rights, except that new foreign bank branches and new joint venture banks must allocate 50% of their loan portfolios to export-related credits.

General banks can be active in all the money markets, although there are some exceptions. State-owned banks tend to buy more of the SBIs offered in the auctions and at times have dominated the purchases completely. They frequently buy the shorter-term (seven-day) SBIs with their excess liquidity and are less active in purchasing thirty- or ninety-day SBIs, despite their significantly higher yields.[16] State-owned banks tend to be the lenders in the interbank markets, and they also issue bills that serve as rediscountable SBPUs. Until the recent regulations restricting net open foreign positions (PAKMAR), state-owned banks generally maintained long foreign exchange positions. Significant proportions of time deposits are held in state-owned banks, even though they have always paid lower interest rates than private banks have.[17]

Private domestic banks have been more active in the auction market for thirty- and ninety-day SBIs and the trading of those issues in the newly emerging secondary market for SBIs. Private banks tend to be the main borrowers in the interbank market. Some private banks are dealers in the SBI auction, and one bank is a broker. In recent years, the growth rate of loans and deposits in the private banks has exceeded that of state-owned banks. The private banks are very active in the foreign exchange markets, arranging their own swaps and forward contracts. They also facilitate and deal in rediscountable SBPUs.

Concentration Among General Banks

State-owned banks[18] have dominated the banking system as well as the entire financial system during this period, although there have been significant inroads into this domination, particularly in the period following PAKTO 27 (October 1988), with the rapid growth of the private banking system and the capital market. The Herfindahl index moved from 0.118 at the end of 1983 down to 0.098 as of the end of June 1989 and is moving steadily downward.[19] The following table gives the actual percentages of total assets held by certain selected categories:

	December 1983	June 1989
State-owned banks	79.5%	73.3%
Other banks	21.5%	26.7%

Regional Development Banks and BPRs

There are twenty-seven regional "development" banks (owned by the provinces) and one national "development" bank—BAPINDO. Regional development banks are not significant players in the money markets except as holders of promissory notes.

BPRs (Bank Perkreditan Rakyat) and other rural financial institutions are wholly owned by Indonesian nationals and serve specific local areas and clientele. There are several thousand of these banks, as would be expected in such a large, geographically spread-out country.[20] They cannot hold demand deposits, deal in foreign exchange, or participate in the payments system. The demand to set up new BPRs since PAKTO 27 has been great. They are not significant players in the money markets.

Other Financial Institutions

In order to help develop the financial markets, in the 1970s the government encouraged the establishment of "nonbank financial institutions" (NBFIs), which now consist of three development finance companies and nine investment finance companies, plus one housing loan institution, Papan Sejahtera. Partial foreign ownership is permitted. Bank Indonesia, state-owned banks, private banks, and private individuals, both foreign and domestic, have participated in the ownership of these institutions (see Table 3.4). They deal in foreign exchange, commercial paper, long-term stocks and bonds, SBIs and SBPUs, and CDs, as well as perform many banking operations. They serve as "agents" for state-owned bank purchases of SBIs and as "market makers" in the SBI market. Ficorinvest, an NBFI 70% owned by Bank Indonesia, is a broker in the SBI market.

Danareksa was established in 1977 by presidential decree as a state-owned "securities company" to foster the growth of the capital market and provide investment funds to broaden the ownership of shares. It completely

Table 3.4. Nonbank Financial Institutions

	Partners	Share (%)
FICORINVEST	Bank Indonesia	70.84
	PT Bina Usaha Indonesia	4.16
	Public	25.00
INDOVEST	Bank Dagang Negara	62.44
	Foreign	37.56
MULTICOR	PT Bank Central Asia	51.00
	Foreign	42.24
	Jardine–Fleming Indonesia Ltd.	6.76
ASEAM	Bank Bumi Daya	51.00
	Foreign	49.00
FINCONESIA	Bank BNI	51.00
	Foreign	49.00
MERINCORP	Bank Ekspor Impor Indonesia	76.00
	Sumitomo Bank Ltd., Japan	24.00
INTERPACIFIC	Bank Rakyat Indonesia	55.00
	Foreign	45.00
I.F.I.	PT Ustrindo	25.91
	BAPINDO	74.09
M.I.F.C.	PT Mutual Promotion Corp., Jakarta	52.50
	Foreign	23.10
	Other	16.90
	PT Pan Indonesia (Panin) Bank Ltd.	7.50
PDFCI	Domestic	65.02
	Foreign	34.98
UPPINDO	Bank Indonesia	75.00
	Netherlands Development Finance Company	25.00
BAHANA	Ministry of Finance	66.70
	Bank Indonesia	33.30
PAPAN SEJAHTERA	Bank Indonesia	20.00
	Other Domestic	50.00
	Foreign	30.00

Source: Ministry of Finance.

dominated the tiny capital market until very recently[21] and still manages the only domestic "investment funds" in Indonesia.[22] Danareksa is not active in the money markets except that its "funds" are invested in time deposits.

There is no insurance law in Indonesia, but insurance companies must be licensed and are regulated through decrees. To date, the insurance industry has not grown noticeably. There is also no pension law, so pension fund activities have proceeded haphazardly. TASPEN, the government employees' pension fund, is the only large single fund. Insurance companies and pension funds (YAYASANs, or nonprofit entities) invest their money mainly in buildings and longer-term time deposits. They are not important in the money markets.

Leasing companies with significant foreign ownership began to spring up in the early 1980s, mainly as a means of circumventing the restrictions on new bank licenses.[23]

Money changers and government-owned pawnshops can be found throughout Indonesia, serving a variety of needs but seeming to play no role in the money markets.[24]

It was only in 1989 that the capital markets began to make an impact on the financial system, and accordingly, there has been an increase in the number of brokers, dealers, and securities companies. The number and value of issues of both debt securities and stocks rose most after January 1989. The capital market is growing very rapidly and has the potential for significant growth in the near future.[25] The development of capital markets may offer alternative sources of funds mobilization for business and should increase the demand for liquid funds by capital market participants and, to the extent they are successful, will affect the money markets.

Other types of financial activity—factoring and raising venture capital, for example—were authorized only with PAKTO 27 and are still insignificant.[26]

THE MONEY MARKETS

The SBI Market

The Sertifikat Bank Indonesia (SBI) is a discount bill, a liability of Bank Indonesia, which was first introduced in 1970, in an attempt to create a money market instrument. It was to be sold to the banking system when BI wanted to reduce liquidity. But this attempt proved premature: Because there was little market interest in the SBI, it was discontinued in 1971. In February 1984 when BI was looking for a new instrument to control the supply of reserve money, it resuscitated the SBI and has been issuing it continuously ever since. Although Bank Indonesia was initially interested in this instrument as an indirect means of reducing reserve money and influencing interest rates, over time the SBI has also become an important instrument for managing liquidity, especially for the state-owned banks.[27] At different times, BI has varied the term of the bill from 7 days to 180 days. The discount rate has been fixed at certain periods and set by auction (as a cutoff rate) in other periods, depending on Bank Indonesia's objectives. From 1984 through 1988, the SBI was sold either directly to banks or indirectly through Ficorinvest (an NBFI).

Since early 1989, the SBI has been sold to or through market makers (banks and NBFIS approved by BI to buy at auction and encouraged by Bank Indonesia to become active in both the primary and secondary SBI markets).[28] A secondary market began to develop only since that time.

Only banks and NBFIs are allowed to participate in the primary auction itself. Theoretically, any domestic investor may deal in the secondary market for SBIs, but in practice so far, only banks and NBFIs are active in this market.[29] The market tends to be concentrated, with only two or three state-owned banks absorbing most of the issues.[30]

As a counterpart to the reduction of the reserve requirements in PAKTO 27 (October 1988), all banks had to buy SBIs up to an amount equal to 80% of their "released" funds.[31] Although the banks were free to sell SBIs, they did not, and these so-called PAKTO SBIs were mostly held for the maximum of three and six months.

With the designation of official brokers and market makers by Bank Indonesia in early 1989, there has been more varied bidding, and the holding of newly issued SBIs has become more widespread. The secondary market in SBIs also grew significantly in 1989, as mentioned previously. Table 3.5 shows data on the secondary market, and Table 3.6 shows the policy types and their effects on this market, as well as the important policy changes for this market.

SBPU Market Bills Rediscounted at Bank Indonesia

The Surat Berharga Pasar Uang (SBPU) is a short-term bill in the form of a promissory note or trade bill cosigned by a bank or NBFI that can be rediscounted at Bank Indonesia either directly or through an appointed agent. Bank Indonesia has stood ready to rediscount these bills since February 1985 when it began to consider these as instruments for providing liquidity to the banking system. (The sales of SBIs could withdraw funds, but because there was no secondary market for SBIs and BI did not do reverse repos, there was no indirect instrument to add to the supply of reserve money.) Ficorinvest (an NBFI, previously 95% owned by BI) served as BI's agent for purchasing SBPUs. The SBPU continued to grow as an instrument of monetary policy from 1985 until mid-1987, but because the rate paid by the banks was not allowed to move freely in response to market forces and at times was held below the equilibrium rate, the banks' excess demand forced BI to impose rediscount ceilings for each bank in order to ration the supply of funds they could obtain through the sale of SBPUs.

Table 3.5. Secondary Market for SBIs, 1989 (in millions of rupiahs, average rates)

	1 Day		2–7 Days		8–27 Days		28+ Days		Total		Total Number of Transactions
	Rate	Volume	Rate	Volume	Rate	Volume	Rate	Volume	Rate	Volume	
January	—	0	—	5,000	—	2,000	—	21,000	—	28,000	13
February	—	2,000	—	382,725	—	156,025	—	13,405	—	554,155	226
March	—	6,500	—	284,350	—	185,475	—	5,750	—	482,075	212
April	13.17	6,000	14.68	185,875	15.76	154,925	15.76	14,600	14.84	361,400	166
May	11.00	2,000	13.37	225,975	14.38	257,675	16.55	16,825	13.83	502,475	162
June	12.71	23,000	13.31	590,350	14.02	376,925	15.48	34,000	13.88	1,024,275	320
July	13.25	6,000	13.61	439,000	14.28	344,500	15.77	17,000	14.23	806,500	242
August	—	0	12.48	685,500	13.64	462,500	15.44	13,000	10.39.	1,161,000	378
September	12.66	39,000	12.88	448,500	13.53	475,000	14.30	13,500	13.34	976,000	293
October	11.50	2,000	12.56	372,000	13.24	417,500	15.50	3,500	13.20	795,000	243
November	11.50	3,500	12.43	499,500	12.78	593,500	14.31	1,000	12.76	1,097,500	297
December	—	0	12.42	248,500	13.17	530,100	—	0	12.80	778,600	209

Source: Bank Indonesia.

Table 3.6. Purpose and Probable Impact of Major Policy Changes on Key Money Markets, 1983–89

Policy Change	Date Effected	Primary Purpose	Foreign Exchange Spot	Foreign Exchange Swap	Interbank Loans (IBs)	SBIs	SBPUs	Time Deposits, Short Term
1. Removal of credit ceilings	June 1983	Improve efficiency of financial system	No major effect	No major effect, subject to ceiling	Promoted to meet imbalance between supply and demand for funds of state and private banks	Not in existence	Not in existence	Gave incentive to all banks to attract more deposits
2. Removal of interest rate ceilings	June 1983	Expand activity and improve efficiency of banks	Encouraged shift from foreign exchange to rupiah deposits and loans repatriation of foreign exchange	No effect	Promoted in same way as Policy 1	Not applicable	Not applicable	Strong stimulus to time deposits especially at state banks; also more rapid expansion of shorter-term deposit funds
3. BI begins issuing SBIs	February 1984	Create a new monetary policy instrument	Not significant	Not significant	Provides alternative asset to IB loan; also a possible reference interest rate	Creates primary market. Direct purchase from IB at set price	Not applicable	Modest stimulus by providing safe short-term use for time deposits

Table 3.6. (*Continued*)

Policy Change	Date Effected	Primary Purpose	Foreign Exchange Spot	Foreign Exchange Swap	Interbank Loans (IBs)	SBIs	SBPUs	Time Deposits, Short Term
4. BI discontinues interest on excess reserves	May 1984	Improve efficiency of banks and effectiveness of monetary policy	Not significant	Not significant	Encourages banks to lend out excess reserves to other banks	Encourages banks to put excess reserves into SBIs		
5. BI accelerates rate of depreciation	August 1984	To realign exchange rate	Heavy pressure on foreign exchange market and loans of BI foreign exchange reserves	Increase in swaps up to ceilings	Very tight interbank market; rate goes to 90%	Demand for SBIs drops	Not applicable	Demand for Rp. time deposit drops
6. Emergency credit from BI	September 1984	Monetary policy to relieve liquidity squeeze	Relieved pressure on banks to sell foreign exchange	Relieves demand for swaps	Sudden increase in liquidity brings IB rates down quickly	Demand increases	Not clear	Not clear
7. BI puts limits on interbank loans to 7.5% of third party liabilities	September 1984	To restrict growth of market instrument to protect solvency of banks	Banks with surplus funds invest in foreign exchange		Alternative to IB loans for deficient banks	Demand increases	Probably reduce use of interbank SBPUs	Forces smaller banks to promote time deposits

	Date	Purpose						
8. Introduction of SBPU and Ficor as market maker	February 1985	Create instrument for monetary policy	Provides banks with alternative source of liquidity to sell foreign exchange	Not significant	Reduced demand for IB loans	Permits expansion of SBIs to offset SBPUs	Gives stimulus to new market	An alternative to time deposits as source of funds
9. Interbank loan limits raised to 15% of total liabilities	August 1985	To encourage instrument's use	No effect	No effect	Substitute for IB loans as source of funds	No effect	No effect	No effect
10. Devaluation of 44%	September 1986	Foreign exchange protection and export stimulus	Led to further pressure on BI's foreign exchange reserves			Not significant	Not significant	Made Rp assets more attractive briefly
11. Removal of ceilings and rise in swap premium	October 1986	Put instrument on market basis	Relieved pressure by providing substitute for foreign exchange holding	Big increase in use of swaps. Greater fluctuations in holdings	Probably reduced demand for IB loans	Substitute for SBIs as investment by banks	No significant effect	Substitute for time deposits as source of funds for banks
12. Rise in controlled swap rate, SBI rate, BI discount rate	May 1987	Monetary policy foreign exchange control	Heavy pressure on foreign exchange market	Heavy demand for swaps even at higher rate	Rise in rate, unclear as to volume	SBIs almost disappeared, controlled rate too slow	Big demand to rediscount SBPUs at low rate	Time deposit rate rose to over 20%
13. Liquidity squeeze	June-July 1987	Foreign exchange control through monetary policy contraction	Caused return flow of foreign exchange	Sharp reduction in swaps	Sharp rise for 1 month interest rate, then sharp fall	No demand for SBIs, then increased demand as squeeze abated	Rediscounting of SBPUs stopped. Market disappeared.	Time deposit rates declined slowly; IDs grew as alternative to foreign exchange

Table 3.6. (*Continued*)

Policy Change	Date Effected	Primary Purpose	Foreign Exchange Spot	Foreign Exchange Swap	Interbank Loans (IBs)	SBIs	SBPUs	Time Deposits, Short Term
14. Stabilize foreign exchange depreciation rate	April 1988	Foreign exchange control, interest rate policy	Reduced speculation	Stabilized demand for swaps	No immediate effect	Helped stabilize SBI rate	Not applicable	No immediate effect; eventually lowered rates
15. PAKTO								
15a. Lower reserve requirements	October 1988	Rules change to help capital market	No effect	No effect	No effect because of 15c	No effect	No effect	Reduced real interest rate cost of TDs for banks
15b. Tax on time deposit interest	October 1988	Equalize treatment of time deposits and securities	No effect	No effect	No effect	No effect	No effect	Lowered net interest income of depositors, raised nominal rate
15c. Forced purchases of SBIs to offset reserve change	October 1988	Mop up excess reserves	Forced sale of foreign exchange to buy SBIs	No effect	Heavy borrowing and some defaulting by private banks	Big increase in stock of 3- and 6-mo. SBIs held by banks	No effect	Stimulated banks to attract TDs and raise rates
15d. Swap rate tied to LIBOR and bank deposit rate	October 1988	Equalize interest rates, control foreign exchange flows	Reduced arbitrage in foreign exchange, stabilized market	Made swap more a hedging instrument rather than arbitrage	No major effect	No effect	No effect	Helped link Rp and $ deposit interest rates

15e. Extended term for swaps to 3 years	Foreign exchange control policy	October 1988	No major effect	Extended hedging role of swap	No effect	No effect	No effect	No effect
15f. Free entry for new banks		October 1988	Brought in new foreign exchange funds and banks. Increased competition	No major effect	Broadened market	No effect	No effect	Increased banks' efforts to attract deposits
15g. Permitted SOEs to deal with private banks	Increase competition and efficiency	October 1988	No effect	No effect	May reduce need for interbank borrowings by private banks	No effect	Created market structure for greater use of SBPUs	Raised interest rates and increased competition for IDs of SOEs
16. BI encourages dealers in SBI market	Market development	January 1989	Reduced demand for foreign exchange assets	Reduced demand for swaps	Supplied high-quality instrument for rediscount and repurchase in interbank market	Increased demand for SBIs, especially for longer term	Reduced potential demand for SBPUs	Possible substitution of SBIs for IDs
17. Limits imposed on net open foreign exchange position of banks	Foreign exchange control, reduce foreign exchange speculation	May 1989	Reduced demand of banks for FX assets	Reduced demand for swaps	Increased use of interbank market to adjust liquidity position	Increased demand for SBIs by banks to hold liquidity	No effect	May have encouraged banks to attract more foreign exchange IDs

In June 1987 the government, facing severe speculation against the rupiah, used the SBPU as a powerful one-shot contraction instrument by suddenly lowering most banks' rediscount ceilings to zero. This extreme measure was taken to reduce liquidity quickly and thereby stem the tide of speculation against the rupiah. Although the impact on foreign exchange speculation was what was desired, a second effect was to undermine the banks' and NBFIs' confidence in the certainty of the funds obtained from a SBPU rediscount with Bank Indonesia and thus in effect to remove it from the arsenal of monetary policy instruments for some time.

The rediscountable SBPU is based on those trade bills and promissory notes that have certain formats and meet certain criteria.[32] These bills can be offered to (rediscounted at) Bank Indonesia in an auction. Bank Indonesia announces its intention to buy SBPUs on the evening before the auction will take place. BI does not state any maximum amount or required price. The banks and NBFIs offer these bills at various prices, and BI either accepts or rejects them, thus establishing their rediscount rate. BI's decisions are based on how much liquidity it wishes to provide and what return it is willing to accept. BI is therefore the initiator of SBPU rediscount activity, and reserve money is thus influenced through this mechanism. Rediscount rates on SBPUs are usually above those of the SBIs. Relevant policy measures are shown in Table 3.6.

The Interbank Loan Market

The interbank loan market is identified as a separate market, even though it is based on several instruments (SBPUs, interbank deposits, SBIs, promissory notes, etc.).[33] This classification is inconsistent with the methodology, but it was determined by the availability of data.

In 1974 Bank Indonesia organized the Jakarta clearing system for the interbank call money market to systematize interbank activity. Bank Indonesia sometimes intervenes in this market: At times it has tried to adjust the level of interbank borrowing by lowering and raising the "ceilings" of third-party liabilities that could be obtained from interbank transactions. Only in October 1988 was the ceiling completely removed.

Banks generally arrange their own interbank loans, either with traditional partners or by telephoning around to learn what is happening in the market. Either a line of credit is available, or the banks use promissory notes or other paper to make the actual transaction (often using an SBPU). There are two "markets" each workday (and one fairly inactive one on Saturday) called the *morning* and *afternoon* markets, followed by *clearings*.

Since early 1989, repurchase agreements (repos) based on outstanding SBIs have begun to underlie some interbank transactions. This secondary market for SBIs had grown to an average of Rp 40 billion to 50 billion per day by mid-1989, out of a total interbank market averaging Rp 200 billion to 300 billion per day and an average level of bank statutory reserves of about Rp 1,200 billion. This new use of the SBI in the interbank loan market contributed to its liquidity and its use as a money market instrument by both private and state-owned banks.

The yield curve for the interbank loan market has traditionally been steeply positive. On those occasions when liquidity is very tight and the interbank rate rises to very high levels, the market tends to become predominantly an overnight market with a negative-sloping yield curve. Then, as the liquidity pressure eases, the rate drops sharply, the maturity of the borrowings gradually lengthens, and the yield curve reverts to a positive slope.

Recently the gap between overnight and longer-term rates has narrowed somewhat, as shown in Table 3.7. Whereas during the last week in February 1989 the spread between the average overnight rate and the average one-month rate was 7.5 percentage points, it had narrowed to 4.9% by the last week of January 1990. This reflects a reduction in the liquidity premium as concerns about a large devaluation had diminished. The continuing, albeit declining, steepness of the yield curve and the concentration in shorter-term loans indicate a very high premium on liquidity rather than expected interest rate changes.

Published data cover the transactions during the afternoon market, often the less active market, which enter the Jakarta clearinghouse. (Interbank markets are significantly larger than these data indicate.) Furthermore, this data series does not distinguish among the terms of the loans. The published interest rates are average rates, weighted by amounts at different transaction rates.[34] The relevant policy measures are shown in Table 3.6.

Bank Indonesia Foreign Exchange Swap Facility ("Swap")

Bank Indonesia introduced the "swap" facility in 1979, ostensibly to eliminate the downside foreign exchange rate risk for foreign investors and domestic borrowers while at the same time providing liquidity for the rupiah. (Banks may also borrow ahead and swap with BI.) "Swaps" are initiated

Table 3.7. Interbank Interest Rates and Amounts Borrowed (weekly volumes in Rp billions; weighted-average interest rates for each maturity)

	Overnight		7-day		27- to 31-day	
	Volume	Rate	Volume	Rate	Volume	Rate
February 20–24, 1989	705.7	12.7	493.3	14.6	20.9	20.3
July 24–29, 1989	516.7	11.7	130.5	13.5	22.3	16.6
January 29– February 2, 1990	568.5	11.0	376.4	12.7	28.0	15.9

Source: Bank Indonesia.

when a party borrows foreign exchange abroad and arranges a swap contract with an onshore bank, whereby the borrower immediately receives the rupiah equivalent at the present exchange rate and locks in the right to exchange the rupiahs for a foreign currency at some specified time in the future at the same exchange rate.[35] The ultimate borrower therefore gets rupiahs with no downside exchange risk.[36] The bank in turn has the right to "reswap" the contract with Bank Indonesia. A "premium" is paid to the bank by the initiator of the swap. Bank Indonesia stands ready to take over the risk of the swap at the premium rate and allows the bank only a small transaction fee that BI has set. If the bank retains the risk, that is, if it does not reswap, then it can earn the full swap premium. In general, the bank risks the "difference " between the premium received and the actual depreciation rate if it does not reswap. If it reswaps with BI, the bank makes only a small percentage (currently one-eighth percentage point per annum). Therefore, banks tend to retain the risk when they have confidence in the rupiah and reswap with BI when they are uncertain.[37]

The effects of a reswap (use of the Bank Indonesia swap facility) on Bank Indonesia's balance sheet are as follows: Spot foreign exchange is sold to BI (increasing its foreign exchange reserves); a forward contract is made by BI with the initiator of the swap (increasing BI's forward commitments); and rupiahs are given to the initiator of the swap (increasing reserves outstanding). If the swap were not available, the person seeking liquidity would simply sell his borrowed foreign currency to a bank, which would increase the foreign exchange reserves of the bank, but not of the central bank. However, the borrower would face an exchange rate risk. So, essentially the use of the swap is as a hedge.

BI can influence the use of the swap by changing its availability (by imposing ceilings) and its price (setting the premium charged).[38] For example, a premium above the "market" rate would make swaps more expensive and cause people to consider more carefully their expectations of the foreign exchange risk. In that case they may simply bring in the foreign exchange and take the risk, or they may not. Rationing, by imposing ceilings on reswapping, might make swaps unavailable and reduce the inflow of foreign currency for those worried about the foreign exchange risk, or if the potential profit from the inflow is sufficient to offset the risk, people may bring in the foreign currency anyway. Therefore, the swap has a rather unclear influence on the inflow of foreign currency. One observation, however, is that when the swap is not rationed by BI and there is speculation against the rupiah, it is used heavily.

In the early years, banks could set and earn the "swap premium." The demand for swaps grew, so in October 1982 Bank Indonesia limited to 2% the portion of the premium that the bank could keep, in the case of a reswap with BI, and gradually reduced this until in February 1983 the structure in the following table was imposed. Ceilings were also placed on the BI swap facilities available to banks.

Swap Period	Bank Premium (%)	BI Premium (%)
30 days	5.00	4.75
90 days	5.25	5.00
180 days	6.00	5.75

Following the September devaluation, in October 1986 BI imposed a single premium for all swap periods and set its swap premium at one-eighth percentage point below the bank swap premium, which was set at a minimum rate of 8%. The ceilings on the BI swap facility were removed.

Removal of the ceiling on bank swaps with BI led to a very rapid increase in BI swaps outstanding.[39] Banks found this an attractive means of speculating against the rupiah while still having rupiah liquidity to lend to their customers. Foreign currency borrowed from abroad could be relieved of any exchange risk and still lent in rupiah at high domestic interest rates.

In May 1987 the minimum bank swap premium was raised to 9%, and BI still allowed only a one-eighth percentage point transaction fee to the banks, in the case of reswap. In October 1988, the bank minimum premium for the use of BI's swap facility was tied to the difference between the average foreign exchange banks' relevant time deposit rate (according to the swaps' terms, which now could be up to three years, with the premium rate renewable each year) and the LIBOR rate on U.S. dollars for the same-term deposit abroad.[40]

LIBOR rates are the London interbank offer rates. The relevant "LIBOR + swap rates" served as the "reference rates" for the Indonesian markets and the measure against which we evaluated their stability. The openness of the foreign exchange system since 1971 and the proximity of Singapore mean that Indonesia's interest rates tend to reflect foreign interest rates, adjusted for depreciation, inflation, and other risks. The SIBOR rate is the Singapore interbank offering rate, which tracks the LIBOR very closely. The relevant policy measures are shown in Table 3.6.

The Foreign Exchange Spot Market

The foreign exchange market as we present it in this chapter represents components of different markets that we have put together. Because there are no detailed data for the components (as is also the case for the interbank loan market), which consist of spot foreign exchange, deposits, and short-term bills, such as U.S. Treasuries. Therefore, in the relevant parts of this chapter, we look at the data that we do have: spot foreign currency transactions by Bank Indonesia, net foreign assets of the deposit money banks, and net foreign assets (international reserves) of Bank Indonesia. We can argue that net foreign exchange assets as a whole, not any specific component, were what interested the holder of the asset during this period. It is the "hedging" or "speculative" aspect and the "liquidity" of the foreign exchange holding that mattered to the holder.

Indonesia has both bourse and off-bourse markets. During the period we are considering the bourse transactions included only Bank Indonesia dollar purchases from and sales to the public and the financial system, that is, spot dollar transactions.[41] Bank Indonesia posted daily its own buying and selling rates for various currencies throughout this period and stood ready to meet all supply and demand at those prices.

Indonesia, as we stated earlier, has an open foreign capital account. In August 1971 the liberal foreign exchange system was put into place, and exchange controls were lifted.[42] But the exchange rate throughout the period was set by Bank Indonesia, and there were three major devaluations. The rupiah was pegged to the U.S. dollar from August 1971 until November 1978, when it was pegged to a "basket of currencies of Indonesia's main trading partners" and there was a substantial devaluation of 51% relative to the dollar. Another major devaluation took place in 1983 (39%). The last major devaluation took place in September 1986 (45%).

On May 1, 1989, limits to the net open foreign exchange position were imposed on the banks, and their external borrowing limits were lifted.[43] These overall limits were imposed for prudential reasons, limiting exposure on the liability side as well as on the assets side, but also freeing up banks to adjust their borrowing portfolios. This regulation also limited the banks' ability to speculate in foreign exchange.

The combination of the liberal foreign exchange regime and the record of devaluations has made the financial system very sensitive to expectations about foreign exchange markets. Thus, policy measures affecting the money markets are greatly influenced by reactions to perceived speculation against the rupiah, as we have noted several times in this chapter.[44] These data series are watched carefully by the monetary authorities. Relevant policy measures are shown in Table 3.6.

Short-Term Time Deposits (One- and Three-Month)

Short-term time deposits serve as the main money market instrument for Indonesia's general public. They are available in both rupiah and foreign exchange and for several terms up to two years, with fixed interest rates payable at specified intervals. All sectors of the economy invested in time deposits throughout the period we studied, and time deposits as a whole have grown rapidly. There are no comprehensive published data regarding the holders of time deposits.

Several important characteristics have made rupiah time deposits very attractive: They are divisible and the most highly liquid instrument with a known return.[45] The interest is usually paid monthly and has been relatively high, and there was no tax on deposits over one month for the entire period, until PAKTO 27 imposed a flat 15% tax on the source. The identity of the holders is also kept secret.

State-owned banks paid lower interest rates on deposits than did private banks throughout the period, but because there is no deposit insurance in Indonesia, the state-owned banks may have appeared "safer" to many depositors. Furthermore, until PAKTO 27 the state-owned enterprises were required to deposit funds with state-owned banks. Table 3.8 shows rupiah time deposits by state-owned and "other bank" categories. State-owned banks dominated through the 1980s in the longer-term deposits, but private banks dominated in the shorter-term categories, even picking up substantially in the last few years. This indicates that state-owned bank depositors were interested more in yield than in liquidity, as compared with private-bank depositors.

One interesting aspect of the time deposit market is that the certificate of deposit (CD) market has not grown very much since its inception in the 1970s. A local banker asserted that the requirements for the CD are "too cumbersome." Especially before PAKTO 27 CDs were highly regulated, requiring at least three directors' signatures, in the unpopular discount form, and of a minimum size. CDs also are in bearer form, which makes their safety a concern. Since PAKTO 27, these requirements have been loosened, but since the time deposit serves almost the same role, but with more flexibility, CDs are not expected to generate much interest. All time deposits and CDs are subject to the same reserve requirements.

Major Players in the Money Markets

Table 3.9 shows the major players in the different money markets. Because of the lack of data, we could give only an impressionistic picture of these players' significance in each market. We distinguished four "degrees" of significance: A blank means no activity or not applicable; L means that the player is limited relative to other players but does play a role; S means that the player is relatively (and in some cases absolutely) significant; and M means that there is one monopolist player only.[46] We also identified the relevant activities within each market, such as underwriter, dealer, issuer, and buyer, and thus could indicate which entities were more significant with respect to the type of activity for that specific money market. Next we briefly discuss some aspects of the players in each market.

The *SBI market* has remained quite limited, with Bank Indonesia as the monopoly issuer (and own underwriter) and with the other players

Table 3.8. Rupiah Time Deposits

Maturity and Bank Category	December 1983			December 1985			December 1987			August 1989		
	Rp billions	Percent of Total Deposit	Percent of That Maturity	Rp billions	Percent of Total Deposit	Percent of That Maturity	Rp billions	Percent of Total Deposit	Percent of That Maturity	Rp billions	Percent of Total Deposit	Percent of That Maturity
State banks	2,831	63.75		5,337	60.05		9,283	60.41		14,472	55.87	
1-month	433	9.75	57.28	613	6.90	49.00	1,617	10.52	50.66	1,198	4.62	31.67
3-month	247	5.56	40.83	694	7.81	49.47	1,879	12.23	56.41	2,396	9.25	44.33
6-month	549	12.36	65.12	726	8.17	48.27	716	4.66	46.40	2,538	9.80	59.70
12-month	886	19.95	70.04	2,795	31.45	71.17	4,213	27.42	69.51	5,220	20.15	63.42
24-month	566	12.74	82.87	411	4.62	76.68	786	5.12	86.37	2,023	7.81	91.87
Other[a]	151	3.40	52.25	99	1.11	37.08	73	0.48	22.19	1,098	4.24	54.06
Other banks	1,610	36.25		3,551	39.95		6,083	39.59		11,431	44.13	
1-month	323	7.27	42.72	638	7.18	51.00	1,575	10.25	49.34	2,585	9.98	68.33
3-month	358	8.06	59.17	709	7.98	50.53	1,452	9.45	43.59	3,009	11.62	55.67
6-month	294	6.62	34.88	778	8.75	51.73	827	5.38	53.60	1,713	6.61	40.30
12-month	379	8.53	29.96	1,133	12.75	28.85	1,849	12.03	30.51	3,011	11.62	36.58
24-month	117	2.63	17.13	125	1.41	23.32	124	0.81	13.63	179	0.69	8.13
Other[a]	138	3.11	47.75	168	1.89	62.92	256	1.67	77.81	933	3.60	45.94
All banks	4,441	100.00		8,888	100.00		15,366	100.00		25,903	100.00	
1-month	756	17.02	100.00	1,251	14.08	100.00	3,192	20.77	100.00	3,783	14.60	100.00
3-month	605	13.62	100.00	1,403	15.79	100.00	3,331	21.68	100.00	5,405	20.87	100.00
6-month	843	18.98	100.00	1,504	16.92	100.00	1,543	10.04	100.00	4,251	16.41	100.00
12-month	1,265	28.48	100.00	3,927	44.18	100.00	6,061	39.44	100.00	8,231	31.78	100.00
24-month	683	15.38	100.00	536	6.03	100.00	910	5.92	100.00	2,202	8.50	100.00
Other[a]	289	6.51	100.00	267	3.00	100.00	329	2.14	100.00	2,031	7.84	100.00

[a] Including matured time deposits.

Source: Bank Indonesia, *Weekly Report*, various issues.

mostly confined to the banks and NBFIs. Occasionally a business holds an SBI. This instrument was designed as a monetary policy instrument by Bank Indonesia, and there has been no major policy effort to extend the market players beyond those who participate in the clearing. The state banks have been the principal buyers.[47] In early 1989, private-sector banks and certain NBFIs became dealers, and one private bank and one NBFI were selected as brokers. Only dealers can participate in the auction. A limited secondary market has developed for SBIs, for their use as collateral in repurchase agreements in the context of interbank borrowing among banks and NBFIs (see Table 3.5).

The *SBPU market*, in this chapter, consists of bills rediscounted at Bank Indonesia. As such, these data include only those bills actually rediscounted by the central bank in its role as the implementer of monetary policy.[48] However, because nonfinancial sectors are issuers of instruments that may qualify as rediscountable SBPUs (when endorsed or accepted by

Table 3.9. Major Players in Money Market Activities, 1989

Markets	Activities	Financial Sectors					
			Banks			Pension	
		BI	State	Private	NBFI	Funds	Insurance
Sertifikat Bank Indonesia (SBI)	Dealer		S	S	S		
	Broker			S	S		
	Agent						
	Buyer		S	L	L		
	Issuer	M					
Surat Berharga							
Pasar Uang (SBPU)	Dealer		S	S	S		
	Broker						
	Issuer		S	S	S		
	Endorser		S	S	S		
	Buyer		S	S	S		
	Rediscounter	M	S	S	S		
Certificates of deposit	Broker						
	Dealer						
	Issuer		S	S	L		
	Buyer					L	L
Foreign exchange spot market	Seller	S	S	S	S	S	S
	Buyer	S	S	S	S	S	S
Foreign exchange swap							
facility (BI)	Seller		S	S			
	Buyer		S	S	L	L	
	Reswap	M					
Short-term time deposits	Depositor					S	S
	Deposit taker		S	S			
Interbank market	Borrower		L	S	L		
	Lender		S	L	L		

Notes: L = limited activity, S = significant activity, M = one player only.

Table 3.9. (*Continued*)

| Markets | Activities | Government | | Nonfinancial Sectors | | |
		Central Government	State Enterprises	Foreign	Business	Individuals
Sertificat Bank Indonesia (SBI)	Dealer					
	Broker					
	Agent					
	Buyer		L			
	Issuer					
Surat Berharga Pasar Uang (SBPU)	Dealer					
	Broker					
	Issuer		S		S	L
	Endorser					
	Buyer					
	Rediscounter					
Certificates of deposit	Broker					
	Dealer					
	Issuer					
	Buyer				S	S
Foreign exchange spot market	Seller	S	S	S	S	S
	Buyer	S	S	S	S	S
Foreign exchange swap facility (BI)	Seller					
	Buyer	S	S	S	S	
	Reswap					
Short-term time deposits	Depositor	S	S	L	S	L/S
	Deposit taker					
Interbank market	Borrower					
	Lender					

Notes: L = limited activity, S = significant activity.

banks and NBFIs), this means that both businesses (state and private) and individual persons are players in this market. These instruments, both promissory notes and trade bills, serve as collateral for loans to these players and as collateral in the interbank market.[49] Banks and NBFIs themselves can also issue bills for rediscount.

The *market for negotiable certificates of deposit* issued in Indonesia by banks and NBFIs has been inactive but may be beginning to emerge. Pension funds and insurance companies are the main buyers, but some nonfinancial sectors also hold these certificates.[50]

The *foreign exchange spot market* is very active, but details of the relative roles of the various market players are not available; hence the S in each cell. The people we interviewed told us that until early 1989 there was not much activity among the banks; rather, it was between the banks and BI, between the banks and their customers, and with the banks acting as agents (off-balance sheet) making arrangements for their customers with banks abroad. Since early 1989, however, there has been more interbank activity.

The *BI foreign exchange swap facility* is available to all Indonesian "investors" who borrow funds abroad, including foreigners investing directly in Indonesia. As a result, the "indirect" users of this facility can be from all sectors. A bank makes the initial swap and then reswaps with Bank Indonesia, sells the contract to another bank, or holds the contract itself. Banks and NBFIs can also use the swap facility based on foreign exchange acquired from their direct borrowing abroad. From our interviews, we found that banks and NBFIs may buy and sell the swap contracts among themselves (not too actively yet, but growing), that they generally buy swap contracts only from other players, that pension funds and insurance companies are limited ultimate users of the facility, and that nonfinancial players, including "foreigners," are significant in the swap market.

Short-term time deposits make up another market in which all sectors play a role, as either a depositor or a deposit taker. Businesses (private and state) especially, use this market as a way to hold excess short-term funds.

The interbank market is, as the name implies, a loan market among banks and NBFIs, and they are the major players. Some of the paper used in the interbank market (promissory notes, SBPUs, etc.) originates in loans to other sectors. The forms of borrowing are call money, commercial paper (a kind of SBPU), nonstandardized bills, lines of credit, and interbank deposits. There is an interbank market among banks in Indonesia and between banks in Indonesia and those abroad. Bank Indonesia clears the market among Indonesian banks; dollar transactions are cleared mainly in New York.

THE CHANGING MONEY MARKET POLICIES

In this section we describe the major subperiods that we identified when examining the effects of government policies on the development of money markets in Indonesia.

Before 1983: Offshore Dollar Money Markets

From 1973 until June 1, 1983, the domestic money markets were relatively small, whereas the offshore, foreign exchange money markets provided much of the liquidity needed by the market participants.[51] The main reason for this was the policy of imposing domestic credit ceilings on all banks as a means of controlling the growth of domestic credit and money supply. High oil revenues during this period contributed to a buoyant economy and ample liquidity in the financial system. This liquidity could not be lent out domestically by the banks because of the credit ceilings and, therefore, was mainly deposited or invested abroad. Suwidjana (1984, Table 1) shows the rapid growth of foreign exchange assets and the net asset positions of the deposit money banks in Indonesia, especially after 1978. Most of the asset growth occurred in the "other" category and reflected a large net foreign asset position. Although the details are not shown, much of this may have been in short-term instruments in the Asian dollar market.

Businesses that needed short-term credit or a place to keep excess liquidity found the offshore markets very accommodating. Most businesses tended to build up deposit balances with banks in Singapore and Hong Kong, not only because the returns were more attractive (because of Indonesia's interest rate controls), but also to serve as guarantees for loans from those foreign institutions. Frequently Indonesian banks helped arrange such deposits and loans with correspondent foreign banks, even for smaller Indonesian businesses. This pattern of financial operations is not well documented because it was off-balance sheet for domestic banks and not reported by either domestic businesses or foreign banks; but when asked, most bankers and businesspeople acknowledge that it was the common practice.

The exchange rate of the rupiah to the U.S. dollar was held constant from August 23, 1971, to November 15, 1978, at which time there was a large (51%) devaluation. Thereafter the rate was periodically depreciated by small amounts until there was another large devaluation on March 30, 1983.[52] The relatively long period of exchange rate stability and the country's generally strong balance-of-payments position led to a perception of limited exchange rate risk in borrowing abroad (see Tables 3.10 and 3.11). Real dollar interest rates paid abroad and in Indonesia were generally positive after 1979, whereas real rupiah interest rates on both deposits and loans of the dominant state-owned banks were consistently negative because of domestic inflation rates that exceeded the interest rate ceilings imposed by the central bank. The stability of the exchange rate and the ceilings on domestic rupiah interest rates encouraged the movement of both short-term and longer-term funds abroad as well as borrowings from abroad.

Private Indonesian and foreign branch banks in Indonesia were not subject to the interest rate ceilings on rupiah deposits and on loans that were imposed on the state-owned banks, but they were subject to credit ceilings, which limited their incentive to work very hard at mobilizing deposits.[53] These banks' main recourse was to the offshore markets either to place any excess liquidity that they were prohibited from lending domestically or to help accommodate any customers whose loan needs they could not meet because of the credit ceilings.

June 1983 to August 1984: Emergence of the Interbank Market

On June 1, 1983, the Indonesian government announced the removal of credit ceilings for all banks and the elimination of most interest rate controls on deposits in state-owned banks. This had been preceded by a 38.5% devaluation of the rupiah in March 1983. A slow exchange rate depreciation policy was followed after June. These new government policies al-

Table 3.10. Dollar Assets and Liabilities: The Size of the Jakarta Dollar Market, 1970–82 (dollar-denominated deposits and loans of foreign exchange banks) (in billions of rupiahs)

End of Year	Deposits				Loans			
	Total	Of Which Rupiah	Of Which U.S. $	%	Total	Of Which Rupiah	Of Which U.S. $	%
1970	172	122	50	29	270	265	5	2
1971	279	216	63	23	408	393	15	4
1972	456	332	124	27	563	512	51	9
1973	641	450	191	30	905	816	89	10
1974	1,069	740	329	31	1,305	1,115	187	14
1975	1,382	1,053	329	24	1,859	1,598	258	14
1976	1,824	1,455	369	20	2,351	2,063	291	13
1977	2,042	1,725	317	16	2,708	2,427	281	10
1978	2,852	1,946	906 [a]	32 [a]	3,458	3,084	374 [a]	11 [a]
1979	3,485	2,463	1,002	29	4,279	3,869	41	10
1980	5,062	3,628	1,434	28	7,880	7,478	402	5
1981	7,406	5,880	1,526	20	10,159	9,754	405	4
1982	9,010	7,113	1,897	21	13,258	12,637	621	5

[a] Revaluated after the November 1978 rupiah devaluation.

lowed the state-owned banks to raise their deposit and loan interest rates. All banks began to take a new interest in mobilizing rupiah deposits to support new lending. The demand for rupiah loans also rose as borrowers came to perceive the higher cost of dollar loans resulting from the steady depreciation of the exchange rate. The private banks soon discovered that they had a comparative advantage over the state banks in lending rather than in mobilizing funds. Private depositors apparently considered the state-owned banks (and perhaps the foreign banks) safer than the private domestic banks and therefore were more willing to deposit funds, even at somewhat lower interest rates, in the state-owned banks than in the private banks. The state-owned banks also had a more extensive branch network. On the other hand, the private banks' lending procedures were quicker and less complicated than those of the state-owned banks, and so private borrowers were willing to borrow from them even at somewhat higher nominal interest rates than those charged by the state banks. All state-owned enterprises were required to deposit only in state-owned banks, which provided state banks with a captive clientele.

This imbalance between the deposit mobilizing and lending capabilities of the two groups of banks created a fertile environment for the development of the interbank money market. Some of the larger private banks also reportedly began to act as informal brokers mediating between the state-owned banks and the smaller private banks.

Table 3.11. Dollar Assets and Liabilities: Foreign Exchange Assets and Liabilities of Deposit Money Banks,[a] 1968–82 (in billions of rupiahs)

End of Year	Assets			Liabilities			Net
	Loans [b]	Other	Total	Deposits [c]	Other [d]	Total	
March 31							
1968	—	22	22	—	32	32	−10
1969	—	24	24	—	57	57	−33
1970	5	N.A.	94	50	30	80	14
1971	15	119	134	63	77	140	−6
1972	51	152	203	124	98	222	−19
1973	89	204	293	191	181	372	−79
1974	187	234	421	329	198	527	−106
1975	258	291	549	329	360	689	−140
1976	291	233	524	369	126	495	29
1977	281	297	578	317	140	457	121
1978	374	402	776	906	153	1,059	−283
1979 [e]	410	714	1,124	1,002	227	1,229	−105
1980	412	1,928	2,340	1,434	313	1,747	593
1981	405	3,233	3,638	1,526	429	1,955	1,683
1982	621	3,392	4,013	1,897	506	2,403	1,610

Note: N.A. = Not Available.

[a] Figures for "Total" and "Other" include, besides foreign exchange banks, other private development and savings banks.

[b] Excludes interbank loans.

[c] Includes demand, time, and savings deposits.

[d] Includes debts and other liabilities.

[e] Revaluated after the November 1978 devaluation of the rupiah.

Source: Bank Indonesia, taken from Njoman Suwidjana, "Jakarta Dollar Market: A Case of Financial Development in ASEAN," *Institute of Southeast Asian Studies Occasional Paper 76,* 1984, Tables 5 and 6.

Data on interbank lending are incomplete, especially for this early period. These partial data indicate that this market grew very rapidly after July 1983 and then collapsed just as quickly after the policies were changed in September 1984. In addition, the weighted average interbank interest rate was relatively volatile but is probably a good indicator of the liquidity conditions in the interbank money market throughout this period.

While the domestic interbank money market was growing in response to "normal" market forces, the monetary authorities became more concerned with creating an "indirect" instrument to influence the total supply of the banking system's reserve money.[54] Bank Indonesia introduced the new money market instrument in January 1984, called a Sertifikat Bank Indonesia, or SBI, which was a short-term liability of Bank Indonesia. This instrument initially had maturities of thirty and ninety days and was sold each week, ostensibly through an auction, but in fact at cutoff discount rates acceptable to Bank Indonesia. The demand for SBIs was limited, as their yield was significantly lower than the rupiah deposit rates or interbank loan rates.

September 1984 to September 1986: Managed Money Markets

In August 1984, the domestic interbank market became very unsettled because of a liquidity squeeze combined with the accelerated rate of the rupiah's depreciation by Bank Indonesia. The normal end-of-month reserve drain, which was usually accompanied by adjustments in the interbank market and some repatriation of foreign exchange, was in this instance compounded by the banks' reluctance to sell foreign exchange in the face of the high and steady rate of depreciation. As one banker remembered, "We no longer had to estimate the rate of depreciation, just to calculate it." The response in the money markets was a sharp rise in the overnight interbank interest rate to a peak of 90% per year in early September 1984 and a moderate outflow of foreign exchange reserves from Bank Indonesia.

In evaluating this crisis, the monetary authorities concluded that activity in the interbank market was contributing to the interbank market speculation against the rupiah, so they reduced ceilings on the amount of interbank borrowings that the banks could undertake (from 15% to 7.5% of their total deposit liabilities).[55] Bank Indonesia also supplied "emergency" credits of up to six months to all banks that were short of liquidity. Most important, the monetary authorities reduced the rate of depreciation of the rupiah, which relieved the speculative pressure. The interbank rate fell back quickly to below the level before the crisis (see Figure 3.3).

Having discovered that a short-term insufficiency of reserve money could be as troublesome as an excess and that the SBI secondary market still was nonexistent, so that it could not be used to supply reserves as well as withdraw them, Bank Indonesia introduced the second new money market instrument in early 1985, called the SBPU, which could be used to supply reserves. The SBPU was essentially a standard bankers acceptance that Bank Indonesia was prepared to purchase at a discount from the banks. The rate of discount was set by Bank Indonesia through a quasi-auction process.

Initially the SBPU was used to replace part of the six-month emergency credits that had been given to many banks in September 1984. But there was a continuing demand for reserve funds, especially from the private banks, whose borrowings were now limited to 7.5% of their total third-party liabilities. On the other hand, the state-owned banks had excess reserve funds that they could not lend directly to the private banks because of the same limit. Instead they put their surplus reserves into Bank Indonesia's SBIs or into dollar deposits abroad. From June 1985 until July 1986, as shown in Figure 3.3, the level of outstanding SBIs rose from practically nothing to Rp 2.4 billion while the level of estimated interbank bor-

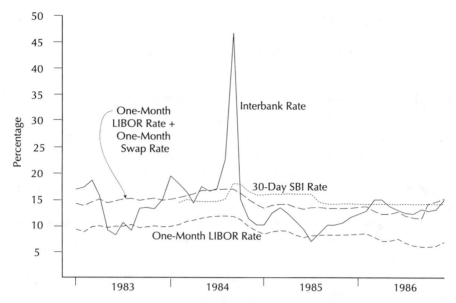

Figure 3.3. Money Market Rates, January 1983–December 1986. *Source:* Bank Indonesia.

rowing declined. The volume of SBPUs rediscounted by Bank Indonesia rose from Rp 89 billion to Rp 368 billion during the same period, indicating the amount of reserve money supplied to the banks by Bank Indonesia through this channel. Finally, the DMBs increased their net foreign exchange holdings by about U.S.$600 million, or Rp 650 billion at the then prevailing exchange rate.

In effect, Bank Indonesia itself played the former role of the interbank market by mopping up excess reserves from the state-owned banks by selling SBIs to them and then lending reserves to the private banks by discounting their SBPUs. In both markets, Bank Indonesia set the interest rates, which accounts for their constancy throughout this period. Bank Indonesia set no specified limits on the amount of SBIs that it would sell to the state-owned banks, but in time it set quotas or ceilings for the amount of SBPUs it would buy from each bank, as a means of controlling the growth of reserve money.

A third money market instrument that Bank Indonesia used during this period was the foreign exchange swap facility Bank Indonesia set the swap premium at 5.25% per year, which was less than the difference between the foreign U.S. dollar interest rates and the domestic rupiah deposit rates on comparable instruments. Using Figure 3.3, it is possible to compare the swap plus one-month LIBOR rate with the one-month state-owned banks' time deposit rate and the SBI rate. There was an excess demand for swaps, fueled by their low price. Bank Indonesia responded to this by "rationing," that is, by putting ceilings on the amount of swap contracts it was willing to accept from each bank.

During this period, therefore, BI set the SBI, SBPU, and swap rates. It rationed the quantity of SBPUs and swaps that it would buy from the individual banks. Since both these instruments were the banks' sources of reserve money, Bank Indonesia essentially rationed the supply of reserve money for the individual banks. It also limited the amount of interbank borrowing by the private banks, and it bought up any excess reserves from the state-owned banks through the open-ended sale of SBIs. Not surprisingly, the volume of interbank borrowing shrank, and movements in the interbank interest rate were erratic and poorly correlated with the rates of either domestic money market instruments or the LIBOR.

The overall effect of these policies was that two of the money market instruments (SBPUs and swaps) were used primarily as quantitative instruments of monetary policy, to control the supply of reserve money, and they were not allowed to develop as flexible means of liquidity adjustment for the financial institutions. The SBI, on the other hand, in this period became a fixed–interest rate instrument of liquidity adjustment primarily for the state-owned banks. Furthermore, since the interest rates on all these instruments were effectively fixed by Bank Indonesia, they provided little information about the overall liquidity conditions or expectations in the money markets.

There was a consistent net outflow of foreign exchange from Bank Indonesia from mid-1984 through August 1986 while at the same time the commercial banks were building up their foreign exchange holdings. The rate of dollar outflow from Bank Indonesia varied from month to month depending on speculation about devaluation. The exchange rate was held fairly steady through this same period, especially after May 1985, which may have contributed to the pressures for and the expectations of a big devaluation in the future.

On September 12, 1986, the monetary authorities implemented a devaluation of 45% against the U.S. dollar. The "timing" of this devaluation came as a surprise to many money market participants, who thought it would occur nearer the end of the year and had therefore held on to larger rupiah assets than they might have, because the rupiah instruments were earning interest rates two to three percentage points higher than the rates (plus swap premium) on comparable U.S. dollar instruments held offshore.

October 1986 to June 1987: Heavy Speculation Against the Rupiah

Following the devaluation, there continued to be speculative surges against the rupiah. In December 1986 the central bank lost $1.7 billion; in May and June 1987 there was an outflow of $1.1 billion. A major cause of these foreign exchange pressures was the sharp drop in world oil prices in 1986/87, which many market participants interpreted as likely to force another large devaluation in order to maintain rupiah budget revenues. But the government authorities concluded that any beneficial effects of a devaluation on the revenue side would be offset by increased rupiah expenditures to service the foreign debt, and so another devaluation could not offer a net gain for the budget. The erratic management of the exchange rate—if viewed relative to the U.S. dollar during this period—gave the impression of uncertainty, although the rate may have looked more stable relative to some basket of foreign currencies.[56] This perception may have added to the speculation.

Concurrent with the devaluation in September 1986, Bank Indonesia removed the ceilings on the swap facility for each bank and raised the swap premium from 5.25% to 8%. Despite the increase in price, swaps outstanding surged, and there was evidence of an apparent substitution of swaps for foreign exchange asset holdings by the DMBs.[57] Interbank rates also continued to rise throughout this period, as the speculative pressure on the rupiah remained severe. In May 1987 the swap premium was raised from 8% to 9%. This increase did not dampen the speculative fever but, instead, probably added to expectations of further devaluation, so that swaps outstanding surged again in May and June. The central bank also raised the interest rate on SBIs and raised the basic discount rate to 19%, but to no avail. The demand for SBIs practically disappeared, and the demand for foreign exchange in both the spot and swap markets continued to be strong.

June to July 1987: Drastic Contraction of Reserve Money

The combination of the steady, heavy loss of foreign exchange reserves, the increasing number of swap contracts, and the sharply higher interbank interest rates finally forced the government to take more direct and drastic action in late June 1987. Rather than impose another devaluation, the government dramatically contracted the rupiah funds.[58] The state-owned banks were the principal "financers" of the speculation against the rupiah by either using their excess liquidity to buy foreign exchange directly or lending to the private banks and customers that could then increase their net foreign exchange positions. Therefore the main attack was on the liquidity position of the banks, especially the state banks. The contraction was accomplished by two specific measures. The first was an instruction to four large state-owned enterprises to transfer part of their time deposit balances at the state-owned banks to holdings of new SBIs issued by Bank Indonesia. The second was a reduction to zero in the ceilings on SBPU rediscounts at Bank Indonesia, in effect forcing all the commercial banks to buy back their outstanding rediscounted SBPUs from Bank Indonesia.

These two measures essentially wiped out, almost overnight, the equivalent of all the available legal reserves of the deposit money banks. The only way in which the banking system could meet its legal reserve requirements was by selling foreign exchange to Bank Indonesia or by borrowing through its discount window. An increase in the discount rate from 20% to 30% was intended to discourage the second alternative and encourage sales of foreign exchange to the central bank.

In July, Bank Indonesia also initiated daily auctions of seven-day SBIs, discontinuing the sale of thirty-day SBIs. The new seven-day SBIs carried market-determined rates, which initially were as high as 20%, but within two months they had dropped below 15% as expectations of another devaluation subsided.

August 1987 to October 1988: Stabilizing Expectations

The effects of the June–July contractionary measures were dramatic. There was a large return flow of foreign exchange to Bank Indonesia, amounting to $1.3 billion from July through November, and a decline of $1 billion in outstanding swap contracts with Bank Indonesia from August through December. The interbank interest rate dropped from an average of 23.5% in June to 11.8% in September (see Figure 3.4). The seven-day SBI auction rates that averaged 18% in July dropped to 14.9% by September. All these changes reflected the changed expectations of another major devaluation in the near future. But the banks' confidence in the use of the SBPU as a source of funds from Bank Indonesia had been severely shaken. The SBI's reputation had also been somewhat tainted by the forced sale to the four public enterprises. The development of these two money market instruments was certainly slowed.

The focus of monetary policy in this period shifted to an attempt to extend the time horizon of stable expectations, especially for the exchange rate, from a few weeks to a few months. The principal instrument used for this purpose was the rate of depreciation of the rupiah against the U.S. dollar. Although the authorities were theoretically adjusting the exchange rate to a basket of currencies, they in effect seemed to be gradually depreciating the rupiah against the U.S. dollar throughout most of 1988. This policy contributed to the effect of extending expectations.[59]

November 1988 to April 1989: Activating the Domestic Money Markets

On October 27, 1988, the Indonesian government announced a broad package of financial reforms designed to free up entry into many types of financial activity and encourage the development of domestic financial markets. The provisions that directly affected the money markets were the following:

1. The removal of specific limitations on interbank borrowing.
2. The introduction of a flexible foreign exchange swap premium based on the difference between the LIBOR rate and the time deposit rates of the state-owned banks.[60]
3. The adoption of a two-day settlement period rather than a same-day settlement for foreign exchange transactions with Bank Indonesia.[61]
4. A reduction in the reserve requirements of banks (and NBFIs) to a uniform rate of 2% of all third-party liabilities.

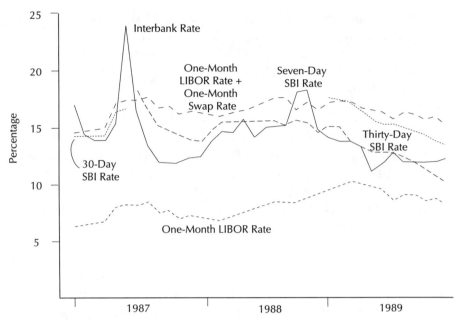

Figure 3.4. Money Market Rates, January 1987–December 1989. *Source:* Bank Indonesia.

5. A "forced sale" at fixed interest rates (16% and 16.5% per year) of three- and six-month SBIs to all banks to absorb 80% of their supposedly freed-up reserves resulting from the reduced reserve requirement.

These policies had the effects of increasing the opportunities and facilities for using the domestic money market instruments and of reducing the relative attractiveness of using foreign exchange for liquidity management purposes.

The fifth measure was particularly interesting. Initially the banks and NBFIs believed that they had to hold the so-called PAKTO SBIs until they matured and that the SBIs could not be traded (see note 28).

The forced purchase of SBIs initially put a severe squeeze on the commercial banks' liquidity position because the reduction in legally required reserves was much greater than the reduction in reserves that the banks believed they needed to meet reasonable liquidity requirements. The level of actual reserves of the banks declined from Rp 3,129 billion to Rp 1,957 billion between the end of October and the end of November 1988. But the banks were required to buy Rp 1,904 billion of SBIs, or Rp 732 billion more than the reduction in their actual reserves. Some banks, faced with this severe liquidity squeeze, had to turn to Bank Indonesia for what turned out to be long-term accommodation. Others managed to adjust by selling foreign exchange holdings or by borrowing abroad and swapping foreign exchange with Bank Indonesia to acquire rupiah.

This liquidity squeeze led to a sharp rise in the interbank interest rate, although most banks managed to meet their legal reserve requirements at the end of the first or second reserve period in November by one means or another. After the dust settled, they began to review their reserve management practices and to work out new ways of meeting the new reserve requirement rules.[62]

After a series of clarifying instructions from, and promotional meetings organized by, Bank Indonesia, the banks and NBFIs began to use the SBIs as tradable paper, mostly under repurchase agreements. By late December, the banks began to sell some of their PAKTO SBIs either outright or under repurchase agreements. In the first part of February, 25% of the PAKTO SBIs, which had a term of ninety days, matured and were redeemed by Bank Indonesia. This helped ease further the banks' liquidity position. In the meantime, the interbank market was becoming more active as a mechanism for redistributing available reserves among the banks.

The prospect of the remaining 75% of PAKTO SBIs' maturing in the first half of May 1989, and thereby supplying new reserve money of Rp 1.2 trillion, led to some concern about the money markets' becoming overly liquid and precipitating a significant loss of foreign exchange. To prevent this, Bank Indonesia further encouraged the development of the secondary and primary markets for SBIs and also took several measures to discourage the holding of foreign exchange for liquidity management purposes.[63]

May 1989 to December 1989: Further Adjustments in Foreign Exchange Operations

On May 1, 1989, a number of additional policy measures took effect that further discouraged the use of offshore foreign exchange deposits for liquidity management purposes, including

1. Setting net open foreign exchange position limits for all foreign exchange banks at 25% of their total capital. However, the definition of capital was extended somewhat.

2. Removing foreign borrowing limits on domestic banks to permit them to acquire more longer-term foreign financing. Before this, NBFIs could borrow up to U.S.$40 million, private banks up to U.S.$7.5 million, and state banks between U.S.$10 million and $15 million.

3. Restricting the definition of capital for branches of foreign banks operating within Indonesia.

4. Restricting the use of foreign exchange swaps with Bank Indonesia by branches of foreign banks.

Then, in November 1989, Bank Indonesia announced that it would begin intervening in the foreign exchange market at its own discretion and would post its buying and selling rates twice a day.[64] The exchange rate continued to depreciate throughout this period at about 4% to 5% per year. Net outstanding swaps were declining, nonoil exports were growing well, and oil prices were steady. The interbank rate and the SBI rates were falling, and ninety-day SBI issues were reintroduced.

The secondary market for SBIs, which was activated only in January 1989, grew quickly into an active and significant market, as shown in Table 3.5. The volume averaged Rp 1 trillion per month from June through December, or a daily average of Rp 40 billion to 50 billion. Most of the activity was in the two- to twenty-seven-day instruments, which were mainly repurchase contracts on SBIs. Several of the SBI market makers were buying longer-maturity SBIs in the weekly auction and then "repoing them out" for shorter periods and earning the spread between the longer and shorter rates. One advantage of this market over the normal interbank market is that the paper is of uniform, high quality so that it can serve as a riskless reference interest rate in the domestic market.

Summary of the Changing Policies

Throughout this period, Indonesia maintained an open foreign exchange capital account, with no restrictions on the transfer of foreign exchange into or out of the country.[65] Before June 1983, the main money market instrument in Indonesia was in foreign exchange, which was held largely in offshore deposits. The freeing up of interest rates and removal of bank credit ceilings in June 1983 led to the rapid development of a significant rupiah interbank money market in Jakarta. But in September 1984 when this market was perceived as reflecting, or possibly contributing to, exchange rate uncertainty, the authorities moved quickly to limit interbank borrowing and replace it with a Bank Indonesia–intermediated and –controlled money market based on SBIs and SBPUs.

Again, in June 1987, in the face of heavy foreign exchange reserve losses, the monetary authorities sacrificed the SBPU and forced government-owned, nonbanking institutions to buy SBIs in order to draw down bank reserves drastically and force a return flow of foreign exchange. These measures clearly set back the development of these domestic money market instruments. Since the financial reforms of October 1988, however, a more consistent set of policies have fostered the development of the rupiah-based money markets in Jakarta. The initial forced sale of SBIs in PAKTO 27 to mop up bank reserves was not, in itself, a market-promoting move, but it did inject a sizable amount of SBIs into the banks' portfolios, and then Bank Indonesia took steps to encourage the trading of those SBIs in the secondary market. Improved exchange rate management and the imposition of net open foreign exchange position limits on the banks further contributed to development of the domestic money markets, as did the removal of restrictions on interbank borrowing and the linking of BI's foreign exchange reswap rate to the difference between domestic and foreign interest rates.

All these measures led to the rapid growth, integration, and flexibility of the domestic money markets. These new and expanded markets were tested by a large outflow of foreign exchange in the first half of 1990. After some initial hesitancy, the monetary authorities used their indirect policy instruments to steer the financial system through the minicrisis without again subjecting the money markets to traumatic shocks.

QUANTITATIVE PERFORMANCE INDICATORS

Efficiency and stability have been suggested by PIFS (1989) as the performance indicators for evaluating the various money markets. Efficiency is evaluated in terms of whether the interest rates of the principal instruments in a given market are free to move in consonance with some reference interest rate, and also whether the spreads between the reference rate and the particular market rate are consistent with reasonable differences in risk or transaction costs. Nonconformity with these patterns suggests that markets are segmented or regulated in ways that distort relative prices and preclude optimal choices.

Stability is measured in terms of the volatility, or variance, of a particular interest rate over time, and again, a comparison with the volatility of some reference rate can provide a standard. This concept of stability assumes some freedom of movement, or free-market-determined rates, not the stability that may result from cartels and government controls. A secondary indicator of stability is in terms of market liquidity—whether a particular market seems to suffer from periodic liquidity crises in which sudden changes in either demand or supply are not met by corresponding changes in supply or demand from other parties. Such liquidity crises are normally reflected in changes in the particular instrument's interest rate, but if the interest rate is controlled, then the volume of transactions may either expand or diminish suddenly, or the market may simply disappear.

A third possible measure of performance, not mentioned in the PIFS guidelines (1989), is the growth of a particular market relative to the average rate of growth of some norm. Rapid growth of the transactions in a particular money market, or in the holdings of a particular money market instrument, normally indicates that the market or instrument is effectively satisfying some demand. This rapid growth may be due to coercive pressure on market participants to buy or hold some particular instrument (such as liquidity requirements to hold government securities), or the price of that instrument may be controlled or distorted to make it especially attractive. But if neither of those conditions holds, then presumably the rapid growth indicates a positive performance.

In seeking some norm against which to measure the relative growth of a particular money market instrument, probably the best choice would be the growth of all money market assets, or of all financial assets. But neither of these aggregative measures is likely to be readily available, especially on a short-term or monthly basis. Since we are dealing with money market instruments, which are close substitutes for money, the best norm, or denominator, which is also readily available for most countries, may be the supply of narrow money (M1).[66]

We therefore decided to use the ratio of the stock of each particular money market instrument to the stock (or supply) of narrow money (M1) as an indicator of the size, or importance, of the money market instrument, and the rates of change in the quantity of one instrument relative to the change in the quantity of narrow money over time as an indicator of that instrument's relative growth. The measure of relative change that seems best for this purpose is based on the concept of elasticity, which compares the percentage change in the particular money market instrument with the percentage change in the narrow money supply over a given period of time. This gives a measure of money-growth elasticity comparable to the notion of income elasticity in relation to income and expenditure analysis.

Growth Indicators

The relative growth indicators for the main money market instruments for which we have reliable data are presented in Table 3.12. Narrow money, or M1, is used as the numeraire, or base, with which the other instruments' growth is compared. Between the end of June 1983 and the end of December 1989, the nominal money supply increased by 152.6%. The value of total time deposits increased during the same period by 801.4%, giving a growth elasticity of total time deposits relative to M1 of 5.25. One-month time deposits had a slightly higher elasticity of 5.3, and three-month time deposits had a growth elasticity of 7.05 relative to M1. This indicates a relative shift from time deposits longer than three months into three-month time deposits.

Data on the stocks of interbank loans, unfortunately, are not available for this period. The best available evidence is the data on average daily transactions in the interbank market, although the coverage of this series may have expanded over the years. The growth for the whole period from June 1983 to December 1989 in reported average daily interbank transactions was 357%, or an elasticity relative to M1 of 2.34. Interbank transactions grew most rapidly between June 1983 and August 1984, when the growth elasticity relative to M1 was 30.3. Thereafter, interbank borrowings were limited, and transactions were depressed until mid-1987. There was another rapid increase since then, following the removal of limits on interbank borrowing in October 1988.

The growth of the deposit money banks' rupiah value of net foreign exchange assets from June 1983 to December 1989 was less than the growth of M1. The elasticity measure is 0.74. The growth of Bank Indonesia's net foreign exchange reserves (measured in rupiah at the current ex-

Table 3.12. Indicators of Relative Growth of Money Market Instruments, 1983–89 (Rp billions, %, elasticities)

	M1	Rupiah Time Deposits	Rupiah 1-Month Time Deposits	Rupiah 3-Month Time Deposits	Net Foreign Assets of DMBs	BI Net Foreign Assets	Swaps Outstanding	SBIs Outstanding	SBPUs Outstanding	Interbank Loans
June 1983	7,506	3,003	497	452	3,547	3,535	3,592[a]	—	—	22.3
August 1984	7,934	5,641	765	804	3,718	6,082	4,017	14	91[b]	60.8
Change 6/83–8/84	5.70%	87.85%	53.92%	77.88%	4.82%	72.05%	11.83%	—	—	172.65%
Elasticity to M1		15.7	9.5	13.7	0.9	12.6	2.1	—	—	30.3
August 1986	10,242	10,479	1,249	1,574	5,618	4,212	4,000	1,551	496	27.2
Change 8/84–8/86	29.09%	85.76%	63.27%	95.77%	51.10%	-30.75%	-0.42%	—	445.1%	-55.26%
Elasticity to M1		2.9	2.2	3.3	1.8	—	—	—	15.3	—
June 1987	11,588	11,798	1,687	1,657	6,423	4,530	6,398	369	515	32.2
Change 8/86–6/87	13.14%	12.59%	35.07%	5.27%	14.33%	7.55%	59.94%	-76.21%	3.83%	18.38%
Elasticity to M1		0.96	2.7	0.4	1.1	0.6	4.6	—	0.3	1.4
October 1988	13,145	20,329	3,395	4,934	7,141	7,881	8,241	796	0	44.2
Change 6/87–10/88	13.44%	72.31%	101.24%	197.77%	11.18%	73.97%	28.81%	115.72%	-100.00%	37.27%
Elasticity to M1		5.4	7.5	14.7	0.8	6.0	2.1	8.6	—	2.8
April 1989	15,146	21,602	3,386	4,777	7,397	8,307	5,540	2,538	210	67.6
Change 10/88–4/89	15.22%	6.26%	-0.27%	-3.18%	3.58%	5.41%	-32.78%	218.84%	—	52.99%
Elasticity to M1		0.4	—	—	0.2	0.4	—	14.4	—	3.5
December 1989	15,959	27,069	4,516	5,312	7,538	9,443	3,019	3,301	0	102.0
Change 4/89–12/89	25.17%	25.31%	33.37%	11.2%	1.91%	13.70%	-45.50%	30.10%	-100.00%	50.89%
Elasticity to M1		1.01	1.33	0.44	0.1	0.5	—	1.2	—	2.0
Change 6/83–12/89	152.6%	801.4%	808.7%	1,075.2%	112.5%	167.1%	-16.0%	—	—	357.40%
Elasticity to M1		5.25	5.30	7.05	0.74	1.10	—	—	—	2.34

[a] Data on swaps outstanding is as of end January 1984.

[b] Data on August 1985, so that the period of SBPUs outstanding change is between August 1985 and August 1986.

Source: Bank Indonesia, *Indonesia Financial Statistics*, and *Weekly Report*, various issues.

change rate) shows a higher elasticity for the period, at 1.10. The outstanding rupiah value of the Bank Indonesia foreign exchange swap facility ("swaps") actually declined from January 1984 to December 1989. Thus there was an overall shift by the banks out of spot foreign exchange assets and holding of swaps at Bank Indonesia, into domestic, rupiah-denominated assets such as SBIs and interbank loans.

The deposit money banks' net foreign exchange holdings had a relatively high growth elasticity of 1.8 between August 1984 and August 1986. They nearly kept pace with M1 growth until October 1988 but since then have declined, especially following the imposition of net open position limits in May 1989. The growth of BI swaps was relatively high from August 1986 until October 1988, reflecting both the devaluation of September 1986 and the removal of ceilings on BI swaps at that time. After October 1988 the outstanding swaps declined absolutely, so the elasticity measure is not meaningful.

In addition to indicating the relative growth of these money market instruments over the six-year period, the elasticity measures show the relative growth during the various subperiods of differing policy regimes. For example, time deposits grew most rapidly from June 1983 to August 1986 and then again from June 1987 to October 1988. Net foreign exchange holdings of the deposit money banks grew at much the same rate as M1 did in all periods except since April 1989, when the imposition of net foreign exchange open position limits curtailed the growth of such holdings. Foreign exchange swaps at Bank Indonesia and SBIs and SBPUs all exhibited a more erratic pattern, rising sharply in some periods and then falling in others. The swaps climbed quickly from August 1986 through June 1987, after the ceilings on them were removed. They continued to grow moderately relative to M1 through October 1988, but since then they have lost popularity. The development of SBIs and SBPUs has depended mainly on whether or not Bank Indonesia was using them actively as monetary instruments.

Stability Indicators

The measure of stability that we used is the standard deviation of the interest rate for the several instruments based on the end-of-month interest rates for each month from June 1983 to December 1989. The means and the standard deviations of the interest rates for seven money market instruments for the whole period and for the several subperiods are shown in Table 3.13. The standard deviation of the one-month LIBOR rate over the whole period was 1.42, which provides a comparative benchmark for a purely market-determined rate. The reference rate that we used for the Indonesian money markets is the one-month LIBOR plus the swap premium. The standard deviation for this combined rate was 1.59, indicating that the changes in the swap rate added to the instability of this rate.

Table 3.13. Indicators of Interest Rate Stability and Correlation with Reference Rate of Money Market Instruments, 1983–89

Period	Sum of 1-Month LIBOR Rate Plus BI Premium			1-Month LIBOR Rate			Weighted Average Interbank Interest Rate			Weighted Average 1-Month Deposit Rate at State Banks			Weighted Average 3-Month Deposit Rate at State Banks			Discount Rate of 7-Day SBIs			Discount Rate of 30-Day SBIs		
	SD	Mean	Corr. Coeff.	SD	Mean	Corr. Coeff.	SD	Mean	Corr. Coeff.	SD	Mean	Corr. Coeff.	SD	Mean	Corr. Coeff.	SD	Mean	Corr. Coeff.	SD	Mean	Corr. Coeff.
Jun. 83–Dec. 89	1.59	15.15	1.00	1.42	8.47	0.45	4.74	13.81	0.36	1.35	14.85	0.66	1.30	15.80	0.67	—	—	—	—	—	—
Jun. 83–Aug. 84	0.80	15.53	1.00	0.80	10.28	1.00	3.97	14.80	0.55	0.38	14.64	0.38	0.39	15.86	0.88	—	—	—	—	—	—
Aug. 84–Aug. 86	1.32	13.62	1.00	1.32	8.37	1.00	7.58	13.37	0.61	0.69	14.15	0.57	1.14	15.33	0.64	—	—	—	1.26	15.09	0.68
Aug. 86–Jun. 87	1.78	14.32	1.00	0.71	6.63	0.82	3.18	14.73	0.68	1.03	13.52	0.53	0.75	14.39	0.74	—	—	—	0.89	14.40	0.74
Jun. 87–Oct. 88	0.58	16.55	1.00	0.62	7.61	0.91	1.80	14.00	0.31	1.64	16.42	0.45	1.15	17.26	0.55	1.05	15.16	0.55	—	—	—
Oct. 88–Apr. 89	0.33	16.85	1.00	0.65	9.32	0.46	2.06	15.07	−0.27	0.54	15.89	0.09	0.79	16.95	0.29	0.82	14.61	0.02	—	—	—
Apr. 89–Dec. 89	0.43	16.05	1.00	0.51	9.12	0.92	0.86	12.15	0.27	0.00	15.13	0.00	0.00	15.17	0.00	1.01	12.07	0.84	0.92	14.91	0.86
Feb. 84–Jun. 87	1.57	14.23	1.00	1.69	8.32	0.70	6.20	14.23	0.56	0.86	14.12	0.51	1.11	15.23	0.55	—	—	—	1.12	14.85	0.41
Jul. 87–Dec. 89	0.58	16.47	1.00	0.99	8.36	0.33	1.84	13.59	0.47	1.32	15.97	0.45	1.28	16.64	0.62	1.69	14.16	0.65	—	—	—

The interbank rate had a very high standard deviation of 4.74 for the whole period. The volatility of this rate was greatest from August 1984 to August 1986, after which it fell considerably. This rate was most volatile during the period when interbank borrowings were most strongly curtailed by Bank Indonesia's restrictions. They may have been used at that time more for emergency purposes, as reflected in the rates' fluctuations.

The two time deposit rates had relatively low standard deviations. Since these were the official, posted rates of the state-owned banks, they are not a good indicator of the variability or level of rates actually paid, because those rates are often subject to negotiation with individual large customers. For example, in the latest period, from April to December 1989, the posted rates did not change at all (the standard deviation is zero), whereas informal information and the actual negotiation of rates on time deposit accounts with a state-owned bank indicated some movement in these rates.

The stability measures for seven- and thirty-day SBIs are available only for the periods when those instruments were being auctioned to the market. The standard deviations of the SBI rates seem quite low relative to the interbank rate. But when compared with either the LIBOR or the LIBOR + swap rates for the same periods, the SBI rates are somewhat more variable. In this instance, variability may have been a virtue, in that it indicates that Bank Indonesia was not controlling the rates excessively. We explore this subject further in the next section.

Efficiency Indicators

The basic measure that we used for indicating the efficiency of a particular money market is the simple correlation coefficient of the interest rate movements in that market with a reference rate. The reference rate that we chose is the LIBOR + swap rate. This rate is reasonable on theoretical grounds for a very open money market such as there is in Indonesia. It would be analogous to using the U.S. Treasury bill rate, plus a forward exchange premium between Canadian and U.S. dollars, as a reference rate for Canadian money market rates. If the markets are working efficiently and freely, then the particular market rate under study would be expected to move with the reference rate.

In the case of Indonesia, the interbank rate was relatively poorly correlated with the reference rate—a coefficient of only 0.36 for the period from June 1983 to December 1989. The correlation of these two rates was somewhat higher for August 1984 to June 1987, but still only in the range of 0.61 to 0.68. This was also a time of great instability in the interbank rate. After the October 1988 reforms, the correlation coefficient was even negative, as the interbank rate was falling from a high level and the U.S. dollar LIBOR was rising in response to the tightening of liquidity in the U.S. and world money markets.

The state-owned bank time deposit rates were better correlated with the reference rate over the whole period (0.66), but the relationship has weakened since the October 1988 reforms. The reason may be that the posted deposit rates of the state-owned banks have been held relatively constant while actual rates paid have been more varied, as we noted earlier.

The thirty-day SBI rate was fairly closely correlated with the one-month LIBOR + swap, especially since its reappearance in April 1989 (a coefficient of 0.86). The seven-day SBI rate also was closely correlated with the reference rate in the most recent period, but before that it moved more erratically.

SUMMARY

No easy generalizations or conclusions emerge from these various performance measures. The growth of the stocks of various money market instruments has been erratic, as has the correlation of the various interest rates with the reference rate of LIBOR+ swap. The time deposits grew most rapidly when their interest rates were above those of the LIBOR + swap rate, for example, from June 1987 to October 1988. Since October 1988, the time deposit rates have not been well correlated with the LIBOR + swap rate, and their growth has slowed.

In the most recent period, since April 1989, the interbank rate has been much more stable than in any previous period, but it has been poorly correlated with the reference rate, because it was dropping rapidly while the reference rate was declining moderately. The volume of interbank borrowing rose rapidly in 1989 while the average term lengthened. This reflects the fact that throughout 1989, concerns about devaluation abated and therefore the gap between most domestic money market rates and foreign rates narrowed. Once these rates are realigned, and if there are no major shocks to the system, the domestic money market rates will probably move more closely in tandem with the LIBOR + swap rate in the future.

Sam Ouliaris, who made an econometric analysis of the data for this book, offered the following comments:

> Efficiency indicators: The simple correlation measures are valid only if the interest rate series are weakly stationary (in the statistical sense). Unfortunately, the Indonesian series were not stationary for the entire sample period. Applying some standard unit root procedures to the data produced the following results:
>
> 1. The interbank rate is definitely a weakly stationary process; that is, it cannot be modeled as a random walk.
>
> 2. The other series cannot be modeled satisfactorily as stationary processes for the sample period.

3. In view of these findings, we have strong evidence opposing the hypothesis of a relationship between the interbank rate and the LIBOR + swap rate, that it is impossible to explain the behavior of a stationary variable (the interbank rate) using a nonstationary variable (LIBOR + swap).

4. Since it is possible to explain a nonstationary variable with another nonstationary variable (i.e., are the variables cointegrated?), we may ask whether the LIBOR + swap variable can explain the time deposit and SBI rates. The statistical analysis suggests that the series did not tend to move together during the entire sample period. This finding invalidates the use of correlation coefficients to analyze the data.

5. On the other hand, if the data are divided into subperiods, applying the theory of cointegration to the data for the period January 1988 to October 1989 reveals that the LIBOR + swap rate is cointegrated with the one-month and three-month time deposit rates and the seven-day SBI rate. The result is subject to reservation because the number of observations in the subperiod is quite small and may adversely affect the power of the cointegration tests to reject the hypothesis of cointegration.

Overall, there appears to be some evidence in favor of the view that the LIBOR + swap rate influenced the one-month and three-month time deposit rates and the seven-day SBI rate from 1988 onward. However, when considering the series over the whole sample period, this relationship is masked by the instability in the middle of the decade (see Chapter 10).

Ouliaris's statistical findings are consistent with the conclusion that the monetary authorities were attempting to control and set rates on key money market instruments from September 1984 until mid-1987 or early 1988 and that thereafter, the markets have been permitted to function with less interference. This has helped the market become more efficient. On the other hand, the interbank rate—which is the rate that is most clearly determined by the market—has not been moving in consonance with the LIBOR + swap rate since 1988 and, in fact, has fallen while the LIBOR + swap rate has remained relatively high.

CONCLUSIONS

The reduction of controls over interest rates, credit ceilings, new entries and branching of banks, along with positive efforts by the government to introduce new market-based instruments enhanced the growth and functioning of the financial system and of the money markets in Indonesia during the decade of the 1980s. A significant part of the growth of the domestic money markets was the result of a reduction in the proportion of money market assets held overseas by domestic financial institutions. The policy measures implemented in 1988 to stabilize the depreciation of the exchange rate, to let the swap rate move in response to differences between domestic and foreign interest rates, to extend the maturities of the primary money market instrument (SBIs), and to encourage a secondary market in SBIs all contributed to expanding and improving the domestic money markets. All these measures were taken in the context of an open foreign capital system and a managed foreign exchange rate. They were effective insofar as they kept domestic financial prices (interest and depreciation rates) consistent with relative levels of and movements in world financial prices. Conversely, when domestic interest rates plus exchange rate expectations got out of alignment with world market rates, the imbalance was reflected in the shifts from domestic to foreign financial asset holdings, or vice versa.

The imposition of net open foreign exchange position limits on banks in May 1989 reinforced the move to repatriate offshore holdings of money market assets. The fact that this policy change coincided with the removal of limits on offshore borrowing by banks suggests that the policy was directed more at moving banks out of foreign exchange speculation and into longer-term intermediation than at limiting foreign exchange transactions, which continued to be totally unregulated.

One of the long-standing debates in Indonesia is over whether the exchange rate should continue to be managed by the central bank or allowed to fluctuate freely in response to market forces. The evidence from our study suggests that when the exchange rate has been managed somewhat erratically or has been allowed to become overvalued or, in the past when oil prices dropped precipitously, there was no corresponding adjustment in the exchange rate, there was a strong tendency for short-term financial asset holdings to move out of the domestic money markets and into the overseas markets. On the other hand, throughout 1988 and 1989, when the managed exchange rate was depreciated relatively steadily at a moderate rate, when the domestic rupiah interest rates were attractive relative to offshore dollar rates, when oil prices were not seriously unstable, and when nonoil exports were growing steadily, then domestic liquidity and domestic money market activity could be allowed to grow rapidly without adversely affecting foreign exchange reserves because of short-term capital outflow.

A second persistent issue relates to the system of determining interest rates on Bank Indonesia's money market instruments, the SBI, the SBPU, and the foreign exchange swap. So far Bank Indonesia has been reluctant to let those rates be freely determined in the market but instead has established cutoff rates for the SBI and SBPU rates in its auctions, and has set the swap premium each day based on the difference between foreign and domestic bank deposit rates. This system of price setting sends signals to the market as to what rates Bank Indonesia thinks are appropriate. If the market participants find these rates unattractive, they can shift over into other, more attractive asset markets. In early 1990, Bank Indonesia lowered interest rates on SBIs by steadily reducing its auction cutoff rate. This led to a reduction in the banks' time deposit rates and in the swap rate. Eventually the market decided that the rates were too low relative to those of other assets and began to shift into foreign exchange assets and other domestic instruments. The loss of foreign exchange was reversed, however, when rupiah interest rates were raised to more attractive levels.

The alternative approach of trying to sell fixed amounts of SBIs or to buy fixed amounts of SBPUs through the auction, and to let market forces determine the appropriate rates, is still apparently considered by Bank Indonesia to be too risky and likely to lead to instability. This response is similar to its position on the flexible foreign exchange rate. The two markets are significantly different, however, in that the central bank has more room to maneuver—to adjust the quantities that it is prepared to buy or sell—in the domestic money markets, whereas in the foreign exchange market there is the possibility of running out of foreign exchange reserves.

Further money market development may be hindered by attempts to push key interest rates out of line with market forces, or the market participants may simply shift to other instruments that have more flexible rates. Not only will this tend to distort the money markets, but, more important, it could make less effective the implementation of monetary policies through the indirect instruments of the money market. Either Bank Indonesia will have to keep its newly created money market instruments attractive, or it will have to find other means for implementing policy.

If, in time, Bank Indonesia can relinquish its remaining controls over these money market interest rates and the markets become deeper and broader so that Bank Indonesia can be more confident of its ability to influence domestic interest rates, then it may also be more willing to consider more flexibility in setting exchange rates.

NOTES

We would like to thank Yuni Budiastuti and Threesye Soemolong for their statistical assistance and Binhadi, John Chant, Phil Wellons, Hal Scott, Lin See-Yan, and Sam Ouliaris for their much appreciated comments. All errors remain our own.

1. It was because of this core function of the money markets that this topic was chosen at the organizing conference held in Bali in January 1988.

2. We leave it to others, or to ourselves at a later stage, to analyze more robustly how well they are serving their functions.

3. All types of controls over foreign exchange receipts and payments were effectively removed in 1970.

4. Certain omissions should be noted: There have been no marketable government debt instruments in the money markets because the government has followed a balanced domestic budget policy and has issued no domestic debt. Negotiable certificates of deposit are discussed only in passing because of their insignificance. Overdrafts and postdated checks are used, but no information on their magnitude and interest rates is available. No "informal" markets are discussed.

The interbank loan market is discussed as a "money market," even though it includes transactions based on several different instruments such as the SBI, SBPU, and interbank deposits. This approach is necessitated by the lack of separate data on the instruments used in the interbank market.

The foreign exchange market includes spot foreign exchange activities and foreign exchange deposits. The role of LIBOR is included in the discussion of this market.

Finally, we also look at longer-term rupiah deposits.

5. Money markets are essentially short-term markets. They respond quickly to exogenous shocks as well as to changes in basic policies or in the policy-instrument variables. If we were dealing with a relatively long time period, during which basic policies had been fairly constant but a limited number of policy instruments had been adjusted frequently in response to changing needs or circumstances, then it would be feasible to fit a meaningful longer-term model to these data. But when the basic policies and instruments have been changing frequently, even within the six-year period from 1983 through 1989, and when the measures have affected the structure in such important ways, it seems more constructive to divide up that time into subperiods reflecting altered policy regimes and to use simpler indicators of association between key variables using monthly, weekly, or even daily data, to try to capture the impacts of the policies.

6. Nonbank financial institutions (NBFIs), similar to merchant banks, also had their limits lifted but were given an indefinite time period to adjust to new limits on their net open position.

7. This section is based on David C. Cole and Betty F. Slade, "Financial Development in Indonesia," Development Discussion Paper 336, Harvard Institute for International Development, Harvard University, April 1990, to be published in a forthcoming book, edited by Anne Booth of the Australian National University.

8. Quasi-money is the sum of time and savings deposits.

9. This could reflect the fact that domestic financial growth was being greatly influenced by financial policy measures and thus was growing more than would be expected by the performance of the real economy. It also suggests that during the years of high economic growth and increases in real income, a significant portion of the increases in savings, which would be expected to be associated with those higher incomes, might have been placed abroad.

10. Deposit money banks include all banks accepting demand deposits. Foreign banks are "branches" of banks incorporated outside Indonesia. National foreign exchange banks include state-owned banks and those private national banks authorized to have foreign exchange operations.

11. As we stated earlier, much of the financial system for Indonesians is offshore. These activities are legal and within the scope of the open capital system. The exact percentage is unknown and unknowable, given the lack of data and information. Many Indonesian banks have close relationships (and even branches and representative offices abroad) with offshore banks and cooperate to arrange, for a fee, for loans, deposits, and other activities abroad. Foreign insurance brokers, securities companies brokers, and other foreign financial asset "salesmen" do an active business in Indonesia. Indonesians and Indonesian financial institutions hold foreign government bills, money market accounts, deposits, stocks, bonds and other types of foreign assets. Borrowing abroad is common, and Bank Indonesia even is willing to "swap" the foreign exchange for rupiah, to eliminate the downside risk for the borrower. This chapter deals with the formal domestic financial system only. It therefore does not do justice to the sophistication of the portfolio holdings of the Indonesian private corporate sector and of many individual persons.

12. Deposit money banks include national foreign exchange banks (private and state-owned commercial banks), foreign banks, joint venture banks, development banks, and national non–foreign exchange banks (smaller commercial banks that are not licensed to have foreign exchange operations). They exclude the State Savings Bank and the nonbank financial institutions as well as small rural and local banks.

13. The Monetary Board, chaired by the minister of finance and consisting of the governor of Bank Indonesia and one or two other economic ministers, has in recent years played an increasingly important role in the formulation of financial and monetary policy.

14. Bank Indonesia sets twice daily the upper and lower limits for the exchange of the rupiah against the dollar and agrees to meet demand and supply at those limits.

15. Before the October 1988 policy reforms known as PAKTO 27, reserve requirements were 15% of banks' third-party liabilities of banks in general. However, state-owned banks had to count two-thirds of their time deposits, and private banks had to count only one-third of their time deposits

when calculating third-party liabilities. Thus the effective reserve requirement was between 8% and 10% for most banks. After the PAKTO 27 reforms, all banks became subject to a uniform 2% reserve requirement on all third-party liabilities.

16. For the state-owned banks, the seven-day SBIs are basically a means of earning some interest on excess reserves.

17. There is no deposit insurance in Indonesia, so state-owned banks appear "safer" to many depositors. Furthermore, until PAKTO, state enterprises were required to deposit funds only with state-owned banks.

18. In particular, Bank Negara Indonesia, Bank Rakjat Indonesia, Bank Bumi Daya, and Bank Dagang Negara are very large.

19. All the state-owned banks, private national and foreign banks, and joint ventures were used to calculate this index.

20. BPRs (Bank Perkreditan Rakyat) are usually small banks limited to non-urban areas. The larger ones tend to cluster on the outskirts of major cities. See Patten and Rosengard 1989.

21. Before PAKDES II (December 1988), Danareksa was given priority to purchase 50% of all new shares sold on the exchange. It actually started selling off some of its portfolio in November 1988 when foreign-based investment funds began to be set up—starting with the Indosuez "Malacca Fund" and the Jardine–Fleming "Indonesia Fund."

22. There are no tax or other regulations for establishing private domestic-based investment funds in Indonesia, other than that for Danareksa. The funds are consolidated with Danareksa's other accounts. There is also no Indonesian regulatory oversight for the foreign-based investment funds.

23. Now that such bank licensing has become easier, it remains to be seen whether growth of leasing companies will continue to grow or whether they will be turned into or affiliated with new banks.

24. In the past, money changers may have joined in the speculative attacks on the rupiah, but they do not have much capital, and therefore their influence in the market is limited.

25. Thirteen foreign-based investment funds have been set up that have begun or intend to invest in Indonesian securities. In September 1989, the government allowed up to 49% foreign participation in all new equity issues, and foreigners can hold up to 49% of all listed shares, except for those of domestic banks. There are no restrictions on long-term bond holdings by foreigners, but there is no secondary market.

26. Data on these activities have not been collected to date. Banks buy up postdated checks, which constitutes a form of factoring.

27. BI can sell SBIs to reduce reserve money and can buy back SBIs to increase reserve money, through so-called reverse repos. BI has only recently begun to use reverse repos.

28. Since Bank Indonesia had used the sale of SBIs to banks as a direct monetary control instrument before November 1988, the banks generally believed that they could not resell, or use SBIs in other ways, because they had been purchased from BI. The banks seemed to believe that SBIs were a kind of reserve requirement. Only a campaign by Bank Indonesia in early 1989 was successful in persuading the banks and NBFIs to use SBIs either under repurchase agreements or through outright sales to manage their liquidity positions.

29. There are tax exemptions for interest received in interbank transactions, whereas others pay the normal marginal tax rate. There are lower returns on the SBIs than on time deposits.

30. This has been changing in the last few months, as market makers have been active in the auction, particularly for longer-term issues. Private banks are also active in the secondary interbank market.

31. The increase in liquidity (excess reserves) caused by the reduction of reserve requirements on November 1, 1988, was offset by "forced purchases" of SBIs.

32. Promissory notes are issued as the counterpart of a bank or NBFI credit or in the framework of interbank borrowing. Trade bills are "acceptances" based on underlying transactions among customers of banks or NBFIs. The ordinary "SBPU" therefore serves the everyday interbank market and other credit functions, but there are no data series that cover this total market. Our study looks at only the SBPUs rediscounted at BI. Note also that the SBPU is part of the interbank loan market.

33. There are no data for promissory notes, ordinary SBPUs, and the like, which serve as the instruments of the interbank loan market. The published series of interbank loan data include volume of transactions based on all instruments and weighted interest rates.

34. These data cover both the morning and the afternoon interbank markets. The data on the morning market may not be complete, but over the past year, they have been much improved and are reasonably indicative of total transactions. The same cannot be said of the market data for earlier years.

35. Previously one to six months; as of October 1988, the available maturity was extended to three years.

36. The assumption here is that the foreign exchange originates from borrowing abroad and is "swapped" for the purpose of hedging the risk of the rupiah's depreciation.

37. Banks can deal in forward contracts and swaps for customers that do not borrow abroad. These tend to be more expensive because the bank must try to hedge. No data are available on these transactions. One observer stated that some customers always wanted to "swap" simply because they were conservative, for example, Japanese companies in joint ventures with Indonesian companies.

38. BI can influence the use of the swap by means of its exchange rate policy and interest rate policy because these affect expectations and relative earnings.

39. Despite the September 1986 devaluation, speculation continued against the rupiah. People who had borrowed abroad but who had not been able to use the swap contract purchased foreign exchange on the BI bourse market, repaid their loans abroad, and, through affiliated companies, borrowed again abroad and obtained a swap.

40. Bank Indonesia recognized the swap as a "set or administered" price. BI wanted to increase the incentives for the development of forward markets in the banking sector itself by giving more flexibility and market orientation to the premium. Indonesian bankers indicate that off-bourse transactions have grown significantly, four or five times the bourse activity. One further point is that if a bank uses borrowed foreign exchange and swaps it, the cost will be the same as through rupiah time deposits. The disadvantage is that the swap adds liquidity (reserve money) at the same time the rupiah is being speculated against, an offset to the spot foreign exchange sales by BI that reduces reserve money. The stickiness of the deposit rate on which the swap premium is based, however, has not given the rate the kind of flexibility that was hoped for, especially in times of pressure against the rupiah.

41. So-called bourse transactions do not include any transactions of the state oil company, Pertamina, or of the government in its budgetary or borrowing and lending operations. These are included in the off-bourse data, and no data are published. BI directly buys from and sells foreign exchange to these public-sector agencies. Other "direct" foreign exchange transactions take place between banks, banks and their customers, and so forth.

42. Indonesia has a liberal foreign exchange system that permits the free allocation and transfer of foreign exchange for the payment of imports, goods, and services. Capital transactions are free of exchange controls. Indonesia has been given Article VIII status by the IMF. Two restrictions are that direct investment by foreigners requires prior approval from the government (BKPM), and foreign loans to a public entity requires prior approval from the government. Banks and NBFIs also had limits imposed on their foreign borrowing until March 1989. Foreign portfolio investment was first opened up to a small extent on the stock exchange in December 1988, and it was further opened up in September 1989. Indonesians were not restricted from holding assets outside Indonesia.

43. Banks cannot have net open positions (as either assets or liabilities) in excess of 25% of their capital.

44. On the other hand, the discipline of the foreign exchange market influences the need to keep discipline in monetary and fiscal policies.

45. Banks stand ready to pay out the time deposit at any time, even though there is a penalty. Large depositors may be able to negotiate early withdrawals at no, or little, penalty.

46. Note, for example, BI in issuing SBIs and granting the foreign exchange reswap facility. Since we have limited data, we drew many of these observations from interviews with the various market players.

47. State enterprises were forced to take up SBIs at one point, and many of these have been rolled over since that date. The state enterprises deal directly with BI.

48. The SBPU was created by Bank Indonesia as an instrument to provide liquidity to the banking system; however, the rediscounted bill is generated from collateral underlying bank loan activity. Data on volume and rates on total bills (which have come to be known as SBPUs) are not available.

49. The interbank overnight market also uses SBPU-type bills, although there is a requirement by BI that these be filled out slightly differently so that they are ineligible for rediscount at BI. These bills clear at the afternoon clearing.

50. Banks are issuing floating-rate, foreign exchange–denominated certificates of deposits outside Indonesia to raise funds. We have not included a detailed study of this market in our study because until very recently it was quite inactive.

51. For a detailed discussion of the role of offshore financing see Suwidjana 1984. He presents data on the foreign exchange assets and liabilities of deposit money banks in Indonesia from 1973 through 1982 and states that by 1981 deposit bank foreign exchange assets were equal to nearly two-thirds of the central bank's foreign exchange assets (US$4.2 billion vs. $6.5 billion). But as he points out (p. 59), this does not include the unrecorded, but probably significant, amount of loans that were booked offshore. Many of these were medium- and longer-term loans, so are not part of our concern with the money markets.

52. The rupiah was no longer pegged to the U.S. dollar. It was linked with a "basket of currencies of Indonesia's major trading partners," but the devaluations reported in this chapter are relative to the U.S. dollar.

53. Bank Indonesia did try to provide incentives by raising the credit ceilings of those banks that were successful in mobilizing deposits, although this may not have been sufficient.

54. Bank Indonesia may have been concerned that the repatriation of foreign exchange holdings could lead to the rapid growth of domestic credit.

55. The speculation actually was being done by both banks and their customers, which in turn put pressure on the banks. The customers withdrew deposits, so the banks began to rely on the interbank market. To cut such dependency, Bank Indonesia further limited interbank borrowings.

56. Bank Indonesia stated that it was adjusting the rupiah to a basket of foreign currencies, but it never specified what currencies were in the basket or how they might be weighted. Actual movements of the rupiah exchange rate were usually measured relative to the U.S. dollar, and expectations were couched in terms of changes against the dollar.

57. There was a shortage of rupiah financing, as reflected in the rising interbank rates. Probably means were found to buy dollars from the central bank and route them to swaps, to obtain rupiah financing. Theoretically, only dollars borrowed abroad were allowed to be swapped for rupiah financing.

58. At the time, a devaluation was not considered necessary for trade and general balance-of-payments purposes. Devaluation was seen as too destabilizing and had not been successful in stemming the tide of speculation in 1986.

59. Other developments that contributed to reduced expectations of devaluation included the following: Exports were increasing rapidly and diversifying. Oil prices were relatively low, but higher than anticipated and relatively stable. Official international reserves were increasing. The presidential elections were smooth, and the new cabinet was expected to continue the "technocrats'" policies.

60. The flexible swap arrangement was intended to set the premium according to market forces and to stop "the act of changing" the premium from being taken as an indicator of "confidence" in the rupiah. That is, if the premium were simply raised by BI without reference to a specified series, it might be construed as a signal that the depreciation would be higher, and vice versa.

61. The change to a two-day settlement put Indonesia in line with most of the rest of the world, which recognizes the need for time to make international payments. However, it also gives the banks a chance to know what their foreign exchange position will be during that day; it enables Bank Indonesia to know in advance one of the elements of reserve money; and immediate changes in the banks' foreign exchange holdings cannot be used to meet rupiah liquidity needs on that day. It should encourage banks to go to the interbank market and, if still short of funds, to the discount window.

62. It turned out that the 2% limit was not seen as a reasonable floor. Most banks have not been able to reduce much lower than 6% their cash and working balances with Bank Indonesia. However, an incentive has been created to make their cash management operations more efficient. One problem is that although banks can take the average liability balances of a two-week previous reserve period (changed from simultaneous to lagged reserve accounting), there can be no "negative balance" days in the reserve period and no negative clearing balances at Bank Indonesia.

63. Notably two-day spot value settlement for foreign exchange transactions.

64. Bank Indonesia buys and sells foreign exchange on the "bourse," but the interbank market has been expanding, perhaps partially because of the two-day settlement.

65. See Cole and Slade 1990 for a discussion of the importance of and reasons for the open capital account system in Indonesia.

66. Broad money (M2) is less satisfactory because it includes time deposits, which here are considered as particular money market instruments. Ouliaris pointed out that using M1 has the same problem, in that M1 is a substitute for some of the money market instruments. He suggested using some measure of real output. Unfortunately, real output data are available only on an annual basis. On the other hand, the ratio of end-of-year M1 to annual GDP has been remarkably stable over the years covered in this study, as shown in Table 3.1. There was undoubtedly some partial substitution of time deposits for demand deposits in 1983/84, but over the whole period, changes in M1 appear to serve as a good surrogate for indicators of growth of total output, and since the M1 data are available on a monthly basis, they can be used to compare changes in other money market variables on other than annual basis.

REFERENCES

Bank Indonesia, *Annual Reports,* various issues.

Binhadi and Paul Meek. 1988. "Implementing Monetary Policy in Indonesia," Chap. 4 of *Visiting Specialist Papers*, 17th Seanza Central Banking course, Sydney, Australia, October–November.

Cole, David C., and Betty F. Slade. 1990. "Financial Development in Indonesia." HIID Discussion Paper 336, April.

Harvard Program on International Financial Systems (PIFS).1987. "Methodology Paper for Regional Research Project on Financial Policy and Performance." December.

———. 1988. "Methodology Paper for Regional Research Project: Guidelines for Study of Money Markets in Asia." May.

———. 1989. "Study of Money Markets in Asia:

Outline for Country Studies." December 1.

Ichimura, S. 1988. "Indonesian Economic Development Issues and Analysis." Japan International Cooperation Agency, March.

Patten, Richard and Jay Rosengard. 1989. "Progress with Profits: The Development of Rural Banking in Indonesia." Harvard Institute for International Development, April.

Sundararjan, V., and Lazaros Molho. 1987. "Financial Reform and Monetary Control in Indonesia." Paper presented at a conference sponsored by the Federal Reserve Bank of San Francisco, September 23–25.

Suwidjana, Njoman. 1984. "Jakarta Dollar Market: A Case of Financial Development in ASEAN." Institute of Southeast Asian Studies Occasional Paper 76.

APPENDIX 3A
INDONESIA: IMPORTANT EVENTS IN MONEY MARKET DEVELOPMENT, 1970–1989

1970	Bank Indonesia first issues SBIs as its own liability. Discontinued.
1971	State banks and several foreign banks licensed to issue rupiah, negotiable certificates of deposit.
Aug. 23, 1971	Rupiah pegged to U.S.$ at Rp415/$.
	Liberal foreign exchange system implemented; no exchange controls.
1974	Bank Indonesia organized an interbank call money market, including a local clearing system.
1975	Exemption of tax on interest from time deposits.
Nov. 15, 1978	Exchange rate no longer simply pegged to U.S.$; peg changed to "basket of currencies of Indonesia's main trading partners" at Rp625/ = U.S.$1.
1979	Introduction of foreign exchange swap facility ("swaps") by Bank Indonesia.
1982	Exporters allowed to sell foreign exchange outside Bank Indonesia.
Oct. 1982	BI takes 2% margin for swaps.
Feb. 1983	BI reduces swap margin to 0.25%.
Mar. 30, 1983	Devaluation of rupiah (39%), Rp703/U.S.$1 to Rp 970/U.S.$1.
June 1983	Deregulation package in which bank credit ceilings are abolished; interest rates of state banks freed up.
Feb. 1984	BI begins to issue SBIs once a week with 30- and 90-day maturities.
	Rediscount Facilities I and II introduced by BI, open to all banks. Limits set on use.
May 1984	BI discontinues interest payments on excess reserves.
Sept. 1984	Pressure on rupiah. Liquidity crisis develops. Interbank call money rate reaches 90%.
	BI sets up "temporary credit" facility with 6- to 12-month repayment facility. Discount rate raised from 16.5% to 26%.
Postcrisis	SBI issued daily and made eligible for rediscount by BI.
	Interbank borrowing limit set at 7.5% of bank third-party liabilities.

Oct. 1984	Interbank rates fall to average 15%.
	Discount rates cut.
	SBIs with 15-day maturity are issued.
Feb. 1985	Introduction of SBPUs with committed lines of credit; 30- to 90-day maturities.
	Ficorinvest, an NBFI and BI affiliate, named as market maker for SBPU.
Mar. 1985	Private Indonesian banks can issue CDs.
May 1985	Fifteen-day maturity SBIs discontinued.
July 1985	SBIs begin to be auctioned daily.
Aug. 1985	Interbank loan limits raised to 15% for rupiah funds from third parties.
	SBPUs' maturity raised to 180 days.
	SBIs issued can be rediscounted at Ficorinvest/BI without penalty.
Aug. 1986	SBIs issued on weekly basis only and eligible for rediscount at BI at penalty rate.
	Rediscount rates on SBIs adjusted.
Sept. 12, 1986	Surprise 45% devaluation of rupiah, Rp1134/U.S.$1 to Rp1644/U.S.$1.
Oct. 1986	Banks' minimum swaps premium raised to 8%.
	Removal of ceiling on swaps.
Dec. 1986 – Jan. 1987	Severe pressure on rupiah. Extensive use of swaps. Interbank rates rise.
May–July 1987: Normal measures	Banks' minimum swaps premium raised to 9%.
	SBI offer rates increased.
	BI basic discount rate raised to 19%.
June–July 1987: Crisis measures	Banks required to repurchase large portions of own SPBUs before maturity.
	Basic discount rate raised to 30%.
	Bank deposits of major state enterprises (BUMN) transformed into SBI holdings.
July 1987: Postcrisis	SBIs limited to 7-day maturities.
	Daily "auctions" for either SBPUs or SBIs at Bank Indonesia's initiative.
	No committed lines for SPBUs.
	Time period for rediscounts reduced.
	NBFIs allowed to use clearing and rediscount facilities.
Jan. 1988	Revolving underwriting facility (RUF) set up whereby underwriter guarantees sale of SBPUs (mainly through Bapindo).
Oct. 27, 1988	October deregulation package (PAKTO 27) issued to reduce government bureaucracy, free up entry and operations of banks and NBFIs, lower reserve requirements, impose tax on interest of time deposits. Large forced issue of SBIs to banks with 3- and 6-month maturities. Swap premium tied to formula. Two-day settlement for FX transactions.
Nov. 1988 – Jan. 1989	Establishment of market makers and brokers in the SBI market. Rules and regulations issued. Commissions given by BI. New special liquidity window set up for market makers.
	Government begins "campaign" to lower interest rates.
	New auction procedures; daily 7-day maturity issues and weekly 30-day maturity issues.

	Beginning of secondary market activity for SBIs with their use as underlying security for repos. Some outright interbank purchases and sales.

Beginning of secondary market activity for SBIs with their use as underlying security for repos. Some outright interbank purchases and sales.

Use of telerate and Reuters screens by BI, brokers, and market makers.

Mar. 1989   Further deregulation measures introduced (PAKMAR). Further measures to clarify and broaden PAKTO.

May 1, 1989   Net open foreign exchange position limits placed on banks equal to 25% of their capital, broadly defined. Sharp reductions in net foreign assets of banking system.

Ceilings on foreign borrowings lifted.

Apr.–May 1989 Deposit rates of state banks begin to be reduced.

BI starts auctioning 7-day and 28-day SBIs on the same day. Also occasionally rediscounts SBPUs on same day as SBI auctions.

May 1989   BI starts auctioning 3-month SBIs.

June 1989   Large increase in secondary market for SBIs through repurchase agreements among banks.

DEREGULATION PACKAGES, OCTOBER 1988–MARCH 1989

PAKTO 27 (OCTOBER 1988)

Banks

1. New entry permitted

   (a) Capital requirements:
   Wholly owned by Indonesian nationals: General banks: Rp 10 billion; Rural banks: Rp 50 million
   Up to 85% owned by foreign banks (joint ventures): General banks: Rp 50 billion
   Branches of foreign banks in Indonesia: No new entry
   NBFIs: No new entry

   (b) Other requirements:
   New joint ventures: Joint ownership by domestic banks and foreign banks (maximum of 85% of shares by foreign partner); Domestic bank must be classified "sound" 20 of last 24 months; Location restricted to seven major cities; Within 12 months, outstanding export credits must equal 50% of total credits outstanding; Foreign bank partner must have representative office in Indonesia, be reputable in country of origin, be from country with reciprocity agreement with Indonesia.

2. New branches

   (a) Banks wholly owned by Indonesian nationals:
   Must have "sound" classification for 20 of last 24 months.
   Can open branches anywhere in Indonesia.

   (b) NBFIs:
   Must have "sound" classification for 20 of last 24 months.
   Can open one branch only in each of seven major cities.

   (c) Existing foreign bank branches in Indonesia:
   Must be classified as sound.
   Can open one sub-branch only in each of seven major cities.
   Within 12 months, outstanding export credits must equal 50% of total credits outstanding.

   (d) Rural banks:
   No restriction on branch office in same district as head office.
   Must be located outside Jakarta, provincial capitals and municipalities; otherwise must move or become a general bank (capital at RP 10 billion).

3. Foreign exchange banks

   (a) Branches of existing foreign exchange banks automatically have right to deal in foreign exchange.

   (b) Domestic nonforeign exchange banks may deal in foreign exchange if classified as "sound" for 20 of last 24 months and total assets greater than Rp 100 billion.

4. Certificates of deposit: All banks, except rural banks, and NBFIs can issue certificates of deposit. (RP1 million and 30-day minimum.)

Money changers: Licenses issued for unlimited period; no specific restrictions on entry

Other measures

1. State enterprises may put 50% of deposits with private national banks, development banks, and NBFIs, up to 20% in one single bank.

2. Maximum legal lending limits imposed on banks and NBFIs (as a % of lender's capital):

   (a) 20% to a single borrower.

   (b) 50% to a group of borrowers.

   (c) Various restrictions on borrowing by Board of Commissioners, shareholders, other affiliates, and staff.

3. Reserve requirements on banks lowered from a nominal 15% to 2% of liabilities to third parties. Lagged reserve accounting adopted; 3-month and 6-month PAKTO SBIs issued.

4. Maximum limit on interbank borrowing eliminated.

5. SBI maturities extended from only 7 days up to 6 months. Auction process strengthened.

6. Final withholding tax of 15% imposed on the interest of time deposits. Exemption allowed for certain "savings" schemes. Anonymity preserved.

7. Banks and NBFIs can issue new shares on capital market.

8. Swap premium of BI made to reflect market conditions. Swap maturity lengthened.

9. Two day settlement for foreign exchange transactions by BI.

PAKDES II (DECEMBER 1988)

1. Allows for establishment of private securities exchanges. Securities can be traded on more than one securities exchange.

2. Priority of Danereksa to purchase 50% of new issues is eliminated. Simple "priority" is retained.

3. Permits licensing of wholly owned Indonesian firms and joint ventures in the financial service activities shown in (4) with up to 85% foreign capital participation. Existing firms must adjust within two years.

4. Licensing of single and multiactivity firms in

   (a) Leasing companies

   (b) Venture capital

   (c) Securities trading

   (d) Factoring

   (e) Consumer finance

   (f) Credit card

5. Banks permitted to set up subsidiaries for 4 (a) and (b), and to engage in (d) through (f) without separate license. Must obtain license for (c).

6. Capital requirements for single activity: Wholly owned by Indonesians:
   (a) Factoring, securities trading, credit card, and consumer finance: Rp 2 billion
   (b) Leasing, venture capital: Rp 3 billion

   Joint ventures:
   (a) Factoring, securities trading, credit card, and consumer finance: Rp 8 billion
   (b) Leasing, venture capital: Rp 10 billion

7. Capital requirements for multiactivity:
   (a) Wholly owned by Indonesians: Rp 5 billion
   (b) Joint ventures: Rp 15 billion

8. Regulations for insurance:
   (a) Joint ventures allowed; up to 80% foreign share.
   (b) Regulations set forth for solvency, admitted assets, retention ratios.
   (c) Supervision strengthened.

PAKMAR (MARCH 1989)

1. Clarifies and interprets PAKTO 27 concerning
   (a) Licensing mergers of banks.
   (b) Definition of "Capital" and "Groups" used to calculate lending limits. "Exempted credits" defined.
   (c) Definition of "Export credits" used in requirements for foreign and joint venture bank operations.
   (d) Shares of foreign banks in joint ventures.

2. Eliminates ceiling on offshore loans by banks and NBFIs.

3. Banks and NBFIs restricted to maximum net open position equal to 25% of capital.

4. Announcement of schedule for removing subsidy on interest rates on export credits within the year.

5. Exempts "existing" rural banks from PAKTO provisions.

6. Elminates existing requirement that medium- and long-term bank loans must be approved by Bank Indonesia.

7. Allows BAPINDO and NBFIs to hold all types of equity.

8. Allows general banks to hold equity in financial activities with certain limits; can hold equity in other firms only with approval of minister of finance.

9. Reaffirms underwriting authority to NBFIs and BAPINDO. Prohibits general banks from underwriting.

PAKJAN (JANUARY 1990)

1. Abolition of Bank Indonesia–subsidized refinancing facilities, which gave credit to banks at (below-market) interest rates from 3% to 14.5%, which then lent to "priority" sectors at below-market interest rates. Insurance was also provided by ASKRINDO, a government-owned agency, for much of this credit at low cost, partially with BI support.

2. PAKJAN 1990 abolished these facilities except for the following: to BULOG for certain food stocks; investment credit for development banks, NBFIs, and estates; working credits for farmers, and certain credits for cooperatives. However, interest rates on these were increased at least to near-market levels, and the insurance scheme was made voluntary and at market rates.

3. National banks were required within one year to allocate a minimum of 20% of their loan portfolio to small business, defined as having assets of less than Rp 600 million, excluding land, with each loan not exceeding Rp 200 million. Failure to make this allocation affects bank's "soundness."

CHAPTER 4
MONEY MARKETS IN KOREA

MOON-SOO KANG

The money market is defined in this chapter to include all financial instruments easily convertible to cash that are used by government, financial, and commercial institutions for short-term funding and placements. The money market brings together economic agents who want to borrow large sums of money for short periods of time and those who want to lend them. The money market instruments created in this process are generally characterized by the safety of their principal. Maturities range from one day to one year.

The money market encompasses the interbank market and a group of short-term credit market instruments and forms an integral part of the Korean financial system. The rates of return on money market instruments tend to fluctuate together because they are close substitutes for one another in many investment portfolios. The major participants are commercial banks, specialized banks, government, corporations, investment and finance companies, merchant banking corporations, other nonbank financial institutions, and the Bank of Korea. In particular, nonbank financial institutions, such as investment and finance companies and merchant banking corporations, have played an important role since the early 1970s in intermediating short-term funds. These institutions offer a number of high-yield short-term savings instruments to the public, thus promoting the flow of private funds from the unorganized financial market to the organized financial market. The money market has been strongly influenced and, in certain instances, controlled by two main monetary authorities, the Ministry of Finance and the Bank of Korea (the central bank).

The size of the money market in Korea is relatively small compared with those of industrialized countries, and its development has been hampered by a long list of regulations that aim primarily to strengthen the stability of the market. In addition, because present Korean money market is limited, it does not satisfy all the needs of its various borrowers and lenders. Notwithstanding these shortcomings in the money market, certain general features in the financial market, such as the steady-state comovements of the interest rate series, stand out in the long-run behavior of various interest rates.

Although in recent years the money market in Korea has been less restricted it is not so open as those in the United States and the United Kingdom. For example, there are indications of market segmentation in the call money market, with some surplus banks lending primarily to nationwide commercial banks. Recently, however, much progress has been made in using the market to transmit monetary policy, mainly through the sale of monetary stabilization bonds in the money market.

In this chapter, we look at recent developments in the money markets and investigate the effects of government policies on particular money market instruments. We also examine the stabilization policy that used the money market to achieve a broader macroeconomic goal. The period of our study is mainly from 1980 to 1989.

THE KOREAN FINANCIAL SYSTEM

The structure of the present financial system in Korea is schematically illustrated in Figure 4.1. It may be divided into two categories, the banking system and the nonbank financial institutions. The banking system consists of the Bank of Korea (the central bank), the commercial banks, and the specialized banks. Currently, Korea's commercial banks number eleven nationwide banks, ten regional banks, and sixty-six branches of foreign banks. The nonbank financial institutions (NBFIs) can be divided into development finance institutions, investment companies, savings institutions, and life insurance companies.

The financial system in Korea grew rapidly between 1975 and 1989, with the financial institutions' total credit increasing from nearly 4 trillion won at the end of 1975 to over 119 trillion won at the end of 1989, a 30-fold rise. The financial institutions' total deposits rose from 3.5 trillion won at the end of 1975 to 160.9 trillion won at the end of 1989, a 46-fold increase, as summarized in Table 4.1. This growth, however, was predominantly among the nonbank financial intermediaries (NBFIs). The share of bank credit in the total financial credit was 73.1% in 1975 but dropped to 52.4% in 1989. The share of the banking institutions' deposits in total financial deposits also fell from 78.9% at the end of 1975 to 41.6% at the end of 1989. The growth of deposits in financial institutions between 1975 and 1989 reflected mainly the increase in the NBFIs' deposits, which recorded a 126-fold increase. Therefore, the NBFIs expanded their share of total financial deposits from 21.1% at the end of 1975 to 58.4% at the end of 1989.

Central bank		Bank of Korea
Banking institutions (deposit money banks)	Commercial banks	Nationwide commercial banks (11) Regional banks (10) Foreign bank branches (66)
	Specialized banks	Industrial Bank of Korea Citizens National Bank Korea Housing Bank National Agricultural Cooperatives Federation National Federation of Fisheries Cooperatives National Livestock Cooperatives Federation
Nonbank financial institutions	Development institutions	Korea Development Bank Export–Import Bank of Korea Korea Long-Term Credit Bank
	Savings institutions	Banking institutions' trust accounts (47) Mutual savings and finance companies (237) Credit unions (4,633) Mutual credits (1,701) Post offices' postal savings
	Investment companies	Investment and finance companies (32) Merchant banking corporations (6)
	Insurance companies	Life insurance companies (17) Local life insurance companies (6) Foreign life insurance company branches (4) Post offices' postal life insurance
Securities markets		Securities Supervisory Board Korea Stock Exchange Securities companies (25) Investment trust companies (3) Local investment trust companies (5) Korea Securities Finance Corporation

Figure 4.1. Korea's Financial System

THE MONEY MARKET

The ideal money market is characterized by four conditions: (1) a wide range of market participants, (2) transactions that are not bilateral but are marketable, (3) free interest rates, (4) and a maturity of one year or less.

Korea's money markets were begun in the 1960s with the issuance of monetary stabilization bonds (1961) and treasury bills (1967), and they now embrace a wide range of financial markets, including those for treasury bills, monetary stabilization bonds (MSBs), commercial paper, negotiable certificates of deposit (CDs), repurchase agreements (RPs), bankers acceptances (BAs), and the call money market (interbank market).

Table 4.1. Movements of Deposits by Type of Institution (end of year) (in billions of won, %)[a]

	1975 (A)	1980	1985	1987	1988	1989 (B)	B/A
Banking institutions	2,779.2	12,421.8	31,022.7	45,720.4	57,484.8	66,917.7	24.1
(deposit money banks)	(78.9)	(70.2)	(53.7)	(47.6)	(45.7)	(41.6)	
Commercial banks	1,923.3	7,752.1	18,157.0	26,131.6	33,807.4	37,880.9	19.7
	(54.6)	(43.8)	(31.4)	(27.2)	(26.9)	(23.5)	
Specialized banks	855.9	4,669.7	12,865.7	19,588.8	23,677.4	29,036.8	33.9
	(24.3)	(26.4)	(22.3)	(20.4)	(18.8)	(18.1)	
Nonbank financial	743.5	5,281.4	26,780.2	50,257.4	68,272.3	93,958.4	126.4
institutions	(21.1)	(29.8)	(46.3)	(52.4)	(54.3)	(58.4)	
Development institutions	28.8	144.8	227.2	454.5	529.3	797.7	27.7
	(0.8)	(0.8)	(0.4)	(0.5)	(0.4)	(0.5)	
Korea Development Bank	28.8	135.8	198.5	402.6	424.6	606.5	
Korea Long-Term							
Credit Bank	—	9.0	28.7	51.9	104.7	191.2	
Investment companies	195.3	1,771.9	9,552.6	17,023.7	22,861.5	30,670.4	157.0
	(5.5)	(10.0)	(16.5)	(17.7)	(18.2)	(19.1)	
Investment and							
finance companies	180.5	902.0	3,238.6	5,217.3	7,091.0	7,423.9	
Merchant banking							
corporations	—	213.2	835.4	1,134.6	1,297.5	1,173.3	
Securities investment							
trust companies	14.8	633.1	5,399.6	10,330.3	14,123.4	22,073.2	
Savings institutions	382.6	2,445.8	10,273.4	20,637.0	28,815.3	41,350.9	108.1
	(10.9)	(13.8)	(17.8)	(21.5)	(22.9)	(25.7)	
Trust accounts at							
banks[b]	86.5	1,042.7	3,928.0	8,741.1	13,453.2	22,119.0	
Mutual savings							
finance companies	50.4	419.5	2,765.4	4,525.4	5,053.7	6,203.2	
Credit unions	7.4	121.9	556.5	1,002.1	1,362.9	1,830.6	
Mutual credit	138.3	861.7	2,814.4	5,660.1	7,782.8	9,976.8	
Postal savings	—	—	209.1	708.3	1,162.7	1,221.3	
Insurance companies	136.8	918.9	6,727.0	12,142.2	16,066.2	21,139.4	154.5
	(3.9)	(5.2)	(11.6)	(12.7)	(12.8)	(13.1)	
Life insurance							
companies	136.8	918.9	6,580.7	11,695.4	15,402.1	20,229.9	
Postal life insurance	—	—	146.3	446.8	664.1	909.5	
Total	3,522.7	17,703.2	57,802.9	95,977.8	125,757.4	160,876.1	45.7
	(100.0)	(100.0)	(100.0)	(100.0)	(100.0)	(100.0)	

[a] Figures in parentheses indicate shares of deposits at each type of institution.

[b] Deposits in won currency on institutions' balance sheets.

Source: Bank of Korea.

The government took measures to channel curb market funds into financial institutions and to organize the short-term financial market. In 1972, with the promulgation of the short-term Financing Business Act and the establishment of investment and finance companies, papers issued by nonfinancial corporate firms and investment and finance companies were first sold. These new instruments were the first step toward the formation of modern money markets in Korea.

Negotiable certificates of deposit were introduced by the commercial banks in 1974. The call money market began in 1975 with the establishment of the Call Transactions Room, in accordance with the Agreement on Call Transactions Room of Banking Institutions. The bankers acceptances (BA) market was established in August 1989. Thus the money market was becoming more diversified.

Along with the increase in the number of financial institutions and the introduction of various new financial instruments such as commercial paper (CP), new types of RPs, CDs, and BAs in the 1980s, there was a seventeenfold increase in the outstanding balance of money market instruments over the last nine years, as shown in Table 4.2.

An overview of the composition and scale of Korea's money markets indicates that in 1980, the commercial paper market was predominant. In addition, there was a relatively small call money market (whose function was to alleviate temporary shortages or surpluses of financial institutions) and a small RP market. The size of the balances of money market instruments relative to nominal gross national product (GNP) was only 6.9% in 1980, whereas the ratio of the balances of money market instruments to M1 was 66.8%.

The scale of the money market has been gradually expanding since 1980. With the reestablishment of the CDs market in June 1984, the volume of CDs issued rose considerably in 1985. Since May 1986 the Bank of Korea has been actively selling monetary stabilization bonds on the market, and so the volume of sales of MSBs grew rapidly as well. In short, the establishment or reestablishment of various short-term money market instruments, together with the rising call money market and commercial paper market balance, accounts for the gradual expansion of the money market from 2.5 trillion won at the end of 1980 to 44.6 trillion won at the end of 1989. The ratio of the balances of money market instruments to nominal GNP increased from 6.9% to 31.6%, and the balances of money market instruments to M1 increased from 66.8% to 311.4%.

The Call Money Market

The call money market was established in 1975 to alleviate very short-term shortages or surpluses of funds among financial institutions. The participants in the call money market are nationwide commercial banks, specialized banks, regional banks, investment and finance companies, merchant banking corporations, investment trust companies, insurance companies, the Korea Securities Finance Corporation, the Credit Insurance Fund, and foreign bank branches in Korea. The government designated six investment and finance companies and the Korea Financial Clearing Institute as dealers in the call money market.

Table 4.2. Money Market Trends (in 100 millions of won)

	1980 Amount	1980 Percent	1985 Amount	1985 Percent	1987 Amount	1987 Percent	1988 Amount	1988 Percent	1989 Amount	1989 Percent	1980–89 Percent Change
Call markets[a]	1,787	7.0	4,327	3.6	4,907	2.1	6,344	1.9	11,523	2.6	544.8
Commercial paper[b]	20,833	81.9	73,958	61.5	95,195	40.4	123,636	36.7	192,042	43.0	821.8
RPs[c]	1,295	5.1	25,627	21.3	27,209	11.5	23,801	7.1	21,460	4.8	1,557.1
Negotiable CDs[d]	—	—	10,809	9.0	16,514	7.0	17,527	5.2	18,477	4.1	70.9[e]
Commercial bills[c]	—	—	464	0.4	30	—	84	—	11	—	
Bankers acceptances	—	—	—	—	—	—	—	—	10,408	2.3	
Treasury bills[d]	1,500	5.9	—	—	10,000	4.2	11,300	3.4	19,237	4.3	1,182.5
MSBs	32	0.1	5,041	4.2	81,745	34.7	153,735	45.7	173,055	38.8	3,332.9[e]
Total (A)	25,447	100.0	120,226	100.0	235,600	100.0	336,427	100.0	446,213	100.0	1,653.5
M1 (B)	38,070		75,578		101,073		121,514		143,290		276.4
M3 (C)	178,108		547,639		920,403		1,181,347		1,507,743		746.5
Nominal GNP (D)	366,723		780,884		1,056,298		1,262,304		1,410,662		284.7
A/B (%)	66.8		159.1		233.1		276.9		311.4		
A/C (%)	14.3		22.0		25.6		28.5		29.6		
A/D (%)	6.9		15.4		22.3		26.7		31.6		

[a] Daily average balances.

[b] Balances of discounts.

[c] Balances of sales.

[d] Balances of issuances.

[e] Percent change for 1985–89.

Source: Ministry of Finance; Bank of Korea.

At present, there are seven types of transactions: overnight loans, three-day loans, five-day loans, seven-day loans, nine-day loans, eleven-day loans, and fifteen-day loans. Call transactions are made in multiples of 100 million won.

The call money market was originally divided into the exchange market (mainly for banks) and the over-the-counter market (mainly for NBFIs). In October 1989, after a transitional period of seven months, the government and the Bank of Korea combined these two markets into a single market in order to improve its operation. The upper limit on applications for call money by each participant in the market, which had been 5% of the participant's average deposit balances, was repealed. Restrictions on the hours of operation also were lifted.

The shares of banks and short-term finance companies in the call money market were 31.0% and 29.3%, respectively, at the end of March 1990, based on outstanding balance. Investment trust companies and insurance companies traditionally have been net lenders in the call money market. At the end of March 1990, the funds provided by investment trust companies and insurance companies amounted to 227.4 billion won, a share of 22.0 percent. Short-term finance companies were the largest borrowers of funds in the call money market, posting a share of 51.2% at the end of March 1990. Call money borrowed by banks reached 248.7 billion won, which was less than the supply of funds by banks in the market. Banks taken as a whole recorded a net demand position of 71.9 billion won (see Table 4.3).

The Commercial Paper Market

Commercial paper are short-term promissory notes issued by eligible non-financial companies, investment and finance companies, and merchant banking corporations. Thirty-two investment and finance companies and six merchant banking corporations are designated as dealers in commercial paper. Only those business firms selected by investment and finance companies can issue commercial paper. These firms usually issue commercial paper as a substitute for short-term bank loans.

There are five kinds of instruments in the commercial paper market:

1. "Own paper," which is issued by the investment and finance companies and merchant banking corporations themselves.
2. Resold notes with recourse, which are issued by business firms and whose payments are guaranteed by dealers.
3. Resold notes without recourse, which are issued by business firms but whose payments are not guaranteed by dealers.
4. Commercial paper (CP), which was introduced in June 1981 with longer maturities and larger minimum denominations than the preceding three instruments.

Table 4.3. Structure of Call Money Transactions, Balances at End of March 1990 (in billions of won)

Call Loans (A)		Call Money (B)					
	Banks	Short-Term Finance Companies	Securities Companies	Insurance Companies	Investment Trust Companies	Others	Total Call Loans
Banks	248.7	67.7	2.0	0	0	2.2	320.6 (31.0)
Short-term finance companies	0	81.6	121.7	0	70.5	29.1	302.9 (29.3)
Securities companies	0	70.4	3.5	0	0	2.0	75.9 (7.4)
Insurance companies	0	51.0	0	0	0	0.7	51.7 (5.0)
Investment trust companies	0	163.1	10.6	0	0	2.0	175.7 (17.0)
Others	0	94.8	5.0	0	0	6.0	105.8 (10.2)
Total call money	248.7 (24.1)	528.6 (51.2)	142.8 (13.8)	0 (—)	0 (—)	42.0 (4.1)	1,032.6 (100.0)
Net position (A − B)	71.9	−225.7	−66.9	51.7	105.2	63.8	

Note: Figures in parentheses indicate institutions' shares of call transactions.

5. Cash management accounts (CMAs), whose yield is linked to the rate of return from pooled commercial paper (accepted by dealers) and other financial assets.

Commerical paper was folded into the category of resold notes without recourse in December 1988. There is no active secondary market in commercial paper, but it can be redeemed from dealers before maturity with a specified loss of interest.

The commercial paper market has been one of the fastest-growing money markets since its establishment in August 1972. It is the largest of the money markets. At the end of 1989, the outstanding balance of commercial paper discounted amounted to over 19.2 trillion won, or 8.8% of external funds raised by the corporate business sector (Table 4.4). At the end of 1989, the outstanding balance of commercial paper sales, including cash management accounts, amounted to 18.6 trillion won, or 27.8% of the deposit money banks' total deposits. Investment and finance companies have been the dominant dealers in the commercial paper market, accounting for 98% of sales and discounts as of the end of 1989.

The Negotiable Certificate of Deposit Market

A negotiable certificate of deposit (CD) is a certificate issued by a bank as evidence that a certain amount of money has been deposited for a fixed

Table 4.4. Commercial Paper Market Trends (in billions of won)

	1980	1985	1986	1987	1988	1989
Discount (A)	2,083.3	7,395.8	9,062.3	9,519.5	12,363.6	19,207.5
CP	—	2,112.1	3,204.8	3,267.3	2,152.5	—
Others	2,083.3	5,283.7	5,857.5	6,245.3	10,211.1	19,207.5
Sale (B)	2,098.4	6,992.4	8,994.4	10,132.3	13,145.1	18,584.4
Commercial paper	1,086.6	3,476.1	4,894.8	4,544.7	5,726.5	10,846.0
CP	—	1,563.5	2,779.2	2,478.8	1,612.6	—
Others	1,086.6	1,912.5	2,115.6	2,065.9	4,113.9	10,846.0
With recourse	186.0	300.6	265.6	325.1	233.5	448.2
Without recourse	900.6	1,611.9	1,850.1	1,740.8	3,880.4	10,398.0
Own paper	1,011.8	1,804.3	1,723.8	1,889.5	2,124.3	1,391.3
CMA	—	1,712.0	2,380.9	3,698.1	5,294.3	6,347.1
Deposits at deposit money banks (C)	12,421.9	31,022.6	35,925.8	45,720.4	57,484.7	66,917.7
External funds raised by corporate business sector (D)	53,878.1	131,461.4	147,587.1	164,131.6	181,421.8	217,637.5
B/C (%)	16.9	22.5	25.0	22.2	22.9	27.8
A/D (%)	3.9	5.6	6.1	5.8	6.8	8.8

Source: Investment and Finance Association of Korea.

period of time and will be redeemed with interest at maturity. The certificate specifies the amount of the deposit, the maturity date, and the interest rate. Because the certificate is negotiable, it can be traded on the secondary market.

After ending the CD business in December 1981 because of poor performance, the nationwide commercial banks, regional banks, and the Korea Exchange Bank reintroduced it in June 1984, and in March 1985, the CD business was opened to all banking institutions. The reintroduction of CDs was designed to enhance the banks' competitiveness with nonbanking financial institutions in attracting short-term deposits, by offering an interest rate higher than that on ordinary time deposits. In addition, the minimum denomination of CDs was lowered from 100 million won to 50 million won in February 1987, and the maturity period was set between 91 days and 180 days.

At first the CD market grew, but then, at the end of October 1989, the outstanding amount of CDs fell to 1,483.4 billion won, from 1,753.3 billion won at the end of 1988. At the end of October 1989 the specialized banks and nationwide commercial banks had shares of 40.3% and 33.5%, respectively, in the CD market.

The relative importance of investor groups shifted between 1984 and 1989. The corporate enterprise buyers' share fell from 60% to 40%, but other groups' shares rose: financial institutions (11% to 21%), government (1% to 8%), and individual persons (29% to 31%).

Investment and finance companies, securities companies, and merchant banking corporations all trade negotiable CDs on the secondary market. In May 1989 the amount of monthly secondary market transactions in the CD market was only 66.5 billion won, or 0.5% of the CDs outstanding (Table 4.5).

The Repurchase Agreement Market

A standard repurchase agreement (RP) refers to the acquisition of immediately available funds through the sale of securities with a simultaneous commitment to repurchase the same securities on a specified date within one year at a specified price, which includes interest. RP transactions have many of the same characteristics of secured lending arrangements, in which underlying securities serve as collateral. Securities eligible for RP transactions are national bonds, local bonds, special bonds, and corporate bonds.

RPs were first introduced in February 1977 when the Korea Securities Finance Corporation made RP transactions with securities companies. Then, in February 1980 and September 1982, respectively, securities companies and banks were given permission to engage in the RP business. Post offices have been allowed to handle RPs since March 1983. But banks and post offices are permitted to handle only the sale of government and public bonds on repurchase agreements.

Table 4.5. Amount of Monthly Transactions in CDs (in billions of won)

	Outstanding Amounts[a] (A)	Secondary Market Transactions[b]		
		(B)	Transactions Intermediaries	Purchased by Intermediated	B/A(%)
1988					
May	14,866	775	771	4	5.2
June	15,351	666.5	666.5	0	4.3
July	14,728	555.5	555.5	0	3.8
August	14,806	702.5	702.5	0	4.7
September	15,117	728	728	0	4.8
October	15,687	458.5	458.5	0	2.9
November	16,771	792	792	0	4.7
December	17,533	918	918	0	5.2
1989					
January	17,147	218	218	0	1.3
February	16,404	138.5	138.5	0	0.8
March	14,523	163.5	163.5	0	1.1
April	13,929	83	83	0	0.6
May	13,202	66.5	66.5	0	0.5

[a] End of period.

[b] Trading volume during month.

Source: Investment and Finance Association of Korea; Bank of Korea.

The major suppliers of bonds—that is, the borrowers of funds—in the RP market are securities companies, banks, post offices, and business corporations. The major demanders—that is, the lenders—are individual investors and nonprofit organizations. The minimum transaction unit is 100 thousand won.

The period of an RP transaction differs with each handling institution. It is less than one year for the Korea Securities Finance Corporation and the securities companies, between ninety-one days and one year for banks, and less than ninety-one days for post offices. For large RPs, the minimum transaction unit is 50 million won, and the period of transaction is between six months and one year. The RP market has grown rapidly in the past nine years, as shown in Table 4.6. The amount of repurchase agreements sold reached more than 2.1 trillion won at the end of 1989, seventeen times the balance at the end of 1980. At the end of 1989 the amount of RP purchases by the Korea Securities Finance Corporation and securities companies was, however, just 3.3% of that of sales.

The Treasury Bill Market

Treasury bills (TBs) are short-term obligations of the Korean government. They are considered to be totally free of default risk and are the most mar-

Table 4.6. RP Market Trends (in billions of won)

	1980	1983	1986	1987	1988	1989
Sales (A)	129.5	1,031.5	2,618.5	2,720.9	2,390.1	2,137.7
Korea Securities Finance Corporation		1.9	31.8	21.9	23.0	28.4
Securities Companies	129.5	219.4	961.8	829.8	566.3	641.9
Banks	757.8	686.9	620.0	338.6	160.6	160.6
Post Offices	52.4	938.0	1,249.2	1,462.2	1,306.8	1,306.8
Purchases (B)	53.0	25.9	107.5	68.8	80.9	69.9
Korea Securities Finance Corporation	18.9	24.9	42.2	60.9	58.4	17.2
Securities Companies	34.1	1.0	65.3	7.9	22.5	52.7
B/A (%)	40.9	2.5	4.1	2.5	3.4	3.3

Source: Ministry of Finance; Bank of Korea *Monthly Bulletin;* Securities Supervisory Board *Monthly Review.*

ketable of all money market instruments. The maximum amount of TBs to be issued in each fiscal year is decided by the National Assembly as part of its annual budget deliberations. Treasury bills must be redeemed within one year.

Since 1967, TBs have been issued as part of Korea's monetary management policy. But in 1981, they were issued to finance a temporary shortage of treasury funds. No TBs were issued from 1983 to 1985.

Since 1987, the government has relied more and more on the sale of treasury bills to absorb excess liquidity in the financial market. At the end of 1989, the balance of treasury bills in the market amounted to 2.5 trillion won, fifty times the balance at the end of 1967. From 1982 to October 1989, treasury bills rose from 0.2% to 5.1% of the bond market, which includes government and public bonds, bank debentures, and corporate bonds.

The government sells TBs at a discount mostly through auctions to banks, insurance companies, securities companies, and other financial institutions. At the end of July 1989, the shares of TBs accepted by banks and the Bank of Korea were 40.7% and 28.8%, respectively, of the TB market. Other investor groups were insurance companies (10.5%), securities companies (8%), and investment trust companies (5.3%).

The minimum denomination of TBs is 10 million won. Before 1983, the maturity periods were mostly 90 days or less, but since 1986, the government has issued only TBs with a maturity period of 364 days.

The Monetary Stabilization Bond Market

Monetary stabilization bonds (MSBs) are liabilities of the Bank of Korea and provide the Bank of Korea with an open market instrument. Since 1986 the Bank of Korea has sold MSBs to absorb the excess liquidity in the financial market that originated mainly from the rapid improvement in the balance of payments. At the end of 1989 the outstanding balance of MSBs reached 17,306 billion won, or 29.5% of the money supply (M2) (see Table

4.7). The outstanding balances of three monetary instruments—MSBs, TBs, and foreign exchange stabilization bonds—were, at the end of October 1989, 20.75 trillion won, or 44% of the bond market. Government and public bonds made up 24%, and corporate bonds took a 33% share.

The Bank of Korea sells MSBs to banks, securities companies, investment and finance companies, investment trust companies, and life insurance companies. The maturity periods are between 14 days and 546 days.

GROWTH INDICATORS AND INTEREST RATES IN MONEY MARKETS

Growth Indicators

The Program on International Financial Systems (PIFS) suggested efficiency and stability as the best performance indicators for evaluating money markets. A third possible measure used by Cole and Slade (1990) is the growth of a particular money market relative to the average rate of growth of some norm. Following their proposal, we adopted the supply of narrowly defined money (M1), which is regarded as a close substitute for money market instruments, as the norm, or denominator. We used the ratio of the stock of each particular money market instrument to the stock (or supply) of narrowly defined money (M1) as an indicator of the size, or importance, of the money market instrument, and relative rates of change in the quantity of that instrument relative to the change in the quantity of narrowly defined money over time as an indicator of that instrument's relative growth performance. As the measure of relative change, we used a measure of money-growth elasticity comparable to income elasticity in relation to income and expenditure analysis, a notion proposed by Cole and Slade.

The relative growth indicators for the money market instruments are presented in Table 4.8. Narrowly defined money, or M1, is the norm against which we compared the growth of the other money market instruments. Between the end of December 1980 and the end of December 1989, the nominal money supply (M1) rose by 276.4%. The value of transactions in the call money market increased by 544.8% during the same period, giving a growth elasticity of call transactions relative to M1 of 1.71. Call transac-

Table 4.7. Issuance of Monetary Stabilization Bonds (in billions of won)

	1985	1986	1987	1988	1989
Balance (A)	504	3,259	8,175	15,374	17,306
Net increase	D59	2,755	4,916	7,199	1,932
M2 (B)	28,565	33,833	40,280	48,939	58,638
A/B (%)	1.8	9.6	20.3	31.4	
29.5					

Source: Bank of Korea *Monthly Bulletin;* Ministry of Finance *Fiscal and Monetary Statistics.*

Table 4.8. Indicators of Money Market Instruments' Relative Growth

Period	Call Market/M1	Commercial Paper/M1	RPs/M1	Negotiable CDs/M1	Bankers Acceptances/M1	Treasury Bills/M1	MSBs/M1
December 1980	0.0469	0.5472	0.0340	—	—	0.0394	—
December 1985	0.0573	0.9786	0.3391	0.1430	—	—	0.0667
Elasticity to M1	1.22	1.79	9.97	—	—	—	—
December 1987	0.0485	0.9418	0.2692	0.1634	—	0.0989	0.8088
Elasticity to M1	0.85	0.96	0.79	1.14	—	—	12.13
December 1988	0.0522	1.0175	0.1959	0.1442	—	0.0930	1.2652
Elasticity to M1	1.08	1.08	0.73	0.88	—	0.94	1.56
December 1989	0.1273	1.3402	0.1498	0.1289	0.0726	0.1343	1.2077
Elasticity to M1	2.44	1.32	0.76	0.89	—	1.44	0.95
December 1980–89 growth rate of money market instrument (%)	921.0	821.8	1,557.1	(70.91)	—	1,182.5	3,332.9[a]
Elasticity to M1	2.71	2.45	4.41	(0.902)	—	3.41	18.11[a]

[a] December 1985–December 1989 for negotiable CDs and MSBs.

tions kept pace with M1 growth until December 1988 but since then have expanded. The value of commercial paper climbed during the same period by 821.8%, giving a growth elasticity of 2.45 for commercial paper relative to M1. The value of repurchase agreements had a very high relative growth elasticity of 9.97 between December 1980 and December 1985 but since then has declined. The monetary stabilization bonds of the Bank of Korea had a very high growth elasticity of 18.11 relative to M1 between December 1985 and December 1989, reflecting the public sale of MSBs to absorb the excess liquidity in the financial market.

Interest Rates in Money Markets

Comparison of Rates

In this section we investigate the movements of various interest rates, including the curb market rate, which is the rate for the unregulated (or unorganized) financial market. We tested for the presence of unit roots in individual series and cointegration between each pair of series. Since the integration and cointegration tests are used to find long-run properties and the power of those tests are limited in a finite sample, a large number of observations and a long sample period are essential for reliable results.

Our sample period begins in September 1976 and ends in March 1990 and is divided into two subperiods: Period I covers the data series from August 1976 to December 1982, and Period II begins in January 1983 when inflation rates fell sharply because of the stabilization policy. The fluctuations of the government bond rates (GBs), corporate bond rates (CPBs), interbank call rates (Calls), interest rates of the unorganized market (RUMs), and inflation rates measured by the Consumer Price Index (CPI) are shown in Figure 4.2. Table 4.9 reports the means and variances of these interest rates during the sample period. As shown in Figure 4.2 and Table 4.9, interest rates were relatively high and volatile in Period I when inflation rates were high and volatile, and real interest rates sometimes became negative during this period. The real curb market rates, however, were always positive. In regard to Period II, with low inflation, interest rates declined and became relatively stable.

One of the interesting findings from Table 4.9 is that the variance of the call market rates was smaller in Period I (but larger in Period II) than those of GBs and CPBs. Short-term interest rates were generally more volatile than long-term rates. The relative stability of the call market rate in Period I might be, at least partially, explained by the collusive behavior of the banks participating in the call market.

Test Results for the Presence of Unit Roots

This section reports the test results for the presence of unit roots in the interest rate series and the monetary stabilization bond rates using $J(p,q)$ statistics (Park and Choi 1988), Phillips $Z(a)$ and $Z(t)$ statistics (Phillips

Table 4.9. Means and Variances of Money Market Rates, August 1976–March 1990 (percent per year)

Interest Rate	Frequency	Mean			Variance		
		Overall	Period I	Period II [a]	Overall	Period I	Period II
Call	Monthly	14.42	18.53	10.79	20.07	7.33	3.26
GB	Monthly	17.82	22.94	13.29	31.07	14.91	1.66
CPB	Monthly	18.25	23.01	14.03	30.21	20.29	1.44
MSB[b]	Monthly	14.17	—	14.17	1.81	—	1.81
RUM[c]	Quarterly	30.78	38.66	23.72	70.42	28.75	2.20

[a] Period II begins in 1983 when the inflation rate declined drastically owing to the stabilization policy.

[b] Sample period: August 1986–March 1990.

[c] Sample period: 1976 III–1990 I.

1987), and the Augmented Dickey–Fuller test (ADF) (Dickey and Fuller 1981, Said and Dickey 1984).[1]

Table 4.10 gives the test results for the presence of unit roots in the interest rate series and the autoregressive coefficient, estimated during the ADF procedure. Here we included four lagged differenced variables, because the ordinary estimates of autoregressive coefficients were not consistent, owing to the nuisance parameter tendency.

If interest rates are determined in a market whose participants are not seriously constrained by liquidity shortages or by some strictly binding regulations and make full use of the information they have, the interest rate series will follow a random walk process. Hence the presence of unit roots can be one of the necessary conditions for an efficient market.[2]

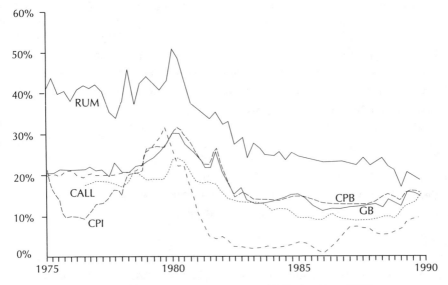

Figure 4.2. Money Market Rates and Inflation Rate (CPI)

Table 4.10. Test Results for Unit Roots

Interest Rate	Period	â	J(p,q)	Z(a)	Z(t)	ADF
Monthly series: August 1976–March 1990						
Call	Overall	0.98	7.455	−3.31	−1.30	−1.37
Call	Period I	0.89	1.857	−5.62	−1.45	−2.16
Call	Period I	0.92	2.914	−7.42	−2.10	−1.50
GBs	Overall	0.98	3.693	−3.14	−1.25	−1.13
GBs	Period I	0.94	2.173	−5.30	−1.41	−0.96
GBs	Period I	0.90	0.740	−9.26	−2.15	−1.89
CPBs	Overall	0.99	2.999	−3.29	−1.25	−1.27
CPBs	Period I	0.96	3.690	−2.90	−1.05	−1.11
CPBs	Period I	0.92	1.040	−9.70	−2.19	−1.91
MSBs		0.88	1.473	−6.39	−1.89	−1.40
Quarterly series: 1976 III–1990 I						
Call	Overall	0.95	8.880	−2.43	−1.15	−0.99
GBs	Overall	0.94	3.696	−3.14	−1.24	−1.29
CPBs	Overall	0.93	2.892	−3.44	−1.27	−1.51
RUM	Overall	0.97	5.400	−2.00	−0.99	−0.66

Notes: â is the estimated autoregressive coefficient allowing four lagged differenced variables to accommodate nuisance parameter dependency. Period II begins in 1983. The sample period for MSBs is from August 1986 to March 1990. The 1%, 5%, and 10% critical values based on the limiting distribution for $J(p,q)$ are 0.112, 0.339, and 0.577; for $Z(a)$, −20.66, −14.10, and −11.25; and for $Z(t)$ and ADF, −3.43, −2.86, and −2.57.

Our test results can be summarized as follows: The presence of unit roots was found to be significant for all series, including the curb market rates, regardless of the sample periods.[3] All the estimated autoregressive coefficients were very close to one (1) except for the MSBs, whose sample period was very short.

Test Results for Cointegration

Cointegrated systems allow individual time series to be integrated on Order 1 but require certain linear combinations of series to be stationary. Evidence that a cointegrating vector exists strongly supports a long-run relationship. In the absence of cointegration, we may question the steady-state representation of the underlying model, because the inherent tendency to return to the equilibrium path is dubious. The test results for cointegration are shown in Table 4.11.

Between each pair of GBs, CPBs, and Calls, the null hypothesis of no cointegration was rejected in favor of cointegration in the sense of Engle and Granger (1987), implying that these series show strong comovements and that the markets of the government bonds, corporate bonds, and inter-bank loans are closely interrelated. The very strong evidence of cointegration between GBs and CPBs suggests that government bonds and corporate bonds, which are usually secured by banks, are close substitutes in the

Table 4.11. Test Results for Cointegration

Variables	$\hat{a}(\hat{u})$	$Z(a)$	$Z(t)$	ADF
Monthly series, overall period: August 1976–March 1990				
GBs, Call	0.74	−48.2	−5.33	−3.56
CPBs, Call	0.85	−24.3	−3.65	−3.30
GBs, CPBs	0.64	−86.1	−7.62	−3.91
August 1986–March 1990				
MSBs, GBs	0.74	−11.1	−2.49	−1.90
MSBs, CPBs	0.74	−11.1	−2.44	−1.76
MSBs, Call	0.79	−8.4	−2.17	−1.88
Quarterly series, overall period: 1976 III–1990 I				
Call, RUM	0.59	−21.4	−3.49	−2.37
CPBs, RUM	0.76	−14.8	−3.18	−1.85
GBs, RUM	0.65	−20.2	−3.57	−2.22

Notes: $\hat{a}(\hat{u})$ is the estimated autoregressive coefficient of the estimated residuals from the cointegrating regression. The null hypothesis is absence of cointegration. The 1%, 5%, and 10% critical values based on the limiting distribution for Phillips $Z(a)$ statistics are −27.90, −20.22, and −16.95; and for $Z(t)$ and ADF are −3.93, −3.34, and −3.05.

Korean financial market. The same testing procedures were applied to Subperiods I and II, and similar results were obtained, though the evidence was slightly weaker than that for the overall period, presumably because of the small sample size. Although they are not given here, the results for the quarterly series are similar to those for the monthly series.

The cointegration between the MSB rates and the other interest rate series is not supported, as reported in Table 4.11, for we think, three reasons. First, the MSB rates do not possess a unit root, as suggested by the integration test results in Table 4.10. Second, because of the small sample size, the power of the test is not high enough to reject the null hypothesis of no cointegration. Third, the monetary stabilization bonds were issued to absorb liquidity and thus to give big shocks, countercyclically, to the financial market; hence their behavior was different from that of other interest series.

Another interesting finding is the test results for cointegration between the curb market rates (RUMs) and other interest rates. The results are mixed. Phillips Z statistics support cointegration, but the ADF procedure does not. Considering the conservative nature of the cointegration test; the relatively small sample size of fifty-five (only a quarterly series is available for the RUMs); the relatively small value of the autoregressive coefficient estimated using the residuals of the cointegrating regression, $\alpha(\mu)$; and the big standard error; we might say that the test results support cointegration between the RUMs and other interest series at least marginally. These results seem to match the findings of Cole and Park (1983), that the regulated and unregulated financial markets interact.

INTEGRATION OF THE CALL MONEY MARKET

Since its establishment in 1975, the net borrowers in the Call Transaction Center, or the exchange market, have been the nationwide commercial banks, which usually are short of funds and the local banks are the net lenders, as shown in the data for July 1989 (Table 4.12). The daily average transaction volume in the exchange market amounted to 473.8 billion won in July 1989.

The call rate, or the interbank rate, was allowed to float freely as of November 1984. In reality, however, it has not fully reflected the market clearing rate and has remained below the market interest rate; primarily because of regulations governing the call money market. The supply of funds by lenders (call loans) is usually not sufficient to meet the demand for funds from borrowers (call money) in the Call Transaction Center. Funds are allocated first to meet the borrowing requirements of the nationwide commercial banks before meeting the requirements of the other financial institutions. The call rates of the nationwide commercial banks have remained below the market-clearing level (see Duk-hoon Lee et al. 1988, p.110).

Regulations in the official exchange market have effectively restricted the NBFIs' competition with the banks for the market's limited funds (see Table 4.12 for the participants in the exchange market and the over-the-counter market). The banks' loan rates are lower (e.g., 10% to 13.5%) than the NBFIs', and they are more tightly controlled than the NBFIs are. These regulations governing the Call Transaction Center limited competition in the market and discouraged and discriminated against nonbank financial institutions such as investment and finance companies, merchant banking corporations, and securities companies. Banks could make short-term fund transactions with banks and nonbank financial institutions through the Call Transaction Center, but the NBFIs, which had overdraft facilities at the banks, could not lend through the Call Transaction Center. The ceiling on borrowing by market participants was limited to 5% of their average deposit balances recorded two months before the transaction.

NBFIs participated in the over-the counter market, going to the unofficial market for additional funds at a higher cost (sometimes as high as 18%). In turn, these NBFIs charged higher lending rates to their clients. Investment and finance companies were the net borrowers of funds in this market. The interest rates in the over-the counter market, which reflected market conditions, were much higher than the interbank interest rates in the exchange market. In July 1989 the monthly average interbank interest rate was 12.1% in the exchange market, and the monthly average interest rate was 15.4% in the over-the-counter market.

The call money market was made into a single market in October 1989 and now has the following features:

Table 4.12. Comparison of Call Market Before and After Integration

	Preintegrated Call Market		Integrated Call Market
	Exchange Market	Over-the-Counter Market (unofficial market)	
Participants	Mainly banks[a]	Nonbank financial institutions[b]	All financial institutions
Transaction by type	Concentrated in the call transaction center	Over-the-counter market	Over-the-counter market through seven brokers[c]
Maturities	1, 3, 7, and 15 days	1, 3, 7, and 15 days	1, 3, 5, 7, 9, 11, and 15 days
Ceiling on call money	Within 5% of average deposits recorded 2 months ago	No restrictions	No restrictions
Transaction time	From Mon. to Fri.: 13:30–16:30, Sat.: 10:00–12:30	No restrictions	No restrictions
Interest rates	Single rate that can implement most transactions	Freely determined rate for each transaction	Freely determined rate for each transaction
Clearing system accounts	Through BOK's reserve accounts for each banks' accounts	Through banks' individual current accounts	Interbank transactions: through BOK's reserve accounts; through transfer of banks' account through broker
Fees	5/100,000%	None	5/100,000%
Collateral	Generally without collateral	Without collateral	Without collateral

[a] Participants in exchange market (official market): banks (including foreign bank branches), National Investment Fund, investment and finance companies (IFCs), merchant banking corporations (MBCs), investment trust companies (ITCs), insurance companies, Korea Securities Finance Corporation (KSFC), and Credit Insurance Fund (CIF).

[b] Participants in the over-the-counter market (unofficial market): IFCs, MBCs, insurance companies, KSFC, CIF, securities companies, lease companies, and mutual savings and finance companies.

[c] The previous call transaction center and the six IFCs are approved brokers.

Source: Ministry of Finance; Bank of Korea.

1. All financial institutions, totaling about 240, are permitted to participate in the integrated call money market.

2. Transactions can be implemented either through the seven dealers or directly between market participants.

3. There are seven types of transactions: overnight loans, three-day loans, five-day loans, seven-day loans, nine-day loans, eleven-day loans, and fifteen-day loans.

4. The ceiling on the maximum amount of borrowing by each participant and the restriction on the hours of transactions were lifted.

5. Two types of clearing systems are permitted:

   a. Reserve accounts at the Bank of Korea can be used when a bank transacts with another bank.

   b. In all other cases, transactions are settled through bank account transfers by notice of the dealers.

6. Call rates were liberalized.

By the end of October 1989 the amount of transactions in the integrated call money market had increased to 903.2 billion won, from 626.6 billion won at the end of August 1989. It continued to rise rapidly; at the end of April 1990, transactions reached 2.2 trillion won. The relative share of the banks and the NBFIs fluctuated widely. In November 1989 the total amount of monthly transactions in the integrated call money market climbed to 23.2 trillion won from 13.7 trillion won in October 1989. In February 1990 the monthly transaction amount reached 38.7 trillion won (Table 4.13). The relative share of direct transactions between banks fell immediately from 33.8% in October 1989 to 11.7% in November 1989, and it decreased further to just 3.2% in March 1990.

There still are two different kinds of call rates in the call money market and a sizable difference between the call rates for transactions between banks and those for call transactions between NBFIs (Figure 4.3). There also are considerable differences between the banks' loan rates and those of the NBFIs. For example, the nationwide commercial banks, who are major borrowers in the call market, are not allowed to charge lending rates higher than 13.5%. Therefore, in the call market, nationwide commercial banks want to protect themselves from the competition with the NBFIs, which can charge a higher lending rate. On the other hand, the NBFIs are quite willing to pay a higher rate in the call money market for additional funds.

These findings show that the government policy of making the call money market into a single market has only partially improved its efficiency and indeed, the call money market has not yet been fully integrated, as the banks are still resisting. The nationwide commercial banks are afraid that

Table 4.13. Monthly Transaction Amounts in Call Money Market After
Integration (in billions of won, %)

	Total	*Intermediated Transactions Among NBFIs*	*Bank-Related Transactions*	
			Intermediated	*Direct*
1989				
October	13,664.8	7,070.7	1,978.2	4,615.9
	(100.0)	(51.7)	(14.5)	(33.8)
November	23,224.4	14,760.0	5,683.7	2,780.7
	(100.0)	(63.6)	(24.5)	(11.9)
December	24,011.7	11,717.0	10,928.5	1,366.2
	(100.0)	(48.8)	(45.5)	(5.7)
1990				
January	35,860.9 8	171.6	26,329.4	1,359.9
	(100.0)	(22.8)	(73.4)	(3.8)
February	38,697.2	7,182.1	28,483.9	3,031.2
	(100.0)	(18.6)	(73.6)	(7.8)
March	20,888.0	9,403.3	10,814.3	670.4
	(100.0)	(45.0)	(51.8)	(3.2)

Note: Figures in parentheses indicate share of transactions.

Source: Bank of Korea.

they may not be able to compete with the NBFIs for short-term funds in a
fully integrated call market unless the considerable differences between the
banks' and the NBFIs' lending rates are reduced. Integration would cause a
considerable rise in the banks' call rate.

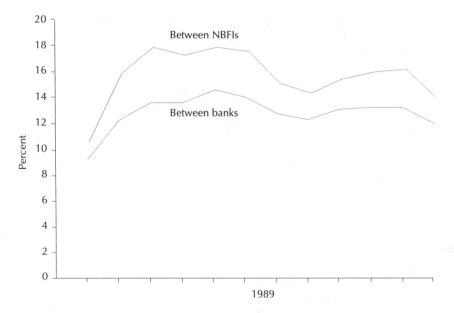

Figure 4.3. Trends of Call Rates in the Call Money Market

COMMERCIAL PAPER MARKET POLICY

The Abolition of Compensating Balances

Investment and finance companies (IFCs) and merchant banking corporations (MBCs) used to adjust the amount of their compensating balances according to the tightness of available funds in the commercial paper market. When IFCs and MBCs discount commercial paper issued by their clients (borrowers), they ask them to set aside a portion of the borrowing and to buy "own paper" or "resold commercial paper without recourse," which offers interest rates lower than the discount rates of the commercial paper. Thus, the compensating balance raises the effective discount rate, or the cost of borrowing from IFCs and MBCs, which is the cause of many of the borrowers' complaints.

On November 14, 1989, the Ministry of Finance (MOF) asked the investment and finance companies, or the short-term finance companies (STFCs), to abolish their practice of requiring their borrowers to deposit compensating balances when they discounted their clients' commercial paper. As a way of underscoring its request, the Ministry of Finance included the abolition of compensating balances as one of the preconditions for allowing the STFCs to open additional business offices, which were vital to their competition with other financial institutions, as well as among themselves.

During the four months from November 1989 to February 1990, the STFCs' compensating balances were reduced by approximately 6 trillion won. Sales of commercial paper without recourse[4] and own paper—which borrowers used as instruments to set aside a portion of their borrowing as compensating balances at the STFCs—declined by 5.6 trillion won and 4.4 billion won, respectively (Table 4.14).

The abolition of compensating balances at the STFCs resulted in the liberalization of the effective interest rates in the commercial paper market. The STFCs began to charge higher market interest rates to borrowers in return for abolishing the compensating balances, and so the commercial paper's interest rate rose to 13.95% at the end of November, from 13.41% at the end of October 1989, to 14.05% at the end of February and 14.32% at the end of April. At present, the commercial paper's interest rate is quoted as an indicator of market interest rates (Figure 4.4).

The Efficiency and Stability of the Commercial Paper Market

Commercial paper is issued by creditworthy firms to raise short-term funds; it is not related to actual commercial transactions. The legal grounds for issuing CP are set forth in the Short-Term Financial Business Law of 1972. The purpose of this law is to draw financial transactions away from the curb markets and to the organized market, as well as to provide a way of raising short-term funds.[5]

Table 4.14. Movements of Outstanding Amounts of Commercial Paper (100 million won)

End of period	1989			1990		
	October (A)	November	December	January	February (B)	Change (B – A)
1. Commercial paper without recourse	134,929	124,726	103,980	90,445	78,591	–56,338
Change		–10,203	–20,746	–13,535	–11,854	
2. Commercial paper with recourse[a]	2,185	2,880	4,480	2,869	4,607	2,422
3. Own paper	16,590	14,529	13,913	13,394	12,147	–4,443
Total (1 + 2 + 3)	153,704	142,135	122,373	107,708	95,345	–58,359
Change		–11,569	–19,762	–14,665	–12,363	

[a] Commercial paper with payment guarantee by IFC or MBC.

Source: Ministry of Finance

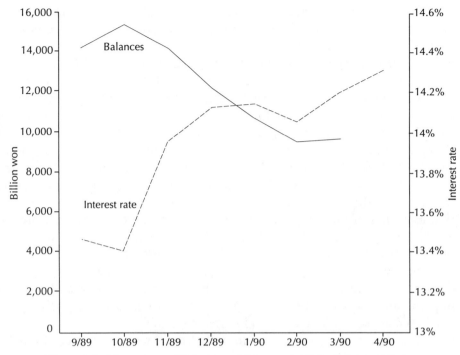

Figure 4.4. Movements of Balances of Commercial Paper's Interest Rates

The designated dealers purchase commercial paper at discounted prices with their own funds and resell it to investors with or without recourse. The dealers are responsible for paying the issuers in the case of resale with recourse. Consequently, the dealers need adequate funds because purchased commercial paper is not fully resold to investors at regulated prices. At present, there are two ways for dealers to obtain funds. The investment and finance companies and merchant banking companies raise funds by issuing and selling their own CP or servicing individual investors' so-called cash management accounts, which are much like deposit accounts.

Commercial paper issued by firms can be divided into two categories. For convenience, let us call the two A/CP and B/CP. A/CP has been traded since 1972, when the CP market was established. The dealers for A/CP are investment and finance companies and merchant banking companies. B/CP, a new type of CP, was created to help lay the groundwork for liberalizing of interest rates in June 1981. Dealers of B/CP are relatively large securities companies, including the dealers of A/CP. The differences between A/CP and B/CP are in the issuing firms, the minimum unit value at which they can be issued, their dates of maturity, the possibility of an investor's reselling them before the maturity date, and whether or not this can be done without recourse to the dealers. Until November 1988, the discounted and resale prices between A/CP and B/CP were different.

The most important characteristic of the Korean CP market is that until November 1988, the interest rates on discounted and resale CPs were strictly controlled and kept below market rates. Until the end of November 1988, the discounted rates of A/CP were fixed at 11.0% to 12.0% (12.0% to 13.0% for dealers working in local areas), and the resale rates of A/CP were fixed at 4.5% to 10.0%. The interest rates of B/CP were freely determined when it was introduced in June 1981. However, the rates were set much higher than the other regulated interest rates, and they also fluctuated sharply, leading to their control after only six months. As of the end of November 1988, the discounted rates for B/CP were under 12.55%, and the resale rates under 11.9%, except for some B/CP over seventy-five points on the credit grading, whose rates were freely determined. With the further liberalization of interest rates in December 1988, the discounted rates of any CP and the resale rates of B/CP worth more than 30 million won in the issued unit were allowed to be determined by market forces.

Next we look at the impact of the government's policies on the performance of the CP market. Table 4.15 shows the major financial policies implemented between 1980 and 1988. The policies are categorized and numbered according to the PIFS (1988) suggestions.

The cash management account (CMA) is a newly invented financial product. Many individual investors who have little specialized investment information but want to invest a small sum deposit it with a dealer. The dealer then can use the funds to buy, for example, discounted CP and subsequently distribute the returns on the funds to each CMA depositor. The CMA business was opened to investment and finance companies in April 1984 and to merchant banking companies in July of the same year. Since that time, the dealers' business boundaries have been expanded, and the public demand for CP has increased. Therefore, we can surmise that the introduction of the CMA has contributed efficiency and stability to the CP market.

Three new dealers were allowed to enter the CP market in 1980, two new dealers in 1981, six new dealers in 1982, and another six dealers in 1983. This policy had the same general impact on the CP market as did the introduction of the CMA. The government has frequently enlisted CP dealers to supply small and medium-size firms with funds by increasing the relative amount of CP or by raising the ceiling on the marketable quantity of discounted CP issued by such industries. We can assume that this government requirement most likely decreases the efficiency of the CP market.

In order to analyze the effect of these policies on the CP market's performance, we need ways to represent efficiency and stability as performance measurements. The methodology paper prepared by PIFS (1988) suggests various ones. But because of data limitations, we used only the following measurements: as indirect measures of operating efficiency, the outstanding volumes of A/CP and B/CP, along with the market share of the four

Table 4.15. Financial Policies for the CP Market, 1980–88

Primary Target	Types	Content	Implementing Date
Financial System	1. Creation of Instrument	New CP CMA	June 1981 April 1984 (ITC) July 1984 (MB)
	4. Fitness and Character	New Entry of Dealers	March 1980 February 1981 June 1982 June 1983
Nonfinancial System	9. Portfolio Composition	Increased Fund-Support for SMI by increasing Discount Ratio and Discount Ceiling	August 1980, April 1981, May 1983, July 1985, July 1986, April 1987, September 1987
Mixed	10. Structural Rules	Ceiling Control of Issuing CP	April 1981, September 1982, April 1983, November 1984
	12. Interest Rate Policy	Changes in Interest Rates	October 1985, January 1986, May 1987
	13. Policies to ward off risk or Failure	Control of Holdings of Financial or Real Assets	April 1981, February 1982, April 1982, August 1983, September 1983, June 1984, July 1984, July 1985, January 1987

Note: Refer to text for details.

largest dealers and the market share of the four largest industry borrowers out of seventeen industries; and as stability measures, coefficients of variances (counted as the standard deviation over the mean) of CP outstanding and outstanding volumes of discounted CP past maturity. We analyzed the effects of the four selected policies on the performance of the CP market using data from 1980 through 1988.

Efficiency Test

The general hypotheses we tested are whether the introduction of new products such as the CMA and the free entry policy made the CP market more efficient and whether the policy of directing the supply of funds to specific segments and issuing monetary stabilization bonds to control the money supply made the market less efficient. In order to test these three hypotheses, we regressed the indirect measures of operating efficiency on the four policies. Dummy variables were the proxies for the policy variables.

Because the authorities strictly managed the interest rates on CP at a level below the market rate during the period analyzed, there was an excess supply of CP. Therefore, because the volume of CP was determined by its demand, we analyzed its effect on efficiency by estimating the CP demand function.

The dummy variable DCMA, which has had only one value since the second quarter of 1984 and a zero value before that time, represents the policy of introducing CMAs. The variable DENT, which represents the system's entry policy, counts the number of dealers in each quarter of the sample periods. The other dummy variable, DSM1, which represents the policy of providing funds to small and medium-size firms, has one value in the initial quarter of implementation and in the following quarter, and otherwise a zero value, on the assumption that the effect of the policy would continue over two quarters. Finally, the dummy variable DMSB, which has had one value since the third quarter of 1986 and a zero value before that time, represents the policy of issuing monetary stabilization bonds. We now estimate the typical demand functions of financial assets from the viewpoint of the dealers and public investors. The demand from the public investors is represented by the demand for CP by dealers. The estimated results are shown in Appendix 4C.

Next, we assumed that the implemented policies affected the efficiency measures, that is, the market share of the four largest dealers (MSD) and the market share of the four largest industry borrowers (MSI) out of seventeen industries. The equations that have MSD (biannual data) and MSI (quarterly data) as dependent variables and the implemented polices as independent variables were regressed, and the results are in Appendix 4C.

The estimated equations show the following results: The introduction of CMAs made the CP market more efficient, since it significantly increased the variables SCP and SCPI and decreased MSI. Similarly, the free-entry policy clearly seems to have increased efficiency. But the policy of directing the supply of funds to specific sectors, that is, to small and medium-size firms, seems to have decreased efficiency, even though the results are not clearly significant.

Finally, issuing of monetary stabilization bonds to control the money supply seems not to have affected the CP market. The policy significantly increased only one of the four efficiency measures we used, namely, the market shares of the four largest dealers. This means that it may have decreased efficiency, which is consistent with our general hypothesis.

Stability Test

The hypotheses to be tested are whether the introduction of the CMA and the policy of supporting funds for small and medium-size firms would make the CP market more stable and whether the free-entry policy and the policy of issuing monetary stabilization bonds would make it less stable.

We assumed that the policy variables DCMA, DENT, DSMI, and DMSB did affect the stability measurements, that is, the coefficient of variances (standard deviation over mean) of CP outstanding (VCP) and the outstanding volumes of discounted CP past maturity (OPM). It is believed that the more unstable the market is, the larger the VCP and OPM will be. The equations that have the implemented policies as independent variables and the stability measurements as dependent variables were regressed, and the results are in Appendix 4C.

The estimated results show that only the policy of issuing monetary stabilization bonds clearly makes the CP market less stable, since it increases variances of the variable CP outstanding (VCP) and the outstanding volumes of discounted CP past maturity (OPM). The effects of other policies are not clear, even though it seems that the policy of CMA introduction and the policy of supporting funds for small and medium-size firms increase stability and the entry policy decreases stability.

Case Study

Since 1980, the most important turning point for the Korean financial market was when interest rates were globally liberalized, in December 1988. Most loan rates and some deposit rates have been freely determined from that time. In the case of the CP market, the discounted rate for all CP was liberalized; the resale rate of CP with more than ninety-one days until maturity and an issuing unit value of more than 30 million won became freely determined. Since then, the difference between A/CP and B/CP has become blurred.

It would be interesting to analyze the behavior of interest rates for CP after their liberalization. In this way, we could test whether the freely determined resale CP rates, the corporate bond yield rates, and the monetary stabilization bond yield rates display the behavior of a cointegrated process, given that the latter two are believed to follow market rate movements. We can conduct this test using the method introduced in the section Interest Rates in Money Markets and daily data for the period from January 4 to June 28, 1989.

The coefficients of the autoregressive variables estimating the autoregressive equations for the three rates are 0.77 (−4.17) for the resale commercial paper rates, 1.00 (−0.04) for the corporate bond yield rates, and 0.99 (−1.29) for the monetary stabilization bond yield rates. The numbers in parentheses are the Dickey and Fuller values. The critical values to reject the hypothesis that the coefficient is 1 are −3.37 and −4.07, under 5% and 1% significance levels, respectively. These results imply that the rates shown still follow a process different from that of the market rates (Table 4.16).

Two of the three rates are regressed, and then the residuals obtained from each of the regressed equations are autoregressed with four lags. The coefficient of the autoregressive residual variables obtained from the regression of the resale CP rates on the corporate bond yield rates is 0.70 (−2.98). A similar coefficient from the regression of the resale CP rates on the monetary stabilization bond yield rates is 0.83 (−2.05). The critical values of the augmented DF are −3.17 and −3.77, under 5 percent and 1 percent significance levels, respectively. These results show that the hypothesis cannot be rejected. Therefore, even though it is believed that the interest rate liberalization policy might make the CP market more efficient, such a short sample of data cannot prove that hypothesis.

THE FOREIGN EXCHANGE MARKET

The Foreign Currency Call Market

There was a gap in the money market in that there was no domestic market for interbank loans in foreign currency. To fill this gap, the foreign currency call market was established in December 1989, for borrowing and lending relatively short term, foreign currency–denominated funds between domestic foreign exchange banks without collateral. The participants in the foreign currency call market are eleven nationwide commercial banks,

Table 4.16. Cointegration Test Results for Case Study of Interest Rate Liberalization

Interest Rates	Autoregressive Coefficient	DF Value or ADF Value	Critical 1% Level	Values 5% Level
Resale CP	0.77	−4.17	−4.07	−3.37
Corporate bonds	1.00	−0.04	−4.07	−3.37
MSBs	0.99	−1.29	−4.07	−3.37
Resale CP on corporate bonds		−2.98	−3.77	−3.17
Resale CP on MSBs		−2.05	−3.77	−3.17

nine specialized banks, ten regional banks, six merchant banking corporations, and fifty-three foreign bank branches. The Fund Brokerage House in the Korea Financial Clearing Institute is designated as an intermediary in the foreign currency call market.

Maturities range from overnight to night the next day, spot next, one week, and twelve months. Transactions are in U.S. dollars, and the minimum amount that can be transacted is U.S.$50,000. Foreign currency call money and loan rates are linked to interest rates in the international financial markets. The minimum unit of fluctuation of interest rates is one-thirty-second percentage point. At present there is no brokerage fee.

An analysis of investors in the foreign currency call market shows that the shares of nationwide commercial banks, specialized banks, and foreign bank branches 28.3%, 24.3%, and 21.6%, respectively, in March 1990 (Table 4.17). Regional banks and foreign bank branches are net fund lenders in the foreign currency call market. Of the borrowers of funds in the foreign currency call market, the nationwide commercial banks were the largest fund borrowers, posting a share of 56.9% in March 1990.

During the first five months of the market's operation, the amount of borrowing considerably increased. From U.S.$907 million in December 1989, the amount of borrowing rose to U.S.$3,119 billion in April 1990.

The interest rates in the foreign currency call market were 0.1 to 0.2 percentage points above the rates for comparable maturities in the Singapore market (SIBOR) in December 1989. In 1990, however, as the amounts

Table 4.17. Structure of Foreign Currency Call Market, February–March 1990 (in U.S.$ million, %)

	Call Loans (A)		Call Money (B)		A – B	
	February	March	February	March	February	March
Nationwide commercial banks	987 (28.5)	639 (28.3)	1,954 (56.0)	1,283 (56.9)	−958	−644
Specialized banks	942 (27.1)	547 (24.3)	647 (18.6)	578 (25.6)	295	−31
Regional banks	622 (17.9)	534 (23.7)	228 (5.6)	249 (11.1)	394	285
Merchant banking corporations	204 (5.9)	48 (2.1)	117 (3.4)	101 (4.5)	87	−53
Foreign bank branches	716 (20.6)	486 (21.6)	534 (15.4)	43 (1.9)	182	443
Total	3,471 (100.0)	2,254 (100.0)	3,471 (100.0)	2,254 (100.0)	0	0

Note: Figures in parentheses indicate share of transactions.

Source: Ministry of Finance.

of foreign currency call transactions increased, the monthly weighted average rates sank slightly lower than the comparable average SIBOR rates (Table 4.18).

Introduction of the Market-Average Exchange Rate Regime

Beginning in 1980, foreign exchange rates in Korea were posted by the Bank of Korea (BOK) on the basis of the special drawing rights (SDR) basket and the trade-weighted basket of five major foreign currencies. Then, on September 20, 1989, as a first step toward reforming Korea's foreign exchange rate policy, the government allowed telegraphic transfer buying and selling rates of U.S. dollars to be freely quoted by foreign exchange banks within a band of plus and minus 0.4% around the BOK's base rate. Exchange rates for cash transactions were determined by foreign exchange banks.

On March 1, 1990, the government introduced the market-average foreign exchange rate system as the next step toward a free-floating regime in the future, replacing the previous multicurrency basket-peg system. The market-average rate is determined by the weighted average of the interbank won–dollar exchange rates for spot transactions on the previous business day. Eighty-nine foreign exchange banks, including the fifty-three foreign bank branches, participate in the interbank foreign exchange market.

A bank's buying and selling rates of U.S. dollars for customers (telegraphic transfer rates) are determined within an upper or lower limit of 0.4% of the market-average exchange rate. The exchange rates of the won against other foreign currencies are set within a range of plus and minus 0.8% around the market-average rate. With the implementation of the market-average foreign exchange rate system in March 1990, the volume of monthly transactions increased to U.S.$3.5 million in March 1990, from $1.1 million in February 1990 and a monthly average of just under $2.0 million dollars in 1989. In April, the volume of monthly transactions rose further, to $4.6 million. The movement of the won–dollar exchange rate and the transaction amounts in March 1990 are shown in Figure 4.5. Movements of the market-average exchange rates and the transaction amounts in April and May 1990 are shown in Figure 4.6. Because each day's base rate

Table 4.18. Foreign Currency Call Market Interest Rates (%)

	December 1989	1990			
		January	February	March	April
Call market interest rate(O/N)	8.76	8.24	8.22	8.27	8.32
SIBOR (O/N)	8.57	8.32	8.25	8.30	8.35
Difference	0.19	−0.08	−0.03	−0.03	−0.03

Source: Ministry of Finance.

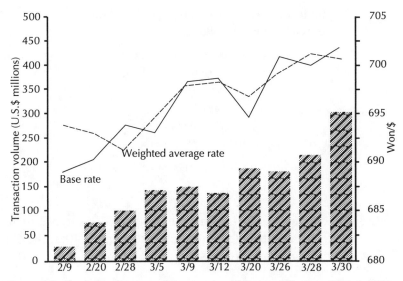

Figure 4.5. Exchange Rates and Transaction Volumes, February–March 1990

is set equal to the weighted-average interbank exchange rate on the previous day, exchange rate movements do reflect market forces.

Variations in the call rates (for NBFIs) determined in the call market were found to be transmitted to the won's market-average exchange rate via arbitrage transactions, as is shown in the estimated equation for the mar-

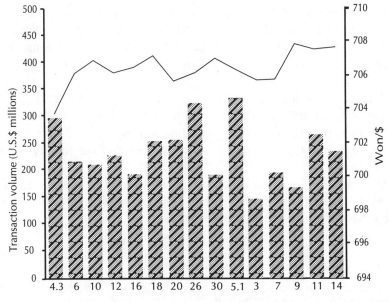

Figure 4.6. Movements of Market: Average Exchange Rates, April–May 1990

Table 4.19. Exchange Rates and Call Rates,
March 2–June 30, 1990

$$Yt = 3.9442 + 0.9966 \, Yt - 1 - 0.0911 \, Callt$$
$$(0.40) \quad (67.38) \qquad (-1.50)$$
$$R2 = 0.9901$$
$$D.W. = 1.18$$
$$S.E. = 0.6621$$

t-values in parentheses

Notes: Y: won's exchange rate with U.S. dollar. Call: call
rates for NBFIs.

ket-average exchange rate during the sample period, March 2 to June 30,
1990 (Table 4.19). The estimated equation also suggests that the exchange
rate followed a random walk process.

MONETARY POLICY AND OPEN MARKET OPERATIONS

In this section we analyze the effects of government policy on the financial
markets' performance. We chose to examine a stabilization policy of using
the financial system to reach a broader macroeconomic goal.

The Setting of Monetary Objectives

In 1979, the monetary authorities in Korea adopted a new technique of setting monetary growth targets (following the lead of the major industrial
countries) as one means of controlling the high rate of inflation. Since
1979 the monetary authorities have always and exclusively used M2 as an
intermediate target variable (Table 4.20).[6] With this approach based on the
monetary growth targets of M2, the monetary authorities presumably managed to bring the inflation rate in Korea under better control than would
otherwise have been possible.

When calculating the annual monetary growth targets, the monetary
authorities normally take into account the following variables: (1) the
expected growth rate of the real gross national product, (2) the anticipated
inflation rate, and (3) the expected development of the money's "velocity
of circulation."

The monetary growth objective is related to the average increase in
M2 during the year in question. Since 1982 the growth rates have been in a
target range of two percentage points (except in 1988), which in recent
years gave the monetary policy the necessary flexibility.

Current Account Surpluses and Monetary Policy

During the long period of current account deficits, the foreign sector continued to absorb liquidity, and the monetary authorities relied on direct

Table 4.20. Money Supply Targets, 1979–1990 (%)

Year	M2 Target Growth Rate	Actual Growth Rate[a]
1979	25.0	26.8
1980	20.0	25.8
1981	25.0	27.4
1982	20.0 – 22.0	28.1
1983	18.0 – 20.0	19.5
1984	11.0 – 13.0	10.7
1985	9.5 – 12.0 – 14.0	11.8
1986	12.0 – 14.0 – 16.0 – 18.0	16.8
1987	15.0 – 18.0 – 20.0	18.8
1988	18.0	18.8
1989	16.0 – 18.0	18.4
1990	15.0 – 19.0	

[a] Based on averages.

Source: Bank of Korea.

controls of bank credit to the private sector to keep the growth of money supply within the annual target range.

Then the current account reversed from a chronic deficit to an ample surplus as a result of a trade surplus and a remarkable improvement in the invisible trade balance since 1986. This signaled a noteworthy change in the flow of money supply: The foreign sector, which had absorbed liquidity

Table 4.21. Korea's Macroeconomic Performance, 1984 – 89 (in U.S.$ billions, annual changes in %)

	1984	1985	1986	1987	1988	1989
GNP growth (%)	9.3	7.0	12.9	12.8	12.2	6.7
GNP deflator (%)	3.8	4.1	2.3	4.0	4.3	4.7
Wholesale prices (%)	0.7	0.9–1.5	0.5	2.7	1.5	
Consumer prices (%)	2.3	2.5	2.8	3.0	7.1	5.7
Current balance	−1.37	−0.89	4.62	9.85	14.16	5.10
Trade balance	−1.04	−0.02	4.21	7.66	11.45	4.51
Exports	26.33	26.44	33.91	46.24	59.65	61.28
Imports	27.37	26.46	29.71	38.58	48.20	56.77
Invisible trade balance and net transfers	−0.34	−0.87	−0.63	0.98	1.27	0.35
Foreign exchange holdings	7.59	7.68	7.91	9.14	12.34	14.98
(change)	(0.83)	(0.09)	(0.23)	(1.23)	(3.20)	(2.64)

Source: Bank of Korea; Economic Planning Board.

until 1985, became a large quantitative contributor to the money supply. The excessive supply of liquidity through the foreign sector has made it difficult to control the money supply (Table 4.21).

The monetary authorities have made great efforts to contain the growth of the money supply within the annual target level. They restricted the entry of foreign capital and encouraged overseas investment and the early repayment of foreign debts. In addition, the Bank of Korea substantially reduced policy loans for export finance and sought tighter control of bank credit to big firms, by adjusting of rediscount rates and ratios.

These policy measures, however, had only limited success in alleviating the pressure of monetary expansion (see Figure 4.7). The Bank of Korea relied more and more on issuing of large amounts of monetary stabilization bonds to absorb the excess liquidity in the financial market.

The shift of the current account into surplus also encouraged further liberalization and internationalization of the financial sector; considerable relaxation of foreign exchange controls to ease payments for invisible transactions and overseas investment; and gradual internationalization of the capital market. Realizing the limits of issuing MSBs as a major instrument of monetary control and the need for more effective instruments, the monetary authorities extensively deregulated interest rates in December 1988 in order to make better use of the price mechanism of interest rates in allocating funds in the market.

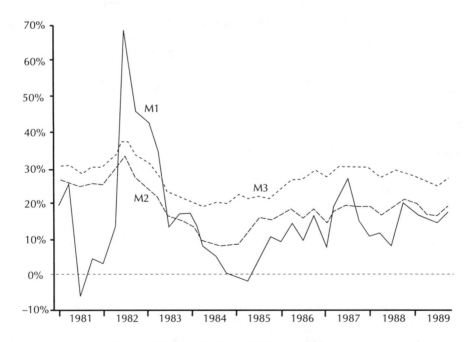

Figure 4.7. Growth Rates of Monetary Aggregates

Open Market Operation Policy

Open market operations have not traditionally been used as a major monetary policy instrument. The most important reason for this is that the government was not anxious in the past to pay market or close-to-market rates of interest on internal public debt. When there was excessive liquidity in the economy, the monetary authorities chose to reduce it not by issuing securities but by using direct credit controls on banks and/or adjusting reserve requirement ratios or the monetary stabilization account. Even though the government was issuing securities and the monetary authorities were trying to develop an active open market, secondary markets for government securities such as treasury bills did not develop, thus denying the Bank of Korea an important monetary policy instrument that would be ideal in a financially liberated environment.

Therefore, in 1986 the Bank of Korea began selling monetary stabilization bonds, a liability of the Bank of Korea, to the public to absorb the increasing excess liquidity in the financial market that primarily originated in the rapid improvement in the balance of payments, and it took several steps that would lead to open market operations (Table 4.22).

During 1986, the Bank of Korea issued MSBs worth a total of 4.4 trillion won (13.1% of M2), and only 1.7 trillion won worth were redeemed or repurchased before maturity. Consequently, the Bank of Korea absorbed a total of 2.75 trillion won in liquidity during 1986.

During 1987, the BOK issued MSBs totaling 9.4 trillion won (23.3% of M2), and the value of those redeemed or repurchased before maturity amounted to 4.4 trillion won, permitting the Bank of Korea to soak up 4.9 trillion won during 1987.

In 1988, the Bank of Korea issued MSBs worth nearly 17 trillion won (34.7% of M2), and 9.77 trillion won worth were redeemed or repurchased before maturity. Consequently, the Bank of Korea absorbed 7.2 trillion won in liquidity during 1988.

Table 4.22. MSBs Open Market Operations (in billions of won)

	1986	1987	1988	1989	January–June 1990
MSBs issued (net)	2,754.5	4,915.9	7,199.0	1,931.9	– 801.4
Issuance	4,435.4	9,383.0	16,966.7	20,148.7	12,707.5
Direct sales	4,102.7	1,239.8	1,574.5	1,684.1	N.A.
Acceptance	332.7	8,143.2	15,324.2	16,401.6	N.A.
Auction	—	—	68.0	2,063.0	—
Redemptions or repurchases (–)	1,680.9	4,467.1	9,767.7	18,216.8	13,508.9

Source: Bank of Korea.

In 1989, the BOK issued MSBs totaling 20.1 trillion won (34.4% of M2), and the value of those redeemed or repurchased before maturity amounted to 18.2 trillion won, permitting the Bank of Korea to soak up 1.9 trillion won during 1989.

The rapid expansion of MSB issuance and assignment to nonbank financial institutions, such as short-term finance companies, investment trusts, securities companies, and life insurance companies, affected their portfolio management and caused distortions in the financial market. Moreover, the growing interest payments on the MSBs themselves caused an additional increase in the monetary base, which limited the effectiveness of issuing MSBs as a major monetary control policy instrument. Although technically providing the Bank of Korea with an open market instrument, MSBs imposed a rather high cost: The interest paid on MSBs in 1989 amounted to over 2 trillion won (Table 4.23).

The monetary authorities have introduced several facilities to absorb large numbers of these MSBs. First, a facility was set up to broaden the ownership of such bonds by encouraging firms to invest in them. With a minimum of 5 million won, businesses can open corporate trust accounts, 80% invested in MSBs and 20% in conventional bank loans.

Second, to achieve a broader and more efficient distribution of MSBs, the monetary authorities introduced a system of primary dealers in 1987, mostly short-term finance companies and securities companies that were already the principal purchasers of MSBs (Table 4.24). The large volume, however, strained the designated dealers' underwriting and portfolio capacity, and so the authorities created a large network of underwriters for such securities. Finally, a bond management fund (BMF) was established jointly by three investment trust companies to underwrite and purchase MSBs and other liquidity control bonds.[7]

Effects of Issuing MSBs and Monetary Targeting

There has recently been much progress in promoting the use of the market for transmitting monetary policy, mainly through the sale of MSBs in open-market operations. A sustained sterilization program, chiefly relying on the public sale of MSBs, however, can, under certain conditions, disrupt domestic money markets. Indeed, domestic interest rates have risen to high levels and at present are higher than international rates, and there are indications of upward pressure on interest rates in the bond market.

The greater supply of MSBs pushed up their yield and influenced interest rates in the bond market (Table 4.25). Investment and finance companies and securities companies, the principal buyers of MSBs, have dumped them on the secondary market to raise funds for their regular lending operations.[8] Foreign bank branches and institutional investors such as pension funds are the secondary market's main investors.

Table 4.23. Issuance of Monetary Stabilization Bonds (in billions of won)

	1981	1982	1983	1984	1985	1986	1987	1988	1989
MSBs issued (net)	—	−25	150.5	408.1	−59.5	2,754.5	4,915.9	7,199.0	1,932.0
MSBs outstanding(A)	30	5	155.5	563.6	504.1	3,258.6	8,174.5	15,373.5	17,305.5
Interest paid on MSBs	175.4	266.9	185.9	355.2	207.6	252.1	735.9	1,469.8	2,015.7
M2(B)	15,671.1	19,904.2	22,938.1	24,705.6	28,565.2	33,833.1	40,279.5	48,938.8	58,638.0
M1(C)	3,982.4	5,799.3	6,783.4	6,820.7	7,557.8	8,808.9	10,151.4	12,151.4	14,329.0
A/B (%)	0.2	0.0	0.7	2.3	1.8	9.6	20.3	31.4	29.5
A/C (%)	0.8	0.1	2.3	8.3	6.7	37.0	80.9	126.5	120.8

Source: Bank of Korea.

Table 4.24. Distribution of MSBs in 1989

Distribution	Amount (billions of won)	Percent
Short-term finance companies	1,858	9.2
Investment trust companies	3,186	15.8
Securities companies	2,723	13.5
Life insurance companies	2,173	10.8
Banks' trust accounts	5,651	28.0
Bank accounts	2,370	11.8
Others	2,188	10.9
Total	20,149	100.0

Source: Bank of Korea.

Quantitative Analysis

In order to investigate the effects of issuing monetary stabilization bonds and to show the effects of the monetary targeting policy, we divided the sample period into two subperiods. Period I covers the period before 1986, and Period II covers 1986 to 1988. As we stated earlier, Korea has been pursuing a published monetary target for M2 since around 1979.

We used MTR (actual M2 growth rates minus the M2 annual target

Table 4.25. Trends of Yields on MSBs and Corporate Bonds (percent per year)

	Monetary Stabilization Bonds		Corporate Bonds[b]
	Issue Market[a]	Trading Market	
1986			
December	12.79	12.98	12.78
1987			
March	12.82	12.81	13.02
June	12.25	12.25	12.66
September	12.47	12.93	13.02
December	12.50	13.23	12.84
1988			
March	12.5	15.32	13.7
June	12.5	15.34	15.1
September	13.0	16.0	15.9
December	12.8	12.86	13.7
1989			
March	13.0	14.68	13.9
June	13.0	15.9	16.3
September	13.0	15.8	15.8
December	13.0	15.5	15.2

[a] Total yields on MSBs with maturity of one year.

[b] Composite yields on corporate bonds.

Source: Bank of Korea.

growth rate divided by the M2 annual target growth rate) as a proxy variable to measure the tightness of the monetary targeting policy during the sample period. When the growth rate of M2 rises to a higher level than the annual targeted growth rate, the monetary authorities increase the public sale of MSBs (and rely on other policy instruments in order to reach the target).

The Interbank Market
The regression for March 1986 to December 1988 shows that the interbank rate was influenced by the tight monetary targeting and the issuance of large amounts of MSBs.

The Monetary Stabilization Bond Market
In regressions for the MSB yield rates for September 1986 to December 1988, the t-statistic of the coefficient of MSB balance (LMSBB) is statistically significant. In order to absorb excess liquidity, the Bank of Korea issued large amounts of MSBs, which raised its yield rate in the market. The MSB yield rate is positively correlated with corporate and government bond yields.

The Government Bond Market
Regressions for the government bond yield rate reveal that it is positively correlated with balances of MSBs and that it is negatively correlated with the money supply. The regression for January 1986 to December 1988 has a higher MSB balance coefficient than does the regression for March 1982 to December 1985.

The Money Demand Function
In the estimated money demand equation for January 1986 to December 1988, the MSB balance coefficient is negative, and its t-statistic is statistically significant. We may conclude that MSBs, which offer market interest rates, partially substituted for money (M2) as a store of value.

The Velocity of Money
Regressions for velocity of money (M2 and M3) for January 1986 to December 1988 show that issuing MSBs tends to increase the velocity of money.

CONCLUSIONS

Korea's money markets have developed considerably in recent years. New instruments were introduced, and the government's control of the money market was gradually relaxed. Along with the introduction of various new financial instruments in the 1980s, the outstanding balance of money market instruments increased seventeenfold between 1980 and 1989. The ratio of the balances of money market instruments to nominal GNP rose from 6.9% to 31.6% during the same period.

   The commercial paper market has been one of the most rapidly developing money markets since its establishment, and it is the largest of Korea's money market. Because the Bank of Korea relies heavily on monetary stabilization bonds (MSBs) to absorb excess liquidity, the monetary stabilization bond market plays a major role in the money market. The rapid expansion of MSB issuance and assignment to nonbank financial institutions has affected their portfolio management and caused distortions in the financial market. The estimated results show that the policy of issuing MSBs makes the commercial paper market less stable. The policy also significantly enlarges the market shares of the four largest dealers, which means that it may lower efficiency.

There continue to be indications of market segmentation in the call money market, with some surplus banks lending primarily to nationwide commercial banks. There remains a sizable difference between call rates for transactions between banks and those for call transactions between NBFIs.

One of the basic functions of a money market is to provide liquidity, but in this area the Korean money market leaves a lot to be desired. Exacerbating the liquidity situation is the fact that many buyers of money market instruments in Korea tend to hold them to maturity, sometimes because of the lack of a well-developed secondary market. The authorities therefore should need to relax the various rigidities that continue to prevail in the market, such as the assignment of MSBs to nonbank financial institutions and the regulations governing the free fluctuation of interest rates.

The government could do several things to develop the money market, such as offering more flexible terms and developing appropriate secondary markets, in which the investment and finance companies could play a useful role.

With the implementation of the market-average foreign exchange rate system in March 1990, variations in the call rates for NBFIs determined in the call market are transmitted to the won's market-average exchange rate via arbitrage transactions. The money market development and liberalization of exchange controls will thus challenge monetary policy management and the stabilization of exchange rates.

It would help the development of the money markets if some of the controls on the terms could be relaxed and more components of the market could be opened up to a wider group of participants, such as nonfinancial businesses and individual persons. It appears likely that in the future the authorities will move toward a greater reliance on market forces and the integration of markets.

NOTES

This chapter was prepared in connection with the Research Project on Money Markets in Asia, organized by the Program on International Financial Systems of the Harvard Law School and the Harvard Institute for International Development. This chapter is not to be circulated, quoted, or cited without the express written approval of the authors.

I am grateful to Dr. Buhmsoo Choi for the cointegration tests and insightful comments on previous drafts.

1. The polynomial order of time trend p is set at zero. The order of superfluous time trend terms q included to calculate $J(p,q)$ is set at 3, as recommended by Park and Choi (1988). In order to estimate the asymptotic variance incorporated in the correction terms of Phillips Z statistics, the Parzen window with eight lags was used, based on fitted residuals from the autoregressive equations, as recommended by Phillips and Perron (1988). To calculate the augmented Dickey and Fuller (ADF) statistics, four lagged differenced variables are included as regressors to accommodate nuisance parameter dependency. As a sensitivity test, we changed the lag truncation numbers (k). For Z statistics, the results are robust for these experiments. The numerical values of ADF change according to k. Regardless of k, the general pictures of the results are similar to those reported later.

2. In advanced financial markets like the U.S. Treasury bill market, interest series are typically integrated processes.

3. Although we could not reject the null hypothesis of integration even with a 90% significance level, it does not absolutely exclude the possibility that those series are a highly autoregressive but stationary process. Because of the limited power of the testing procedures for unit roots in a finite sample, a clear distinction between integration and highly autoregressive stationarity is very difficult.

4. Commercial paper without recourse means commercial paper without a payment guarantee by investment and finance companies (IFC) or merchant banking corporations (MBC). Commercial paper with recourse has such a payment guarantee.

5. The main reason that the curb markets drew financial transactions away from the organized markets is the regulation of the interest rates. For example, the nominal interest rates on general bank loans (with one-year maturity) were 17.7%, and the interest rates on the curb market loans were 39%.

6. M2 is the currency in circulation and the total deposits of banking institutions.

7. Individual persons and institutional investors can participate in the Bond Management Fund by purchasing beneficiary certificates.

REFERENCES

Bank of Korea. 1985. *Financial System in Korea.* Seoul: Bank of Korea.

———. 1989a. *Annual Report.* Seoul: Bank of Korea.

———. 1989b. *Financial System and Monetary Policy in Korea.* Seoul: Bank of Korea.

Cho, Y. J., and D. C. Cole. 1986. "The Role of the Financial Sector in Korea's Structural Adjustment." Working Paper 8607. Seoul: Korea Development Institute.

Cole, D. C., and Y. C. Park. 1983. *Financial Development in Korea 1945–1978.* Cambridge, MA: Harvard University Press.

Cole, D. C., and B. F. Slade. 1990. "Development of Money Markets in Indonesia." Cambridge, MA: Harvard Institute for International Development, February. Photocopy.

Dickey, D. A., and W. A. Fuller. 1981. "Likelihood Ratio Statistics for Autoregressive Time Series with a Unit Root." *Econometrica* 49: 1057–72.

Duk-hoon, Lee, et al. 1988. *Financial Market Changes and Policy Strategy for Developing the Money Market and Short-Term Financial Institutions* (in Korean). Seoul: Korea Development Institute.

Emery, R. F. 1984. *The Japanese Money Market.* Lexington, MA: Heath.

Engle, R. F., and C. W. J. Granger. 1987. "Cointegration and Error Correction: Representation, Estimation and Testing." *Econometrica* 55: 251–76.

Federal Reserve Bank of Richmond. 1986. *Instrument of the Money Market.* Richmond, VA: Federal Reserve Bank of Richmond.

Harvard Program on International Financial Systems (PIFS). 1988. "Methodology Paper for Regional Research Project: Guidelines for Study of Money Markets in Asia." Cambridge, MA: PIFS, May.

Japan Center for International Finance. 1988. "The Past and Present of the Deregulation and Internationalization of the Tokyo Money and Capital Market." JCIF Policy Study Series 10. Toyko: JCIF, April.

Meek, Paul. 1982. *U.S. Monetary Policy and Financial Markets.* New York: Federal Reserve Bank of New York.

Ministry of Finance. 1990. *MOF Bulletin.* 79. Gwachon, Korea: February.

Park, J. Y., and B. Choi. 1988. "A New Approach

to Testing for Unit Roots." Center for Analytic Economics Working Paper 88–23. Ithaca, NY: Cornell University.

Phillips, P. C. B. 1987. "Time Series Regression with Unit Roots." *Econometrica* 55: 277–302.

Phillips, P. C. B., and P. Perron. 1988. "Testing for a Unit Root in Time Series Regression." *Biometrica* 75: 335–46.

Roh, Choong-Hwan. 1989. "The Money Market Development in Korea." *Monthly Review.* Korea Exchange Bank, December.

Said, S. E., and D. A. Dickey. 1984. "Testing for Unit Roots in Autoregressive-Moving Average Models of Unknown Order." *Biometrica* 71: 594–607.

World Bank. 1987. *Korea: Managing an External Surplus: Monetary and Trade Issues.* Washington, DC: World Bank, December.

APPENDIX 4A

IMPORTANT EVENTS IN THE DEVELOPMENT OF THE MONEY MARKET IN KOREA

1961	The Bank of Korea (BOK) issues monetary stabilization bonds.
1967	Treasury bills are first issued.
1972	The short-term Financing Business Act is promulgated, and investment and finance companies are established.
1974	Negotiable certificates of deposits are introduced at commercial banks.
1975	Call transactions are systemized by the establishment of the Call Transactions Room.
1977	The Korea Securities Finance Corporation initiates bond trading on repurchase agreements with securities companies on a short-term basis.
February 1980	Securities companies gain permission to engage in the RP business.
June 1981	Commercial paper (CP) is introduced with longer maturities and larger minimum denominations.
December 1981	The CD business is discontinued.
September 1982	Banks gain permission to engage in the RP business.
February 1984	The Cash Management Account (CMA) is introduced at investment and finance companies and merchant banking corporations.
June 1984	The CD business is reintroduced.
May 1986	The Bank of Korea begins to activate the sale of monetary stabilization bonds to absorb excess liquidity.
November 1986	The Bank of Korea designates ten securities companies and seven investment and finance companies as counterparts for open market operations and introduces a system of primary dealers.
1987	The Bond Management Fund is established jointly by three investment trust companies to underwrite and purchase MSBs and other monetary control bonds.
February 1987	The minimum denomination of CDs is lowered from 100 million won to 50 million won, and the maturity period is set between 91 days and 180 days.
January 1988	The Monetary Board of the Bank of Korea increases the ceiling of MSB issuances from within 25 percent of money supply (M2) to within 35 percent of M2.

August 1988   The Monetary Board of the Bank of Korea increases the ceiling of MSB issuances from within 35 percent of M2 to within 50 percent of M2.

December 1988 The CP is integrated into the category of "resold note without recourse."

December 1988 Monetary authorities implement an extensive deregulation of interest rates. Interest rates of CP and CDs are deregulated.

February 1989   MSBs with a maturity of 546 days are introduced.

May 1989   Monetary authorities adopt a marginal reserve requirement system. Banks are required to hold 30 percent of any increase in average deposit balances as reserves.

August 1989   Trade bills, similar to bankers acceptances, are introduced.

October 1989   The call money market, originally divided into the exchange market (mainly for banks) and the over-the-counter market (mainly for NBFIs), is integrated into a single market.

November 1989   The Ministry of Finance (MOF) asks investment and finance companies to abolish the practice of requiring their borrowers to deposit de facto compensating balances when they borrow funds.

December 1989 The foreign currency call market is established.

March 1, 1990   The government introduces the market-average foreign exchange rate system and replaces the previous multicurrency basket-peg system.

APPENDIX 4B
REGRESSION RESULTS FOR INTERBANK AND GOVERNMENT BANK MARKETS

CALL = Call market rate
MTR = 100 * {(M2 growth rates – annual target)/annual target}
RMSBB = MSBB/M2
   M2 = Currency in circulation + total deposits of banking institutions
   LM2 = ln (M2)
RBOKL = BOK loans to banks/M2
   GPB = Government bond yield
   CPB = Corporate bond yield
RCBB = CBB/M2
   CBB = Balance of corporate bonds
LMSBB = ln(MSBB)
   ( ) = t-value

Table 4B.1. Estimated Equations for Interbank Rate

---

1. March 1984–December 1985

$CALL_t =$ 156.13 + 0.02 MTR_{t-1} + 33.97 $RMSBB_t$ –7.42 $LM2_t$
      (4.27)   (2.33)   (0.86)   (– 0.73)

      –7.99 $LM2_{t-1}$ + 9.20 $RBOKL_t$ + 0.64 $CALL_{t-1}$
       (–0.67)   (2.20)   (4.38)

      $R^2 = 0.8797$ D.W. = 2.31

2. March 1986–December 1988

$CALL_t =$ 16.26 + 0.03 MTR_{t-1} + 4.90 $RMSBB_t$ + 13.03 $LM2_t$
      (0.28)   (2.07)   (0.95)   (1.53)

      –14.56 $LM2_{t-1}$ + 10.17 $RBOKL_t$ + 0.57 $CALL_{t-1}$
       (–1.37)   (1.19)   (3.98)

      $R^2 = 0.4837$ D.W. = 2.24

3. March 1986–December 1988

$CALL_t =$ 73.12 + 0.04 MTR_{t-1} + 8.37 $RMSBB_t$ + 12.10 $LM2_t$
      (2.11)   (2.31)   (1.95)   (1.42)

      –18.81 $LM2_{t-1}$ + 0.53 $CALL_{t-1}$
       (–1.86)   (3.78)

      $R^2 = 0.4567$ D.W. = 2.22

Table 4B.2. Estimated Equations for Government Bond Rate

1. *March 1982–December 1988*

   GPBt = 25.27 + 0.76 CPBt – 2.15 LM2t –9.19 RCBBt
   　　　 (4.31)　 (10.49)　　 (–3.38)　　 (–2.27)

   　　　 +0.34 LMSBBt– 0.0013 MTRt–1
   　　　　 (4.55)　　　　 (– 0.34)

   　　　 r(AR(1)) = 0.11 (0.98)

   　　　 R2 = 0.8341　　 D.W. = 2.02

2. *March 1982–December 1985*

   GPBt = 25.13 +0.84 CPBt –2.28 LM2t–7.17 RCBBt
   　　　 (1.08)　　 (8.68)　　 (– 0.93)　　 (– 0.7)

   　　　 +0.29 LMSBBt – 0.015 MTRt–1
   　　　　 (3.50)　　　　 (– 0.35)

   　　　 r(AR(1)) = 0.12 (0.74)

   　　　 R2 = 0.8690　　 D.W. = 2.02

3. *January 1986–December 1988*

   GPBt = 33.97 + 0.55 CPBt –2.88 LM2t –10.24 RCBBt
   　　　 (0.75)　　 (3.33)　　 (– 0.70)　　 (– 0.30)

   　　　 +0.57 LMSBBt +0.0008 MTRt–1
   　　　　 (1.23)　　　　 (0.07)

   　　　 r(AR(1)) = – 0.03 (– 0.16)

   　　　 R2 = 0.5832　　　　 D.W. = 1.96

REGRESSION RESULTS FOR COMMERCIAL PAPER MARKET

SCP = Outstanding volume of A/CP and B/CP
RTD = Rate on bank time deposits (%, average of period)
RCPB = Average discount yield of B/CP (%, average of period)
INF = Inflation rate
GNPN = Nominal GNP
TIM = 1, 2, 3, . . .
DCMA = Dummy variables
DENT = Dummy variables
DSMI = Dummy variables
DMSB = Dummy variables
SCPI = Outstanding volume of CP bought by investors
RCPBS = Resale yield of B/CP (%)
VCP = Variance of commercial paper outstanding
MSI = Market share of four largest borrowers
MSD = Market share of four largest dealers
OPM = Outstanding volume of discounted CPs past maturity
CP Rate = Commercial paper resale rate
CB Rate = Corporate bank yield rate
MSB Rate = MSB yield rate
( ) = t-value

Table 4C.1. Regression Results

1. Dealer's Demand Function:
  Sample Period: January 1982–December 1988

$$\ln SCP = 2.46 - 0.08\ RTD + 0.10\ RCPA - 0.02\ INF + 0.09\ \ln GNPN$$
$$(1.90)\quad(-2.15)\qquad(2.64)\qquad(-2.60)\qquad(0.85)$$

$$+\ 0.18\ DCMA + 0.02\ DENT - 0.05\ DSMI - 0.01\ DMSB$$
$$(2.28)\qquad\quad(2.97)\qquad\quad(-1.70)\qquad\quad(-0.27)$$

$$+\ 0.03\ TIM + 0.34\ \ln SCP\ (-1)$$
$$(2.99)\qquad\quad(2.61)$$

$$R = 0.98 \quad SSE = 0.05 \quad DW = 2.08$$

Table 4C.1. (*Continued*)

2. *Investor's Demand Function:*
   Sample Period: January 1982–December 1988

In SCPI = $1.47 - 0.14$ RTB $+ 0.13$ RCPBS $- 0.05$ INF $+ 0.28$ln GNPN
$\qquad$ (0.61) $\quad$ (−1.73) $\qquad$ (2.20) $\qquad\quad$ (−2.46) $\qquad$ (1.28)

$\qquad + 0.19$ DCMA $+ 0.03$ DENT $- 0.06$ DSMI $- 0.02$ DMSB
$\qquad\qquad$ (1.14) $\qquad\quad$ (2.09) $\qquad\quad$ (−1.15) $\qquad$ (0.19)

$\qquad + 0.02$ TIM $+ 0.22$ ln SCP (−1)
$\qquad\quad$ (1.25) $\qquad\quad$ (1.26)

$\qquad$ R = 0.85 $\quad$ SSE = 0.11 $\quad$ DW = 2.56

3. *Market Share of Four Largest Dealers:*
   Sample Period: July 1980–December 1988

MSD = $87.80 + 1.21$ DCMA $- 1.66$ DENT $- 0.08$ DSMI $+ 2.81$ DMSB
$\qquad$ (18.35) $\quad$ (0.72) $\qquad\quad$ (−10.91) $\qquad$ (−0.07) $\qquad$ (2.13)

$\qquad$ R = 0.94 $\quad$ SSE = 1.98 $\quad$ DW = 2.34

4. *Market Share of Four Largest Borrowers:*
   Sample Period: April 1982–December 1988

MSI = $63.84 - 1.37$ DCMA $- 0.16$ DENT $- 0.18$ DSMI $- 0.53$ DMSB
$\qquad$ (16.72) $\quad$ (−1.99) $\qquad\quad$ (−1.45) $\qquad$ (−0.36) $\qquad$ (−0.97)

$\qquad$ R = 0.42 $\quad$ SSE = 1.16 $\quad$ DW = 1.76

5. *Stability Measures:*
   VCP: Sample Period: January 1982–December 1988

VCP = $0.06 - 0.05$ DCMA $+ 0.03 \times 10$ DENT $- 0.04$ DSMI $+ 0.06$ DMSB
$\qquad$ (0.40) $\quad$ (−1.20) $\qquad\qquad$ (0.08) $\qquad\qquad$ (−1.27) $\qquad$ (1.78)

$\qquad + 0.91$ VCP (−1)
$\qquad\quad$ (6.93)

$\qquad$ R = 0.87 $\quad$ SSE = 0.06 $\quad$ DW = 2.14

6. *Stability Measures: OPM:*
   Sample Period: July 1980–December 1988

OPM = $-5{,}173.02 + 120.31$ DCMA $+ 925.78$ DENT $- 3{,}042.59$ DSMI
$\qquad$ (−0.24) $\qquad\quad$ (0.20) $\qquad\qquad$ (1.33) $\qquad\qquad$ (−0.63)

$\qquad + 34{,}425.64$ DMSB
$\qquad\qquad$ (5.71)

$\qquad$ R = 0.80 $\quad$ SSE = 9.026.18 $\quad$ DW = 2.47

CHAPTER 5
MONEY MARKETS IN MALAYSIA

LIN SEE-YAN
CHUNG TIN FAH

The money market is made up of intermediaries and instruments for short-term funds and forms an integral part of Malaysia's financial system. It provides a ready source of funds for market participants who require funding and investment outlets for those with temporary surplus funds. Operations in the money market can be divided into two broad categories: placing time or fixed deposits and borrowing against time, and purchasing and selling money market papers. This chapter examines the financial flows and instruments in the money market as well as the impact of policy on the performance of the money market so that resources can be effectively deployed to assist the development of the economy. Such an examination is both desirable and timely given that the financial markets in Malaysia have radically changed over time. In order to avoid any structural problems relating to the pre-1979 fixed interest rates, we will look at the period after the interest rate liberalization program of 1978, covering the decade from 1979 to the second quarter of 1989.

The openness of the central bank's policy in the 1980s resulted in little intervention in the operations of the Malaysian money market. Our findings indicate that the Malaysian money market functions efficiently and that there was no market segmentation. There is some positive causality between deposit rates and interbank rates, and the interbank rates themselves had a stable term structure during the period. An analysis of the efficiency of each money market instrument's rates, namely, the interbank rates, treasury bill rates, bankers acceptance rates, and U.S. dollar–Malaysian ringgit exchange rates revealed a general randomness of movement between 1979 and 1984, thus indicating that the Malaysian money market is efficient. However, some signs of market inefficiency were evident in 1985/86, a period when the Malaysian economy was beset with recession and the financial system underwent structural changes. The central bank's recuperative measures implemented during this period, while improving the stability of the market, inevitably affected its efficiency.

THE FINANCIAL SYSTEM AND THE REGULATORY FRAMEWORK GOVERNING ITS OPERATIONS

In Malaysia's money market, the players are the major financial institutions, and the developments in the financial system and the money market are closely interrelated. Basically, the financial system can be divided into the banking system and the nonbank financial intermediaries.

The banking system in Malaysia, which is the major component of the financial sector, consists of Bank Negara Malaysia, serving as the central bank; thirty-eight commercial banks; Bank Islam Malaysia Berhad; forty-seven finance companies; twelve merchant banks; seven discount houses; and eight money and foreign exchange brokers, all of which are regulated and supervised by the central bank.

The nonbank financial institutions are mainly supervised by other government agencies. These institutions can be divided into five groups, the development finance institutions, the savings institutions, the savings and pension funds, the insurance companies, and other financial intermediaries, that is, building societies, unit trusts, and several special investment agencies. According to the Banking and Financial Institutions Act of 1989, these institutions can be further subdivided into scheduled and nonscheduled institutions, which, if deemed necessary by the minister of finance, can come under the supervision of Bank Negara Malaysia. The central bank took over the supervision of the insurance companies on April 1, 1988.

The financial system in Malaysia grew rapidly over the previous two decades, deepening and innovating apace. As summarized in Table 5.1, the total resources of the financial system increased from RM3.553 billion at the end of 1960 to RM11.622 billion at the end of 1970, an average annual growth of 12.6%. Between 1971 and 1980, this growth accelerated to an average annual rate of 20.4% before moderating to 15% from 1981 to 1988.

At the end of 1988, the financial system's total resources amounted to RM226.7 billion. The growth of its assets between 1971 and 1988 reflected mainly the increase in the size of the banking system, which expanded at an average annual rate of 18.3%. As a group, therefore, the banking system increased its share of the financial system's total assets, from 66.3% at the end of 1960 to 68.5% at the end of 1988, resulting from the banking institutions' success in mobilizing a larger share of the private-sector deposits. Although the number of nonbank financial intermediaries rose, especially during the 1970s, their aggregate share of the financial system's total

Table 5.1. Assets of the Financial System (in RM millions)

Sector	As of End of			
	1960	1970	1980	1988
Banking system	2,356	7,455	54,346	155,142
Monetary institutions	2,346	6,882	45,180	120,932
Central bank	184	2,227	12,994	26,482
Currency Board[a]	930	195	—	—
Commercial banks	1,232	4,460	32,185	94,450
Nonmonetary institutions	10	573	9,166	34,210
Finance companies	10	531	5,635	24,286
Merchant banks	—	—	2,229	7,026
Discount houses	—	42	1,292	2,210
Credit Guarantee Corporation	—	—	10	688
Nonbank financial intermediaries	1,197	4,167	19,807	71,487
Provident, pension and insurance funds	836	3,156	13,846	47,490
Employees Provident Fund	633	2,265	9,481	36,454
Other provident funds	100	452	1,889	4,007
Life insurance funds	83	324	1,657	5,363
General insurance funds	20	115	819	1,666
Development finance institutions[b]	1	133	2,193	5,478
Savings institutions[c]	267	645	2,463	8,750
Other financial intermediaries[d]	93	233	1,305	9,769
Total	3,553	11,622	74,153	226,629

[a] Malaysia's estimated share of assets of the Currency Board. The Currency Board ceased to function as of November 30, 1979, following its liquidation and the final distribution of its assets to the participating governments of Malaysia, Singapore, and Brunei.

[b] Including Malaysian Industrial Development Finance Berhad (MIDF), Agriculture Bank of Malaysia, Borneo Development Corporation, Sabah Development Bank Berhad, Sabah Credit Corporation, Development Bank of Malaysia, and Industrial Development Bank of Malaysia Berhad.

[c] Including National Savings Bank, Bank Kerjasama Rakyat, and the cooperative societies.

[d] Including unit trusts, building societies, and Pilgrims Management and Fund Board.

assets declined over the period, from 33.7% at the end of 1960 to 31.5% at the end of 1988. This was due mainly to the slower growth of their total assets, at an average annual rate of 15.8% during the period, compared with 16.1% for the banking system. To a large degree, the banking sector was stimulated by the greater monetization of the economy, including the spread of the bank branch network and the inculcation of banking habits. The aggressive credit policies adopted by the banks were also an important factor.

Within the banking system, the monetary institutions (principally the central bank and the commercial banks) dominated the overall growth, although their relative share of the financial system's total assets fell from 66% at the end of 1960 to 53.4% at the end of 1988, mainly because of the significant growth of the finance companies and the merchant banks in the 1970s. Among the major groups of nonbank financial institutions, the savings, pension, and insurance funds remained the largest, accounting for 21% of the financial system's total assets at the end of 1988. Another noticeable trend was the growing significance of the development finance institutions, following the establishment of several new institutions, such as the Development Bank of Malaysia, the Sabah Development Bank, and the Industrial Development Bank of Malaysia, in the second half of the 1970s. The development banks as a group increased their share of the financial system's total assets to 2.4% in 1988, compared with a negligible share at the end of 1960 and 1.1% at the end of 1970. Conversely, the performance of the savings institutions was weak, with their relative share of the financial system's total assets dropping from 7.5% to only 3.9% at the end of 1988.

The monetization and financial deepening in Malaysia was significant compared with other ASEAN countries between 1975 and 1988. With the exception of Singapore, Malaysia performed relatively better than its ASEAN colleagues. The use of money by Malaysians is comparable to that in Singapore. Nominal and real M1 at the end of 1988 were 4.2 and 4.6 times higher, respectively, than the levels at the end of 1975. The currency-to-M1 ratio at 50% in 1988 was the same as that in Singapore. As is true among the other ASEAN countries, M2 in Malaysia increased more significantly than M1 did, as seen in the rise of the M2/GNP ratio from 0.46 to 0.70 between 1975 and 1988. The ratio at the end of 1988 was, however, lower than the corresponding ratio in Singapore (0.84). The M2/GNP ratios in Indonesia, the Philippines, and Thailand were lower than in Malaysia because of the slower penetration of the commercial banking system in these economies. Another observation about the M2/GNP ratio is that in the developed economies, the ratio was relatively more stable compared with Malaysia's rising ratio, reflecting the more rapid monetization process in Malaysia. This can also be seen in its high M2/M1 ratio of 3.34 at the end of 1988. The degree of monetization in Malaysia is also indicated by the holdings of M2 per capita and total bank deposits per capita, which rose from U.S.$349 to U.S.$1,361 and from U.S.$283 to U.S.$5,004, respectively, between 1975 and 1988. The levels at the end of 1988 were high relative to those in the Philippines, Thailand, and Indonesia, although noticeably lower than Singapore's.

The process of deepening in the Malaysian financial system can be seen in the relationship between the total assets of the financial system and the nation's gross national product (GNP). The ratio of financial assets to GNP rose from 1.23 in 1975 to 2.62 in 1988. Although this is second only to Singapore in the ASEAN region, there still is a wide gap between the financial development in the two nations, especially if the offshore Asian dollar market is included in Singapore's financial system when computing the financial assets/GNP ratio. This reflects the fact that Singapore has become a major international financial center. The dominance of the banking system in the Malaysian financial system is evident, as the banking system's assets/GNP ratio of 1.79 in 1988 represented almost 70% of the ratio of 2.62 for the whole financial system. Furthermore, the commercial banks alone accounted for 41% of the financial system's total assets at the end of 1988.

The Banking System

Currently, the institutions in the banking system are differentiated on the basis of the types of deposits they are legally allowed to mobilize, the types of assets they can hold, and other regulatory constraints imposed on their operations. Because the distinctions among banking institutions are continuing to blur, such a demarcation might not be necessary in the future.

Commercial Banks

The commercial banks represent by far the largest component, accounting for about 41.7% of the financial system's total assets at the end of 1988. The commercial banks provide the normal banking services, including accepting deposits, granting loans and advances, discounting trade bills and bankers acceptances, dealing in foreign exchange, and providing business investment advisory services. Although other financial institutions in Malaysia perform similar functions, the commercial banks have the additional advantage of being able to offer a wider range of ancillary facilities. Apart from Bank Islam Malaysia, they are the only group of financial institutions in the country licensed by the central bank as check-paying banks. They are also the only group (apart from Bank Islam Malaysia) authorized to deal in foreign exchange. Over the years, the role of the commercial banks has evolved from the simple traditional one of mobilizing deposits and using them to finance trade and commerce to that of agents of change in the country's economic development.

In regard to portfolio restrictions, commercial banks are not allowed to accept deposits of less than one-month maturity. They are required to keep 6.5% of their eligible liabilities[1] as statutory reserves at Bank Negara Malaysia, on which no interest is paid, and to invest 17% of these liabilities in liquid assets.[2] Moreover, for the domestic banks, the ratio of shareholders' funds to total assets (both shorter-term investments) must not fall below 4%. For foreign banks, the ratio of net working funds to total assets (both shorter-term investments) must not be below 6%. This capital adequacy requirement, however, was amended on September 1, 1989, in accordance with the recommendation of the Basel Committee, based on a risk-weighted approach. Under this new system, the commercial banks had to comply with a capital adequacy ratio of 7.25% (9.25% in the case of foreign banks) by the end of 1990 and to increase it further to 8% (10% in the case of foreign banks) by the end of 1992. Their investments in shares (trustee shares, Malaysian Airline System and Malaysian International Shipping Corporation shares, manufacturing companies, unit property trusts, and fixed assets) are subject to an overall limit of 50% of the banks' capital base (net of investments in subsidiaries and in other financial institutions). In addition, the commercial banks' loan portfolios are subject to lending guidelines designed to channel credit to certain sectors, considered as priority sectors on the basis of socioeconomic factors. At the same time, loans to a single customer cannot exceed 30% of the bank's capital.

The growth of the commercial banks stemmed mainly from the growth of their deposit base, which rose at an average annual rate of 11.9% from 1981 to June 1989 and accounted for 60.3% of the banks' total resources at the end of June 1989. Throughout the 1980s, 38 banks operated in Malaysia, of which 22 were domestic incorporated banks with a total of 927 branches throughout the country. The banks also maintain correspondent relationships with most of the world's major financial centers. The commercial banking system is dominated by two government-owned commercial banks, accounting for 35.8% of the total assets of all commercial banks as of the end of June 1989; their branch network of 327 offices represented more than 35% of the total branch network of commercial banks. In addition to the 2 large banks, there are 9 medium-size banks and 27 smaller banks of different sizes, 16 of which are branches or subsidiaries of foreign banks. Most of the foreign banks operate no more than 1 office each. As a group, the banks accounted for 66.1% of the financial system's aggregate deposits and provided the largest proportion of the aggregate credit extended by the financial system to the private sector. The total resources of the commercial banks amounted to RM104.6 billion at the end of June 1989.

Bank Islam Malaysia Berhad

A milestone in the evolution of the banking system in Malaysia was the incorporation of Bank Islam Malaysia Berhad on March 1, 1983. Bank Islam Malaysia was created for Malaysian Muslims who wanted the services of a modern banking system but did not want to pay or receive interest, as their religion forbids receiving interest. The bank offers all the conventional banking services based on Islamic principles and is also required to maintain statutory reserves with the central bank (at present, the ratio is 6.5% of its total eligible liabilities). In addition, it is also required to observe a first liquid assets ratio of 10% on its total eligible liabilities, excluding investment account liabilities, and a ratio of 5% on its investment account liabilities.

After more than five years in operation, Bank Islam Malaysia Berhad has proved to be a viable banking institution. Its total resources rose from RM171 million at the end of 1983 to RM1.449 billion at the end of June 1989, of which deposits accounted for RM1.272 billion, or 87.8% of its total resources.

Financing extended by Bank Islam increased from RM41 million at the end of 1983 to RM728 million at the end of June 1989. However, Bank Islam does not participate directly in the money market, as the money market operates on the basis of interest rates.

The operations of the finance companies, merchant banks, and discount houses, which also are important financial institutions in the Malaysian financial system, complement and supplement the activities of the commercial banks.

Finance Companies

The finance companies are the second-largest group of deposit-taking institutions in Malaysia. They operate in the medium-term credit market and derive their resources mainly from savings and fixed deposits. They are prohibited from accepting demand deposits and fixed deposits of less than three months' maturity, dealing in gold or foreign exchange, and granting overdrafts. Loans extended by the finance companies were mainly installment-plan loans, leasing finance, housing loans, and loans for a variety of other purposes, particularly for the purchase and development of real estate. The finance companies grew during the 1980s, with their numbers rising from 39 to 47, and although no finance companies had assets reaching M$1 billion in 1981, 10 companies exceeded this amount in 1989. By 1989, 11 finance companies were wholly owned by domestic commercial banks; 2 were subsidiaries of merchant banks; and 5 were foreign controlled (4 being subsidiaries of foreign banks). At the end of June 1989, the finance companies as a group operated a total of 486 offices throughout Malaysia, with their total resources amounting to RM25.967 billion. In terms of assets, the finance companies are much smaller in size than the commercial banks and are more evenly distributed.

The finance companies are differentiated from the commercial banks by the regulations on the types of deposits and assets. The statutory reserve for finance companies is 6.5%, which is similar to that for commercial banks. However, the liquidity ratio is lower, at 10% of their eligible liabilities. The finance companies' capital adequacy ratio is defined in terms of risk assets, which cannot exceed fifteen times the shareholders' funds. However, as of September 1, 1989, the finance companies were required to comply with a risk-weighted capital adequacy ratio of 7.25% by the end of 1990 and 8% by the end of 1992. This is meant to equalize the assessment of capital adequacy among the three groups of banking institutions. Finance companies are subject to lending guidelines that are broadly similar to those of commercial banks.

Merchant Banks

Merchant banks in Malaysia are licensed to operate as specialized financial intermediaries in the money and capital markets. Since their emergence at the beginning of the 1970s, the merchant banks have expanded their scope of operations by providing a wide range of specialized services, including issuing-house and underwriting facilities, corporate financing, financial investment, management advice, and portfolio investment management. The merchant banks are allowed to accept term deposits from financial institutions with a minimum maturity of one month and in the amount of RM250.000 per deposit, except in the case of deposits from corporations, for which the minimum amount is RM1 million per deposit. The merchant banks are also allowed to accept foreign currency deposits from nonresidents (the minimum equivalent to RM250,000 per deposit) and to make direct loans to their clients. Other activities include money market operations, trading of money market instruments in secondary markets, and related banking functions. At the end of June 1989, there were twelve merchant banks with a total of seventeen offices operating in the country. The total resources of the merchant banks amounted to RM8.116 billion at the end of June 1989.

Merchant banks are subject to a reserve requirement of 6.5% on their eligible liabilities and a minimum liquidity ratio of 10% (12.5% for those merchant banks allowed to issue negotiable certificates of deposit, or NCDs). Their loan operations are not subject to lending guidelines, but at least 30% of the total income of each merchant bank must be from fee-based activities. The merchant banks are required to observe two gearing ratios: (1) Their domestic borrowings must not exceed fifteen times their shareholders' funds, and (2) their domestic borrowings and contingent liabilities must not exceed twenty times their shareholders' funds. Under the new capital adequacy requirement, which went into effect on September 1, 1989, the merchant banks were required to achieve a risk-weighted capital ratio of 7.25% by the end of 1990 and 8% by the end of 1992. On the whole, each merchant bank is permitted to invest up to 10% of its paid-up capital and published reserves in the shares of a single enterprise or up to 10% of the paid-up capital of the enterprise in which it invests, whichever is lower. In the aggregate, a merchant bank may invest in shares valued at up to a total of 50% of its paid-up capital and published reserves. Although the merchant banks are relatively small, accounting for only 3.8% of the financial system's total assets, they are significant market players because of their money market activities and in the competition they provide in making loans to customers.

Discount Houses

There are currently seven discount houses in Malaysia. Their role has changed substantially over the years. When the discount houses were first created in the 1960s and 1970s, their role was envisaged to be that of "keepers of liquidity." The overnight deposits and call money placed by the financial institutions with the discount houses qualified as first-line liquid assets, and this privilege enabled the discount houses to mobilize funds at below-market rates. Moreover, they were the only financial institutions allowed to accept corporate deposits of less than one-month maturity. The funds mobilized by the discount houses were invested in Malaysian government paper (at least 75%), bankers acceptances (BAs), and negotiable certificates of deposit (NCDs) (not more than 25%).

Various actions were taken over the years to change the discount houses' role from that of being merely "keepers of liquidity" to that of being bona fide securities dealers. Before October 1987, the discount houses had to invest at least 85% of their portfolios in government paper, whereas the permissible maximum holdings of BAs and NCDs was only 15%. The ratio was changed to 75:25 in October 1987. The maximum permissible maturity of the instruments held by the discount houses was lengthened to five years, from the previous three years in January 1989. In June 1990, the maturity period was further lengthened to ten years. Another important change made in June 1990 was the discontinuation of the 75:25 ratio and its replacement with a risk-weighted capital adequacy ratio so as to provide as much flexibility as possible for the discount houses to hold the permissible assets in whatever proportion they wished, subject only to the risk-weighted capital adequacy constraint.

Given the special status of the discount houses in the Malaysian financial system, it is not surprising that their operations have expanded rapidly since the early 1960s. Their total deposits rose from RM19 million at the end of 1964 to RM3.474 billion at the end of June 1989. Apart from placing deposits, companies, public authorities, and other financial institutions also entered into repurchase agreements with the discount houses. The marked expansion in the volume of funds received by discount houses by way of repurchase agreements is a reflection of the growing demand by the corporate sector for a short-term investment vehicle for funds that are temporarily in surplus. By the end of July 1988, the volume of outstanding repurchase agreements of the seven discount houses amounted to RM1.179 billion, which was mainly transacted with financial institutions and corporations.

Nonbank Financial Intermediaries

Malaysia's nonbank financial intermediaries accounted for 31.9% of the financial system's total assets at the end of 1988. The largest institution in this group is the Employees Provident Fund (EPF), which mobilizes contractual savings in the form of savings and pension fund contributions and invests the funds mainly in government securities. The other institutions in this group are relatively small. The insurance companies, development finance institutions, savings institutions, and other intermediaries each accounted for less than 5% of the financial system's assets at the end of 1988. Nevertheless, these institutions are expected to perform an increasingly important role in the financial system in the coming years.

The financial system is served by the sophisticated money and foreign exchange markets, which have strengthened monetary control by the central bank and aided in the process of financial deepening in the country.

THE MONEY MARKET

The money market consists of the interbank market, where short-term funds are lent and borrowed, and the market for short-term money market instruments, that is, Malaysian government securities, treasury bills, mortgage bonds, bankers acceptances, negotiable certificates of deposit, and repurchase agreements.

We subdivided the market that we studied into (1) the primary market for short-term deposits and loans (overdrafts), (2) the secondary market for short-term deposits and loans, (3) the short-term government securities market, (4) the commercial bills market, and (5) the foreign exchange market. Although a substantial portion of the government securities have longer maturities and do not form part of the money market, the shorter-maturity securities are an integral part of it. We felt that a fuller treatment of the government securities market was necessary because of its linkage with other components of the money market. In addition, we discuss the foreign exchange market, since the developments in both the money and foreign exchange markets are closely related; that is, conditions in the foreign exchange market are reflected in the money market, and vice versa.

The development of the money and foreign exchange markets in Malaysia has been largely influenced by the structure of the banking system, the openness of the economy to the capital flows, the portfolio regulations of the banking institutions, and the rediscount policies of the central bank.

The diversity of financial institutions in terms of their size and branch network has led to the emergence of surplus and deficit centers within the financial system, and especially within the commercial banking sector. The larger domestic commercial banks were able to expand their branch network nationwide and, hence, have a large deposit base. They usually are net lenders in the interbank market. The smaller banks have fewer branches, and the foreign banks are not allowed to open new branches in Malaysia. Consequently, the small domestic banks and the foreign commercial banks have limited opportunities to attract deposits. Although foreign banks have access to their headquarters' funds, such access may be restricted by the prudential exposure limits set by the parent institutions. Therefore, these banks have come to rely substantially on the surplus resources of local financial institutions. Finally, since the merchant banks' deposit base is limited to deposits from corporations (a minimum of RM1 million per deposit) and approved financial institutions (a minimum of RM250,000 per deposit), most of them are net borrowers in the money market.

The supply of and demand for funds in the money market have also been affected by the hedging and arbitrage activities in the foreign exchange market. In Malaysia, the exchange control regime is liberal, and foreign currencies may be freely bought or sold. Transactions in the foreign exchange market, especially in forward and swap transactions, can be covered from the interbank market and thereby influence interest rates in the money market. Since early 1974, the standard value date was changed from "value today," that is, when reciprocal transfers took place on the day of the deal, to "spot value," when the transfers were made on the second business day following the day of the deal. The move to spot value gave the market dealers and other participants more time and flexibility to cover their foreign exchange transactions in the money market when the standard value date was "value today." It also allowed them to arbitrage. The role of the central bank was to ensure an orderly market, to protect the market from overexposure to exchange risks. As a matter of policy, the central bank intervened in the foreign exchange market very rarely, and even then only to moderate day-to-day fluctuations in the value of the ringgit and not to "fight" the underlying trends dictated by the market. It was also the bank's responsibility to ensure that conditions in the market were conducive to the orderly trading of the ringgit. These conditions included the availability of continuous quotations as well as the avoidance of expectations of excessive short-term changes in the exchange rate.

To minimize the commercial banks' foreign exchange exposure, the "open" position of each bank was also regulated. This position was defined by the central bank as the amount in a foreign currency that a bank could hold in an uncovered exchange risk. The rationale for regulating the commercial banks' "open" positions was to ensure that a measure of prudence prevailed in the foreign exchange deals, to be consistent with operational needs. An "open" position limit for the ringgit vis-à-vis all currencies was set for the individual banks by the central bank, taking into account a variety of factors, including the resources of the bank, the volume of its foreign exchange business, and its expertise in foreign exchange dealings. In practice, the open position for each bank was normally set at a generous level, in order to provide sufficient flexibility for each bank to be effective in "making" a market without undue restrictions on its exchange exposure.

Since its inception, the central bank has promoted the development of a domestic money market. Besides building institutions to facilitate a greater degree of financial intermediation, its efforts were also directed at deepening the money market and strengthening the transmission mechanism of monetary policy. The major policies that were implemented were the deregulation of interest rates; the introduction of new financial instruments; the reform of the structure of liquidity requirements and the composition of liquid assets; a more efficient payments system, such as the Day-1 interbank settlement system, the electronic interbank funds transfer system, and a computerized book-entry system for transactions in government papers and mortgage bonds; and the participation of more actors in the money market. To make open market operations a more effective tool of monetary policy, the central bank had encouraged not only the commercial banks and, later, the other financial institutions to hold treasury bills but also the government to issue securities of three- and five-year maturities in order to give investors a wider range of choices for short-term investment. Of the RM984 million in securities outstanding at the end of 1960, only RM28 million represented five-year securities. The issue of three-year securities, for a total of RM13 million, began only in 1965. By the end of June 1989, outstanding securities with an original maturity of three years rose to RM250 million, and those with a five-year maturity climbed to RM1.850 billion. Before August 1973, treasury bills were made available only "on tap"; that is, they were issued on demand. The rates of discount for these bills were predetermined by the government, on the recommendation of the central bank. A further improvement in the method of issuing bills was introduced by the central bank on August 20, 1973, in order to promote greater competition in the market and to encourage a wider range of potential investors. On this date, treasury bills were sold by regular weekly tenders, with 91-day bills offered weekly, 182-day bills every fortnight, and 364-day bills every four weeks. Tenders are conducted weekly at the bank, attended by representatives of the central bank, the treasury, and the auditor-general's office.

In addition, the central bank has encouraged market dealings in treasury bills and other government securities by offering rediscounting facilities for these instruments at relatively attractive rates. The central bank also stands ready to buy and sell treasury bills and other government securities in the interest of stabilizing the market. The bank issues a price list at the end of each month for all outstanding government securities, which is published in the monthly journal of the Kuala Lumpur Stock Exchange. As of January 31, 1976, the following changes were made in the list: (1) Only middle prices are quoted, whereas previously the actual buying and selling prices at the end of the month were quoted; (2) the middle prices are only indicative; (3) the prices exclude accrued interest, whereas previously they included such interest; and (4) the securities are listed in the order of remaining maturity, whereas previously they were listed in the order of the coupon rate of interest.

Other, more recent, major developments in the government securities market are the adjustments in the coupon rates of Malaysian government securities (MGS) and the yields posted by the central bank in line with market rates, the issuance of more shorter-term maturity MGS, the increased frequency of issues, the primary use of government securities (up to ten years maturity) based on the auction, the establishment of a network of principal dealerships, and the change in the central bank's intervention procedure for MGS to give the market a greater role.

In 1987, the central bank made its first move to issue MGS with market-related coupon rates. Although the rate of return on the MGS had been regulated by the government and had historically been lower than the yields on comparable nongovernment financial assets, the adjustments during 1987 significantly narrowed this gap. For example, whereas the posted yield on MGS with a one-year maturity was reduced from 5% to 4% during 1987, the fall in the one-year fixed deposit rate was much larger. The policy of market-related rates has been maintained even in the current environment of higher interest rates, when the first loan of 1990 was issued on a higher yield curve. Over the years, the yield differentials between the short and long ends of the market have been narrowed from 3.6 to 2.05 percentage points.

In addition, the central bank no longer stands ready to buy and sell MGS within narrow margins around the posted yield curve. Instead, it uses the posted yields only to indicate middle prices and accepts bids or offers only at prices based on market yields. The objective is to allow a greater role for the market and to encourage secondary trading in MGS.

In order to develop further the secondary trading in MGS, the central bank introduced a principal dealership system for MGS on January 1, 1989. A total of eighteen principal dealers were appointed to underwrite the primary issues of MGS and to provide two-way quotations in the secondary market. (This number was increased to twenty-three in 1990.) Under this system, only the principal dealers have access to the central bank's rediscount window, and the bank's open market operations are conducted through these dealers only. Accordingly, the central bank's role in the money market changed to one of maintaining liquidity in the system as a whole and no longer just responding to the needs of each institution. Individual financial institutions that have excess liquidity or are short of funds must square their position in the market and not with the central bank. Institutions and individual persons wishing to purchase MGS from primary issues must do so through the principal dealers.

In general, securities with maturity periods of up to ten years are now issued by auction through the principal dealers, and so the central bank no longer accepts advance subscriptions. However, the Employees Provident Fund (EPF) and the National Savings Bank (NSB) are allowed, for the time being, to purchase longer-dated government securities in the primary market by way of advance subscription.

As a further measure to develop the treasury bills market, all twenty-three principal dealers were appointed on June 1, 1990, as principal dealers also for the Malaysian treasury bills. (Previously, only the discount houses were principal dealers for treasury bills.) They underwrite the treasury bills issue, provide a two-way price, and promote secondary trading in treasury bills.

The central bank was also instrumental in introducing new money market instruments and establishing new institutions, including building the financial infrastructure to develop and deepen the money market. In May 1979, two new instruments, BAs and NCDs, were introduced. Then, in December 1986, a national mortgage corporation, Cagamas Berhad, was established and began issuing mortgage-backed Cagamas bonds in October 1987. A variation of the NCDs, floating-rate NCDs, were introduced in June 1988, with the objective of giving Malaysian investors a wider range of available instruments and thereby adding depth to the money market.

In Malaysia, the rediscount operations have had only a limited influence on the money market. The central bank does not announce in advance a discount rate in order to influence the money market rates. Rather, the discount rate on various instruments are determined by market conditions in that, in line with the central bank's policy at a particular moment, they are generally set in accordance with the prevailing money market rates in order to stabilize any fluctuations in them.

The central bank attempts to influence interbank rates by intervening in the money markets—by making funds available to or withdrawing them from the money market participants. The purpose of such intervention is mainly to even out sharp erratic fluctuations in the interbank rate. The central bank uses swap operations and movements in government deposits to influence bank liquidity.

Swap operations work as follows: If the liquidity situation in the money market is tight, the commercial banks (particularly the foreign banks) can bring in foreign currencies to be swapped into ringgit proceeds with the central bank. The commercial banks use the ringgit proceeds for funding loans, thus alleviating the tight liquidity in the money market. Swaps are considered a temporary liquidity-injecting measure, although they can be renewed on maturity. A swap transaction is attractive to the commercial banks if the swap rate is lower than the interbank rate plus statutory reserve and liquidity costs.

Movements in government deposits, dubbed *recycling of government deposits*, work as follows: The federal government maintains its accounts with the central bank. Because of the lag between receipts and payments by the government, the central bank recycles the funds back into the banking system in the form of short-term deposits, thereby allowing the central bank to manage the government's cash reserve. In this way, it also ensures consistency of monetary policy, compared with the situation in which the government manages its cash position independently (sometimes at cross-purposes with monetary policy). Swap operations are short term and self-liquidating, enabling the central bank to influence liquidity for specific periods. The central bank can signal to the banking system that the move is only temporary and that in the event the market conditions change, the market mechanism will be allowed to work. Recycling of government deposits influences money market conditions on a day-to-day basis.

The Primary Market for Short-Term Deposits and Loans

In the primary market for short-term funds, the participants are both the initial suppliers and the final users. The suppliers are mainly individual persons; large enterprises; plantation houses; international trading companies; savings, pension, and other trust funds; and public authorities and government departments. They normally keep their surplus money in short-term deposits with the various financial institutions such as the commercial banks, merchant banks, finance companies, and discount houses. The movement of funds by big corporations, especially the oil corporations, can affect liquidity conditions and hence influence interest rates in the money market. The role played by any particular group of financial institutions in the market depends on the scope of its deposit-taking activity, as prescribed by the central bank.

Short-Term Deposits

In Malaysia, the thirty-eight commercial banks and Bank Islam are allowed to accept demand deposits, savings deposits, and time deposits, whereas the forty-seven finance companies are allowed to accept only savings deposits and time deposits of not less than three months maturity. The twelve merchant banks are allowed to accept only time deposits. The minimum size of each deposit accepted by the merchant banks must be at least RM250,000 in the case of deposits from the financial institutions and RM1 million in the case of corporations. The commercial banks have been allowed to issue NCDs since 1979, and the merchant banks, since 1987. In addition, both the commercial banks and the merchant banks are permitted to accept foreign currency deposits from nonresidents.

These primary sources of deposits are the main sources of liquidity for the banking institutions, which contribute to the supply of funds in the money market. All deposits grew from RM3.4 billion in 1970 to RM53.1 billion in 1988; of this, the domestic banks' share rose from 39% to 75%. The thirty-eight commercial banks mobilized about 70% of total deposits placed with the banking system. Over the years, there has been a distinct change in the volume and type of deposits placed with the commercial banks. Although demand deposits accounted for 50.6% of total deposits in 1960, their growth at an average rate of 11.7% per year, from RM477 million in 1960 to RM11.182 billion at the end of June 1989, was slower than for fixed and savings deposits. By the end of June 1989, demand deposits accounted for only 17.7% of total deposits, reflecting the greater income consciousness of depositors with regard to their surplus funds and the growing sophistication of business enterprises in the management of their funds.

In contrast with the behavior of demand deposits, fixed deposits with the commercial banks assumed a larger share of the total deposits. These deposits rose at an average rate of 16.9% annually from RM352 million, or 37.4% of total deposits, at the end of 1960 to RM30.026 billion, or 47.6%, by the end of June 1989. The rapid growth in fixed deposits—which reflected mainly the general increase in income levels, the spread of the savings habit, and the generally higher interest yield—was marked by a distinct preference for deposits of longer maturity. Before 1971, fixed deposits accepted by the banks were confined to those with maturity periods of up to one year, although the Association of Banks in Malaysia allowed its member banks to accept fixed deposits with maturities of more than one year as of January 2, 1971. As a result, fixed deposits with maturities exceeding one year amounted to RM14.651 billion, or 48.8% of total deposits, at the end of June 1989, compared with a share of only 5.2% at the end of 1971. The rates on deposits exceeding one year are negotiable. At the end of June 1989, of the total fixed deposits, 21.7% were those with maturities of three months or less.

The growth in savings deposits, the main medium of savings for small savers, has been moderate over the years. These deposits rose from RM113 million, or 12% of total deposits, at the end of 1960 to RM12.386 billion, or 19.6% of the total, by the end of June 1989, that is, at an average annual rate of 17.9%. The steady rise in savings in this form reflected mainly the growth in incomes and the marketing of various savings schemes, including the establishment of automatic teller machines (ATMs), flexibility in withdrawals while earning a reasonable return, and the rapid expansion of the commercial banks' branch network into nonurban areas. The computerization of banks, starting on January 1, 1986, also made it easier to calculate interest on savings deposits on a daily basis.

Since NCDs, basically negotiable fixed deposits, were introduced in May 1979, they have become an increasingly important instrument for the commercial banks to mobilize savings, particularly from the corporate sector. Gross NCDs issued grew from RM167 million at the end of June 1979 to RM8.629 billion, accounting for 13.7% of total deposits, at the end of June 1989. The domestic banks accounted for the bulk of the gross NCDs issued, with a share of 92.1% at the end of June 1989.

In general, the seven discount houses are the only institutions in the country allowed to accept interest-earning deposits for periods of less than one month from the general public, banks, and nonbank financial institutions. The only restriction pertains to the minimum size of each deposit, which is set at RM50,000. In practice, the discount houses mainly receive deposits "at call" or "overnight," although they also sometimes accept term deposits for a specific time period. Deposits at call may be withdrawn on demand (i.e., on call), provided that a notice of the withdrawal is received by the discount house not later than 11.30 A.M. on the day of the withdrawal. Overnight deposits are only for one day but may be "rolled over" (i.e., redeposited), but the interest rate must be renegotiated at each rollover. Between 1971 and June 1989, deposits placed with the discount houses grew from RM70 million to RM3.474 billion, or at an average annual rate of 25%.

Short-Term Loans (Overdrafts)

Overdrafts are short-term loans with no fixed repayment period, and they are subject to an annual review by the lending institutions. Overdrafts are more suitable for financing trade and working capital, although for the prime customers, the overdraft facilities are often renewed annually and for all practical purposes represent long-term credit. In Malaysia, only the commercial banks are allowed to grant loans in the form of overdrafts. In the 1960s, the bulk of the commercial bank credit was extended as overdrafts and short-term financing for periods of less than one year. For the prime customers, the overdraft facilities were often renewed annually and therefore were as good as long-term credit. But in terms of efficient cash management, the adoption of term lending to finance industrial and business investment and development has advantages over the traditional overdraft arrangement, which may be better for financing trade and working capital. Since the late 1960s, therefore, with the continuing encouragement of the central bank, the commercial banks have stepped up their term lending. As a result, the proportion of overdrafts and short-term financing by the commercial banks has fallen significantly, from 79.2% of total loans at the end of 1969 to 43.8% at the end of June 1989.

The Secondary Market for Short-Term Deposits and Loans

The secondary market in short-term deposits refers to the dealing activities of the banks and other financial institutions among themselves. The hub of activities is the interbank market, where the commercial banks, merchant banks, finance companies, and discount houses trade in short-term funds.

The Interbank Market

The interbank market is basically a "wholesale" market, providing a ready source of funds for financial institutions temporarily short of funds and a ready outlet for institutions with temporary surplus funds. This helps the borrowing institutions meet their various loan and investment commitments and even their minimum statutory reserve and liquidity requirements. The interbank market enables the lending institutions to earn a return on their surplus funds while waiting for a more permanent use of them, for example, loans to corporate customers.

These short-term interbank funds consist of overnight and seven-day money and short-term deposits or loans with maturities of one to six months. The participants are the commercial banks, merchant banks, selected finance companies, discount houses, and the National Mortgage Corporation. Before October 1987, the finance companies were not permitted to participate in the interbank transactions except to place fixed deposits. Since October 1987, however, well-capitalized finance companies (with shareholders' funds of at least RM30 million) were allowed to participate in the interbank market. The borrowings of the finance companies in the interbank market, however, are subject to a limit of RM50 million or the size of their shareholders' funds, whichever is lower. The reason for allowing the finance companies to participate in the interbank money market is to increase the number of participants in the market and thereby to increase the depth and breadth of the market. The reason for limiting the finance companies' borrowing in the interbank market is to ensure that they do not rely too much on this temporary funding vehicle to lend long term.

The discount houses participate in the interbank market mainly by accepting overnight and call money and investing in short-term government papers, BAs, NCDs, and Cagamas bonds. The other financial institutions, such as the Employees Provident Fund and Agricultural Bank, also place funds in the interbank market through their agent banks. In addition, deposits outside the interbank market are also made daily by these three groups of institutions. Apart from placing deposits, companies, public authorities, and other financial institutions also place funds by way of repurchase agreements. Such an agreement is made when a company, a public authority, or a financial institution enters into an agreement with another financial institution to buy money market papers at today's price and simultaneously to sell them for value on a specified future date at a price agreed on today. The agreed-price differential should yield a sufficiently attractive return for the buyer. Such an agreement enables the buyer to lend money for short periods against the security of money market papers and in turn enables the seller to finance with short-term funds an investment in money market papers.

Generally, the lenders in the interbank market are the larger commercial banks, with a wide network of branches throughout the country, which gives them a large deposit base. The borrowers, on the other hand, are the branches of the foreign banks and the smaller domestic banks, which normally do not have a sufficiently large deposit base to fund their loans. Borrowings in the market are also made by banks seeking temporary funds to meet their statutory reserve and the minimum liquidity requirements of the central bank. The interbank market is also an important source of short-term funds for the merchant banks, which are generally net borrowers in the market.

Eight money brokers serve the interbank market, and their role is to match the needs of the lenders and the borrowers. More than 50% of the interbank transactions are made through these brokers. The brokers' fees are reviewed every two years and are negotiated by the associations of banks and finance companies and the brokers' association. Activities in the interbank market are generally influenced by the central bank's monetary policy, especially its decisions to inject or withdraw liquidity from the system. In addition, the interbank market's imposition of an informal limit of a 20% total funding requirement for each bank ensures the orderly development of the market, by preventing undue reliance on the interbank market to fund long-term investments.

Over the last thirty years, the size of the market has expanded rapidly, reflecting, to a large extent, the better management of funds among the banks and the other financial institutions. Banks usually record a higher loan-to-deposit ratio and rely more on the interbank market for any necessary adjustments in their liquidity and reserve positions. The average monthly borrowings in the domestic interbank market rose from RM15 million in 1964 to RM107 million in 1967 and RM9.3 billion in 1985, and subsequently doubled to RM18.6 billion in 1986. The increase in volume during 1986 was due mainly to the active demand for funds by banks in the face of sluggish growth in deposits in the banking system relative to the rapid increase in loans. In addition, speculative pressures stemming from expectations of a sharp currency (ringgit) depreciation further contributed to the sharp increase in short-term borrowings, particularly overnight and seven-day money, in the interbank market. Transactions regarding longer-term money remained relatively stable and declined during the last two months of the year when the liquidity situation improved significantly. As a result, whereas the volume of transactions for overnight and seven-day money more than doubled in 1986, that for one- to four-month money actually fell. In 1987, as the liquidity situation continued to improve and the demand for loans slackened significantly, money market activity was more subdued, with the average monthly volume of funds transacted declining to RM7 billion. Subsequently, in 1988, as the economic recovery and the demand for loans from the banking system gathered momentum, coupled with the entry of well-capitalized finance companies into the interbank market, the monthly volume of interbank transactions rose again to average RM12.6 billion.

Until the end of 1986, placing deposits and borrowing against time predominated because the range of money market papers available was narrow and the market for them was limited. Moreover, the yield of available papers was relatively low. But this situation changed in 1987. A surplus of liquidity in the market during the year led to a sharp decline in the interest rates, which in turn induced the financial institutions and corporations to move some of their funds to higher-yielding money market papers, especially government bonds. During this year, Cagamas bonds were also introduced to give investors a wider range of instruments to structure their investment portfolios.

The interbank market has developed into an important source of short-term funding for the banking institutions. They resort to this method of funding usually during periods of tight liquidity in the interbank money market. Although most of the deals in the interbank market are for overnight money, seven-day money, and deposits for one, two, and three months, funds for maturities of up to six months are not uncommon. In recent years, overnight borrowing accounted for 70% to 80% of the total volume of interbank transactions. The minimum amount for an interbank transaction is RM50,000, but the usual amount per transaction for overnight money is RM5 million or higher, whereas for other maturities, the normal amount is RM1 million. The interest rates in the interbank money market are free to fluctuate in response to market forces.

Over the years, the interbank market has developed to serve the financial community well. Funds in the market, often supplemented by discounting short-term papers and borrowing from banks outside Malaysia, have generally been adequate to meet the industry's needs. The ample supply of funds is apparent in the relative stability of the interbank interest rates, which are determined freely in the market. However, there have been occasions, such as in 1984 and 1986, when the interbank rates rose to double digits, exceeding for a sustained period the commercial banks' prevailing minimum lending rate for their prime customers. For example, in 1984 the seven-day call money rate rose from 7.663% in April to 16.166% in October and then fell to below 9% by year end. These were periods when the money market was very tight, owing to the sharp increase in demand for funds in the presence of speculative pressures in the foreign exchange market, due to expectations of an impending currency (ringgit) depreciation, which never happened.

Apart from the interbank market, the commercial banks and finance companies often place deposits with the merchant banks. The merchant banks, to some extent, depend on these funds to finance their lending activities. In conditions of relatively easy liquidity, the commercial banks and finance companies place significant amounts of funds with the merchant banks, whereas in tighter conditions, these funds are withdrawn and the merchant banks must compete directly for corporate deposits. At the end of June 1989, the deposits of the commercial banks and finance companies with the merchant banks amounted to RM1.379 billion, or 26% of their total deposits with the merchant banks. In addition, the finance companies also place deposits with the commercial banks, which amounted to RM1.309 billion at the end of June 1989.

The Government Securities Market

The government securities market in Malaysia has two parts: the market for treasury bills, consisting of bills with original maturities of one year or less, issued on a discount basis through tenders; and the market for Malaysian government securities (MGS), consisting of coupon issues with maturities of more than one year. Until December 1988, the MGS issues were sold at par on a subscription basis with preannounced coupons. Then, on January 1, 1989, MGS with maturities of up to ten years were issued by auction through the principal dealers. Although government securities have generally longer maturities and represent part of the capital market, we will examine this market here because of its linkage with money market activities. The yield on treasury bills and MGS is one of the factors for determining the interest rate at which the central bank provides credit to the financial institutions. The other two government papers—the Malaysian government investment certificates (which are based on Islamic principles) and the central bank certificates—are issued to meet specific needs and are usually not traded in the secondary market.

Treasury Bills

The government began issuing treasury bills in 1955, and until August 1973, they were made available "on tap"; that is, they were issued on demand. The discount rates of these bills were determined by the government, on the recommendation of the central bank. However, since August 20, 1973, treasury bills have been sold though regular weekly tenders in order to promote greater competition in the market and to encourage a wider range of potential investors. Three series of treasury bills are issued, with maturities of 91, 182, and 364 days. The 91-day bills are offered weekly, the 182-day bills every fortnight, and the 364-day bills every four weeks. Tenders are conducted weekly at the bank, attended by representatives of the bank, the treasury, and the auditor-general's office. There are now twenty-three principal dealers for treasury bills, consisting of nine commercial banks, seven merchant banks, and seven discount houses. The principle dealers underwrite the primary issues, and they are also required to make a secondary market for the treasury bills.

The minimum denomination for a treasury bill is $10,000, and it is issued on a discount basis. Since treasury bills fall under the category of "liquid assets," so that the financial institutions can maintain minimum liquid asset ratios, and since discount houses are required to invest their investable funds in short-term government paper (including treasury bills) and other money market papers, treasury bill rates usually are reflected in the call money rates offered by the discount houses. Because treasury bills are issued by the government and are regarded as risk-free assets, the discount rates are slightly lower than other interest rates on other money market papers. The yield on treasury bills is one of the factors for determining the interest rate at which the central bank provides credit to the financial institutions, including discounting trade bills by financial institutions. The central bank does not preannounce the discount rate, but the commercial banks, finance companies, merchant banks, and discount houses can either rediscount treasury bills and eligible short-term bills or obtain an advance secured by government securities, treasury bills, or other papers eligible for rediscounting at the central bank, such as BAs or any other collateral acceptable to the central bank.

The central bank acts as an agent for the government (through the Ministry of Finance) and manages the issuance and redemption of treasury bills as well as other government papers. The main purchasers of treasury bills are the commercial banks and discount houses, although the finance companies also purchased a significant amount in recent years. The central bank also holds treasury bills, purchased through the discount window, especially in times of tight liquidity in the banking system.

The rediscounting facilities provided by the central bank for treasury bills and the eligibility of treasury bills as liquid assets for satisfying the liquidity requirements of the banking institutions provided strong incentives for these institutions to hold treasury bills. As a result of the legal provisions prescribing minimum holdings of liquid assets, the marked expansion in the banking institutions' deposits has also led to an increase in their holdings of treasury bills and other government securities. The commercial banks' holdings of treasury bills and other government securities, of which treasury bills accounted for a large amount, have risen substantially since 1960. At the end of June 1989, the commercial banks' holdings of treasury bills and other government securities amounted to RM11.243 billion, of which treasury bills accounted for RM2.447 billion, or about 21.8%. The commercial banks have been the largest holders of treasury bills, accounting for 87% of the total outstanding in 1985, followed by discount houses, which held 6% (see Table 5.2). By comparison, the commercial banks' holdings of treasury bills amounted to only RM29 million at the end of 1964 and RM106 million at the end of 1965. Mainly as a result of more purchases by the commercial banks, the total amount of treasury bills outstanding rose sharply from RM113 million at the end of 1960 to RM450 million at the end of 1965 and to RM4.32 billion at the end of June 1989. In order to keep up with the demand for treasury bills, the maximum limit for their issue was raised from RM150 million in March 1955 to M$600 million in June 1965. Later this was raised to RM1 billion in December 1966, RM1.5 billion in September 1971, RM2 billion in August 1975, RM3 billion in September 1977, and to the limit of RM5 billion in October 1987. The Treasury Bill Act (Local), 1946 (Section 2.1) sets the legal ceiling on the amount of outstanding treasury bills that can be issued, currently at RM5 billion. The ceiling generally depends on the fed-

Table 5.2. Distribution by Holder of Treasury Bills Outstanding as of the End of the Year (in RM millions)

	1980	1985	1986	1987	1988	June 1989
Commercial banks	1,202.3	2,441.9	2,384.5	2,755.2	2,533.2	2,446.8
Bank Negara Malaysia	67.4	133.6	0.0	279.9	110.0	188.0
Discount houses	200.5	174.2	594.8	641.5	247.3	1,126.1
Finance companies	9.3	21.0	0.6	268.9	280.8	134.6
Others	10.5	19.3	20.1	54.5	1,148.7	424.5
Total	1,490.0	2,790.0	3,000.0	4,000.0	4,320.0	4,320.0

eral government's short-term financing needs and the market demand for treasury bills. The legal ceilings did not, in the past, restrain the growth of the treasury bill market, since the ceiling could be adjusted upward, depending on the demand (see Table 5.3).

Malaysian Government Securities

The Malaysian government securities (MGS) market is the largest component of the Malaysian capital market in terms of primary funds raised. The share of net funds raised by the public sector in the domestic capital market has generally exceeded 80% of the total net funds raised domestically. This is reflected in the size of the federal government's domestic debt — excluding government-guaranteed debt—which more than doubled from about RM18.6 billion (37% of GNP) at the end of 1980 to RM55.8 billion (65% of GNP) at the end of 1988. The government's domestic debt grew particularly quickly between 1980 and 1982, when budget deficits were large, but it has slowed since then, because of ongoing fiscal adjustments. The size of the government's debt is subject to statutory ceilings, which, however, have been raised from time to time to accommodate the government's borrowing needs. The Loan (Local) Ordinance, 1959 (Section 3.3) specifies the statutory ceiling for the amount of MGS outstanding. The present ceiling is RM90 billion.

Most government securities are held by social security institutions and the banking system, and the distribution of holdings by the various

Table 5.3. Discount Rates on Treasury Bills as of the End of the Year (% per year)

	1980	1985	1986	1987	1988	June 1989
3-month	4.047	4.732	4.125	2.676	3.485	5.419
6-month	4.321	4.954	3.510	2.939	3.617	5.553
12-month	4.458	5.036	4.308	3.109	3.730	5.542

groups of institutions has remained generally unchanged. The Employees' Provident Fund (EPF), the largest savings fund in Malaysia, has been the principal investor in MGS, absorbing 57.3% of the total outstanding securities at the end of June 1989; the banking institutions (commercial banks, finance companies, and merchant banks) held 18%; and the nonbank financial institutions and Petronas, the state-owned petroleum company, held the balance. Among the other institutions, discount houses absorbed 2.2% of the total outstanding, and the smaller savings funds and insurance companies together held 4.6%. Following the sharp increase in domestic financing requirements in the early 1980s, Petronas entered the MGS market for the first time in 1981 and had invested about RM4 billion (6.8% of the total) by the end of June 1989. Part of this investment was funded by converting Petronas's external assets.[3]

The distribution of government securities by their holders is in accord with the portfolio regulations, which require various financial institutions to hold specified percentages of their assets or liabilities in government securities. The EPF is legally required to hold at least 70% of its funds in government securities. Its actual holdings varied from 86% to 90% in recent years, and the share is being brought down to the required minimum through diversification into other, higher-yielding assets. The National Savings Bank (NSB) is required to hold 65% of its assets in government securities, and the insurance companies, 25%.[4] In addition, the commercial banks, merchant banks, and finance companies must hold at least 10% to 17% of their eligible liabilities in specified liquid assets, whose major component is government securities. Other instruments include Cagamas bonds, bankers acceptances with maturities of less than ninety days, and call deposits with discount houses.

Previously, the discount houses were required to invest 75% of their portfolios in government paper, mainly government securities with maturities up to five years. Since June 1990, the discount houses have been free to invest in any eligible paper (MGS, Malaysian treasury bills, central bank certificates, government investment certificates, mortgage bonds, BAs, and NCDs) on the basis of risk-weighted ratios. Given the selective risk weights, however, it is expected that the discount houses will continue, as they have done in the past, to invest a sizable portion of their investable funds in shorter-term government paper, in addition to investing in treasury bills, mortgage bonds, central bank certificates, BAs, and NCDs.

Associated with the captive nature of the market, the rate of return on government securities has been regulated by the government, and until the mid-1980s, was usually lower than yields on comparable nongovernment financial assets. Between 1985 and 1988, the rate of return on government securities was more attractive. Adjustments in coupon rates on MGS have been infrequent, despite substantial fluctuations in market interest rates following the deregulation of interest rates in the banking system.

In regard to the maturity of government debt, most of the new issues are in longer-term maturities. The EPF is effectively permitted to buy only longer maturities because of the political commitment to maintain its annual dividend at 8% or more. Other captive holders would also prefer the higher-yielding, fifteen- to twenty-year maturities, but these are not generally available to them, as they are allocated mainly to the EPF through closed subscription. The remainder of the new debt is in medium-term maturities, to even out the schedule of redemptions.

The secondary market in MGS and treasury bills has, until recently, been thin but is picking up in tandem with the developments in the financial markets. Until recently, the market for government securities was limited to individual institutions obtaining their preferred maturities from other institutions in order to meet liquidity requirements. For example, with most new MGS issues allotted to the EPF, commercial banks would typically buy from the EPF the older issue with a remaining maturity of ten to fifteen years. Commercial banks would generally hold these securities until the remaining maturity reached two or three years and then sell them to discount houses or to the central bank for liquidity purposes. Secondary trading was more active in the short-term papers and was generally influenced by the liquidity position of the MGS holders. Although MGS with a remaining maturity of one year or less made up only a small percentage (2.1% at the end of 1989) of the total MGS outstanding (see Table 5.4), they were, nevertheless, an important element of the money market, both for the central bank to influence liquidity through open market operations and for the financial institutions to discount and alleviate temporary shortages in liquidity. The discount houses, which were required to hold government securities of five years or less, strongly preferred MGS, since their yield was higher than that of treasury bills. This enabled arbitrage in the markets for commercial banks' primary and secondary liquid assets, with very little risk and a generous spread. In practice, therefore, the secondary market activity in coupon issues was concentrated in maturities of under five years (which constituted 18.9% of the total MGS outstanding at the end of 1989), reflecting the regulations governing the discount houses and banks. The thinness of a secondary market in MGS is evident from the limited number of transactions, which averaged about nine hundred per year.

The recent changes in the issue and trading of government securities and the liberalization of the discount houses' activities should lead to significant improvements in the secondary market activities for government securities. The introduction of benchmark issues in 1989 also has this objective. Benchmark issues are meant to have liquidity, as they are issued in sizable amounts (M$1 billion per issue). The principal dealers must provide two-way quotations for these issues at all times. The movement in the prices of the benchmark issues immediately reflects market conditions. As

Table 5.4. Malaysian Government Securities by Remaining Maturity

Remaining Years to Maturity	As of End of					
	1980	1985	1989	1980	1985	1989
	(RM $ millions)			(% of total)		
1	873.9	702.5	1,243.0	5.2	1.9	2.1
2	986.8	878.7	1,552.0	5.9	2.4	2.7
3	330.7	477.5	2,841.0	2.0	1.3	4.9
4	728.0	1,160.4	2,224.0	4.3	3.2	3.8
5	689.0	322.0	3,149.0	4.1	0.9	5.4
6	702.5	343.0	2,250.0	4.2	0.9	3.9
7	428.7	1,571.5	2,100.0	2.6	4.3	3.6
8	694.9	2,028.5	2,228.0	4.1	5.5	3.8
9	1,345.0	1,797.0	2,600.0	8.0	4.9	4.5
10	741.0	1,071.0	4,176.0	4.4	2.9	7.2
11	1,322.0	1,909.0	4,150.0	7.9	5.2	7.1
12	1,990.9	1,048.0	3,100.0	11.9	2.8	5.3
13	1,624.5	1,350.0	3,400.0	9.7	3.7	5.8
14	1,149.0	1,226.0	3,400.0	6.9	3.3	5.8
15	452.0	1,950.0	4,000.0	2.7	5.3	6.9
16	2,800.0	3,350.0	0.0	7.6	5.8	
17	328.0	3,400.0	3,850.0	2.0	9.2	6.6
18	3,400.0	3,850.0	0.0	9.2	6.6	
19	426.0	3,500.0	4,250.0	2.5	9.5	7.3
20	1,950.0	3,350.0	500.0	11.6	9.1	0.9
21	2,500.0	0.0	6.8	0.0		
Total	16,762.9	36,785.1	58,213.0	100.0	100.0	100.0

of 1989, RM2.8 billion of benchmark government securities had been issued, of which RM1.4 billion was for five years and another RM1.4 billion for ten years.

Investment Certificates
Investment certificates, which were introduced in July 1983, are non–interest-bearing instruments issued by the government to enable Bank Islam Malaysia and other institutions to invest their liquid funds according to Islamic principles. The returns are declared by the government on the anniversary date of the certificates' issue. The volume of outstanding investment certificates with original maturities of one, two, and five years increased from RM100 million at the end of 1983 to RM1 billion at the end of June 1989.

Central Bank Certificates
Central bank certificates have been used as a monetary instrument since the end of 1979 to mop up excess liquidity in the system and to rechannel funds to finance new productive investments. So far the certificates have been used to help fund the Malaysian Industrial Development Finance

(MIDF) and the New Investment Fund (NIF). These certificates were issued at par on a subscription basis and carried a coupon rate of interest with maturities ranging from one to five years. The issues were not open to the public but were, instead, placed with selected financial institutions. There was not much trading in this paper in the secondary market. On maturity, they were redeemed at par by the central bank. The volume of the central bank certificates issued is shown in Table 5.5. By the end of 1989, all the central bank certificates had matured.

The Commercial Bills Market

By 1979, the money market had reached a stage at which the supply of treasury bills and other shorter-term government securities was no longer sufficient to meet the growing and diverse needs of the investors. There was, therefore, more interest in buying trade bills, which usually yield a better return than bank deposits, treasury bills, or shorter-dated government securities. However, the secondary market in trade bills did not succeed because of the higher perceived credit risk attached to the bills. As a result, a joint committee of representatives from the central bank, the Association of Commercial Banks, the Association of Finance Companies, the Association of Merchant Banks, and the discount houses was convened to study the feasibility of introducing two new instruments, bankers acceptances and negotiable certificates of deposit, as additional tools for the more effective mobilization of savings and the efficient channeling of funds for productive use. The two new instruments were launched in May 1979.

Bankers Acceptances

A bankers acceptance (BA) is a bill of exchange drawn on and accepted by either a commercial bank or a merchant bank. For the market in Kuala Lumpur, BAs are to be drawn only for short-term trade financing and therefore are limited only to periods of thirty to two hundred days. They are drawn by the importer, exporter, buyer, or supplier who requires financing. BAs are payable in multiples of a thousand ringgit, with a minimum denomination of RM30,000. The yields on BAs are determined by the market and have generally been higher than fixed deposit rates. BA rates are negotiable and are basically a function of the drawer's creditworthiness,

Table 5.5. Volume, Maturity, and Interest Rates of Newly Issued Central Bank Certificates (in millions of RM)

Year	Interest Rate (%)	Volume Issued	Maturity
December 15, 1980	6.5	30	3 years
December 15, 1983	6.5	30	3 years
December 15, 1983	6.5	30	3 years
July 1, 1987	4.4	500	2 years
September 25, 1987	4.0	280	1 year

the quality of collateral provided, and the interest rates prevailing in the country and abroad.

BAs were introduced to provide an additional source of trade financing for businesses. They are used by business enterprises engaged in international and domestic trade and are issued only by commercial banks and merchant banks. Other financial institutions are allowed to trade in BAs, through either rediscounting or repurchase agreements. The main purchasers of BAs are commercial banks, merchant banks, discount houses, corporations, savings and pension funds, finance companies, and individual persons. Most of the transactions in BAs, in the form of rediscounting or repurchase agreements, are carried out directly between the buyer and the seller, although the eight money market brokers help bring buyers and sellers of BAs together.

The development of a secondary market in BAs was supported by the various policies introduced by the central bank since the BAs were launched. First, BAs with a remaining maturity of not more than twenty-one days may be rediscounted with the central bank. Second, banking institutions were allowed to include BAs (up to a maximum of 5% of the institution's eligible liabilities) as liquid assets to satisfy the requirements imposed by the central bank. And third, the portfolio regulations governing the discount houses were amended to allow them to hold BAs and NCDs.

The volume of outstanding BAs increased significantly over the years. At the end of 1979 the total amount of BAs outstanding was only RM825 million. At the end of 1980 this rose to RM1.135 billion and, at the end of September 1986, to RM2.959 billion, indicating the success of this new instrument (see Table 5.6). However, the outstanding volume of BAs issued by the banks has since remained at around that level (RM2.5 billion at the end of June 1989). In particular, the outstanding volume of BAs issued by the merchant banks declined continuously since the last quarter of 1986 when the liquidity situation in the money market improved significantly and the economic recovery gathered momentum. It was also during this time, in mid October, that the pilot test of the Phase II revisions to the Export Credit Refinancing (ECR) scheme was begun, to promote backward linkages in the export industries and to extend the ECR to a wide range of indirect exports. There was, therefore, less need for local suppliers to resort to BA financing.

BAs were also actively discounted and rediscounted in the secondary market and were traded under repurchase agreements. The secondary market BA rates generally reflected the liquidity condition in the money market (see Table 5.7) and were discounted at competitive rates.

The foreign banks, however, were more aggressive and, with their vast international connections with multinationals, were able to charge higher rates that were not necessarily competitive. When the BAs first entered the market, in order to promote public confidence in their use, the central bank provided a last-resort facility for them and imposed a limit on

Table 5.6. Outstanding Volume of Bankers
Acceptances (in millions of RM)

	Commercial Banks	Merchant Banks	Total
1983			
Mar.	1,254.9	538.4	1,793.3
Jun.	1,303.2	557.9	1,861.1
Sep.	1,525.6	675.1	2,200.7
Dec.	1,603.2	677.2	2,280.4
1984			
Mar.	1,642.9	646.2	2,289.1
Jun.	1,641.0	638.6	2,279.6
Sep.	1,785.8	665.0	2,450.8
Dec.	1,593.2	608.8	2,202.0
1985			
Mar.	1,869.6	648.0	2,517.6
Jun.	1,944.2	647.0	2,591.2
Sep.	2,064.3	680.4	2,744.7
Dec.	2,166.5	593.8	2,760.3
1986			
Mar.	2,144.0	626.7	2,770.7
Jun.	2,067.9	544.3	2,612.2
Sep.	2,317.0	641.5	2,958.5
Dec.	1,889.0	560.5	2,449.5
1987			
Mar.	1,402.5	524.2	1,926.7
Jun.	1,806.1	445.1	2,251.2
Sep.	1,853.9	494.7	2,348.6
Dec.	1,784.2	408.9	2,193.1
1988			
Mar.	1,765.7	434.6	2,200.3
Jun.	2,053.9	453.7	2,507.6
Sep.	2,163.1	410.4	2,573.5
Dec.	2,136.5	443.7	2,580.2
1989			
Mar.	1,920.2	212.1	2,132.3
Jun.	2,297.8	241.7	2,539.5

the amount of "own BAs" that each accepting bank could place in the secondary market. Accordingly, whatever was allowed to be circulated in the secondary market was assured of liquidity, that is, of being rediscountable at the Central Bank (subject to a remaining maturity period of not more than twenty-one days and bearing the endorsement of a financial institution other than the accepting bank). By February 1980, the market for BAs had grown significantly, with outstanding BAs amounting to RM957 million, of which RM581 million was circulating in the secondary market. It was clear that public confidence in the use of this instrument had grown. In order that the BAs would not stifle the natural growth of the secondary market, the limit imposed on own BAs was removed completely on May 5,

Table 5.7. Local and Foreign Banks' Rates for Secondary-Market Bankers Acceptances (% per year)

	1-Month	*2-Month*	*3-Month*
1979			
Jun.	4.00/4.00	4.25/4.25	4.50/4.50
Sep.	4.25/4.25	5.00/5.00	5.25/5.25
Dec.	4.25/4.25	5.00/5.00	5.25/5.25
1980			
Mar.	5.00/5.00	5.50/5.50	5.85/5.85
Jun.	6.70/6.80	7.00/7.10	7.50/7.60
Sep.	9.40/9.50	10.5/10.75	10.90/11.00
Dec.	7.90/8.00	8.20/8.35	8.30/8.75
1981			
Mar.	8.00/8.40	8.50/8.70	8.80/9.00
Jun.	8.90/9.00	9.30/9.50	9.60/9.80
Sep.	9.50/10.25	10.70/10.90	11.25/11.50
Dec.	8.50/9.25	9.00/9.50	9.60/9.75
1982			
Mar.	7.90/8.50	8.50/9.50	9.00/9.50
Jun.	7.80/8.50	8.50/9.10	9.00/9.30
Sep.	8.00/8.80	8.50/9.20	9.00/9.30
Dec.	7.60/8.10	8.00/8.30	8.40/8.60
1983			
Mar.	6.90/7.00	7.10/7.20	7.30/7.40
Jun.	8.00/8.10	8.20/8.25	8.30/8.45
Sep.	8.00/8.30	8.20/8.50	8.80/8.90
Dec.	8.90/9.00	9.00/9.10	9.20/9.25
1984			
Mar.	7.60/8.20	7.90/8.30	8.25/8.35
Jun.	8.20/9.30	8.70/9.30	8.90/9.40
Sep.	8.40/9.10	8.70/10.00	10.10/10.20
Dec.	8.40/8.90	8.80/9.10	9.00/9.70
1985			
Mar.	8.40/8.90	9.00/9.30	9.40/10.00
Jun.	8.00/8.50	8.80/9.10	9.20/9.80
Sep.	7.40/7.50	7.75/7.95	8.00/8.20
Dec.	7.50/7.70	7.60/7.80	7.90/8.10
1986			
Mar.	6.80/8.35	8.10/8.50	8.30/8.65
Jun.	7.80/8.30	8.00/8.40	8.50/9.00
Sep.	7.70/8.80	8.75/9.00	9.00/9.20
Dec.	4.80/5.00	5.10/5.75	5.50/6.00
1987			
Mar.	2.10/2.50	2.30/2.70	2.50/2.90
Jun.	2.60/2.80	2.70/2.90	2.80/3.00
Sep.	2.40/2.50	2.50/2.60	2.60/2.70
Dec.	3.00/3.00	3.10/3.10	3.20/3.20
1988			
Mar.	3.35/3.35	3.45/3.45	3.55/3.55
Jun.	3.60/3.60	3.80/3.80	3.90/3.90
Sep.	3.50/3.50	3.60/3.60	3.70/3.70
Dec.	4.20/4.20	4.30/4.30	4.40/4.40
1989			
Mar.	5.30/5.30	5.60/5.60	5.70/5.70
Jun.	5.10/5.10	5.60/5.60	5.70/5.70
Sep.	4.90/4.90	5.00/5.00	5.10/5.10

1980. At the same time, a limit on the number of each accepting bank's BAs in the central bank's portfolio was imposed in order to promote the growth of an active secondary market in BAs.

The central bank's refinancing facilities for BAs are a last resort; that is, they are provided for liquidity purposes and not as a source of continuous funding to support the accepting banks' lending activities. These facilities are a privilege, not a right, as the terms and conditions for access to them are based on monetary policy objectives. The BAs were bought and sold with minimal reliance on the central bank.

Negotiable Certificates of Deposit

A negotiable certificate of deposit (NCD) is a receipt for a time deposit in ringgit placed with a commercial bank. Unlike the receipts for ordinary "fixed deposits," the NCD is negotiable. The name of the depositor is not stated on the NCD, and the issuer pays the principal sum of the deposit to whoever is the bearer of the NCD on the date of maturity. NCDs are issued in multiples of three months to five years, in denominations of RM50,000 to RM1 million. When NCDs were first introduced in May 1979, the minimum denomination was RM100,000, and the maturities ranged from six months to three years. Then, to make the NCDs more popular and encourage secondary trading, the minimum denomination was reduced to RM50,000 in December 1981 and at the same time, the minimum maturity of NCDs was reduced to three months. In June 1988, the maximum maturity was extended to three to five years together, and floating-rate NCDs were introduced.

NCDs were introduced to develop further and improve the efficiency of the money market by offering business enterprises, financial institutions, and individual people greater flexibility in the management of their funds. In order to encourage the holding and trading of NCDs, the portfolio regulation of the discount houses was amended to allow discount houses to invest in NCDs. When NCDs were introduced in May 1979, only commercial banks were authorized to issue them. Eight years later, in February 1987, merchant banks with shareholders' funds of RM30 million or more were also permitted to issue NCDs. In line with merchant banks' wholesale banking activities, these NCDs had to be in denominations of at least RM1 million for corporations and RM250,000 for approved institutions. In addition, those merchant banks allowed to issue NCDs were also required to maintain a higher liquidity ratio of 12.5% (10% for the other merchant banks). More recently, finance companies with shareholders' funds of more than RM30 million were also allowed to issue NCDs. The amount of NCDs that each institution can issue is subject to a limit set by the central bank, based on its capital funds and deposit base (generally not more than three times its capital funds, or 30% of total deposits, whichever is lower).

The buyers of and investors in NCDs are business enterprises, financial institutions (including banking institutions and discount houses), statutory authorities, savings and pension funds, the government, and individual persons. NCDs can be used as collateral for borrowing, but they cannot be rediscounted at the central bank for liquidity purposes. Nevertheless, NCDs have been traded fairly actively in the secondary market and were commonly used as the underlying asset in repurchase agreements (repos) because of their higher liquidity compared with fixed deposits. In addition, NCDs' yields are also generally higher than those of fixed deposits offered by the financial institutions, and NCD rates can be negotiated between the issuer and the buyer. Interest on NCDs with a maturity of one year or less is paid in full at maturity, together with the principal, whereas for NCDs with a maturity greater than one year, interest is paid on each anniversary of the date of issue and on maturity, together with the principal.

As in the case of BAs, the volume of NCDs has grown significantly since their introduction in May 1979. The outstanding amount of NCDs at the end of June 1989 was RM9.146 billion, compared with RM200 million at the end of 1979 and RM931 million at the end of 1980 (see Tables 5.8 and 5.9).

Cagamas Bonds and Floating-Rate Negotiable Certificates of Deposit

In June 1988, two other new instruments were introduced, Cagamas bonds and floating-rate negotiable certificates of deposit (FRNCDs). The aim was to broaden the money market and give Malaysian investors more instruments for their portfolios.

Cagamas Bonds. The National Mortgage Corporation (Cagamas Berhad) was established in December 1986 as an intermediary between the primary lenders of housing loans and the investors of long-term funds. Its Cagamas bonds (mortage bonds) are issued at auction through a system of principal dealers.

The mortgage bonds are in bearer form and can be used by financial institutions to meet their liquidity requirements. In addition, transactions in these bonds are exempt from stamp duties, which made them relatively more attractive than corporate bonds before all stamp duties were abolished in October 1988. These bonds have attractive yields and are of shorter maturities (up to five years), thus filling an important gap in the term structure of available financial assets in the Malaysian market. The mortgage bonds are transacted in the same network of principal dealers for MGS, and their primary issues are offered through auction. The majority of these bondholders now are financial institutions, but the goal is to attract a larger number of corporations and individual persons to hold the bonds.

At the end of June 1989, the Mortgage Corporation had bought RM2.4 billion worth of housing loans from the banking system and the government. To date, it has offered six unsecured bearer bond issues, amounting

Table 5.8. Outstanding Volume of Negotiable
Certificates of Deposit (in millions of RM)

	Commercial Banks	Merchant Banks	Total
1983			
Mar.	2,040.7		2,040.7
Jun.	1,983.9		1,983.9
Sep.	2,651.7		2,651.7
Dec.	3,305.6		3,305.6
1984			
Mar.	3,473.3		3,473.3
Jun.	4,370.4		4,370.4
Sep.	4,581.3		4,581.3
Dec.	4,332.4		4,332.4
1985			
Mar.	4,031.6		4,031.6
Jun.	3,836.0		3,836.0
Sep.	3,351.2		3,351.2
Dec.	5,141.3		5,141.3
1986			
Mar.	4,502.4		4,502.4
Jun.	5,845.1		5,845.1
Sep.	7,397.3		7,397.3
Dec.	6,101.3		6,101.3
1987			
Mar.	3,372.9	146.0	3,518.9
Jun.	5,781.8	255.7	3,518.9
Sep.	5,067.4	343.1	6,037.5
Dec.	7,295.1	355.2	5,410.5
1988			
Mar.	7,484.1	365.9	7,850.0
Jun.	7,946.2	377.3	8,323.5
Sep.	7,493.9	450.2	7,944.1
Dec.	7,599.6	527.3	8,126.9
1989			
Mar.	5,665.6	529.8	6,195.4
Jun.	7,295.1	517.4	7,812.5

to RM2.2 billion (see Table 5.10). The attached coupon rates are market related, and the terms of maturity are from two to five years. Trade in the mortgage bonds, which is conducted through the same set of principal dealers as for MGS, has been encouraging, with the daily turnover averaging between RM40 million and RM50 million. Their success is due mainly to the bonds' attractive features, such as their shorter maturity in line with market preferences, their eligibility as liquid assets for banking institutions, their exemption from the stamp duties that apply to corporate securities, the market-related selling techniques for the primary issue, and the existence of a dealer network.

Table 5.9. Rates of Secondary-Market Negotiable
Certificates of Deposit (% per year)

	1-Month	2-Month	3-Month	6-Month
1987				
Jan.	4.00	4.50	4.75	5.00
Feb.	2.50	3.00	3.20	3.75
Mar.	2.10	2.30	2.50	3.40
Apr.	2.60	2.80	2.85	3.80
May	2.50	2.65	2.75	3.60
Jun.	2.60	2.70	2.80	3.30
Jul.	2.55	2.65	2.70	3.40
Aug.	2.60	2.70	2.75	3.30
Sep.	2.45	2.50	2.60	2.80
Oct.	2.90	2.95	3.05	3.30
Nov.	3.00	3.20	3.35	4.25
Dec	3.30	3.90	3.50	3.90
1988				
Jan.	3.05	3.35	3.35	3.70
Feb.	3.30	3.35	3.45	3.90
Mar.	3.30	3.35	3.40	3.80
Apr.	3.10	3.40	3.50	3.70
May	3.20	3.50	3.50	3.80
Jun.	3.40	3.60	3.70	3.90
Jul.	3.20	3.30	3.50	3.70
Aug.	3.50	3.40	3.60	4.00
Sep.	3.40	3.50	3.60	3.90
Oct.	3.80	3.80	3.90	4.10
Nov.	3.90	3.90	3.90	4.10
Dec.	4.00	4.10	4.20	4.50
1989				
Jan.	5.40	5.60	5.80	5.90
Feb.	5.50	5.70	5.70	5.80
Mar.	5.50	5.70	5.70	5.80
Apr.	5.60	6.70	5.80	5.90
May	5.50	5.60	5.60	5.80
Jun.	5.60	5.70	5.70	5.80
Jul.	5.40	5.50	5.50	5.80
Aug.	5.30	5.40	5.40	5.60
Sep.	5.00	5.20	5.30	5.40

Floating-Rate Negotiable Certificates of Deposit. The floating-rate negotiable certificates of deposit (FRNCDs) were introduced in June 1988.
They have a specified tenure similar to that of the NCDs, but their interest
rates are refixed every three or six months based on the Kuala Lumpur
interbank offered rates (KLIBOR). A special feature of the FRNCDs is the
adjustable rate, which minimizes the interest rate risk for investors while
giving the issuers longer-term funds with shorter-term interest rates.

Repurchase Agreements (Repos)
The repo market came into existence in 1979, soon after the introduction of
BAs and NCDs. Repos were initiated by financial institutions in need of

Table 5.10. Volume, Maturity, Interest Rates, Price, and Yield of Cagamas Bonds

Issue Date	Volume (RM millions)	Interest Rates	Price	Yield	Maturity
Oct. 19, 1987	50	4.5	100.05–100.10	4.43–4.36	2 years
Jan. 20, 1988	300	5.3	102.12–100.20	4.53–4.51	4 years
Oct. 19, 1987	50	5.4	102.36–100.42	4.71–4.69	5 years
Jun. 22, 1988	500	5.4	102.48–100.53	4.77–4.76	5 years
Nov. 29, 1988	400	5.4	102.29–100.33	4.87–4.86	5 years
Feb. 28, 1989	500	6.1	100.28–100.33	6.02–6.00	5 years
Apr. 4, 1989	400	5.7	N.A.	N.A.	3 years

liquidity to fund their operations. They were introduced without much government support, except that repos were not included in the financial institutions' eligible liabilities and were therefore not subject to the statutory reserve and liquidity requirements imposed by the central bank. The definition of eligible liabilities, however, was revised in 1989 to include repos when it became increasingly clear that they were being used as deposit substitutes to mobilize funds.

A repurchase agreement is a short-term deposit or loan backed by a collateral of securities. It involves a borrower who needs short-term funds, ranging from overnight to a few months, and an investor with surplus funds to invest. In a typical repo transaction, a borrower enters into a contract to sell a security and agrees to buy it back at the end of the contracted period at a predetermined price. Even though the borrower sells the asset for a fixed period with an agreement to buy it back when the term expires, the borrower continues to receive interest from the asset. The transactions in repos can be for very short as well as for odd periods, thereby offering flexibility to the financial institutions to structure the maturity periods of their assets and liabilities as they wish.

The instruments commonly used in repo transactions are Malaysian government securities, BAs, and NCDs, although other instruments such as Treasury bills, Cagamas bonds, Malaysian government investment certificates, central bank certificates, and other trade bills have also been transacted. The outstanding volume of repos with the banking system had increased markedly from RM120 million at the end of 1979 to RM7.224 billion by the end of June 1989, or at an average annual rate of 53.9% (see Table 5.11). For the commercial banks for which data on instruments are available, MGS accounted for 45.7% of the total repos outstanding at the end of June 1989, with the balance being in NCDs (27.1%), BAs (21.2%), and other instruments (6%).

The major borrowers of funds through repos are commercial banks, merchant banks, finance companies, and discount houses, although data on repos transacted through discount houses are not readily available. At the

Table 5.11. Total Volume of Repos Outstanding in Banking System (in RM millions)

Year	Commercial Banks					Finance Companies	Merchant Banks	Total
	BAs	NCDs	MGS	Others	Subtotal			
1979	25.5	3.3	9.5	52.0	90.3		29.4	119.7
1980	190.9	6.9	80.1	61.9	339.8		118.5	458.3
1981	233.1	19.3	24.7	125.6	402.7		217.8	620.5
1982	174.7	18.1	4.9	54.1	251.8		433.8	685.6
1983	466.5	269.1	271.0	64.5	1,071.1		737.3	1,808.4
1984	462.6	380.3	924.6	77.4	1,844.9		554.0	2,398.9
1985	669.1	322.0	1,010.6	14.0	2,015.7		800.0	2,815.7
1986	764.5	389.7	1,138.1	37.5	2,329.8	17.7	864.8	3,212.3
1987	1,058.4	745.7	1,473.4	20.3	3,297.8	77.8	888.5	4,264.1
1988	1,247.5	530.6	786.5	2,033.8	4,598.4	814.9	1,017.0	6,430.3
Jun. 1989	1,245.0	1,591.8	2,685.6	355.3	5,877.7	625.2	721.0	7,223.9

end of June 1989, the commercial banks had contributed 81.4% of the total outstanding volume of repos with the banking system. The balance was transacted through the merchant banks (10%) and finance companies (8.6%). The lenders or suppliers of funds in the repo market are business enterprises, financial institutions, individual persons, and the government (including the federal and state governments, statutory autorities, and local governments). At the end of June 1989, for the commercial banks, for which data are available, business enterprises accounted for 73.7% of the repo transactions, financial institutions (11.1%), government (8.6%), and individual persons (6.6%).

The growth of repos has enabled the commercial banks and merchant banks to compete with discount houses in the shortest end of the money market (less than one month maturity) by offering investment opportunities to corporate clients. Although the commercial banks and merchant banks cannot legally accept deposits for less than one month maturity, there is no such restriction in the case of repos. The discount houses responded to this competition by increasing their own volume of repos, mainly on BAs and NCDs. They were dependent on BAs and NCDs for two reasons: (1) Because BAs and NCDs had a higher yield than government papers did, this enabled the discount houses to give a higher yield to the clients in the repo transaction, and (2) because (under the accounting system then) BAs and NCDs sold under repos were taken off their balance sheets, they were able to "hold" more than the 25% allowed under the guidelines for the two papers.

The net effect was that a large part of the transactions in the money market was in the form of repos. Over time, they evolved as a significant deposit substitute in the Malaysian banking community. Nevertheless, repos became a major instrument of the central banks' monetary control only in February 1987. Since late 1986, when the rising volume of excess liquidity in the banking system contributed to the sharp fall in interest rates, the monetary policy shifted to absorbing liquidity and containing the fall in interest rates. For this purpose, the range of monetary policy instruments was expanded to include repos in government securities and the issuance of central bank certificates. (Foreign exchange swaps and the recycled government deposits were allowed to mature and be phased out.) The central bank began selling MGS under repurchase agreements in February 1987 as a technique to offset the buildup of short-term reserves, to contain the downward movement in money market rates, and to create a repo market in MGS. The approximate length of the repos contract (varying from overnight to several weeks) was determined using rough projections of treasury cash flows, foreign exchange transactions, and the movement of currency held by the public. The central bank stood ready to accept repos of specified maturities at preannounced rates. The repos rates quoted by the central bank serve as a lower boundary on short-term money market rates and are fixed flexibly in line with monetary policy considerations.

Private Corporate Bonds
The market for private corporate bonds is currently small, and the extent of trading in this market is quite limited. A total of twelve issues (valued at RM1.2 billion) came to the market between January 1987 and June 1989.

In order to develop an active corporate bond market, the government took a number of steps, including exempting corporate bonds from stamp duties. Among the measures considered for the future are exempting individual holders of corporate bonds from paying income tax on the interest income earned, similar to the exemption given to individual holders of MGS, and lessening the rigorous prospectus requirements for public issues.

To facilitate the orderly development of both the primary and the secondary markets for private debt securities, the central bank published new "Guidelines on the Issue of Private Debt Securities" in December 1988. The guidelines listed the criteria that must be met for issuing private debt securities, including making a viable secondary market in such instruments. These guidelines form the framework for bond financing and have the objective of encouraging companies to raise funds through this channel. Any company wishing to issue bonds must obtain the approval of the central bank.

The Foreign Exchange Market

In Malaysia, all dealings in foreign currency must be conducted through one of the thirty-eight commercial banks or Bank Islam Malaysia, the only authorized dealers in foreign exchange under the Exchange Control Act of 1953. There are, in addition, more than three hundred money

Table 5.12. Volume, Maturity, and Interest Rates of Promissory Notes

Approval Date	Volume (RM millions)	Maturity	Interest Rates	Issuer
Jan. 31, 1987	25	3 years	6.5%	Shell Malaysia
Dec. 16, 1987	200	3 years	6.5%	Sarawak Shell
Apr. 19, 1988	100	3 years	6.9%	MISC
Jun. 27, 1988	100	2 years	0.375 above 6-month KLIBOR + cost of reserve (maximum of 7%)	Pernas
Jul. 28, 1988	100	Revolving period of 5 years	.5% over KLIBOR + cost of liquidity reserves or .5% above individual underwriting bank's BLR, whichever is lower	Esso
Aug. 3, 1988	100	5 years	7%	MISC
Sep. 9, 1988[a]	50	5 years	6.1%	MIDF
Oct. 1, 1988	100	5 years	6.9%	Sarawak Shell
Oct. 3, 1988	19	5 years	7.5%	Lions Plantation
Oct. 8, 1988	50	5 years	6.75%	Sarawak Shell
Oct. 14, 1988	25	3 years	6.5%	Syt. Perumahan
	15	5 years	6.75%	Pegawai Kerajaan
Dec. 23, 1988	10	3 years	6.5%	Perbadanan
	20	4 years	6.75%	Kemajuan Ekonomi
	20	5 years	7%	Negeri Johor
Dec. 28, 1988	140	3 years	At a discount, determined by tender process	Sarawak Shell
	49.2	5 years	8%	General Corporation
Jan. 24, 1989	50	3 years	6.75%	System Televisyen Malaysia Berhad
May 11, 1989	90	3 years	0.375 above 3-month KLIBOR + cost of reserve	Pernas
May 22, 1989	36	5 years	1st—& 0.25%	MISC
	64		2nd—7.5%	
May 31, 1989[b]	100	5 years	At a discount, determined by tender process	Malaysian Mining Corporation
Jun. 1, 1989	50	5 years	7%	Boustead
Jul. 3, 1989	100	3 years	7.3%	System Televisyen
Jul. 4, 1989	90	4 years	7.4%	Malaysia Berhad
Jul. 5, 1989	70	5 years	7.5%	
	60	6 years	7.6%	
Aug. 23, 1989	50	3 years	7.25%	MOCCIS

[a] Bond issue.

[b] Issue date.

changers that are licensed under this act to buy and sell foreign currency notes and coins.

Transactions in foreign exchange among commercial banks form the core of the foreign exchange market. Exchange transactions are made on both "spot" and "forward" bases. Swap transactions in the foreign exchange market—which are spot sales of foreign exchange for ringgit, matched by forward purchases of foreign exchange at a negotiated premium or discount—help facilitate capital flows. The major foreign currency used for swap transactions is the U.S. dollar, and the transactions take place both among commercial banks, which are the only financial institutions eligible for swap transactions, and between the central bank and the commercial banks.

The foreign exchange market in Malaysia was established initially to service the large turnover of foreign trade. It expanded gradually to include corporations remitting profits or dividends abroad, businesspersons making overseas payments for services rendered by enterprises, payments by travelers, and remittances to support overseas education. Except for travelers making transactions in foreign currency notes and coin, all foreign exchange dealings must be conducted through the authorized banks. Exporters must bring foreign currency to a bank in Malaysia to exchange for ringgit within six months in order to comply with the exchange control regulations.

Until June 21, 1973, the transactions of the commercial banks with nonbank customers were made at rates of exchange determined by the Association of Banks for twenty-two foreign currencies. A freely floating Malaysian dollar regime was introduced in the country on June 21, 1973. After that date, exchange rates of foreign currencies against the Malaysian dollar for all amounts were allowed to float in accordance with the dictates of market forces. The other important policy decision that had a significant impact on the foreign exchange market in Malaysia was the termination, on May 8, 1973, of the interchangeability of the Singapore dollar at par with Malaysian currency.

The two major monetary changes in 1973 radically altered the nature and depth of foreign exchange operations in Malaysia. The termination of interchangeability and the decision to float the ringgit opened the way for Malaysia to pursue an independent course in the foreign exchange market, dictated only by its economic conditions and prospects in relation to the rest of the world. The central bank refrains from interfering in basic market forces, and it does not prevent the exchange rate from reflecting the underlying trend in the market. It intervenes in the foreign exchange market only when necessary to even out erratic fluctuations in the value of the ringgit and to maintain orderly market conditions.

The interbank foreign exchange market in Kuala Lumpur has expanded rapidly since 1973. The average monthly volume of foreign exchange business rose from less than RM300 million in the first half of 1973 to about RM600 million in the second half. By 1975, the monthly turnover exceeded RM2 billion and averaged about RM2.6 billion in 1977. In 1987, the average monthly volume was more than RM20.7 billion.

KEY ECONOMIC EVENTS

Structural Adjustment Period

Following two decades of rapid growth in the 1960s and 1970s, the Malaysian economy entered the 1980s marked by sharply falling commodity prices. The Malaysian authorities attempted to stimulate domestic real growth through an aggressive expansion of public spending to support an ambitious program to build up the infrastructure and accelerate industrialization. This policy did contribute to real growth in the early 1980s, but by 1983, it was clear that it could not be sustained over the medium term. Sustaining growth at a time of global sluggishness had its costs in the marked increase in the fiscal deficit and the deteriorating current account in the balance of payments. By the end of 1982, Malaysia was faced with two deficits: a federal budget deficit equivalent to nearly 18% of GNP and a current account deficit equivalent to 14% of GNP, as compared with 7.2% and an insignificant 1.2%, respectively, in 1980. A recourse to external borrowings to prop up sagging government revenues and to finance the large current account deficit led to a significant accumulation of external debt, from RM10 billion in 1980 (19.5% of GNP) to RM24.3 billion (40.7% of GNP) at the end of 1982.

It was clear that by mid-1982, the extremely expansionary fiscal policy stance could not be sustained. Structural adjustment policies were implemented in mid-1982. To control the deficits in the current accounts of the external sector and the budget, public-sector spending, especially on development, was cut by more than RM1 billion a year between 1983 and 1985. In addition, measures to consolidate and rationalize the activities of the nonfinancial public enterprises (NFPEs) were implemented.

The Collapse of Commodity Prices, 1985–86

Commodity prices, which had been on the decline since mid-1984, collapsed in the third quarter of 1985. Total export income fell by 1.6% and 6.2% in 1985 and 1986, respectively. As a result, Malaysia's real GDP contracted by 1% in 1985. At the same time, nominal income declined by 2.9% in 1985 and by another 8% in 1986. The sharp deflation of 1985/86 was the most severe that the Malaysian economy had experienced since the post–Korean War collapse of rubber and tin prices. The consequences of the domestic deflation were that the cash flow of many companies sharply contracted; share prices fell by 60% from their peak in 1984; and in December 1985, the Kuala Lumpur and Singapore Stock Exchange actually closed for a few days because of the failure of a large public company, Pan Electric. Property prices fell by over 30%. The combination of tight liquidity, low inflation, and a sharp decline in share and property prices exposed the financial overcommitments of many entrepreneurs. Their problems were quickly revealed in the balance sheets and profitability of the banking system.

Speculative Runs on Banks and the Failure of the Twenty-four DTCs

In July 1985, the failure of the Overseas Trust Bank (OTB) in Hong Kong led to a spate of rumors regarding a large domestic bank in Malaysia. Although the run was quickly stopped, it was the first time in nearly twenty years that there had been a run in Malaysia. In September 1985, the first deposit-taking institutions failed, causing further depositor anxiety and leading to isolated runs against a number of branches of licensed finance companies. These were quickly stopped, but when commodity prices plunged in the fourth quarter, the failure of a large, public-listed company in Singapore, Pan-Electric, led to the closure for three days of the Kuala Lumpur and Singapore Stock Exchange. There was then a run on a medium-size finance company associated with a businessman with interests in Pan-Electric. This run subsided after liquidity was provided by Bank Negara and an experienced professional was appointed to manage the finance company. Then began a spell of sporadic runs throughout 1986 against the weaker financial institutions, culminating in the failure of the deposit-taking cooperatives in mid-1985, which made the dangers of contagion in the financial system a real possibility.

EFFICIENCY OF THE MONEY MARKET

The money market provides a way for the financial system to economize on the use of cash and other liquid assets. A well-functioning market facilitates the rapid distribution of the financial system's temporary surplus funds to those institutions experiencing liquidity shortages, at the lowest transaction costs, thus reducing the need for recourse to the central bank's facilities. A money market is considered efficient when prices and interest rates of money market instruments correctly reflect available information. The test of efficient markets usually hypothesizes not only that investors' expectations are rational but also that investors know how the economy "really" works and are able to use what they know. Therefore, in an efficient market, in which prices are set competitively, the available information on the asset being traded is fully reflected in current prices, and an investor cannot earn additional profits by following different trading rules or investment strategies. In short, one cannot beat the market.

Deregulation of Loan and Deposit Rates

The one policy measure that has affected the efficiency of the money market most is the deregulation in 1978 of the banks' interest rate determination. Before October 23, 1978, the central bank, in consultation with the commercial banks, determined the minimum rates on loans and advances and the ceiling rates on deposits. The central bank then began to liberalize deposit rates for commercial banks in the early 1970s, by means of the following steps:

1. Fixed deposits with maturities of more than four years, introduced at commercial banks in 1971, carried market-determined interest rates.
2. As of January 1972, ceilings were lifted on the rates of all commercial bank deposits with maturitities of more than one year.
3. The phaseout of the administered interest-rate regime was completed on October 23, 1978, when the commercial banks were allowed to determine their own interest rates on deposits. Under this new regime, the commercial banks were also allowed to determine the minimum lending rates they charged their most creditworthy customers. The objective of the interest-rate deregulations was to increase the responsiveness of bank loan and deposit rates to market forces.

In order to test whether this objective of deregulating interest rates was achieved, we conducted a regression analysis. The research methodology and results are discussed and presented in Appendix 5A. We examined the effectiveness of the interest rate deregulation for the period before October 1978 and following the deregulated regime. The results of the tests indicate that the deregulation of interest rates in 1978 significantly increased the responsiveness of the loan and deposit rates to market forces, that is, to the interbank rate. In each case, the results show that the average lending rate became more responsive to the changes in the average deposit rate after deregulation, which in turn was more responsive to the changes in the interbank rates.

The greater responsiveness of interest rates to market forces facilitated financial flows and trading of money market instruments in the secondary market, thereby promoting greater and more sophisticated financial intermediation and improving the markets' efficiency. Therefore, in our tests of the overall efficiency of the money market, we concentrated on the period after the liberalization in 1978 of commercial banks' interest rates.

Determination of Interbank, Deposit, and Lending Rates

To test for the overall efficiency of the money market, one could test the responsiveness of domestic financial institutions to market conditions in general and to monetary policy in particular, and the extent to which the commercial banks' market power influences interest-rate determination. In an open economy like Malaysia's, domestic interest rates are expected to be significantly influenced by international rates and exchange rate expectations. The immediate impact of foreign disturbances (e.g., changes in international interest rates or exchange rate expectations) or shifts in domestic monetary policy is likely to be felt in the money market. These effects then spread through the system, as individual commercial banks adjust their lending and deposit rates in line with the changes in liquidity, interest rate expectations, and the rate-of-return objective. In an efficient market, the transmission mechanism from the interbank to deposit and the loan markets works fairly rapidly through the system, and the adjustments quickly show up in the interest rates in all markets.

A discussion of the methodology and its results is presented in Appendix 5B. The equations were regressed using quarterly data for 1979–84 and 1979–89:2Q periods. The reason for regressing two separate periods of time series data is to test whether the efficiency of the market had been significantly affected by the recession of 1985/86, with the consequent impact on the financial system.

On the whole, the results indicate that the domestic interbank rates were influenced by the banks' excess liquidity, with international rates playing a significant role. They generally exhibited pronounced seasonal increases in the third quarter, primarily reflecting tightness in liquidity due to the payments of corporate taxes. Bank deposit rates seemed to follow the conditions in the money market, and banks in the aggregate did not seem to have any market power on the deposit side of the market to alter deposit rates, beyond that dictated by money market conditions. There are no indications of market segmentation. Deposit rates generally increased during periods of tight liquidity and declined when liquidity improved. Even between October 1985 and January 1987 when deposit rates of one- to twelve-month maturities were pegged to the two lead banks' rates, banks competed for funds by raising interest rates for longer-term deposits. Lending rates are primarily determined on a cost-plus basis, with some adjustments to reflect the supply of credit in relation to demand. However, the response of both deposit and lending rates to underlying market conditions is sluggish. The results also indicate that the efficiency of the money market was affected by the economic recession of 1985/86. In all the equations, the lagged dependent variable became more significant when the end period of the regression was extended to 1989 from 1984.

The banks' ability to pass on the cost of funds by the full amount to their borrowers suggests that banks do have market power in the loan markets and that they strive to obtain a target rate of return. The degree of concentration in the commercial banking industry, as measured by the Herfindahl–Hirschman index, is high (Table 5.13), and individual commercial banks vary significantly in their total assets and branch network. Although no new banks are allowed to enter the Malaysian financial system and foreign banks are not allowed to expand their branch network, the

Table 5.13. Concentration in the Commercial Banks

	1980	1981	1982	1983	1984	1985	1986	1987	1988	1989
Share of five largest banks in commercial banks' total assets (%)	57.1	56.7	55.9	55.5	52.2	50.2	52.2	54.2	53.2	54.0
Herfindahl concentration index (H)[a]	0.076	0.080	0.082	0.086	0.066	0.061	0.063	0.070	0.070	0.077
Number of banks of equal size producing the same H ratio[b]	13.16	12.50	12.20	11.63	15.15	16.39	15.87	14.29	14.29	12.99

a. Calculated as $H = \sum_{i=1}^{n} \zeta_i^2$, where ζ_i = share of bank i in total assets and n = number of banks.

b. Calculated as $1/H$.

Source: Data provided by Bank Negara Malaysia.

concentration in the banking industry was falling until 1985, as shown in the decline in both the share of the five largest banks and the Herfindahl–Hirschman index (since 1984). Later, it moved up marginally, demonstrating the strength of the larger banks to compete with the weaker ones during recessionary years.

Notwithstanding the high degree of concentration of the commercial banks, the available evidence suggests that the money market in Malaysia functions efficiently. The flow of information through the money market appears to be sufficient, with eight brokers serving as major centers for the dissemination of information on surpluses and deficits. There are no indications of market segmentation, with some surplus banks lending only to a subgroup of institutions. The commercial banks' ratio of cash in total liquid assets and primary assets fell between 1975 and 1985/86 (Table 5.14). The higher ratios in the subsequent years were merely a reflection of higher liquidity in the system and slower expansion in bank credit. Since the commercial banks are the largest component of the financial system, the

Table 5.14. Cash Holdings of Commercial Banks, Merchant Banks, and Finance Companies (%)

Cash Holdings as a Ratio of	As of End of								
	1975	1978	1981	1983	1984	1985	1986	1987	1988
Liquid assets									
Commercial banks	6.46	5.15	5.29	5.38	5.65	5.21	5.45	4.91	5.25
Finance companies	0.34	0.33	1.04	1.24	1.03	1.19	1.73	1.26	1.20
Merchant banks	N.A.	N.A.	1.27	1.46	1.14	1.31	1.08	3.27	1.74
Primary liquid assets									
Commercial banks	10.53	9.34	11.50	10.82	12.31	10.43	9.78	11.30	11.08
Finance companies	0.39	0.36	2.16	2.47	2.05	2.45	3.68	2.41	3.61

decline in their cash holdings since 1975 may be an indication that the money market has become more efficient.

Changes in Yields of Money Market Instruments

A thorough analysis of the efficiency of the money market requires an examination of the market for each instrument, broken down into specific maturities. In an efficient market, in which prices are set competitively, the available information relevant to the asset being traded should be fully reflected in the current prices, and an investor would not be able to earn additional profits by following different trading rules or investment strategies. Therefore, in an efficient market, changes in yields on a particular instrument of specific maturity fluctuate randomly.

The test of efficiency, presented in Appendix 5C, is based on the notion that changes in yields exhibit random behavior in efficient markets, leaving no additional scope for making profits based on anticipated price developments.[5] Therefore, in an efficient market, changes in yields on a particular instrument of specific maturity fluctuate randomly. We applied the standard statistical tests of efficiency—based on this criterion of randomness—to money market rates. We divided the data series into two periods, 1979–84 and 1979–89, since the recession of 1985 had affected the economy severely, and the financial system had undergone a period of disinflation and adjustments. The runs and failures of a few banking institutions as well as the failure of the twenty-four deposit-taking cooperatives (DTCs) also occurred during this period. These events, together with the measures and regulations introduced, affected the efficiency of the money market and therefore warranted our running the tests on two separate time periods. The results suggest that the market for these instruments was generally efficient from 1979 to 1984. However, between 1979 and 1989, the tests indicate that the efficiency of most of the instruments was affected by the economic recession of 1985/86.

CONCLUSIONS

There were significant developments in the money market in Malaysia over the past three decades. The available information suggests that the money market in Malaysia functioned efficiently. The flow of information through the money market appears to be sufficient, with eight brokers serving as major centers for the dissemination of information on surpluses and deficits. There are no indications of market segmentation, in which some surplus banks lend only to a subgroup of institutions. In addition, there was a close link between the deposit rates and the interbank rates (which reflect money market conditions). As a group, commercial banks do not appear to have market power in the deposit market to change deposit rates beyond that dictated by money market conditions. The key money market rates, such as the interbank rates for different maturities and the discount yields on bankers acceptances of different maturities, also moved closely together, with a stable term structure during most of the periods under review.

We also analyzed the efficiency of each money market, by computing the serial correlation coefficients of each instrument's yield movements and testing them for randomness. The results generally indicate that the movements of interbank rates, treasury bill rates, bankers acceptance rates, and U.S. dollar–Malaysian ringgit exchange rates fluctuated randomly between 1979 and 1984. This means that the money market was efficient, leaving no additional scope for making profits based on anticipated price developments. However, in the intervening period of 1985/86 when the Malaysian economy was severely affected by the recession, its financial system underwent a period of disinflation and adjustments, which made the money market less efficient. The runs on a number of banking institutions, together with the failure of the twenty-four DTCs, led to the introduction of some new measures and regulations that while decreasing the efficiency of the money market also made it more stable, as shown in the smaller variances of yields of money market instruments.

POLICY IMPLICATIONS

Although the Malaysian money market functions efficiently, the evidence suggests that further deregulation of the banking institutions would enhance competition and strengthen the linkages among money market rates, deposit rates, and loan rates. In particular, such policies should be directed at liberalizing structural rules, allowing more institutions to participate in the interbank market, and encouraging product innovations and diversification. Because the banking institutions differ widely in terms of size, a policy of encouraging mergers and acquisitions of the banking institutions would also enhance competition and lead to the more active participation of these institutions in the market and, in the process, help build up an efficient and resilient money market.

At the same time, money market efficiency could be further improved by introducing, when appropriate, new institutions and instruments, as the range of money market papers available in the country is still fairly limited. There is also room to improve the conditions under which the financial infrastructure operates. In this regard, the proposal to establish an independently run credit rating agency is timely. It would be an important step toward creating a short-term commercial paper market and permitting highly rated corporations access to cheaper funds. At the same time, it would provide a new outlet for the public to invest their short-term funds.

1. Comprise total deposits, net amounts due to other commercial banks, the finance companies and the merchant banks, negotiable certificates of

deposit, net repurchase agreements (repos), and instruments discounted/rediscounted under repurchase agreements.

2. Liquid assets are defined to comprise cash, money at call with discount houses in Malaysia, federal government treasury bills, and federal and state government securities as well as Cagamas bonds.

3. Risk assets are defined to include all assets other than liquid assets and reserves with Bank Negara Malaysia.

4. The same effect could have been achieved by placing the central bank's own funds in the system, but the basic central banking law did not permit the central bank to do so. The law was subsequently amended in January 1987 to allow such deposits, thereby giving the central bank an additional instrument to manage bank liquidity.

5. The changes in the ceiling required parliamentary approval of amendments to the act.

NOTES

The authors acknowledge the comments made by Phil Wellons and Sam Ouliaris on an earlier version of the study. Their comments were incorporated in the study wherever possible, but they are in no way responsible for any errors or limitations.

1. An exceptional year was 1984, when equity issues by the private sector witnessed a boom, thereby reducing the share of funds raised by the public sector.

2. The EPF had a membership of 5.3 million workers in 1988, or 80% of the total employed labor force. Given the sizable contribution rate—9% of wages by the employee and 11% by the employer—the EPF's total assets grew rapidly, with the total contributors' balances reaching M$35.8 billion in 1988.

3. Petronas was set up under the Petroleum Development Bill of 1974. Under this act, the entire ownership and exclusive rights of exploring and exploiting petroleum in Malaysia are vested in a corporation known as Petroleum Nasional Berhad, or Petronas. In the past, Petronas invested its proceeds in foreign assets. Some of these overseas investments have now been converted to government securities.

4. In 1984, in order to enable the NSB to be more competitive with banks following deregulation, the required share of investment in government paper was lowered from 70% to 65%, and the NSB was also allowed to issue fixed deposits. The required share of insurance companies was raised gradually from 20% to 25% between 1978 and 1982.

5. See P. A. Samuelson, "Proof That Properly Anticipated Prices Fluctuate Randomly," *Industrial Management Review* 6 (Spring 1965): 41–50. Note that randomness is a sufficient but not a necessary condition for this concept of efficiency, because market friction such as transaction costs may prevent earning of additional profits even if prices do not fluctuate randomly. Thus, if prices do not fluctuate randomly, it must be shown that profits can actually be earned before the hypothesis that the market is efficient can be rejected.

REFERENCES

Bank Negara Malaysia. 1978–1988. *Annual Reports*. Kuala Lumpur: Bank Negara Malaysia.

———. 1989. *Money and Banking in Malaysia*. 3rd ed. Kuala Lumpur: Bank Negara Malaysia.

Davidson, R., and J. G. McKinnon. Several Tests for Model Specification in the Presence of Alternative Hypotheses. *Econometrica* 49, 791–83.

Dickey, David A., William R. Bell, and Robert B.

Miller. 1986. "Unit Roots in Time Series Models: Tests and Implications." *American Statistician* 40 (February): 12–26.

Evans, G. B. A., and N. E. Slavin. 1981. "Testing for Unit Roots: 1." *Econometrica* 49: 753–79.

Fuller, Wayne A. 1976. *Introduction to Statistical Time Series,* New York: Wiley.

Lin, S. Y. 1989a. "Malaysia: Developing Securities Markets." Paper presented at the roundtable entitled Innovations in Foreign Financing: Country and Debt Conversion Funds, Venture Capital Funds and Limited Recourse Financing. Stratford-upon-Avon, United Kingdom, June.

————. 1989b. "Malaysia: Issues in Capital Market Development." Paper presented at the Tenth Economic Convention, The Malaysian Economy Beyond 1990: An International and Domestic Perspective. Kuala Lumpur, August.

Phillips, P. C. B. 1987. "Time Series Regression with a Unit Root." *Econometrica* 55 (March): 277–301.

Samuelson, P. A. 1965. "Proof That Properly Anticipated Prices Fluctuate Randomly." *Industrial Management Review* 6 (Spring): 41–50.

Sundararajan, V., R. Vaez-Zadeh, and In-su Kim. 1985. "A Study of Interest Rates in Malaysia: Deregulation, Its Consequences, and Policy Options." Washington, D.C.: International Monetary Fund, Central Banking Department, February.

APPENDIX 5A

REGRESSION ANALYSIS OF INTEREST RATE LIBERALIZATION

We used a direct empirical testing procedure relating the bank deposit rate to a money market interest rate (which is representative of the marginal cost of bank funding and the marginal return on short-term assets) to test the effectiveness of the interest rate deregulation. We chose the interbank interest rate as the most appropriate market rate for this purpose. The deposit rate (R_d) is assumed to be linearly dependent on the current and lagged values of the interbank rate (R_{iB}):

$$R_d = \alpha_1 + D(L) R_{iB} + U_1$$
$$= \alpha_1 + \beta_0 R_{iB} + \beta_1 R_{iB}(-1) + \cdots$$
$$\beta_k R_{iB}(-k) + U_1 \tag{1}$$

where $D(L)$ is a polynomial of degree k in the lag operator (i.e., $L_k R_{iB} = R_{iB}(-K)$) so that

$$D(L) = \beta_0 + \beta_1 L_1 + \beta_2 L_2 + \ldots + \beta_k L^k$$

α_1 and β_i $(i = 0, \ldots, k)$ are parameters, and U_1 is an error term.

The functional form of Equation 1 is assumed to apply to both the administered rate regime before October 1978 and the subsequent deregulated regime. However, the coefficients on the current and lagged interbank rate would be expected to change across regimes if the deregulation in fact altered the responsiveness of the deposit rate to market forces. In particular, the lag distribution would be expected to have a larger weight on the lower-degree terms in $D(L)$ after October 1978. Before the October 1978 regime,

Equation 1 can be viewed as a rate-setting relationship in which the central bank, in consultation with the commercial banks, relied on information about the current and lagged interbank rate to establish the deposit rate.

The average loan rate is assumed to depend on the expected cost of bank funds. This assumption is reasonable, given that funding costs are central to loan pricing, and lending rates should be consistent with the cost of funds. For empirical testing, two alternative specifications, based on marginal and average-cost pricing, were used. For the case of marginal-cost pricing, the average loan rate is related to the money market cost of funds represented by the interbank interest rate. For the average-cost pricing case, the average loan rate is related to the average cost of deposit funds. In either case, the cost variables must reflect the effective cost of bank funds and, therefore, must be adjusted for the statutory reserve holdings that arise from acquiring funds in either the interbank market or the deposit market. The relevant cost variables are the time deposit rate and the interbank rate adjusted for the statutory reserve requirement:

$$R_d = \frac{R_d}{(1-k)}$$

and

$$R_{iB} = \frac{R_{iB}}{(1-k)}$$

where k is the statutory reserve ratio.

The average loan rate (RL) is specified as dependent on a distributed lag, the adjusted time deposit rate (R_d), or a distributed lag of the adjusted interbank rate (R_{iB}). The alternative specifications are as follows:

$$\begin{aligned} RL &= \alpha_2 + D(L)\, R_d + U_2 \\ &= \alpha_2 + \beta_0\, R_d + \beta_1\, R_d(-1) + \ldots + \\ &\quad \beta_p\, R_d(-p) + U_2 \ldots \end{aligned} \tag{2}$$

and

$$\begin{aligned} RL &= \alpha_3 + D(L)\, R_{iB} + U_3 \\ &= \alpha_3 + \beta_0\, R_{iB} + \beta_1\, R_{iB}(-1) + \ldots + \\ &\quad \beta_m\, R_{iB}(-m) + U_3 \ldots \end{aligned} \tag{3}$$

where $D(L)$ in Equations 2 and 3 denote polynomials in the lag operator of degrees p and m, respectively; α_2 and β_i $(i = 0, \ldots, p)$ and α_3 and β_i $(i = 0, \ldots, m)$ are parameters; and U_2 and U_3 are error terms.

Equations 1, 2, and 3 were estimated using quarterly data for the 1971–89:2Q period, resulting in thirty-two sample observations for the 1971:1–1978:4 subsample before deregulation and forty-two observations for the 1979:1–1989:2Q subsample. The regression results for Equation 1 are shown in Table 5A.1, and those of Equations 2 and 3 are given in Table 5A.2.

For each sample period in Equation 1, the estimated optimal lag structure involved three lags on R_{iB} as regressors in the R_d equations. When we used the standard F-test for structural change (i.e., the Chow test), we detected significant parameter changes across regimes. According to the results in (1.2) and (1.3) in Table 5A.1. the responsiveness of R_d to R_{iB} appears to have increased after the liberalization of interest rates, based on a comparison of both the size and the signficance (t-values) of the estimated coefficients on current and lagged R_{iB} in the two regimes.

Estimates of the loan rate equations (Equations 2 and 3) for each sample period are shown in Table 5A.2. In each case, the optimal lag structure was estimated to include two lags on the adjusted deposit rate and three lags on the adjusted interbank rate in the alternative specifications for Equations 2 and 3. For each specification, the Chow test indicated noticeable structural shifts in parameters across regimes. The results for RL regressed on R_d show a larger weight on current R_d after 1978, as seen by comparing (2.2) and (2.3) in Table 5A.2. Similarly, for the RL equations involving R_{iB}, the weight for the current R_{iB} was also larger in the 1979–89:2Q period, as shown in (2.5) and (2.6). This shows that after the liberalization of interest rates, changes in interbank and deposit rates were reflected in the bank-lending rates much faster than they were before the liberalization of interest rates.

The nonnested hypothesis-testing procedures suggested by Davidson and McKinnon (1981) was adopted to determine whether the distributed-lag terms involving R_d were more significant than the distributed lag on R_{iB} in explaining RL. These testing procedures, called J-tests, use separate regressions to test two alternative sets of regressors that are postulated to be possible determinants of the single dependent variable, y. If we denote one of the regression models as the null hypothesis (H_0) and the other model as the alternative hypothesis (H_1), the hypotheses will be

$$H_0: y = X\beta_1 + W\beta_2 + e_1$$

and

$$H_1: y = ZY_1 + WY_2 + e_2$$

where X and Z denote the alternative sets of regressors and W denotes one or more regressors that are common to both hypotheses. In our problem, y is the loan rate, X refers to the current and lagged values of R_d, Z refers to the current and lagged values of R_{iB}, and W includes only the intercept term. The J-test consists of the estimation of a compound model,

$$y = (1 - \alpha)(X\beta_1 + W\beta_2) + y$$

where y is the fitted value of y obtained from estimating H_1, and the examination of the significance of the parameter on y. If it is insignificant, the

Table 5A.1. Determinants of the Time Deposit Rate

	Estimation Period	Intercept	R_{iB}	$R_{iB}(-1)$	$R_{iB}(-2)$	$R_{iB}(-3)$	ϕ	η_1	η_2	D.W.
(1.1)	1971:1–1989:2	3.78	0.12	0.16	0.06	0.05	0.76	0.73	0.35	2.02
		(4.50)	(3.36)	(4.72)	(1.59)	(1.34)				
(1.2)	1971:1–1978:4	4.61	0.06	0.09	0.07	0.04	0.82	0.53	0.34	1.25
		(5.52)	(1.73)	(2.52)	(1.91)	(1.08)				
(1.3)	1979:1–1989:2	3.07	0.16	0.23	0.05	0.04	0.70	0.82	0.43	2.08
		(2.62)	(2.69)	(4.11)	(0.86)	(0.73)				

Note: Dependent variable = weighted average time deposit rate (R_d); R_{iB} = interbank rate.

Absolute values of t-statistics are in parentheses: η_1 is the coefficient of the determination so that the explained sum of squares includes the explanatory contribution of the first-order serial correlation term, $\phi\mu\tau-1$, where ϕ is the estimated first-order serial correlation coefficient and $\mu\tau-1$ is the lagged residual; ϕ_2 denotes the coefficient of determination based on the estimates excluding the explanatory contribution of $\phi\mu\tau-1$.

Table 5A.2. Determination of the Loan Rate Based on Finite Lag, Distribution of the Time Deposit Rate, and Interbank Rate

	Estimation Period	Intercept	R_d	$R_d(-1)$	$R_d(-2)$	R_{iB}	$R_{iB}(-1)$	$R_{iB}(-2)$	$R_{iB}(-3))$	ϕ	RL	D.W.
(2.1)	1971:1–1989:2	6.00	0.33	0.15	0.12					0.90	0.63	1.73
		(9.26)	(6.89)	(3.15)	(2.42)							
(2.2)	1971:1–1978:4	5.59	0.23	0.29	0.07					0.73	0.97	1.22
		(20.22)	(4.91)	(5.14)	(1.63)							
(2.3)	1979:1–1989:2	5.96	0.35	0.13	0.11					0.69	0.75	1.48
		(5.89)	(5.63)	(2.12)	(1.69)							
(2.4)	1971:1–1989:2	8.07				0.07	0.08	0.07	0.04	0.90	0.51	1.38
		(10.23)				(3.29)	(4.14)	(3.85)	(1.75)			
(2.5)	1971:1–1978:4	7.95				0.06	0.05	0.06	0.05	0.88	0.57	0.73
		(16.66)				(4.06)	(3.13)	(3.68)	(3.04)			
(2.6)	1979:1–1989:2	7.71				0.08	0.11	0.07	0.02	0.71	0.73	1.29
		(6.53)				(2.37)	(3.54)	(2.36)	(0.69)			

Note: Dependent variable = average loan rate (*RL*); R_d = time deposit rate; R_{iB} interbank rate; k = reserve requirement; $R_d = R_d/(1-k)$ $R_{iB} = R_{iB}/(1/k)$. See Note for Table 5A.3.

model in H_1 will be rejected against the combined evidence of the data and H_0. The J-test is reversed, resulting in the estimation of the model under H_1, augmented with the fitted value of y under H_0 as an additional regressor, and testing of the significance of the parameter on fitted y. If this parameter is significant, the H_0 hypothesis will not be rejected in favor of H_1. The J-test was derived for situations in which the error terms under each hypothesis are serially uncorrelated. However, the procedure was extended to cover the case of AR(1) errors, which were detected in our regression results in Table 5A.2, under the assumption that the parameters of the AR(1) process are identical for the specifications in H_0 and H_1.

The J-test and reverse J-test results for the loan rate equations are shown in Table 5A.3 for the entire sample period and the subsamples corresponding to the interest rate regimes. In all cases, both hypotheses are not rejected (i.e., significant parameters on fitted y values in both the J-test and the reverse J-test). However, the t-values of all parameters in the reverse J-test turned out to be more significant, leading us to accept H_0 (i.e., the RL specifications involving R_d and its lagged values) and to reject H_1, the RL relationships involving R_{iB} and its lags. The assumption that the AR(1) parameters are identical under H_0 and H_1 weakens the J-test results reported in Table 5A.3. The estimated AR(1) parameters for the two regression models were sufficiently close, however, to give us some confidence in these test results, particularly for the tests involving the 1979–89:2Q estimation period, for which the estimated AR(1) parameters were -0.07 and -0.005 for the models under H_0 and H_1, respectively. Even for the earlier sample period, the estimated AR(1) parameters of 0.40 and 0.32 were sufficiently close to yield some confidence in the tests.

These results support the proposition that the interest rate deregulation in 1978 significantly increased the responsiveness of the loan and deposit rates to market forces, that is, the interbank rate. In each case, the results indicate that the average deposit rate became more responsive to the changes in the interbank rate after deregulation. At the same time, the results also show that RL was more responsive to R_d across regimes.

Table 5A.3. J-Test Results for the Determinants of the Loan Rate

	Test Period	J-Test			Reverse J-Test			Estimate of ϕ	
		Null	Alternative	α	Null	Alternative	α	Under H_0	Under H_1
(3.1)	1971:1–1978:4	H_0	H_1	0.34 (3.57) [0.002]	H_1	H_0	1.02 (24.88) [0.0001]	0.40	0.32
(3.2)	1979:1–1989:2	H_0	H_1	0.90 (14.36) [0.0001]	H_1	H_0	0.98 (16.97) [0.0001]	−0.07	−0.005
(3.3)	1971:1–1989:2	H_0	H_1	0.95 (24.23) [0.0001]	H_1	H_0	1.05 (37.10) [0.0001]	0.06	−0.10

Notes: Null: H_0: $RL = \beta_0 + \beta_1 R_d \times + \beta_2 R_d(-1) + \beta_3 R_d(-2) + \mu\tau$; $\mu\tau = \phi\mu\tau - 1 + e\tau$.

Alternative: H_1: $RL = \gamma_0 + \gamma_1 R_{iB} \times + \gamma_2 R_{iB} \times(-1) + \gamma_3 R_{iB} \times(-2) + \gamma_4 R_{iB} \times(-3) + V\tau$; $V\tau = \phi V\tau - 1 + e\tau$.

α denotes the estimated coefficient on the predicted value from the alternative hypothesis, where this predicted value is entered as an addition variable in the specification of the null hypothesis. Absolute values of t-ratios for the α estimates are in parentheses. Probabilities of type I errors (incorrect rejection of the null hypotheses) are in square brackets.

263

APPENDIX 5B

REGRESSION ANALYSIS OF EFFICIENCY IN THE MONEY MARKET

For empirical testing, we used the following regressions:

1. Determination of interbank rates

$$R_{iB} = a_0 + a_1(R_f + e/e) + a_2 EL + i = 1 a_3 iD_i + u + a_4 R_{iB}(-1)$$

where

R_{iB} = weighted daily average interbank rates for seven-day money

EL = commercial banks' excess liquidity ratio

D = seasonal factors

u = random shocks

$R_{iB}(-1)$ = previous interbank rates, to allow for the partial adjustment of interbank rates to changes in international rates or in the stance of monetary policy

R_f = foreign interest rates (SIBOR three-month rates)

e/e = expected depreciation of exchange rates.

2. Determination of banks' deposit rates

$$R_d = b_0 + t = o\, b_{it}\, R_{iB}\,(-t) + b_2 R_d(-1)$$

where

R_d = weighted average fixed and savings deposit rates

$R_{iB}(t)$ = interbank rate prevailing t periods earlier

$R_d(-1)$ = distributed lag in interbank rates representing expected level of interbank rates.

3. Determination of banks' lending rates

$$RL = C_0 + C_1 R_d + C_2 g_D + C_3 RL(-1)$$

where

RL = average lending rates

R_d = deposit rates

g_D = growth in real deposits to reflect the supply of credit

or

$$ALR = a_0 + a_1 ACF + a_2 SD/D + a_3 FD/D + a_4 G_L$$

where

ALR = commercial banks' average lending rates

ACF = commercial banks' average cost of deposit funds

SD/D = savings deposits' share of total deposits

FD/D = fixed deposits' share of total deposits

G_L = growth in loans at each bank during 1988.

These equations were regressed using quarterly data for the 1979–84 and 1979–89:2Q periods. The reason for regressing two separate periods of time-series data is that the efficiency of the market had been greatly affected by the recession of 1985/86. This had resulted in a sharp and severe disinflation in the financial system, exposing weaknesses in credit and asset management in various financial institutions. In mid-1985, runs on a large domestic bank and a number of branches of licensed finance companies first appeared in Malaysia after a run-free period of nearly twenty years. This was followed by sporadic runs throughout 1986 against the weaker financial institutions, culminating in the failure of the deposit-taking cooperatives (DTCs) in July and August. The financial institutions also began to face the specter of more nonperforming loans and bad and doubtful debts. Later the central bank had to rescue a few ailing banks and finance companies. All these events had led to the introduction of some prudential and solvency regulations that helped stabilize the markets, but at the cost of sacrificing their efficiency. The empirical results of these equations are shown in Tables 5B.1 and 5B.2.

Interbank Rates

The regression results presented in Tables 5B.1 and 5B.2—Equations 1(a) and 1(b)—suggest that domestic interbank rates were influenced by the banks' excess liquidity. They generally exhibited a pronounced seasonable increase in the third quarter, a result of the seasonal tightness in liquidity due to the payment of corporate taxes. The speed at which the interbank rates adjusted to changes in foreign interest rates and in monetary policy (as reflected in excess liquidity) was fairly slow, as is evident from the size of the coefficient of the lagged dependent variable, which is statistically different from zero at 5% significance level.

Table 5B.1. A Model of Interest Rate Determination, 1979–84

1. Interbank rates

(a) $R_{iB} = 3.87 + 0.04\, R_f - 0.39\, \text{EL} + 0.96\, \text{DUM}$
       (2.25) (0.55)   (–3.15)   (1.56)
       $+ 0.54\, D_2 + 1.91\, D_3 + 0.53\, R_{iB}(-1) \ldots (1a)$
       (0.88) (3.17)   (2.83)
       $R^2 = 0.77, H = 1.33$

(b) $R_{iB} = 4.30 + 0.004\, R_f + 0.07\, R_f \text{DUM} - 0.40\, \text{EL}$
       (2.37) (0.05)   (1.45)   (–3.17)
       $+ 0.52\, D_2 + 1.90\, D_3 + 0.57\, R_{iB}(-1) \ldots (1b)$
       (0.82)   (3.09)   (3.08)
       $R^2 = 0.78, H = 1.02$

2. Deposit rates

    $R_d = -0.60 + 0.18\, R_{iB} + 0.21\, R_{iB}(-1) + 0.13\, R_{iB}(-2) +$
      (1.03)   (3.08)   (2.54)   (1.56)
    $0.12\, R_{iB}(-3) - 0.14\, \text{DUM} + 0.47\, R_d(-1)$
    (1.40)   (–0.54)   (2.80)
    $R^2 = 0.96, H = -0.94$

3. Lending rates

(a) $R_L = 0.48 + 0.13\, R_d + 0.03\, g_D + 0.88\, R_L(-1)$
     (0.76)   (2.73) (1.00)   (13.26)
     $R^2 = 0.95, H = -0.20$

(b) $R_L = 0.61 + 0.37\, R_d + 0.03\, g_D + 0.68\, R_L(-1)$
     (1.42) (6.03)   (1.38)   (11.17)
     $R^2 = 0.97, H = -0.32$

Note: R_f = weighted average fixed deposit rates; R_d = weighted average fixed and savings deposit rates.

Table 5B.2. A Model of Interest Rate Determination, 1979–89

1. Interbank rates

(a) $R_{iB} = 2.70 + 0.21\, R_f - 0.46\, \text{EL} + 1.34\, \text{DUM} + 0.68\, D_2$
     (2.00) (3.04)   (–3.53)   (1.83)   (1.40)
     $+ 1.25\, D_3 + 0.42\, R_{iB}(-1)$
     (2.53)   (3.57)
     $R^2 = 0.70, H = 0.74$

(b) $R_{iB} = 4.14 + 0.13\, R_f + 0.12\, R_f \text{DUM} - 0.49\, \text{EL}$
     (3.43) (2.47)   (2.28)   (–3.82)
     $+ 0.59\, D_2 + 1.16\, D_3 + 0.39\, R_{iB}(-1)$
     (1.25)   (2.36)   (3.36)
     $R^2 = 0.72, H = 0.75$

2. Deposit rates

    $R_d = 0.31 + 0.15\, R_{iB} + 0.07\, R_{iB}(-1) - 0.15\, R_{iB}(-2)$
     (1.06) (2.34)   (0.83)   (–1.71)
    $- 0.03\, R_{iB}(-3) - 0.34\, \text{DUM} + 0.95\, R_d(-1)$
    (–0.51)   (–1.87)   (9.87)
    $R^2 = 0.96, H = 0.07$

3. Lending rates

(a) $R_L = 0.72 + 0.15\, R_d + 0.03\, g_D + 0.84\, R_L(-1)$
     (1.65) (4.72) (1.44)   (17.52)
     $R^2 = 0.95, H = 0.21$

(b) $R_L = 0.92 + 0.19\, R_d + 0.01\, g_D + 0.79\, R_L(-1)$
     (2.05) (5.67) (0.70)   (15.72)
     $R^2 = 0.95, H = 0.40$

When the data were extended to 1989:2Q, foreign interest rates (SIBOR three-month rates) became significant in influencing domestic interbank rates. The Malaysian financial system had been affected by the economic recession of 1985/86 and the financial crises involving the failure of the twenty-four DTCs, the runs and failures of a few banks and finance companies, the large buildup of nonperforming loans of financial institutions, and the slow growth of loans. These events affected the depositors' confidence and had a noticeable impact on the banks' performance.

The regression results also show that the domestic interbank rates responded more quickly to foreign interest rates after the banks introduced the BLR system in late 1981. This was evident from the reduction in the standard error when the dummy variable representing the introduction of BLR was entered multiplicatively with foreign interest rates—Equation 1(b) in Tables 5B.1 and 5B.2.

Deposit Rates

The adjustment of deposit rates to changes in money market conditions (represented by the interbank rates) was sluggish. The coefficient for the lagged dependent variable for Equation 2 in Tables 5B.1 and 5B.2 is fairly large and quite different from zero at 5% level for both periods 1979–84 and 1979–June 1989. Only a small percentage of the increase in the expected interbank rate is reflected in the increase in the deposit rate during that quarter, although in the long run the full amount of the increase in interbank rate is shown. The lagged dependent variable is especially large (0.95) when the data series was extended to June 1989. As mentioned earlier, the slowdown in the speed of adjustment reflects mainly the period of recession (1985/86) and subsequent financial crises that affected the performance of the financial system. Deposit rate adjustments in the aggregate were not greatly influenced by the controls on the prime lending rate that prevailed before the BLR system was introduced. This can be seen in the insignificance of the BLR dummy.

Lending Rates

The lending rate is basically determined by the cost of funds (represented by the deposit rate), although the lending rates adjusted very slowly—Equations 3(a) and 3(b) in Tables 5B.1 and 5B.2. Only a small percentage change in the deposit rate was passed on to lending rate within the same quarter, whereas in the long run, the full amount of the increase was reflected in the lending rate.

The relatively sluggish response of deposit and lending rates to market forces probably was a result of imperfections in the deposit and loan markets, the oligopolistic structure of the banking system, and the lead bank system in determining deposit and lending rates.

APPENDIX 5C

SERIAL CORRELATION TEST FOR EFFICIENCY OF SELECTED MONEY MARKET INSTRUMENTS

Before using the serial correlation test for efficiency of money market instrument we tested the data for unit root behavior. Only when the data exhibit nonstationary behavior could we proceed to test for efficiency, using the serial correlation test. We used the Dickey–Fuller test for unit root behavior.

The test estimates an equation of the form

$$y = \alpha + \beta y_{t-1} + i\,\Delta y_{t-1} + e_t$$

To test whether the y process contains a unit root, we must determine whether $\beta = 1$. However, under the null hypothesis that the process generating y contains a unit root, the ratio of the estimated value of β to its standard error does not have the usual t-distribution. The critical values to be used in this case were tabulated by Fuller (1976) (Table 5C.1). The table shows that we were unable to reject the null hypothesis of a unit root for all the money market instruments.

Methodology for Testing Efficiency

The test of randomness in yield movements was based on the serial correlation coefficient of log yield relatives, defined as the logarithm of yield in period $t + 1$ relative to the yield in period t. If yield movements follow a random walk, this correlation coefficient will not be significantly different from zero; we used the log yield relative to eliminate skewness in the yield distribution. Formally, let

Table 5C.1. Dickey–Fuller Unit Root Test for Selected Money
Market Instruments (sample period: January 1979–June 1989)

Instrument	$y_t = \beta_0 + \beta_1 {}_{t-1} + i\,\Delta y_{t-1} + u_t$	
Interbank deposits/loans		
Overnight money	0.9063	−0.6188
7-day call money	0.7549	−1.4168
1-month money	1.0434	0.1824
3-month money	1.1544	0.6709
Treasury bills		
91-day TB		0.6483–1.9253
182-day TB		0.7192–1.8299
364-day TB		0.7680–1.6070
Bankers acceptances		
1-month BA		0.8589–0.9192
2-month BA		0.8350–1.0224
3-month BA		0.8397–1.0092
Foreign exchange rates		
M$/US$ rates	1.0015	0.0243

Notes: This is the *t*-test of the hypothesis that ß=1, and its critical values are from Fuller
(1976). The critical value for the 0.05 level is –3.50 for sample size 50.

$$V_t = \log \frac{y_{t+i}}{y_t}$$

where V_t = log yield relative and y_t = yield at time t.
   The serial correlation is given by

$$\rho = \text{covariance} \ \frac{V_t,\ V_{t+i}}{\text{VAR}(V_t) \cdot \text{VAR}(V_{t+i})}$$

where $\text{VAR}(V_t)$ = variance of V_t.
   Because of the small number of observations, our calculations were
based on time lags of one and two periods only, that is, i = 1,2. The serial
correlation coefficient was calculated for

1. Interbank deposits/loans: Overnight, 7-day, 1-month, and 3-month money,
   using the quarterly daily weighted-average interbank rates for the periods
   1979–84 and 1979–June 1989.
2. Treasury bills: Quarterly auction yields on 91-day, 182-day, and 364-day
   treasury bills for the periods 1974–84 and 1979–June 1989. The appropriate
   analysis should be based on yields in the secondary market, data for which
   are not available. However, the secondary market yields differ from the primary auction yield usually by a small margin of +0.02 percentage point.
3. Bankers acceptances: The quarterly yields on bankers acceptances of 1-
   month, 2-month, and 3-month maturities during the periods June 1979–
   December 1984 and June 1979–June 1989.

4. Foreign exchange rates (US$/RM): The quarterly average U.S. dollar/ Malaysian ringgit exchange rates for the periods 1979–84 and 1979–June 1989.

Empirical Findings for Interbank Deposits and Loans

The serial correlation coefficient estimates for the interbank rates were computed and tabulated (Table 5C.2). During the period 1979–84, in only one case was the correlation coefficient quite different from zero. However, when the period was extended to cover 1979–June 1989, the serial correlation coefficient estimates turned out to be relatively significant. This does not mean that the interbank market is inefficient; rather, the reason was that Malaysia underwent a period of severe structural adjustment that, together with declining commodity prices, resulted in a sharp and severe disinflation in the financial system in 1985/86. Sporadic runs of a few banks and finance companies, culminating in the failure and freeze of twenty-four DTCs, also affected the efficiency of the interbank market. Although the various monetary and regulatory measures introduced during this period stabilized the financial markets, the efficiency of the system was hurt.

To measure the effects of the policy measures on the stability of the interbank rate, given that the interbank rate has a unit root, we calculated the variance of the first difference of the interbank rate and compared the periods before and after the new policy measures were implemented.

In general, the interbank rates stabilized with the implementation of new policy measures and the greater development of the market. In particular, before the unpegging of deposit rates and the averaging of the banking institutions' liquidity requirements on February 1, 1987, the interbank rates were volatile. These measures therefore offered greater flexibility to these institutions in the management of their portfolios. As a result, the efficiency of the market, although it had been hurt, is expected to improve in the long run.

Treasury Bills

We also computed the serial correlation coefficient estimates of Malaysian treasury bill discount rates for two periods, 1979–84 and 1979–June 1989. For the treasury bills market, except for the shorter-term maturity bills of ninety-one days, the correlation coefficient estimates for other maturities

Table 5C.2. Interbank Rates

	1979–84				1979–June 1989			
	Overnight	7-Day	1-Month	3-Month	Overnight	7-Day	1-Month	3-Month
One-period lag	−0.498[a]	−0.316	−0.045	−0.127	0.267	0.206	0.479[a]	0.450[a]
Two-period lag	0.150	0.127	0.371	0.386	0.571[a]	0.531[a]	0.640[a]	0.650[a]

[a] Coefficient is significantly different from zero at 5% level.

Table 5C.3. Variance of the First Difference of the Interbank Rate

	Overnight	*7-Day*	*1-Month*	*3-Month*
December 1984	3.911	0.198	0.457	0.391
December 1985	0.486	0.174	0.261	0.203
December 1986	0.109	0.112	0.033	0.008
March 1987	0.117	0.257	0.025	0.019
June	0.009	0.002	0.002	0.003
September	0.048	0.023	0.001	0.012
December	0.032	0.014	0.016	0.003
March 1988	0.015	0.018	0.004	0.002
June	0.208	0.010	0.005	0.004
September	0.080	0.080	0.022	0.007
December	0.132	0.026	0.013	0.005
March 1989	0.264	0.012	0.010	0.005
June	0.291	0.020	0.010	0.002
September	0.371	0.087	0.010	0.002
December	0.159	0.008	0.002	0.001
March 1990	0.297	0.012	0.008	0.008

turned out to be relatively significant for both periods, mainly reflecting the government's policy limiting the supply of treasury bills in relation to the demand for them by captive holders. Historically, the discount yield on treasury bills fluctuated between 4% and 5% per year. However, the discount yield on Treasury bills fell in 1987 to average between 2% and 3% per year before picking up again toward the end of 1988, reflecting the movements in interest rates and the liquidity situation of the country. With the establishment of the principal dealership network on January 1, 1989, the efficiency of the treasury bills market is expected to improve in the coming years.

Bankers Acceptances

The serial correlation coefficient estimates of the discount yields on bankers acceptances during June 1979–84 and June 1979–June 1989 are shown in Table 5C.5. For the one-period lag, none of the serial correlation

Table 5C.4. Treasury Bill Discount Rates

	1979–84			*1979–June 89*		
	91-Day	*182-Day*	*364-Day*	*91-Day*	*182-Day*	*364-Day*
One-period lag	– 0.344	0.480[a]	0.461[a]	0.191	0.379[a]	0.377[a]
Two-period lag	0.094	0.290	0.656[a]	0.525[a]	0.643[a]	0.654[a]

[a] Coefficient is significantly different from zero at 5% level.

Table 5C.5. Discount Yields on Bankers' Acceptances

	June 1979–84			1979–June 1989		
	1-Month	2-Month	3-Month	1-Month	2-Month	3-Month
One-period lag	0.107	−0.070	−0.032	0.247	0.186	0.225
Two-period lag	0.508[a]	0.391	0.381	0.597[a]	0.571[a]	0.580[a]

[a] Coefficient is significantly different from zero at 5% level.

coefficient estimates is much different from zero, indicating that the BA market is efficient. Historically, the discount yields on BAs and interbank rates of different maturities moved closely together, with a stable term structure during most of the periods under review.

Foreign Exchange Market

We also calculated the serial correlation coefficient estimates of US$/M$ (Table 5C.6). Except for the two-period lag between 1979 and June 1989, the other correlation coefficients are not significantly different from zero, indicating that the changes in US$/RM exchange rates fluctuate randomly. This is an indication that the Malaysian foreign exchange market is efficient and that there is no additional scope for making profits based on anticipated exchange rate movements.

Table 5C.6. Foreign Exchange Markets

	1979–84	1979–June 1989
One-period lag	0.066	0.086
Two-period lag	0.329	0.450[a]

[a] Coefficient is significantly different from zero at 5% level.

CHAPTER 6
MONEY MARKETS IN THE PHILIPPINES

JOSEF T. YAP
MARIO B. LAMBERTE
TEODORO S. UNTALAN
MA. SOCORRO V. ZINGAPAN

In this chapter we relate policies of the central bank to the behavior of the money market. The money market is defined as the short-term financial market for instruments that are close substitutes for money. By convention, only instruments with a maturity of less than sixty days are analyzed, although we present data for instruments with longer maturities.

We analyze four major instruments in the money market: interbank call loans (IBCL), deposit substitutes, commercial paper, and government securities. Deposit substitutes include promissory notes, repurchase agreements (government and private), and certificates of assignment. The relative importance of these instruments in the money market have changed during the period under study (1975 to 1988). The IBCLs became increasingly important, with their use by financial institutions evolving from reserve adjustment to general liability management similar to the use of deposit substitutes. Treasury bills and other government instruments also grew in importance since 1983, as the government began to rely more on domestic borrowings to finance its deficit and to prevent the private accumulation of substitute foreign assets. Likewise, private securities, which generally carried lower interest rates than T-bills did in the mid-1980s, despite being more risky, declined in relative importance.

The government is involved in the money market as a regulatory authority and, since 1983, as a major borrower. Through the central bank, the government started to regulate the market heavily in 1974. Regulation was in the form of capping the interest rates of the IBCLs and deposit substitutes, imposing a transactions tax, prescribing the minimum placement, and placing the nonbank investment institutions under its regulatory purview. The objectives were to instill discipline in the market, which had not been regulated since its inception in the mid-1960s, and to slow the flow of surplus funds into short-term assets, which was considered detrimental to the real sector's performance. The period of heavy regulation lasted until 1981, at which time liberalization policies were introduced. The liberalization period, which still is continuing, features a mix of free-market and administered market policies. The free-market policies are the lifting of all interest rate ceilings, the reduction in minimum placements, and the promotion of universal banking. Administered policies refer to the imposition of higher reserve requirements and other forms of taxation. Meanwhile, the government became involved as a major borrower in the market after 1981, because of the growing instability of its balance-of-payments position.

Originally, we performed a regression analysis of money market variables against the suggested typology of central bank policies, but this yielded unsatisfactory results (PIFS 1988). Instead, we did a qualitative analysis of three measures of operating efficiency: (1) the spread between the price of the funds in the market under study and the reference rate, (2) the liquidity of the market or the range of prices in the market, and (3) the concentration of financial institutions in the market. The last two are indirect measures of efficiency, and the liquidity of the market was also used as an indicator of stability. The reference rate used for the spread, the ninety-one day treasury bill rate, was identified through the unit root test.[1] This test, which we also applied to other alternative rates, was used to determine whether the behavior of a particular market followed a random walk.

Based on our observation of these performance measures, we concluded that the regulations before 1981 produced a less efficient but more stable market. During the liberalization period, the behavior of the money markets was significantly affected by the Dewey Dee crisis in 1981 and the balance-of-payments crisis in 1983, which led to the 1984/85 recession. Since the central bank did not provide data for the money market for 1981, our assessment of the key events is limited to the effect of the balance-of-payments crisis. The central bank's main policy instruments during the crisis were the introduction of the controversial "Jobo" bills which carried artificially high interest rates to arrest capital outflows. The monetary system was stabilized, but at the expense of operating efficiency. Transactions in the money market instruments, excluding treasury bills and interbank call loans, declined rapidly between 1983 and 1985 and have not yet recovered.

OVERVIEW

An overview of the present structure of the Philippine financial system is given in Figure 6.1. Its development can be divided into three phases. During the first phase, 1956 to 1973, ceilings on deposit and lending rates were imposed, and rediscounted loans were provided at concessional rates. This state of affairs did not encourage savings and thus paved the way for the emergence of new financial assets and also new financial institutions outside the purview of the central bank's regulations. In turn, this signaled the beginning of the money market. Because of the attractive yields that these new instruments offered, resources were drawn away from traditional deposits while at the same time increasing the level of savings. Moreover, the existence of the money market instruments eased the central bank's control over the flow of funds into the real sector.

Instead of liberalizing the traditional assets' interest rates, the authorities responded to the rise in money market assets and intermediaries by (1) placing the nonbank financial institutions engaged in short-term lending under its authority, (2) enforcing specialization among various types of financial entities, and (3) imposing interest rate ceilings and taxes on money market transactions. This set of regulations ushered in the next phase in the development of the Philippine financial system, 1974 to 1981.

The regulations imposed during the second phase were an attempt to reverse the flow of funds from short-term instruments to long-term financial assets. This effort, however, was undermined by two factors. First, the financial system was still segmented, which was underscored by the enforced specialization among the financial institutions, and second, there existed a general state of repression which resulted in a mismatch between assets and liabilities in terms of maturity.

In 1981 a financial liberalization program was initiated that featured the removal of interest rate ceilings and the introduction of universal banking (actually a year earlier). The progress of this liberalization scheme was affected by two crises: one in 1981 when a businessman fled the country leaving a debt of billions of pesos, and the other between 1983 and 1985 when the country was plunged into a balance-of-payments crisis. The 1981 crisis served to highlight the reactive nature of the central bank's supervisory function. More recently, the Philippine financial system has been more stable, although it is widely perceived that it functions in an oligopolistic manner, primarily because of the restrictive policies the central bank imposed on bank branching and entry.

In regard to the money market, we came up with the following findings:

1. Deposit substitutes were the most popular instrument until about 1984. They served to increase the commercial banks' resources, as traditional deposits were subject to interest rate ceilings. The popularity of deposit substitutes declined later on as time deposits offered close to market rates and also because government securities carried more attractive rates. In addition, the desire of the commercial banks to avoid the high reserve requirement ratios prompted them to make long-term time deposits, which carried a much lower reserve requirement ratio (5% versus 20%). Another reason for the attractiveness of time deposits was in the form of informal agreements by which the client could terminate the time deposit early without incurring penalties. As a percentage of total domestic liquidity, deposit

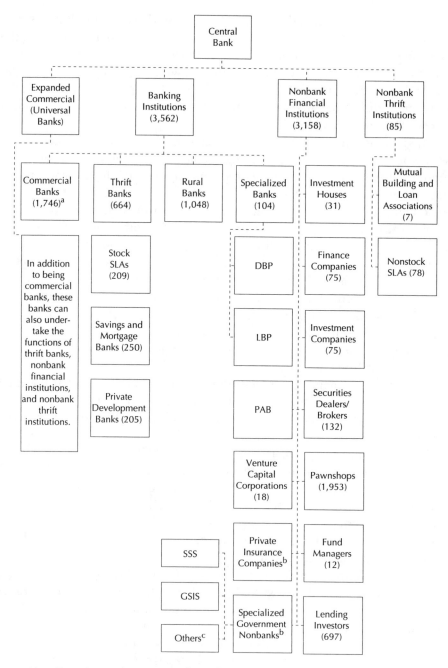

Figure 6.1. The Philippine Financial System

substitutes reached a high of 33% in 1975, but in 1988 this figure was a mere 1.3%.

2. Interbank call loans rose significantly during three periods: in 1979, shortly after the 1981 liberalization program, and shortly after the BOP crisis began in 1983. In the first case, the failure of a major bank caused a liquidity crunch. The second jump was due to a similar liquidity squeeze caused by the Dewey Dee crisis, in which the loss of confidence caused depositors to terminate their deposits early and transfer them to safer banks. The volume of interbank call loans also grew shortly after the BOP crisis, as a result of the increase in the reserve requirement ratio. During the past several years the interbank call loan market has also become a semipermanent source of investable funds for banks.

3. The volume of government securities rose rapidly after the BOP crisis began, because of the government's macroeconomic policy, which we would describe as elitist. For example, the tax policy and exchange rate policy have been conducted so as to benefit the upper-income segment of society.

4. The financial system has displayed a great deal of innovativeness which can be traced to the bankers' "regulation-avoiding" attitude. We suspect, however, that the costs of avoiding central bank regulations have outweighed the benefits. Recently, this behavior has somewhat diminished as a result of the 1981 crisis and also because of the prevailing high interest rates.

5. Based on statistical tests and also some existing practices, we chose the ninety-one-day treasury bill rate as a reference rate. Using this result in our data analysis, we found that there was a trade-off between efficiency and stability.

As for the oligopolistic structure of the financial system, a holistic analysis of the problem would reveal that it is only a reflection of the general state of Philippine society, which is characterized by a highly skewed income distribution. Since the development of the real sector has been hampered by "special privileges," it is no surprise that a similar condition should filter into the financial system. Any solution to the problem should be made part of a more comprehensive liberalization program.

THE PHILIPPINE FINANCIAL SYSTEM

History and Current Developments

The Philippine financial system has grown rapidly in size and variety, albeit at uneven rates, since the establishment of the central bank in 1949. Before this, the system consisted of only seven commercial banks, three savings banks, a government-owned agricultural bank, seven branches of foreign banks, and a small stock exchange. The banking sector since then has evolved into a sophisticated system, and various nonbank financial institutions (NBFIs) such as financing companies and investment houses have appeared. (Figure 6.1 presents the structure of the financial system and the number of financial agencies as of 1988. Tables 6.1 and 6.2 show the total resources of the institutions and their relative importance from 1970 to 1988.)

The banking sector had total assets of P360 billion as of year-end 1988, representing a 63% real growth over its resources in 1970. The sector consists of commercial banks (KBs), thrift banks, rural banks, and specialized government banks. Most of the banking offices are concentrated in the National Capital Region (Metro Manila), as the bank density ratio in this area (9.9) is much higher than the next region of importance (2.3).[2]

The commercial banks form the dominant group in the financial system, consistently accounting for more than 50% of its gross assets over the years. At present, the group is composed of twenty-nine banks, of which nine have expanded commercial banking functions, including the government-owned Philippine National Bank (PNB).[3] Four of these are branches of foreign banks (Citibank N.A., Bank of America, Hongkong and Shanghai Banking Corporation, and Standard Chartered Bank). The PNB is the biggest of the banks, with total assets of P38.8 billion as of 1988, or three times more than the average-size KB. The PNB, along with the Development Bank of the Philippines, underwent a massive rehabilitation in 1986. The program called for the transfer of the PNB's liabilities, amounting to P53 billion, to the national government and its nonperforming assets to the Assets Privatization Trust. The effect of this on the commercial banking structure can clearly be seen, starting in 1986 when PNB's historical share in KB resources of more than 25% dipped to only 14% in 1986 and further to 12% in 1988 (Table 6.3). Apart from the PNB, the next five largest banks (Bank of the Philippine Islands, Far East Bank, Metrobank, Citibank, and Philippine Commercial and Industrial Bank) chalked up 40% of the KBs' total assets in 1988. However, compared with commercial banks in other countries, Philippine banks are among the smallest. As of 1986, the PNB and the BPI ranked only eighty-second and ninety-ninth, respectively, among the largest KBs in Asia (World Bank 1988). Nevertheless, the stickiness of the nominal interest rate for deposits and the fact that entry into the sector has been discouraged by the central bank since 1972 have led to speculation that the KB structure is essentially oligopolistic. Tan points out that the indices of concentration for the commercial banks, excluding the PNB, rose rather quickly from 1982 to 1988 (Tan 1989). The Herfindahl or H index of 0.045 (which means 22.2 equally sized banks comprising the industry) in 1982 increased by 64% to 0.074 in 1988.[4]

Although from the start the banking system has dominated the financial system, other nonbank financial intermediaries (NBFIs) have appeared. The largest of these are the insurance companies, which are in turn dominated by the two government-owned insurance systems, the Social Security System (SSS) and the Government Service Insurance System (GSIS).

Table 6.1. Financial System's Assets as of December 31, 1970, 1975, 1980–88 (in billions of pesos)

	1970	1975	1980	1981	1982	1983	1984	1985	1986	1987	1988
Central bank	6.0	26.0	65.4	71.6	91.7	130.4	206.0	251.6	313.9	325.2	349.9
Banking system	18.8	69.9	193.3	226.6	276.9	330.8	408.1	394.3	289.0	313.2	360.1
Commercial banks	14.1	53.2	144.1	168.9	205.3	248.2	303.5	285.7	236.5	259.8	299.3
Private	8.3	35.1	84.0	100.5	118.0	134.7	167.2	165.7	164.4	179.4	224.6
Government	4.6	18.1	41.4	47.6	60.7	73.1	89.5	76.1	35.0	31.3	38.8
Foreign	1.2	—	18.7	20.8	26.6	40.4	46.8	43.9	37.1	49.1	35.9
Thrift banks	0.9	2.1	10.6	9.7	12.6	16.1	15.0	15.1	17.6	19.5	24.9
Savings and mortgage banks	0.7	1.4	7.4	5.0	5.9	7.4	7.6	6.8	8.1	10.6	14.2
Private development banks	0.2	0.4	1.6	2.6	3.7	4.6	4.6	5.1	5.6	5.4	6.7
Stock savings and loan associations	—	0.3	1.6	2.1	3.0	4.1	2.8	3.2	3.9	3.5	4.0
Rural banks	0.7	2.8	5.5	6.5	8.0	9.3	8.8	8.6	9.1	9.7	10.7
Specialized government banks	3.1	11.8	33.1	41.5	51.0	57.2	80.8	84.9	25.8[a]	24.2[a]	25.2
Nonbank financial intermediaries	6.1	26.8	60.3	62.0	73.6	91.3	97.7	105.6	111.8	119.2	132.8
Insurance companies	5.9	11.9	29.5	33.3	40.7	44.6	50.0	60.8	70.8	79.2	90.9
Government[b]	4.0	7.7	19.5	22.0	27.0	30.9	35.9	42.7	50.5	53.8	61.2
Private	1.9	4.2	10.0	11.3	13.7	13.7	14.1	18.1	20.3	25.4	29.7
Investment institutions	0.0	10.3	25.5	23.5	25.6	28.9	27.3	23.8	23.3	20.8	21.4
Financing companies	3.5	11.9	12.1	12.9	11.8	9.6	6.2	5.6	7.0	7.4	
Investment companies	2.0	5.0	5.5	5.9	9.9	10.2	11.0	10.2	4.8	5.6	
Investment houses	4.8	8.6	5.9	6.8	7.2	7.5	6.6	7.5	9.0	8.4	
Trust operations (fund managers)	2.6	1.7	0.8	1.1	1.5	1.9	1.6	1.3	1.6	1.8	
Other financial intermediaries	0.2	2.0	3.6	4.4	6.2	16.3	18.5	19.4	16.4	17.6	18.7
Total	30.9	122.7	319.0	360.2	442.2	552.5	711.8	751.5	714.7	757.6	842.8
Percentage of GNP	75.7	107.3	120.6	118.6	131.8	145.9	135.0	125.7	116.3	107.7	102.4
Total without CB	24.9	96.7	253.6	288.6	350.5	422.1	505.8	499.9	400.8	432.4	492.9
Percentage of GNP	61.0	84.5	95.9	95.1	104.5	111.5	95.9	83.6	65.2	63.0	60.8
Memo Item: GNP	40.8	114.4	264.5	303.6	335.4	378.7	527.4	597.7	614.7	703.4	822.7

[a] After transfer of certain assets and liabilities to the government.

[b] GSIS and SSS.

Sources: World Bank Report (1988) for data on insurance companies from 1970 to 1986; *Philippine Financial Fact Book* (1988); Insurance Commission for data on insurance companies in 1987 and 1988; Government Corporate Monitoring and Coordinating Committee for assets of SSS and GSIS in 1988.

Table 6.2. Distribution of Financial System's Assets (excluding central bank) as of December 31, 1970, 1975, 1980–88 (percent)

	1970	1975	1980	1981	1982	1983	1984	1985	1986	1987	1988
Banking system	75.5	72.3	76.2	78.5	79.0	78.4	80.7	78.9	72.1	72.4	73.1
Commercial banks	56.6	55.0	56.8	58.5	58.6	58.8	60.0	57.2	59.0	60.1	60.7
Private	33.3	36.3	33.1	34.8	33.7	31.9	33.1	33.1	41.0	41.5	45.6
Government	18.5	18.7	16.3	16.5	17.3	17.3	17.7	15.2	8.7	7.2	7.9
Foreign	4.8	—	7.4	7.2	7.6	9.6	9.3	8.8	9.3	11.4	7.3
Thrift banks	3.6	2.2	4.2	3.4	3.6	3.8	3.0	3.0	4.4	4.5	5.1
Savings and mortgage banks	2.8	1.4	2.9	1.7	1.7	1.8	1.5	1.4	2.0	2.5	2.9
Private development banks	0.8	0.4	0.6	0.9	1.1	1.1	0.9	1.0	1.4	1.2	1.4
Stock savings and loan associations	—	0.3	0.6	0.7	0.9	1.0	0.6	0.6	1.0	0.8	0.8
Rural banks	2.8	2.9	2.2	2.3	2.3	2.2	1.7	1.7	2.3	2.2	2.1
Specialized government banks	12.4	12.2	13.1	14.4	14.6	13.6	16.0	17.0	6.4[a]	5.6[a]	5.1
Nonbank financial intermediaries	24.5	27.7	23.8	21.5	21.0	21.6	19.3	21.1	27.9	27.6	26.9
Insurance companies	23.7	12.3	11.6	11.5	11.6	10.6	9.9	12.2	17.7	18.3	18.4
Government[b]	16.1	8.0	7.7	7.6	7.7	7.3	7.1	8.5	12.6	12.4	12.0
Private	7.6	4.3	3.9	3.9	3.9	3.2	2.8	3.6	5.1	5.9	6.0
Investment institutions	—	10.7	10.1	8.1	7.3	6.8	5.4	4.8	5.8	4.8	4.3
Financing companies	—	3.6	4.7	4.2	3.7	2.8	1.9	1.2	1.4	1.6	1.5
Investment companies	—	2.1	2.0	1.9	1.7	2.3	2.0	2.2	2.5	1.1	1.1
Investment houses	—	5.0	3.4	2.0	1.9	1.7	1.5	1.3	1.9	2.0	1.7
Trust operations (fund managers)	—	2.7	0.7	0.3	0.3	0.4	0.4	0.3	0.3	0.4	0.4
Other financial intermediaries	0.8	2.1	1.4	1.5	1.8	3.9	3.7	3.9	4.1	4.1	3.8
Total without CB	100.0	100.0	100.0	100.0	100.0	100.0	100.0	100.0	100.0	100.0	100.0

[a] After transfer of certain assets and liabilities to the government.
[b] GSIS and SSS.

The former was the country's largest financial institution as of 1988, with its assets accounting for around 9% of the financial system's gross assets. However, the insurance sector has declined in importance during the past two decades: Its share in the total financial system's assets of 23.7% in 1970 dropped to 11.7% in 1980 and reached only 18.4% in 1988.

Investment institutions such as investment companies, investment houses, and financing companies as well as trust operations (fund managers) were formed in the mid-1960s through the 1970s. Their importance in the 1980s declined, however, as a result primarily of the Dewey Dee crisis in 1981, which triggered a loss of confidence in the short-term funds markets and, in the process, precipitated the downfall of several finance companies and investment houses, including the nation's two largest investment houses (Atrium Capital Corporation and Bancom). The number of investment institutions licensed to engage in quasi-banking functions (i.e., to issue deposit substitutes) had been trimmed from twenty-six in 1980 to thirteen as of year-end 1989. Likewise, as of 1988, investment institutions accounted for a mere 4.3% of the financial system's total assets, compared with their share of 10.7% in 1975. Similarly, smaller NBFIs such as pawnshops, lending investors, venture capital corporations, and nonbank thrift institutions have not sustained their phenomenal growth in 1983 and are now relatively unimportant.

A noteworthy characteristic of the Philippine financial system is the prevalence of interlocking directorates, that is, the simultaneous holding of a position on the board of directors of several financial as well as nonfinancial institutions. This is a feature that is implicitly encouraged by the universal banking law; that is, universal banks are permitted to make equity investments in allied and nonallied financial institutions (see note 3). The purpose of the policy is ostensibly to reduce the fragmentation of financial intermediaries, to increase competition and economies of scale in order to make the financial system more efficient. But in the money markets, such interlocking with investment institutions increases the relative importance of certain banks and consequently makes these (money markets) less diversified. For example, as of year-end 1988, four commercial banks (Metrobank, Citytrust, Citibank, and BPI) directly accounted for only 13.32% of the total deposit substitutes of all financial institutions with quasi-banking licenses (Table 6.4). Their affiliates' total share of 34.73% clearly underscores the effect of interlocking directorates on the concentration of these markets.

Policy Framework, 1956–Present

The Philippines' financial institutions (FIs) (except the insurance companies, which are supervised by the Philippine Insurance Commission) are regulated by the central bank. Although the policies are set by the Monetary Board via circulars and memoranda, the Supervision and Examina-

Table 6.3. Commercial Banking System's Assets, as of Year-Ends 1980, 1985–88

Commercial Bank (KB)	1980 Millions of Pesos	1980 Percent Share	1985 Millions of Pesos	1985 Percent Share	1986 Millions of Pesos	1986 Percent Share	1987 Millions of Pesos	1987 Percent Share	1988 Millions of Pesos	1988 Percent Share
Universal banks	79,204	54.85	178,042	62.31	136,885	57.88	142,488	54.83	180,467	60.31
Government										
PNB	38,652	26.77	76,157	26.65	35,022	14.81	31,268	12.03	38,758	12.95
Private	40,552	28.08	101,885	35.66	101,863	43.07	111,220	42.80	141,709	47.36
Allied	7,257	5.03	9,131	3.20	6,672	2.82	7,290	2.81	9,470	3.16
BPI	6,442	4.47	16,201	5.67	18,333	7.75	20,662	7.95	26,280	8.78
Citytrust	1,482	1.03	5,124	1.79	5,663	2.39	6,867	2.64	8,098	2.71
Equitable	2,890	2.01	4,069	1.42	5,632	2.38	6,826	2.63	8,190	2.74
FEBTC	4,345	3.02	12,490	4.37	15,430	6.52	19,246	7.41	28,093	9.39
Metro	5,506	3.82	16,368	5.73	15,943	6.74	19,202	7.39	25,729	8.60
PCIB	4,781	3.32	16,510	5.78	14,269	6.03	17,151	6.60	19,676	6.58
UCPB	4,645	3.22	13,898	4.86	10,564	4.47	13,976	5.38	16,173	5.40
Manila Bank[a]	3,204	2.22	8,094	2.83	9,357	3.96				
Other domestic KBs	46,469	32.18	63,774	22.32	62,501	26.43	68,224	26.25	82,848	27.69
Government										
Veterans[b]	2,745	1.90								
Private	43,724	30.28	63,774	22.32	62,501	26.43	68,224	26.25	82,848	27.69
Associated	1,624	1.13	2,583	0.90	2,623	1.11	2,509	0.97	2,518	0.84
Boston (ex Combank)	2,413	1.49	1,944	0.68	1,900	0.80	1,751	0.67	2,150	0.72
China	3,542	2.46	4,684	1.64	4,518	1.91	5,097	1.96	6,015	2.01
Interbank	1,641	1.14	5,491	1.92	4,225	1.79	5,208	2.00	7,274	2.43

PBCom	2,744	1.90	3,157	1.10	2,889	1.22	3,551	1.37	5,010	1.67
Philbanking	2,204	1.53	2,735	0.96	3,290	1.39	3,482	1.34	3,699	1.24
Philtrust	917	0.64	2,335	0.82	2,672	1.13	3,035	1.17	3,938	1.32
Pilipinas	1,054	0.73	1,738	0.61	1,632	0.69	1,596	0.61	1,425	0.48
Producers	1,417	0.98	2,618	0.92	2,619	1.11	2,778	1.07	3,121	1.04
Prudential	2,178	1.51	4,878	1.71	5,672	2.40	6,255	2.41	7,879	2.63
Republic Planters	4,880	3.39	5,928	2.07	5,732	2.42	6,330	2.44	7,604	2.54
RCBC	3,720	2.58	5,492	1.92	6,430	2.72	8,221	3.16	11,169	3.73
Security	2,587	1.79	6,030	2.11	4,657	1.97	4,811	1.85	4,666	1.56
Solidbank (ex Consolidated)	2,979	2.07	5,368	1.88	6,501	2.75	6,596	2.54	8,837	2.95
Traders	3,758	2.61	4,825	1.69	3,724	1.57	3,408	1.31	3,853	1.29
Union	3,968	1.39	3,417	1.44	3,596	1.38	3,690	1.23		
IBAA[c]	2,721	1.89								
Pacific[b]	3,345	2.32								
Foreign bank branches	18,730	12.97	43,902	15.37	37,096	15.69	49,154	18.92	35,912	12.00
Bank of America	3,602	2.50	11,439	4.00	10,176	4.30	12,793	4.92	8,868	2.96
Std. Chartered	865	0.60	2,602	0.91	2,382	1.01	3,414	1.31	2,843	0.95
Citibank	12,637	8.77	26,382	9.23	20,985	8.87	27,801	10.70	19,916	6.66
Hongkong-Shanghai	1,626	1.13	3,479	1.22	3,553	1.50	5,146	1.98	4,285	1.43
Total	144,403	100.00	285,718	100.00	236,482	100.00	259,866	100.00	299,227	100.00

[a] Closed in 1987.

[b] Closed in 1985.

[c] Absorbed by PCIB in December 1985.

Source: PNB Annual Report on the Commercial Banking System, various years.

tion Sector of the central bank acts as the operational arm for supervision purposes.

The Monetary Board is composed of the central bank's governor as chairman, five representatives of the national government (the secretaries of the Departments of Finance, and Budget and Management; the chairman of the Board of Investments, who is concurrently the secretary of the Department of Trade and Industry; and the director-general of the National Economic and Development Authority), and two representatives of the private sector who are appointed by the president. The preponderance of national government representatives on the board has been rationalized by the need for effective coordination among the economic, financial, and fiscal policies of the government and the monetary, credit, and exchange policies of the central bank.[5] Thus, all central bank policies are, in essence, formulated in consultation with the heads of the economic agencies.

The central banks' regulations of FIs include (1) asset creation (e.g.,

Table 6.4. Share of Top Three Conglomerations in Total Money Market Balances of Banks and NBQBs as of Year-end 1988

	Percent Share	
Conglomeration	Deposit Substitutes [a]	Trading Account Securities [b]
Metrobank[c]	0.01	11.09
First Metro Investment Corp.[d]	29.29	3.83
Subtotal	29.30	14.92
Citytrust[c]	0.03	1.68
Citibank	9.97	4.62
Citytrust Investment Phil., Inc.[d]	0.36	0.05
Citytrust Finance Corp.[e]	0.58	0.00
Subtotal	10.94	6.35
Bank of the Philippine Islands[c]	3.31	6.09
AEA Development Corp.[d]	1.04	0.34
BPI Credit Corp.[e]	2.57	0.17
BPI Family Savings[f]	—	0.89
Subtotal	6.92	7.49

[a] Deposit substitutes are borrowings from the money markets in the form of promissory notes, certificates of participation assignments, and repurchase agreements.

[b] Trading account securities include government and private securities and commercial papers purchased for money market trading.

[c] Universal banks.

[d] Investment houses.

[e] Finance companies.

[f] Thrift bank.

Source: Published financial statements; *Philippine Financial Fact Book* (1988).

single borrower's limit, lending for agricultural and agrarian reform, DOSRI [directors, officers, stockholders, and related interests] accounts), (2) liability creation (e.g., type of deposits, borrowings from CB); and (3) equity (e.g., minimum equity). However, the crises that struck the financial system, especially those originating in the money markets in 1981, demonstrated the central bank's generally slow reaction to practices that disregarded its rules and regulations. Lamberte states that the central bank's measures regarding money market transactions such as the prohibition against the attachment of postdated checks to "without recourse" transactions came in too late, after the money market already collapsed (Lamberte 1989).[6]

In addition to the central bank, the Securities and Exchange Commission acts as the principal supervisory body for the securities market. Its Money Market Operations Department oversees the registration of short- and long-term commercial papers, financing companies, and investment houses. Although the SEC's regulations are aimed at "investors' protection," it does not judge the worth of the securities or the issuing companies. "Investors' protection" is mainly requiring the issuers to submit certain information for dissemination to prospective investors. The central bank and the SEC coordinate their formulation and implementation of policies affecting commercial papers. For instance, the rules of registration for commercial papers were approved first by the Monetary Board's chairman before they were promulgated by the SEC. Also, all applications for a certificate of authority to open a branch, an extension office, or an agency with quasi-banking functions are filed with the SEC, which refer them to the central bank's Department of Financial Intermediaries for comments and recommendation. The cental bank's recommendations are generally based on the applicant's compliance with its laws, rules, and regulations such as capital adequacy and solvency, profitability, and liquidity position.

Information on the creditworthiness of borrowers in the financial markets is augmented by the Credit Information Bureau, Inc. (CIBI), which was established by the central bank after the 1981 crisis to coordinate information on all issuers of commercial papers. As of 1988, it has collected data, such as outstanding loans, on some 25,000 companies and 6,000 individual persons, most of which are used by commercial banks.

Notwithstanding the sophistication of the Philippine financial system, it remains one of the least developed vis-à-vis its neighboring Asian economies. The highest ratio of M2 to GNP, 27.5%, was recorded in 1967 but has never been duplicated or approached since, even during the financial liberalization starting in 1981 (Table 6.5). The same ratio was merely 22% in 1987, in contrast with the 31% of Indonesia (Table 6.6). Malaysia and Thailand have much higher intermediation levels. Almost all studies of this phenomenon agree that the Philippine government's repression of asset prices in the intermediation markets as well as its subsidized equity

Table 6.5. Financial Development Indicators, 1956–88 (percent)

	M2 GNP[a]	M3 GNP[b]	Savings Deposits	Time Deposits	Secured Loans (61–90 days)	91-Day T-Bills	Deposit Substitutes

I. Period of managed interest rates of traditional assets with de facto free-market forces operating in money markets, 1956–73

	M2 GNP[a]	M3 GNP[b]	Savings Deposits	Time Deposits	Secured Loans (61–90 days)	91-Day T-Bills	Deposit Substitutes
1956	19.4	19.4	2.0	2.5	12.0		
1957	19.4	19.4	3.0	3.5	12.0		
1958	20.4	20.4	3.0	3.5	12.0		
1959	20.5	20.5	3.0	3.5	12.0		
1960	20.4	20.4	3.0	4.0	12.0		
1961	23.5	23.5	3.0	4.0	12.0		
1962	25.1	25.1	3.0	4.0	12.0		
1963	26.0	26.0	3.5	4.5	12.0		
1964	24.1	24.1	4.0	5.0	12.0		
1965	23.4	23.4	5.8	6.5	12.0		
1966	24.8	24.8	5.8	6.5	12.0	6.5[c]	
1967	27.5	27.5	5.8	6.0	12.0	6.4[c]	
1968	25.7	25.7	5.8	6.0	12.0	6.7[c]	
1969	26.2	26.2	6.0	7.0	12.0	8.1[c]	
1970	23.0	23.0	6.0	7.0	12.0	13.1	
1971	21.2	21.2	6.0	7.0	12.0	11.9	13.30
1972	21.2	21.2	6.0	7.0	12.0	11.9	13.90
1973	19.4	25.0	6.0	7.0	12.0	9.4	9.40
Average	22.8	23.2					

II. Period of rising but managed interest rates in all markets

	M2 GNP[a]	M3 GNP[b]	Savings Deposits	Time Deposits	Secured Loans (61–90 days)	91-Day T-Bills	Deposit Substitutes
1974	16.8	24.3	6.0	9.5	12.0	10.0	31.8
1975	16.8	25.2	6.0	9.5	12.0	10.3	13.8[d]
1976	18.6	26.8	7.0	10.0	12.0	10.2	13.1[d]
1977	21.2	28.7	7.0	10.0	12.0	10.9	12.5[d]
1978	22.8	29.3	9.0	10.0	14.0	10.9	10.6[d]
1979	20.8	26.3	9.0	12.0	14.0	12.2	12.0[d]
1980	21.0	25.6	9.0	14.0	14.0	12.1	12.2[d]
Average	19.7	26.6					

III. Liberalization period

	M2 GNP[a]	M3 GNP[b]	Savings Deposits	Time Deposits	Secured Loans (61–90 days)	91-Day T-Bills	Deposit Substitutes
1981	21.6	27.0	9.8	14.6	16.0	12.6	15.9[d]
1982	23.5	28.4	9.8	14.5	17.1	13.8	15.0[d]
1983	25.3	29.8	9.7	13.4	18.4	14.1	16.6[d]
1984	20.8	23.0	9.9	20.1	29.2	30.5	23.8[d]
1985	20.8	22.0	10.8	18.8	27.5	26.8	21.0[d]
1986	22.2	23.0	8.0	11.0	17.5	14.4	13.6[d]
1987	22.1	22.6	4.5	7.4	13.4	11.4	9.7[d]
1988	23.0	24.1	4.1	12.9	16.2	12.1	—
Average	22.4	25.0					

[a] M2 = currency + deposits (demand, savings, and time).

[b] M3 = M2 + deposit substitutes.

[c] As of December.

[d] Interest on promissory notes.

Sources: Mario B. Lamberte, "Financial Liberalization and the Internal Structure of Capital Markets," Philippine Institute for Development Studies (PIDS), 1985; Edita A. Tan, "Philippine Monetary Policy and Aspects of the Philippine Market: A Review of Literature," PIDS, 1980; *CB Statistical Yearbook.*

programs for selected institutions (rural banks and private development banks) before 1981 are to blame for this. After 1981, a host of new factors contributed to maintaining the stickiness of savings deposit rates, among them the oligopolistic character of the commercial banking system that is further nurtured by the central bank's aversion to the entry of new players in the sector.

The formal financial system has gone through three periods of policy environment promoted by government (see also Lamberte 1985). In the first period, 1956–1973, government policies replaced market forces in the intermediation of surplus funds through the banking system while "allowing" free-market forces to operate in new markets, that is, money markets. During the second period, 1974–1981, the central bank's authority was broadened to include the pricing of assets and structure of all financial institutions involved in credit allocation, such as the so-called nonbank financial intermediaries with authority to engage in quasi-banking functions (NBQBs). Thus the money markets became heavily regulated. The intention was to close the gap between the yields of short-term and long-term funds. The third period, which started in 1981 and continues to the present, is the period of liberalization. A mix of free- and administered-market policies are being promoted, the former demonstrated by the lifting of all interest rate ceilings and the latter implemented through the imposition of record-high reserve requirements and taxes on deposit transactions.

Period of Rigid Financial Repression: 1956–73

The period of rigid financial repression, 1956–73, featured a mix of central bank policies aimed at increasing the supply of credit at subsidized rates to broad-based, government-identified priority areas. Lending rates were governed by the Usury Act of 1916, which prescribed ceilings of 12%

Table 6.6. M2/GNP in Selected Asian Countries[a]

Country	1975	1980	1981	1982	1983	1984	1985	1986	1987	1988
Indonesia	0.16	0.18	0.19	0.19	0.21	0.22	0.26	0.30	0.31	—
Malaysia	0.46	0.54	0.58	0.63	0.63	0.62	0.67	0.81	0.75	—
Philippines	0.17	0.21	0.22	0.24	0.25	0.21	0.21	0.22	0.22	0.23
Singapore	0.60	0.66	0.70	0.72	0.70	0.66	0.70	0.78	0.85	0.84
Thailand	0.34	0.39	0.39	0.45	0.50	0.56	0.60	0.63	0.67	0.66
Korea, Rep. of	0.31	0.34	0.35	0.39	0.39	0.37	0.39	0.40	0.41	0.43
Taiwan	0.56	0.64	0.64	0.75	0.86	0.92	1.08	1.17	1.32	1.44

[a] M2 = M1 + saving deposits + time deposits.

Source: Key Indicators of Developing Member Countries of ADB, vol. 17, July 1987; vol. 14, April 1983; vol. 18, July 1988, vol. 19, July 1989, cited in Edita A. Tan, "Bank Concentration and the Structure of Interest." University of the Philippines School of Economics Discussion Paper No. 89–15, October 1989.

and 15% for secured and unsecured loans, respectively. Interest ceilings on deposits were imposed starting in 1956 and were adjusted upward but at long time intervals and in smaller steps. Deposits were further taxed by reserve requirements imposed on commercial banks' savings and time deposits, which were gradually raised from 5% in 1959 to 20% in 1970. Preferential or concessional rediscount rates were extended to a broad range of activities such as rice production and small-scale industrial loans. The wide margins between the prescribed loan rates and the central bank's rediscount rates plus the subsidized entry of rural banks and small private development banks facilitated the rise of banking institutions that relied more on the central bank's support than on funds intermediation. The development of other forms of financial intermediation was neglected. The market for government securities did not prosper, owing to their unattractive yields which were fixed in at par. The equity market likewise remained underdeveloped, primarily because of the low loan rates.

The repression of the banking system's deposit and lending rates paved the way for the emergence of new financial institutions that introduced new financial assets outside the purview of the central bank's regulations. Soon after, the existing KBs also started issuing unregulated short-term instruments. Money market instruments began to be traded in the mid-1960s. An interbank call market, which operated on a limited scale and a day-to-day basis, was augmented by the trading by few investment houses of short-dated debt instruments of banks and prime corporate names (Licuanan 1986). The prices of these instruments inevitably drew resources away from traditional deposits. From 1965 to 1974, the private sector's deposit substitutes holdings amounted to P7.5 billion, almost double the amount of demand deposits (P3.9 billion). The average M3/GNP ratio during the entire period of financial repression was 23.2%. In regard to the banking sector's increasing use of deposit substitutes, Tan explains that this was partly a move "to price discriminately between small and large lenders. Instead of paying a uniform rate on all deposits, banks maximize profits by paying regulated rates to ordinary small depositors, borrowing from the CB part of its funds and offering deposit substitutes to large depositors" (Tan 1980, p. 200).

Even though new financial institutions emerged to expand the domestic financial system, their integration into the international markets was not encouraged by the central bank. Although foreign investments in the short-term funds market have not been prohibited, residents are not allowed to purchase foreign securities or maintain bank balances overseas, although they may deposit foreign currencies in authorized domestic banks. These policies prevail up to the present. (Even the purchase of Philippine debt papers in foreign currencies by local banks requires the central bank's approval.)[7]

These policies were not intentionally designed to protect the domestic financial system from competition but, rather, functioned as exchange controls. The exchange controls were imposed in view of the limited (rather than full) flexibility of the exchange rate system, which started in 1970.[8] Limited flexibility, which is encountered in the purchase and sale of foreign exchange by the central bank and other exchange controls,[9] is a consequence of the central bank's mandate "to maintain the stability of the exchange rate," notwithstanding the official policy that "all exchange transactions [should] take place in a free market."[10]

Prohibiting investments in foreign assets abroad is thus seen as an important complementary strategy. Nevertheless, recent evidence shows that the practices of some local residents (some of whom were government officials) were effectively eviscerating the policy. The more infamous transgressors of the policy, the family of then President Ferdinand Marcos, reportedly maintained multimillion-dollar deposits in Swiss banks. Boyce and Zarsky (1988) provide a list of the mechanics used by residents to export capital illegally: (1) cash transfers via personal smuggling, the use of hired couriers, the mails, and wire transmission services;[11] (2) false invoicing of exports and imports;[12] (3) kickbacks on import contracts;[13] and (4) interbank transfers. The total capital flight from the Philippines from 1962 to 1986 has been estimated at U.S.$10.3 billion, which is one-third the total increase in the outstanding external debt of U.S.$27.9 billion during the same period (Boyce and Zarsky 1988).

Instead of liberalizing the traditional assets' interest rates, that is, deposits, the authorities responded to the rise in money market assets and intermediaries by (1) placing under its authority the nonbank FIs engaged in short-term lending, (2) enforcing specialization among various types of financial entities, and (3) imposing interest rate ceilings and taxes on money market transactions. These policies came with the reforms introduced in 1972/73 via amendments in the General Banking Act and the Central Bank Act. The other major reforms besides those previously mentioned are

1. The reduction of bank classifications into three main categories: commercial, thrift, and rural banks.

2. The adoption of policies to improve the efficiency of existing banks. Entry into the commercial banking system was to be halted by preferring branch over unit banking while consolidations, mergers, and foreign equity participation in domestic banks were promoted. An increase in minimum paid-in capital to P100 million was imposed.

3. The redefinition of the central bank's mission to exclude promotion of economic growth, which was to be the domain of the government-planning agencies. Thus, the central bank was given more flexibility in exercising powers consistent with maintaining monetary stability.

4. The financial institutions—that is, "banks," "banking institutions," and "nonbank financial institutions"—were redefined to indicate the extent to which each type was subject to the central bank's regulations.

5. The Monetary Board was given the authority in 1973 to prescribe maximum lending rates, which virtually repealed the Usury Act of 1916.

Period of Repression in the Money Markets: 1974–80

Within the framework of these reforms, the period 1974 – 80 featured interest rate reforms that were intended to reverse the flow of funds from short-term instruments (essentially money market instruments) to long-term financial assets. At the outset, however, these were undermined by the segmentation of the financial system, which was underscored by the enforced specialization among the FIs; for example, investment banking activities were assigned solely to investment houses and were set apart from regular banking activities.

Although rates on long-term deposits were deregulated, the ceilings of shorter-term instruments remained but changed from time to time. For instance, ceilings on short-term time deposits were raised from 6.5%– 8.0% to 8%–11% in 1974; on savings deposits, from 6% to 7% in 1976. Intermediation in the money markets was penalized by: (1) a 17% interest ceiling on short-term deposit substitutes, (2) an increase in the minimum placement on deposit substitutes to P200,000 for maturities of 730 days or less and P100,000 for maturities of more than 730 days, (3) a reserve requirement of 20% on deposit substitutes of commercial banks and nonbank financial institutions; and (4) a 35% transactions tax on all primary borrowings in the money market.

Notwithstanding these regulations, we should note that the M3/GNP ratio increased during this period, reaching an average of 26.6%, in contrast with the 23.2% during the period of repression. The attractiveness of deposit substitutes was emphasized by the fact that the M2/GNP ratio declined from 22.8% to 19.7%. Tan explains the seemingly minimal effect of the regulations on the issuers' ability to arrange their portfolios "so that those of relatively low risk and transactions cost are issued in known money market papers with rates at or below the ceiling, while those with market rates above the ceiling are issued as new papers and therefore not covered by regulations (Tan 1981, p. 135)." The NBQBs also evaded the central bank's regulations by engaging in transactions falling outside the latter's terms of reference. Specifically, they engaged in "without recourse" transactions in which they attached their own postdated checks according to a paying-agency agreement reinforced with verbal commitments to buy back the paper (Lamberte 1989).

Period of Liberalization: 1981–Present

The financial liberalization program initiated in 1981 included reforms of pricing policies for the various financial assets as well as reforms of the structure of the financial system, with the objective of encouraging competition and making medium- and long-term funds more available to deficit units. First, the interest rate ceilings on all types of deposits and loans were lifted, and the rediscounting privileges were scaled down. Minimum placements on deposit substitutes were also reduced to P50,000, irrespective of their maturity. Second, the differentiation among banks and nonbanks performing quasi-banking functions was narrowed with the introduction of universal banking. Under universal banking, commercial banks whose capitalization reached P500 million are authorized to perform a broad range of activities, including underwriting, securities dealing, and equity investments in both allied and nonallied undertakings. Clearly, the focus was on bigness, which was thought to help ensure the stability of the banking system.

On the other hand, regulations of other aspects of intermediation were made more stringent. The reserve requirement ratios for deposits and deposit substitutes of KBs, which were supposed to be scaled down to reduce the cost of intermediation, were instead jacked up to 24% in 1984, the highest since the establishment of the central bank. (These ratios were later brought down to 21% in 1986.) Moreover, two taxes were imposed in order to generate revenue: a 5% tax on gross receipts of banks and a 20% tax on deposit and money market earnings of depositors and investors. One estimate showed that both taxes comprised 25% to 39% of the banks' average intermediation cost (defined as the difference between the average cost of funds and the average interest rate on loans and investments other than reserve requirements) between 1983 and 1986 (World Bank 1988, p. 67).

Despite the freeing up of all interest rates, M3/GNP ratios were generally lower than those during the earlier periods of repression, although the M2/GNP ratios were slightly higher. Aside from these policies, other factors brought about these dismal records. First, the government's continued high deficit spending fueled double-digit inflation rates for most years, especially during the 1984/85 recession, resulting in negative real returns on deposits, which remained sticky. Second, savings deposit rates have beem extremely low since 1985, even lower than those set by the authorities during the regulated regimes. This, together with the abnormal bank margins among commercial banks of 5.8% (versus the 4.4% average of other countries), seems to indicate a monopolistic banking structure (Tan 1989). Third, trust accounts, which are banks' off–balance sheet borrowings, have been absorbing an increasing portion of funds from large depositors. Between 1984 and 1988, these funds reached P181 billion, of which only around 10% was held as cash and deposits in banks. Most of these funds are lent and invested in money market instruments, especially high-yielding government securities. Last, it is felt that the Dewey Dee crisis in 1981 had a lasting impact on confidence, causing large depositors to invest their funds in more stable assets, for example, trust accounts.

THE DEVELOPMENT OF THE PHILIPPINE MONEY MARKET

The evolving needs of an expanding economy set the stage for the development of the Philippine money market. Faced by the changing structure of a developing economy in the 1960s, from predominantly extractive industries into a diversifying economy in which manufacturing concerns played an increasing role, the financial system had to respond by developing in a similar fashion.

New ways had to be found to mobilize untapped financial resources, especially at a time when the administration was lowering the rates on traditional instruments. This became a take-off point for emerging financial concerns trying to meet the financial requirements of new industrial ventures by raising funds through the trade of short-term debt papers whose rates were not regulated by the authorities. In 1963, Private Development Corporation of the Philippines, an investment company, was created, offering financial services through underwriting and loan syndication. Shortly thereafter, in 1964, Bancom, the first investment house, was established. This new form of financial intermediation has attracted others, especially among the established commercial banks. Since then, the money market has put its mark on Philippine finance.

There are no official figures regarding the value of transactions from money market activities during the early period, but an unofficial estimate placed it at around P32M at the end of 1966 (Licuanan 1986).

Before the 1972 banking reforms, the Philippine money market was not regulated. Because of its novelty and the relatively higher returns compared with ordinary deposits, many investors were attracted to it, which contributed to its exceptional growth. By 1972, consistent with the task of the Philippine Central Bank to supervise and regulate the financial system, it began supervising the operations of nonbank financial institutions as well. The need to rein in this new form of financial intermediation, that is, the marketing of short-term debts, became a necessity, as it was challenging to the central bank's effectiveness in directing the allocation of financial resources and in pricing financial instruments.

In 1973, the investment house law was enacted, which became the basis for the establishment, operation, and regulation of investment houses. Accordingly, the borrowings of investment houses and other nonbank financial institutions from twenty or more lenders at any one time for the purpose of relending or purchasing receivables and other obligations were placed under the central bank's regulation and were also known as *quasi-banking* functions. The borrowing instruments allowed by the central bank are those introduced under Central Bank Circular 438 in 1974 and are collectively called *deposit substitutes*. Such instruments are repurchase agreements, certificates of assignment, certificates of participation, and dealer promissory notes.

By 1975, the Securities Act was amended to place all debt instruments under the supervision of the Philippine Securities and Exchange Commission (PSEC). All commercial paper had to be registered and comply with the minimum requirements for issuance by the PSEC. For the rest of the 1970s, various laws were passed to regulate the money market, such as requiring firms to obtain authority to issue debt instruments, determining the qualifications of officers of quasi banks, imposing a transaction tax on all money market borrowings, and prescribing reserve requirements for interbank loans and deposit substitutes, among others.

Between 1973 and 1979, the money market became as highly regulated as the rest of the financial system was. Nonetheless, the volume of money market transactions—meaning the sales and purchases of money market instruments—increased from the official figure of P142B in 1975 to P304B in 1980 (Table 6.7).

A second set of bank reforms was enacted in 1980, which liberalized the financial system and introduced the concept of universal banking. Commercial banks could now engage in investment banking and own allied and nonallied enterprises. The investment banks' functions were also expanded to include foreign exchange operations and trust functions. Underlying these reforms was the need to strengthen the condition of the financial intermediaries to meet the growing need for financial services. As a prerequisite for expansion, banks were required to increase their capital-

Table 6.7. Volume of Money Market Transactions,[a] 1975–88 (in millions of pesos)

Year	Nominal	Real	As Percentage of M3
1975[2]	142,263.76	84,887.47	5.50
1976	190,449.00	104,072.77	5.95
1977	210,520.97	107,122.27	5.32
1978	238,094.40	110,933.01	5.07
1979	295,488.10	119,476.02	5.55
1980	303,739.92	106,246.61	5.08
1981	329,558.00	103,896.62	4.37
1982	462,822.23	134,581.25	5.28
1983	600,561.87	156,377.59	5.97
1984	505,810.94	87,900.01	4.48
1985	505,742.25	74,343.03	4.14
1986	523,417.46	76,212.38	4.03
1987	460,855.74	62,112.87	3.26
1988	780,052.00	95,794.52	4.59

[a] Sum of monthly trading.

[b] First-quarter data not available.

Source: Central Bank of the Philippines.

ization or encouraged to merge with other allied financial institutions. The improvement in these banks' financial standing permitted them to assume broader operations, particularly in packaging financial services. The latter provided incentives for these banks to mobilize more funds for bigger operations. The benefits were translated into a greater flow of savings into the system for the requirements of medium- and long-term borrowers made possible through the transformation of terms.

Since lending long and borrowing short could create liquidity problems, the central bank instituted safeguards, among which was its lender-of-last-resort facility. Obviously, however, the money market functioned not only as an important source of funds for financial intermediaries but also as an essential counterweight for illiquidity, as this provided a ready mechanism for intermediaries to raise short-term funds.

From that time on, the volume of money market transactions has grown, surviving the liquidity crisis in 1981 and then reaching a peak at the onset of the economic crisis of 1983. After that, it ballooned to a volume of P780 billion in nominal terms by the end of 1988. The money market has since become an important form of financial intermediation.

A Survey of the Philippine Money Market

The Philippine money market is made up of the interbank loans (also known as the interbank call loans market) and the deposit substitutes, the commercial paper, and the government securities markets. These markets are functionally classified according to the major players, usually the borrowers, in each market.

Interbank loans and deposit substitutes are the markets for financial intermediaries' funds. On the other hand, the market for debt instruments of private corporations and of other financial institutions without quasi-banking functions are included in the commercial paper market. Finally, the market for the government securities includes the issues by the central bank, the national government, and the various government corporations and government financial institutions.

Interbank Call Loans

Interbank call loans are very short term—normally not more than twenty-four hours—bank-to-bank accommodations to cover reserve deficiencies by banks and non-bank quasi banks. Interbank loans are made by means of fund transfers among lending and borrowing financial intermediaries carried each day in the central bank's books when the clearing results are known.

Since interbank call loans are bank-to-bank accommodations for funds, the players in this market are banks and nonbanks granted quasi-banking licenses, that is, investment houses and finance companies. The biggest borrowers in the market usually are commercial banks. Between 1983 and 1987, commercial banks were consistently the sole users of funds for this market (see Table 6.8), mainly to cover reserve deficiencies for their deposits and deposit substitutes.

The lending side of this market has a more diverse composition. Although commercial banks were also the biggest lenders, with an average share of 85% between 1983 and 1988 (see Table 6.9), other major lenders in the market were the government financial institutions (the Development Bank of the Philippines and the Land Bank) (10%), the investment houses (0.4%), and the finance companies (0.2%). The interbank market is also a ready market for rural and thrift banks' investable funds (3.7%).

In the 1970s, interbank call loans comprised less than 10% of the total volume of money market transactions. Between 1975 and 1979, the interbank market had an average share of 9% of total money market transactions, compared with its average share of 33% in the 1980s (Table 6.10). This market rapidly expanded in the 1980s, and the volume of transactions by 1988 accounted for almost 40% of total money market transactions.

There was evidence even as early as 1979 that banks used the funds in this market not only for their reserve deficiencies but also for their regular operations. During 1979, despite a new reserve requirement of 5% for interbank borrowings imposed in 1978, the volume of interbank loan transactions almost doubled. This may be traced to the persistent demand for short-term funds by enterprises hit by the oil price shock that year.

Given the favorable business climate in the banking sector, starting with the lifting of interest restrictions on long-term loans in 1981 and on short-term loans in 1982, the need for more funds for the expanded banking, mainly among commercial banks, necessitated the increase in the volume of funds sourced through this market. Such funds were, likewise, relatively more attractive than deposit substitutes, which carried higher reserve requirements. The required reserves for interbank funds were lowered from 5% to 1% in 1980.

The growth of this market in the 1980s can also be traced to the demand for reserves, especially among banks, owing to the increase in their deposit liabilities resulting from the newly liberalized deposit rates. Banks resorted to interbank borrowings to cover up their reserve deficiencies whenever they felt the pinch of high reserve requirements for deposit liabilities, which reached as high as 24% in 1984. The rash of failures among banks and quasi banks in the early 1980s, which dictated the need for these financial intermediaries always to remain liquid, may also have contributed to the emerging importance of this market as a ready and immediate source of funds among banks.

Deposit Substitutes

Deposit substitutes are alternative means by which financial intermediaries, specifically banks and nonbanks with quasi-banking licenses (NBQBs), raise funds other than through traditional deposits.[14] Transac-

Table 6.8. Volume of Interbank Call Loan Transactions[a] by Type of Borrower, 1983–88 (in millions of pesos)

Borrower	1983 Volume	1983 Percent	1984 Volume	1984 Percent	1985 Volume	1985 Percent	1986 Volume	1986 Percent	1987 Volume	1987 Percent	1988 Volume	1988 Percent
Commercial banks	198,100.97	100.0	178,116.70	100.0	226,380.02	100.0	200,691.76	99.6	172,614.10	99.9	282,381.51	93.0
Investment houses	—	—	—	—	—	—	—	—	—	—	8,392.72	2.8
Financing companies	—	—	—	—	—	—	—	—	—	—	10,997.57	3.6
Savings banks	—	—	—	—	—	—	732.00	0.4	173.50	0.1	1731.77	0.6
Other banking institutions	—	—	—	—	—	—	—	—	—	—	—	—
Total	198,100.97	100.0	178,116.70	100.0	226,380.02	100.0	201,423.76	100.0	172,787.60	100.0	303,503.57	100.0

[a] Sum of monthly trading; no breakdown as to borrower before 1983.

Source: Central Bank of the Philippines.

Table 6.9. Volume of Interbank Call Loan Transactions[a] by Type of Investor, 1983–88 (in millions of pesos)

Borrower	1983 Volume	1983 Percent	1984 Volume	1984 Percent	1985 Volume	1985 Percent	1986 Volume	1986 Percent	1987 Volume	1987 Percent	1988 Volume	1988 Percent
Commercial banks	172,933.6	87.3	160,817.9	90.3	169,796.8	75.0	194,353.0	96.5	149,353.0	96.5	149,691.5	74.1
Commercial banks	172,933.6	87.3	160,817.9	90.3	169,796.8	75.0	194,353.0	96.5	149,691.5	86.6	22,4829.6	74.1
Other banking institutions	20,350.6	10.3	10,189.4	5.7	51,405.2	22.7	2,356.8	1.2	13,806.0	8.0	3,4625.9	11.4
Investment houses	1,349.0	0.7	2,748.1	1.5	280.9	0.1	73.0	0.0	4,303.7	2.5	1,6184.5	5.3
Rural/thrift banks	3,166.4	1.6	3,351.8	1.9	4,888.6	2.2	4,640.9	2.3	4,002.8	2.3	2,7518.4	9.1
Finance companies	301.4	0.2	1,009.6	0.6	8.5	0.0	—	—	983.6	0.6	345.2	0.1
Total	198,101.0	100.0	178,116.7	100.0	226,380.0	100.0	201,423.8	100.0	172,787.6	100.0	30,3503.6	100.0

[a] Sum of monthly trading; no breakdown as to borrower before 1983.

Source: Central Bank of the Philippines.

Table 6.10. Volume of Money Market Transactions[a] by Type of Instrument, 1975–88 (in millions of pesos)

Instrument	1975[b] Volume	Percent	1976 Volume	Percent	1977 Volume	Percent	1978 Volume	Percent	1979 Volume	Percent	1980 Volume	Percent	1981 Volume	Percent
Interbank call loans	10,340.8	7.3	17,818.0	9.4	17,819.1	8.5	18,371.0	7.7	42,268.2	14.3	50,509.3	16.6	66,969.3	20.3
Deposit substitutes	121,486.5	85.4	160,873.6	84.5	181,340.6	86.1	208,791.1	87.7	241,903.4	81.9	242,083.7	79.7	237,776.3	72.2
Promissory notes	80,750.3	56.8	119,469.6	62.7	140,451.1	66.7	160,891.5	67.6	151,203.5	51.2	144,463.2	47.6	189,531.8	57.5
Repurchase agreements	39,799.6	28.0	41,048.9	21.6	40,304.1	19.1	47,392.3	19.9	90,084.7	30.5	95,660.0	31.5	47,818.5	14.5
Certificates of assignments	806.6	0.6	278.0	0.1	385.5	0.2	180.1	0.1	55.6	0.0	1,065.2	0.4	230.2	0.1
Certificates of participation	130.0	0.1	77.1	0.0	200.0	0.1	327.2	0.1	559.6	0.2	895.3	0.3	195.8	0.1
Commercial paper	8,387.5	5.9	10,228.5	5.4	8,958.7	4.3	7,980.5	3.4	9,763.4	3.3	10,466.0	3.4	23,922.8	7.3
Nonfinancial	7,723.7	5.4	9,660.5	5.1	8,196.0	3.9	7,232.4	3.0	7,928.8	2.7	8,575.9	2.8	20,464.1	6.2
Financial	663.8	0.5	568.0	0.3	762.7	0.4	748.1	0.3	1,834.6	0.6	1,890.0	0.6	3,458.7	1.0
Government securities	2,049.0	1.4	1,528.9	0.8	2,402.5	1.1	2,951.8	1.2	1,553.1	0.5	680.9	0.2	889.6	0.3
DBP bonds and other securities	182.9	0.1	86.4	0.0	118.5	0.1	162.0	0.1	226.7	0.1	55.1	0.0	150.8	0.0
CBCIs	1,729.4	1.2	1,320.3	0.7	2,165.1	1.0	1,948.6	0.8	1,027.9	0.3	478.5	0.2	674.3	0.2
Treasury bills	136.7	0.1	122.2	0.1	118.9	0.1	841.2	0.4	298.5	0.1	147.3	0.0	64.5	0.0
Total	142,263.8	100.0	190,449.0	100.0	210,521.0	100.0	238,094.4	100.0	295,488.1	100.0	303,739.9	100.0	329,558.0	100.0

Table 6.10. (*Continued*)

Instrument	1982 Volume	1982 Percent	1983 Volume	1983 Percent	1984 Volume	1984 Percent	1985 Volume	1985 Percent	1986 Volume	1986 Percent	1987 Volume	1987 Percent	1988 Volume	1988 Percent
Interbank call loans	133,593.6	28.9	198,101.0	33.0	178,116.7	35.2	226,380.0	44.8	201,423.4	38.5	172,787.6	37.5	303,503.6	38.9
Deposit substitutes	286,290.5	61.9	363,604.2	60.5	258,192.7	51.0	184,372.4	36.5	213,764.4	40.8	135,087.2	29.3	108,420.3	13.9
Promissory notes	238,308.0	51.5	244,043.0	40.6	183,831.3	36.3	156,798.6	31.0	158,656.1	30.3	131,084.3	28.4	104,075.7	13.3
Repurchase agreements	47,413.3	10.2	119,291.7	19.9	73,930.3	14.6	27,573.7	5.5	54,054.5	10.3	3,765.5	0.8	4,344.3	0.6
Certificates of assignments	328.2	0.1	259.0	0.0	409.2	0.1	0.1	0.0	7.6	0.0	0.1	0.0	0.3	0.0
Certificates of participation	241.0	0.1	10.6	0.0	22.0	0.0	—	—	1,046.2	0.2	237.2	0.1	—	—
Commercial paper	34,655.3	7.5	23,997.7	4.0	23,390.8	4.6	20,164.1	4.0	15,650.8	3.0	18,535.8	4.0	16,950.4	2.2
Nonfinancial	22,761.7	4.9	8,948.8	1.5	13,085.3	2.6	19,912.5	3.9	15,650.4	3.0	18,440.5	4.0	16,833.4	2.2
Financial	11,893.6	2.6	15,048.9	2.5	10,305.5	2.0	251.6	0.0	0.4	0.0	95.3	0.0	117.0	0.0
Government securities	8,282.9	1.8	14,859.0	2.5	46,110.7	9.1	74,825.7	14.8	92,578.9	17.7	134,445.2	29.2	351,177.7	45.0
DBP bonds and other securities	1,213.9	0.3	6,098.6	1.0	23,821.7	4.7	36,063.4	7.1	36,875.4	7.0	37,882.5	8.2	55,911.1	7.2
CBCIs	5,809.5	1.3	3,861.3	0.6	603.8	0.1	13.7	0.0	23.5	0.0	2.2	0.0	—	—
Treasury bills	1,259.5	0.3	4,899.1	0.8	21,685.2	4.3	38,748.5	7.7	55,680.0	10.6	96,560.5	21.0	295,266.7	37.9
Total	462,822.2	100.0	600,561.9	100.0	505,810.9	100.0	505,742.3	100.0	523,417.5	100.0	460,855.7	100.0	780,052.0	100.0

a Sum of monthly trading.
b First-quarter data not available.

Source: Central Bank of the Philippines.

tions in deposit substitutes may either be through the issuance of a debt paper by the bank or quasi bank or through the sale or the transfer to a third party of existing instruments in their portfolio for purposes of raising funds. The debt paper is a primary issue that we will refer to as a *dealer promissory note* because it is the intermediary itself that issues the debt instrument. The third-party instruments may not, however, be considered secondary instruments, since they are sold or transferred with recourse to the original subscribers. The banks or NBQBs must redeem such issues at some specified date in the future. Strictly speaking, there is no secondary market for their debt instruments.

The following instruments make up the deposit substitutes market:

1. *Repurchase agreements* are existing instruments in a financial intermediary's portfolio sold in the money market with recourse, meaning that by mutual agreement with the buyer, the bank or quasi bank will buy back the instrument sometime in the future. The underlying instruments are both private and government issues.

2. *Certificates of assignment* are instruments that may be transferred from the financial intermediary to the assignee, in which case the latter can claim credit or interest on the instrument at some agreed time in the future. The underlying instruments also are both private or government securities.

3. *Certificates of participation* are instruments certifying the holder's share of investment or participation in the instrument, on which interest is payable at some future time. This enables the financial intermediary to retail debt instruments denominated in large amounts, which can be either private or government securities.

4. *Dealer promissory notes* are debt instruments issued by the banks and quasi banks to investors, payable at some agreed time in the future.

Between 1975 and 1984, deposit substitutes accounted for more than 50 percent (see Table 6.10) of total money market transactions, even averaging as much as 75% during this period. This reflects the importance of this market as a secondary source of funds relative to deposits for financial intermediaries with quasi-banking functions.

The deposit substitutes market has been dominated by commercial banks, the largest borrowers, which at the same time are also the largest investors (see Tables 6.11 and 6.12). As borrowers they accounted for an average share of 55% of total deposit substitute borrowings between 1983 and 1988, although this share has been declining. As lenders, they accounted for an average share of 46% of this market during the same period.

As the second-largest group of borrowers, investment houses increased their borrowings through this market from 13.6% in 1983 to 39% in 1988 (see Table 6.11). The finance companies increased their share from 9.9% in 1983 to 21% in 1988. Together these institutions accounted for about 39% of total borrowings through deposit substitutes between 1983 and 1988.

Table 6.11. Volume of Deposit Substitute Transactions[a] by Type of Borrower, 1983–88 (in millions of pesos)

Borrower	1983		1984		1985		1986		1987		1988	
	Volume	Percent	Volume	Percent	Volume	Percent	Volume	Percent	Volume	Percent	Volume	Percent
Commercial banks	265,251.8	73.0	185,636.5	71.9	114,080.1	61.9	117,520.0	55.0	38,028.2	28.2	42,823.0	39.5
Investment houses	49,382.2	13.6	33,874.6	13.1	34,146.3	18.5	42,733.9	20.0	50,134.1	37.1	42,268.5	39.0
Financing companies	36,174.5	9.9	22,423.2	8.7	19,510.7	10.6	29,862.7	14.0	39,237.3	29.0	22,884.2	21.1
Savings banks	7,456.4	2.1	10,955.5	4.2	1,101.0	0.6	10,064.3	4.7	7,251.6	5.4	444.7	0.4
Other banking institutions	5,339.4	1.5	5,303.0	2.1	15,534.3	8.4	13,583.0	6.4	435.9	0.3	—	—
Total	363,604.2	100.0	258,192.8	100.0	184,372.5	100.0	213,764.0	100.0	135,087.2	100.0	108,420.4	100.0

a Sum of monthly trading; no breakdown as to borrower before 1983.

Source: Central Bank of the Philippines.

Table 6.12. Volume of Deposit Substitute Transactions[a] by Type of Investor, 1983–88 (in millions of pesos)

	1983		1984		1985		1986		1987		1988	
Investor	Volume	Percent	Volume	Percent	Volume	Percent	Volume	Percent	Volume	Percent	Volume	Percent
Commercial banks	134,473.0	37.0	112,024.1	43.4	88,786.5	48.2	126,564.2	59.2	71,060.5	52.6	36,483.8	33.7
Individuals	23,217.9	6.4	20,660.5	8.0	21,590.1	11.7	21,154.7	9.9	30,788.9	22.8	31,851.5	29.4
Private corporations	52,100.8	14.3	47,554.3	18.4	23,225.7	12.6	12,866.9	6.0	10,102.6	7.5	13,222.9	12.2
Other banking institutions[b]	52,305.5	14.4	16,506.8	6.4	21,480.1	11.7	11,601.4	5.4	1,546.7	1.1	3,433.6	3.2
Investment houses[c]	35,309.5	9.7	16,134.7	6.2	815.3	0.4	901.9	0.4	12,535.4	9.3	15,984.7	14.7
Trust/pension funds	12,764.8	3.5	7,111.7	2.8	4,814.8	2.6	3,131.7	1.5	3,340.2	2.5	3,995.3	3.7
Rural/thrift banks	14,608.7	4.0	6,246.7	2.4	7,150.2	3.9	16,200.3	7.6	2,615.1	1.9	2,023.8	1.9
Government corporations	12,591.4	3.5	14,043.5	5.4	7,725.7	4.2	6,994.7	3.3	342.1	0.3	1,221.4	1.1
Finance companies	20,093.1	5.5	11,812.2	4.6	421.3	0.2	717.8	0.3	1,874.0	1.4	42.8	0.0
Investment companies[c]	1,151.0	0.3	983.7	0.4	925.7	0.5	133.7	0.1	139.5	0.1	31.7	0.0
Private insurance companies	2,712.0	0.7	1,640.8	0.6	387.5	0.2	101.1	0.0	307.3	0.2	77.5	0.1
Government insurance companies[d]	35.3	0.0	867.1	0.3	5,105.4	2.8	13,346.5	6.2	387.2	0.3	—	—
Lending investors[e]	751.6	0.2	1,522.0	0.6	56.0	0.0	45.8	0.0	3.6	0.0	51.0	0.0
Security dealers	1,459.2	0.4	3.2	0.0	—	—	3.1	0.0	34.6	0.0	0.3	0.0
National government	30.5	0.0	1,081.3	0.4	1,888.3	1.0	0.3	0.0	9.5	0.0	—	—
Local government	—	—	—	—	—	—	—	—	—	—	0.1	0.0
Total	363,604.2	100.0	258,192.8	100.0	184,372.4	100.0	213,764.0	100.0	135,087.2	100.0	108,420.4	100.0

[a] Sum of monthly trading; no breakdown as to investor before 1983.

[b] Development Bank of the Philippines and Land Bank of the Philippines.

[c] Investment houses are engaged in guaranteed underwriting, and investment companies are primarily engaged in investing, reinvesting, or trading in securities.

[d] Social Security System and Government Service and Insurance System.

[e] Persons who use their capital to extend all types of loans, often without collateral.

Source: Central Bank of the Philippines.

After the commercial banks, individuals and private corporations are two of the largest lenders in this market, accounting for an average market share of 15% and 12%, respectively, between 1983 and 1988 (see Table 6.12). Investment houses and finance companies accounted for only 6.5% and 2%, respectively, of total investments in deposit substitutes between 1983 and 1988.

Dealer promissory notes are the most popular debt instruments among all deposit substitutes, accounting for an average of 77% of the total volume of all deposit substitutes traded between 1975 and 1988. Repurchase agreements are the second most popular, averaging 23%. Financial intermediaries seemed to prefer borrowing directly by issuing their own instruments rather than raising funds using other securities as underlying instruments.

Starting in 1975, when deposit substitutes had already been formally introduced through quasi banking, the deposit substitute market averaged 62% of the total volume of money market transactions. Despite this large share, the share of this market in the total volume of money market transactions began to fall, from 82% in 1979 to only 14% in 1988 (see Table 6.10).

There seems to be a shift in the preference of sourcing funds, notably among banks. The liberal deposit rates that came during the 1980 financial reforms saw the expansion of funds coming from traditional deposits. From a peak in 1981, total outstanding deposit substitutes among commercial banks declined, showing negative growth rates from 1984 onward, whereas outstanding deposits grew, with an average growth rate of 43% for the same period (see Table 6.13). Banks find it convenient to obtain funds through de-

Table 6.13. Amount of Outstanding Deposits and Deposit Substitutes of Commercial Banks and Quasi Banks (in millions of pesos)

	KBs		Quasi Banks Deposit Substitutes
	Deposit Substitutes	Deposits	
1978	11,493	43,625	6,731
1979	11,950	55,997	8,907
1980	12,371	72,630	11,327
1981	16,452	29,261	8,598
1982	16,565	93,230	9,590
1983	17,106	116,227	8,438
1984	11,275	134,552	6,401
1985	8,608	143,017	5,434
1986	4,874	138,026	6,086
1987	3,605	151,794	7,885
1988	2,543	192,125	7,131

Source: Central Bank of the Philippines.

posits rather than issue their own promissory notes, given the stringent rules instituted after the collapse of a few investment and finance companies at the start of the 1980s. Arguably, the decline in the volume of deposit substitutes by way of repurchase agreements was also due to the decline in the use of private commercial papers as underlying instruments (Table 6.10).

The preference for sources of funds other than deposit substitutes can also be explained by the increasing reserve requirements imposed on this group of instruments, from 20% in 1980 to as high as 24% during the 1984 financial crisis. Despite the same reserve requirements imposed on deposits, sourcing funds through deposit substitutes involves more paperwork, in compliance with the minimum legal requirements of issuing debt instruments in the money market. The growth of banks' funds sourced through traditional deposits and through interbank loans may, therefore, have come at the expense of deposit substitutes.

Commercial Paper

The commercial paper market is defined here as the market for debt instruments issued by private corporations (nonfinancial) and financial corporations without quasi-banking licenses. This market consists of debt instruments issued and sold outright in the market, through the financial intermediaries, for an investor's account.[15]

Intermediation in the commercial paper market takes one of three forms. First, commercial paper may be traded as underlying instruments in deposit substitutes. This form of activity, as defined in quasi banking, occurs when financial intermediaries buy these debt instruments, keep them in their loan portfolios, and later use them as underlying instruments. Or the instrument may be traded when the original transaction involves commercial paper as a primary issue, which the financial intermediary buys and later sells outright and without recourse, as in dealership. Last, the borrowers and the investor may be brought together, in which case intermediation takes the form of brokerage.

The nonfinancial corporate sector has used this market more often than have the financial institutions (without a quasi-banking license) to obtain funds through issuances of commercial paper. The data available between 1983 and 1988 show nonfinancial corporations accounting for an average share of 82% against 18% for financial corporations in the total volume of outright sales of commercial paper in the money market (see Table 6.14). Between 1985 and 1988, nonfinancial corporate borrowers had almost a 100% share of the market, and financial corporate borrowers had a negligible share. On the other hand, the major investors were individual persons, accounting for an average of 54% share of investment on commercial paper sold without recourse, followed by private corporations, with 29%. Investments through trust and pension funds accounted for 11% of the total investment in these instruments (see Table 6.15).

Table 6.14. Volume of Commercial Paper Transactions[a] by Type of
Borrower, 1983–88 (in millions of pesos)

Borrower	1983		1984		1985	
	Volume	*Percent*	*Volume*	*Percent*	*Volume*	*Percent*
Nonfinancial	9,049.1	37.7	13,085.3	55.9	19,912.5	98.8
Financial	14,948.6	62.3	10,305.5	44.1	251.6	1.2
Total	23,997.7	100.0	23,390.8	100.0	20,164.1	100.0

Borrower	1986		1987		1988	
	Volume	*Percent*	*Volume*	*Percent*	*Volume*	*Percent*
Nonfinancial	15,650.4	100.0	18,440.5	99.5	16,833.3	99.3
Financial	0.4	0.0	95.3	0.5	117.0	0.7
Total	15,650.8	100.0	18,535.8	100.0	16,950.3	100.0

[a] Sum of monthly trading; no breakdown as to borrower before 1983.

Source: Central Bank of the Philippines.

The popularity of commercial paper as an investment alternative for those with surplus funds enabled it to stand out from the rest of the money market. In fact, the Philippine money market had almost become synonymous with the commercial paper market. Yet the volume of transactions involving commercial paper issues sold outright averaged only 4.2% of the total volume of money market transactions from 1975 to 1988 (Table 6.16).

The high profile of the commercial paper market from the inception of the money market to the time it was regulated in 1972 deserves a closer look. Through the years, the commercial paper market has been the focus of some important banking regulations.

In the 1970s, most private corporations turned their efforts to sourcing their fund requirements through the money market. The growing number of these firms prompted the need to regulate the issuance of commercial papers in order to protect investors and to achieve monetary targets. In 1975, the Philippine Securities and Exchange Commission (PSEC) required all corporate issuers to seek its approval before issuing commercial papers. In November of the same year, the central bank required all banks and non-bank quasi banks to observe the PSEC's rules of registration regarding commercial paper. At the start of 1976, the central bank sent a circular to all banks and quasi banks requesting evidence of authority when issuing instruments and/or requiring from corporate issuers this authority before selling or buying their commercial paper.

Despite the regulations introduced in 1975/76, the volume of transactions involving issues of commercial paper sold without recourse increased by 12%. Somehow the high-yielding debt instruments were still attracting investors.

Table 6.15. Volume of Commercial Paper Transactions[a] by Type of Investor, 1983–88 (in millions of pesos)

Investor	1983 Volume	1983 Percent	1984 Volume	1984 Percent	1985 Volume	1985 Percent	1986 Volume	1986 Percent	1987 Volume	1987 Percent	1988 Volume	1988 Percent
Commercial banks	150.4	0.6	24.2	0.1	55.3	0.3	53.7	0.3	497.4	2.7	801.2	4.7
Individuals	14,689.4	61.2	13,528.5	57.8	11,260.2	55.8	7,207.6	46.1	9,915.1	53.5	8,140.9	48.0
Private corporations	6,305.4	26.3	6,094.6	26.1	4,922.1	24.4	4,218.0	27.0	5,815.4	31.4	6,301.1	37.2
Other banking institutions	0.5	0.0	1.0	0.0	2.7	0.0	—	—	22.3	0.1	2.5	0.0
Investment houses	5.0	0.0	18.8	0.1	1.2	0.0	30.0	0.2	135.6	0.7	129.3	0.8
Trust/pension funds	1,187.0	4.9	3,133.6	13.4	3,514.2	17.4	2,693.5	17.2	853.7	4.6	964.7	5.7
Rural/thrift banks	55.7	0.2	379.6	1.6	222.2	1.1	76.4	0.5	54.1	0.3	87.9	0.5
Government corporations	13.0	0.1	92.4	0.4	5.5	0.0	0.7	0.0	151.1	0.8	31.2	0.2
Finance companies	1,130.3	4.7	59.7	0.3	32.3	0.2	16.3	0.1	149.0	0.8	87.6	0.5
Investment companies	1.1	0.0	1.0	0.0	34.8	0.2	422.3	2.7	82.6	0.4	165.1	1.0
Private insurance companies	277.4	1.2	38.9	0.2	108.7	0.5	821.8	5.3	629.1	3.4	238.6	1.4
Government insurance companies	—	—	—	—	—	—	—	—	—	—	—	—
Lending investors	178.9	0.7	17.7	0.1	4.9	0.0	110.2	0.7	20.6	0.1	0.2	0.0
Security dealers	0.5	0.0	1.0	0.0	—	—	0.4	0.0	1.3	0.0	—	—
National government	3.0	0.0	—	—	—	—	—	—	208.5	1.1	—	—
Local government	—	—	—	—	—	—	—	—	—	—	—	—
Total	23,997.7	100.0	23,390.8	100.0	20,164.1	100.0	15,650.8	100.0	18,535.8	100.0	16,950.4	100.0

[a] Sum of monthly trading; no breakdown as to investor before 1983.

Source: Central Bank of the Philippines.

Table 6.16. Volume of Money Market Transactions[a] by
Instrument, 1975–88 (in millions of pesos)

Instrument	Volume (pm)	Percent
Interbank call loans	1,638,001.55	29.52
Deposit substitutes	2,943,986.921	53.05
Promissory notes	2,203,557.97	39.71
Repurchase agreements	732,481.284	13.20
Certificates of assignment	4,005.66	0.07
Certificates of participation	3,942.003	0.07
Commercial paper	233,052.236	4.20
Nonfinancial	185,413.86	3.34
Financial	47,638.38	0.86
Government securities	734,335.943	13.23
DBP bonds and other securities	198,849.018	3.58
CBCIs	19,658.08	0.35
Treasury bills	515,828.84	9.30
Total	5,549,376.65	100.00

[a] First-quarter data for year 1975 not available.

Source: Central Bank of the Philippines.

Despite the regulations on the money market brought about by the 1972 banking reforms, the central bank's ability to allocate financial resources through credit was severely challenged. First, commercial paper sold outright or without recourse is outside the scope of quasi banking and remains unregulated by the central bank. Furthermore, the central bank's authority regarding the origin or issuer of the commercial paper is limited to financial intermediaries, for example, banks and nonbank quasibanks, and not private corporations.[16]

The popularity of commercial paper, which promised fast and high returns, also came at the time when the financial system was repressed. Savers, particularly investors, had more reason to shift their savings from deposits, which carried negative real rates, to such investment alternatives as commercial paper.

In 1977, realizing this disparity of yields between ordinary deposits and commercial paper, the authorities imposed a 35% transaction tax on all primary borrowings. On the same year, the volume of transactions involving commercial paper sold outright dropped by 18.4%.

The money market continued to be very active in the second half of the 1970s, with the emergence of some aspiring corporate giants associated with the administration. These firms extensively used the money market for their funding requirements. Most of them turned to the money market because they could no longer obtain credit from the banking system, either because they had overborrowed or there were not enough investment funds for lending by the financial system, given the repressed regime (Lamberte 1989). Some of these expanding corporations even acquired their own investment houses and finance companies in order to acquire funds through this market.

These investment houses and the finance companies affiliated with these corporate giants became virtual "cash cows," owing to the large loans awarded to their parent companies or their use as conduits for investors' funds. Following the collapse in 1977 of a commercial bank that had extensive exposure to its sister investment company, the central bank acted to prevent similar cases in the future and to restore the public's confidence in the financial intermediaries.

In 1977, the central bank issued a circular limiting the credit accommodations by nonbanks to their directors, officers, stockholders, subsidiaries, and affiliates. This was followed in 1978 by another regulation regarding interlocking directorates and officerships in banks and nonbank quasi banks. Despite these regulations, the commercial paper market maintained nearly the same trading volume from 1978 to 1980. In fact, its share of the total volume of transactions on the entire money market was fairly constant (Table 6.10).

During the first quarter of 1981, just when investors' confidence was about to be restored, a businessman with hundreds of millions of pesos owed by his firms through the money market fled the country, directly affecting thirteen commercial banks and eleven investment houses and finance companies. A massive early termination ensued, heavily damaging the nonbank quasi banks, which were highly dependent on the money market for funds. Among the first to fold were the so-called financing arms of the corporate giants.

In 1981, the volume of newly issued commercial paper by corporations fell from its level in the first quarter (see Table 6.17). In 1981 and 1982, the intermediaries, mainly commercial banks, in an obvious maneuver to extricate themselves from this mess, sold commercial paper in the market on a without-recourse basis instead of using it as an underlying instrument in deposit substitutes. The volume of transactions involving the outright sale of commercial paper rose relative to the volume of repurchase agreements involving private instruments (see Table 6.10). Table 6.18 shows that the volume of deposit substitute transactions involving private securities in repurchase agreements dropped drastically by 31% in 1981 from its level in 1980. This volume decreased further in 1982. On this basis, the volume of commercial papers sold outright without recourse remained high during 1981 and 1982.

Table 6.17. Total Commercial Paper Issuances by Registered
Issuers, 1979–82 (in millions of pesos)

	1979	1980	1981	1982
January	2,874	3,036	3,945	2,663
February	2,369	3,475	3,609	2,259
March	2,591	3,374	4,295	2,404
April	2,652	3,711	3,699	2,023
May	2,844	4,227	3,160	2,182
June	2,840	3,430	3,226	1,979
July	3,033	3,311	3,467	1,781
August	3,483	3,579	2,709	1,420
September	3,259	4,493	2,821	1,477
October	3,252	3,355	2,791	961
November	3,189	3,661	2,360	940
December	3,002	3,673	2,148	663
Total	35,388	43,325	38,230	20,752

Source: V. S. Licuanan, *An Analysis of the Institutional Framework of the Philippine
Short-Term Financial Markets* (PIDS), 1986.

Before the year ended, with a looming liquidity crisis threatening to
affect the entire system, the central bank issued various circulars to enhance the market's stability in general and to protect investors in particular: Among them were

Table 6.18. Volume of Money Market Transactions[a] by Instrument, 1980–82 (in
millions of pesos)

	1980		1981		1982	
Instrument	Volume	Percent	Volume	Percent	Volume	Percent
Interbank call loans	50,509.3	16.6	66,969.3	20.3	133,593.6	28.9
Deposit substitutes	242,083.7	79.7	237,776.3	72.2	286,290.5	61.9
Promissory notes	144,463.2	47.6	189,531.8	57.5	238,308.0	51.5
Repurchase agreements (priv.)	60,369.7	19.9	20,610.7	6.3	13,840.5	3.0
Repurchase agreements (gov't.)	35,290.3	11.6	27,207.8	8.3	33,572.8	7.3
Certificates of assignment	1,065.2	0.4	230.2	0.1	328.2	0.1
Certificates of participation	895.3	0.3	195.8	0.1	241.0	0.1
Commercial paper	10,466.0	3.4	23,922.8	7.3	34,655.3	7.5
Nonfinancial	8,575.9	2.8	20,464.1	6.2	22,761.7	4.9
Financial	1,890.0	0.6	3,458.7	1.0	11,893.6	2.6
Government securities	680.9	0.2	889.6	0.3	8,282.9	1.8
Total	303,739.9	100.0	329,558.0	100.0	462,822.2	100.0

[a] Sum of monthly trading.

Source: Central Bank of the Philippines.

1. Fully disclosing a corporate issuer's financial standing and performance before it is given the authority to issue commercial paper.

2. Limiting a corporate issuer's outstanding liabilities to at most 300% of its net worth.

3. Requiring a corporate issuer to secure at least a 20% credit line from an authorized bank before it can issue commercial paper.

4. Providing incentives to commercial banks that issue credit lines to prospective commercial paper issuers, through special credit accommodations by the central bank.

Also during 1981, to prop up the market, the central bank extended a massive bailout to some of these banks and nonbank quasi banks. To discourage early terminations, the early-termination clause as an option of the lender was removed from the commercial paper. In 1982, the central bank also helped set up a credit-rating agency to furnish information on corporations' creditworthiness.

The drastic drop in the volume of transactions in 1983 was expected. The fifteen-month transition period granted by the central bank to some corporations, during which they could issue commercial paper without the necessary credit line, had already expired. With the application to all corporate issuers of the credit line requirement in 1983, the number of firms intending to issue commercial paper suddenly dropped. A political crisis also began to grip the economy at that time.

From 1983 to 1988, the share in the volume of money market transactions of commercial paper sold outright averaged only 3.6%, compared with 4.5% in the second half of the 1970s. The total volume of pesos also showed a constant decline.

Government Securities

Instruments in the government securities market consist of issues of the central bank (e.g., Central Bank Certificates of Indebtedness (CBCIs) and CB bills), the national government (e.g., treasury bills), and debt instruments of government corporations and financial institutions (e.g., DBP bonds). The scope of the government securities market discussed here includes only the marketable securities traded in the market and not some special CB issues, such as those used by banks and nonbank quasi banks for branching requirements. Normally, government securities are relegated to their institutional roles as a tool for monetary and fiscal policies, such as for the control of money and the allocation of credit, and as instruments for public-sector debt. Nevertheless, the government securities market grew in importance relative to the entire money market, especially in the 1980s, owing to the greater acceptance of these instruments as an alternative investment.

In the 1970s, the primary government securities sold without recourse to investors were the CBCIs and the treasury bills. But owing to their unattractive yield relative to other money market instruments such as commercial papers, the combined market share of all government securities of the total volume of money market transactions averaged only 1%. Likewise, the growth rates of this type of market were negligible.

In most cases, issues of government securities, especially CBCIs, ended up on the balance sheets of financial intermediaries as required investments in accordance with the government's credit policies, such as in agricultural and agrarian credit programs. In 1975, repurchase agreements with the central bank on the holdings of CBCIs and other government securities by banks and nonbank quasi banks were allowed mainly as a means of controlling credit. Most of these instruments were also used as collateral by financial intermediaries with CB's rediscount window.

With the banking reforms in the 1980s, a rationalization program for government securities was instituted by the monetary authorities, to make them competitive in the market. First, starting in 1981, the CBCIs were slowly phased out (although there were reissues in 1983 and 1984). With treasury bills being made the main instrument of public debt and at the same time a primary open-market tool by the central bank. Second, a securities dealership network was instituted, which included nine commercial banks and six nonbank quasi banks.

The share of this market in the total volume of money market transactions markedly increased in 1982 with the entry of the dealership network of these fifteen financial intermediaries. During the same year, new treasury bills at competitive market rates were issued to replace maturing CBCIs. Between 1982 and 1988, the share of this market averaged 17% (Table 6.19). Particularly during the financial crisis in 1984, the total volume of transactions involving government securities more than doubled from the previous year's level, owing to the higher yields of these instruments, which were intended to moderate the liquidity expansion at that time. From 1983 to the third quarter of 1986, the central bank both auctioned and negotiated the sale of primary government securities such as the CBCIs and treasury bills. During the 1980s, the dominant share of this market, particularly for treasury bills, gave the monetary authorities a way of influencing the rates of other instruments in the market.

The biggest investors in government securities, based on their average share between 1983 and 1988, were private corporations (29%), commercial banks (17%), and individual persons (13%) (see Table 6.19a). By instrument, for treasury bills, the top three investors were private corporations, commercial banks, and individual persons (see Table 6.19b). For DBP bonds and other government securities, the top investors were private corporations, other banking institutions, and commercial banks (see Table 6.19c). The phased-out CBCIs attracted investments from trust pension funds, government corporations, commercial banks, private corporations, and private insurance companies (see Table 6.19d).

Table 6.19. Volume of Government Security Transactions[a] by Type of Borrower, 1983–88 (in millions of pesos)

Borrower	1983		1984		1985		1986		1987		1988	
	Volume	Percent	Volume	Percent	Volume	Percent	Volume	Percent	Volume	Percent	Volume	Percent
Treasury bills[b] (national government)	4,899.1	33.0	21,685.2	47.0	38,748.5	51.8	55,680.0	60.1	96,560.5	71.8	295,266.7	84.1
CBCIs[b] (central bank)	3,861.3	26.0	603.8	1.3	13.7	0.0	23.5	0.0	2.2	0.0	—	—
DBP bonds	111.7	0.8	350.7	0.8	20.0	0.0	—	—	262.1	0.2	136.8	0.0
Other government institutions	5,986.9	40.3	23,471.0	50.9	36,043.4	48.2	36,875.4	39.8	37,620.4	28.0	55,774.4	15.9
Total	14,859.0	100.0	46,110.7	100.0	74,825.7	100.0	92,578.9	100.0	134,445.2	100.0	351,177.8	100.0

[a] Sum of monthly trading; no breakdown as to borrower before 1983.

[b] All maturities.

Source: Central Bank of the Philippines.

Table 6.19a. Volume of Government Security Transactions[a] by Type of Investor, 1983–88 (in millions of pesos)

Investor	1983 Volume	1983 Percent	1984 Volume	1984 Percent	1985 Volume	1985 Percent	1986 Volume	1986 Percent	1987 Volume	1987 Percent	1988 Volume	1988 Percent
Commercial banks	2,751.7	18.5	6,443.1	14.0	8,001.9	10.7	8,022.3	8.7	26,304.2	19.6	87,049.8	24.8
Individuals	1,242.6	8.4	6,286.9	13.6	11,182.0	14.9	19,047.7	20.6	14,153.8	10.5	38,376.7	10.9
Private corporations	1,311.9	8.8	11,790.1	25.6	23,331.6	31.2	34,706.9	37.5	53,634.0	39.9	119,024.2	33.9
Other banking institutions	3,826.3	25.8	8,462.5	18.4	11,537.4	15.4	6,858.0	7.4	3,714.8	2.8	7,842.8	2.2
Investment houses	192.8	1.3	1,309.1	2.8	532.4	0.7	48.9	0.1	832.3	0.6	22,009.7	6.3
Trust/pension funds	1,499.2	10.1	2,984.3	6.5	5,029.4	6.7	10,252.1	11.1	13,055.7	9.7	27,696.6	7.9
Rural/thrift banks	168.9	1.1	290.7	0.6	6,220.9	8.3	2,059.0	2.2	3,993.7	3.0	12,888.1	3.7
Government corporations	1,672.5	11.3	2,519.6	5.5	2,175.5	2.9	2,342.2	2.5	4,466.2	3.3	12,475.3	3.6
Finance companies	36.5	0.2	83.5	0.2	128.5	0.2	496.2	0.5	3,207.7	2.4	4,595.8	1.3
Investment companies	78.0	0.5	81.2	0.2	826.1	1.1	1,688.2	1.8	3,004.4	2.2	3,705.4	1.1
Private insurance companies	2,050.9	13.8	5,843.3	12.7	5,846.2	7.8	5,875.4	6.3	3,789.2	2.8	4,464.6	1.3
Government insurance companies	—	—	1.9	0.0	10.4	0.0	979.8	1.1	3,769.8	2.8	9,676.7	2.8
Lending investors	—	—	14.3	0.0	2.0	0.0	59.4	0.1	90.1	0.1	606.7	0.2
Security dealers	27.8	0.2	0.4	0.0	1.3	0.0	110.0	0.1	124.0	0.1	473.0	0.1
National government	—	—	—	—	—	—	32.7	0.0	305.3	0.2	287.2	0.1
Local government	—	—	—	—	—	—	—	—	—	—	5.0	0.0
Total	14,859.0	100.0	46,110.7	100.0	74,825.7	100.0	92,578.9	100.0	134,445.2	100.0	351,177.7	100.0

[a] Sum of monthly trading; no breakdown as to investor before 1983.

Source: Central Bank of the Philippines.

Table 6.19b. Volume of Treasury Bill Transactions[a] by Type of Investor, 1983–88 (in millions of pesos)

Investor	1983		1984		1985		1986		1987		1988	
	Volume	Percent	Volume	Percent	Volume	Percent	Volume	Percent	Volume	Percent	Volume	Percent
Commercial banks	1,480.8	30.2	4,936.7	22.8	4,617.7	11.9	6,954.7	12.5	18,878.4	19.6	78,112.6	26.5
Individuals	636.1	13.0	3,618.4	16.7	7,021.7	18.1	15,102.0	27.1	11,444.8	11.9	35,425.4	12.0
Private corporations	517.6	10.6	7,538.9	34.8	14,768.7	38.1	18,432.5	33.1	33,339.3	34.5	90,103.0	30.5
Other banking institutions	535.8	10.9	318.4	1.5	138.8	0.4	276.9	0.5	2,714.6	2.8	5,824.4	2.0
Investment houses	92.3	1.9	1.6	0.0	264.9	0.7	40.7	0.1	783.3	0.8	19,457.2	6.6
Trust/pension funds	261.5	5.3	994.7	4.6	1,962.8	5.1	6,036.2	10.8	11,043.8	11.4	25,567.5	8.7
Rural/thrift banks	38.4	0.8	221.0	1.0	4,631.9	12.0	1,217.0	2.2	3,248.1	3.4	11,691.8	4.0
Government corporations	1.0	0.0	—	—	703.5	1.8	2,174.4	3.9	2,647.5	2.7	9,056.9	3.1
Finance companies	2.5	0.1	50.6	0.2	105.8	0.3	287.9	0.5	2,811.4	2.9	4,143.2	1.4
Investment companies	67.8	1.4	—	—	151.6	0.4	858.8	1.5	2,960.2	3.1	3,541.5	1.2
Private insurance companies	1,265.4	25.8	4,005.1	18.5	4,368.4	11.3	4,180.5	7.5	3,110.7	3.2	3,538.0	1.2
Government insurance companies	—	—	—	—	9.4	0.0	7.0	0.0	3,203.5	3.3	7,744.9	2.6
Lending investors	—	—	—	—	2.0	0.0	2.8	0.0	52.2	0.1	604.7	0.2
Security dealers	—	—	—	—	1.3	0.0	108.5	0.2	77.2	0.1	435.3	0.1
National government	—	—	—	—	—	—	—	—	245.4	0.3	15.2	0.0
Local government	—	—	—	—	—	—	—	—	—	—	5.0	0.0
Total	4,899.1	100.0	21,685.2	100.0	38,748.5	100.0	55,680.0	100.0	96,560.5	100.0	295,266.7	100.0

[a] Sum of monthly trading; no breakdown as to investor before 1983.

Source: Central Bank of the Philippines.

Table 6.19c. Volume of DBP Bonds and Other Government Security Transactions[a] by Type of Investor, 1983–88 (in millions of pesos)

Investor	1983 Volume	1983 Percent	1984 Volume	1984 Percent	1985 Volume	1985 Percent	1986 Volume	1986 Percent	1987 Volume	1987 Percent	1988 Volume	1988 Percent
Commercial banks	780.5	12.8	1,322.6	5.6	3,379.4	9.4	1,067.7	2.9	7,423.7	19.6	8,937.2	16.0
Individuals	297.0	4.9	2,640.8	11.1	4,159.0	11.5	3,945.7	10.7	2,709.0	7.2	2,951.3	5.3
Private corporations	386.5	6.3	4,019.3	16.9	8,558.4	23.7	16,251.4	44.1	20,294.5	53.6	28,921.2	51.7
Other banking institutions	3,255.4	53.4	8,142.1	34.2	11,398.6	31.6	6,581.1	17.8	1,000.2	2.6	2,018.5	3.6
Investment houses	46.1	0.8	1,307.5	5.5	267.5	0.7	8.2	0.0	49.0	0.1	2,552.4	4.6
Trust/pension funds	204.9	3.4	1,920.4	8.1	3,066.6	8.5	4,215.9	11.4	2,011.9	5.3	2,129.0	3.8
Rural/thrift banks	106.1	1.7	20.3	0.1	1,587.9	4.4	841.9	2.3	745.6	2.0	1,196.3	2.1
Government corporations	821.1	13.5	2,519.6	10.6	1,472.0	4.1	167.8	0.5	1,818.7	4.8	3,418.5	6.1
Finance companies	34.0	0.6	21.9	0.1	22.8	0.1	208.3	0.6	396.3	1.0	452.6	0.8
Investment companies	10.2	0.2	81.2	0.3	674.5	1.9	829.4	2.2	44.2	0.1	163.9	0.3
Private insurance companies	129.0	2.1	1,809.9	7.6	1,475.8	4.1	1,694.4	4.6	678.4	1.8	926.7	1.7
Government insurance companies	—	—	1.9	0.0	1.0	0.0	972.8	2.6	566.3	1.5	1,931.8	3.5
Lending investors	—	—	14.3	0.1	—	—	56.6	0.2	37.9	0.1	2.0	0.0
Security dealers	27.8	0.5	—	—	—	—	1.5	0.0	46.8	0.1	37.7	0.1
National government	—	—	—	—	—	—	32.7	0.1	59.9	0.2	272.0	0.5
Local government	—	—	—	—	—	—	—	—	—	—	—	—
Total	6,098.6	100.0	23,821.7	100.0	36,063.4	100.0	36,875.4	100.0	37,882.5	100.0	55,911.1	100.0

[a] Sum of monthly trading; no breakdown as to investor before 1983.

Source: Central Bank of the Philippines.

Table 6.19d. Volume of CBCI Transactions[a] by Type of Investor, 1983–88 (in millions of pesos)

Investor	1983		1984		1985		1986		1987		1988	
	Volume	Percent	Volume	Percent	Volume	Percent	Volume	Percent	Volume	Percent	Volume	Percent
Commercial banks	490.4	12.7	183.8	30.4	4.9	35.3	—	—	2.1	95.1	—	—
Individuals	309.5	8.0	27.7	4.6	1.4	9.8	—	—	—	—	—	—
Private corporations	407.8	10.6	231.8	38.4	4.5	32.9	23.0	97.9	0.1	4.9	—	—
Other banking institutions	35.1	0.9	2.0	0.3	—	—	—	—	—	—	—	—
Investment houses	54.4	1.4	—	—	—	—	—	—	—	—	—	—
Trust/pension funds	1,032.8	26.7	69.3	11.5	—	—	—	—	—	—	—	—
Rural/thrift banks	24.5	0.6	49.5	8.2	1.0	7.3	—	—	—	—	—	—
Government corporations	850.4	22.0	—	—	—	—	—	—	—	—	—	—
Finance companies	—	—	11.0	1.8	—	—	—	—	—	—	—	—
Investment companies	—	—	—	—	—	—	—	—	—	—	—	—
Private insurance companies	656.4	17.0	28.2	4.7	2.0	14.6	0.5	2.1	—	—	—	—
Government insurance companies	—	—	—	—	—	—	—	—	—	—	—	—
Lending investors	—	—	—	—	—	—	—	—	—	—	—	—
Security dealers	—	—	0.4	0.1	—	—	—	—	—	—	—	—
National government	—	—	—	—	—	—	—	—	—	—	—	—
Local government	—	—	—	—	—	—	—	—	—	—	—	—
Total	3,861.3	100.0	603.8	100.0	13.7	100.0	23.5	100.0	2.2	100.0	—	—

a Sum of monthly trading; no breakdown as to investor before 1983.

Source: Central Bank of the Philippines.

The Foreign Exchange Market

A total of twenty currencies make up the basket of foreign currencies traded at official rates in the foreign exchange market. Of the twenty, twelve form part of the official reserves of the Philippines, led by the U.S. dollar.[17] The U.S. dollar is considered the principal currency mainly because of the traditional ties of the peso to the dollar. After the shift from a fixed–foreign exchange rate regime to a "managed" floating rate in February 1970, the U.S. dollar has been the main currency for intervention in the foreign exchange market by monetary authorities.

Trading in the foreign exchange market involves both forward and spot transactions. The peso–dollar exchange rate is based on the results of the previous day's trading by banks at the FOREX Trading Center.[18] The rates of the peso against the other currencies are based on the New York rates as well as the existing peso–dollar exchange rate. Beginning in the 1970s, the central bank directly controlled the movement of the peso against the U.S. dollar by intervening on the trading floor. Starting in 1972, there was a marked increase in the cental bank's intervention. Pante points out that as a percentage of foreign exchange transactions among commercial banks, the cental bank's purchases and sales of dollars climbed from 9.4% in 1970 to 60% in 1972 (Pante 1983).

For the rest of the 1970s, the monetary authorities followed the official policy of defending the peso against the dollar, quite a formidable task given the persistent current account deficit experienced by the economy during this period.[19] The peso was devalued between 1973 and 1981, but only by a minimal amount. Between 1973 and 1981, the peso depreciated by only 20.1%, compared with 64% between 1970 and 1973. Much of the effort to prop up the value of the peso during this period, characterized by difficulties in the balance of payments due to the 1973/74 oil crisis, was focused on the massive foreign borrowings by monetary authorities. These were intended mainly to build up international reserves in order to shield the peso against undue speculation, given the worsening current account balance. Bautista explains that the authorities adopted this policy because of the scare brought about by the unexpected current account deficit in 1974 and the perceived instability in the world market at that time (Bautista 1978).

This resulted in an overvalued peso that penalized exports but rewarded imports, further aggravating the current account deficit. A drastic devaluation was inevitable when the country experienced a severe balance-of-payments crisis in 1983. Between 1983 and 1984, the peso was devalued twice, mainly to discourage imports. Likewise, several exchange rate control measures were implemented,

1. Requiring all nonbank authorized foreign exchange dealers to sell to the central bank U.S.$100,000 a month.

2. Instituting a dollar-pooling scheme for priority uses, by requiring all banks to sell all dollar receipts to the cental bank.

3. Imposing a 10% excise tax on all foreign exchange sold by the central bank or any of its authorized foreign exchange dealers.

4. Giving banks access to the central bank's special credit facility for sales to it of any of the acceptable foreign currencies and/or deposits of U.S. dollars.

The central bank also imposed stricter standards in approving all foreign borrowings and guarantees limiting these to high-priority projects and the refinancing of maturing obligations and of working capital only for overseas projects. The amount of foreign exchange allowed Philippine overseas companies was reduced and the private sector's debt obligations were monitored, requiring monthly reports of all foreign obligations.

The BOP crisis of 1983/84 unmasked the inherent weakness of the peso vis-à-vis the dollar. The Philippines was no stranger to unfavorable trade developments in the 1980s, since the country had also experienced balance-of-payment difficulties in the 1970s. The only difference was that earlier the peso had been artificially strengthened by a strong capital account.

Starting in 1980, the strong dollar, the recession in most industrial economies, and the Philippines' debt service began to exact a toll on the country's reserves. The monetary authorities tried to prevent speculation on the peso–dollar rate by steadily but gradually allowing the peso to depreciate. Debtors and traders sought forward exchange cover through swaps. Financial intermediaries, notably the commercial banks, also were active participants in the market. Table 6.20 shows that the total amount of dollars bought from the central bank exceeded the amount sold in the future exchange market, indicating that the banks were profiting from the dollar trade. In effect, the central bank was giving these banks dollar subsidies.

Table 6.20. Outstanding Volume[a] of Forward Exchange Contracts by Commercial Banks, 1978–88 (in millions of pesos)

	1978	1979	1980	1981	1982	1983
Bought	7,566	13,693	20,902	25,131	34,265	49,574
Sold	4,368	9,013	15,281	19,493	24,537	34,146
Total	11,934	22,706	36,183	44,624	58,802	83,720

	1984	1985	1986	1987	1988
Bought	70,518	31,976	24,140	23,945	26,781
Sold	48,489	10,570	9,227	10,970	12,561
Total	119,007	42,546	33,367	34,915	39,342

[a] Year-end figures.

Source: Central Bank of the Philippines.

Realizing the futility of further defending the peso as well as the need to let the peso find its real value, all exchange controls were lifted in 1984. The cental bank also finally stopped accommodating forward exchange covers resulting from heavy losses when a brief unrestricted trading sharply depreciated the peso from P14.002 in October 1983 to P18.002 in June 1984.

Developments in the foreign exchange market also influenced the money market. The intensified marketing of CBCIs and T-bills, a strategy used during 1983/84 to mop up excess liquidity, was adopted partly to minimize speculations on the dollar. At present, however, the central bank still has the option of intervening in the flow of trade at the FOREX Center as a way to maintain the existing rate and/or prevent severe fluctuations in the pursuit of monetary and economic targets.

Key Events

In early 1981 the Philippine economy experienced a major financial crisis when Dewey Dee, a prominent Filipino-Chinese businessman, suddenly fled the country, leaving behind P635 million (or 2.7% of the country's money supply) in unpaid debts. The sources of these debts were unsecured loans from several financial institutions, overborrowing from the money market, and loans from foreign banks with central bank approval. When this scandal surfaced, the public reaction was instantaneous: Money market placements were terminated early, and deposits were withdrawn to be placed in what were believed to be safer repositories, such as the local branches of foreign banks. In the wake of this crisis, several institutions that had actively participated in the money market went bankrupt. Subsequently there was a decline in the commercial paper market and in the importance of investment houses and financial institutions as money market institutions. On the whole, however, money still grew by 8.5% in 1981, which was only slightly lower than the 1976–80 average growth rate of 12%.

The most recent economic crisis was in 1983 when the Philippines experienced severe balance-of-payments difficulties. Although this particular BOP crisis had long historical roots, it was the Aquino assassination and the central bank's disclosures regarding its international reserves that precipitated it. During this period, international lending institutions ceased further lending to the Philippines and called in their maturing loans in the second half of 1983.

The response to the crisis in the monetary sector was generally restrictive and deflationary. Reserve requirements were increased; the central bank rediscounting window was nearly closed; and the CB bills, which carried relatively high interest rates, were introduced to help mop up excess liquidity. Although the unprecedentedly high rates offered on these bills seemed to have arrested capital outflows that might have put further pressure on the peso, they led to high interest rates in the whole system, resulting in a massive decline in trade and inventory financing.

THE EFFECT OF POLICY ON THE MONEY MARKET'S PERFORMANCE

Performance Measures

We analyzed the behavior of the money market along two dimensions, efficiency and stability. We evaluated efficiency according to whether the interest rate of the principal instruments in a given market moved in tandem with some reference interest rate and also whether the spreads between the reference rate and the particular market rate were consistent with reasonable differences in risk or transactions cost (definition from Cole, Slade, et al. 1990). A more rigorous definition states that a market is considered efficient when the prices and interest rates of money market instruments correctly reflect the available information.

In order to identify a reference rate, we applied a unit root test to the rates of various instruments. (The test and the results are presented in the Appendix.) The first difference of those rates that were determined to have unit roots was then checked to see whether they exhibited a pattern closely following the assumptions of independent and identically distributed error terms (i.i.d.). The objective of such a combination of tests is to determine whether the behavior of a particular market follows a random walk. If it does, then the market is considered to be efficient, since a random walk indicates that all information is being fully utilized by the agents involved, effectively discounting the possibility of arbitrage resulting in economic profits.

Many rates were considered as the possible reference rate, the ninety-one-day treasury bill rate, the interbank call loan rate, promissory notes (selected maturities), government repurchase agreements (selected maturities), and private repurchase agreements (selected maturities) . Although several rates qualified as the reference rate, we decided to use the ninety-one-day treasury bill rate for this purpose, for the following reasons: First, it is the most widely quoted rate, as bankers use it as a basis for setting their lending rates. Second, government-issued securities are mostly in the form of ninety-one-day treasury bills. Last, in different econometric studies of the linkage between real and financial sectors, the ninety-one-day treasury bill rate consistently turned out to be a significant transmission mechanism.

A direct measure of operating efficiency is the spread between the price of funds in the market in our study and the reference rate. If r is the market rate, the spread is computed to be $r - \delta$, where δ is the reference rate. We computed the monthly spreads for a selected subset of instruments and then computed an annual average (equal to $\Sigma(r - \delta)/12$). We call this measure the *spread average*.

An indirect measure of operating efficiency is liquidity. A market for an intermediated instrument is considered liquid, or deep and broad, if it has many suppliers and borrowers over a wide range of prices. We simplified our analysis by using as a measure of liquidity the monthly range of interest rates, averaged over a whole year. The range is defined to be the difference between the highest rate and the lowest rate accepted by the seller of the instrument.[20] We call this measure the *range average*. However, in our later analysis we observed that this measure could also be an indicator of the market's stability, especially since the range, like the variance, is a measure of dispersion.

A second indirect measure of operating efficiency is the concentration of financial institutions in the market. A small number of financial institutions in the market would reduce efficiency by permitting collusion in the pricing of financial services. We counted the number of institutions that held approximately 55% of the market share and compared it across time.

Stability was relatively difficult to measure for this study. We tried using the variance between the price and the volume as an indicator of stability, with a smaller variance indicative of greater stability in the money market. However, data on the variance of a particular instrument's rate over a monthly period was not readily available. An alternative was to compute the variance across a twelve-month period, although such a figure is of limited usefulness compared with an average monthly variance.

The Effect of Policy

At its inception, the money market was allowed to develop in a relatively unregulated atmosphere until its rapid expansion was deemed detrimental to the growth of the real sector. Beginning in 1973, the money market was subjected to various regulations and controls, culminating in the central bank's policy of 1977, in which the different instruments were slapped with a 35% tax and ceilings were imposed on the interest rates of deposit substitutes. It has been hypothesized that controls on pricing within the money market decreases the efficiency, but may increase the stability, of those markets.

This hypothesis cannot be effectively tested because we do not have complete data for the period 1975–81 (in fact, the data for 1981 is missing for almost all the instruments). The available data are presented in Table 6.21. Note that the range average fell markedly from 1975 to 1977 and again from 1977 to 1980. Granted that the range average is a measure of liquidity, the downward movement in the figures implies a narrower band within which interest rates fluctuated and hence shows a decline in efficiency. But this analysis is not supported by the direct indicator of operating efficiency, which is the spread average.

The figures for 1977 and 1980 in Table 6.21 are smaller in absolute value than those of 1975. Assuming that these years are representative of the general trend, it would seem that efficiency in the money market generally increased. But such a conclusion may be misleading, since even the ninety-one-day T-bill rate experienced a similar decrease in its range aver-

Table 6.21. Spread and Range Average Before 1981

Instrument	1975	1976	1977	1978	1979	1980
Spread average						
Interbank call loans	1.362	1.225	1.076	−0.397	1.319	−0.266
Promissory notes (demand)	4.306	—	1.690	—	—	0.072
Promissory notes (1- to 7-day maturity)	2.228	—	2.432	—	—	0.621
Promissory notes (8- to 15-day maturity)	3.060	—	1.358	—	—	1.216
Promissory notes (31- to 45-day maturity)	4.519	—	1.972	—	—	2.726
Government repurchase agreements (demand)	4.870	—	2.177	—	—	0.154
Government repurchase agreements (1- to 7-day maturity)	2.294	—	2.610	—	—	−0.279
Government repurchase agreements (8- to 15-day maturity)	2.431	—	1.969	—	—	1.767
Government repurchase agreements (16- to 30-day maturity)	3.657	—	1.167	—	—	2.143
Private repurchase agreements (demand)	6.009	—	2.793	—	—	−0.270
Private repurchase agreements (1- to 7-day maturity)	4.036	—	1.107	—	—	−1.621
Private repurchase agreements (31- to 45-day maturity)	5.298	—	2.958	—	—	3.193
Commercial paper (nonfinancial)	5.441	3.904	2.668	0.537	2.084	3.922
Commercial paper (financial)	4.252	4.307	3.094	0.383	3.143	5.276

Table 6.21. (*Continued*)

Instrument	1975	1976	1977	1978	1979	1980
Range average						
Interbank call loans	12.357	—	13.800	—	—	10.096
Promissory notes (demand)	38.821	—	15.111	—	—	11.118
Promissory notes (1- to 7-day maturity)	30.000	—	10.333	—	—	1.644
Promissory notes (8- to 15-day maturity)	22.357	—	15.111	—	—	2.388
Promissory notes (31- to 45-day maturity)	19.107	—	14.106	—	—	4.445
Government repurchase agreements (demand)	32.786	—	13.778	—	—	8.900
Government repurchase agreements (1- to 7-day maturity)	20.518	—	5.361	—	—	2.746
Government repurchase agreements (8- to 15-day maturity)	13.821	—	7.722	—	—	1.488
Government repurchase agreements (16- to 30-day maturity)	15.221	—	7.750	—	—	1.634
Private repurchase agreements (demand)	38.143	—	13.611	—	—	6.755
Private repurchase agreements (1- to 7-day maturity)	28.861	—	8.367	—	—	1.499
Private repurchase agreements (31- to 45-day maturity)	17.786	—	9.409	—	—	2.792
Commercial paper (nonfinancial)	26.357	—	22.636	—	—	9.529
Commercial paper (financial)	15.036	—	12.525	—	—	10.803

Source: Central Bank of the Philippines.

age (please refer to Figure 6.2.). We may surmise that the repression prevailing in the financial system at that time led to a general narrowing of the range within which interest rates could fluctuate, whether or not the latter were from an efficient market.

The range average could also be interpreted to mean that there was greater stability in the market. This is likely, since this measure took a big jump in 1982 compared with the figures for 1980. This is readily observed when comparing Table 6.21 with Figure 6.3. Right in the middle of these two years came the Dewey Dee crisis. It is highly probable that the scandal induced greater instability in the market, which was then reflected in the data.

A slight complication arises though, because it was during the same year of the financial crisis that the central bank began implementing its liberalization program. Although this may also have contributed to the significant increase in the market's instability, theoretically efficiency should have also been enhanced. Following the definition of a liquid market and its relation to efficiency, the rise in the range average could also be attributed to the increase in efficiency. The latter could also be gleaned from the relatively low spread average for instruments with an on-demand maturity[21] (see Table 6.22).

From this discussion we conclude that the range average is an indicator of both stability and efficiency. As for the spread average, in a regime of controlled interest rates, it ceases to be a reliable gauge of efficiency. One could also look at Figures 6.3 and 6.4 and observe data points during the crisis year of 1984 for instruments with on-demand maturities. There is a high correlation (albeit negative) between the spread average and the range average.

Thus far, we have presented adequate evidence to support the hypothesis that controls on pricing lead to a decline in efficiency but an increase in stability. During the time that the money market was effectively regulated,

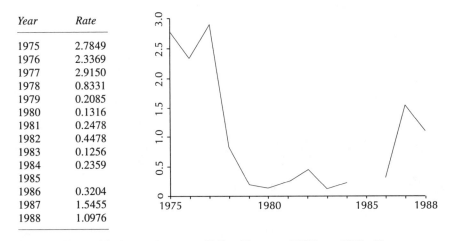

Year	Rate
1975	2.7849
1976	2.3369
1977	2.9150
1978	0.8331
1979	0.2085
1980	0.1316
1981	0.2478
1982	0.4478
1983	0.1256
1984	0.2359
1985	
1986	0.3204
1987	1.5455
1988	1.0976

Figure 6.2. Range Average: 91-Day Treasury Bill Rate, 1975–88

Table 6.22. Money Market Transactions[a] by Maturity of Paper Volume and Share, 1975–88

Maturity	Volume	Percent
Demand (interbank call loans)	1,573,651.1	34.35
Demand	1,311,159.3	28.62
1- to 7-day maturity	204,195.2	4.46
8- to 15-day maturity	175,859.3	3.84
16- to 30-day maturity	431,397.2	9.42
31- to 45-day maturity	440,328.0	9.61
46- to 60-day maturity	184,480.7	4.03
61- to 90-day maturity	164,456.2	3.59
91- to 120-day maturity	38,562.8	0.84
121- to 180-day maturity	21,545.6	0.47
181- to 730-day maturity	22,782.6	0.50
Over 730-day maturity	12,441.7	0.27
Total	4,580,859.7	100.00

[a] First-quarter data for year 1975 not available.

Source: Central Bank of the Philippines.

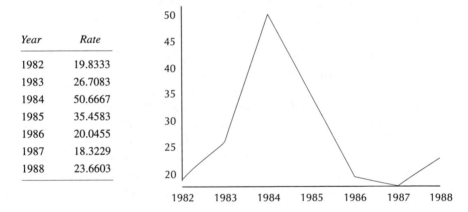

Year	Rate
1982	19.8333
1983	26.7083
1984	50.6667
1985	35.4583
1986	20.0455
1987	18.3229
1988	23.6603

Figure 6.3a. Range Average: Interbank Call Loan Rate

Year	Rate
1982	24.5417
1983	28.9063
1984	52.8500
1985	37.2500
1986	22.0455
1987	17.8342
1988	21.9671

Figure 6.3b. Range Average: Promissory Notes (Demand)

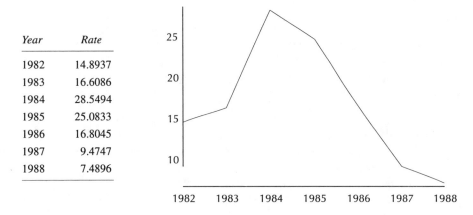

Year	Rate
1982	14.8937
1983	16.6086
1984	28.5494
1985	25.0833
1986	16.8045
1987	9.4747
1988	7.4896

Figure 6.3c. Range Average: Promissory Notes (1- to 7-Day Maturity)

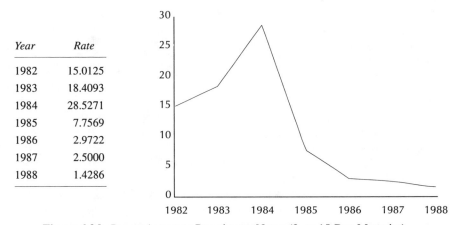

Year	Rate
1982	15.0125
1983	18.4093
1984	28.5271
1985	7.7569
1986	2.9722
1987	2.5000
1988	1.4286

Figure 6.3d. Range Average: Promissory Notes (8- to 15-Day Maturity)

Year	Rate
1982	14.5400
1983	16.1583
1984	27.0412
1985	14.1154
1986	9.8973
1987	6.2646
1988	4.3542

Figure 6.3e. Range Average: Promissory Notes (31- to 45-Day Maturity)

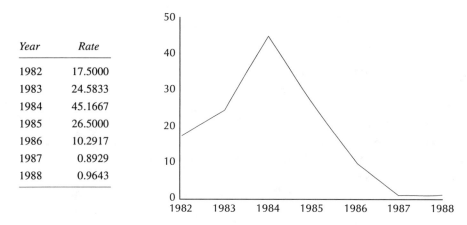

Year	Rate
1982	17.5000
1983	24.5833
1984	45.1667
1985	26.5000
1986	10.2917
1987	0.8929
1988	0.9643

Figure 6.3f. Range Average: Government Repurchase Agreements

Year	Rate
1982	8.4715
1983	8.7509
1984	16.0490
1985	2.0000
1986	0.1166
1987	1.0000
1988	2.0000

Figure 6.3g. Range Average: Government Repurchase Agreements (1- to 7-Day Maturity)

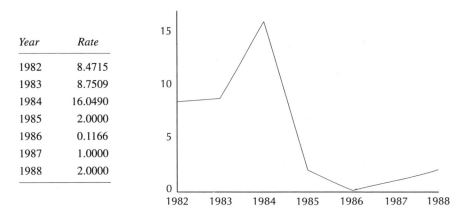

Year	Rate
1982	5.8125
1983	8.4163
1984	17.8875
1985	11.0000
1986	0.6580
1987	0.1000
1988	0.0000

Figure 6.3h. Range Average: Government Repurchase Agreements (8- to 15-Day Maturity)

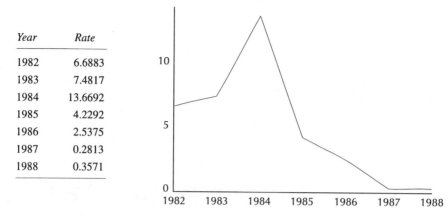

Year	Rate
1982	6.6883
1983	7.4817
1984	13.6692
1985	4.2292
1986	2.5375
1987	0.2813
1988	0.3571

Figure 6.3i. Range Average: Government Repurchase Agreements (16- to 30-Day Maturity)

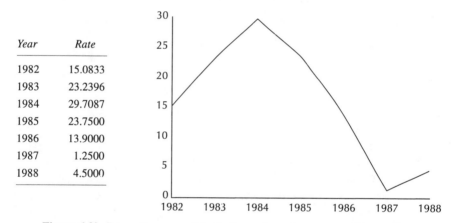

Year	Rate
1982	15.0833
1983	23.2396
1984	29.7087
1985	23.7500
1986	13.9000
1987	1.2500
1988	4.5000

Figure 6.3j. Range Average: Private Repurchase Agreements (Demand)

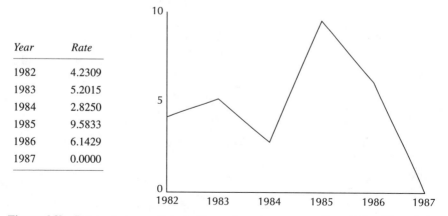

Year	Rate
1982	4.2309
1983	5.2015
1984	2.8250
1985	9.5833
1986	6.1429
1987	0.0000

Figure 6.3k. Range Average: Private Repurchase Agreements (1- to 7-Day Maturity)

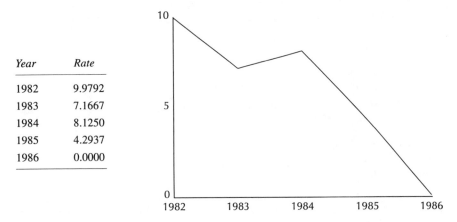

Year	Rate
1982	9.9792
1983	7.1667
1984	8.1250
1985	4.2937
1986	0.0000

Figure 6.3l. Range Average: Private Repurchase Agreements (31- to 45-Day Maturity)

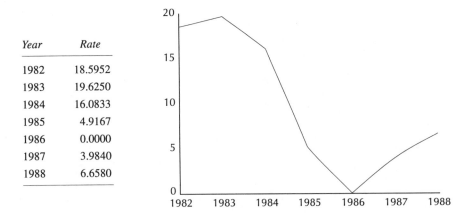

Year	Rate
1982	18.5952
1983	19.6250
1984	16.0833
1985	4.9167
1986	0.0000
1987	3.9840
1988	6.6580

Figure 6.3m. Range Average: Commercial Paper Without Recourse (Financial)

Year	Rate
1982	16.0173
1983	12.6250
1984	23.0833
1985	25.3187
1986	8.8125
1987	8.0167
1988	8.6231

Figure 6.3n. Range Average: Commercial Paper Without Recourse (Nonfinancial)

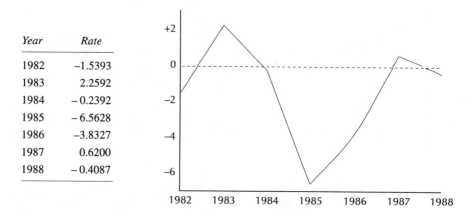

Year	Rate
1982	−1.5393
1983	2.2592
1984	−0.2392
1985	−6.5628
1986	−3.8327
1987	0.6200
1988	−0.4087

Figure 6.4a. Spread Average: Interbank Call Loan Rate

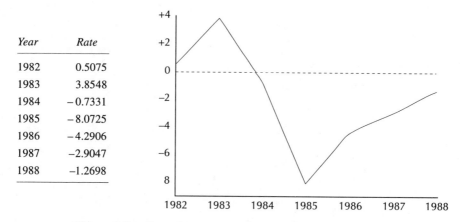

Year	Rate
1982	0.5075
1983	3.8548
1984	−0.7331
1985	−8.0725
1986	−4.2906
1987	−2.9047
1988	−1.2698

Figure 6.4b. Spread Average: Promissory Notes (Demand)

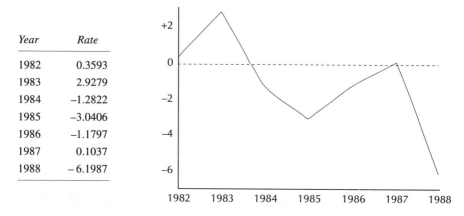

Year	Rate
1982	0.3593
1983	2.9279
1984	−1.2822
1985	−3.0406
1986	−1.1797
1987	0.1037
1988	−6.1987

Figure 6.4c. Spread Average: Promissory Notes (1- to 7-Day Maturity)

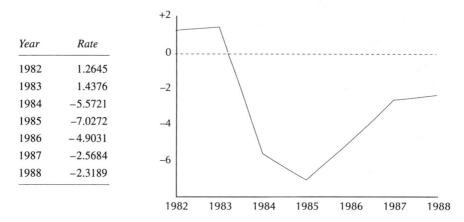

Year	Rate
1982	1.2645
1983	1.4376
1984	−5.5721
1985	−7.0272
1986	−4.9031
1987	−2.5684
1988	−2.3189

Figure 6.4d. Spread Average: Promissory Notes (8- to 15-Day Maturity)

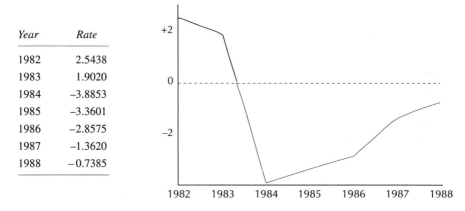

Year	Rate
1982	2.5438
1983	1.9020
1984	−3.8853
1985	−3.3601
1986	−2.8575
1987	−1.3620
1988	−0.7385

Figure 6.4e. Spread Average: Promissory Notes (31- to 45-Day Maturity)

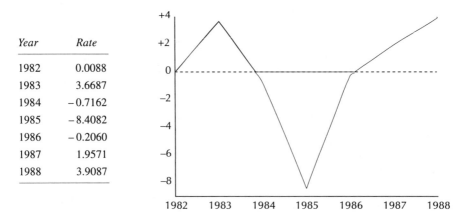

Year	Rate
1982	0.0088
1983	3.6687
1984	−0.7162
1985	−8.4082
1986	−0.2060
1987	1.9571
1988	3.9087

Figure 6.4f. Spread Average: Government Repurchase Agreements (Demand)

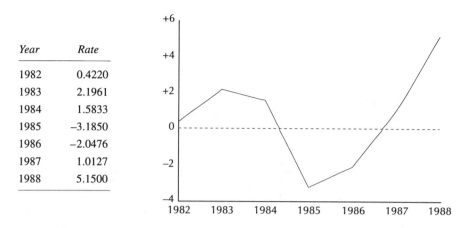

Year	Rate
1982	0.4220
1983	2.1961
1984	1.5833
1985	−3.1850
1986	−2.0476
1987	1.0127
1988	5.1500

Figure 6.4g. Spread Average: Government Repurchase Agreements (1- to 7-Day Maturity)

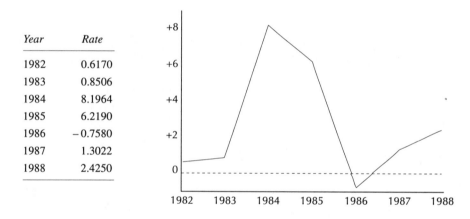

Year	Rate
1982	0.6170
1983	0.8506
1984	8.1964
1985	6.2190
1986	− 0.7580
1987	1.3022
1988	2.4250

Figure 6.4h. Spread Average: Government Repurchase Agreements (8- to 15-Day Maturity)

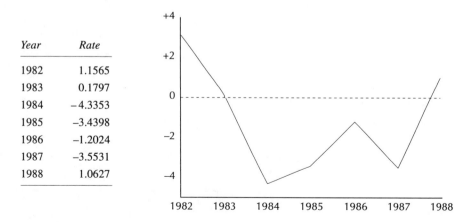

Year	Rate
1982	1.1565
1983	0.1797
1984	− 4.3353
1985	−3.4398
1986	−1.2024
1987	−3.5531
1988	1.0627

Figure 6.4i. Spread Average: Government Repurchase Agreements (16- to 30-Day Maturity)

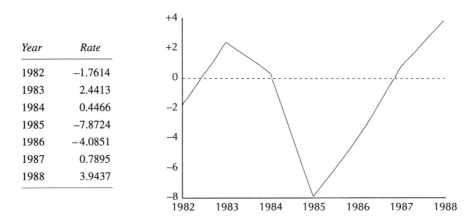

Year	Rate
1982	−1.7614
1983	2.4413
1984	0.4466
1985	−7.8724
1986	−4.0851
1987	0.7895
1988	3.9437

Figure 6.4j. Spread Average: Private Repurchase Agreements (Demand)

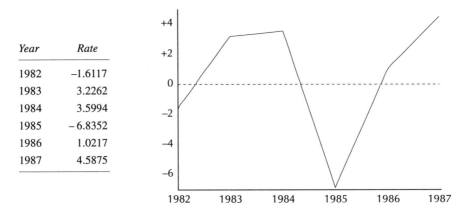

Year	Rate
1982	−1.6117
1983	3.2262
1984	3.5994
1985	−6.8352
1986	1.0217
1987	4.5875

Figure 6.4k. Spread Average: Private Repurchase Agreements (1- to 7-Day Maturity)

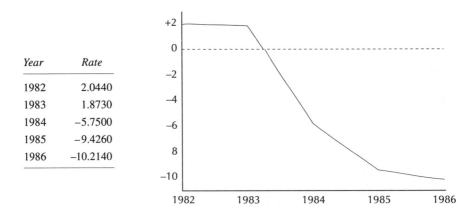

Year	Rate
1982	2.0440
1983	1.8730
1984	−5.7500
1985	−9.4260
1986	−10.2140

Figure 6.4l. Spread Average: Private Repurchase Agreements (31- to 45-Day Maturity)

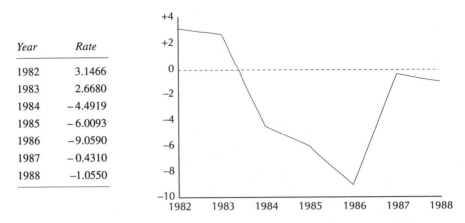

Year	Rate
1982	3.1466
1983	2.6680
1984	−4.4919
1985	−6.0093
1986	−9.0590
1987	−0.4310
1988	−1.0550

Figure 6.4m. Spread Average: Commercial Paper Without Recourse (Financial)

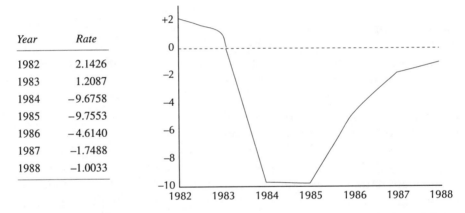

Year	Rate
1982	2.1426
1983	1.2087
1984	−9.6758
1985	−9.7553
1986	−4.6140
1987	−1.7488
1988	−1.0033

Figure 6.4n. Spread Average: Commercial Paper Without Recourse (Nonfinancial)

the range average declined. After the liberalization program in 1981, the range average increased, accompanied by low values for the spread average. Further support for this conjecture is provided by running cointegration tests using the reference rate and various market rates. If two or more variables are cointegrated in the sense of Engle and Granger (1987), there will be an equilibrium condition among them.

Table 6.23 shows the result of the cointegration tests. For almost all rates, especially for those with on-demand maturity, and when using all years for which data are available, we find that the market rates are cointegrated with the reference rate. On the other hand, if we divide the sample period into two subsets, one before 1981, when financial reforms were introduced, and the other after 1981, we obtain mixed results. The latter shows that a market rate may not be cointegrated with the reference rate before 1981 but is cointegrated later on, but not the other way around. This

Table 6.23. Testing for Cointegration with 91-Day Treasury Bill Rate

Instrument	All Years	Before 1981	After 1981
Interbank call loans	Coint	N.A.	Coint
Promissory notes (demand)	Coint	Not coint	Coint
Promissory notes (1- to 7-day)	Coint	Not coint	Coint
Promissory notes (8- to 15-day)	Not coint	Not coint	Not coint
Government repurchase agreements (demand)	Coint	Not coint	Coint
Government repurchase agreements (1- to 7-day)	Coint	Coint	Coint
Government repurchase agreements (8- to 15-day)	Not coint	Not coint	Not coint
Government repurchase agreements (16- to 30-day)	Coint	Not coint	Coint
Private repurchase agreements (demand)	Coint	Not coint	Coint
Private repurchase agreements (1- to 7-day)	Coint	Not coint	Not coint
Private repurchase agreements (8- to 15-day)	Not coint	Not coint	Not coint
Private repurchase agreements (31- to 45-day)	Not coint	Not coint	Not coint

outcome supports the hypothesis that distortions were introduced by the imposition of interest-rate ceilings and other forms of control. These, however, were reduced with the introduction of the liberalization program.

In 1980 the central bank fundamentally altered the structure of the financial system by introducing the concept of universal banking. By imposing a minimal capital requirement of P500 million to qualify as a universal bank, this reform act effectively regulated the number of participants and granted a privilege to a select group of financial institutions. The original objective of this act was to reduce specialization and thus eliminate market segmentation, to increase allocative efficiency, and to enhance the stability of the financial system. It is hypothesized, however, that the operational efficiency will decrease because of the potential oligopolistic structure. In this case, a more appropriate measure of efficiency would be the concentration ratio, defined earlier.

Table 6.24 lists the specific financial institutions that comprise 55% of the market share in trading account securities.[22] In 1979, fourteen institutions contributed to 55% of the market share. In 1985 the list was pruned down to eight, a figure that reached a low of five in 1987. What is more striking is that investment houses and financing companies were eased out completely from the picture from 1985 onward and that during the recovery years of 1986–88 it was mostly universal banks that dominated the scene. Judging from these data, we can conclude that to the extent that greater concentration is a measure of less efficiency, there was a decline in the money market's operating efficiency.

Analysis of Key Events

The effect of government policy on the behavior of the money market can also be observed by analyzing specific key events, the response of the gov-

Table 6.24. Trading Account Securities of Bank and Nonbank Financial
Intermediaries, Selected Years

Institution	Volume (PM)	Percent	Institution	Volume (PM)	Percent
1979			*1980*		
Allied[a]	762	7.12	Atrium	1,004	8.10
RCBC[a]	666	6.22	Allied[a]	786	6.34
Ayala Invt.	567	5.30	PNB[a]	761	6.14
Metro Bank[a]	555	5.18	Ayala Invt.	755	6.09
Citibank[a]	430	4.02	State Ihi	571	4.61
China[a]	396	3.70	Union[a]	569	4.59
Bancom	392	3.66	China[a]	429	3.46
Filinvest	385	3.60	Asia-Pacific	415	3.35
Inv & Underwrite	375	3.50	Pacific[a]	382	3.08
Bpi[a]	347	3.24	BPI[a]	380	3.07
Pacific[a]	320	2.99	PCIB[a]	350	2.82
State Ihi	297	2.77	Metro Bank[a]	348	2.81
PBCOM[a]	288	2.69	Bancom	314	2.53
Phil-Am	275	2.57			
1985			*1986*		
Allied[a]	2,514	15.12	FEBTC[a]	2,481	13.76
BPI[a]	1,391	8.37	BPI[a]	2,420	13.42
FEBTC[a]	1,242	7.47	Metro Bank[a]	1,752	9.71
PCIB[a]	1,131	6.80	Citytrust[a]	1,252	6.94
Solid[a]	873	5.25	BPI Family[a]	1,157	6.42
Citytrust[a]	798	4.80	Solidbank[a]	1,100	6.10
UCPB[a]	779	4.69			
Security[a]	758	4.56			
1987			*1988*		
PNB[a]	3,203	18.42	PNB[a]	5,249	20.80
FEBTC[a]	2,945	16.94	Metro Bank[a]	2,800	11.09
PCIB[a]	1,750	10.07	PCIB[a]	2,181	8.64
Metro Bank[a]	1,210	6.96	BPI[a]	1,537	6.09
UCBP[a]	1,166	6.71	FEBTC[a]	1,529	6.06
			Interbank[a]	1,337	5.30

[a] Banks; otherwise, NBQBs.

Source: Published financial statements.

ernment to any instability caused by these events, and the resulting reaction of the money market. The events we analyze here were described earlier.

The first key event is the Dewey Dee scandal in 1981. However, a rigorous analysis of this crisis is not possible, for two reasons. First, data for the money market for 1981 were not provided by the central bank. And second, data after 1981 were influenced by major policies instituted in 1980 and 1981.

Instead, we focus on the balance-of-payments crisis in 1983, triggered by the assassination of a key political figure. Looking at Figure 6.3, we observe that the range average for almost all instruments peaked in 1984 (this is true for all instruments with on-demand maturity). Simultaneously, the spread average dropped to negligible levels (again true for all instruments with on-demand maturity). However, the spread average bottomed out in 1985, and in most cases the absolute value was greatest between 1982 and 1988.

The substance of these figures becomes apparent in the sequence of policies that took effect. Because of the increase in market instability, the government sought to control the transactions involved. Although these efforts met with some success, it was only at the cost of reduced efficiency. What is left unanswered is the response to the policy.

During the last quarter of 1984, the central bank began to sell the much-celebrated "Jobo" bills, which carried a much higher rate than did other instruments.[23] The main objective for floating these attractive bonds was to arrest the outflow of capital. In addition, the high interest rates reduced domestic absorption, thus freeing resources that were used to meet external debt obligations. At this time also, the government required that all public offices invest all their surplus funds in CB bills or treasury bills.

Other policy responses by the government to the crisis were three major currency devaluations, accompanied by severe foreign exchange restrictions and wide-ranging import controls. These included the creation of a foreign exchange pool for priority import payments, by requiring banks to sell 100% of their foreign exchange receipts to the central bank and setting up priorities in the allocation of foreign exchange. The money supply was also tightened by raising reserve requirements.[24]

That the portfolio restriction contributed to the decline in operating efficiency is a hypothesis supported by the data. However, one critical factor that gave rise to the larger spread between the reference rate and the yields of other instruments is that the former was held at an artificially high level. The central bank achieved its objective of slowing speculation and financial instability, by effectively choking off expenditure demand and suppressing the other sectors of the money market. Transactions in money market instruments, excluding treasury bills and interbank call loans, declined rapidly between 1983 and 1985 and have not yet recovered (see Table 6.10).

The government's financial and fiscal policies following the BOP crisis of 1983 have not been fundamentally altered; the former, because of the lack of a better term, can be described as *elitist*. A basic macroeconomic identity as modified by Cohen (1987) can be used as a reference to describe the government's general policy.

Assuming that there is no capital accumulation and that all external debt is government debt (which closely approximates reality in the Philippines), the following identity can be derived:

$$TB = (T - G) + D - (1 + \tau)D_{-1}$$

The trade balance, *TB,* is the sum of the government's primary surplus (taxes, T, less government spending, G, which includes repayments on the external debt) and of the net new savings drained from the domestic financial markets; τ is the domestic interest rate.

The government's primary surplus in turn can be decomposed into resources from money creation or the seigniorage tax, S, and the primary surplus due to an excess of tax revenue, Z. The revised identity thus reads as

$$TB = S + Z + D - (1 + \tau)D_{-1}$$

The increase in money supply has generally been maintained at controllable levels. Inflation since 1985 reached a maximum of 14 percent. It can be assumed that the inflation tax has been used to the limit allowed by the IMF. The tax system has been described as regressive, with the government relying heavily on indirect taxes to generate additional revenues. Estimates have also shown the tax system to be inelastic.

Putting aside the option of a currency devaluation, in order to restrain the current account deficit (caused primarily by a currency estimated to be 22% to 25% overvalued), the government must resort to domestic savings. It can do this (and as a matter of fact has done it) by making government financial instruments more attractive than other money market instruments. This in turn has led to a significant degree of crowding out that has maintained real interest rates at a very high level, which in fact are the highest in Asia. As can be observed from Table 6.25 in 1986, real interest rates reached their highest level in five years. The rise in the variable G due to the external debt overhang only exacerbated the situation.

This process, of course, cannot be pursued indefinitely. The government, however, has generally not varied its policy. It avoids implementing stronger measures that would raise direct taxes while at the same time it intervenes in the exchange rate market to prevent a drastic drop in the value of the peso. The main beneficiaries of an overvalued currency are the import-substituting industries, which are themselves heavily dependent on imports. These sectors have been favored with protectionist measures. Likewise, most of the additional direct taxes would come from the upper-income brackets. A high interest rate policy, on the other hand, would benefit large savers and, of course, the large commercial banks. Small savers are restricted to savings deposits, which offer ridiculously low yields. Smaller banks, which are relatively more dependent on income from loans, are faced with a lower demand for credit. It goes without saying that high real interest rates slow down economic growth by discouraging real consumption and investment expenditures.

The net result of this combination of macroeconomic policies is a more skewed income distribution that forms a symbiotic relationship with the banking system's oligopolistic structure. For example, smaller banks hard pressed to generate income from loans, would hesitate to compete with larger banks by offering a higher savings deposit rate. The larger

Table 6.25. Real Interest Rates 1970–89 (in percent)

Year	91-Day T-Bill Rate	Inflation Rate	Real Interest Rate
1970	13.13	14.85	−1.71
1971	11.95	21.90	−9.95
1972	11.92	8.23	3.69
1973	9.43	16.50	−7.07
1974	10.05	34.16	−24.12
1975	10.34	6.78	3.56
1976	10.19	9.23	0.96
1977	10.90	9.93	0.97
1978	10.89	7.29	3.60
1979	12.25	16.51	−4.26
1980	12.14	17.60	−5.46
1981	12.61	12.39	0.22
1982	13.81	10.21	3.60
1983	14.17	10.17	4.01
1984	30.53	50.35	−19.81
1985	26.81	23.10	3.71
1986	14.43	0.75	13.68
1987	11.39	3.79	7.60
1988	14.67	8.76	5.91
1989	19.33	10.60	8.73
1990 [a]	26.00	13.00	13.00

[a] January to May 1990.

Source: Central Bank, Department of Economic Research.

banks would simply match their rates, thus negating any possible increase in the flow of savings deposits to the smaller banks. In the end, the latter would have, at most, the same volume of deposits but at a lower spread, a condition that could prove disastrous. The smaller banks must simply be content to follow the actions of their bigger counterparts.

We may conclude from this brief analysis that the government's macroeconomic policy has created inefficiencies in the financial system in general and the money market in particular.

SOME BROAD CONCLUSIONS

Apart from the hypotheses that we proved, one point stands out in the analysis: There is a trade-off between operating efficiency, on the one hand, and stability, on the other. Policies designed to bring stability to the financial system have met with success only at the cost of operating efficiency, and vice versa.

It seems that the central bank has placed greater weight on the role of stability and that this attitude has created an oligopolistic structure in the financial system that could have led to rent-seeking activity. As a result, both the development of the money market and the overall financial deepening of the economy has stagnated. There could have also been adverse effects on the income distribution, but empirical studies have to be conducted to prove this. It is now up to the policymakers to design reforms that will ensure a more efficient structure, but not at the cost of a financial collapse.

NOTES

1. The unit root test followed Dickey and Fuller 1981.

2. The bank density ratio is the ratio of banking offices to total cities and municipalities as of December 31, 1988.

3. Expanded commercial banks (also called *universal banks*) are allowed to offer a host of banking and nonbanking services, such as investment or merchant banking and own voting shares in allied and nonallied enterprises. Allied undertakings include other commercial banks (up to 30% of total voting shares) and investment institutions (up to 100%). Nonallied undertakings include insurance agencies (up to 35%).

4. The H index is derived by squaring and summing the market shares of the banks in the KB sector.

5. The central bank is also referred to as a *quasi-fiscal agent*; that is, it is primarily responsible for the marketing and stabilization of government securities, and it acts as the financial adviser of the government. The government, through the secretary of finance, must request the Monetary Board's opinion before borrowing from the domestic and international markets.

6. As of July 1993, the Monetary Board of the Bangko Sentral ng Pilipinas (the new name of the central bank) will be composed of the following: the BSP governor as chairman, five representatives from the private sector, and a representative from the government. Unlike the previous Monetary Board, which was composed mostly of cabinet secretaries, the new Monetary Board is dominated by private sector representatives to ensure its independence from the executive branch of government.

7. The central bank began deregulating the foreign exchange markets in a gradual manner in 1991. Presently, the foreign exchange markets are already liberalized. For instance, foreign exchange earners may now retain and use 100 percent of their foreign exchange receipts; authorized agent banks may sell foreign exchange without limit and without prior central bank approval for any payment on any foreign exchange transaction such as travel, educational expenses, medical expenses, and other invisible transactions; and the ban against deposits abroad of residents was lifted.

8. Before 1970, a fixed–exchange rate system was in force.

9. Other exchange controls include quantitative limitations on invisible payments, such as those for travel abroad, educational expenses of students abroad, and maintenance of dependents.

10. Central Bank of the Philippines, "Trade and Payments Systems of the Philippines," June 30, 1980 (mimeo).

11. Wire transmission services were used by blackmarketeers in Manila's Binondo district (also known as the Binondo Central Bank). Binondo bankers bought dollars in the Philippine black market and smuggled them abroad for deposit in major banks. Philippine residents bought these deposits by giving pesos to an intermediary in exchange for the latter's instruction to the major bank to wire dollars to the Philippine resident's overseas account.

12. Exporters are required to surrender their foreign currency receipts to the central bank's authorized agent banks for conversion to pesos. They can understate their invoice value and deposit the difference abroad.

13. Kickbacks for the contract's go-between are paid abroad but are eventually paid in dollars from the Philippines, obtained via higher prices of the goods.

14. This class of instruments was created under Central Bank Circular 438, dated November 1974. Only these instruments, classified under deposit substitutes, are allowed in quasi banking.

15. This does not include commercial paper used as underlying instruments in deposit substitutes in repurchase agreements or by certificates of participation or assignment. The latter were already part of the deposit substitutes market. For functional segregation, all commercial paper issues by financial institutions with or a without quasi-banking license, for example, banks and nonbank quasi banks for purposes of raising funds for their own use, are classified under deposit substitutes. We referred to these earlier as dealer promissory notes or simply promissory notes.

16. The Philippine Securities and Exchange Commission, as the registrar of all corporations, public or private, financial (with or without a quasi-banking license) or nonfinancial, supervises the activities of all corporations. The central bank's role is limited to supervising the operations of financial institutions in relation to its monetary goals, and it does not act as a corporate watchdog.

17. Currencies that are official reserves: U.S. dollar, Japanese yen, pound sterling, Canadian dollar, Swiss franc, Deutsche mark, French franc, Dutch guilder, Austrian schilling, Hong Kong dollar, Singapore dollar, Belgian franc.

18. The central bank allows all authorized foreign exchange dealers to quote spot-buying and -selling rates by a certain percentage below and above the guiding rate. The guiding rate is the weighted average of the rates for all sales made off the trading center floor and is posted daily at the beginning of each day.

19. Central Bank, *Annual Report,* 1970: "Generally, the Central Bank (or an agent acting on its behalf) stands ready to provide foreign exchange at the current rate to maintain the stability of the exchange rate."

20. Most of the rates presented are those of primary issues. Thus high and low rates are bidders' offers accepted by the sellers. Technically this would not reflect a high and low rate for a particular transaction but, rather, for a particular period of time.

21. We chose to emphasize the behavior of instruments with an on-demand maturity, since these accounted for more than 60% of the transactions (refer to Table 6.2). One could also observe from the graphs in Figures 6.4g and 6.4h that between 1982 and 1988 these instruments generally behaved in the same manner.

22. Owing to limitations in the data, we are able to present only the figures for 1979/80 and 1985–88. However, these may be assumed to be representative periods, since the 1981–85 period was one in which the financial sector experienced a number of convulsions.

23. The central bank introduced the CB bills (or "Jobo" bills) under MB Resolution 416, dated March 16, 1984, but began stepping up sales of these instruments only in September. Thus the main effects were not felt until 1985. During this period, transactions in treasury bills at auction were suspended, and instead, rates were determined on a negotiated basis. Hence, although the ninety-one-day treasury bill rate remains the reference rate for the period September 1984–October 1986, its value generally followed the trend of the CB bills.

24. For a more detailed and exhaustive discussion of the government's response to the balance-of-payments crisis, see Lamberte et al. 1985.

REFERENCES

Bautista, R. M. 1978. "Balance of Payments Adjustment Process in the Philippines." Paper presented at the UNCTAD/UNDP Round Expert Group Meeting on the BOP Adjustment in Developing Countries.

Boyce, J. K., and L. Zarsky. 1988. "Capital Flight from the Philippines, 1962–1986." *Journal of*

Philippine Development 152: 191–222.

Cohen, D. 1987. "External and Domestic Debt Constraints of LDCs: A Theory with a Numerical Application to Brazil and Mexico," In *Global Macroeconomics.* Edited by R.C. Bryant and R. Portes. New York: Macmillan.

Cole, D. C., B. F. Slade, et al. 1990. "Development of Money Markets in Indonesia." Photocopy. January.

Dickey, D. A., and W. A. Fuller. 1981. "Likelihood Ratio Statistics for Autoregressive Time Series with a Unit Root." *Conomietrica* 49 (July): 1057–72.

Engle, R. F., and C. W. J. Granger. 1987. "Co-Integration and Error Correction Representation, Estimation and Testing." *Econometrica* 55 (March): 251–76.

Hall, S. G., and S. G. B. Henry. 1988. *Macroeconometric Modelling*. Amsterdam: Elsevier Science.

Lamberte, M. B. 1985. "Financial Liberalization and the Internal Structure of Capital Markets." *Philippine Institute for Development Studies Staff Paper Series 85–07*.

———. 1987. "Comparative Bank Study: A Background Paper. "*PIDS Working Paper Series 87–04*, April.

———. 1989. "Assessment of the Problems of the Financial System: The Philippine Case." *PIDS Working Paper 89–18*, August.

———. Forthcoming. "Assessment of the Problems of the Financial System: The Philippine Case." *Philippine Institute for Development Studies Working Paper Series*.

Lamberte, M. B., et al. "A Review and Appraisal of the Government Response to the 1983–84 Balance-of-Payments Crisis." *PIDS Monograph Series 8*. Makati: Philippine Institute for Development Studies, October.

Licuanan, V. S. 1986. *An Analysis of the Institutional Framework of the Philippine Short-Term Financial Markets*. Makati: Philippine Institute for Development Studies.

Pante, Filologo, Jr. 1983. "Exchange Rate Flexibility and Intervention Policy in the Philippines, 1973–1981." *PIDS Staff Paper Series 83–01*, February.

Program on International Financial Systems (PIFS). 1988. "Methodology Paper for Regional Research Project: Guidelines for Study of Money Markets in Asia." Harvard Institue for International Development, May.

Tan, E. A. 1980. "Philippine Monetary Policy and Aspects of the Financial Market: A Review of the Literature." *Survey of Philippine Development Research I*. Makati: Philippine Institute for Development Studies.

———. 1981. "The Structure and Growth of the Philippine Financial Market and the Behavior of Its Major Components." *PIDS Working Paper Series 81–06*, June.

———. 1989. "Bank Concentration and the Structure of Interest. "*University of the Philippines School of Economics Discussion Paper No. 8915*, October.

World Bank. 1988. *Philippine Financial Sector Study*. Report No. 7177–PH, August.

———. 1989. *World Development Report*.

APPENDIX 6A
MAJOR BANKS AND NONBANKS WITH QUASI-BANKING FUNCTIONS

Commercial Banks (KBs)
  Expanded KBs (EKBs)
        Philippine National Bank (Government)   PNB
        Allied Banking Corporation   Allied
        Bank of the Philippine Islands   BPI
        Citytrust Banking Corporation   Citytrust
        Equitable Banking Corporation   Equitable
        Far East Bank and Trust Company   FEBTC
        Metropolitan Bank and Trust Company   Metrobank
        Philippine Commercial International Bank   PCIB
        United Coconut Planters Bank   UCPB
  Non-EKBs
        Associated Bank   Associated
        Boston Bank   Boston (formerly Combank)
        China Banking Corporation   China Bank
        International Corporate Bank   Interbank
        Philippine Bank of Communications   PBCom
        Philippine Banking Corporation   Philbanking
        Philippine Trust Company   Philtrust
        Pilipinas Bank   Pilipinas
        Producers Bank of the Philippines   Producers
        Prudential Bank and Trust Company   PBTC
        Republic Planters Bank   Republic
        Rizal Commercial Banking Corporation   RCBC
        Security Bank   Security
        Consolidated Bank and Trust Company   Solidbank
        Traders Royal Bank   Traders
        Union Bank of the Philippines   UBP
        Family Bank   Family
  Foreign Banks
        Bank of America   BA
        Standard Chartered   Chartered
        Citibank   Citibank
        Hongkong and Shanghai Banking Corporation   Hongkong-Shanghai

Thrift Banks

Asiatrust Development Bank	Asiatrust
Banco de Oro and Mortgage Bank	Banco de Orod
Bank of the Philippine Islands Family Bank	BPI Family Bank

Special Government Banks

Land Bank of the Philippines	LBP
Development Bank of the Philippines	DBP

Nonbanks with Quasi-Banking Licenses (NBQBs)

Investment Houses

AEA Development Corporation	AEA
Anscor Capital and Investment Corporation	Ascor
Citytrust Investment Philippines	Citicorp
First Metro Investment Corporation	First Metro
Multinational Investment Bancorporation	Multinational
Private Development Corporation of the Philippines	PDCP
State Investment House Incorporated	State IHI
Philippine Pacific Capital Corporation	PPCC
First Pacific Capital Corporation	FPCC
PCI Capital Corporation	PCIC

Finance Companies

Bank of America Finance Corporation	BA Finance
BPI Credit	BPIC
Cebu International Finance Corporation	CIFC
Citytrust Finance Corporation	Citytrust Finance
General Credit Corporation	GCC
First Malayan Leasing and Finance Corporation	Malayan
Paramount Finance Corporation	Paramount
Anscor Finance Corporation	Anscor Finance

PESOS PER U.S. DOLLAR RATE,[a] 1975–89 MONTHLY AVERAGES

Period	January	February	March	April	May	June
1975	7.0664	7.0522	7.0261	7.0177	7.0178	7.0150
1976	7.4856	7.4693	7.4583	7.4354	7.4304	7.4309
1977	7.4279	7.4272	7.4262	7.4109	7.4049	7.3981
1978	7.3715	7.3715	7.3735	7.3668	7.3635	7.3632
1979	7.3762	7.3767	7.3777	7.3796	7.3783	7.3739
1980	7.4167	7.4179	7.4259	7.4434	7.5095	7.5209
1981	7.6323	7.6676	7.7303	7.7904	7.8504	7.9360
1982	8.2542	8.2831	8.3405	8.3792	8.4161	8.4509
1983	9.2865	9.4644	9.6057	9.8693	10.0316	10.3846
1984	14.0020	14.0020	14.0020	14.0020	14.0020	17.4020
1985	18.9794	18.2557	18.4778	18.4841	18.4800	18.4727
1986	19.0417	20.4608	20.7810	20.5045	20.5002	20.5520
1987	20.4629	20.5252	20.5625	20.5048	20.4732	20.4564
1988	20.8461	20.9030	21.0277	21.0296	20.9540	20.9487
1989	21.3421	21.3574	21.3388	21.4136	21.5622	21.6569

Period	July	August	September	October	November	December	Average
1975	7.2719	7.5018	7.5091	7.5001	7.4975	7.4992	7.24790
1976	7.4298	7.4297	7.4290	7.4283	7.4282	7.4282	7.44026
1977	7.3961	7.3940	7.3934	7.3892	7.3869	7.3791	7.40283
1978	7.3609	7.3617	7.3613	7.3590	7.3650	7.3712	7.36576
1979	7.3706	7.3717	7.3722	7.3709	7.3718	7.4110	7.37755
1980	7.5432	7.5562	7.5622	7.5669	7.5802	7.5942	7.51143
1981	7.9491	7.9516	7.9920	8.0641	8.1009	8.1312	7.89966
1982	8.4878	8.5293	8.6380	8.7664	8.8752	9.0594	8.54001
1983	11.0017	11.0016	11.0018	13.7016	14.0020	14.0020	11.11273
1984	18.0020	18.0020	18.0020	19.1482	19.9590	19.8593	16.69871
1985	18.5810	18.6047	18.6157	18.7039	18.7368	18.8963	18.60734
1986	20.4542	20.4316	20.5092	20.4372	20.4360	20.5198	20.38568
1987	20.4500	20.4387	20.6005	20.7062	20.8171	20.8148	20.56769
1988	21.0247	21.0591	21.2485	21.3616	21.3771	21.3560	21.09470
1989	21.8614	21.89	21.9398	21.9483	22.0626	22.3352	21.72569

[a] Per Bankers Association of the Philippines reference rate, starting December 13, 1984.

Source: Central Bank of the Philippines.

APPENDIX 6C
DETERMINING AN APPROPRIATE REFERENCE RATE

One requirement of our study is to identify a reference rate, which is the price of a short-term low-risk instrument in a free, liquid market. Since this reference rate has been used as a basis to measure efficiency in other markets, we simplified the process by determining which particular interest rate followed a random walk. We did this by applying the unit root test developed by Dickey and Fuller (1981) and later determining whether the first difference of the rate or rates with unit roots exhibited a pattern similar to error terms that are independent and identically distributed (i.i.d.). As we stated in the text, a random walk implies that all information pertinent to the market is being fully utilized, thereby effectively discounting the possibility of arbitrage resulting in economic profit.

The unit root test for a particular interest rate r is based on the following model:

$$r = \delta r_{-1} + u$$

where u is a stochastic disturbance term representing white noise. The null hypothesis is that $\delta = 1$, with the alternative hypothesis that the series is stationary (for the case that $|\delta| < 1$) or explosive (for the case that $|\delta| > 1$).

Using the Augmented Dickey–Fuller test to guard against error terms (u in our model) that are not i.i.d., the actual model estimated using ordinary least squares is

$$r = \alpha + \beta r_{-1} + \tau_1 r_{-1} + \tau_2 r_{-2} + \cdots + \tau_p r_{-p} + u$$

This is done in order to generate consistent estimates. If β is insignificant, then the null hypothesis cannot be rejected, and we conclude that the series has a unit root. On the other hand, if β is negative and significant, the null hypothesis is rejected in favor of the alternative that the series is stationary. A positive and significant coefficient for β is indicative of an explosive series.

We ran the model for $p = 2$ and $p = 4$, with the choice of the regression equation based on a higher-adjusted coefficient of determination.

The results for the various interest rates are presented in Tables 6C.1 and 6C.2. To show that an interest rate, r, has a unit root, it must not be integrated of order zero, and its first difference must be integrated of order zero (i.e., r must be $I[1]$). The critical region for the test of significance was obtained from the tables generated by Dickey and Fuller.

Based on the results, we conclude that almost all interest rates have unit roots. The behavior of the first difference of the ninety-one-day treasury bill rate is plotted against time, and its behavior reasonably approximates white noise (please refer to Figure 6C.1). Because of this result and also because of reasons cited in the text, the ninety-one-day treasury bill rate is used as the reference rate.

In addition, we conducted a cointegration test between a particular market rate and the reference rate δ. Following the Granger two-step procedure (Hall and Henry 1988), we first regressed r against δ. If the resulting residual terms were stationary or $I(0)$ (determined by using an augmented Dickey–Fuller test), we could conclude that the two variables were cointegrated.

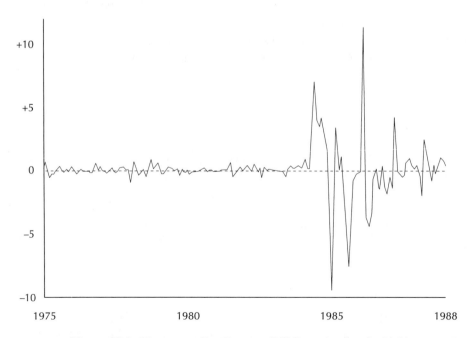

Figure 6C.1. Ninety-one-Day Treasury Bill Rates (testing for i.i.d.)

Table 6C.1. Determination of Order of Integration (Test for I [0]).

Dependent Variable Δx_t	α	x_{t-1}	Explanatory Variables			
			Δx_{t-1}	Δx_{t-2}	Δx_{t-3}	Δx_{t-4}
Interbank call loans	2.420	−0.149	−0.168	−0.157	−0.249	−0.23
	−1.83	−1.94	−1.44	−1.42	−2.32	−0.22
Promissory notes (demand)	1.814	−0.121	−0.214	−0.269	−0.248	−0.194
	−1.58	−1.72	−2.02	−2.63	−2.49	−2.0
Promissory notes (1- to 7-day)	1.723	−0.108	−0.470	−0.370	−0.424	−0.035
	−1.45	−1.53	−4.23	−3.43	−4.12	−0.37
Promissory notes (8- to 15-day)	2.067	−0.133	−0.523	−0.166	−0.130	−0.013
	−1.74	−1.81	−4.47	−1.29	−1.03	−0.11
Government repurchase agreements (demand)	3.534	−0.198	−0.111	−0.195	−0.172	−0.75
	−2.17	−2.15	−0.90	−1.65	−1.53	−0.68
Government repurchase agreements (1- to 7-day)	1.598	−0.090	−0.423	−0.023	−0.222	−0.314
	−1.21	−1.16	−4.01	−0.21	−1.98	−3.81
Government repurchase agreements (8- to 15-day)	2.63	−0.141	0.102	0.112		
	−1.94	−2.20	−0.79	−0.87		
Government repurchase agreements (16- to 30-day)	1.459	−0.088	0.151	−0.004	−0.359	0.187
	−1.76	−1.82	−1.38	−0.04	−3.67	−1.28
Private repurchase agreements (demand)	3.824	−0.223	−0.192	−0.248	−0.248	−0.023
	−1.97	−2.05	−1.40	−1.92	−2.07	−0.20
Private repurchase agreements (1- to 7-day)	4.751	−0.319	−0.127	−0.096		
	−2.36	−2.58	−0.76	−0.75		
Private repurchase agreements (8- to 15-day)	16.51	−1.148	1.041	0.874	0.736	0.742
	−4.64	(4.57)[a]	−3.81	−3.16	−3.08	−3.72
Private repurchase agreements (31- to 45-day)	2.386	−0.144	−0.282	0.054	0.139	0.293
	−1.84	−1.94	−2.18	−0.41	−1.07	−2.46
91-day treasury bill rate	0.712	−0.047	0.373	−0.039		
	−2.22	−2.35	−4.81	−0.50		

[a] Significant at the 5% level.

347

Table 6C.2. Determination of Order of Integration (Test for I/[1])

Interest Rate: X_t; $Z_t = \Delta x_t$ Dependent Variable ΔZ_t	α	Z_{t-1}	Explanatory Variables			
			ΔZ_{t-1}	ΔZ_{t-2}	ΔZ_{t-3}	ΔZ_{t-4}
Interbank call loans	0.029	-1.778	0.523	0.298		
	-0.06	$(8.73)^a$	-3.36	-2.97		
Promissory notes (demand)	-0.041	-1.994	0.711	0.395	0.123	0.082
	-0.10	$(6.07)^a$	-2.57	-1.79	-0.77	-0.83
Promissory notes (1- to 7-day)	0.021	-2.377	0.848	0.438		
	-0.05	$(12.06)^a$	-5.73	-5.16		
Promissory notes (8- to 15-day)	0.018	-1.728	0.108	-0.112		
	-0.05	$(6.44)^a$	-0.54	-1.07		
Government repurchase agreements (demand)	0.175	-1.721	0.498	0.225		
	-0.36	$(8.03)^a$	-3.10	-2.12		
Government repurchase agreements (1- to 7-day)	-0.379	-2.118	0.541	0.276		
	-0.70	$(7.84)^a$	-2.77	-2.79		
Government repurchase agreements (8- to 15-day)	-0.023	-1.035	0.074	0.120		
	-0.03	$(4.75)^a$	-0.41	-0.92		
Government repurchase agreements (16- to 30-day)	0.031	-1.435	0.459	0.395		
	-0.11	$(8.72)^a$	-3.49	-4.10		
Private repurchase agreements (demand)	0.110	-1.996	0.662	0.314		
	-0.15	$(8.90)^a$	-3.97	-2.93		
Private repurchase agreements (1- to 7-day)	-0.053	-1.764	0.329	0.087		
	-0.08	$(5.32)^a$	-1.37	-0.71		
Private repurchase agreements (8- to 15-day)	0.196	-1.386	0.494	0.486	0.323	
	-0.49	$(3.50)^a$	-1.13	-1.21	-1.07	
Private repurchase agreements (31- to 45-day)	-0.05	-1.44	0.049	0.023		0.618
	-0.21	$(5.48)^a$	-0.24	-0.19		-3.0
91-day treasury bill rate	0.029	-0.746	0.103	0.047		
	-0.22	$(6.98)^a$	-1.11	-0.59		

[a] Significant at the 5% level.

CHAPTER 7

MONEY MARKETS IN SINGAPORE

M. ARIFF
B. K. KAPUR
A. TYABJI

The principal markets in short-term (up to a year) funds in Singapore are the markets for bank deposits, overdrafts and commercial bills, interbank loans, and foreign exchange. These funds are issued by a variety of institutions: full, restricted, and offshore commercial banks; merchant banks; finance companies; the Post Office Savings Bank; money brokers; and others. These financial institutions can be grouped into, on the one hand, a national banking system, made up of institutions (or departments within institutions) whose transactions are mainly in Singapore dollar–denominated instruments or involve exchanges between such instruments and those denominated in other currencies, and, on the other hand, an offshore system, made up of institutions (or departments) whose transactions are mainly in and among foreign currency–denominated instruments. Much of the analysis in this chapter will be devoted to the national banking system, as our focus is on money markets operating directly under the regulatory and policy aegis of the monetary authorities.

INSTITUTIONAL DEVELOPMENT AND POLICY CHANGES IN THE MONEY MARKETS SINCE THE 1970s

Throughout much of its history, financial activities in Singapore revolved around its role as the premier regional entrepôt. With the structural changes during the 1960s and the growing importance of manufacturing, commercial banks added industrial financing to their loan portfolios. But these activities mainly serviced domestic trade and industry and, to a lesser extent, the region.

Even during the colonial period up to 1959, Singapore was well provided with banking and other financial institutions. There was a money market (interbank) and a foreign exchange market whose activity was limited to squaring positions by commercial banks. Activity was generally thin. Until early 1973, Singapore, like much of the rest of the world, was on a fixed–exchange rate regime; its exchange rate was determined by a (bank) cartel system. A division of the Ministry of Finance oversaw monetary affairs until 1971, when an independent monetary authority with primary responsibility for supervising the financial system was established.

Since the late 1960s, Singapore's development strategy has become more outward looking; that is, the export of goods and services has become the focal point of policy. Financial activities, which were until then largely domestic centered, were directed toward offshore activities. As a first step, the now well-known Asian dollar market (ADM) was launched in 1968. The goal of developing Singapore as an international financial center has since been nurtured by the government and the monetary authorities, with fiscal incentives and new financial institutions, instruments, and markets. The visible hand of the government has taken the role not only of supervisor, regulator, and policymaker but also of direct participant, especially through the various innovative changes introduced by the Development Bank of Singapore and the Post Office Savings Bank.

Because this study concentrates on the money markets, we will review the institutional and policy changes that have taken place in these markets since the 1970s. We will identify institutions, instruments, and the regulatory environment of each of these institutions. The money market participants are listed in Table 7.1, and a calendar of financial events is provided in Appendix 7A. The calendar of events for Singapore is a chronology of how the monetary regime changed from a fixed-rate, exchange-controlled system to a managed-float system with virtually no exchange controls.

Table 7.1. Money Market Institutions in Singapore, 1970–89

	1970	1980	1989
Banks			
Full license	36	37	35
Restricted license	—	13	14
Offshore license	—	43	85
ACUs	14	109	191
Merchant banks	—	37	65
Finance companies	361	34	30
National saving bank (POSB)	12	1	1
Discount houses	43	4	—
International money brokers	54	7	8

Source: MAS, *Annual Report,* various years.

Commercial Banks

Commercial banks are by far the largest group of money market institutions in Singapore (Table 7.2). Furthermore, they and the Post Office Savings Bank are the only institutions allowed to offer checking facilities. As part of the strategy to develop Singapore as a financial center, many new banks have been permitted entry since the 1970s (see Table 7.1). Before 1971 there was only one type of commercial bank in Singapore, the full-license bank permitted to offer the whole range of banking services. (Of the thirty-five-full-license banks in 1989, thirteen were local and the remainder foreign, like the Bank of America.)

Banks other than those with a full license (both local and foreign) have been permitted entry since 1971, to add breadth to the offshore money market launched in 1968. The 20% liquidity requirement for ACUs (Asian currency units, banking departments engaged in offshore transactions) was lifted, effective in January 1972. The differentiation began in 1971 with the issue of the first restricted license to a foreign bank. Although these banks may offer the whole range of domestic banking business, they cannot accept time (fixed) deposits below S$250,000 (or the equivalent) per deposit from nonbank customers; they cannot operate savings accounts; and they may not open branches.

Yet another type of license was introduced in 1973, again to expand the activities of the offshore (international) market. In addition to the restrictions imposed on the restricted-license banks, offshore-license banks may not accept any interest-bearing deposits from resident non-

Table 7.2. Assets of Money Market Institutions in Singapore, 1975–89 (in millions of S$)

	1975	1980	1989	Annual Average Growth Rate
Commercial banks				
Domestic operations	14,417	33,316	127,207	16.8
Domestic and offshore	43,041	131,253	586,215[a]	22.2
Merchant banks				
Domestic operations[b]	290	1,183	7,631	26.3
Domestic and offshore	1,840	13,300	34,046	23.2
Finance companies	1,430	3,075	10,137	15.0
Discount houses	492	950	2,458[c]	15.7
National savings bank[d]	554	2,786	13,201	25.4

[a] At end of 1988.

[b] Figures do not reflect corporate financial advisory services, underwriting, and operations in the gold market.

[c] Discount houses were discontinued in 1986.

[d] Total depositors' balances.

Source: MAS, The Financial Structure of Singapore, 1980 and 1990 editions.

bank customers and cannot extend credit to them in excess of S$50 million.

The restrictions imposed on both the fourteen restricted- and eighty-five offshore-license banks suggest that competition among the three types of commercial banks is limited to some extent to domestic banking activities but liberalizes their offshore activities. This separates the national banking activities from international activities so that (1) monetary policies can be executed through the national banking system, over which the monetary authorities wish to maintain a certain degree of influence (especially in the short run), and (2) overbanking, in an economy that is relatively small, can be avoided.

The approval of the Monetary Authority of Singapore (MAS) is required for transactions in the Asian dollar market, in which transactions are confined to offshore currencies. In 1989, all the restricted- and offshore-license banks and twenty-five of the full-license banks were permitted to operate in the ADM through their Asian currency units, licensed separately as separate accounting units.

The changing share of selected assets and liabilities of the different banks is depicted in Table 7.3. These share include both domestic and ACU operations. The restrictions pertain to domestic, not offshore, banking activities. In view of this and the large influx of offshore banks since the early 1970s, the picture in Table 7.3 should not be surprising.

As the premier financial institutions, the commercial banks are major participants in the money market. Has the drive toward financial internationalization changed their activities to any significant extent? An answer may be found by examining the commercial banks' consolidated balance sheets over time (presented in Table 7.4). In the aggregate, the balance

Table 7.3. Distribution of Selected Assets/Liabilities by Type of Commercial Banks in Singapore[a] (%)

		Local Banks	Foreign— Full and Restricted	Offshore
Total assets/liabilities	1970	41.1	58.9	—
	1980	13.6	43.6	42.8
	1988	8.4	29.0	62.6
Deposits	1970	40.8	59.2	—
	1980	26.3	57.9	15.8
	1988	25.5	46.6	27.9
Loans and advances	1970	40.3	59.7	—
	1980	20.9	46.6	32.5
	1988	11.8	26.6	61.6

[a] Includes domestic as well as ACU operations.

Source: MAS, *The Financial Structure of Singapore* (Singapore, 1989), Table 12.

Table 7.4. Singapore Commercial Banks: Assets and Liabilities

Items	1970 Amount ($m)	%	1989 Amount ($m)	%
Excluding Asian Currency Units				
Assets				
Cash at hand	43	0.8	401	0.3
Balances with MAS	129	2.5	3,314	2.6
Amount due from banks	941	18.7	57,238	45.0
Money at call with discount houses	—	—	—	—
S$NCDs held	—	—	283	0.2
Investments in securities and equities	921	18.3	10,818	8.5
Loans and advances (including bills)	2,722	54.0	50,786	39.9
Other assets	286	5.7	4,644	3.7
Total assets	5,042	100.0	127,202	100.0
Liabilities				
Capital and reserves	292	5.8	7,972	6.3
Deposits of nonbank customers	3,195	63.4	53,351	41.9
S$NCDs issued[a]	—	—	1,428	1.1
Amount due to banks	1,046	20.7	57,475	45.2
Other liabilities	509	10.1	6,982	5.5
Total liabilities	5,042	100.0	127,202	100.0
Including Asian Currency Units				
Assets				
Cash at hand	43	0.7	590	0.1
Balances with MAS	129	2.1	2,371	0.4
Amount due from banks	2,017	32.7	380,953	65.0
Money at call with discount houses	—	—	—	—
S$NCDs held	—	—	2,660	0.5
Investments in securities and equities	921	14.9	25,616	4.4
Loans and advances (including bills)	2,764	44.7	160,293	27.3
Other assets	303	4.9	13,731	2.3
Total assets	6,177	100.0	586,215	100.0
Liabilities				
Capital and reserves	355	5.7	8,058	1.4
Deposits of nonbank customers	3,941	63.8	125,469	21.4
S$NCDs issued[a]	—	—	5,106	0.9
Amount due to banks	1,420	23.0	427,544	72.9
Other liabilities	461	7.5	20,037	3.4
Total liabilities	6,177	100.0	586,215	100.0

[a] Singapore dollar negotiable certificates of deposit (S$NCDs) first issued by banks in May 1975.

Source: MAS, *The Financial Structure of Singapore* (Singapore, 1989), Tables 9 and 11.

sheet items grew rapidly: Total assets grew at an annual average rate of 18.5% without ACUs from 1970 to 1989 and 28.8% with ACUs between 1970 and 1989. On both the assets and liabilities sides, the most rapid growth is for "Amounts due from and to banks," with or without ACUs, which indicates the importance—indeed, the predominance—of interbank and offshore financial activities. This is supported by the changing share of balance sheet items. For example, the share of loans and advances in 1970 was 54.0% without ACUs and 45% with ACUs. By 1988 this had declined to 43 and 27%, respectively. Likewise, "Amount due from banks" rose to 18.7% without ACUs in 1970 and 32.7% with them. By 1989, this share had risen to 45.0% (65.0% with ACUs in 1988).

As might be expected, these changes are mirrored on the liabilities side: a sharply increased share of "Amount due to banks" and a smaller share of "Deposits of nonbank customers." This indicates the growing importance of the banks' liability management.

Two balance sheet items deserve further examination. In regard to the structure of commercial bank loans and advances (Table 7.5), the clearly discernible change is the growth of term loans and the drop in overdrafts. Term loans constituted only 26% of loans and advances to nonbank customers in 1977 but increased to 53% in 1989. This suggests that perhaps maturity transformation was more prominent in the 1980s than in the 1970s.

An examination of the composition of deposits over the same period reveals, first, the growing importance of interest-bearing deposits (see

Table 7.5. Structure of Commercial Banks' Loans and Advances (%)

				Term Loans		
Year	Bills Financing	Overdrafts	Trusts Receipts	Up to 1 Year	1–3 Years	3 or More Years
1977	23.1	39.8	10.9	9.5	3.9	12.7
1978	23.1	39.9	12.1	9.1	3.7	12.0
1979	24.7	39.0	11.0	9.2	3.6	12.6
1980	20.0	42.2	11.7	8.6	3.4	14.0
1981	15.8	41.0	10.6	11.8	4.2	16.6
1982	13.9	42.8	9.2	10.8	5.2	18.1
1983	11.5	45.4	9.0	11.3	5.6	17.3
1984	11.2	43.8	8.7	13.6	5.9	16.8
1985	9.7	43.0	7.7	17.8	5.5	16.2
1986	11.5	37.9	8.2	20.1	5.8	16.5
1987	9.5	32.9	8.1	26.7	6.0	16.9
1988	8.6	27.2	7.4	24.9	4.9	14.5
1989	8.9	30.9	7.3	27.9	7.2	17.7

Source: Computed from MAS, *Monthly Statistical Bulletin,* various years.

Table 7.6). Second, the S$NCD (negotiable certificates of deposit) is not a significant source of funds for banks.[1] Third, the falling share of demand deposits is closely paralleled by the rising share of savings deposits. This may be attributed to the enhanced liquidity of savings deposits in the 1980s, due especially to technological change.

The operations of all banks (indeed, of most financial institutions) are supervised and regulated by the MAS as administrator for the relevant legislation (the Banking Act as amended in 1984).[2] Supervision takes the form of field inspections, guidelines and notices, reviews of statistical returns, and internal and external audit reports. Periodic returns are required for annual income and expenditure statements, monthly balance sheet data, and schedules of loans to directors, employees, and related companies. Foreign exchange positions are monitored by requiring returns on foreign currency positions. Since April 24, 1986, the following information is required daily by the MAS from banks, merchant banks, and the Post Office Savings Bank: Singapore dollar transactions for new interbank deposits, outstanding interbank deposits, S$NCDs, new swaps on foreign currencies against the Singapore dollar, outstanding swaps of foreign currency against the Singapore dollar, new spot transactions of foreign currency against the Singapore dollar, and maturing transactions of foreign currencies against the Singapore dollar (MAS, Notices to Banks, MAS 1104, April 10, 1986).

The major regulation provisions of the Banking Act pertain to capital adequacy, minimum liquidity requirements (a 6% minimum cash balance and an 18% liquid assets ratio in 1989), and other balance sheet restric-

Table 7.6. Structure of Commercial Bank Deposits (%)

Year	Demand Deposits	Fixed Deposits	S$NCDs	Savings and Other Deposits
1977	28.6	54.9	2.0	14.4
1978	28.3	54.7	2.4	14.6
1979	27.8	55.8	2.6	13.8
1980	23.2	62.9	1.1	12.8
1981	23.7	62.3	1.3	12.7
1982	22.1	62.2	1.2	14.5
1983	20.2	61.0	1.0	17.9
1984	18.9	60.9	0.1	20.1
1985	17.3	58.9	0.1	23.7
1986	18.5	53.4	1.5	26.6
1987	17.7	55.0	2.4	24.9
1988	16.5	57.9	2.3	23.2
1989	14.7	64.2	2.1	19.0

Source: Computed from MAS, *Monthly Statistical Bulletin,* various years.

tions. Some of the relevant prohibitions are that a bank may not grant more than 30% of its capital funds to a single borrower; credit may not be granted against the security of its own shares; unsecured credit to directors, related companies, and employees cannot exceed S$5,000; a bank may not hold more than 40% of its capital funds in any financial, commercial, agricultural, or industrial undertaking (an exception is made for the Development Bank of Singapore),[3] although this excludes interest in another bank or subsidiary company established to carry out nominee, executor, trustee, or other business incidental to banking business; and finally, a bank may not hold more than 40% of its capital funds in immovable property (with the exception of the DBS), and its loans for or against immovable property cannot exceed 30% of its deposits.

Merchant Banks

Merchant banks are perhaps the most heterogeneous of the money market institutions owing to the lack of uniformity in their functions, though they appear to be active money and capital market participants. In Singapore, there is no special legislation regarding their activities. Although merchant banks are incorporated under the Companies Act, the MAS's approval is necessary. Like other financial intermediaries, their activities are supervised by the MAS, especially since most have been granted ACU licenses. Their domestic operations are regulated through directives, notices, and guidelines issued by the MAS.

Unlike other financial intermediaries, merchant banks in Singapore are not allowed to accept deposits from the public, "to avoid unnecessary competition with commercial banks and finance companies" (MAS 1989, p. 37). They also are not allowed to raise funds by issuing promissory notes, certificates of deposit (CDs), or commerical paper. They may, however, obtain funds from banks, other approved financial institutions, and shareholders and companies related to shareholders, and, with the approval of the MAS, they may engage in the foreign exchange and the Asian dollar market.

In regard to their sources and uses of funds, much of the merchant banks' activity is with the ADM and the interbank market. Their share of the ADM's assets and liabilities is estimated by the MAS to have been 6% in 1988 (MAS 1989, pp. 34–35). Comprehensive guidelines for their domestic currency operations in Singapore were issued by the MAS in late 1985, and the main features are as follows:

1. The issued and paid-up capital of merchant banks incorporated in Singapore must at all times be equal to S$3 million. For a branch, the head office's net funds in Singapore for domestic operations must never drop below S$3 million.

2. Loans to any single or group of borrowers may not exceed 30% of capital

funds. The limit may be raised to 100% provided that the excess facilities are guaranteed by its head office.

3. They cannot acquire more than 20% equity of any company except under special circumstances.

4. Annual approval from the MAS is necessary for the appointment of an external auditor.

5. The MAS's approval is required for credit exceeding S$5 million to non-residents or for use outside Singapore. This applies also to syndicated loans, bond issues, and other financial paper denominated in Singapore dollars.

These guidelines replicate the spirit and substance of the Banking Act as applied to this category of financial organizations not covered by the Banking Act.

Finance Companies

Among private-sector financial institutions, finance companies rank second after commercial banks in deposit-taking activities. Their rapid growth, especially in the mid-1960s, can be attributed to two factors. First, the (bank) cartelization of interest rates prevented banks from offering higher interest rates to attract deposits, and so several banks established finance companies (as subsidiaries) to circumvent the cartelization. (The bank cartel was abolished in July 1975.) Second, the finance companies were able to satisfy their need for installment plan finance, an area in which the banks are not involved. It is thus not surprising that of the thirty finance companies in 1989, fifteen were affiliated with commercial banks. In 1988, the shares of these bank-affiliated finance companies amounted to 55% of total assets, 58% of total deposits collected, and 53% of total loans extended (MAS 1989, p. 36). As a result of the mergers and takeovers during the 1980s, most of the large finance companies are owned by six major finance groups, of which four are the Big Four local banks (Tan 1988, pp. 85–87). This suggests increasing concentration, as there is stiff competition among the various groups (particularly the Big Four local banks) to maintain, if not increase, their market shares.

All the finance companies are locally incorporated and licensed and regulated by the MAS. Similar to those for banks and other financial intermediaries, specific regulations differentiate the financial companies' activities somewhat. On the one hand, the finance companies may collect fixed and savings deposits and make loans (see Table 7.7). But on the other hand, they cannot offer current accounts, issue NCDs, deal in gold and foreign exchange, or grant unsecured loans of more than S$5,000.

Governed by the Finance Companies Act (amended in 1984), finance companies are required to hold minimum capital and reserve fund requirements and to maintain a minimum cash ratio of 6% and a liquid assets ratio

Table 7.7. Singapore Finance Companies: Sources and
Uses of Funds (%)

	1970	1980	1989
Uses			
Reserves with MAS	2.7	4.1	4.0
Deposits with			
Financial institutions	33.0	13.2	17.4
Loan and advances	56.6	77.0	70.8
Securities and equities	3.5	3.3	5.5
Other	4.4	2.5	2.2
Sources			
Capital and reserves	17.1	15.5	13.1
Deposits	76.8	69.0	72.8
Fixed	70.1	63.8	64.2
Savings	2.1	2.1	3.0
Other	4.6	3.1	5.6
Borrowings	0.6	4.7	2.2
Other liabilities	5.6	10.8	11.8

Source: Computed from MAS, *Annual Report,* various issues.

of 10% of their liabilities base. Supervision by the MAS, as in the case of banks, takes the form of field inspections, reviews of regular returns, and consultation. The MAS's approval is required for takeovers and mergers with other finance companies. Again similar to banks, the MAS's approval is required for loans of more than S$5 million to nonresidents or to residents for use outside Singapore.

Unlike banks, finance companies have, from the outset, determined their own borrowing and lending rates. With the freeing of bank interest rates in 1975, spreads between the two have narrowed. This, combined with the banks' ability to issue NCDs and the Post Office Savings Bank's (POSBank) mobilization of savings deposits, has affected their share of deposits. Their loan activities have been affected adversely to some extent by measures to restrict the growth of car ownership and availability of housing finance from other intermediaries, especially the Central Provident Fund and Credit POSBank, a subsidiary of the POSBank. The competition, especially in the housing loan market, has had an impact on loan rates.

Discount Houses

Discount houses, numbering four, have had a rather short history as money market institutions, as they functioned only from 1972 to May 3, 1987, when they were phased out to make way for the revamped government securities market. (The revamping was to activate the market.) The discount houses were established to develop secondary activities in the money market, which until then was a market for short-term interbank funds with maturities ranging from overnight, eight days call, to one to three months. Discount houses accepted short-term deposits (minimum S$50,000) from banks and other financial institutions and invested them in treasury bills, other short-dated government securities, bills of exchange, and NCDs. Since February 1980, individual discount houses have been free to quote their own call rates; before that they were fixed by a cartel-like agreement among them. They also facilitated the rediscounting of these instruments and served as acceptance houses for export bills. With the establishment of the discount houses, the MAS ceased rediscounting treasury bills for banks and finance companies. In 1979, around 50% of the discount houses' trading volume was in commercial bills, 38% in Singapore government bonds, 6% in NCDs, and the remainder in treasury bills (MAS 1980, p. 27).

In 1973, with the advent of the discount houses, the weekly (ninety-one-day) treasury bill issue was changed from a tap to a tender system.[4] In fact, the discount houses guaranteed they would underwrite the whole weekly treasury bill issue. This enabled the monetary authorities to bring in market forces through indirect dealing with the national banking units. It was hoped that the discount houses would help develop a liquid money market in time, but they did not.

The need to balance their books at the end of each trading day provided the nexus between the discount houses and the MAS. Deficits could be handled by either rediscounting money market papers or borrowing from the MAS, the choice depending on their asset ratios. Surpluses could be utilized by purchasing money market instruments from the MAS, including overnight treasury bills. In this regard, it is interesting that in February 1977, the discount houses' purchases of overnight treasury bills were limited to 50% of their daily closing surplus funds, followed by a suspension of the sale of overnight treasury bills to them. The reason for these developments was "to develop the market for term papers and improve expertise in rate quotation and position taking on short dated Treasury bills" (MAS 1980, p. 69).

Although they were not governed by specific legislation, the discount houses operated according to the MAS's guidelines, made up of a gearing ratio and an asset ratio. The former restricted the discount houses' borrowing in relation to their equity and reserves. For example, this ratio was 30 in 1972. Like other financial institutions, they, too, had to submit returns to the MAS, in particular reporting daily their principal assets and liabilities (MAS 1984).

The asset ratio pertained to the proportion of various assets held by the discount houses. In 1972, the ratio for government securities was 85, and that for commercial paper was 15. This was changed to 70:30 when

S$NCDs were introduced in 1975. Both these ratios were prudential in nature.

As a postscript, we should mention the new Singapore government securities market (SGSM), as it has affected the role of the discount houses. Two of the four discount houses were absorbed by local banks, and the other two operate as subsidiaries of local banks, with their equity enlarged to S$25 million each. These subsidiaries and three major local banks have become the first primary dealers to trade in government securities.[5] Three others were subsequently added.

Modeled on the U.S. Treasury bond market, the new SGSM had a gross issue of S$36 billion with maturities up to ten years from 1987 to 1992. The securities are auctioned through primary dealers in the SGSM and carry a market-determined interest rate rather than a preset one, as they did previously.[6] As market makers, the dealers buy and sell, giving two-way quotes.

One reason that the SGSM was restructured was to activate the secondary market in government bonds. Such activity increased from an average of S$8 million (daily turnover) in 1986 to S$450 million in 1988. The daily turnover, however, fell to S$250 million in 1989. Trading in repos has remained at higher levels, with the daily turnover moving from S$700 million in 1988 to S$790 million in 1989 (MAS 1990, p. 39).

The Post Office Savings Bank

Unlike banks and financial institutions, the POSBank is a statutory organization established in 1972 (although from 1952 to 1972 the Post Office system operated a less active savings scheme). Its chief objective is to encourage thrift and mobilize funds for public-sector development. It introduced current accounts in 1984, traveler's checks in 1986, and a current/savings account facility in 1988, similar to other ATS schemes. Interest from POSBank savings deposits is tax exempt; savings deposits below S$100,000 are paid a higher rate compared with those. This two-tiered interest rate was introduced in September 1978. In the early years, POSBank's share of savings deposits relative to those of commercial banks was only 19%, but by 1987, this had increased to 57% (Tan 1988, p. 262).

As it does not come under the aegis of the Banking Act, the POSBank is not required to observe the minimum cash and liquid assets ratios.[7] It does, however, face other restrictions: It cannot accept corporate deposits, finance foreign trade, or engage in foreign exchange transactions. At the time of POSBank's establishment, at least 50% of its assets had to be invested in government securities. Since then, the range of permissible assets has been considerably expanded. By 1977, the POSBank had begun to participate in the money market by depositing overnight funds with banks and discount houses. It introduced a nonbank savings account (the passcard account) in November 1980. In 1988, 55% of the POSBank's funds were redeposited in the banking system (in fixed deposits and S$NCDs), 24% were in term loans (including housing loans), and 9% were in government securities (MAS 1989, p.16).

On account of the POSBank's special status, banks in particular regard it as an unwelcome competitor. Nonetheless, the POSBank has shown itself to be a robust and innovative institution, in terms of the services it provides, such as GIRO (prearranged service charge payments), computerization, enhanced liquidity of its savings deposits (through such measures as the availability of ATMs and higher daily withdrawal limits), its participation with the Big Four local banks in the electronic funds transfer system (EFTPOS, introduced in January 1986), attractive housing loan schemes, and diversification of activities through subsidiary and associate companies.

Money Brokers

International money-broking companies appeared in the early 1970s along with other financial institutions. Because they provide intermediation between financial institutions, they are active in various money markets. As of January 1986, brokerage rates between banks and brokers became freely negotiable. In 1988, 25% of foreign exchange transactions were channeled through money brokers.

THE MONEY MARKETS

Sizes and Market-Clearing Rates

The volumes and the rates clearing the money markets indicate the levels of activities in those markets (see Table 7.8). The volumes in 1989 in the money markets are as follows: S$8.0 billion in demand deposits, S$10.0 billion in savings deposits, S$35.0 billion in fixed deposits, $18.2 billion in overdrafts and commercial bills, and S$8.8 billion in interbank transactions. The treasury bills market is valued at S$5.7 billion, and the foreign exchange transactions are estimated at S$120 billion per day.

Based on the size of the seven money markets described in Table 7.8, the total deposits of the national banking system of about S$53 billion are about equal to Singapore's GNP, at S$55 billion. The treasury bills market is about one-tenth the size of the GNP. The overdrafts/bills market, which is an important source of finance for commercial firms, is a third of the size of the economy. The foreign exchange market dominates the money markets, as Singapore is an important foreign exchange center.

Of more interest to the market participants are the market-clearing rates for each of these instruments. The rates clearing the markets are very low in Singapore (relative to those of other countries). The deposit rates in the deposit market are 2.95% per year (savings) and 4.27% (fixed deposits) over the study period. The interbank rate is 5.19%, and the yield on trea-

Table 7.8. Volume and Market-Clearing Rates on Money Market Securities in Singapore, 1989

	Size of Money Market (millions)	Market-Clearing Rates at End of 1989	Rates Relative to GNP of S$55 Million in 1989 (ratio)
Treasury bills	S$5,760.0	3.93%	0.105
Demand deposits	S$8,019.2	nil	0.146[a]
Savings and NCDs deposits[b]	S$9,952.2[c]	2.95%[c]	0.181[a]
Fixed deposits	S$34,972.0	4.27%	0.636[a]
Overdrafts/bills	S$18,249.0	5.84%	0.332
Interbank: overnight	S$8,833.0	5.19%	0.161
Spot foreign exchange rate to U.S. unit per day	S$120,000.0	S$1.9660[d]	2.182

[a] Total deposits-to-GDP ratio is 0.963.

[b] The average size for savings deposits and NCDs refers to 1978–88.

[c] Interest rates only on normal savings deposits.

[d] Exchange rate as of end of 1989.

Source: MAS publications, various years and ongoing research files.

sury bills is 3.93%. At the prime rate of 5.84% in 1989, the spread between the lending rate and the savings deposit rate was 289 basis points: 157 basis points relative to the fixed-deposits rate. These differences were large, demonstrating that the money-market lending rates are quite substantial. Figure 7.1 shows the volumes and the 1989 rates in the national money markets.

Short-Term Deposits

Short-term deposits in 1989 in Singapore commercial banks (i.e., the full-license banks) amounted to S$54.5 billion, 16% in the form of savings deposits, 12% as demand deposits, 48% as fixed deposits, and a meager 2% as NCDs (see Table 7.9). The remaining savings deposits of S$13.0 billion were deposits in the POSBank (which is not a commercial bank): This represented an additional deposit, constituting 22% of total deposits. Further details of the short-term deposits, including their ratios to GDP, are given in Table 7.9.

Total commercial bank deposits grew from S$7.6 billion in 1975 to S$55.5 billion in 1989, a growth rate of 18% per year. POSBank's deposits grew at a compound annual rate of more than 20% during this period, the POSBank having embarked on a more active expansion program in 1978. From 1975 to 1989, the savings-to-GDP ratio climbed from a low of 0.341 (1975) to 0.636. Demand deposits appeared to be stable at 15% relative to the GDP.

The market-clearing rates based on returns from the top ten commer-

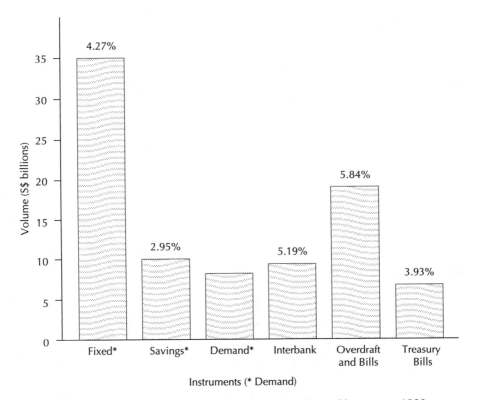

Figure 7.1. Volume and Rates in Money Markets, Singapore, 1989

cial banks—the top six banks and the POSBank account for three-fourths of all deposits—are summarized in Table 7.10.

The prime lending rates (PLR) are given for a comparison with the minimum rates that banks are likely to make on the safest loan portfolios. For the fifteen-year period, the average savings deposit rate was 5.00%, followed by the POSBank rate of 5.26%, and 6.53% for NCDs. The differences between the prime lending rate of 7.99% and the various deposit rates are substantially higher than those found in some major markets but are below the figures for several newly developed and developing countries. The spread between the PLR and the savings deposit rate was fairly stable over these years, whereas that between the PLR and the fixed deposit rate widened somewhat. One would have expected competition and technological advance to have reduced the spreads, although as countervailing factors, there were increases in wages, rentals, and other costs that increased the spread. As Table 7.10 shows, the share of demand deposits fell, and that of savings deposits increased. The openness of the financial system also limited the permissible width of the spreads.

Regarding the small proportions of NCDs at 2% of all commercial bank deposits (see Table 7.9), the difference between the interest rates on

Table 7.9. Value of Short-Term Deposits in Commercial Banks and the POSBank in Singapore, 1978–89

| | Savings | | | Demand Deposits | |
Year	Savings	Fixed	Demand Deposits	Negotiable Certificates of Deposit	Savings Deposits in POSBank
Absolute values (S$ millions)					
1960	131.9	304.4	386.2	Nil	20.0
1970	412.9	1,818.3	947.7	Nil	45.1
1975	890.6	4,565.9	2,111.1	527.6	554.5
1976	999.2	5,062.4	2,378.2	617.8	1,000.4
1977	1,069.5	5,328.3	2,513.9	513.4	1,535.7
1978	1,211.2	6,045.3	2,732.1	455.3	2,029.0
1979	1,394.8	7,473.0	3,244.3	515.0	2,525.2
1980	1,692.5	10,788.4	3,484.0	331.9	2,756.7
1981	2,168.1	13,315.4	4,441.0	404.5	3,265.9
1982	2,917.4	15,619.7	4,781.4	428.0	5,058.4
1983	4,079.0	17,099.6	4,982.7	471.6	6,240.9
1984	4,870.1	18,191.5	4,856.7	300.7	7,287.3
1985	5,982.8	17,940.8	4,700.2	263.6	9,129.4
1986	7,426.1	17,609.6	5,422.9	696.4	10,558.3
1987	8,482.0	21,008.6	6,657.9	896.8	11,165.3
1988	9,024.7	26,507.5	6,636.2	992.6	12,139.8
1989	9,952.2	34,972.0	8,019.2	1,421.1	13,049.7
Relative to GDP					
1975[a]	0.067	0.341	0.158	—	—
1980[a]	0.070	0.446	0.144	0.015	0.114
1989[a]	0.181	0.636	0.146	0.026	0.237

[a] GDPs of the respective years were S$13,373, S$24,200, and S$55,000 (est.).

Source: Singapore, Monthly Digest of Statistics, various issues.

NCDs and on fixed deposits was about 127 basis points (or 1.27%), a substantial difference during the fifteen-year period. Later the difference widened (e.g., to 197 basis points), which probably accounts for the accelerated increase in NCD volume.

Tables 7.11 and 7.12 offer data on the deposit rates of banks and finance companies in Singapore. The rates of the Big Four local banks (and their affiliates)—Overseas Chinese Banking Corporation (OCBC), United Overseas Bank (UOB), Overseas Union Bank (OUB), and the semigovernmental Development Bank of Singapore (DBS)—tend to be close to one another. It is generally believed that the DBS's presence has enhanced the competitiveness of the banking system, in terms of the narrowing spread between lending and deposit rates.

Table 7.10. Average Annual Rates for Savings and Demand Deposits in Singapore, 1978–89 (%)

Year	Prime Lending Rate	Savings Deposit Rate	Negotiable Certificates of Deposit: 3 Months	Fixed Deposits: 3 Months
1970	8.00	3.50	4.00	5.50
1975	7.08	3.50	5.50	4.31
1976	6.78	3.52	5.50	3.76
1977	7.02	3.68	5.00	4.54
1978	7.65	4.20	7.44	5.29
1979	9.48	6.38	8.74	7.14
1980	13.60	9.52	13.00	11.22
1981	11.83	7.90	7.50	7.43
1982	9.33	6.43	8.38	6.16
1983	8.98	6.30	7.56	6.53
1984	9.40	6.53	6.19	6.00
1985	7.20	5.18	5.38	4.58
1986	6.10	3.08	4.00	2.88
1987	6.10	3.03	3.13	2.90
1988	6.13	2.83	5.31	2.95
1989	6.23	2.95	5.25	3.28
Mean (1975–89)	7.99	5.00	6.53	5.26

Source: MAS publications and Department of Statistics publications.

Overdrafts and Commercial Bills

Overdrafts are the principal form of borrowing by commercial enterprises in Singapore, as they represent 42% of all nonbank borrowing over the period we studied (see Table 7.13). Commercial paper is extremely limited, as firms can obtain cheap funds as rolling lines of credit or bill financing. Occasionally one or two public-listed firms may issue commercial paper, but their contribution to the money market (in relative terms) is insignificant. The data on overdrafts and commercial bills are given in Table 7.13.

Currently, overdrafts account for 30% of all loans. The figure for bill financing is 9%. These figures are low by historical standards, but overdrafts have grown in volume over the years, from S$4.8 billion to S$13.9 billion. The growth rate was 10% per year, close to that of the GDP over this period. Bill financing rose slowly at 4% per year. In the eyes of the borrowers, the convenience of the overdraft facility appears to outweigh the marginally higher interest rates for overdraft borrowing (at 6.23% in 1989, against 5.44% for bills).

Table 7.11. Commerical Bank Deposit Rates in Singapore, 1990 (%)

	Savings				Fixed Deposits			
	Daily Interest	1 Month	3 Months	6 Months	9 Months	12 Months	24 Months	36 Months
ABN Bank	3.25	3.625	4	4.25	4.375	4.5	—	—
Asia Commercial Bank	3.25	4.25	4.25	4.5	4.75	5	5.5	—
Ban Hin Lee Bank	3.75	4	4.25	4.5	4.75	5	5	—
Bangkok Bank	3.25	3.375	3.625	4	4.5	4.625	—	—
Bank of America	4.ᵃ	4	4.25	4.5	4.75	5	—	—
Bank of China	3.25	3.75	3.75	4.5	4.5	5	5.25	5.25
Bank of East Asia	3.25	4	4.25	4.5	4.75	4.75	—	—
Bank of India	4.25	4.5	4.75	5	5	5.25	—	—
Bank of Singapore	3	3.5	3.5	4	4.25	4.75	5	—
Bank of Tokyo	3	3.25	3.25	3.5	3.75	3.75	—	—
Banque Indosuez	2.25	3.25	3.25	3.75	4.25	4.75	—	—
Chase Manhattan Bank	2.75	3.5	3.75	4.5	4.75	5	—	—
Chung Khiaw Bank	2.75	4	4	4.5	4.5	5	5.25	5.25
Citibank	2.5	3	3.5	4	4.5	5	5.5	5.5
DBS Bank	2.75	3.75	3.75	4.25	4.5	5	5.25	—
Far Eastern Bank	2.75	4	4	4.5	4.5	5	5.25	5.25
Four Seas Bank	3	3.5	3.5	4	4.25	4.75	5	5.
Hongkong Bank	2.25	3	3.25	3.75	4.25	4.5	4.5	4.63
Indian Bank	4.25	4.5	4.75	5	5	5.25	—	—
Indian Overseas Bank	4.25	4.25	4.5	4.75	5	5.25	—	—
Ind & Commercial Bank	3.5ᵃ	4.25	4.25	4.75	4.75	5	5.25	5.25
Int Bank of Singapore	3.25	3.5	3.5	4	4.5	4.75	—	—
Kwangtung Prov'l Bank	3	3.75	4	4.5	4.75	5.125	5.25	5.25
Lee Wah Bank	2.75	4	4	4.5	4.5	5	5.25	5.25
Malayan Banking	2.75	4	4	4.5	4.75	5	5.25	5.25
Mitsui Bank	3.5	3.5	3.75	4	4.25	5	—	—
OCBC Bank	3	3.5	3.5	4	4.25	4.75	—	—
Overseas Union Bank	2.75	3.75	3.75	4.25	4.5	5	5.25	5.25
Sec Pac Asian Bank	4	4	4.125	4.125	4.5	5.25	—	—
Sid Chartered Bank	2.5	3.5	3.5	3.875	4	4.25	4.375	4.5
Tat Lee Bank	3.25	3.75	3.75	4.25	4.5	5	5.25	—
UCO Bank	4.ᵃ	4.5	4.75	4.75	5	5.25	5.5	—
UMBC	2.75	3	3	3.75	4	4.5	4.75	—
United Overseas Bank	2.75	4	4	4.5	4.5	5	5.25	5.25

ᵃ Interest rates are computed monthly as of February 15, 1990.

Source: Business Times, February 17–18, 1990.

Table 7.12. Finance Company Deposit Rates in Singapore, 1990 (%)

	Savings				Fixed Deposits			
	Daily Interest	1 Month	3 Months	6 Months	9 Months	12 Months	24 Months	36 Months
Asia Building Society	3.75	4.5	4.75	4.75	4.75	5.375	5.5	—
Asia Comm'l Finance	3.75	4.25	4.25	4.5	4.75	5	—	—
Credit Corporation (S)	—	4	4.25	5	5	5.5	5.5	5.5
DBS Finance	3.5	4	4.25	4.5	4.75	5.125	5.375	—
Far East Finance	4.[a]	4.25	4.5	4.75	4.75	5.25	5.375	—
Focal Finance	4.[a]	4.25	4.5	5	5.125	5.375	5.5	—
Golden Castle Finance	4.[a]	4.25	4.5	4.75	4.75	5	—	—
Great Pacific Finance	3.5	4	4.25	4.5	4.75	5.125	5.25	5.38
Hong Leong Finance	4	4.125	4.375	4.375	4.625	4.75	5	5.25
Island Finance	4.25[a]	4.25	4.25	4.5	4.75	5.4	5.5	—
Keppel Finance	4	4.25	4.5	5	5	5.25	5.375	—
Kiaw Aik Hang Finance	4.[a]	—	4	4.5	—	5.25	—	—
Lian Huat Hang Finance	4.[a]	—	2.75	3	—	5.38	—	—
Maybank Finance	4	3.75	4	4.25	4.75	5	5.25	5.5
Nanyang Finance	4.25	—	4.5	4.75	5	5.25	—	—
OCBC Finance	3.25	4	4.25	4.5	4.5	5	5.25	—
Overseas Union Trust	4.[a]	4.25	4.5	4.75	5	5.25	—	—
Public Finance	4	—	4.25	4.5	4.75	5	—	—
Sing Investments & Fin	3.5	4.375	4.625	4.625	4.875	5.125	5.375	5.63
Singapore Finance	4	4.125	4.375	4.375	4.625	4.75	5.25	—
Singapura Building Soc	3.5	4.25	5.5	4.5	5	5	4.5	—
Soon Teck Finance	—	—	4.65	4.75	5	5.4	5.5	—
Std Chartered Finance	—	3.5	4	4	4.5	5	5	5.
Tat Lee Finance	3.5	—	4.25	4.5	4.75	5	5	—
Tong Bee Finance	—	—	4.5	4.75	5	5.25	—	—
UMBC Finance	3.5[a]	4	4	4.5	4.75	5.125	5.6	—
United Overseas Finance	3	4.25	4.25	4.75	4.75	5.25	5.5	5.5
Wayfoong Mortgage & Fin	2.5	3.25	3.5	4	4.75	5.25	5.75	6.

[a] Interest rates are computed monthly as of February 15, 1990.

Source: Business Times, February 17–18, 1990.

From the foregoing discussion we suggest that (1) firms tend to rely on overdrafts (a money market instrument, as its maturity is equal to or less than one year), which form a principal and predominant form of financing by commercial banks for Singapore's commercial activities and (2) the importance of bills and/or commercial paper financing in Singapore is secondary to overdrafts. Financing firms' working capital requirements through these two forms of financing appears to have grown at a rate fairly close to that of the GDP over the study period.

Table 7.13. Total Loans and Short-Term Loans to Nonfinancial Firms in
Singapore, 1978–89

Year	Total Loans (S$ millions)	Overdraft S$ millions (%)	Rate	Bill Financing S$ millions (%)	Rate
Absolute value					
1972	4,292.8	2,549.2 (59%)	7.50	727.6 (17%)	N.A.
1973	6,271.2	3,421.4 (54%)	9.00	1,124.7 (18%)	N.A.
1974	6,930.4	3,614.2 (52%)	10.25	1,233.4 (18%)	N.A.
1975	7,829.3	3,758.5 (48%)	7.08	1,326.2 (17%)	4.50
1976	8,894.2	3,787.9 (43%)	6.78	1,622.5 (18%)	3.81
1977	10,183.0	4,058.1 (40%)	7.02	2,352.2 (23%)	5.44
1978	12,226.4	4,883.9 (39%)	7.65	2,827.5 (23%)	7.44
1979	10,184.0	6,241.3 (38%)	9.84	3,948.3 (24%)	10.38
1980	20,206.9	8,536.2 (39%)	13.60	4,049.3 (25%)	14.06
1981	25,229.9	10,336.7 (42%)	11.83	3,979.4 (20%)	8.50
1982	29,442.9	12,589.6 (41%)	9.33	4,107.3 (16%)	8.50
1983	39,045.8	15,466.3 (43%)	8.98	3,900.4 (14%)	8.50
1984	36,876.5	16,140.0 (45%)	9.40	4,124.8 (11%)	7.06
1985	37,403.1	16,089.2 (45%)	7.20	3,628.1 (11%)	5.81
1986	35,792.0	13,578.8 (38%)	6.10	4,113.0 (9%)	4.13
1987	37,868.0	12,445.5 (32%)	6.10	3,599.6 (9%)	3.25
1988	41,848.0	13,002.0 (31%)	6.13	4,096.9 (10%)	5.63
1989	50,785.9	15,761.9 (31%)	6.23	4,533.9 (9%)	5.44
Relative to GDP					
1972[a]	.526	.320		.089	
1975	.585	.281		.100	
1980	.835	.353		.167	
1989	.923	.287		.082	

[a] GDP = S$8,156 million.

Source: MAS publications and *Yearbook of Statistics,* various years.

The total number of loans by national banking system to nonbank customers (i.e., mainly firms) was dominated by overdraft agreements, a form
of money market instrument. However, the proportion of this instrument
declined from a high of 59% of all loans in 1972 to 31% in 1989. Total
loans increased in relation to the GDP, from about 53% of GDP in 1972 to
92% of GDP in 1989.

The Interbank Market

The interbank market until recently had two components, the interbank
market proper and the discount market, the latter ceasing to exist as a separate entity after May 1987. In the interbank market, as the name sug-

gests, the major participants are the commercial banks, which are legally required to observe reserve requirements. Generally, the local banks, with their larger deposit bases, are the net lenders, and the foreign banks are the net borrowers. As our earlier discussion of the commerical banks' balance sheets indicated, interbank transactions are a major component of the total. Loans between banks are unsecured, but the lending is limited. The other players are the merchant banks, which usually are borrowers, the POSBank, which is a lender, and, to a lesser extent, the finance companies. The money brokers act as intermediaries. The instruments employed here are overnight money and term loans of one to three months. The market appears to be a rather liquid one, judging from the number of participants, the volume of transactions, and the absence of any quantitative credit controls.

Recourse to the interbank market by the various institutions is obviously related to liquidity needs, especially for commercial banks' cash reserve requirement. Banks' domestic liquidity conditions arise from such factors as changes in their cash holdings, net amount of treasury bills and other government securities issued, the government's financial transactions, foreign exchange transactions, and the maturity and rediscounting of commercial bills. The activities of one other institution not discussed previously—because it is not a money market institution—should be mentioned here: the Central Provident Fund (CPF), Singapore's compulsory savings scheme for retirement, which drains private-sector liquidity as contributions still outdistance withdrawals. The savings mobilized by the CPF are to a large extent invested in longer-dated government securities. Since such securities are issued only periodically, the CPF money is channeled to the MAS as advance deposits (before the purchase of government securities). The CPF-induced liquidity drain is compensated by offsetting actions by the MAS.

Activity in the interbank market affects short-term interest rates which were determined by a bank cartel arrangement until mid-1975 (when the cartel was abolished). With the introduction of the Singapore dollar NCD in the same year, all other interest rates were liberalized. And with the removal of exchange control in June 1978, domestic interest rates became more sensitive to international rates. Among other things, the two-way flows of interbank funds between ACUs and banks engaged in domestic banking activities helped facilitate this.

Interbank rates are closely monitored by the MAS. For the short term, the MAS's intervention is directed at smoothing out large fluctuations in interest rates. Because the long-term objective is sustained noninflationary growth of the economy, its intervention seeks to provide a monetary environment that will complement its relatively stable exchange rate policy and help achieve the growth objective. Since the early 1980s, liquidity has been influenced mainly by the MAS's intervention in the interbank and foreign exchange swap markets. Before the deregulation of exchange (in 1978) and interest rates (in 1975), the authorities relied on interest rate adjustments and changes in the reserve and liquid assets ratios to influence liquidity. Since then, in addition to the foreign exchange swaps, the other instruments employed have been borrowing and lending in the interbank market and repos and outright purchases and sales of government securities. Although not a monetary policy, the export bills–rediscounting scheme also affects liquidity in the money market. The domestic interest rate response to international interest rate changes is smoothed through swap activities in the foreign exchange markets.[8]

We turn now to the other component of the domestic money market, the discount market, which functioned until May 1987. As we noted earlier, discount houses were established in 1972 to develop secondary activities in the money market. In this market, besides the discount houses, the participants were the money market institutions, with the MAS as the lender of last resort to the discount houses. Discount houses helped the regulators deal with commercial banks at arm's length, but they did not create liquidity.

Other than accepting short-term funds from commercial banks (the national banking system) and investing in primary issues of treasury bills, the discount market traded in and discounted money market instruments such as treasury bills, S$NCDs, bills of exchange, short-dated commercial paper, and government securities. As we indicated earlier, in 1987 the discount market was reconstituted as the SGSM, with the intent of further fostering market transactions in government bonds. In this case, the monetary authorities would have to rely on the money markets to conduct their monetary policies, without recourse to discount houses as the intermediaries.

Estimates of the levels of activity in the money market are presented in Table 7.14. The data suggest two things: First, in the aggregate, activity in the market more than quadrupled. Second, between 1984 and 1986 the discount market stagnated, whereas generally the more important of the two, the interbank market, was more robust.

The Treasury Bill Market

The treasury bill market has not developed to the same extent it has in several other countries. The market has grown steadily, but not at spectacular rates, as in the more developed money markets, in which the treasury bill market is the mainstay of the short-ended markets (see Table 7.15). The outstanding securities are of three-month, six-month, nine-month, and twelve-month durations: The three-month securities form the bulk of the market and are auctioned every week on Thursday, with the dealers in the SGSM participating. The total value of these securities was about S$5.7

Table 7.14. Estimated Size of Key Money Markets in Singapore (in millions of S$)

End of Period	Interbank Market[a]	Discount Market	Total
1975	584	494	1,088
1976	799	552	1,351
1977	1,264	619	1,883
1978	1,616	685	2,301
1979	1,987	764	2,751
1980	2,757	950	3,707
1981	4,196	1,604	5,800
1982	3,728	2,051	5,779
1983	3,699	2,248	5,947
1984	4,088	2,563	6,651
1985	5,342	2,469	7,811
1986	6,694	2,444[b]	9,160
1987	9,271	—	9,271
1988	8,833	—	8,833

[a] Measured as amounts due from banks in Singapore.

[b] Started in 1972 and ceased operation in June 1986.

Source: MAS, *The Financial Structure of Singapore* (Singapore, 1989).

billion (for the year 1988); auctions in 1989 were at an average yield of 3.93%. They were resold or discounted at a slightly higher yield when commercial banks (and, since June 1988, individual persons through their brokers) resold the securities later in the secondary market. The twelve-year average auction rate between 1978 and 1989 was 3.59%, and the resale rate was 3.97%, a thirty-eight basis point difference in the secondary market, which is higher than the spread in more liquid and developed markets.

The Foreign Exchange Market

Until the early 1970s, activity in the foreign exchange market was confined to banks squaring their foreign exchange positions arising from transactions with nonbank customers. There was, as in the case of interest rates, a cartel system of foreign exchange rate quotations by banks. Although the banks were free to quote their own rates for interbank transactions, they were required to quote in minimum changes of S$0.0025. This and other restrictions were partially removed in June 1972 when banks were free to quote exchange rates for amounts in excess of S$250,000, that is, a wholesale market–negotiated commission. Further liberalization came with the floating of the Singapore dollar in mid-1973. Removal of exchange controls in June 1978 freed the market even more.

The liberalization of exchange controls had various consequences.

Table 7.15. Treasury Bill Market Size and Yield in Singapore, 1979–89 (in millions of S$)

Years	Number of Issues	Treasury Bill Market	Mean Rates (%)	Yield on 3-Month T-Bills (%)[a]
1978	64	1,610	3.56	4.12
1979	63	1,915	5.14	6.12
1980	61	3,280	7.18	6.88
1981	59	6,365	6.43	2.25
1982	52	7,145	3.45	2.75
1983	59	6,685	2.76	2.63
1984	58	6,990	3.00	2.88
1985	63	5,720	2.99	3.00
1986	59	6,610	2.47	2.00
1987	60	9,540	3.06	2.77
1988	24	5,760	3.73	3.75
1989	N.A.	N.A.	N.A.	3.93
Mean per year	56	5,601.8	3.97	3.59

[a] Internal yield based on market prices.

Source: Current study under way.

Individual persons and corporations won the option of keeping their export and other proceeds overseas (previously such proceeds had to be brought back within six months); merchant banks became free to engage in foreign exchange transactions, whereas previously, specific approval was necessary; and offshore banks, which before had been restricted to dealing with banks and approved financial institutions, could now deal with resident nonbank customers. And residents became free to deal with ACUs. Thus capital mobility has become almost perfect. The remaining restriction is the prohibition against lending more than S$5 million to nonresidents or residents for use outside Singapore without prior consultation with the monetary authorities.

These developments, coupled with the 1968 abolition of the withholding tax on interest for nonresidents, have given a tremendous impetus to the foreign exchange market. Singapore's location offers a time zone advantage (also enjoyed by Hong Kong), which has also contributed to larger trading volumes, as has the financial liberalization in Tokyo since 1987. The average daily turnover (spot and forward, including swaps and arbitrage) increased from U.S.$336 million in 1974 to U.S.$61 billion in 1989. The activity was dominated by spot transactions (64%), followed by swap (33%) and forward transactions (3%). The increased competition is reflected in the finer margins, which were as high as forty basis points in July 1973 but dropped to an average of five or fewer basis points in 1988 (MAS 1989, p. 63).

Until June 1972, the pound sterling was the most widely traded currency in the Singapore foreign exchange market, since the Singapore dollar was pegged to it. With the switch to the U.S. dollar as the intervention currency, the American dollar has replaced sterling as the most widely traded currency.

Participants in this market are the commercial banks, ACUs, merchant banks, international money brokers, central banks, and multinational corporations. The MAS intervenes in the market to manage the float of the Singapore dollar.

The Asian Dollar Market

The Asian dollar market (ADM), based in Singapore, is an international money and capital market. Our concern here is only with the former. The ADM, like its counterpart the Eurodollar market, is a market for offshore currencies, mainly the U.S. dollar, deutsche mark, Japanese yen, pound sterling, and Swiss franc.

In the early 1960s the U.S. dollar and other currency holdings of residents in Asia could be pooled and used in the same way as in the Eurodollar market in London. Singapore appeared to have the potential to develop an Asian dollar market, given its location with a time zone advantage, sound financial infrastructure, good communication network, and political stability.

The first bank to be given permission to start an Asian currency unit (ACU), in 1968, was the Bank of America; this also heralded the separation between national and international banking in Singapore. The ACU, a separate bookkeeping unit for offshore currency transactions, is permitted to accept deposits from and make loans to other ACUs, authorized banks, and nonresidents.[9] Until 1978, transactions with residents were restricted, but with the removal of exchange controls in that year, such restrictions became redundant. Their other activities include investing in foreign currency securities, dealing in third currencies, and making foreign exchange transactions.

The growth and development of the ACUs have been carefully nurtured by government policies, which provide a preferential tax and regulatory environment. There is no withholding tax on nonresidents' interest earnings from the ACU. The income of ACUs and other offshore activities are taxed at 10%, compared with the 1989 company tax rate of 32%. In addition, ACUs are not required to observe reserve requirements—an important reason to consider them as part of offshore banking. ACUs are, however, regulated and supervised by the MAS. They are governed by the Banking Act with the exemptions noted. As a condition for obtaining an ACU license, the head office of the bank or institution must prove to the MAS that it will be responsible for the liquidity of the unit. The maximum size of each ACU as measured by its assets/liabilities is stipulated by the MAS, but application may be made for increases in limits.

The number of ACUs rose from 1 in 1968 to 187 twenty years later, and their total assets/liabilities increased from U.S.$31 million in 1968 to U.S.$280 billion at the end of 1988 (MAS 1989, p. 25). It is estimated that in 1989, spot transactions in foreign currencies amounted to about U.S.$60 billion per day, placing Singapore in fifth place, at about 8% of the world's foreign currency transactions. Concomitantly with global changes, new financial instruments have been employed as well, such as revolving underwriting facilities (RUFs), note-issuing facilities (NIFs), fixed-rate notes (FRNs), floating-rate notes, and Asian commercial paper.

In regard to the sources and uses of ACU funds (Table 7.16), at first nonbank customers supplied the bulk of the funds, but this was not sustained. Nonbank depositors include individual persons, multinational corporations (MNCs), and regional central banks. Interbank funds now account for almost four-fifths. Among interbank funds, the share of banks in Singapore, though it has doubled, cannot be regarded as significant.

On the uses side, the share of loans to nonbank customers (MNCs, securities firms, resident companies engaged in the export trade, and foreign governments) increased six and a half times, whereas that of interbank funds fell from 95% in 1970 to 68% in 1989. Again, the share of banks in Singapore is insignificant. The maturities for both sources and uses are largely at the short end of the market, that is, three months.

There is a fairly close link between domestic banking activities and offshore activities, since banks without ACUs may borrow from ACUs to fund their operations as well as deposit money with them. Similarly, ACUs may place deposits or loans in the interbank market (domestic money mar-

Table 7.16. Asian Dollar Market in Singapore: Sources and Uses of Funds (%)

Items	1970	1980	1989
Total assets	100.0	100.0	100.0
Loans to nonbank customers	3.6	22.8	25.7
Interbank funds	95.0	72.7	68.0
Singapore	3.4	2.0	2.2
Outside Singapore	91.6	70.7	65.8
Other assets	1.4	4.5	6.4
Total liabilities	100.0	100.0	100.0
Deposits of nonbank customers	62.5	17.1	16.3
Interbank funds	36.2	75.2	80.1
In Singapore	1.5	2.4	3.7
Outside Singapore	34.7	72.8	76.4
Other liabilities	1.3	7.7	3.6

Source: MAS, *The Financial Structure of Singapore* (Singapore, 1989), p. 54.

ket), depending on the interest differentials, which at times can be quite significant, and exchange rate expectations. The ACUs' participation in the foreign exchange market is similar.

OTHER REGULATIONS

Short-Term Deposits

The segregation of the financial units into those that can accept deposits and those that cannot accept deposits of less than S$250,000 from residents in Singapore is designed to protect the domestic banks from what some observers have termed *overbanking*.[10] Although the offshore banks, the merchant banks, and the ACUs (in all, 349) play the important role of internationalizing Singapore's banking activities, the restrictions placed on them ensure that the thirteen local banks and twenty-two foreign banks dominate the domestic deposit markets. The full-license banks (except the POSBank), having a free hand in the short-term markets, are subject to the minimum cash ratio of 6% and the liquid asset ratio of 18% of deposit liabilities, and this remained the same from 1971 to 1989 except for minor changes.

The separation of domestic banking from international banking resulted in some protection for the full-license banks, which are the thirteen locally incorporated and twenty-two foreign-incorporated banks. Moreover, four of the thirteen local banks account for 70% of the deposits. Under a regulation issued pursuant to Section 12 of the Banking Act, banks are required to apply for approval to open a branch or an ATM, and since 1987, they also have to pay a fee of S$100,000 per year per branch and per ATM.

The separation of national banking helps reduce the exposure of the national banking system to sudden shocks from abroad. It also enables the authorities to enact short-run monetary policies fairly effectively without restricting the international offshore banks to what are national priorities. A fully open system would have given the monetary authorities less room—perhaps no room, as in Hong Kong—for monetary intervention.

The banks' supervision by the authorities is generally perceived to be adequate and professional by all the senior bankers we interviewed, in that the regulations are regarded as not being cumbersome and, more important, that recent efforts have progressed toward less supervision and more self-regulation, including reliance on the work of internal and external auditors. Banks are required to submit statistics and returns periodically as well as whenever special information is required.[11] The recent development of *supervision by exception* when a particular issue crops up appears to be well received by bankers. The returns are required under Section 22 of the Banking Act.

Other significant supervisory regulations are worth noting. One (MAS 606) mandates banks to provide adequate provisions under Section 19 of the act for bank loans that are unlikely to be recovered to be written off expeditiously (except in the case of writing off loans to banks' related parties, which require case-by-case approval). Another (MAS 611) makes it mandatory to seek approval for credit facilities for directors, staff, and related concerns. Banking secrecy is provided for in Section 42 of the act and is regulated by MAS 614. Finally, "as an added protection, all foreign banks' head offices are required by the MAS to give an undertaking to provide financial support to their operations in Singapore, including their ACUs, in times of need" (Peat, Marwick, Mitchell and Co. 1986; Price Waterhouse 1987).

Another regulatory issue pertains to the role of the POSBank, which is a public-sector institution whose deposits are guaranteed by the government: There is no national insurance for bank deposits. Interest paid on POSBank savings deposits is exempt from income tax, an exemption that other banks and finance companies do not enjoy. On occasion, the issue is raised as to whether in the light of changing circumstances, this exemption should continue. Given the healthy state of public-sector finances in Singapore, the role of the POSBank in mobilizing funds for developmental purposes appears to be less important at the moment. To the extent that lending on concessionary terms to various bodies and for various purposes (such as buying a house) is deemed to be desirable, such lending could continue even if the tax-exempt status were removed (with the requisite interest subsidies being financed out of the revenue raised by the tax on interest paid on POSBank savings deposits). Moreover, with the current efforts to foster a market in government securities, the reliance on the POSBank as a purchaser of a large amount of securities would be lessened.

It has also been argued that removing the tax-exempt status would lead to a flow of funds out of Singapore. This argument overlooks the fact that the POSBank would presumably raise the interest rates it pays if the tax exemption were removed. As the next section suggests, there is a "risk premium" in favor of the Singapore dollar, at least for domestic residents, and so the POSBank would not have to raise its rates all the way to equality with foreign rates.[12]

The primary advantage of removing the tax-exempt status is that other commercial banks would be able to compete for deposits with the POSBank on a "level playing field." The resulting intensified competition might well induce greater innovativeness in meeting depositors' needs, and any increases in deposits placed with other banks may also enable them to service their borrowers better. At the same time, consideration should also be given to associating the removal of the tax-exempt status with the POSBank's increased access to the market for commercial loans.

Overdrafts and Commercial Bills

There are no restrictions on domestic and foreign borrowing by firms with local or foreign interest, except that borrowing more than S$5 million by residents or nonresidents for use outside Singapore requires prior approval by the monetary authorities. The main reason for this is the regulators' desire to prevent the Singapore dollar from becoming an international currency.

Because of the persistently low interest rates in the local money markets, firms have not found it necessary to raise working capital directly from the public through paper issues. As a result, the commercial paper market has been nonexistent except for one or two forays into the market by very large firms. Accordingly, the commercial paper (and even bills) money markets have not developed appreciable liquidity.

The Interbank Market

In regard to the interbank loan market, the regulator's task is to maintain liquidity and intervene temporarily during times of excess demand for cash and during end-of-month large cash flows on account of wages and compulsory payments into the Central Provident Fund (CPF). The discount houses were created in 1972 as the third party for dealing in discounting bills and for creating a more liquid market for bills. However, given the banks' underlying ability to manage their funds without recourse to frequent discounting activities, the five discount houses did not contribute significantly to liquidity management, and they did not create active secondary markets in the instruments held. The discount market expanded to S$2.4 billion in 1986 after a decade and a half. The presence of the discount houses meant that the regulators could not directly intervene in the market without going through a third party. So, in May 1987, the discount houses were discontinued, and the central banking authorities began to engage in repurchase activities directly with the commercial banks daily at the central clearinghouse facility. The repo market that was born out of this change has been in operation since 1987. Its role to date appears to be subsidiary to that of the MAS's foreign exchange swap activities regarding the regulation of liquidity.

The Treasury Bill Market

The same problem has beset the treasury bill market; that is, there was little demand for borrowing by the state during our study period, given the large budgetary surpluses. Indeed, the situation was so favorable that the government did not issue long-dated treasury bonds between 1984 and 1986. The issuance of government securities is motivated by the regulators' desire to obtain market-clearing rates as yardsticks on the term structure of interest rates. This helps provide benchmarks for intervention by making decisions based on some market indicators.

In May 1987, the issuing authority adopted a series of reforms in the market, adopting the U.S. Federal Reserves' procedures. Discount bills of three, six, nine, and twelve months and securities of two or more years' maturity, with half-yearly coupons, are issued regularly, though not in large volumes. Bids are required by primary dealers (there are eight in this category) on designated auction dates. The dealers are also responsible for making a liquid market in these instruments. These securities are issued under the Treasury Bills Act. There were about sixty bill auctions (predominantly for three-month maturities) per year over the subsequent period. The primary dealers have begun to sell these securities to individual persons, by lowering their denominations to $5,000 for bills and $1,000 for bonds. Yet the secondary market is still not substantially more active than it was before the 1987 change.

The Foreign Exchange Market

Singapore, as the fifth-largest foreign exchange center (after London, Chicago, Frankfurt, and Tokyo, in that order) has a large and active foreign exchange market. It also has an active forward market. The market offers value today (settlement two days later) as well as fixed and odd-dated forward contracts in major and regional currencies. There are no restrictions on the types, amount, or time (maturity) of forward cover transactions. Residents and nonresidents alike can hold deposits in any currency in the 191 ACUs (1989), except that an offshore market in Singapore dollars does not exist, since institutions are reluctant to oppose the desire of the monetary authorities not to internationalize the Singapore dollar.

Two interesting events occurred after 1978, when the exchange controls were completely lifted. The first was the "round-tripping" episode in 1982. It was discovered that a number of banks were accepting from domestic residents deposits denominated in Singapore dollars for placement with their Hong Kong offices (where such deposits, being "offshore," were not subject to reserve requirements), and then in effect "borrowing" these moneys from those offices for domestic lending (hence the term *round-tripping*). By avoiding the reserve requirements "tax," these banks could offer more favorable rates to their depositors and/or lenders. Being opposed to the internationalization of the Singapore dollar[13] and probably also the resulting diminution of its domestic monetary control, the MAS took a critical view of this and imposed various penalties on the banks concerned, and the practice has since been discontinued.

Theoretically, there still exists the possibility of round-tripping, through the medium of a foreign currency. In other words, a domestic resident could place an offshore deposit, say in U.S. dollars, by opening an ACU account or an account in restricted banks, and the receiving bank could convert the deposit to Singapore dollars and use the proceeds for domestic lending. Such a bank could presumably provide forward cover by offering an equivalent forward currency (to obviate the exchange risk) to the domestic resident on favorable terms, since it would have a corresponding asset (its loan) denominated in Singapore dollars. It appears that the MAS's supervisory practices discourage a close matching of such deposits and loans, although on an aggregate basis, there are large two-way flows of funds, given the openness of the financial system.

There still remains the larger issue that the existence of a reserve requirement tax places the domestic banking system at a disadvantage vis-à-vis the offshore system or a system such as that of Hong Kong or the Cayman Islands. Although the reserve requirements ratio is only 6%, the continually increasing sophistication of the financial markets may result in the tax's having more consequences for the domestic monetary base as time progresses. The situation therefore requires regular monitoring, and it may be necessary at some point for interest to be paid on the required reserves held by banks.[14]

The second event was in 1985 when, perhaps due partly to the recession that the economy was in at that time, the Singapore dollar came under intense pressure, reaching S$2.31 to one U.S. dollar in mid-September of that year. The local dollar was supported heavily when the MAS spent an estimated S$400 million in the market to stabilize the exchange rate around S$2.10 to S$2.15. A statement issued at that time declared, "Those who must speculate on currencies are well advised to leave the Singapore dollar alone" (*Strait Times*, September 19, 1985).

This event makes it clear that owing to their large foreign exchange reserves, the Singapore monetary authorities are better positioned than are the authorities in some other developing countries that also have open capital accounts to deal with short-term speculative pressures. As a consequence, the Singapore authorities also are likely to have somewhat greater leeway for short-run monetary management, although in practice such management appears to be exercised primarily to minimize undue fluctuations in short-run monetary conditions.

THE OPERATIONS OF THE MONEY AND FOREIGN EXCHANGE MARKETS

Policy

Given the small size of the domestic money market (relative to markets elsewhere, though not to the economy) and the absence of exchange controls, any discussion of the modus operandi of the domestic money market must include a consideration of its links with the foreign exchange market. Moreover, any discussion of the latter market must include the policy framework in which it operates.

For this purpose, the following quotations are instructive. First, on the objectives of exchange rate policy:

How is the exchange rate managed and set? The Singapore dollar exchange rate is managed against a trade-weighted basket of currencies of its major trading partners. The trade-weighted Singapore dollar is allowed to float within a target band. The MAS keeps the trade-weighted dollar within the band through foreign exchange interventions. The U.S. dollar is the currency of intervention. . . . The level at which the trade-weighted Singapore dollar is set is determined by what world inflation and domestic inflation are expected to be. Generally, the aim is to reduce imported inflation in domestic prices by appreciating the trade-weighted dollar.

Second, on the execution of policy:

The actual operation of monetary policy has been influenced by the institutional arrangement of the CPF (Central Provident Fund) and government surpluses being deposited with MAS. Such action has the effect of reducing liquidity in the banking system and if not offset, would cause the Singapore dollar to appreciate. MAS' actions to restore this liquidity largely take the form of unsterilized foreign exchange interventions, in which U.S. dollars are purchased by MAS through the creation of bank reserves. The extent of this intervention is determined by what is needed to keep the exchange rate within the target band.

Domestic money market operations are undertaken in the main to complement exchange rate policy. They are tactical in nature, to add to or mop up temporary liquidity to offset seasonal or technical factors, or to smooth out short-term interest rate movements with a minimum of impact on the exchange rate. These operations are carried out primarily through foreign exchange currency swap transactions (in which Singapore dollars are swapped for U.S. dollars or vice versa), and through short-term borrowing and lending in the interbank market. With the development of a secondary market for Singapore government securities in May 1987, MAS has also begun to enter into overnight repurchase agreements in government securities (repos).

To date, however, open market operations in government securities have not been used as an instrument of monetary policy (Teh 1988, pp. 9–11; see also Lim et al. 1988, chap. 11).

Statistical Analysis

The fact that, as Teh indicated, the Singapore dollar "is allowed to float within a target band" suggests that generally the behavior of the Singapore dollar–U.S. dollar exchange rate might well be described by a random walk or, slightly more generally, by a unit root process.[15] Our formal analysis of the time-series properties of the logarithm of the spot exchange rates at successive monthly intervals supported this.[16]

With this finding, we proceeded to examine the relationship among various domestic interest rates (on Singapore dollar–denominated instruments) and a "representative" foreign interest rate. The domestic interest rates we selected were the one-month interbank rate (denoted OMITR), the one-month fixed deposit rate (OMFDR), and the prime lending rate (PLR), and the foreign rate was the one-month interbank rate in the Singapore Asian dollar market (in U.S. dollars), denoted SIBOR.

As a first step, we examined whether the foregoing interest rates were characterized by unit root behavior, and the answer in all four cases was yes. As such, a conventional regression analysis would have been inappropriate, and so we undertook a cointegration analysis instead.[17] Detailed results are presented in Table 7.17.[18] Our tests revealed that the SIBOR was a significant determinant of all three domestic rates, indicating the sensitivity of domestic monetary conditions to external influences. The long-run responsiveness to a unit change in the SIBOR was highest for OMITR (at 0.6), and for OMFDR and PLR, it was 0.42. Again, these results are plausible, although the result for PLR may not be very accurate, since it is not solely a one-month lending rate: however, data constraints prevented a more precise "matching."

Table 7.17. Unit Roots and Cointegration Tests Between Exchange Rate and Selected Interest Rates: Singapore

Interest Rates	$G(p,q)$	Test Statistic	p-value	Finding
Unit roots test results[a]				
SIBOR[b]	0,4	17.996	0.001	Unit root
PLR[c]	0,4	18.690	0.001	Unit root
OMFDR[d]	0,4	17.162	0.002	Unit root
OMITR[e]	0,4	17.832	0.001	Unit root

Exchange rate with interest rates	Constant	Coefficients		$h(0,3)$	Findings
		1	2		
Cointegrating regression of exchange rate with interest rates[f]					
Regression number 1:	0.601	1.240	−1.456	5.775	Cointegrated
with OMITR and SIBOR	(6.546)	(0.925)	(−1.325)	$p = 0.22$	
Regression number 2:	0.622	3.225	−4.326	5.675	None
with OMFDR and SIBOR	(2.346)	(1.370)	(−2.042)	$p = 0.07$	
Regression number 3:	0.627	0.627	−2.613	7.696	None
with PLR and SIBOR	(3.176)	(2.754)	(−1.532)	$p = 0.10$	

[a] Unit roots tests revealed that the interest rates possess unit roots.

[b] Singapore interbank offer rate.

[c] Prime lending rate.

[d] One-month fixed deposit rate.

[e] One-month interbank rate.

[f] Cointegration tests show that the exchange rate series is cointegrated with the one-month interbank rates and the interbank offered rates over the test period: regression number 1.

It is noteworthy that the long-run responsiveness of OMITR was less than unity. Over the sample period, the average value of the SIBOR (on an annual basis) was 10.63%, and that of OMITR was 7.0%. This difference is unlikely to be attributable to exchange rate expectations, given our unit root finding. It is likely, therefore, to be attributable largely to a risk premium—which is consistent with the MAS's policy of seeking to maintain stability in the real value of the Singapore dollar. Moreover, the difference widened when the SIBOR went up, probably because, in the 1980s at least, high foreign interest rates were viewed as indicative of greater turmoil in world financial markets. All in all, our results suggest that in the extremely open Singapore economy, the SIBOR serves as a relevant reference rate for the domestic economy but also that astute macroeconomic management has enabled the domestic economy to enjoy somewhat lower real interest rates (in Singapore dollars) because the local currency is viewed by domestic residents as somewhat "safer" than the U.S. dollar.

CONCLUSIONS

The focus of this chapter was on the development of activity in the principal markets for short-term funds in Singapore. The most important policy changes were the shift to a floating–exchange rate system in June 1973, the gradual but complete removal of exchange controls by 1978, and the deregulation of commercial bank interest rates in 1975. The unleashing of competitive forces through these policy changes did not lead to financial instability. The close supervision of the regulators and the generally tight regulatory (prudential) framework contributed to this stability, despite important structural changes.[19]

Despite the removal of exchange controls—suggesting the freedom to borrow and lend in any currency—the restriction on lending in Singapore dollars in excess of S$5 million to nonresidents and for use outside Singapore remains. This is aimed at preventing the internationalization of the Singapore currency and the implied instability that such a development may generate throughout the financial system.

Side by side with these policy changes, Singapore has, since the late 1960s, been nurturing offshore financial activities. A preferential regulatory and tax framework has been employed as a policy instrument. However, to minimize the loss of monetary control and to distinguish domestic financial activities from offshore financial activities, new banks wishing to operate in Singapore have, in almost all cases, been issued only restricted and offshore licenses rather than full licenses. This has curtailed their activities to some extent in regard to the domestic money market, especially for nonbanking entities, given the size of the economy, which in any case is small. Also, policy changes, such as removing exchange controls, which allow residents to transact in any currency, and lowering the limits of loans by offshore banks to residents, helped intensify competition.[20]

Given its openness and the close links between domestic and offshore markets, we would expect that domestic interest rates would be influenced by rates in international markets. After all, both domestic and offshore activities take place in close proximity, and such a result is guaranteed. And this was confirmed by our tests, which revealed that the SIBOR was a significant determinant of all three domestic interest rates we chose.

An interesting feature of the Singapore system is that although the banking system is well developed, open market operations in government securities have not been viewed as an important monetary policy instrument. Liquidity is managed mainly through foreign exchange purchases and sales, both directly and via swap operations. Care is taken to ensure that these activities do not interfere with attaining the main objective of the exchange rate policy, which is to minimize imported inflation. This is facilitated by the fact that swap activities per se appear to have only a minor, if not negligible, effect on the exchange rate. Liquidity management through foreign exchange intervention is facilitated by Singapore's large foreign exchange holdings, although it is conceivable that if the government securities market were to take off, open market operations would also be used as an instrument of monetary policy.

NOTES

We would like to express our gratitude to a large number of money market observers, discussions with whom yielded extremely helpful information and insights. We also wish to thank Sam Ouliaris for his invaluable help with the econometric analysis reported in this chapter.

1. This instrument, with maturities ranging from three months to three years, has been issued since 1975. The minimum denomination for each certificate is S$100,000, and the maximum is S$1 million, in multiples of S$50,000, except for restricted-license banks, in which case the minimum is S$250,000. The volume has not been very large, for several reasons. First, because banks have a flexible attitude toward the release of money from fixed deposits, customers tend to prefer them. Second, the thin secondary market makes it difficult to resell S$NCDs. Third, customers appear to prefer commercial bills. See Hendrie 1986.

2. Generally, the official explanation for the 1984 amendments to the Banking Act, and similar amendments to the Finance Companies Act at the same time, rests on the lapse of time since their first enactment (in the late 1960s and early 1970s) and the ensuing changes in the financial sector. Their broad purpose is to strengthen and tighten prudential regulation. The proximate reason for their timing may be related to global and regional developments, such as the debt crisis in 1982, the spate of banking and finance company problems in Hong Kong in 1982 (attributed by many to a failure of supervision), and similar problems in Malaysia.

3. The Development Bank of Singapore was established by the government in 1968 to operate as a development finance institution to serve the needs of the growing manufacturing sector. Because the DBS has been expected to support government policies and programs, some of the provisions of the Banking Act make an exception for it. Although it was established as a development finance institution, the DBS has been active in commercial, international, and merchant banking. Especially in the 1980s the DBS was active in providing new financial instruments such as RUFs (revolving underwriting facilities) and NIFs (note-issuing facilities) to corporate clients. In consumer banking, the DBS was the first to introduce Saturday afternoon banking and ATS accounts (DBS autosave: interest-

bearing savings accounts with checking facilities). At the end of 1988, the government, through a holding company, owned 47% of its equity.

4. Whereas 182-day treasury bills are issued monthly, 273- and 364-day bills are issued intermittently.

5. Primary dealers operating from within banks are subject to the provisions of the Banking Act, whereas the rest operate under the MAS's directives. The latter are subject to the following requirements: (a) a minimum net adjusted capital of S$20 million, (b) a gearing ratio of 20, and (c) a minimum of 40% of assets made up of Singapore government securities (SGS), repurchase agreements of SGS, cash with MAS, and commercial bills (not exceeding 10% of total assets).

6. In the past, treasury bills were generally issued on a tender basis, and longer-term government securities were taken up mostly by the Central Provident Fund and the Post Office Savings Bank on a "tap" basis.

7. However, it is required to submit daily returns on some of its transactions to the MAS, according to its directive, MAS 1104 (April 10, 1986), referred to earlier.

8. It is common knowledge that the principal intervention by regulators is through swap activities in the foreign exchange market. But little is revealed about the details of how they do this: The kind of weekly and monthly reporting by regulators so common in the U.S. Congress is not required in Singapore.

9. NCDs (fixed and floating rate) in the ACU were in minimum denominations of U.S.$50,000 and ¥10 million. The minimum deposit size has declined. Currently, most major banks offer deposits as low as U.S.$5000 for ACU accounts. Maturities run from a minimum of one month to a maximum of five years. Forward deals are not permitted. Yen NCDs have been allowed only since December 1984.

10. At the end of 1989, the 4 big local banks and 4 big foreign banks (out of the 35 full-license banks) had a total of 1,214 branches and ATMs. With the population of 2.65 million living in 627 square kilometers, this works out to 1 branch/ATM per 2,200 persons. The 8 banks would account for three-fourths of the branches/ATMs.

11. See MAS 610 (1983) for the extensive classification/format of required reports.

12. Removal of the tax-exempt status would in all likelihood also entail removal of the current "two-tier" interest rate structure, according to which individual POSBank deposits in excess of S$100,000 receive a lower interest rate than do those that are less than S$100,000.

13. One of the main reasons for this opposition is the view that internationalization would make the domestic monetary situation susceptible to the unsettling consequences of foreign financial shifts.

14. We are indebted to Professor Ronald McKinnon of Stanford University for discussions on this point.

15. It appears that in the short run, the exchange rate is even permitted to move temporarily outside the target band in response to sudden pressures and that the band itself is gradually adjusted over time in response to secular developments.

16. The Augmented Dickey–Fuller, or ADF, statistic (Said and Dickey 1984) for a ten-year series ending in January 1989 was -0.971, and the $G(p,q)$ statistic (Park and Choi 1988) was 141.05, both within the unit root acceptance region. We are greatly indebted to Sam Ouliaris, National University of Singapore, for conducting the unit root and cointegration analyses reported in this part of the chapter.

17. An excellent summary of this methodology, with references to the literature, may be found in S. M. Leong and S. Ouliaris, "Evaluating the Long-Run Effectiveness of Advertising on Sales: Theory, Methodology, and Application of Cointegration," Working Paper, Faculty of Business Administration, National University of Singapore, February 1990. Also see Ouliaris's analysis in Chapter 10.

18. The upper part of the table presents the results of the unit root analysis, and the lower part, the cointegration analysis. The "Order" on the first line refers to the order of the polynomial adopted for the unit root examination; it was not found necessary to include a time trend. The CCR estimator is developed by J. Y. Park, "Canonical Cointegrating Regressions" (hence CCR) (1988). For each CCR estimation in the table, the betas refer to the coefficients of the SIBOR, the constant term, and the

time trend, respectively, and the t-statistics, to their respective t-ratios. The H-statistic, also developed by Park, as well as the G-statistics, together with the associated probability values, indicates in each case that the domestic interest rate and the SIBOR are cointegrated.

19. It would appear that a good regulatory system, among other things, obviates the need for a system of deposit insurance, which (in conjunction with fixed insurance premiums) tends to induce excessive risk taking by banks. See Kareken and Wallace 1978 and Kareken 1986, both of which are cited in Penati and Protopapadakis 1988.

20. There is, of course, room for further improvement in the system, indicated by the fact that Singapore's "financial sector's productivity is slightly ahead of Hong Kong's, but only one-third that of Japan's" (Pillay 1989, p. 4). It would be interesting to know whether Singapore's financial system is at the "technology frontier" in terms of the range of instruments being traded and, if not, whether further enhancing the degree of competition domestically (either from domestic institutions such as the POSBank or by allowing somewhat greater scope for foreign institutions to compete) would stimulate more rapid financial innovation and better terms for customers. Improved terms would, of course, also be a result if increased competition reduced possible oligopolistic profit margins.

REFERENCES

Hendrie, A., ed. 1986. *Banking in the Far East: Structures and Sources of Finance*. London: Financial Times Business Information.

Kareken, J. 1986. "Federal Bank Regulatory Policy: A Description and Some Observations." *Journal of Business* 59: 3–49.

Kareken, J., and N. Wallace. 1978. "Deposit Insurance and Bank Regulation: A Partial Equilibrium Exposition." *Journal of Business* 51: 379–413.

Leong, Siew Mun, and S. Ouliaris. 1990. "Evaluating the Long-Run Effectiveness of Advertising on Sales: Theory, Methodology, and Application of Cointegration." Working Paper, Faculty of Business Administration, National University of Singapore, February.

Lim, Chong Yah, et al. 1980. *Policy Options for the Singapore Economy*. Singapore: McGraw-Hill.

MAS. 1980. *Annual Report*. Singapore: Monetary Authority of Singapore.

———. 1984. *Notice to Discount Houses*. MAS 909, February 24. Singapore: Government Gazette Notification.

———. 1986. *Notices to Banks*. MAS 1104, April 10. Singapore: Monetary Authority of Singapore.

———. 1989. *Annual Report*. Singapore: Monetary Authority of Singapore.

———. 1990. *MAS 1989–1990 Annual Report*. Singapore: Monetary Authority of Singapore.

Park, J. Y. 1988. "Canonical Cointegrating Regressions." Working Paper, Department of Economics, Cornell University.

Park, J. Y., and B. Choi. 1988. "A New Approach to Testing for a Unit Root." Working Paper 88–23, Department of Economics, Cornell University.

Peat, Marwick, Mitchell and Co. 1986. *Banking in Singapore*. Singapore: Peat, Marwick, Mitchell and Co.

Penti, A., and A. Protopapadakis. 1988. "The Effect of Implicit Deposit Insurance on Banks' Portfolio Choices with an Application to Investment Overexposure." *Journal of Monetary Economics* 21: 98–107.

Pillay, J. Y. 1989. Speech delivered as managing director of the Monetary Authority of Singapore, at the Association of Banks in Singapore's annual dinner, June 28.

Price Waterhouse. 1987. *International Banking—Singapore*. Singapore: Price Waterhouse.

Said, S. E., and D. A. Dickey. 1984. "Testing for Unit Roots in Autoregressive Moving Average Model of Unknown Order." *Biometrika* 71: 599–607.

Tan, Chwee Huat. 1984: *1988 Financial Markets in Singapore*. Singapore: National University Press.

Teh, Kok Pong. 1988. "Monetary Policy in an Open Economy: Singapore." Speech given at the 17th SEANZA Central Banking Course, Reserve Bank of Australia, Sydney.

CALENDAR OF SIGNIFICANT
FINANCIAL EVENTS

Jan. 1, 1972	The 20% liquidity requirement on ACUs is abolished.
Feb. 20, 1972	The stamp duty on NCDs, bills of exchange, and promissory notes transacted through banks is abolished.
Jun. 25, 1972	A switch is made from the pound sterling to the U.S. dollar as the intervention currency.
Jul. 12, 1972	The MAS frees rates for foreign exchange transactions of S$250,000 or more.
Aug. 25, 1972	The MAS liberalizes exchange control of Singapore companies regarded as Singapore residents.
Jan. 22, 1973	Treasury bills are issued on a tender basis.
Jun. 21, 1973	The Singapore dollar is floated.
Aug. 30, 1973	The stamp duty on contact notes relating to Singapore government securities is remitted.
Mar. 29, 1975	Singapore dollar NCDs are issued.
May 1, 1975	The MAS rediscount facility begins operation.
Jul. 1, 1975	The MAS permits flexible banking hours subject to a minimum of twenty-seven hours per week.
Jul. 15, 1975	The bank cartel for interest rates is abolished.
Feb. 14, 1976	Exchange controls are liberalized further.
Nov. 19, 1977	The MAS makes available to banks a S$120 million swap facility for periods of one, two, and three months.
Jan. 3, 1978	Banks are authorized to issue fixed-rate U.S.$NCDs.
Jun. 1, 1978	The MAS lifts all exchange control regulations.
Jun. 15, 1978	The MAS permits merchant banks to deal in gold and foreign exchange.
Jul. 1, 1978	The MAS allows offshore banks to extend credit facilities to Singapore residents without the need to extend a qualifying term loan. The total credit facilities extended by each offshore bank to residents cannot exceed S$30 million at any one time.
Sep. 1, 1978	The MAS makes available to banks a S$60 million swap facility for a one-month period.
Sep. 1, 1978	The Post Office Savings Bank introduces a two-tier interest rate structure.
Jan. 2, 1980	Individual discount houses are free to quote their own call deposit rates. Previously, rates were fixed by agreement among the discount houses.

Jan. 7, 1980	The Development Bank of Singapore introduces auto-save.
Sep. 25, 1980	The Overseas Union Bank introduces silver passbook accounts and the sale of silver kilobars.
Nov. 24, 1980	The Post Office Saving Bank launches Singapore's first nonbook savings account—a passcard account system.
Jan. 2, 1981	The United Overseas Bank and the Overseas Union Bank introduce gold passbook accounts.
Jul. 20, 1981	The Development Bank of Singapore introduces NCDs denominated in SDRs.
Sep. 1, 1981	The Association of Banks in Singapore allows its members to decide various charges and minimum payments for each domestic transaction of S$40,000 and above.
Jan. 1, 1982	A system of quantity discounts is implemented, in which banks are entitled to discounts on their monthly foreign exchange bills exceeding specified amounts.
May 13, 1982	Finance companies are allowed to use commercial bills of exchange, S$NCDs, and floating-rate certificates of deposit issued by banks in Singapore as liquid assets to make up the 10% liquid asset ratio requirement they must observe.
Jan. 26, 1983	The Association of Banks in Singapore agrees formally to allow its members to calculate interest on savings accounts on a daily basis.
Mar. 1, 1983	Citibank launches a U.S. dollar savings account.
Mar. 4, 1983	The Banking (Amendment) Bill is passed. It is designed to improve the standard of banking secrecy in Singapore.
Jan. 17, 1984	The Banking (Amendment) Bill of 1984 is passed. The amendments cover a wide range of subjects, relating to operations, loan portfolios, equity structures, responsibility of directors, and gearing of banks. Penalties for violations are substantially increased.
Apr. 7, 1984	The Singapore Clearing House Association launches the Interbank GIRO System to facilitate the paperless transfer of funds between customers of any participating bank.
Sep. 21, 1984	The MAS (Amendment) Act goes into effect. The act gives the authority wider powers in regulating the financial system and in playing its role as banker and adviser to the government.
Oct. 19, 1984	The Finance Companies (Amendment) Bill of 1984 is passed, bringing the act in line with the amended Banking Act.
Dec. 1, 1984	The MAS allows the ACUs of banks and merchant banks to issue NCDs denominated in Japanese yen.
Feb. 6, 1985	Members of the Association of Banks in Singapore are free to determine commissions and fees charged for banking transactions.
Jan. 18, 1986	The electronic funds transfer system at point of sale (EFTPOS) is launched.
Mar. 26, 1987	Parliament authorizes the minister of finance to borrow up to S$6 billion through treasury bills. This paves the way for launching the revamped government securities market.
May 4, 1987	The Singapore government securities market is launched.
Jul. 1, 1988	The ceiling on lending to residents by offshore banks is raised from S$30 million to S$50 million.
Nov. 24, 1988	The big four local banks and their subsidiaries launch their shared ATM network.

CHAPTER 8
MONEY MARKETS IN PREWAR JAPAN

JURO TERANISHI

The purpose of this chapter is to analyze the operations and development of money markets during the prewar period in Japan, 1915 to 1930. The financial system of this period was plagued with serious problems related to information asymmetry and a lack of long-term capital. Consequently, the system was highly unstable, with chronic bank runs. It was difficult for money markets to fulfill their role as a device for adjusting liquidity, as a proper conduit of monetary policy, or as a source of information about the cost of short-term funds.

Instability is a typical and frequently the most serious problem faced by the financial systems of developing countries. Both the liquidity risk and the solvency risk are responsible for this. Since the nonbanks' supply of assets is usually short term, reflecting their small amount, financial systems often suffer from liquidity risk when they transform maturities in order to meet the industrial sector's need for long-term funds. On the other hand, because ownership and management are not separate, the loans of related firms often result in nonperforming assets, endangering the banks' deposit absorption capability and eventually their solvency. Apparently, the role of the money markets is closely related to the degree of instability. Although liquidity could be adjusted by changing liquid assets or through bank borrowing and trade credits in the case of nonbanks and by central bank borrowing in the case of banks, a well-functioning money market is best for adjusting liquidity and alleviating the financial system's liquidity risk. However, for many developing countries, the smooth working of the money market is frequently handicapped by the system's solvency risk. First, the quantity of money market funds becomes inelastic whenever some members of the banking sector suffer from solvency risk. In order to compensate for the deterioration of their deposit-raising capability, those banks are likely to use money market funds as a source of long-term loans to related firms. Since the funds used in this way are related to fixed investments, the demand for money market funds becomes quite inflexible, and as a result, interest rates become unnecessarily volatile. Second, government policy regarding the solvency problem sometimes discourages the development of money markets. If the government tried to regulate deposit interest rates in order to alleviate the interest rate battle often waged by banks in difficulties, money markets would have to remain closed to nonbanks, since the availability to nonbanks of money market instruments whose interest rates on deposits are regulated would cause an all-or-nothing shift of portfolios between assets, depending on the interest rates. If the central bank, on the other hand, resorted to offering an excess amount of credit, especially short-term credit, to banks in difficulties, the money market's liquidity function could be replaced by central bank credits, and thus money markets would not spontaneously develop.

The efficient functioning of the money markets is enhanced by the nonbanks' participation in both the diversification of shocks to the market and the increase in the depth of the market. However, such participation is not easy for most developing countries. As suppliers of money market funds, nonbanks usually do not have large enough asset portfolios to reduce effectively the risk of investing in the money market by means of diversified asset holdings. Rather, they tend to use money market funds as a source of fixed investments. Moreover, the lack of disclosure, owing to the minimal ownership and management, causes a serious information problem concerning the quality of the nonbank participants in the markets.

OVERVIEW

The Macroeconomy

The period covered in this chapter is the approximately fifteen years from the beginning of World War I to the aftermath of the great financial crash in 1927. The experience in this period is typical of the relationship between the instability of the banking sector and the development of the money markets.

World War I (July 1914 –November 1918) brought an unprecedented boom to Japan. The chronic balance-of-payment deficits before the war was suddenly wiped out, and Japan accumulated huge current account surpluses during the war. Its foreign reserves increased from ¥516 million in 1915 to ¥2,179 million in 1920 (Table 8.1), and the GNP showed enormous growth owing to the expansion of exports (Table 8.2). Indigenous industries thrived on the expansion of exports, and new heavy and chemical industries were established, substituting for both exports and imports.

After World War I, the macroeconomic situation changed drastically; the trade balance returned to deficit; and the indigenous sectors encoun-

Table 8.1. Trade Balance (Mainland Japan) and Foreign Reserves (in millions of yen)

	Trade Balance			Foreign Reserves	
	Export	Import	Net Export	Absolute Values	Change
1915	793	634	157	516	(175)
1916	1,252	884	368	714	(198)
1917	1,793	1,201	591	1,105	(391)
1918	2,177	1,902	275	1,588	(483)
1919	2,444	2,501	−57	2,045	(457)
1920	2,267	2,682	−415	2,179	(134)
1921	1,503	1,941	−438	2,080	(−99)
1922	1,885	2,261	−331	1,830	(−250)
1923	1,966	2,394	−695	1,653	(−177)
1924	7,121	2,972	−851	1,501	(−152)
1925	2,987	3,109	−422	1,413	(−88)
1926	2,432	2,923	−492	1,357	(−56)
1927	2,399	2,715	−315	1,273	(−84)
1928	2,425	2,747	−321	1,199	(−74)
1929	2,621	2,766	−145	1,343	(−144)
1930	1,888	2,006	−118	960	(−383)

Source: BOJ, *One Hundred Year History,* vol. 2 (Tokyo: BOJ, 1983).

Table 8.2. Money Supply and GNP (in millions of yen)

	Money Supply	M2	GNP at Current Prices	Currency/ GNP (%)	M2/GNP (%)
1915	382	2,501	4,991	7.7	50.1
1916	510	3,338	6,148	8.3	54.3
1917	668	4,800	8,592	7.8	55.9
1918	918	6,638	11,839	7.6	56.1
1919	1,224	8,314	15,453	7.9	53.8
1920	1,171	8,435	15,893	7.4	53.4
1921	1,272	9,115	14,886	8.5	61.2
1922	1,377	9,352	15,573	8.8	60.1
1923	1,375	9,443	14,924	9.2	63.3
1924	1,302	9,718	15,576	8.4	62.4
1925	1,275	10,453	16,265	7.8	64.3
1926	1,224	10,934	15,975	7.7	68.4
1927	1,307	11,010	16,293	8.0	67.6
1928	1,311	11,535	16,506	7.9	69.9
1929	1,331	11,711	16,286	8.2	71.9
1930	1,197	11,335	14,671	8.2	77.3

Source: GNP from *Long-Term Economic Statistics,* vol. 1 (Tokyo: Toyo keizai shinposha, 1974), and money supply from S. Fujino, "Nikon no money-stock 1871–1940" (Tokyo: Institute of Economic Research, Hitotsubashi University Discussion Paper 222, February 1990). Money supply data as of end of year.

tered serious difficulties owing to the fall of demand, both domestic and foreign. Newly established modern industries endured several difficult years as a result of severe competition from abroad. Nominal and real GNP were stagnant, staying at almost the same level during this period (Table 8.2).

Following the United States, Japan formally suspended its adherence to the gold standard in September 1917 and did not return to it until 1930. Nonetheless, Japan continued to intervene into the foreign exchange market. Until 1920, it tried to prevent the appreciation of the exchange rate and actively purchased foreign exchange reserves, with the consequent undervaluation of the real exchange rate (Figure 8.1). The money supply increased rapidly during the period (Table 8.2). After 1921, Japan tried to prevent the yen's depreciation and intervened in the market by selling accumulated foreign reserves. The real exchange rate remained considerably overvalued until 1930 (Figure 8.1). The money supply (M2) showed a slow increase, reflecting the expansion of domestic credits (Table 8.2).

The Financial System

The financial system of prewar Japan can be characterized as follows.

The bank-dominated system. As Table 8.3 shows, the most important financial institutions were banks, although their share declined continuously. The banking sector was made up of commercial banks and special banks. The latter consisted of two development banks (the Japan Hypothec Bank and the Industrial Bank of Japan), one foreign trade–financing bank (Yokohama Specie Bank), two colonial banks (Taiwan Bank and Chosen Bank, Hokkaido Takushoku Bank), and prefectural agricultural banks.

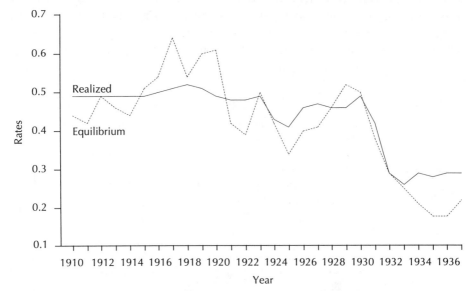

Figure 8.1. Realized and Equilibrium Exchange Rates

Table 8.3. Percentage Share of Financial Institutions

| | Banks | | Insurance | Trust | Postal Saving | Credit | |
	Commercial	Special	Cos.	Fund Cos.	System	Coops.	Total
1900	83.8	8.4	1.8	—	5.9	—	91.3
1910	72.1	14.9	2.9	—	9.6	0.5	86.0
1920	78.2	10.4	3.3	—	6.1	2.0	88.6
1930	49.8	15.3	7.3	6.5	14.9	6.2	65.1
1940	46.2	9.8	8.8	5.7	22.1	7.3	56.0

Note: Share refers to total loans and security investments. Commercial banks are ordinary and saving banks.

Source: J. Teranishi, *Nihon no keizai hatten to kinyu* (Tokyo: Iwanami shoten, 1982), pp. 392–93.

Two development banks, the Hokkaido Takushoku Bank, and the prefectural agricultural banks could obtain funds by issuing financial debentures and accepting deposits. The Yokohama Specie Bank (YSB), whose main source of funds was private deposits, acted as the sole agent for the Bank of Japan (BOJ) and the central government for foreign exchange transactions, and it could borrow from the Bank of Japan on special terms, by means of the so-called foreign exchange financing loans (FEFLs).

Weak international linkage. Overall, international financial linkage was weak in the prewar period. But with respect to long-term finance, international linkages became relatively stronger after World War I. Table 8.4 reports the results of regressing Japanese long-term interest rates on the weighted average of short-term interest rates, U.S. long-term interest rates, and the expected change in the exchange rate. U.S. interest rates were quite influential after World War I. We also tested the uncovered interest parity condition with respect to Japan's short-term interest rates and the United States' assuming static expectations. The result was unsatisfactory, indicating the isolation of Japanese short-term interest rates from the international financial market.

Table 8.4. Regression of Long-Term Interest Rates

| | Independent Variables | | | | | |
| | Const. $\Sigma\omega_i\rho_s$ | | | Expected μ | R2 | DW |
Period						
October 1900–March 1914	0.049	0.139	−0.144	−0.007	0.50	0.23
	(7,05)	[0.03]	(−1.04)	(−1.55)		
January 1925–February 1937	0.015	0.111	0.969	0.007	0.79	0.18
	(6.98)	[0.03]	(11.39)	(4.13)		

Note: $\Sigma\omega_i\rho_s$ shows the distributed lag of short-term interest rates (bank bill–discounting rate). A three-degree polynomial Armon lag is assumed; ρ_{ex}long-term interest rate in the United States is the yield of high-grade railroad bonds. Expected μ (rate of change of exchange rate) is assumed to be equal to the rate of change of the WPI in Japan minus that in the United States. Figures in parentheses show *t*-values except for those under $\Sigma\omega_i\rho_s$, which give the sum of the standard errors of lagged variables.

A free-market system with increasing intervention. The prewar financial system essentially operated on the principles of a free market. Entry into the banking industry was almost completely free before 1918, and even after 1918 anyone who met the minimum capital requirements could set up a new bank. However, after the enactment of the Bank Act in 1927, the government used minimum capital requirements to promote bank mergers. Interest rates were virtually free to move before 1918, but after 1918, a cartel agreement on the maximum deposit rate was introduced in the major urban regions. Although violations in the form of under-the-table payments were common, the ceiling was effective at least for large prestigious banks who led the agreement and for special banks which the government supervised strictly.

The Banking Sector

Owing to the minimal separation of ownership and management, lending among related firms was common among banks in prewar Japan and was a frequent source of serious risk for the banks. When a firm slumped, the related-firm loans were increased and invariably became overdue. To finance these fixed loans, the banks offered high interest rates to attract deposits, and the higher interest costs often necessitated making further high-risk loans in order to earn acceptable spreads.

Such risky behavior was the principal characteristic of small- and medium-size banks, which were connected to indigenous industries or whose clients were less diversified. Large banks such as *zaibatsu* banks, on the other hand, had well-diversified portfolios and had none of these problems.

Consequently, the prewar financial system had a dual structure: large banks with a high deposit-raising capability and small and medium-size banks with a low deposit-raising capability, as shown in Table 8.5. For small and medium-size banks with paid-in capital of less than ¥10 million, both their deposit rate and their lending rate were high, whereas their lending and

Table 8.5. Differences in Banks' Performance, by Size, 1925

	Size by Paid-in Capital (in millions of yen)			
	1–3 (131)	3–5 (27)	5–10 (30)	10– (18)
Operating cost/deposits	0.012	0.015	0.011	0.010
Average lending rate	0.122	0.134	0.128	0.110
Average deposit rate	0.087	0.093	0.092	0.074
Lendings/deposits	0.996	0.906	1.033	0.784
Borrowings/total assets	0.066	0.063	0.091	0.009
Cash/deposits	0.073	0.068	0.089	0.086
Net interbank call money/deposits	0.036	0.029	0.004	0.023

Note: Based on sample of 206 banks in 1925. Numbers in parentheses show the size of the sample for each category. The category with paid-in capital greater than ¥10 million includes five large banks.

deposit ratios remained low because they depended greatly on loans, mostly from Bank of Japan. These small and medium-size banks were a major source of the prewar financial system's instability. Table 8.6 shows that between 1920 and 1930, the average number of bank bankruptcies each year was 43.5. Table 8.7 lists the relative sizes of the deposits of large commercial banks, small and medium-size banks, and special banks. The share of special banks' deposits decreased considerably after 1918. Before 1918, they had tried to absorb deposits by offering high interest rates, with the consequent stagnation of commercial banks' deposits. After 1918, the special banks were forced to rely heavily on funding at the interbank call market. The share of the large banks generally rose during this period.

The Money Markets

The prewar Japanese financial system had the following money markets:

1. The *interbank call market* was the only viable and significant money market during this period. It was created by the pioneering bankers around the turn of the century when the government tried to reduce the banks' dependence on borrowing from the Bank of Japan. The size of this market relative to deposits is shown on Table 8.8, together with the Bank of Japan's loans and deposits. The size of the interbank call market is comparable, though slightly smaller than the BOJ's lending to commercial banks.

2. With the export boom during World War I, the Ministry of Finance and the BOJ tried to create a *trade bill market* in Japan, with the ambitious aim of making Tokyo the "London of the Far East." But this market, created in 1919, was only temporarily active and disappeared after several years.

3. Although neglected by the existing literature, prewar Japan did have a type of *commercial paper market*. When the bill brokers prospered in the World War I boom, they began a new business—-buying bills from banks at their own risk and selling them to other banks or nonbanks. These bills, both financial and commercial, were mostly without collateral and were endorsed by the bill brokers. They were like the present-day commercial paper, although this market did not expand much.

Table 8.6. Changes in the Number of Commercial Banks

| | *Number of Banks* | | *Annual Average* | | |
| | *At Beginning of Period* | *At End of Period* | *Increase Due to Establishment* | *Decrease Due to* | |
				Bankruptcy	*Mergers*
1902–19	2,334	2,001	15.8	24.6	9.9
1920–32	2,001	625	19.6	43.5	88.0
1933–45	625	65	4.2	7.8	39.5

Source: J. Teranishi, *Nihon no keizai hatten to kinyu* (Tokyo: Iwanami shoten, 1982), p. 299.

Table 8.7. Deposits and Financial Debentures of Banks' Value and Percentage Share (in millions of yen)

| | Deposits of Commercial Banks | | | | Special Banks | | | |
| | Five Large Banks | | Other Banks | | Deposits | | Financial Debentures | |
	Value	%	Value	%	Value	%	Value	%
1915	407	(12.2)	2,229	(67.0)	331	(10.0)	360	(10.8)
1916	584	(13.2)	2,945	(66.5)	511	(11.5)	387	(8.7)
1917	860	(13.4)	4,167	(65.0)	993	(15.5)	389	(6.1)
1918	1,252	(13.9)	5,928	(65.7)	1,304	(14.4)	545	(6.0)
1919	1,485	(13.7)	7,522	(69.5)	1,174	(10.8)	643	(5.9)
1920	1,570	(14.1)	7,670	(68.9)	1,097	(9.9)	793	(7.1)
1921	1,579	(13.2)	8,391	(70.3)	1,029	(8.6)	933	(7.8)
1922	1,517	(12.7)	8,452	(70.7)	1,016	(8.5)	967	(8.1)
1923	1,981	(15.6)	8,499	(67.1)	1,111	(8.8)	1,076	(8.5)
1924	2,007	(15.0)	8,887	(66.6)	1,256	(9.4)	1,196	(9.0)
1925	2,106	(14.9)	9,632	(68.3)	1,092	(7.7)	1,277	(9.1)
1926	2,233	(15.2)	10,247	(69.5)	925	(6.3)	1,332	(9.0)
1927	2,818	(18.4)	10,129	(66.0)	1,012	(6.6)	1,385	(9.0)
1928	3,130	(19.4)	10,581	(65.4)	987	(6.1)	1,474	(9.1)
1929	3,210	(19.4)	10,714	(64.6)	1,125	(6.8)	1,537	(9.3)
1930	3,187	(25.4)	6,552	(52.2)	1,152	(9.2)	1,657	(13.2)

Note: Figures in parentheses show percentage shares in total deposits and financial debentures. Special banks are YSB, Japan Hypothec Bank, Japan Industrial Bank, Taiwan Bank, and Korea Bank.

Source: Shinichi Goto, *Nihon no kinyu tokei* (Tokyo: Toyo keizai shinposha, 1970), pp. 94–115, 205–62.

Prewar Japan did not have a treasury bill (TB) market. Although the government issued short-term financing bonds, with maturities of one to twelve months, all of them were purchased by the BOJ (after 1905) and in turn were sold to banks in order to control the money supply. Since the quantity of this bond market was small and unstable (Table 8.8), the bonds purchased by banks were held until maturity, and a secondary market never developed.

THE INTERBANK DEPOSIT MARKET

Demand and supply in the interbank deposit market mirrored its dual structure. Large banks with a strong deposit-raising capability, owing to their perceived safety, always were on the supply side of the market. Many of the small and medium-size banks with overdue loans to related firms were hindered by their low deposit-raising capability and invariably

Table 8.8. Interbank Deposits, BOJ Loans and Deposits, and Government Short-Term Financing Bonds as Ratios to Commercial Bank Deposits (%)

	Interbank Deposits	BOJ Loans to Commercial Banks	Commercial Bank Deposits in BOJ	Government Short-Term Financing Bonds
1914	—	5.7		—
1916	(1.3)	8.4	1.2	—
1918	(2.2)	12.4	1.0	1.1
1920	(2.6)	4.0	1.2	2.6
1922	(1.5)	7.1	0.9	2.0
1924	4.3 (2.3)	9.0	0.7	1.9
1926	5.2 (2.3)	6.4	0.6	1.1
1928	1.7 (0.9)	9.1	0.9	—
1930	2.6 (1.7)	8.6	1.3	2.1

Note: Figures for interbank deposits in parentheses refer to only the Tokyo area.

Source: Shinichi Goto, *Nihon no kinyu tokei* (Tokyo: Toyo keizai shinposha, 1970); *Kinyujiko sankosho* of various years, and Toyo keizai shinposha, *Nihon no Keiki-hendo* (Tokyo: Toyo keizai shinposha, 1931).

stood at the demand side. Special banks were also on the demand side of the market because their ability to attract deposits was low compared with their need for funds. This was especially true of such special banks as Yokohama Specie Bank and two colonial banks whose other main source of funds was deposits.[1]

The relationship between the demand and supply of the interbank deposit market and the dual structure of the banking industry was clearest in the period before the great financial crash, which occurred in the spring of 1927. Table 8.9 shows this relationship for November 1926 and November 1927. The small and medium-size banks and special banks tended to regard the interbank deposits as a substitute for time deposits and used them to finance long-term loans to related firms. Conversely, the large banks considered their deposits in the interbank market not as a temporary abode for liquidity but as lucrative investments.

As a result of this situation, two characteristics emerged. First, the maturity of interbank deposits lengthened. Table 8.10 shows that at the end of November 1926, 56.3% of interbank deposits were long term—usually one to three months and even up to six months. Second, the quantity of deposits became inelastic, with a consequent increase in the volatility of interest rates. Accordinly to Table 8.11, the variability of interbank deposits was smaller than that of other reserve assets such as cash holdings or BOJ deposits and larger than that of BOJ loans or bill discounting, alternative methods of financing between 1924 and 1927. At the same time, the interbank deposit rate was much more volatile than the other interest rates.

Table 8.9. Interbank Deposits by Various Economic Units (in millions of yen)

	November 1926	November 1927
Supply		
Four large commercial banks	188	55
Other banks and security companies	149	76
Total	337	131
Demand		
Special banks	241	34
Bill brokers	33	14
Security companies	20	48
Commercial banks	42	34
Total	337	131

Note: Demand for interbank deposits by bill brokers comprise net dealings. The four large banks are Mitsui, Mitsubishi, Daiichi, and Yasuda.

Source: Nihon kinyushi shiryo (Meiji–Taisho hen) vol. 22.

The Great Financial Crash and the Interbank Market

The dual structure of the banking industry was a manifestation of both the instability of the banking system and the two characteristics of the interbank deposits market—long maturity and interest volatility or quantity inelasticity. Therefore, when some of the banks that relied heavily on financing through long-term interbank deposits fell into difficulty, the whole system of interbank deposits market was affected. This occurred at the time of the great financial crash, when a number of small and medium-size banks were hit by bank runs and the Taiwan Bank was beset by a huge amount of overdue loans to Suzuki shoten.

Table 8.10. Percentage Composition of Interbank Deposits Handled by Bill Brokers Before and After Financial Crash

	November 1926	November 1927
Collateral		
With collateral	12.2	55.9
Without collateral	87.7	44.0
Maturity		
Overnight	16.6	46.7
Long term	56.3	21.1
Others	26.8	32.0

Note: "Others" refers to unconditional and ordinary interbank deposits.

Source: Nihon kinyushi shiryo (Meiji–Taisho hen), vol. 22.

Table 8.11. Coefficient of Variation of Banks' Interest Rates, Assets, and Liabilities

	January 1924–January 1927	June 1927–June 1930
Interest rates		
Lending rate	0.016	0.048
Bill discounting rate	0.035	0.083
Time deposit rate	0.003	0.080
Interbank deposit rate	0.099	0.100
Assets and liabilities		
Lendings	0.059	0.025
Deposits	0.052	0.052
Security holdings	0.077	0.140
Cash holdings	0.193	0.138
Interbank deposits	0.123	0.182
BOJ lending	0.270	0.100
BOJ deposits (private sector)	0.207	0.298
BOJ bill discounting	0.237	0.103

Note: Coefficient of variation is standard deviation/mean.

Source: Interest rates are from S. Fujino and R. Akiyama, *Shoken kakaku to rishiritsu* (Tokyo: Institute of Economic Research, Hitotsubashi University, 1977); and banks' assets and liabilities are from Toyo keizai shinposha, *Nihon no keiki-hendo* (Tokyo: Toyo keizai shinposha, 1931).

After the virtual collapse of the interbank deposit market, bankers tended to avoid long-term and noncollateralized interbank deposits (Table 8.10). The Ministry of Finance endorsed this tendency by adding a clause to the operating rules of the new Bank Act excluding uncollateralized interbank deposits with maturities of more than seven days.

THE UNDERDEVELOPMENT OF THE OPEN MONEY MARKETS[2]

One significant effect of the unprecedented World War I export boom was the emergence of large business corporations as huge asset holders (Table 8.12). The increase in inventory reflects the inflation and excess demand for commodities at that time. Most noteworthy was the rapid accumulation of financial assets between 1916 and 1919, which had the following results: First, banks competed fiercely for corporate deposits and eventually established a deposit rate cartel in 1918. Second, corporations sought profitable instruments for their investments, which led to the emergence of the commercial paper market. Third, the Bank of Japan used this situation to create "open" money markets in Japan and tried to introduce trade bill markets.

The Creation and Failure of the Trade Bill Market

The BOJ said that it had two reasons for creating a trade bill market. The first was to improve the method of trade financing. Before trade bills were

Table 8.12. Liquid Asset Holdings by Large Corporations

	Liquid Assets/ Total Assets	Inventories/ Total Assets	Financial Assets/ Total Assets
1914	27.2	11.5	15.7
1915	26.8	12.1	14.7
1916	33.7	16.0	17.7
1917	38.5	14.0	24.6
1918	43.9	14.3	29.6
1919	50.5	15.6	34.9
1920	52.4	18.1	34.3
1921	43.9	10.3	33.5
1922	38.1	7.3	30.7
1923	33.4	7.4	26.0
1924	32.5	7.1	25.4
1925	32.4	8.1	24.3
1926	30.0	7.4	22.6
1927	30.1	5.8	24.2
1928	29.7	5.4	24.3
1929	28.9	5.3	23.7
1930	28.7	5.3	23.4

Note: The sample size is about 50 to 70 large companies. Liquid assets are the sum of inventories and financial assets.

Source: Jigyo gaisha keiei koritsu no kenkyu (Tokyo: Toyo keizai), various issues.

introduced, trade financing was mainly funded by BOJ loans (known as foreign exchange financing loans, or FEFLs) to the Yokohama Specie Bank (YSB). As the trade surplus grew during World War I, the BOJ felt the need to sterilize the foreign reserve flow and tried to do this by inducing the YSB to fund itself through interbank deposits. However, this policy had the side effect of lengthening the maturity of interbank deposits, and so the BOJ had to introduce an alternative method of trade financing. The BOJ's second purpose was to make Tokyo "the London of the Far East." The BOJ traditionally viewed Great Britain's financial system as the ideal, and it was the long-cherished desire of the BOJ's leaders to have well-functioning open money markets in Japan.

Two kinds of trade bills were created. For imports, every commercial bank was allowed to issue letters of credit and finance imports through yen-denominated bankers acceptances, which could be sold on the domestic bill discounting market. For exports, for example, to the United States, export bills bought by the YSB were kept at the New York branch of the BOJ until maturity, preventing the YSB from rediscounting them on the New York bill market. The YSB was, instead, allowed to issue yen-denominated "stamp" bills up to the amount of the yen value of the export bills, which could then be sold on the domestic bill market.[3] However, unlike a bankers acceptance, the stamp bills could not be sold to the general public, owing to the banks' opposition. The stamp bills issued by the YSB were guaranteed by the BOJ, so the asset was highly attractive to such nonbanks as large business corporations and insurance companies. Since the maximum deposit rate was regulated by cartel agreements and at least the large prestigious banks obeyed the rule, they pressured the Ministry of Finance and the BOJ to prevent the stamp bills from being sold directly to nonbanks.

In order to promote the stamp bills, the BOJ gave the YSB an incentive for financing through them by revising the rate of interest on its FEFLs. Before revision, it was 0.178 per mil (daily rate) for loans of more than ¥35 million, whereas the new rate was 0.18 per mil for loans between ¥35 million and ¥100 million, 0.2 per mil between ¥100 million and ¥200 million yen, and 0.22 per mil over ¥200 million.[4] Since the average interbank call rate (opportunity cost for funds of surplus banks) was 0.196 per mil in August 1918, the stamp bills were issued at the comparative rate (taking the risk premium into consideration).[5] The stamp bills were expected to reduce the FEFLs to less than ¥200 million, whereas they were actually ¥352 million by the end of July 1918. This happened because immediately after the stamp bills were introduced the interbank call rate began to climb rapidly, reaching a high of 0.287 per mil in March 1920 (Table 8.13), causing the YSB to turn to the FEFLs again. As Table 8.14 indicates, the balance of FEFLs began to increase toward the end of 1919.

Bankers acceptances (BAs) were introduced in May and stamp bills in August 1919. As Table 8.14 shows, both bills developed quite quickly at first. But after the severe recession in the spring of 1920, both trade bills became inactive and had almost disappeared within a few years.

The following three points account for the failure of the trade bills: First, in regard to BAs, the commercial banks lacked expertise in dealing with trade credits, and so those banks that suffered when importers defaulted became reluctant to issue letters of credit. Second, in regard to the stamp bills issued by the YSB, the regulation that closed the market to the public seems to have been responsible for its underdevelopment. Moreover, after World War I ended, the trade balance changed from surplus to deficit (Table 8.1), and therefore the role expected of stamp bills in financing the trade surplus was reduced. Third, the demand for money market instruments did not grow much. Since the export boom was caused by an external demand shock, not by increased international competitiveness, it was short lived, and the rise of corporate sector as a significant financial asset holder ended, being only a temporary phenomenon.

The Bill Brokers and the Nascent CP Market

During the boom period of World War I, the proliferation of bill brokers was remarkable. Table 8.15 shows the movement over time in the main items of the balance sheet of the two largest bill brokers—Fujimoto and Masuda

Table 8.13. Trade, Prices, and Interest Rates, 1919/1920

	Export/Import Ratio		Stock Price Index	Interbank Call Rate[b]	BOJ Discount Rate[b]	WPI (Tokyo)
	Actual	Adjusted [a]				
1919						
May	0.84	1.05	100	1.43	1.80–2.10	100
Jun.	0.86	1.03	105	1.80		106
Jul.	1.25	1.14	112	1.41		115
Aug.	1.01	0.83	115	1.96		116
Sep.	0.88	0.67	126	1.93		119
Oct.	1.25	0.86	136	2.26	2.00–2.30	130
Nov.	1.19	1.01	130	2.00	2.20–2.50	133
Dec.	1.23	1.06	132	2.31		137
1920						
Jan.	0.86	1.12	131	1.97		143
Feb.	0.64	0.93	135	3.52		149
Mar.	0.59	0.88	140	2.87		153
Apr.	0.73	0.92	121	2.51		143
May	0.65	0.80	96	1.24		129
Jun.	0.84	0.99	85	1.25		118
Jul.	0.98	0.89	78	0.97		114
Aug.	1.42	1.16	76	1.23		112
Sep.	1.31	1.00	77	0.98		109
Oct.	1.24	0.87	72	0.83		107
Nov.	0.97	0.82	75	0.91		105
Dec.	0.83	0.71	75	1.10		98

[a] Seasonal variation adjustment is based on data for 1910–14 and 1919–26.

[b] Daily %/100.

Source: BOJ, *One Hundred Year History,* vol. 2 (Tokyo: BOJ, 1983); and Toyo keizai shinposha, *Nihon no keiki-hendo* (Tokyo: Toyo keizai shinposha, 1931).

(which went bankrupt in 1920). The main business of the bill brokers was brokering interbank deposits. As of the end of November 1926, the total amount of interbank deposits absorbed by the four largest bill brokers (Fuji-moto, Hayakawa, Yanagida, and Tanaka) was ¥347 million, and the total balance of the interbank deposits of all commercial and special banks was ¥569 million, which means that about 61% of interbank deposits were handled by the four big bill brokers. Out of this ¥347 million, the bill brokers redeposited ¥313 million in other banks, and the difference of ¥33 million was used for their dealing business. The net dealing ratio was 10%. The similar ratios for the two largest brokers are given in the last column of Table 8.15.

Highly intriguing is the way that the bill brokers handled their own deals. They bought commercial and finance bills of various firms (in such industries as cotton spinning, railways, sugar refineries, electricity, ship-

Table 8.14. Trade Bill and BOJ Credits Between 1919 and 1928
(in millions of yen)

	Trade Bills			BOJ Loans to Private Sector	
	Stamp Bill		BAs	Non-FEFLs	FEFLs
Jun. 1919	—	(—)	1	(1)	152	374
Jul. 1919	—	(—)	0	(0)	132	352
Aug. 1919	39	(2)	1	(1)	168	330
Sep. 1919	103	(10)	2	(1)	182	250
Oct. 1919	99	(30)	3	(0)	179	271
Nov. 1919	60	(17)	19	(5)	199	266
Dec. 1919	19	(6)	32	(11)	358	358
Jan. 1920	59	(26)	N.A.		251	324
Feb. 1920	66	(28)	N.A.		280	340
Mar. 1920	57	(29)	N.A.		389	287
Apr. 1920	26	(16)	N.A.		513	321
May 1920	36	(3)	N.A.		400	327
Jun. 1920	52	(2)	45	(16)	365	295
Dec. 1920	85	(9)	0	(1)	158	77
Dec. 1921	3	(2)	0	(0)	290	76
Dec. 1922	31	(3)	5	(0)	344	206
Dec. 1923	23	(0)	2	(0)	641	212
Dec. 1924	42	(0)	1	(0)	524	200
Dec. 1925	20	(0)	1	(0)	464	234
Dec. 1926	22	(0)	2	(0)	518	69
Dec. 1927	12	(0)	2	(0)	815	78
Dec. 1928	—	(0)	2	(0)	760	88

Note: Figures in parentheses show bills rediscounted by BOJ.

Source: M. Ito, *Nihon no taigai kinyu to kinyu* seisaku (1914–1936) (Nagoya: Nagoya daigaku shuppankai,1989); BOJ, *One Hundred Year History,* vol. 2 (Tokyo: BOJ, 1983), p. 529; and *Kinyu jiko sankosho,* various issues.

building, and foreign trade) from banks with low deposit-absorbing capabilities and from nonbanks. Most of the bills had no collateral, and so the bill brokers had to be able to judge their quality. The brokers endorsed the bills they bought and then sold them to their clients with surplus funds. Fujimoto's clients in 1909 were eighty-four banks and forty-one individuals and companies (Tsurumi 1978).

There was fierce competition between the large banks with surplus funds and the bill brokers for bills issued by blue-chip firms such as the cotton-spinning companies. Moreover, such high-quality bills as those issued by the *zaibatsu* firms were increasingly monopolized by large banks in the same *zaibatsu* (family-based conglomerate). In regard to low-

Table 8.15. Selected Assets and Liabilities of Bill Brokers (in millions of yen)

	Liabilities		Assets		Net Dealing Ratio (%) $\frac{(a) - (b)}{(a)}$
	Interbank Deposits (a)	Bill Rediscounting	Interbank Deposits (b)	Bill Discounting	
1912	4.0	2.0	2.8	11.6	30
1913	6.3	6.0	5.4	19.8	14
1914	15.0	10.6	14.4	16.4	4
1915	23.3	12.2	11.5	22.8	51
1916	15.1	9.9	12.5	9.4	17
1917	57.1	13.2	52.1	26.3	9
1918	67.4	13.4	34.1	32.6	49
1919	65.4	34.0	48.1	46.5	26
1920	50.4	48.7	18.3	59.6	66
1926	85.8	88.9	72.5	143.8	16
1927	3.5	26.0	8.2	43.3	-134
1928	9.6	11.7	6.4	6.0	32
1936	42.6	10.0	10.7	10.9	75

Note: Assets and liabilities of two largest bill brokers (Fujimoto and Masuda). After 1920, the data refer to only Fujimoto.

Source: S. Tsurumi, "Daiichijitaisenki tankikinyu shijo no hatten to bill broker no keieikido," *Keizai shirin* 51 (1983): 29–63; S. Goto, *Nihon tankikinyu shijo hattatsushi* (Tokyo: Nihon keizai hyoronsha, 1986); and *Nihon Okinyushi shiryo* (*Showa hen*), vol. 30.

quality bills, because the bill brokers' expertise did not grow fast enough, business on that front was limited. After the great financial crash in 1927, the aversion of nonbanks to uncollateralized bills grew stronger, and the bill brokers lost even more business. Although the spontaneous rise of the commercial paper market in prewar Japan was remarkable in itself, the market never developed.

MONETARY POLICY AND THE MONEY MARKETS, 1919–20

One of the important roles of money markets is as an effective conduit or arena of monetary policy. In prewar Japan, when the economy was moving into a state of speculative boom, the BOJ was expected to dampen it by raising its lending rate. The higher borrowing cost from the BOJ would first lead the deficit banks to rely more on interbank call loans, and then the consequent rise in the call rate would cause the surplus banks to reduce their lending activities because of the rise in the opportunity cost. As this process continued, the interbank rate would gradually rise, and the increased cost of funds for deficit banks would finally curtail their lending activities.

This theoretical mechanism did not work, however, in late 1919 when the BOJ tried to stem the speculation. This episode provides an interesting insight into the effectiveness of monetary policy in the presence of a dual structured banking system.[6] It seems that monetary policy, though quite effective as an expansionary policy, was an impotent contractionary policy.

With the end of World War I in November 1918, the Japanese economy faced great general uncertainty and discouraging prospects for aggregate demand growth. But six months later, the economy moved into an expansionary boom again. There are several reasons for this. First, partly owing to the increased demand for silk from the United States, the trade balance for this year was still good, as seen in Table 8.13. Since the trade balance in prewar Japan had a clear seasonal pattern—a deficit during the early months of the year and a surplus after June or July—the seasonally adjusted export/import ratio in the second column rather than the first is more relevant. Exports were greater than imports from May through July and after November. Second, together with this favorable trade balance situation, the nontrade balance, especially transportation and interest income from abroad, recorded a large surplus, with a consequent surplus in the overall current account. This continued the accumulation of foreign reserves (Table 8.1) and expanded the money supply (Table 8.2) during 1919. Third, the ruling government (Prime Minister Kei Hara, and Minister of Finance Korekiyo Takahashi) took the rather aggressive position of trying to make the Japanese economy into a great power. This policy was reinforced by the public's spending its financial savings accumulated during World War I.

But the boom was both temporary and speculative. When the price level and stock prices recorded a large climb in October (Table 8.13), the authorities finally decided to step in, and the BOJ raised its discount rates twice, in October and November 1919 (Table 8.13). As Table 8.14 shows, however, the BOJ's lending did not show any definite signs of slowing, and the economy crashed in March–May 1920 despite the BOJ's policy. Why did it fail to prevent the disaster? Why did the official discount rate policy fail to stop the speculation?

We believe that the BOJ was reluctant to raise the official rates sufficiently to stop the crisis, for fear of angering its customers.[7] To understand this, note that the dual structure of the banking industry meant that the rate of return on assets of small and medium-size (deficit) banks (1) was greater than the deposit rate of small and medium-size banks, (2) equaled the interbank call rate, (3) equaled the rate of return on assets of large (surplus) banks, and (4) was greater than the deposit rate of large banks.

Since the official discount rate was kept close to the interbank rate, which was higher than the deposit cost to large banks, the larger and healthier banks were reluctant to borrow from the BOJ, and in spite of the BOJ's efforts to expand its lending, the ratio of BOJ loans to the private sector (excluding FEFLs) to total commercial bank loans fell from 0.12 in 1900, 0.06 in 1910, to 0.02 in 1920.[8] Again, I suspect that the BOJ hesitated to raise the discount rate too high because that would turn away customers.

The speculative boom was led by the small and medium-size banks. The total lending of the five large banks increased by 20%, from ¥1,027 million at the end of 1918 to ¥1,267 million at the end of 1919, whereas that of other commercial banks increased by 39%, from ¥3,553 million to ¥4,941 million, during the same period. Probably because of inflationary expectations, the small at-risk banks continued to borrow from the BOJ despite the increase in official discount rates. The reason was that the revised BOJ rates, kept at a level sufficiently low to induce the relatively sound banks to continue borrowing, were still attractive to most of the at-risk banks.

To sum up, the BOJ at that time seemed to have faced the following dilemma: If it had raised the official lending rates sufficiently high, only the at-risk borrowers would have remained as its customers. But if it had not raised its rates, it would have eventually ended up with a portfolio of rescue credits acquired to bail out the failed borrowers.

I should also note that the BOJ governor, Junnosuke Inoue, did insist on limiting of the effects of the interest rate policy and did try to cool the speculative boom by means of moral suasion.[9] This view was later endorsed by Kamekichi Takahashi (1954), who argued that it would have been quite difficult to stop the speculation merely by raising the interest rate, which explains why the BOJ did not raise it further. Here, it seems to be necessary to take into consideration both the costs and the benefits of the BOJ's policy. Even if the effect of interest rate on speculative behavior is small, it is definitely nonnegative, so that in order to understand the BOJ's attitude, we must look at the other side of the coin, the cost of the policy. Thus, even without referring to the existence of cost in the form of losing customers (positive and greater than the benefit in absolute value), it would be difficult to give a full explanation of the BOJ's behavior at that time.

Incidentally, we should add that the BOJ at that time had no effective way of directly mopping up liquidity other than by reducing its lending. Although the stamp bills had just been introduced, the YSB was reluctant to issue them in view of the relative low rate of the FEFLs, and the public was excluded from the market owing to the existence of the deposit rate cartel. And the secondary market for government bonds was too small to be effective (Table 8.16). The reason was that most of the government bonds—the only genuinely safe asset at that time—were kept until maturity by banks and other organizational investors.

THE EFFECTS OF GOVERNMENT POLICIES

We have already discussed the government policies used directly to create money markets and the related issues of macromonetary policy. The following three policy issues pertain to the growth of money markets in prewar Japan.

Table 8.16. (Domestic) Government Bonds (in millions of yen)

	Outstanding Volume	Annual Transactions at Tokyo Stock Exchange	Volume Held by BOJ
1915	2489	42	44
1916	2468	46	37
1917	2699	55	32
1918	3052	32	29
1919	3278	5	37
1920	3777	34	53
1921	4077	267	64
1922	4342	184	94
1923	4730	146	157
1924	4863	198	175
1925	4999	289	196
1926	5157	212	200
1927	5398	474	148
1928	5831	1012	141
1929	5959	456	155
1930	5956	381	165

Source: K. Shimura, ed., *Nihon koshasai shijoshi* (Tokyo: Tokyo University Press, 1980); and BOJ, *One Hundred Year History,* vol. 2 (Tokyo: BOJ, 1983).

The Deposit Rate Cartel

When small and medium-size banks make risky loans to related firms, the competition for deposits through interest rates is likely to lead to a banking crisis. When the competition for deposits intensified during World War I, Minister of Finance Korekiyo Takahashi persuaded the bankers' associations to make cartel agreements on the maximum deposit rate.

This 1918 deposit rate agreement—the first cartel agreement with a penalty clause for violation—seems to have had the following two effects on the development of money markets, to the extent that the banks abided by the agreement. First, it reinforced the structural pattern of demand and supply of interbank deposits by further reducing the deposit absorption capability of the at-risk banks. Actually, the deposits of special banks grew much less slowly after 1919, leading to their heavier reliance on longer-term interbank deposits. Second, because of this agreement, the BOJ could not open the stamp bill market to nonbanks.

The Bank Merger Policy

After the great financial crash, the Ministry of Finance focused its banking policy on promoting mergers and used the newly enacted Bank Act for this purpose. In the 1930s, mergers were first encouraged through administrative guidance, and after 1937, through military coercion. The result of these policies can be seen in Table 8.6.

Since mergers of weak banks should strengthen them, it should in turn weaken the dual structure. Accordingly, the original structural characteristics of the interbank deposits markets were weakened, and the volatility of interest rate should have been reduced to that extent.

The Bank of Japan's Rescue Credits

During the slump of 1920, the Bank of Japan increased its supply of rescue credits, as can be seen from its special loans to the private sector (Table 8.17). Since these credits were long term, the weak small and medium-size banks cut back their reliance on long-term interbank deposits.

This factor seems to have increased the elasticity of the quantity of interbank deposits, with a concomitant decline in the volatility of interest rates. The figures in Table 8.11 seem to be consistent with these observations: The interbank deposit rate became less variable relative to other interest rates. Also, the increase in the BOJ's credit did not have the effect of replacing the money market. Since the credit was long term, the variability of the BOJ's loans was smaller than that of interbank deposits, and after 1927 liquidity seems to have been adjusted mainly through interbank deposits, with some BOJ deposits.

CONCLUSIONS

The history of the money market in prewar Japan was rather depressing: The commercial paper market did not develop; the bankers acceptance market failed; and the interbank call market was frequently a source of crisis in the banking system. The reasons for this bad performance—a serious information asymmetry in the bank-lending markets and too great a demand for long-term funds—were eliminated for the most part after World War II, partly owing to the improved financial environment, such as the greater accumulation of financial assets and the wider separation between the ownership and the management of corporate firms and partly

Table 8.17. Bank of Japan Credits (in millions of yen)

	Special Loans to Private Sector	Other Loans to Private Sector	Credits to Government Sector
1910	—	112	87
1915	—	58	66
1920	37	198	214
1925	148	550	295
1930	585	169	799
1935	498	345	1079

Source: S. Goto, *Nihon no kinyu tokei* (Tokyo: Toyo keizai shinposha, 1970); and Bank of Japan, *One Hundred Year History,* vol. 3 (Tokyo: BOJ, 1983).

owing to the government's intervention. But there is some evidence that the postwar government's concern about stabilizing the financial system was excessive and the postwar financial system suffered from the inefficiency, instead of the instability, of the banking system (Teranishi 1990).

NOTES

1. Moreover, since trade credits take a few months for transportation, the demand for interbank call loans by the YSB was rather long, about two to three months.

2. Nonbanks participate in the money markets.

3. Sumitomo Bank and Taiwan Bank were also allowed to issue stamp bills, but the amount was very small.

4. In order to alleviate the YSB's burden, the revised rate was temporarily lowered in the actual application. See Bank of Japan 1983, chap. 4; and Yokohama Specie Bank 1981, p. 203.

5. Of 0.1875 per mil for the sixty-day bill and 0.19 per mil for the ninety-day bill (as of August 21, 1919).

6. The 1920 crash is of vital importance in understanding the Japanese economy in the interwar period, as the economic conditions and policy pattern at that time were carried over to successive crashes. On this point, see Kamekichi Takahashi 1954. Regarding the confusion of economic policy in the interwar period, see Hugh Patrick 1972.

7. This point was also taken up in the Diet on January 26, 1920. See Takahashi 1932, p. 594.

8. The BOJ tried to attract new customers, to reduce the limitation on the eligibility of collateral (bonds and stocks), and even to attract (nonbank) individual merchants.

9. Refer to his speeches on December 3 and January 27 (Bank of Japan 1958).

REFERENCES

Bank of Japan. 1958. *Honpozaikai doyoshi*. Originally published around 1925. Reprinted in *Nihonkinyushi shiryo Meiji–Taisho hen*. Vol. 22. Tokyo: Bank of Japan.

———. 1983. *One Hundred Year History*. Vol. 2. Tokyo: Bank of Japan.

Engle, Robert F., and Clive W. J. Granger. 1987. "Co-integration and Error Correction: Representation, Estimation, and Testing." *Econometrica* 55: 251–76.

Fuller, Wayne A. 1976. *Introduction to Statistical Time Series*. New York: Wiley.

Goto, Shinichi. 1970. *Nihon no kinyu tokei*. Tokyo: Toyo keizai Shinposha, 1970.

———. 1986. *Nihon tanki kinyu shijo hattatsushi*. Tokyo: Nihon keizai-hyoronsha, 1986.

Ito, Masanao. 1989. *Nihon no taigai kinyu to kinyu seisaku (1914–1936)*. Nagoya: Nagoya daigaku shuppankai.

Okura, Masanao, and J. Teranishi. 1989. "Senkanki makuro-kinko to kawase-reto." *Keizaikenkyu* 40 (October): 313–25.

Patrick, H. 1972. "The Economic Muddle of the 1920s." In *Dilemmas of Growth in Prewar Japan*. Edited by James W. Morley. Princeton, NJ: Princeton University Press.

Phillips, Peter C. B. 1987. "Time Series Regression with a Unit Root." *Econometrica* 55: 277–301.

Takahashi, K., ed. 1932. *Zaisei keizai 25 nenshi*. Vol. 1. Tokyo: Jitsugyo no sekaisha.

———. 1954. *Meiji–Taisho zaikai hendoshi*. Tokyo: Toyo keizai shinposha.

Teranishi, Juro. 1982. *Nihon no keizai hatten to kinyu*. Tokyo: Iwanami shoten.

———. 1990. "Financial System and the Industrialization of Japan: 1900–1970." Banca Nazional del Lavaro, *Quarterly Review*, September, pp. 309–41.

Toyo keizai shinposha. 1931. Nihon no keiki-hendo. Tokyo: Toyo keizai shinposha.

Tsurumi, Seiryo. 1978. "Seiritsuki Nihon shinyokiko no ronri to kozo." *Keizai shirin* 46: 133–76.

———. 1983. "Daiichijitaisenki tankikinyu shijo no hatten to bill broker no keieikido." *Keizai shirin* 51: 29–63.

Yokohama Specie Bank. 1981. *Yokohama shokin zenshi*. Vol. 2. Tokyo: YSB.

APPENDIX 8A
KEY EVENTS

Dec. 1918	Cartel agreements on deposit interest rates are established in Tokyo, Osaka, and Nagoya.
May 1919	BOJ introduces BA rediscounting system.
Aug. 1919	BOJ introduces stamp bill system.
Aug. 1919	Interest rate of FEFLs is revised.
Apr. 1920	Frequent bank runs occur throughout Japan.
May 1920	BOJ rescue credits are started.
Dec. 1922	Frequent bank runs occur throughout Japan.
Sept. 1923	Great Kanto earthquake strikes.
Apr. 1925	A cartel for interbank call rates is established by five large banks.
Mar. 1927	Bank Act is promulgated (enacted in January 1928).
Mar.–May 1927	Great financial crash hits the country, and frequent bank runs occur throughout Japan.

TESTING THE COINTEGRATION HYPOTHESIS REGARDING PREWAR JAPAN'S INTEREST RATES

with YASUHIKO TAKEI (FUJI UNIVERSITY)

The cointegration hypothesis has been found to be very useful in characterizing the long-run equilibrium of Japan's prewar economic system, which consisted of integrated processes. Two time series are said to be cointegrated if both have unit roots but a linear combination of these series is stationary. Since the interest rate data for prewar Japan suggest the presence of unit roots, we tried to understand the long-run relationship of these interest rates by testing the cointegration hypothesis on them. We had six interest rates: loan rate ($R1$), bill discount rate ($R2$), overdraft rate ($R3$), demand deposit rate ($R4$), time deposit rate ($R5$), and call rate ($R6$). Only one interest rate ($R6$) was a money market rate in our test. We used three periods to test the cointegration hypothesis: Period 1 started in August 1910 and ended in November 1918; Period 2 started in November 1918 and ended in February 1927; and Period 3 started in June 1927 and ended in September 1935. Figures 8B.1, 8B.2, and 8B.3 show their behaviors during each period. We used the Dickey-Fuller test and the Augmented Dickey–Fuller test to test whether these rates were integrated processes. The Dickey–Fuller test uses the following regression:

$$r_t = a\, r_{t-1} + ct + d + ut$$

where t is a time trend. The null $H_0 : a = 1$ is tested by constructing

$$\tau_\tau = \frac{a-1}{[s^2\, r_{11}]}$$

where s is the standard error from our regression and r_{11} is the first element on the principal diagonal of $(X'X)^{-1}$, where X is the matrix of independent variables. Fuller (1976) provided the table of critical values. The Augmented Dickey–Fuller regression can be written as

$$\Delta r_t = a\, r_{t-1} + \sum_{i=1}^{m} b_i \Delta r_{t-i} + ct + d + u_t$$

and the statistic for testing the null $H_0 : a = 0$ is

$$ADF = \frac{a}{[s^2\, r_{11}]^{1/2}}$$

Table 8B.1 shows our results where τ_τ is the Dickey–Fuller statistics without time trends, and ADF shows the Augmented Dicky–Fuller statistics for the case that $m = 4$. These results suggest the presence of the unit root except for the call rate ($R6$). The cointegration regression, which can be written as

$$r_t^i = k\, r_t^i + d + u_t$$

was conducted, and the residuals

$$\bar{u}_t = r_t^i - \bar{k}\, r_t^j - \bar{d}$$

were obtained.

We tested the null of the cointegrated system by examining $H_0 : \bar{u}_t \cong I(0)$. We used the Augmented Dickey–Fuller test :

$$\Delta \bar{u}_t = \phi\, \bar{u}_{t-1} + \sum_{i=1}^{n} b_i \Delta \bar{u}_{t-i} + \varepsilon_t,\ H_0 : \phi = 0$$

Although Engle and Granger (1987) proposed several methods, the Augmented Dickey–Fuller test was generally the best. Table 8B.2 summarizes our results. We observed the cointegration between the loan rate ($R1$) and the overdraft rate ($R3$) for Period 1, between the bill discount rate ($R2$) and the time deposit rate ($R5$) for Period 1, between the overdraft rate the ($R3$) and the call rate ($R6$) for Period 2, and between the time deposit rate ($R5$) and the call rate ($R6$) for Period 2. However, the last two cases are not reliable because the Dickey–Fuller tests suggest the nonexistence of the unit root for the call rate ($R6$). Figure 8B.4 shows the movements of the loan rate ($R1$), the bill discount rate ($R2$), and the overdraft rate ($R3$) for Period 1. See Figure 8B.5 for Period 2. Residuals from the "cointegration regression" are depicted in Figures 8B.6, 8B.7, 8.B8, and 8B.9. The stationary residuals are depicted in Figure 8B.9. Other processes could not be regarded as stationary (Figures 8B.6, 8B.7, 8B.8, and 8B.9), which suggests that the null hypothesis should be rejected.

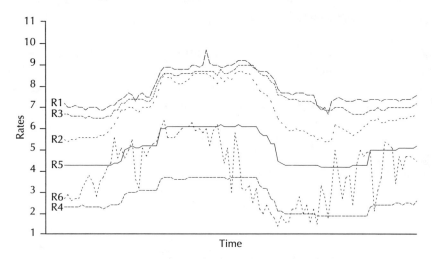

Figure 8B.1. Interest Rates, Period 1

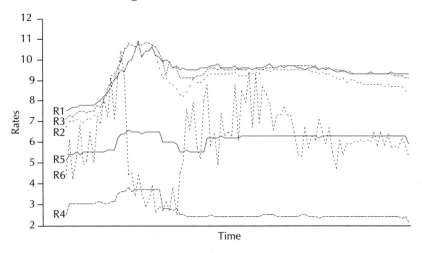

8B.2. Interest Rates, Period 2

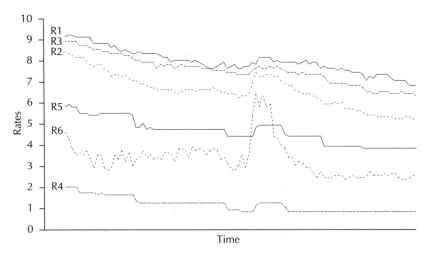

Figure 8B.3. Interest Rates, Period 3

Table 8B.1. Unit Root Test

Period	τ_τ	τ_μ	ADF
Loan rate			
1	−1.3221	−1.2750	−1.5348
2	−2.3029	−2.9518	−2.5174
3	−2.5755	−1.1623	−1.8016
Bill discount rate			
1	−1.2884	−1.1460	−1.7426
2	−2.1935	−2.7575	−2.9001
3	−1.8387	−1.4744	−2.2000
Overdraft rate			
1	−1.0848	−0.9789	−1.4964
2	−2.2442	−2.9031	−2.9688
3	−2.3306	−0.9520	−1.9305
Demand deposit rate			
1	−1.3144	−0.9812	−1.8023
2	−2.9785	−1.3028	−3.0089
3	−2.4931	−2.3120	−2.6907
Time deposit rate			
1	−1.2462	−1.1960	−1.6281
2	−2.4798	−3.0543	−2.8785
3	−2.6453	−1.4886	−2.7389
Call rate			
1	−3.3313	−3.2677	−1.7021
2	−4.3676	−4.3889	−2.7675
3	−2.4707	−2.3212	−3.5912

Table 8B.2. Augumented Dickey–Fuller Statistics for Residuals of Cointegration Regression

	1	2	3
R1–R2	−1.6927	−1.5541	−1.9081
R1–R3	−3.4660	−1.9495	−2.2387
R1–R4	−1.8942	−2.5617	−1.4202
R1–R5	−2.0022	−1.8207	−2.4036
R1–R6	−1.2600	−2.8013	−1.3919
R2–R3	−1.3274	−2.3536	−2.0470
R2–R4	−2.5664	−2.6241	−0.7341
R2–R5	−3.6600	−2.3583	−2.1010
R2–R6	−1.4211	−3.0097	−2.8650
R3–R4	−1.4173	−2.6730	−1.0431
R3–R5	−1.0476	−1.7992	−2.5310
R3–R6	−1.3279	−3.1775	−1.6561
R4–R5	−0.7031	−1.1849	−1.9067
R4–R6	−1.6396	−1.6119	−1.7795
R5–R6	−1.7834	−3.1980	−1.688

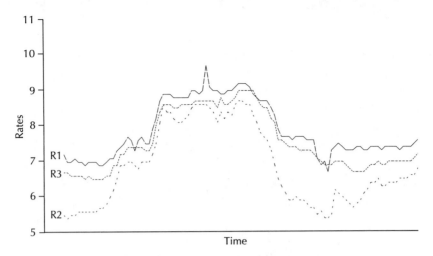

Figure 8B.4. Interest Rates ($R1$–$R3$), Period 1

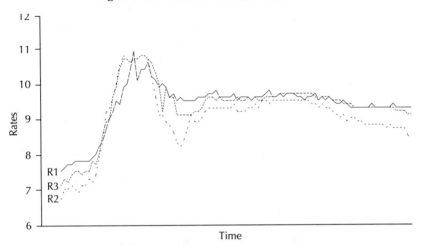

Figure 8B.5. Interest Rates ($R1$–$R3$), Period 2

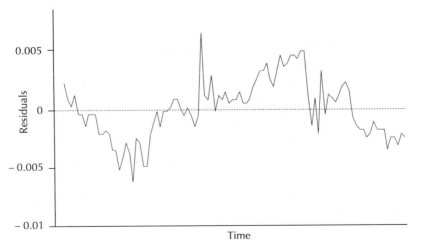

Figure 8B.6. Residuals of $R1$–$R2$ Regression, Period 1

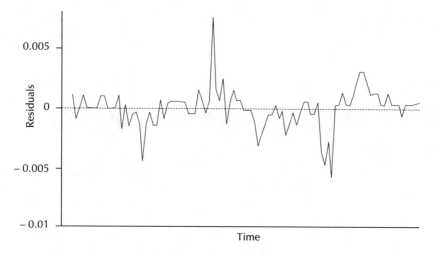

Figure 8B.7. Residuals of $R1$–$R3$ Regression, Period 1

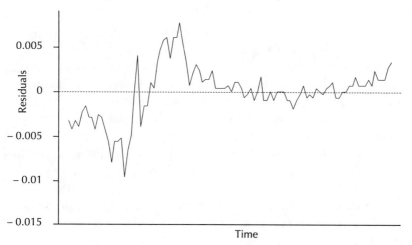

Figure 8B.8. Residuals of $R1$–$R2$ Regression, Period 2

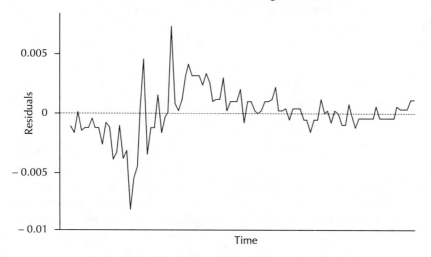

Figure 8B.9. Residuals of $R1$–$R3$ Regression, Period 2

CHAPTER 9
MONEY MARKETS IN POSTWAR JAPAN

SHOICHI ROYAMA

This chapter surveys the evolution of money markets in Japan during the high economic growth period since its recovery from World War II up to 1975 and thereafter. We examine the roles and operation of money markets in the past as well as the present Japanese financial system, particularly in the light of the Bank of Japan's (BOJ) monetary policy.

Money markets are defined as markets in which assets with a maturity of less than one year are traded. They are separated into two types, the interbank money markets, whose only participants are financial institutions, and the open markets, in which there are no restrictions on participation. In the real world, not all the types of money markets have developed evenly. In Japan, the first money market was established in the early 1900s as a call money market among banks. Bill brokers started businesses to intermediate between the demand for and the supply of short-term funds among both commercial and financial entities, although their major clients were banks. Since then, Japan's money markets have developed as interbank call markets. The evolution and development of open money markets had to wait until the 1970s when Japan's economic growth had subsided.

THE FLOW OF FUNDS AND THE MONEY MARKET IN THE PERIOD OF HIGH ECONOMIC GROWTH

The Japanese financial system through the period of high economic growth after its recovery from World War II was characterized by a simple flow of funds. The major borrower of funds in the economy was the corporate sector, which relied on borrowing from banks and other financial intermediaries. The major lender of funds was the personal sector, including nonincorporated businesses. The lender preferred bank deposits and other indirect securities to direct financing instruments such as stocks and bonds. Equities were actively traded in the secondary market; the primary market for equities had only a minor role in corporate financing, as shown in Tables 9.1 and 9.2.

The market for both loans and deposits is characterized by the long-term relationship between borrower and lender. In theory, a market dominated by a long-term customer relationship is not flexible in the short run, as it cannot adapt quickly to changes in the market's environment. Accordingly, the Japanese financial system was impervious to the various changes in the economic environment throughout the period of high economic growth. In other words, the financial system could not have been economically efficient if it had been dominated only by the sticky network of long-term customer relationships through banks and other financial intermediaries. But because the call money market among financial institutions in fact efficiently allocated financial resources through indirect financial intermediation, this was not the case.

The money market in that period was not available to all economic entities. Only banks and other officially recognized financial institutions could participate in it. Through the banks and other financial institutions, the interbank money market fulfilled the short-term demand for financing

Table 9.1. Funds Raised by Domestic Sectors, Annual Averages as % of Total

	1965–69	1970–74	1975–79	1980–84	1985–89[a]
By sector					
Corporate business	60.4	58.4	33.1	39.9	57.1
Personal	18.4	20.1	20.5	17.3	24.2
Public	21.3	21.5	46.4	42.8	18.8
By instrument					
Borrowings	76.5	79.1	61.7	63.7	69.2
From private institutions	63.0	64.1	40.1	44.4	57.5
From public institutions	13.5	15.0	21.6	19.3	11.7
Securities	22.2	18.4	37.7	36.6	25.8
of which bonds	15.7	14.1	31.2	30.0	16.2
CP	—	—	—	—	2.9
Others[b]	1.3	2.5	0.6	−0.3	2.1
Total (¥100 billion)	103.3	271.8	451.8	571.8	800.8
as percentage of GNP	21.6	26.7	23.8	21.0	22.6

[a] Periods are fiscal years except 1985–89.

[b] Others include foreign borrowings.

Sources: Yoshio Suzuki, ed., *The Japanese Financial System* (Oxford: Clarendon Press, 1987), p. 15. Bank of Japan, *Flow of Funds* table, annual (Tokyo: Bank of Japan).

Table 9.2. Funds Provided by Domestic Sectors, Annual Averages as % of Total

	1965–69	1970–74	1975–79	1980–84	1985–89 [a]
By sector					
Corporate business	26.3	26.7	18.2	23.0	35.2
Personal	64.4	64.3	69.6	68.6	56.7
Public	9.3	9.0	12.2	8.4	8.1
By instrument					
Cash and demand deposits	21.0	22.1	14.1	6.3	6.8
Saving deposits and CDs	46.4	44.8	47.5	43.6	42.4
Trusts[b]	5.5	5.3	5.9	6.9	16.8
Insurance	9.4	8.5	9.9	13.5	18.5
Securities[c]	8.1	9.5	12.6	14.1	–1.4
CP	—	—	—	—	—
Foreign claims	2.0	2.5	1.6	5.7	9.2
Total (¥100 billion)	99.9	262.6	439.1	579.4	1002.8
as percentage of GNP	20.9	25.8	23.2	21.2	28.4

[a] Periods are fiscal years except 1985–89.

[b] Securities investment trusts are included for 1985–89 period.

[c] Securities investment trusts are included for periods other than 1985–89.

Sources: Yoshio Suzuki, ed., *The Japanese Financial System* (Oxford: Clarendon Press, 1987), p. 15. Bank of Japan, *Flow of Funds* table, annual (Tokyo: Bank of Japan).

and investment by nonfinancial entities. There are two types of interbank money markets in Japan: the call money market and the bills market. Before May 1971 only the call money market existed, for very short term transactions and also slightly longer term transactions such as over-the-month trade. In May 1971 the slightly longer term transactions were shifted to the newly established bills market. The call money market then returned to trading only of very short term funds.

The call money market and the bills market are composed of lenders, borrowers, and specialized intermediaries known as *tanshi gaisha* (money market dealers). Only recognized financial institutions can lend and/or borrow money in the markets. The Bank of Japan also participates in the bills market. Money market dealers borrow funds from lender financial institutions with surplus reserves and lend them to borrower institutions with a temporary shortage of reserves.

The three types of call money are half-day, unconditional, and fixed date, which are distinguished by the time limit on their settlement. The half-day money is subdivided into morning money and afternoon money. The morning money is for financial institutions that need funds early in the morning, and it is settled by the time of clearing at a clearinghouse (13:00 in Tokyo on weekdays). The afternoon money is demanded after the daily clearing and is settled by the end of the business day. The half-day money is transacted in checks drawn on the Bank of Japan without collateral.

The unconditional money is, in principle, settled on the day after the date of transaction, but when neither party to the transaction requests repayment or collection at that time, it is automatically extended. The old next-day call money abolished in April 1979 did not have this characteristic of extendability. One type of unconditional call money is called *morning repayment money*, which is settled at 9:00 A.M. the morning after the transaction.

The fixed-date call money may be outstanding for a fixed period longer than two days, including the date of transaction. Besides the two-, three-, four-, five-, and seven-date call moneys in this group, two- and three-week moneys were introduced in August 1985 (Suzuki 1987, p. 113).

Two types of bills are traded in the bills market. One is eligible bills such as high-grade commercial and industrial bills, trade bills, high-grade promissory notes, and yen-denominated fixed-term export and import bills. The other is bills of exchange, or *cover (hyoshi) bills*. For example, a financial institution uses a bundle of eligible bills as collateral for the bill of exchange that the institution itself underwrites and whose payee is a money market dealer. Most transactions are in the form of cover bills, as the underlying bills do not always make up an adequate amount. The maturities of these bills vary from one to six months. In addition, resale bills may be used. The five- and six-month bills were introduced in June 1985 in order that the bills' maturities would correspond to those of the new open market instruments such as certificates of deposit (CDs) and Euroyen deposits (Suzuki 1987, p. 114).

Bills transacted in the bills market are of a high grade so that the transaction does not need any collateral. In call money transactions, however, the borrower must provide collateral to secure the transaction. Collateral has been required in the call money market since the financial panic of 1927, which was caused by the Bank of Taiwan's borrowing call money without collateral and consequently going bankrupt (Bank of Japan 1983, p. 221). This requirement was maintained until July 1985, when uncollateralized call money transactions were begun.

For transactions without collateral, money market dealers can act only as brokers. They may trade on their own account for collateralized transactions, but in fact, such transactions have never been popular.

The interbank money market provides a reference rate for every financial institution. When extending loans to borrowers, the financial institution considers the interbank market rate as the standard with regard to whether or not the loan can be extended. This use of the interbank money market rate is reinforced by the fact that all rates of interest on bank deposits and other indirect instruments issued by financial institutions are strictly controlled by government regulation, which is often termed the *artificial low rates of interest* policy. Under this policy, banks and other financial institutions have few means of competing in the short run in the market for deposits. In principle, banks and other financial institutions cannot control their own deposits in the short run. Rather, they must accept the depositors' portfolio preferences. In practice, the banks and other financial institutions allocate their funds to various loans and investment opportunities, including the interbank money market. Some banks, particularly the big banks, with plenty of profitable opportunities to offer loans but with fewer means for accepting deposits, prefer the negative holding of interbank money market claims. This means that the big banks borrow funds from other financial institutions through the interbank money market. Other banks and nonbank financial institutions have opposite lending and deposit opportunities, and so they take a positive position in the interbank money market. Thus the operation of the interbank money market among banks and other financial institutions is as a sort of permanent conduit from smaller financial institutions to big banks, owing to the differences in their loan-extending and deposit-taking opportunities (see Tables 9.3 and 9.4).

Table 9.3. Major Participants in the Call Money Market, Annual Average Outstanding Balance (%)

	1965	1970	1975	1980	1985
Supply side					
City banks	0.1	0.1	0.0	0.0	1.5
Regional banks	12.4	15.3	17.9	12.5	7.7
Trust banks[a]	24.1	23.1	19.5	26.7	48.5
Long-term credit banks	3.9	2.9	6.3	4.9	1.7
Foreign banks	1.1	0.4	3.3	4.3	2.7
Sogo banks	3.4	4.7	10.4	8.9	6.2
Zenshinren, shinkin banks	18.1	16.6	11.0	10.8	9.2
Agricultural institutions	25.3	20.2	9.4	13.5	8.5
Securities houses, etc.	2.1	5.4	4.8	3.9	3.5
Insurance companies	4.6	8.6	10.0	10.0	7.0
Others	4.9	2.7	7.4	4.5	3.5
Total	100.0	100.0	100.0	100.0	100.0
Demand side					
City banks	87.3	85.4	84.9	72.5	51.8
Regional banks	1.5	0.9	3.2	7.3	11.8
Trust banks	1.1	1.4	1.2	0.7	3.1
Long-term credit banks	0.3	0.2	0.1	0.0	3.6
Foreign banks	—	—	1.2	3.3	11.6
Securities houses, etc.	5.9	0.7	—	—	1.3
Others[b]	3.9	11.4	9.4	16.2	16.8

[a] Investments in the call money market by securities investment trusts are included, occupying the major part of the figures in this row.

[b] Almost all portions are of securities finance companies.

Source: Bank of Japan, *Wagakuni no kin'yu seido* (*The Japanese financial system*) (Tokyo: Bank of Japan, 1986), pp. 165–66.

Table 9.4. Major Participants in the Bill Discount Market, Annual Average Outstanding Balance (%)

	1972	1975	1980	1985
Supply side				
City banks	0.0	0.0	0.0	0.2
Regional banks	11.7	4.5	2.7	3.2
Trust banks[a]	18.1	4.3	13.5	10.7
Long-term credit banks	2.0	1.1	1.3	1.5
Foreign banks	1.0	0.6	4.3	5.7
Sogo banks	2.0	3.6	1.8	1.6
Zenshinren, Shinkin banks	7.2	14.3	12.9	16.8
Agricultural institutions	36.2	5.2	4.5	25.7
Securities houses etc	0.0	0.1	0.0	0.2
Insurance companies	0.8	1.1	2.8	1.0
Others[b]	21.0	65.2	56.2	33.4
Total	100.0	100.0	100.0	100.0
Demand side				
City banks	98.0	94.4	90.5	83.7
Foreign banks	—	5.4	9.2	2.9
Others	2.0	0.2	0.3	13.4

[a] Investments in the call money market by securities investment trusts are included, occupying the major part of the figures in this row.

[b] Almost all portions are of the Bank of Japan.

Source: Bank of Japan, *Wagakuni no kin'yu seido* (*The Japanese financial system*) (Tokyo: Bank of Japan, 1986), pp. 165–66.

The crucial working of the interbank money market in the Japanese financial system through the period of high economic growth is revealed in the fact that the money provided by the banking system was dependent on the level of the call money market rate. The coefficient of the call rate in the regression equation of money supply over the GNP and the call rate was significantly higher between 1969 and 1973 than later (see Tables 9.5 and 9.6).

Table 9.5. Marshallian k and the Call Money Market Rate, 1969–88

	(¥ billion)		(%)	
	GNP Nominal	Money Supply (M2+CD)	Marshall k: Money Supply Relative to GNP	Call Money Market Rate
1969	574,872	388,385	67.56	7.49
	604,604	407,069	67.33	7.12
	628,933	422,242	67.14	7.96
	666,261	447,751	67.20	8.38
1970	693,606	459,065	66.19	8.38
	715,605	481,070	67.23	8.25
	746,543	497,190	66.60	8.50
	763,668	524,784	68.72	8.13
1971	777,001	541,916	69.74	7.38
	794,460	575,604	72.45	6.63
	815,924	607,560	74.46	6.25
	829,910	650,500	78.38	5.54

Table 9.5. (*Continued*)

| | (¥ billion) | | (%) | |
	GNP Nominal	Money Supply (M2+CD)	Marshall k: Money Supply Relative to GNP	Call Money Market Rate
1972	870,190	670,608	77.06	5.14
	897,232	710,055	79.14	4.82
	938,362	742,731	79.15	4.45
	978,595	805,544	82.32	4.57
1973	1,046,180	830,241	79.36	5.19
	1,093,259	878,162	80.33	6.13
	1,135,841	906,528	79.81	7.88
	1,203,788	945,654	78.56	9.44
1974	1,231,327	966,485	78.49	12.08
	1,316,095	998,761	75.89	12.17
	1,375,529	1,011,507	73.54	13.04
	1,412,518	1,051,016	74.41	12.87
1975	1,415,637	1,074,652	75.91	12.86
	1,463,924	1,111,023	75.89	11.27
	1,496,106	1,143,871	76.46	10.45
	1,540,016	1,199,839	77.91	8.10
1976	1,590,246	1,243,615	78.20	7.09
	1,644,612	1,286,164	78.20	6.80
	1,693,400	1,320,683	77.99	7.13
	1,719,521	1,374,061	79.91	6.88
1977	1,792,090	1,398,265	78.02	6.90
	1,831,603	1,431,564	78.16	5.51
	1,870,387	1,470,541	78.62	5.46
	1,920,010	1,524,217	79.39	4.85
1978	1,977,984	1,549,002	78.31	4.74
	2,016,834	1,607,298	79.69	4.10
	2,069,397	1,650,670	79.77	4.36
	2,110,070	1,711,721	81.12	4.23
1979	2,154,579	1,740,920	80.80	4.43
	2,200,880	1,802,435	81.90	5.11
	2,234,566	1,842,388	82.45	6.43
	2,267,138	1,885,848	83.18	7.46
1980	2,315,266	1,919,960	82.93	9.18
	2,368,411	1,955,967	82.59	12.47
	2,429,337	1,987,504	81.81	12.06
	2,476,055	2,027,239	81.87	10.01
1981	2,524,559	2,053,990	81.36	8.52
	2,539,974	2,132,530	83.96	7.12
	2,583,632	2,169,780	83.98	7.25
	2,613,724	2,237,977	85.62	6.85
1982	2,647,987	2,296,573	86.73	6.61
	2,689,832	2,325,607	86.46	7.17
	2,722,631	2,371,275	87.09	7.12
	2,724,907	2,428,719	89.13	6.84
1983	2,762,048	2,452,283	88.78	6.64
	2,782,790	2,493,897	89.62	6.19
	2,828,569	2,552,111	90.23	6.46
	2,847,453	2,582,514	90.70	6.28
1984	2,908,509	2,645,732	90.97	6.18
	2,960,648	2,689,187	90.83	5.84

Table 9.5. (*Continued*)

	(¥ billion)		(%)	
	GNP Nominal	*Money Supply (M2+CD)*	*Marshall k: Money Supply Relative to GNP*	*Call Money Market Rate*
	3,004,223	2,743,936	91.34	6.15
	3,056,316	2,793,208	91.39	6.22
1985	3,099,127	2,856,772	92.18	6.25
	3,148,794	2,908,520	92.37	6.07
	3,191,807	2,960,432	92.75	6.25
	3,247,132	3,019,662	92.99	7.28
1986	3,251,178	3,102,336	95.42	6.05
	3,304,390	3,146,655	95.23	4.44
	3,341,128	3,228,873	96.64	4.56
	3,352,845	3,303,889	98.54	4.12
1987	3,386,708	3,381,351	99.84	4.00
	3,391,365	3,468,922	102.29	3.28
	3,487,934	3,562,502	102.14	3.25
	3,533,762	3,644,520	103.13	3.52
1988	3,632,206	3,796,748	104.53	3.49
	3,591,603	3,830,174	106.64	3.33
	3,704,523	3,981,792	107.48	3.78
	3,726,328	4,197,323	112.64	3.89

Table 9.6. Regression of M2 over GNP and the Call Rate (in terms of logarithm)

	GNP	*Call Rate*
1969–88		
Constant	−1.08128	
Standard error of *y* estimate	0.019786	
R squared	0.995349	
Number of observations	80	
Degrees of freedom	77	
X coefficients	1.173345	−0.10607
Standard error of coefficient	0.010097	0.015893
1969–73		
Constant	−1.62491	
Standard error of *y* estimate	0.008897	
R squared	0.995373	
Number of observations	20	
Degrees of freedom	17	
X coefficients	1.273054	−0.15173
Standard error of coefficient	0.023666	0.021398
1974–88		
Constant	−0.02778	
Standard error of *y* estimate	0.006635	
R squared	0.994474	
Number of observations	22	
Degrees of freedom	19	
X Coefficients	0.995052	−0.05720
Standard error of coefficient	0.064562	0.026934

THE EVOLUTION OF OPEN MONEY MARKETS

Since the mid-1970s the structure of the Japanese financial system has drastically changed. The development of open money markets is one of the most remarkable of these changes, as it has altered the roles of money markets in the financial system which itself is in the process of changing. How the Japanese money markets have evolved is an interesting topic for analysis.

In the middle of the 1970s the Japanese economy suffered from a series of events—demand–pull inflation, the oil price shock, a recession after severe deflationary policies, and reflation with massive issues of government bonds—after which the period of high economic growth ended. The change in economic conditions also transformed the Japanese financial system into a more open, flexible, and internationalized structure with liberalized financial markets (Cargill and Royama 1988). The most remarkable among these changes is that government bonds have become the standard open market asset in the portfolio of every entity of the financial system.

As government bonds were being added to the portfolios of individual persons, corporations, and financial institutions, the money market underwent a major change. At the same time, the money market transmitted the influence of the massive issue of government bonds to the whole financial system.

THE GENSAKI MARKET

The emergence and evolution of the *gensaki market* and its impact on the other sectors of the financial system are remarkable examples of the changes in Japan's financial system.

It is often said that market innovations played a less important role in the structural change in Japan's financial system since the mid-1970s. Instead, it is believed, regulatory reform preceded the changes. The need to fund the large government deficits that emerged after 1975 was the main reason that the regulatory authorities initiated a series of reforms that started the liberalization process.

In 1976, the Ministry of Finance (MOF) officially recognized the already-existing competitive money market for repurchase agreements in bond securities, known as the *bond gensaki market*. A gensaki transaction is the purchase and sale of securities for which there is a prior promise either to repurchase or to resell the same securities after a fixed period of time and at a fixed price. In other words, the gensaki market is a repurchase market for securities. The market had been in existence among securities houses since the late 1940s, though it was of minor importance until the early 1970s. At that time the market expanded in response to the large increase in the market rates of interest, reflecting the inflation and the growing volume of government bonds. The newly emerged gensaki market was the first free and open money market since the end of World War II. Any corporation, financial or nonfinancial, may participate in the market. However, an MOF directive prohibits the participation of individual persons, because it is difficult for them to determine creditworthiness and because the market should be reserved for corporate fund-raising and portfolio investment (Cargill and Royama 1988).

In 1978 the BOJ altered the procedures for purchasing, at favorable prices, government bonds held by financial institutions. Previously, the BOJ had bought government bonds held by financial institutions, one year after their issue, and the price that the BOJ paid for government bonds was quite beneficial to financial institutions. By introducing this new procedure, the BOJ removed an important subsidy to financial institutions holding government bonds. Consequently, the financial institutions tried to find another way to deal with the huge number of government bonds that they were forced to accept, at least at the time of their issue. The gensaki trade was the best place for financial institutions to deal with this problem, and so the gensaki market rose to the fore. After the official recognition of the gensaki market, measures were taken to liberalize it, as shown in Table 9.7.

THE DIVERSIFICATION OF OPEN MONEY MARKETS

Japan's Ministry of Finance was forced to become more sensitive to market forces in funding the growing budget deficits and in developing money markets. The case of the gensaki market shows that the evolution of the money markets was indispensable to the eventual financial liberalization.

The Certificate of Deposit Market

Not only the regulators but also the banks and other financial institutions reacted to the development of the gensaki money market. Corporate investors shifted their portfolios to the gensaki market, as the gensaki rate

Table 9.7. Liberalization of the Gensaki Market

March 1976	Official recognition of the gensaki trade.
October 1978	Ceiling of the gensaki sales outstanding imposed on city banks enlarged from ¥5 billion to ¥20 billion.
April 1979	The same measure, from ¥20 billion to ¥50 billion.
May 1979	Nonresidents' participation allowed.
April 1980	Ceiling of gensaki sales imposed on city banks abolished.
April 1981	City banks allowed to purchase gensaki.

Source: Shin'ichi Goto, *Tanki kin'yu shijo no chishki* (Information on short-term financial markets) (Tokyo: Nihon keizai shinbunsha, 1985), pp. 36–38.

was more attractive under free market conditions. Banks were urged to give to their investors instruments more competitive than traditional deposits and those with regulated rates of interest. In 1979 this need resulted in CDs (certificates of deposit) with market-determined interest rates.

Even though the rates of interest on CDs were freely determined, their minimum denomination, maturity term, and maximum amount were regulated, although those limitations were gradually relaxed (see Table 9.8). The U.S. government had an important role in deregulating the CD market. For instance, after talks on November 10, 1983, Donald Regan (then secretary of the treasury) and Takeshita (then finance minister) announced that the minimum denomination of CDs would be lowered from ¥0.5 billion to ¥0.3 billion yen as of January 1984 and that the bank issue ceiling would be raised from 75% to 100% of banks' own capital as of April 1984.

Following this agreement, the so-called yen–dollar talks made liberalization of the CD market one of the key issues, because it was expected to lead to further liberalization of the bank deposit market.

The Bankers Acceptance Market

Responding to the U.S. government's demand for financial liberalization, Japan seriously considered a market for bankers acceptances (BA) in the early 1980s. It also was believed that the BA market would promote the internationalization of the yen. A yen-BA is a yen-denominated, fixed-term bill of exchange underwritten by a bank after being issued originally by an exporter or importer for the purpose of settling a trade transaction (Suzuki 1987, p. 123). In June 1985 this market was activated. Since then,

Table 9.8. Deregulation of CD Market

	Minimum Denomination (¥ billion)	Maturity	Issue Ceiling (% of own capital)
May 1979	0.5	3–6 months	10
January 1980			25
April 1981			50
January 1984	0.3		75
April 1985	0.1	1–6 months	100
October 1985			150
April 1986		1–12 months	200
September 1986			250
April 1987			300
October 1987			abolished
April 1988	0.05	2 weeks–2 years	

Source: Bank of Japan, *Wagakuni no kin'yu seido* (The Japanese financial system) (Tokyo: Bank of Japan, 1986), pp. 165–66.

several measures have been taken to improve its performance, but the market has remained quite stagnant, and BAs have never been attractive to investors.

The Commercial Paper Market

In May 1981 when the new Banking Law was enacted, the Committee on Treasury in the Lower House of the Diet recommended establishing a commercial paper (CP) market for the purpose of diversifying financial instruments (Federation of Bankers 1981, app. 30). This was the first official statement regarding the CP market in Japan, but it took years before the market finally started up, in November 1987. The reason for the delay was the conflict of vested interests concerning CP among the industries.

First, there was a disagreement between the banking industry and the nonfinancial industries. The nonfinancial industry believed that the CP market would provide a good substitute for bank loans and that it would lower the cost of short-term financing. The banking industry opposed the introduction of a CP market, asserting that because commercial paper was issued without collateral, it would violate the principle of collateral in markets, damage the banks' health, and expose the investors. In addition, the banks were reluctant to introduce CP, as it would further weaken the close relationship between them and their customers (Suzuki 1987, p. 123).

Second, the securities and the banking industry did not agree on how to introduce CP. Commercial paper is a security that can be traded among anonymous investors in an open market, and so the market needed some kind of institutional framework to protect the investors. The Japanese Securities and Exchange Law, however, applies to a list of securities that does not include commercial paper, and accordingly, the securities industries wanted commercial paper to be added to this list in an amendment to the Securities and Exchange Law. If this had been done, the industry could have monopolized the CP business, because banks were prohibited from handling securities, by Article 65 of the Securities and Exchange Law. The banking industry tried to circumvent Article 65 by getting into the commercial paper business; thus the debate. The banks and the securities companies reached an agreement in 1987 that the commercial paper business could be shared by both the banking and the securities industry. To protect investors, a set of MOF directives determined that the minimum denomination should be ¥0.1 billion and that CP should be sold only to institutional investors, not to individual persons.

The commercial paper market expanded quickly after its introduction, reflecting the strong demand by business corporations for different kinds of short-term funding. Some of its development can be traced to the fact that arbitrage gains can be secured by investing funds raised by issuing CP in large-denominated bank deposits.

Now the commercial paper market has become the core of the Japanese money markets, and in May 1989 even the Bank of Japan began participating.

The Short-Term Government Debt Market

Two types of government debts are issued by Japan's central government. The first is short-term government securities issued for the purpose of synchronizing budgetary expenditures and tax receipts. The second kind of debt is short-term securities issued to finance the redemption of government bonds. The first kind of debt is short-term government securities (later renamed financing bills, FBs), and the second one is treasury bills (TBs). The market for TBs and FBs depends on the MOF's and the BOJ's feelings about the market mechanisms through which the market for short-term government debts has developed.

The BOJ has been anxious about the absence of an open short-term government securities market, because of its continuing need to absorb short-term government securities in the market. Specifically, the BOJ wishes to have flexible open market operations in a broad maturity spectrum of government securities as a major policy instrument.

Before February 1986, the MOF offered only one short-term instrument (two-month maturity), now referred to as the FB; however, this instrument was used for cash management of the government budget rather than for new funds or for budgetary refunding. The FBs were priced significantly above market levels, and as a result, the BOJ was required to absorb almost every issue. The system of issuing debt instruments with a fixed rate to the public, with the BOJ having to underwrite any remaining debts, is quite favorable for the MOF. Indeed, in prewar days, this system was used even for long-term government bonds. But after World War II, it was used only for short-term government securities. The BOJ objected to this procedure for two reasons: (1) The FBs accounted for an increasingly large part of the supply of high-powered money, and (2) the absence of an open short-term securities market denied the BOJ a policy instrument more consistent with a financially liberated system in which interest rates played a more important role in allocating credit.

In February 1986 the MOF began issuing TBs with a six-month maturity, for debt-refunding purposes. They are auctioned on a competitive basis. The amount of TBs outstanding as of March 1987 had already increased to 18% of the amount of CDs outstanding and the amount of trading in TBs has equaled or exceeded CD trading in the secondary market.

The new TB instrument has not yet provided the BOJ with a full-fledged short-term government debt market environment in which to conduct flexible open market operations. But the new instrument does represent a step toward establishing a competitive short-term government securities market. Such a market would have major implications for Japan's financial system as well as the BOJ's policy.

THE FURTHER LIBERALIZATION OF THE MONEY MARKETS

Japan's money markets have grown significantly since the official recognition of the gensaki market in 1976 and the authorization of banks to issue large-denomination CDs in 1979. The authorization in 1987 to issue commercial paper is also contributing to the future expansion of the money market. Table 9.9 gives a statistical summary of the evolution and development of money markets in Japan. Despite these developments, the lack of a well-developed short-term government debt market, TBs or FBs or both, has sharply limited the evolution of the money market as a major conduit for transferring funds from lenders to borrowers. The market for TBs and/or FBs would provide a highly liquid asset with no default risk to

Table 9.9. Development of Money Markets in Japan (outstanding balance at end of year, ¥ trillion)

	Interbank Money Market	Call Money Market	Bill Discount Market	Open Money Market
1970	1.8	1.8	—	0.6
1975	6.7	2.3	4.4	1.8
1979	9.8	3.5	6.3	5.8
1980	9.8	4.1	5.7	6.9
1981	8.7	4.7	4.0	7.8
1982	9.9	4.5	5.4	8.6
1983	11.3	4.5	6.8	10.0
1984	13.0	5.0	8.0	12.1
1985	19.8	5.1	14.7	14.0
1986	23.7	10.2	13.5	19.3
1987	29.1	16.0	13.1	22.5
1988	33.7	15.7	18.0	35.2
1989	45.3	24.5	20.8	44.0

	Open Money Market	Gensaki in Securities	CDs	BAs	CPs	TBs	FBs
1970	0.6	0.6	—	—	—	—	—
1975	1.8	1.8	—	—	—	—	—
1979	5.8	4.0	1.8	—	—	—	—
1980	6.9	4.5	2.4	—	—	—	—
1981	7.8	4.5	3.3	—	—	—	—
1982	8.6	4.3	4.3	—	—	—	—
1983	10.0	4.3	5.7	—	—	—	—
1984	12.1	3.6	8.5	—	—	—	—
1985	14.0	4.6	9.4	0.03	—	—	—
1986	19.3	7.1	9.2	0.0	—	2.1	0.9
1987	22.5	6.9	10.3	0.0	1.7	2.7	0.9
1988	35.2	7.4	15.5	0.0	9.3	2.0	1.0
1989	44.0	6.3	20.6	0.9	bn	13.1	4.0

Source: Bank of Japan, *Economic Statistics Annual,* each year.

a broad spectrum of market participants. A TB and/or FB market would become the pivotal element for determining interest rates in other direct and intermediation markets; it would provide a secondary reserve asset for financial institutions; it would greatly contribute to the internationalization of the yen; and it would give the BOJ a powerful and flexible policy instrument. The establishment of a competitive market for short-term government debt combined with the existing competitive long- and medium-term government bond market would be a major step toward a liberated financial system and would enable the BOJ to operate in a flexible open market.

In February 1986, the MOF took the first step toward an open and competitive short-term government debt market by introducing the six-month TB. There is some reason to believe that this will lead to the establishment of a broad and active short-term government debt market. The BOJ, the securities companies, and the United States all have pressured the MOF to expand the short-term government debt market. The BOJ sees a TB and/or FB market as providing a more effective and flexible environment for monetary policy. The securities companies see the market as a way of further expanding direct and open-market transactions. The United States and other countries see the market as contributing to the further internationalization of the Japanese financial system and the yen.

Thus despite the reform efforts to expand the money markets in Japan, the actual accomplishments fall short of open, competitive, and broad-based securities markets. The lack of a complete TB and/or FB market remains the most serious problem in this regard.

MONETARY POLICY AFTER THE DEVELOPMENT OF THE MONEY MARKET

During the period of high economic growth in Japan, the BOJ conducted its monetary policy by controlling the call money market rate, in turn by lending to the big banks. In order to make the BOJ's lending more attractive than the call money market rate, various interventions in the latter's movement were instituted. In addition, the BOJ took direct control of the banks' loan extension, in the name of *window guidance*. Thus the BOJ could successfully control bank credit, which in turn produced a well-controlled money supply under the specific flow-of-funds conditions during that period.

Monetary control operations have changed drastically since the evolution of open money markets. First, borrowers have access to sources of funds other than borrowing from banks and other financial institutions: They now can raise funds in open markets. The liquidity constraints of real expenditures have been relaxed. Expenditures are now more interest elastic since being freed from bank lending. Second, lenders have alternatives to bank deposits. The demand for money has become more elastic with regard to interest rates. Third, the banks and other financial institutions have had many opportunities to make investments other than loans and in the interbank call money market.

Under these new circumstances, the monetary authorities had to make reforms in the money markets, including the interbank money market. In November 1988 they implemented three measures to get rid of the old intervention, and this made the money market interest rates more flexible.

First, the maturity terms of commercial bills and unsecured call money contracts were expanded. Second, a bid–offer system of pricing was introduced for the interbank money market transactions with maturities equal to or longer than one week. Third, the BOJ commenced operation by means of commercial bills with maturities shorter than one month.

Further reforms of money markets were implemented in January 1989. First, the minimum unit of interest rate quotation was reduced in the interbank market from 1/16% to 1/32%. Second, the minimum holding period required for banks before reselling purchased commercial bills was shortened from one month to one week. Third, a bid–offer price quotation system was established for unsecured call money transactions with maturities shorter than one week.

In April 1989, the third series of reform measures were enacted. Maturities were expanded for commercial bills and unsecured call contracts, and the brokerage fee was lowered from 1/16% to 1/25% for commercial bills and unsecured call transactions.

In May 1989, the BOJ started purchasing commercial paper. Thus it succeeded for the first time in acquiring a policy instrument for overnight market operations.

There is no clear evidence that all these measures have had much effect on monetary control, because the BOJ has not yet tackled the urgent need for an active monetary policy. But it is believed that the transmission mechanism of the BOJ's monetary policy was improved. The money markets, particularly the interbank markets, have assumed their anticipated role as conduits for short-term funds and flexible interest determination, as they should have. The BOJ's day-to-day operations now run more smoothly, as reflected in the market rates, which market participants watch carefully. The BOJ has obtained better control of money market rates.

In addition to reforms of the money markets, measures for determining interest rates on bank loans and deposits have increased the effectiveness of transmitting money market rates to the lending and borrowing nonfinancial private sectors. The closer link between the banks' prime rates and the leading banks' money market rates is one of these measures. The other is the money market certificates of deposit (MMCs), whose interest rates are linked to money market rates.

CONCLUSIONS

It is too early to say whether the development of money markets has improved the performance of the Japanese financial system and whether the BOJ has made its monetary policy more effective. The Japanese economy has not yet experienced serious monetary and financial constraints. With regard to macromonetary issues, the discount rate at the BOJ rose from the all-time low level of 2.50% in February 1987 to 3.25% in May 1989, after which it was raised four times, to reach 6.0% at the end of August 1990. But the growth of money supply was kept high. The BOJ decided on the serial increase in the discount rate in 1989 and 1990 to avoid too great an increase in stock and land prices. Because the economy has kept production, employment, and prices in good condition, the BOJ has not instituted an active monetary policy. The BOJ may have been able to adjust the day-to-day money supply more smoothly since it made the series of money market reforms. Indeed, Japan's financial system has changed from a paradigm of credit to one of money. The evolution of open money markets had a crucial role in this transformation. The monetary authorities have done their best to reform the policy environment, but the time has not yet come to judge whether their efforts have helped the economy.

REFERENCES

Bank of Japan. Annual. *Economic Statistics*. Toyko: Bank of Japan.

———. Annual. *Flow of Funds Tables*. Toyko: Bank of Japan.

———. 1983. *Nippon ginko hyakunenshi* (The-centennial history of the Bank of Japan). Vol. 3. Toyko: Bank of Japan.

———. 1986. *Wagakuni No kin'yo seido* (The Japanese financial system). Toyko: Bank of Japan.

Cargill, Thomas F., and Shoichi Royama. 1988. *The Transition of Finance in Japan and the United States: A Comparable Perspective*. Stanford, CA: Stanford University, Hoover Institution.

Federation of Bankers Associations of Japan. 1981. *Ginkoho kaisei ni kansuru kokkai rongi shu* (Collection of discussions in the Diet on the amendment of the Banking Law). Tokyo: Federation of Bankers Associations of Japan.

Goto, Shin'ichi. 1985. *Tank kin'yu shijo no chishki* (Information on short-term financial markets). Tokyo: Nihon keizai shinbunsha.

Money Market Study Group of the Ministry of Finance and the Bank of Japan. 1990. *Wagakkuni tanki kin'yu shijo no genjo to kadai* (Japan's short-term money market and its issues). Tokyo: Kin'yu zaisei jijo kenkyukai.

Suzuki, Yoshio. ed. 1987. *The Japanese Financial System*. Oxford: Clarendon Press.

CHAPTER 10
AN ECONOMETRIC ANALYSIS OF ASIAN MONEY MARKETS

SAM OULIARIS

This chapter provides an econometric analysis of Asia's emerging money markets. We consider the money markets of five countries: Singapore, Malaysia, Korea, Indonesia, and the Philippines. We also examine Japan's prewar money market. For each of these countries, we want to determine the time-series properties of returns payable on short-term money market instruments. In particular, we test whether each interest rate can be modeled as a unit root process driven by weakly dependent innovation sequences, that is, $y_t = y_{t-1} + \varepsilon_t$, where ε_t is drawn from the ARMA (p,q) class. The alternative hypothesis is that each series is a stationary process drawn from the ARMA (p,q) class. Note that when ε_t is statistically independent over time, the "unit root" model is in fact a "random-walk." The latter is commonly associated with the efficient market hypothesis literature. Also, the unit root hypothesis implies that each shock affects the level of the series permanently. It follows that a unit root process, in contrast with a stationary process, does not display mean-reverting behavior (or reversion to the mean).

Assuming that the data are consistent with the unit root hypothesis, we also want to determine whether the individual money markets are efficient. Here efficiency is defined as whether or not there is a reference rate that dictates the long-run movement of returns paid by other money market instruments. Put in another way, assuming the data are consistent with the unit root hypothesis, we want to determine whether the reference rate is cointegrated with other returns available in the market. Cointegration occurs whenever a linear combination of two or more integrated processes (in this case, money market interest rates) is stationary. If the reference rate is cointegrated with other market rates, then there is strong evidence that the interest rate series are comoving over time.[1] The reason is that a linear combination of integrated processes is normally nonstationary, and such behavior would clearly invalidate the use of any of the unit root series as a reference rate.

We find considerable evidence in favor of the unit root hypothesis in the Singapore, Malaysian, Indonesian, and prewar Japanese money markets. We can also find a reference rate for each of these markets. However, we found the interest rates in Korea and the Philippines to be stationary processes, reflecting considerable volatility in the rates of return around their mean. In many cases, this volatility can be attributed to interference by the monetary authorities attempting to manipulate the money market independently of the forces of supply and demand, thereby preventing the market from operating efficiently.

EMPIRICAL RESULTS

Singapore

Figures 10.1, 10.2, and 10.3 plot Singapore's one-month interbank rate, fixed deposit rate, and prime lending rates against the SIBOR between January 1979 and January 1989 (i.e., the interbank rate paid on U.S. dollars in the Singapore Asia dollar market). The comovement between the three series and the SIBOR rate is immediately apparent, particularly from January 1983 onward. This comovement, of course, is due to Singapore's being a price taker in the market for U.S. dollar–denominated funds and its very open capital markets. Thus Singapore's monetary conditions are extremely sensitive to external influences. It is also clear from the plots that the money markets have imputed exchange rate movements in the return on SIBOR deposits. The exchange rate premium has been consistently positive, reflecting depositors' expectation of the Singapore dollar's appreciating against its U.S. counterpart. It is also noteworthy that Singapore's money market rates have become much less volatile since January 1983. This is probably due to the Federal Reserve's switch from monetary to interest rate targets in the fall of 1982, which reduced the variance of the SIBOR.

Table 10.1 reports some unit root statistics for the interest rate data plotted in Figures 10.1 through 10.3. We also consider the Singapore/U.S. dollar exchange rate, since we will use it in our in regressions. The following statistics are provided: (1) Phillips (1987) $Z_t(\mu)$ statistic[2] for the null hypothesis that the first-order autocorrelation coefficient is unity (see column 1); (2) the Said and Dickey (1984) Augmented Dickey–Fuller ADF(μ) statistic, which uses the same null hypothesis as the $Z_t(\mu)$ statistic (see column 2); and (3) the Park and Choi (1988) G (p,q) statistic for the null hypothesis that the data are stationary (see column 3) and its corresponding p-value (see column 4). The unit root statistics are applied to both the levels and the first differences of the interest rate data.

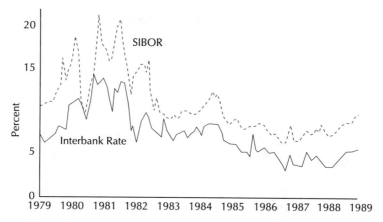

Figure 10.1. Singapore Money Market: Interbank Rate vs. SIBOR

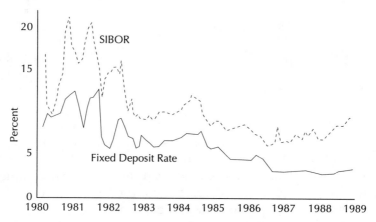

Figure 10.2. Singapore Money Market: Fixed Deposit Rate vs. SIBOR

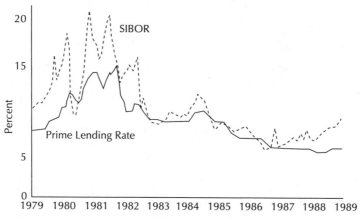

Figure 10.3. Singapore Money Market: Prime Lending Rate vs. SIBOR

Table 10.1. Monthly Unit Root Statistics for the Singapore Money Market, January 1979 to January 1989

Series		$Z_t(\mu)$ [a]	$ADF(\mu)$ [b]	$G(0,4)$	p-value
SIBOR	Level	−2.0082	−1.3956	8.9391	0.0626
	Difference	−9.9106	−5.9410	2.5023	0.6442
PLR [c]	Level	−1.1598	−0.6134	9.5226	0.0492
	Difference	−5.9681	−4.7200	5.3996	0.2487
FDR [d]	Level	−1.2601	−0.9921	8.7996	0.0663
	Difference	−6.8120	−10.0327	3.8970	0.4201
ITR [e]	Level	−1.8650	−1.1986	8.9847	0.0614
	Difference	−12.5647	−7.0186	1.7223	0.7866
Spot rate	Log–Level	−1.8721	−1.2907	15.7827	0.0003
	Difference	−11.8855	−5.1036	3.2998	0.5089
Critical values		−2.76	−2.76	9.49	

[a] $Z_t(\mu)$ computed using 10 autocorrelation terms.

[b] $ADF(\mu)$ statistic computed using 5 lags.

[c] Prime lending rate.

[d] Fixed deposit rate.

[e] Interbank rate.

The basic conclusion to be drawn from the statistics is that the null hypothesis of a unit root cannot be rejected for the interest rate data. We also detected a unit root in the Singapore/U.S. dollar exchange rate. Note that the unit root finding implies that the series exhibit nonstationary behavior and can be modeled as integrated processes (i.e., $y_t = y_{t-1} + \varepsilon_t$) driven by weakly dependent innovation sequences (i.e., ε_t can be drawn from the ARMA (p,q) class). It also implies that the data possess a long memory; in other words, random shocks to the interest rate and exchange rate will affect the level of the data for a very long period of time.

Table 10.2 shows the results of regressing the money market rates against the SIBOR and the expected rate of depreciation in the Singapore/U.S. dollar exchange rate, which is proxied here by the observed change in the exchange rate. The regressions are motivated by the interest rate parity equation,

$$i_D = \beta_1 i_F + \beta_2 \pi^e + \varepsilon_t$$
$$H_0: \beta_1 = 1, \beta_2 = 1 \tag{1}$$

where i_D is the domestic interest rate, i_F is the foreign interest rate, and π^e is the expected rate of depreciation of the domestic currency relative to the base currency (in this case the U.S. dollar). The method of estimation is Park's CCR (1988) regression procedure for cointegrated systems, which,

Table 10.2. Cointegration Regressions for the Singapore Money Market Interest Rate Parity Equation

Dependent Variable	Period[a]	Constant	SIBOR	ln(S$/U.S.$)	Speed of Adjustment	H–Stat (p–value)
			Explanatory Variable			
ITR[b]	1	−0.0073	0.6894	0.4164	0.4534	5.7372
		(0.0335)	(10.7829)	(7.8176)		(0.2196)
	2	−0.01827	1.0479	0.0334	0.5073	6.3141
		(0.1082)	(8.2561)	(0.2927)		(0.1768)
F statistic for structural change: 10.7891** (5% critical value = 3.07)						
FDR[c]	1	0.2751	0.7207	0.3039	0.6101	8.6785
		(0.7715)	(6.9964)	(4.4629)		(0.0696)
	2	−0.0229	0.9907	−0.1926	0.5321	6.1251
		(0.0678)	(3.8385)	(1.3706)		(0.1899)
F statistic for structural change = 15.6564** (5% critical value = 3.09)						
PLR[d]	1	0.0086	0.5647	0.0551	0.8966	7.7162
		(0.0207)	(5.7596)	(0.6387)		(0.1025)
	2	−0.0179	0.8497	−0.2052	0.4852	6.1695
		(0.0562)	(3.4969)	(1.4446)		(0.1868)
F statistic for structural change = 6.5653** (5% critical value = 3.07)						

[a] Period 1: Jan. 1979 to Jan. 1989; 2: Jan. 1983 to Feb. 1989.

[b] Interbank rate.

[c] Fixed deposit rate.

[e] Prime lending rate.

in contrast with ordinary least squares (OLS), yields centered t-statistics for the parameter estimates. The t-statistics reported in Table 10.2 may, therefore, be interpreted in the usual way. Note that the estimated coefficients for the SIBOR measure the long-run responsiveness of domestic rates to the SIBOR. In contrast, the coefficients on the expected rate of depreciation, a stationary variable, estimate a short-run, or transitory, response. These coefficients were estimated from a regression of the residuals from the cointegrating regression against the inflation rate.

An important component of Park's (1988) procedure is a test for stationarity or comovement between the domestic interest rate and, in this case, the SIBOR. This test is provided by the H (p,q) statistic, which simply tests for stationarity (or mean reversion) in the residuals of the cointegrating regression (see Appendix 10A for a description of the H (p,q) statistic). If the residuals of the cointegrating regression are stationary, then there is very strong evidence of comovement between the dependent variable, i_D, and the independent variables, i_F. The empirical results support the hypothesis of stationarity and thus comovement between the three domestic money market rates and the SIBOR. Over the whole sample period, the long-run responsiveness of the fixed deposit rate and the interbank rate to a unit change in the SIBOR was 0.69 and 0.72, respectively. For the prime lending rate, it was approximately 0.56.

An interesting issue is whether the interest rate parity equation is actually satisfied for Singapore. For this to be the case, the coefficients on the SIBOR and the expected rate of depreciation should be unity. Between January 1979 and January 1989, this condition was clearly violated. When the interest rate parity equation is estimated for after January 1983, domestic rates appear to move almost 1:1 with movements in the SIBOR. However, the coefficients on the expected depreciation rate fall to zero in this period, thus violating the interest parity equation. Therefore, the evidence is very much against the interest parity equation.

We speculated that there was a structural break in the data around March 1982, when the Federal Reserve moved from money targets to interest rate targets. It is possible to test the hypothesis of structural change more formally using the usual F-statistic. (The appropriate F-statistics are given in Table 10.2.) They all are significant at the 5% level, implying that the null hypothesis of no structural break in the sample period can be rejected. It appears that the Federal Reserve's movement from money growth targets to interest rate targets had a significant impact on the volatility of interest rates in Singapore.

Estimates of the speed of the domestic interest rates' adjustment to movements in the SIBOR are also provided in Table 10.2. The estimates are derived from the first-order autocorrelation coefficients implicit in the residuals of Equation 1 for each of the three interest rates. Note that the autocorrelation coefficient measures the rate at which states of disequilibrium (i.e., a residual) influence the time path of the dependent variable. The speed of adjustment toward equilibrium increases as the autocorrelation coefficient approaches zero (from unity). Our estimates suggest that the speed of adjustment in the money market appears to be quite rapid, of no more than three months for the period after January 1983.

An important issue is whether or not the various interest rates in the money market move together over time. If the money market is truly efficient, then variations in the opportunity cost of funds should affect the levels of all the interest rates in the market. In short, we should observe comovement or cointegration among the individual series in the money market. Table 10.3 estimates, using Park's CCR technique, the relationship among the interbank rate, the fixed deposit rate, and the prime lending rate for the Singapore market over the two sample periods. Three different regressions were computed: (1) the fixed deposit rate against the interbank rate, (2) the prime lending rate against the interbank rate, and (3) the prime lending rate against the fixed deposit rate. Again, we used Park's $H(p,q)$ statistic to test the hypothesis of comovement among the three interest rate series. The H (p,q) statistics (see the last column of Table 10.3)

Table 10.3. Cointegrating Regressions for the Singapore
Money Market, Comovement in Domestic Interest Rates

Dependent Variable	Explanatory Variable		H Statistic (p-value)
Jan. 1983 to Jan. 1989			
PLR	= −0.00526 + 0.73755	ITR	6.3359
	(0.0275) (5.4785)		(0.1754)
FDR	= −0.00756 + 0.8825	ITR	6.6393
	(0.0402) (6.6413)		(0.1562)
PLR	= 0.0027 + 0.8855	FDR	6.0856
	(0.0693) (37.1085)		(0.1928)
Full period: Jan. 1979 to Jan. 1989			
PLR	= 0.01434 + 0.7834	ITR	8.4262
	(0.0686) (9.4128)		(0.0771)
FDR	= 0.1720 + 0.9177	ITR	8.408
	(1.1804) (16.1902)		(0.0777)
PLR	= 0.00841 + 0.8897	FDR	10.5156
	(0.0783) (20.8897)		(0.03258)
Structural change tests			
	PLR/ITR	FDR/ITR	PLR/FDR
F statistic	1.52	1.24	10.5158**
Critical value	3.07	3.09	3.09

indicate that the residuals of the CCR regressions are stationary, implying comovement among the three interest rates. The comovement was particularly strong between January 1983 and January 1989. The parameter estimates indicate that a percentage point change in the interbank rate produces, on average, a 0.88 percentage point change in the fixed deposit rate and a 0.73 percentage point change in the prime lending rate. We were unable, however, to reject the null hypothesis of no structural change for the whole sample period, implying that the relationship among these rates was stable. This means that interest rates in the Singapore market moved together even during the volatile period between January 1979 and March 1982, which was characterized by excessive volatility in the SIBOR. The existence of comovement among domestic interest rates despite high volatility in foreign rates of return suggests that Singapore possesses a mature and efficient money market.

Overall, the results indicate that the interbank rate is a very good predictor of domestic interest rates in Singapore. Moreover, since the interbank rate is cointegrated with the SIBOR rate, either the SIBOR or the interbank rate could serve as a reference rate for Singapore's money market.

Malaysia

We now consider the behavior of interest rates in Malaysia for the period between January 1979 and February 1989, at the beginning of which the monetary authorities deregulated their money markets. Given that Malaysia is an open economy highly dependent on trade and capital flows for economic development, we would expect the foreign return on capital to have an important influence on domestic money market rates. Any unwarranted divergence between the foreign and domestic rates of return would result in potentially disruptive capital inflows and/or outflows.

Figures 10.4, 10.5, and 10.6 depict the empirical relationship between the ex-post rate of return on foreign currency–denominated assets (proxied by the SIBOR plus the actual depreciation in the Malaysian ringgit) and the Malaysian interbank rate (Figure 10.4), its deposit rate (Figure 10.5), and its average lending rate (Figure 10.6) between January 1979 and January 1989 (data permitting). Figure 10.4 suggests a fairly close relationship between the ex-post foreign return and the interbank rate; however, the ex-post foreign return is obviously more variable than the domestic interbank rate. Figure 10.5 shows a relationship between the deposit rate and the foreign rate; however, the deposit rate appears relatively unresponsive to movements in the foreign rate when compared with the interbank rate. A similar conclusion can be made about the average lending rate, which is virtually unresponsive to changes in the ex-post foreign rate of return. Given that the interbank rate may be viewed as the marginal cost of funds in the money market, the differences in the variability of these rates is indicative of imperfections in the money market. The sluggish behavior of the average loan rate would be indicative of some monopoly power of the Malaysian banks.

Table 10.4 reports the usual unit root statistics for the Malaysian interest rate series. As in the case of Singapore, the unit root statistics provide strong support for the null hypothesis of a unit root (using a 10% level of significance). The statistics also suggest that the first differences of the data are stationary (as required).

It follows that the issue of comovement among the various money market rates amounts to the question of whether or not the interest rate series are cointegrated processes. The relevant cointegrating regressions, estimated using Park's (1988) CCR technique, are given in Table 10.5.

The first three regressions estimate the interest parity equation. Each market rate is regressed on the ex-post foreign rate (the SIBOR + depreciation of the Malaysian ringgit). The H(0,4) statistics imply that each of the interest rate series is cointegrated with the ex-post foreign rate. However, the actual influence of the ex-post foreign rate is rather small; note that all the estimated coefficients on the ex-post foreign rate are numerically small and statistically insignificant. Thus, although there appears to be some

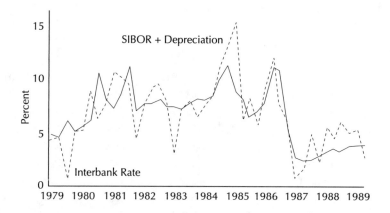

Figure 10.4. Malaysian Money Market: Interbank Rate vs. Foreign Rate

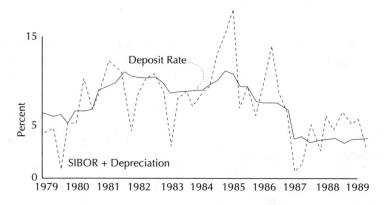

Figure 10.5. Malaysian Money Market: Deposit Rate vs. Foreign Rate

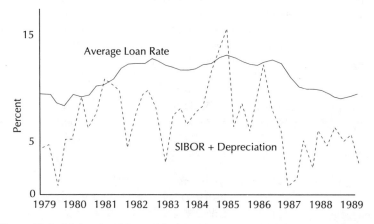

Figure 10.6. Malaysian Money Market: Average Loan Rate vs. Foreign Rate

Table 10.4. Unit Root Statistics for the Malaysian Money Market, January 1979 to February 1989

		Code	$Z_t(\mu)$[a]	$ADF(\mu)$[b]	$G(0,4)$	p-value
Interbank rate	Level	R_{IB}	−2.2793	−0.9237	8.2763	0.0819
	Difference		−6.6948	−3.5918	1.9017	0.7538
Deposit rate	Level	R_D	−0.9810	−1.2965	9.1064	0.05841
	Difference		−5.6376	−2.2950	5.0364	0.2835
Loan rate	Level	R_L	−1.4214	−0.9196	9.9962	0.0404
	Difference		−4.0309	−4.0402	6.4721	0.1665
SIBOR	3-month	SIBOR	−1.8503	−1.5933	8.6780	0.06961
	Difference		−6.0371	−3.5625	2.4836	0.6476
Depreciation rate		DEP	−7.0446	−3.5902	0.8877	0.9263
Critical values			−2.76	−2.76	9.49	

[a] $Z_t(\mu)$ computed using 10 autocorrelation terms.

[b] $ADF(\mu)$ statistic computed using 5 lags.

comovement between the money market rates and the ex-post foreign rate in the long run, the empirical relationship is not very strong. Also, there is very little support for the interest parity equation, since the estimated coefficients are different from unity (see Equation 1).

Table 10.5. Quarterly Cointegrating Regressions for the Malaysian Money Market, January 1979 to February 1989

				$H(0,4)$	Speed of Adjustment
1.	R_{IB}	= 6.5882 (7.0857)	+ 0.0308 (SIBOR + DEP) (0.2418)	0.8696 (0.9288)	N.A.
2.	R_D	= 5.8110 (9.5570)	+ 0.0905 (SIBOR + DEP) (1.0930)	3.4796 (0.4809)	N.A.
3.	R_L	= 11.4255 (13.2280)	+ 0.0642 (SIBOR + DEP) (0.5631)	0.3387 (0.9871)	N.A.
4.	R_D	= 1.7032 (2.3446)	+ 0.6963 RIB (6.7846)	6.4300 (0.1692)	0.3416
5.	R_L	= 8.9150 (1.5802)	+ 0.3034 RIB (6.5761)	5.8282 (0.2123)	0.8413
6.	R_L	= 7.1848 (10.2781)	+ 0.5575RD (5.6919)	11.9028 (0.0108)	0.9197
7.	R_F on IB: $\hat{e}_t$	= 0.3420 $\hat{e}_t$ (2.2503)	+ 0.003644EL + V_t (0.0997)	N.A.	N.A.
8.	R_L on IB: $\hat{e}_t$	= 0.8416 $\hat{e}_{t-1}$ (9.6248)	− 0.001367EL + V_t (−0.07217)	N.A.	N.A.
9.	R_L on R_D: $\hat{e}_t$	= 0.9197 $\hat{e}_{t-1}$ (15.9196)	− 0.0004EL + V_t (0.0465)	N.A.	N.A.

Regressions 4 through 6 of Table 10.5 provide statistical evidence regarding the long-run relationship among the interbank rate, the deposit rate, and the average loan rate. Again, the H(0,4) statistics support the cointegration or comovement hypothesis for the three rates. Thus there is strong evidence for comovement among the three interest rate series. This follows from the results that the estimated residuals are stationary, even though the interest rate series have unit roots. The long-run response of the deposit rate to a percentage point change in the interbank rate is approximately 0.69, and that for the average loan rate is 0.30.

Because the residuals of the cointegrating regressions represent stationary or mean-reverting deviations from the long-run path (in this case, dictated by the interbank rate), we can infer the speed of adjustment toward equilibrium from the estimated residual series itself simply by fitting an ARMA (p,q) model to the estimated residuals. Also, we may partially explain the residuals using a proxy for the excess liquidity of the banks over the sample period.

Table 10.5 also shows the appropriate regressions needed to infer the speed of adjustment. Again, we fit a first-order autoregressive model to the residuals from the cointegrating regression. The regression also includes a proxy for the excess liquidity of the Malaysian banking system. The expected sign for the excess liquidity variable is negative. If the deposit rate were above the interbank rate during a period of excess liquidity, we would expect the excess liquidity to contribute to a reduction in the deposit rate relative to the interbank rate (the marginal cost of funds).

The empirical estimates suggest that the deposit rate adjusted fairly rapidly to the interbank rate. The speed of adjustment was approximately three quarters. In contrast, the average loan rate took about five quarters and was thus much less sensitive to movements in the marginal cost of funds. The coefficient on the excess liquidity variable proxy was small and statistically insignificant for both the deposit rate and the average loan rate.

Overall, the statistical analysis for Malaysia suggests that the ex-post foreign return on short-term funds had little, if any, significant influence on the three money market rates. But the interbank rate appears to be a good candidate for a reference rate. Although comovement between the interbank rate and the deposit and lending rates was indeed present, the relationship weakened significantly when we moved from the deposit rate to the lending rate. Thus the marginal cost of funds seems to have been an important determinant of the deposit rate, but not as important for explaining movements in the average loan rate. The average loan rate seems to have been influenced more by the need to maintain a margin above the deposit rate itself. The long-run existence of this wedge between the marginal cost of funds and the average loan rate is indicative of some monopoly power in the Malaysian banking system.

Korea

Figure 10.7 depicts the behavior of Korea's money market rates between August 1986 and December 1988. Four rates are plotted: the interbank rate (CALL), the rate paid on government monetary stabilization bonds (MSB), the government bond rates (GB), and the rate paid on certificates of deposit (CD). The four rates were largely determined by the market during the sample period. The plots suggest that three (the GB, CD, and MSB) of the four interest rates moved together over time. These rates, however, appear to have moved independently of the interbank rate—which is indicative of market imperfections in the money market.

Table 10.6 provides the usual unit root statistics for the Korean data. The results are mixed and rather difficult to interpret. The $Z_t(\mu)$ and ADF(μ) statistics support the null hypothesis of a unit root for all the interest rate series. However, the G(0,4) statistic, which uses stationarity as its null hypothesis, favors the stationarity hypothesis (using a 5% level of significance). We feel that the stationarity hypothesis is more likely to be correct. The point estimates for the unit root parameters are 0.7955 (CALL), 0.8401 (GB), 0.9040 (MSB), and 0.9110 (CD). Since these estimates are quite far from 1.00 (the unit root hypothesis), it would be very difficult to accept the implications of the $Z_t(\mu)$ and ADF(μ) statistics. Moreover, the $Z_t(\mu)$ and ADF(μ) statistics are notorious for their lack of power (i.e., their ability to reject the unit root hypothesis when it is incorrect).

Because unit root behavior is a characteristic typical of interest rates in an efficient financial market, these results suggest that the Korean money market is not very efficient. Since the interest rate data are stationary, we can use standard econometric procedures to investigate the relationship among the four interest rate series. This analysis is reported in Kang and Choi 1990.

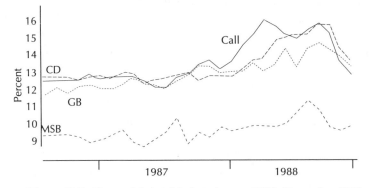

Figure 10.7. Korean Money Market, August 1986–December 1988

Table 10.6. Monthly Unit Root Statistics for the Korean Money Market, August 1986 to December 1988

	$Z_t(\mu)$	$ADF(\mu)$	$G(0,4)$	p-value
Interbank rate	−2.5614	−1.0712	8.4011	0.1354
	−7.8217	−4.8643	0.8773	0.9277
Government bond rate	−1.8797	−1.2332	9.3297	0.0966
	−8.0460	−3.6587	4.5450	0.3372
Monetary stabilization rate	−1.4617	−1.3526	9.6998	0.0842
	−2.7372	−2.0538	9.5369	0.0489
Certificates of deposit	−2.2916	−2.2916	9.9486	0.0367
	−1.4340	−1.4340	10.962	0.0269
Critical value (5%)	−2.7600	−2.7600	9.49	

Indonesia

World interest rates are likely to be a prime determinant of Indonesian interest rates. Like Singapore, Indonesia operates a fairly open foreign exchange market. Figure 10.8 plots the Indonesian interbank rate against the LIB1SWAP rate between January 1983 and December 1989.[3] The periodicity of the data is monthly. The LIB1SWAP is equal to the LIBOR interest rate payable on one-month deposits plus the premium payable on one-month swap contracts (see Cole and Slade 1990 for a complete description of the LIB1SWAP rate). It is a measure of the rate of return on foreign currency deposits offered to Indonesian residents. The Indonesian interbank rate is obviously a very erratic series compared with the LIB1SWAP rate. Surprisingly, there is little indication of comovement between the two series.

Figure 10.9 plots the interest rate payable on one-month and three-month deposits offered by state banks (SBDEP1 and SBDEP3, respectively) against the LIB1SWAP rate. In contrast with the interbank rate, the

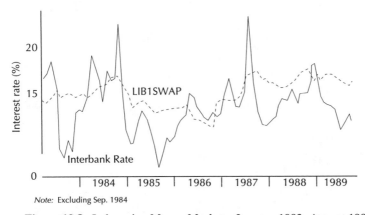

Note: Excluding Sep. 1984

Figure 10.8. Indonesian Money Markets, January 1983–August 1989

LIB1SWAP rate appears to be a good reference rate for the deposit rates paid by the state banks, except for the middle of the sample period, during which the SBDEP1 and SBDEP3 rates were often held constant. Note that the SBDEP1 and SBDEP3 series moved together over time.

Table 10.7 gives the usual unit root statistics for the four interest rate series between January 1983 and December 1989. Only the interbank rate appears to be a stationary process, confirming the unique behavior of the interbank rate (see Figure 10.8). For the remaining three series, the unit root statistics strongly supported the unit root hypothesis. We also found that the first differences of the data are stationary processes (as required when the level of the data possess a unit root).

Stationarity in the interbank rate is probably an outcome of the fact that the interbank market was highly regulated by the Indonesian authorities, resulting in periodic imbalances between the demand and the supply for short-term funds and thus an extremely volatile interbank rate. It follows that the interbank rate is a poor candidate for a reference rate.

Table 10.8 reports the usual cointegrating regressions for the interest rates, which we found to be consistent with the unit root hypothesis. The cointegrating regressions yield strong evidence in favor of the hypothesis that the LIB1SWAP is a reference rate. Note that the $H(0,4)$ statistics support the null hypothesis that the SBDEP1 and SBDEP3 rates are individually cointegrated with the LIB1SWAP rate (using a 5% level of significance). The point estimates from the cointegrating regression suggest that a percentage point change in the LIB1SWAP rate results, on average, in a 0.57 point change in the SBDEP1 rate and a 0.55 point change in the SBDEP3 rate in the long run. The speed of adjustment, as implied by the first-order autoregressive coefficient of the residuals of the cointegrating regression, of the deposit rates to the LIB1SWAP rate was fairly rapid. SBDEP3 appears to have taken approximately three months; SBDEP1 adjusted slightly faster (nearly two months).

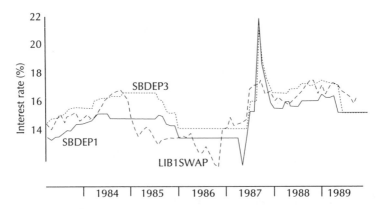

Figure 10.9. Indonesian Money Markets, January 1983–August 1989

Table 10.7. Monthly Unit Root Statistics for the Indonesian Money Market, January 1983 to December 1989

	$ADF(\mu)$	$Z_t(\mu)$	$G(0,4)$	p-value
Interbank rate	−3.0118	−5.5561	3.9597	0.4114
	−5.7628	−14.237	0.1059	0.9986
LIBOR + SWAP	−1.8112	−1.7523	9.4623	0.0505
	−3.9107	−8.2200	2.5422	0.6371
SBDEP1	−2.1707	−3.3588	9.1072	0.0585
	−5.2174	−11.5595	0.5994	0.9631
SBDEP3	−2.2046	−2.7579	10.2774	0.0360
	−4.2539	−10.6034	1.7723	0.7775
Critical value (5%)	−2.76	−2.76	9.46	

These results also imply that SBDEP1 and SBDEP3 are cointegrated. The latter hypothesis can be tested explicitly by regressing SBDEP1 against SBDEP3 (see regression 3 in Table 10.8). The H(0,4) statistic supports the null hypothesis of cointegration between SBDEP1 and SBDEP3. The point estimates imply that a percentage point change in SBDEP3 is associated, on average, with a 0.70 point change in SBDEP1.

The Philippines

Table 10.9 provides the unit root statistics for the Philippine money market between January 1982 and July 1988 (using monthly data). We looked at five broad classes of money market instruments: (1) the interbank market, (2) promissory notes, (3) government repurchase agreements, (4) private repurchase agreements, and (5) treasury bills. Figure 10.10 provides a plot of the return on promissory notes (eight to fifteen days), the interbank rate, and the rate paid on government repurchase agreements. Unfortunately, the data were incomplete for many of the series considered in Table 10.9. To compensate for this problem and thus to provide continuous data over

Table 10.8. Cointegrating Regression for the Indonesian Money Market, January 1983 to December 1989

	Speed of Adjustment	$H(0,5)$
$R_{SBDEP1} = 6.0482 + 0.5778\, R_{LIB1SWAP}$		5.6489
$\qquad\quad\ (3.9226)\quad (5.6811)$	0.5446	(0.3419)
$R_{SBDEP3} = 7.5097 + 0.5481\, R_{LIB1SWAP}$	0.6918	9.8013
		(0.0876)
$R_{SBDEP1} = 5.4077 + 0.7010\, R_{SBDEP3}$	0.8000	6.6752
$\qquad\quad\ (2.9676)\quad (5.6993)$		(0.2549)

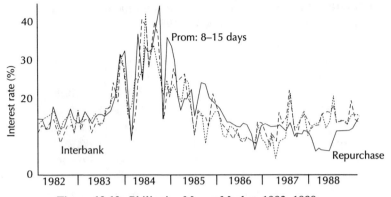

Figure 10.10. Philippine Money Market, 1982–1989

the sample period, we used the most recently observed value of the series to estimate the missing data points. This procedure for removing missing values is acceptable if the null hypothesis is a unit root and it is correct; however, it is extremely unsound when the null hypothesis is stationarity. For these reasons, we report only the ADF(μ) and $Z_t(\mu)$ statistics for the series, since the G (p,q) statistic uses a null hypothesis of stationarity. Note, how-

Table 10.9. Summary Statistics for the Philippines Money Market Monthly Data, January 1982 to July 1989

	$ADF(\mu)$	$Z_t(\mu)$
Interbank call rate	−2.0064	−3.8630
	−5.4936	−13.5083
Promissory notes		
Demand	−1.6846	−3.6949
	−5.0678	−13.4879
1–7 days	−1.4425	−5.1297
	−4.4064	−19.9360
8–15 days	−2.0802	−3.2228
	−4.4505	−15.6420
Government repurchase agreements		
Demand	−1.6762	−3.4386
	−5.1501	−15.9727
1 – 7 days	−1.7315	−3.0866
	−4.8798	−15.0738
8 – 15 days	−2.0113	−1.6878
	−3.2901	− 6.2187
16 – 30 days	−2.2583	−1.7272
	−3.2937	− 6.1245
Private repurchase agreements	−2.1054	−3.2810
	−4.6235	−10.228
Treasury bill rate	−2.5091	−2.004
	−3.551	− 6.603

ever, that the procedure we adopted to estimate the missing data biased the results in favor of the unit root hypothesis.

Unfortunately, the results for the $Z_t(\mu)$ and ADF(μ) statistics are not consistent. The ADF(μ) statistic provides very strong evidence in favor of the unit root hypothesis. This inference, however, is not supported by the $Z_t(\mu)$ statistic, which strongly supports the stationarity hypothesis for all the interest rates except for government repurchase agreements (eight to fifteen and sixteen to thirty days) and the treasury bill rate. The statistics are in agreement for the treasury bill rate. Given that the data for government repurchase agreements are incomplete and that the corrections probably biased the results toward the unit root model, we feel that the treasury bill rate is the only series that can be modeled as an integrated process. As such, we can propose the treasury bill rate as a reference rate for the Philippines' money market. But in view of the stationarity finding for the remaining interest rate series in the money market, we can immediately conclude that the treasury bill rate is not a significant determinant of money market rates in the Philippines. This result follows from the fact that it is not possible to explain a stationary process using an integrated or unit root variable.[4]

Prewar Japan

We now consider the behavior of interest rates in Japan's money market between 1910 and 1936. Following Teranishi (1990), we examined six interest rates series, all available on a monthly basis between 1910 and 1936: a loan rate (denoted by $R1$), a bill discount rate ($R2$), an overdraft rate ($R3$), (4) a demand deposit rate ($R4$), a time deposit rate ($R5$), and an interbank call rate ($R6$). We looked at the series for three separate subperiods: (1) August 1910 to November 1918 (denoted as Period 1), (2) December 1918 to February 1927 (Period 2), and (3) June 1927 to September 1935 (Period 3).

Figures 10.11 and 10.12 plot the data for the 1910–1935 period. The loan rate, the bill discount rate, and the overdraft rate (see Figure 10.11) moved together for most of the prewar period. In contrast, the demand and time deposit rates remained relatively constant, suggesting that Japanese banks, presumably because of their monopoly power, were able to maintain a wedge between the marginal cost of funds and their lending rates (see Figure 10.12). The interbank call rate was by far the most volatile interest rate during the prewar period. The plots indicate that the interbank rate did not comove with the loan rate and the overdraft rate.

Table 10.10 reports the unit root statistics for the data. We cannot reject the unit root hypothesis for most of the interest rate series. The only exception occurs in Period 2, in which all the statistics imply that the interbank rate was a stationary process. It follows that the interbank rate should not be used as a reference rate in Period 2, since the remaining interest rates are integrated processes.

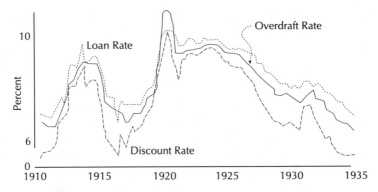

Figure 10.11. Prewar Japanese Money Market, August 1910–September 1935

Table 10.11 gives the cointegrating regressions for the Japanese money market for the three subperiods. For each possible pair of interest rates, we estimated the regression

$$r_{jt} = \alpha + \beta r_{kt} + \varepsilon_t, j \neq k$$

and tested the null hypothesis of comovement or cointegration using the H(0,4) statistic. Table 10.11 reports the estimates and their corresponding *t*-statistics for the set of regressions found to be cointegrated (using a 5% level of significance). The parameters were estimated using Park's (1989) CCR regression technique.

Comovement was evident among most of the interest rates across the three subperiods. Moreover, the estimates for β are uniformly large and significantly different from zero. The loan rate ($R1$), the discount rate ($R2$), and the overdraft rate ($R3$) are cointegrated across the three sample periods. The point estimates imply that a percentage point change in the bill discount rate was associated, on average, with a 0.70 to 0.77 percentage point change in the loan rate. Also, a percentage point change in the overdraft rate was associated with a 0.85 to 0.92 change in the loan rate.

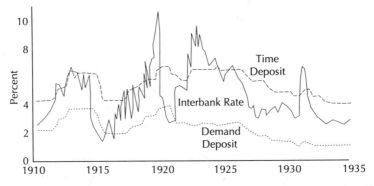

Figure 10.12. Prewar Japanese Money Market, August 1910–September 1935

Table 10.10. Unit Root Statistics for Prewar Japan's Money Market

	$ADF(\mu)$	$Z_t(\mu)$	$G(0,5)$	$p\text{-}value$
Period 1: Aug. 1910 to Nov. 1918	−1.5936	−1.6143	20.7050	0.0009
	−2.2022	−1.6133	20.7090	0.0009
	−1.8848	−1.6218	21.3880	0.0006
	−1.6652	−1.6164	20.3540	0.0010
	−2.0279	−1.7578	20.2430	0.0011
	−1.8037	−3.7791	19.7410	0.0014
Period 2: Nov. 1918 to Feb. 1927	−2.7201	−2.3209	20.9160	0.0008
	−3.0745	−2.3875	17.7590	0.0032
	−3.1642	−2.3405	19.0960	0.0018
	−1.8261	−1.7379	18.0220	0.0029
	−3.0661	−2.5861	18.491	0.0023
	−3.2144	−4.6778	8.8620	0.1147
Period 3: Jun. 1927 to Sep. 1935	−0.5858	−0.9070	24.0670	0.0002
	−1.3574	−1.3605	23.8740	0.0002
	−0.6365	−1.1949	24.1330	0.0002
	−2.4771	−10.271	13.1560	0.0219
	−1.0627	−1.6942	23.5950	0.0002
	−2.5585	−2.3737	19.958	0.0013
Critical values	−2.76	−2.76	11.07	0.0500

A notable exception to the comovement hypothesis is provided by $R6$ (the call rate), which was not cointegrated with most of the interest rates during the prewar period. It follows that the interbank rate, usually a proxy for the marginal cost of funds, would be a very poor reference rate for pre-

Table 10.11. Cointegrating Regressions for the Prewar Japanese Money Market

	Period 1 Aug. 1910 to Nov. 1918		Period 2 Nov. 1918 to Feb. 1927		Period 3 Jun. 1927 to Sep. 1935	
		$H(0,4)$ $(p\text{-}value)$		$H(0,4)$ $(p\text{-}value)$		$H(0,4)$ $(p\text{-}value)$
R1–R2	0.6976	5.8737	0.7677	8.7647	0.70229	9.2896
	(18.84)	(0.2087)	(16.825)	(0.0672)	(18.591)	(0.0542)
R1–R3	0.9258	2.3342	0.8538	8.7668	0.8466	6.9901
	(27.695)	(0.6745)	(26.558)	(0.0672)	(25.517)	(.1364)
R1–R4	1.0755	9.2241	0.48210	8.3333	Not cointegrated	
	(8.7310)	(0.0557)	(1.0540)	(0.0801)		
R1–R5	Not cointegrated		1.8000	8.0436	0.9538	9.1805
			(6.6266)	(0.0899)	(17.061)	(0.0567)
R1–R6	Not cointegrated		Not cointegrated		Not cointegrated	

Table 10.11. (*Continued*)

| | Period 1 Aug. 1910 to Nov. 1918 | | Period 2 Nov. 1918 to Feb. 1927 | | Period 3 Jun. 1927 to Sep. 1935 | |
	H(0,4) (p-value)		H(0,4) (p-value)		H(0,4) (p-value)	
R2–R3	Not cointegrated		1.0415	6.1197	1.1636	6.9315
			(32.760)	0.1903	(18.046)	(0.1395)
R2–R4	1.5794	9.2244	0.8955	7.6763	Not cointegrated	
	(12.780)	(0.0557)	(1.3872)	(0.1042)		
R2–R5	1.4631	7.5013	2.2239	7.6133	1.3281	6.6275
	(22.586)	(0.1116)	(0.1068)	(16.546)	(0.1569)	
R2–R6	Not cointegrated		Not cointegrated		Not cointegrated	
R3–R4	Not cointegrated		0.7566	7.7171	Not cointegrated	
			(1.3366)	(0.1431)		
R3–R5	Not cointegrated		2.1467	6.8656	1.1298	8.2158
			(7.5752)	(0.1432)	(26.130)	(0.0839)
R3–R6	Not cointegrated		Not cointegrated		Not cointegrated	
R4–R5	0.87216	10.263	Not cointegrated		0.6603	2.2758
	(12.4710)	(0.0362)			(4.4133)	(0.6851)
R4–R6	0.2814	7.6374	Not cointegrated		0.35823	6.3371
	(2.0256)	(0.0469)			(2.4441)	(0.1753)
R5–R6	0.3085	9.5989	Not cointegrated		0.6231	9.8683
	(1.9864)	(0.0477)			(4.4821)	(0.0427)

war Japanese money markets. This long-run divergence between the marginal cost of funds and the loan and deposit rates would be indicative of the Japanese banks' monopoly power.

NOTES

1. Since the theory of cointegration and cointegrated processes is relatively new, the interested reader is referred to the technical appendix of this chapter, which provides a brief survey of the field.

2. The symbol $Z_t(\mu)$ means that we are computing the Z_t statistic from a fitted regression with a constant term: $y_t = \ + y_{t-1} + \varepsilon_t$.

3. The plot excludes the data for September 1984, when the interbank rate rose to 46%.

4. The missing data problem makes it virtually impossible to analyze the data more formally.

REFERENCES

Brillinger, David R. 1981. *Time Series Data Analysis and Theory.* San Francisco: Holden-Day.

Campbell, John Y., and Robert J. Shiller. 1987.

"Cointegration and Tests of Present Value Models." *Journal of Political Economy* 95 (October): 1062–88.

Cochrane, John, and Argia M. Shordone. 1988. "Multivariate Estimates of the Permanent Components of GNP and Stock Prices." *Journal of Economic Dynamics and Control* 12 (June–September): 255–96.

Cole, David C., and Betty F. Slade. 1990. "Development of Money Markets in Indonesia." Harvard Institute of International Development. Photocopy.

Engle, Robert F., and Clive W. J. Granger. 1987. "Cointegration and Error Correction: Representation, Estimation, and Testing." *Econometrica* 55 (March): 251–76.

Fuller, Wayne A. 1976. *Introduction to Statistical Time Series*. New York: Wiley, 1976.

Granger, Clive W. J., and Paul Newbold. 1974. "Spurious Regressions in Econometrics." *Journal of Econometrics* 2 (July): 111–20.

Hannan, Edward J. 1963. "Regression for Time Series." In *Time Series Analysis*. Edited by M. Rosenblatt. New York: Wiley.

Johansen, Soren. 1988. "Statistical Analysis of Cointegrating Vectors." *Journal of Economic Dynamics and Control* 12 (June–September): 231–54.

Kang, Moon-Soo, and Jang-Bong Choi. 1990. "Money Markets in Korea." Mimeo.

Nelson, Charles R., and Charles I. Plosser. 1982. "Trends and Random Walks in Macroeconomic Time Series." *Journal of Monetary Economics* 10 (September): 139–62.

Ouliaris, Sam, Joon Y. Park, and Peter C. B. Phillips. 1989. "Testing for a Unit Root in the Presence of a Maintained Trend." In *Advances in Econometrics*. Edited by Baldev Raj. Amsterdam: Kluwer Academic Publishers.

Park, Joon Y. 1988. "Canonical Cointegrating Regressions." Working Paper, Department of Economics, Cornell University.

Park, Joon Y., and Bhumsoo Choi. 1988. "A New Approach to Testing for a Unit Root." Working Paper 88–23, Department of Eco-

nomics, Cornell University.

Park, Joon Y., and Peter C. B. Phillips. 1988. "Statistical Inference in Regressions with Integrated Processes: Part 1." *Econometric Theory* 4 (December): 468–98.

———. 1989. "Statistical Inference in Regressions with Integrated Processes: Part 2." *Econometric Theory* 5 (April): 95–132.

Phillips, Peter C. B. 1986. "Understanding Spurious Regressions in Econometrics." *Journal of Econometrics* 13 (December): 311–43.

———. 1987. "Time Series Regression with a Unit Root." *Econometrica* 55 (March): 277–301.

———. 1988a. "Optimal Inference in Cointegrated Systems." Cowles Foundation Discussion Paper 866R, Yale University.

———. 1988b. "Spectral Regression for Cointegrated Time Series." Cowles Foundation Discussion Paper 872, Yale University.

Phillips, Peter C. B., and Steven N. Durlauf. 1986. "Multiple Time Series with Integrated Variables." *Review of Economic Studies* 53 (August): 473–96.

Phillips, Peter C. B., and Bruce Hansen. 1990. "Statistical Inference in Instrumental Variables Regressions with I(1) Processes." *Review of Economic Studies* 57: 99–125.

Phillips, Peter C. B., and Sam Ouliaris. "Asymptotic Properties of Residual Based Tests for Cointegration." *Econometrica*.

Said, Said E., and David A. Dickey. 1984. "Testing for Unit Roots in Autoregressive Moving Average Model of Unknown Order." *Biometrika* 71 (December): 599–607.

Stock, James H. 1987. "Asymptotic Properties of Least Squares Estimators of Cointegrating Vectors." *Econometrica* 55 (September): 1035–56.

Teranishi, J. 1990. "Money Markets in Prewar Japan." Working Paper, Institute of Economic Research, Hitotsubashi University.

APPENDIX 10A
COINTEGRATION THEORY

Econometric procedures for evaluating and estimating cointegrated systems were proposed by Engle and Granger (1987), Phillips and Durlauf (1986), Park and Phillips (1988, 1989), and Phillips and Ouliaris (forthcoming), among many others. Much of the theoretical work builds on the seminal paper by Phillips (1987), in which he used a univariate invariance principle to derive the asymptotic distribution of the ordinary least squares (OLS) estimator for the unit root model, namely, $y_t = y_{t-1} + \varepsilon_t$. Considered as a whole, these papers derive the asymptotic distributions of standard estimators and diagnostics applied to cointegrated systems. More recently, a number of papers proposed estimators for cointegrated systems which, unlike OLS, yield chi square (χ^2) asymptotics for conventional t- and F-statistics (Park 1988, Phillips 1988b, Phillips and Hansen forthcoming).

Cointegrated systems have been found to be very useful in characterizing economists' notions of long-run equilibrium in theoretical models involving integrated processes. For instance, Cochrane and Shordone (1988) demonstrated that the permanent income hypothesis implies that consumption and income are cointegrated, and Campbell and Shiller (1987) show that the present value relation implies that stock prices and dividends are cointegrated. Furthermore, the evidence is mounting that key macroeconomic time-series variables such as gross national product are best modeled as integrated processes (see Nelson and Plosser 1982). We now present a review of the econometric results for cointegrated systems.

Theory

The econometric theory of cointegration distinguishes between cointegrated and noncointegrated systems of variables. A cointegrated system may be defined as a linear regression equation in which the dependent and explanatory variables are integrated processes (e.g., random walks), yet the residuals are mean reverting (i.e., a variable that returns to its mean in the long run). It may also be defined as a linear combination of integrated variables that are stationary.

Since a linear combination of integrated variables would normally be an integrated process, the existence of a cointegrated system suggests a stochastic equilibrium between the integrated variables. A noncointegrated system, on the other hand, is a linear regression equation in which the residuals are nonstationary and thus not mean reverting. From an econometric and modeling perspective, it is important to show that a set of integrated variables form a cointegrated system, since a noncointegrated system can be viewed as a nonequilibrium system and thus a misspecified regression equation. It also falls into the Granger and Newbold (1974) class of "spurious regressions." In the absence of cointegration, the conditional variance of the dependent variable is not stable, thus raising considerable doubt about specification of the regression line.

For the purpose of explication, we follow Phillips (1988b) and let D_t^* be an $n \times 1$ vector of integrated processes of order one ($I(1)$) generated according to:

$$D_t^* = \omega(\otimes, t) + D_{t-1}^* + \zeta_t = \sum_{i=0}^{t} (\omega(\otimes, i) + \zeta_i) \tag{1}$$

In Equation 1, ζ_i is an $n \times 1$ vector process drawn from the set of stationary variates, and $\omega(\otimes, t)$ is the deterministic part of the process (e.g., its mean). For example, ζ_i may be drawn from the class of stationary ARMA(p,q) models (using standard Box–Jenkins terminology). Let $n = m + 1$, and partition D as $[y, x^*]$, where x is an $m \times 1$ vector and y is a scalar. We now assume that the following relationship holds among the components of D purged of $\omega(\otimes, t)$, which we will denote by D_t:

$$y_t = \beta' x_t + v_t \tag{2}$$

$$\Delta x_t = u_{2t} \tag{3}$$

where
$$D_t = \begin{bmatrix} y_t \\ x_t \end{bmatrix} = D_{t-1} + u_t, \text{ and}$$

$$u_t = \begin{bmatrix} u_{1t} \\ u_{2t} \end{bmatrix} {}_m^1$$

Again, we allow v_t to be a stationary process in Equation 2. Contemporaneous correlation between the components of u_t is also permitted.

Since Equation 2 possesses stationary residuals, it is, in the terminology of Engle and Granger (1987), a "cointegrated system" with cointegrating vector $\alpha' = (1, -\beta')$. We may call $\beta' x_t$ the long-run component of y_t, whereas v_t represents the short-run influences on y_t. The v_t process is meant to capture the dynamic behavior of the temporary influences on the dependent variable, y_t.

Engle and Granger (1987) argue that cointegrated systems provide an ideal framework for modeling the long-run behavior of time-series variates, which follow an $I(1)$ process. Specifically, cointegrated systems allow for a very broad class of data-generation processes for y_t and x_t, because ζ_t and v_t may be drawn from the very large class of stationary variates. The Engle and Granger (1987) framework therefore provides a significant relaxation of the standard assumptions for OLS, since it is no longer necessary to restrict v_t in Equation 2 to an independent, normally distributed random variable.

Cointegrated systems also distinguish between the short-run and long-run behavior of the model. In a noncointegrated system, in which the error term is an integrated process with infinite variance, that is, $\psi = \psi_{t-1} + \varepsilon_t$, deviations from the long-run path will affect the level of the series permanently, thus confusing the distinction between the short run and the long run. According to Engle and Granger (1987), irrespective of the time-series properties of the data, a properly formulated regression model involving $I(1)$ variables must ensure that the deviations from the long-run path are mean reverting. If these deviations (residuals) are integrated processes, there is no guarantee that the model will return to its long-run path (i.e., $\beta'x_t$), and claims of a relationship among the integrated variables are obviously suspect.

The econometric methodology pertaining to cointegrated systems yields significant advantages over conventional econometric methodology (such as OLS applied to the first difference of Equation 2). Stock (1987) and Park and Phillips (1988) proved that when OLS is applied to Equation 2, the OLS estimates converge to the true long-run vector, β, at the rate T (sample size) rather than $T^{1/2}$ (the conventional case). This result occurs because the moments of the long-run component, $\beta'x_t$, are an order of magnitude larger (by a factor of T) than the moments of v_t. This so-called superconsistency property of OLS holds even in the presence of correlation in v_t, simultaneity between y_t and x_t, and stationary measurement error in y_t and x_t. The superconsistency of OLS also implies that it is not necessary to specify and estimate the short-run dynamics influencing y_t to estimate the long-run parameter vector, thereby enormously simplifying the specification problem.

The superconsistency result ceases to hold if y_t and $\beta'x_t$ are not cointegrated. Equation 2 becomes a "spurious" regression in this case (see Granger and Newbold 1974). As proved by Phillips (1986), application of OLS to a noncointegrated system will result in a situation in which the empirical size of conventional hypothesis tests greatly exceeds their nominal setting, irrespective of the actual values of β. Thus, conventional hypothesis tests will consistently reject the null hypothesis even when it is true. Phillips (1986) also proved that the Durbin–Watson statistic has a probability limit of zero in noncointegrated systems and that R^2 is random in the limit, thereby undermining the usefulness of most diagnostics for applied work.

METHODOLOGY

A standard applied methodology now exists for estimating cointegrated systems. It is as follows:

Step 1: Pretest the time-series data to determine whether the data are consistent with the $I(1)$ hypothesis. A number of statistics are now available to test this hypothesis formally. We shall restrict ourselves to a subset of those statistics that allows for a general process to drive the innovation sequence vector, ζ_t.

If the null hypothesis is Equation 1, we may use Said and Dickey's (1984) Augmented Dickey–Fuller (ADF) statistic, which allows $\omega(\otimes,t) = 0$, μ, $\mu + \pi t$. (See also Ouliaris, Park, and Phillips (1989) for models that allow $\omega(\otimes,t)$ to be a polynomial trend of arbitrary order.) To test the unit root hypothesis using the ADF procedure, we estimate the following regression equation using OLS:

$$D_{i,t} = \omega(\otimes,t) + \alpha D_{i,t-1} + \sum_{j=1}^{k} \rho_j \Delta D_{i,\,t-j} + \kappa_{i,t}, \ i = 1, 2, \ldots, n \qquad (4)$$

where $\kappa_{i,t}$ is $iid(0,\sigma^2)$, and test the null hypothesis that $\alpha = 1$ using the conventional t-statistic. Note that the ADF statistic allows for ARMA (p,q) innovation sequences by including lagged innovation sequences (i.e., $\Delta D_{i,t-j}$) in the fitted regression.

The form of $(\otimes,t)$ is dictated by the need to purge the integrated vector D_t of its deterministic part. For example, if the integrated variable D_t possesses a mean, so that $\omega(\otimes,t) = \mu$, we must set $(\otimes,t) = \mu + \pi t$ to purge the integrated process of the influence of $\omega(\otimes,t)$. When the initial value of the integrated process (i.e., $D_{i,0}$) is not equal to zero, it is necessary to set $(\otimes,t) = \mu$—and $\omega(\otimes,t) = 0$—in order to ensure that the asymptotic distribution of the statistic is invariant to the value of $D_{i,0}$ (an unknown quantity in practice).

The limiting distribution of the ADF statistic is nonstandard (see Phillips 1987 for an explicit representation); the critical values for a given level of significance depend on the form of the deterministic part, $\omega(\otimes,t)$. Critical values for $\omega(\otimes,t) = 0$, $\omega(\otimes,t) = \mu$, $\omega(\otimes,t) = \mu + \pi t$ are reported in Fuller 1976, and critical values for higher polynomials may be found in Ouliaris, Park, and Phillips 1989. The null hypothesis of a unit root is rejected if the computed value of the statistic is smaller than the critical value of the test.

If the null hypothesis for the data is stationarity, with an alternative of a unit root, we may use the G (p,q) statistic, $q > p$, developed in Park and Choi 1988. Consider the least squares regressions

$$D_{i,t} = \sum_{0}^{p} \alpha_k t^k + e_t \tag{5}$$

$$D_{i,t} = \sum_{0}^{q} \alpha_k t^k + e_t \tag{6}$$

and let $W(p,q)$ be the standard Wald statistic for the null hypothesis that a subset of the higher order time polynomials are zero (i.e., $\alpha_j = 0$, $j = p + 1$, ..., q). Let σ^2 denote the variance of $_t$ in Equation 6. Define

$$G(p,q) = \left(\frac{\sigma^2}{\varphi^2}\right) W(\alpha_{p,q}) \tag{7}$$

where φ^2 is the "long-run" variance of ε_t. Park and Choi (1988) proved that the $G(p,q)$ statistic for stationarity possesses a χ^2_{q-p} distribution asymptotically.

The long-run variance, φ^2, may be estimated in a number of ways. For our purposes, we can restrict ourselves to the class of estimators that can be expressed as

$$\varphi_\gamma^2 = \sum_{1}^{T} \varepsilon_t^2 + \sum_{2/t}^{\gamma} C_\gamma(k) \sum_{t=k+1}^{T} \varepsilon_t \varepsilon_{t-k} \tag{8}$$

where the lag truncation number, $\gamma = o_p(n^\delta)$, $0 \le \delta \le$, and the weights, $c_\gamma(k)$, are less than one in absolute magnitude. Note that the estimator of the long-run variance is simply the conventional estimator for the variance of ε_t plus a weighted average of the lagged covariances of ε_t from $k = 1$ to $k = \gamma$.

Step 2: Formulate the long-run regression equation for the integrated variables and show that the regression is a cointegrated system. This step is normally carried out by estimating the long-run regression using OLS. Under the null hypothesis of no cointegration, the residual vector will possess a unit root, that is, will be an $I(1)$ variable. If the cointegrating regression is estimated by OLS, we can use the ADF statistic to test the null hypothesis of no cointegration. The critical values of the ADF statistic for this case are provided in Phillips and Ouliaris (forthcoming). If the null hypothesis is that the residuals are cointegrated, we may use the H(p,q), $q > p$, statistic developed by Park (1988), a generalization of the G(p,q) statistic discussed earlier. Like the G(p,q) statistic, this statistic uses q^{th} order time polynomials in the cointegrating regression and is a modified Wald statistic for the hypothesis that a subset of the time polynomials (say those from $p+1$ to q) are irrelevant. Park (1988) proved that the H(p,q) statistic possesses χ^2_{q-p} distribution asymptotically.

Step 3: Reestimate the cointegrating regression using the efficient regression estimators proposed by Park (1988) or Phillips (1988b).[1] This step is necessary because the asymptotic distribution of the OLS estimator applied to cointegrating regressions depends on nuisance parameters, resulting in nonstandard distributions for the t- and F-statistics (see Park and Phillips 1988 and 1989) for explicit representations of the asymptotic distributions). Phillips's (1988b) methodology involves transforming an error correction model (ECM) representation of the cointegrating regression into the frequency domain, which induces errors that are asymptotically independent across frequencies. Efficient estimation of the ECM requires generalized least squares (GLS) in the frequency domain. Phillips (1988b) proved that the application of spectral estimation techniques to Equation 2 produces unbiased and efficient estimates for β. Moreover, unlike OLS, the spectral estimator allows the use of conventional asymptotics to test linear restrictions on the cointegrating vector. Park's (1988) approach centers on adjusting the original data to remove the nuisance parameters from the limiting distribution of the OLS estimator. Park (1988) refers to his estimator as the canonical cointegrating regression technique.

NOTES

1. Phillips and Hansen (1990) and Park (1988) also developed estimators for cointegrated systems that yield conventional asymptotics for cointegrated systems. The estimators share the same asymptotic distribution as Phillips's (1988b) spectral regression estimator. The Phillips and Hansen (1990) and Park (1988b) estimators use complex "GLS-type" corrections to the data, followed by the application of OLS.

INDEX